LOOKING THROUGH IMAGES

COLUMBIA THEMES IN PHILOSOPHY,
SOCIAL CRITICISM, AND THE ARTS

COLUMBIA THEMES IN PHILOSOPHY,
SOCIAL CRITICISM, AND THE ARTS

....

Lydia Goehr and Gregg M. Horowitz, Editors

Advisory Board

Carolyn Abbate

J. M. Bernstein

Eve Blau

T. J. Clark

John Hyman

Michael Kelly

Paul Kottman

In memoriam: Arthur C. Danto

Columbia Themes in Philosophy, Social Criticism, and the Arts presents mono-
graphs, essay collections, and short books on philosophy and aesthetic theory. It
aims to publish books that show the ability of the arts to stimulate critical reflection on modern and contemporary social, political, and cultural life. Art is not
now, if it ever was, a realm of human activity independent of the complex realities
of social organization and change, political authority and antagonism, cultural
domination and resistance. The possibilities of critical thought embedded in the
arts are most fruitfully expressed when addressed to readers across the various
fields of social and humanistic inquiry. The idea of philosophy in the series title
ought to be understood, therefore, to embrace forms of discussion that begin
where mere academic expertise exhausts itself; where the rules of social, political,
and cultural practice are both affirmed and challenged; and where new thinking
takes place. The series does not privilege any particular art, nor does it ask for the
arts to be mutually isolated. The series encourages writing from the many fields of
thoughtful and critical inquiry.

For a complete list of titles, see page 393.

LOOKING THROUGH IMAGES

A PHENOMENOLOGY OF VISUAL MEDIA

EMMANUEL ALLOA

Translated by Nils F. Schott

AFTERWORD BY ANDREW BENJAMIN

Columbia University Press

New York

Columbia University Press
Publishers Since 1893
New York   Chichester, West Sussex
cup.columbia.edu

Das durchscheinende Bild
copyright © 2011 diaphanes, Zürich-Berlin
Copyright © 2021 Columbia University Press
All rights reserved

Library of Congress Cataloging-in-Publication Data
Names: Alloa, Emmanuel, author. | Schott, Nils F., translator. |
Alloa, Emmanuel. Durchscheinende Bild.
Title: Looking through images : a phenomenology of visual media /
Emmanuel Alloa ; translated by Nils F. Schott.
Other titles: Durchscheinende Bild. English
Description: New York : Columbia University Press, [2021] | Originally presented as the
author's thesis (doctoral)—Université de Paris I: Panthéon-Sorbonne and Freie Universität
Berlin, 2009) under the title: Das durchscheinende Bild : Konturen einer medialen
Phänomenologie. | Includes bibliographical references and index.
Identifiers: LCCN 2020056481 (print) | LCCN 2020056482 (ebook) |
ISBN 9780231187923 (hardback) | ISBN 9780231187930 (trade paperback) |
ISBN 9780231547574 (ebook)
Subjects: LCSH: Phenomenology. | Image (Philosophy) |
Visual communication—Philosophy.
Classification: LCC B829.5.A5513 2021 (print) | LCC B829.5 (ebook) | DDC 128/.3—dc23
LC record available at https://lccn.loc.gov/2020056481
LC ebook record available at https://lccn.loc.gov/2020056482

Cover design: Milenda Nan Ok Lee
Cover image: Léon Foucault, *Solar Spectrum*, daguerreotype (1844), 12.8 x 9.4 cm.
Société française de photographie, Paris.

We find certain things about seeing puzzling, because we do not find the whole business of seeing puzzling enough.

—Ludwig Wittgenstein, *Philosophical Investigations*

Ineluctable modality of the visible . . . Limits of the diaphane. But he adds: in bodies. Then he was aware of them bodies before of them coloured. How? By knocking his sconce against them, sure. Go easy. Bald he was and a millionaire, *maestro di color che sanno*. Limit of the diaphane in. Why in? Diaphane, adiaphane. If you can put your five fingers through it, it is a gate, if not a door. Shut your eyes and see.

—James Joyce, *Ulysses*

Contents

Preface to the English Edition

Seeing one's book translated into another language a decade after it was first published is both flattering and terribly discomforting. It is flattering inasmuch as it tends to prove that the book, initially written in German, can have a life of its own, slowly but steadily making a place for itself in contemporary debates. The fact that this English edition coincides with translations into other languages seems to indicate that the ideas it advances have a certain momentum. Yet the prospect of having one's book transposed into another language is also terribly discomforting inasmuch as, in retrospect, its author sees all its flaws and shortcomings. Many ideas, especially in the later, more experimental sections, are merely sketched and will have to be spelled out in more detail. The temptation is considerable to rewrite it in light of all the developments the field of visual studies and media philosophy has seen since the book first came out. This temptation, though, is stopped dead in its tracks by the realization that it would not mean writing the book differently but writing a different book altogether. *Pace* my perfectionist instincts: I have kept interventions in the text to a bare minimum, just enough to dare present the book to a foreign audience.

The next temptation, then, if the content cannot be changed altogether, is at least to provide a guide to reading the book, explaining the text with some sort of paratext, an explanatory vestibule, as it were, to frame the entry into the real thing. But again, that would be tragically to overestimate the role of the author: once published, a book is no longer in the hands of the one who wrote it, and it should be left to readers to make their way through it as they see fit. Suffice it to say that I always envisioned the book as a phenomenologically inspired archaeology of the Western engagement with images. Yet in any archaeological endeavor, diggers never know what they will find.

In that respect, the table of contents is less a table than a topographical map that points the way to all sorts of paths and shortcuts across a vast excavation site.

I will thus leave it at that and instead highlight the crucial role several people played in seeing this volume to publication.

First and foremost, I would like to express my gratitude to Lydia Goehr and Gregg Horowitz, who decided to include this book in their prestigious series: I could not think of a more desirable setting. Second, I'm indebted to Andrew Benjamin, with whom I have discussed matters of image philosophy for many years now. He has been one of the most penetrating readers of the book, probably because he looks at it from a distance from where its author is. Third, my thanks go to Wendy Lochner at Columbia University Press for her precious support throughout the entire process: such editors have become rare in publishing today. But if there is anyone who deserves credit for this book coming into being, it clearly is Nils F. Schott. Not only has he checked every source and chased down technical translations where they existed in remote libraries or suggested his own where they didn't. More important, he has achieved something that seems half a miracle, namely, turning a text written in baroque academic German into a readable English text. At least I like to think so. Should anything remain that seems stiff or obscure, the blame lies not with the translator but with the author alone.

———

The volume epigraph is from Ludwig Wittgenstein, *Philosophical Investigations*, trans. G. E. M. Anscombe, P. M. S. Hacker, and Joachim Schulte, ed. P. M. S. Hacker and Joachim Schulte, 4th ed. (Chichester: Wiley, 2009), 2.251:224^e; and James Joyce, *Ulysses* (London: Penguin, 2000), 45.

Introduction

In the early seventeenth century, Tommaso Campanella, in his utopian dialog, *The City of the Sun*, describes his vision of an ideal city-state that—particularly remarkable from today's perspective—is pervaded by images: inner and outer walls, streets, every house and every available surface is used as a bearer of images.[1] In this regard, at least, Campanella's vision of the future proves to be prophetic. It seems to anticipate our own present, which is inconceivable without images. Our late-modern cities are primarily pictorial architectures, gigantic surfaces for projecting optical messages of all kinds. Since Campanella's day, images have become even more supple and adaptable and find a place on even the most precarious media support, albeit often for just a short moment before others take their spot. Be it as an official mural or merely as graffiti quickly painted over, as feature presentation on the silver screen or as transient image on an itself mobile screen—all these images are united by one thing: the promise to be understood immediately and by everyone.

This likely was what fascinated the utopian Campanella, and today, now that we have reached the end of the Gutenberg age, it is easier than ever to understand this fascination. Going beyond alphabetizing human minds, the society of informed and free citizens promised by Renaissance thinkers demands seeing for oneself, and this, precisely, is what images seemed to offer: Campanella sought an *orbis pictus*, a world of images, or, more exactly, an imaged world that would no longer keep any secrets from viewers but would be self-evident. The architecture of the *City of the Sun* is thus an architecture of insight, and the images on its walls herald a complete and immediate view onto the world.

Campanella's *orbis pictus* seems strangely familiar today, in a time subject to a general visual imperative. Images, to be sure, have long come off the walls and the vertical to adopt all other places and formats as well. There is hardly a domain in which we do not notice an exponential increase in images: in science and education, in politics, the economy, law, and media, but also in quotidian practices and processes, we notice an ever stronger push toward visualization. Even in Campanella's day, the production of images was still reserved for specific corporations: to wield the brush, one had first to seek admission to the painters' guild. And it was not that long ago that to have one's picture taken, one went to see the photographer. Today, the democratization of image technologies turns everyone into a potential image expert.

That we are familiar with images, however, does not yet mean that we understand how they work. Nor do we need to, just as we do not need to understand how a car functions in order to drive it. Although we produce, consume, and reproduce images on a daily basis, we would hardly be able to describe their functioning in detail if asked to do so. While we do have an intuitive understanding of what counts as an image for us, we would be hard-pressed to name what exactly it is that makes images images. The sheer ubiquitous presence of images in our everyday world should make us all image experts, but instead, this ubiquity seems to be inversely proportionate to our grasp of what images are.

What is an image? The question leaves us at a loss. It seems to be as tricky as the problem Augustine confronted in trying to define what, exactly, time is. Augustine's answer, then, holds for the image as well: "If no one asks me, I know what it is. If I wish to explain it to him who asks me, I do not know."[2] For a long time, however, the very possibility to ask what an image is was far from self-understood. Just how recent the concern with the image is, at least in academia, is evident in the fact that it was only at the beginning of the 1990s that theorists, independently of each other, first spoke of a "pictorial turn" (W. J. T. Mitchell) or an "iconic turn" (Gottfried Boehm).[3] Moreover, the status of this turn toward the image remains peculiarly unstable: its proclamation did not specify whether it was meant to describe the situation or articulate a wish. The pictorial or iconic turn, which set out to take over from the linguistic turn that had dominated the social sciences and humanities in the twentieth century, seemed to do the exact inverse of the preceding paradigm. While the turn toward analyzing the linguistic-grammatical constitution of our access to the world had already taken place around 1900, it was not conceptualized as such until the 1960s (most prominently in the anthology *The Linguistic Turn*, edited by Richard Rorty). In the case of the pictorial or iconic turn, while the description was quickly given, the reality it was meant to capture was longer in coming.

Nonetheless, much has fortunately happened since the pictorial turn was first proclaimed some thirty years ago. While in the Anglo-American context, new research fields such as visual studies emerged, in Europe—and primarily in the German-speaking countries—the so-called *Bildwissenschaften* or image studies developed. What was at stake here, on the model of earlier formations of disciplines (of, say, sociology as the science of the social or psychology as a scientific exploration of the soul), was nothing short of establishing a new—albeit interdisciplinary—study of what images are, of how they produce meaning, and of how social practices are thereby reflected. Even where no one saw any need for founding a new discipline, the effects of a paradigm shift within the existing canon of disciplines gradually became manifest. From visual ethnography via political science to reflection in historical studies on images as historical sources, from film anthropology via historical epistemology to research on medical imagineering, in recent years few disciplines have not undergone a process of reflecting on what they owe to images. Philosophy, too, has not remained untouched by this and has increasingly confronted the paradox that in its history, philosophy has again and again taken recourse to images but at the same time has been shaped by an ambivalent relationship toward images that often turned into a downright iconophobia (more on that in a moment). Not even art history is an exception here: although the analysis of images is one of its core tasks, it has rarely—at least in the eyes of its critics in image studies, whose founders often started out as art historians—addressed the pictoriality of images. There is thus, generally, little reflection on the use made of visual media, even among those who have made the exploration of visuality their goal. Images primarily remain purveyors of information through which we look at something else but which do not deserve to be looked at in their own right. As supposedly transparent media, they are usually overlooked.

This book is conceived as a phenomenology of the way we deal with visual media and as a rehabilitation of images as irreplaceable agents of our everyday opening up of world. Images present things to us that would otherwise not be accessible to us. They endow with visibility states of affairs we would have passed over without them. Images bring back what has been forgotten, they provide orientation, they succinctly present otherwise impenetrable correlations, and they allow for anticipating what is yet to come. What shows itself in images, shows itself in such and in no other way. Iconic sense, in other words, cannot be translated into other dialects of sense (into a verbal description, for example) without losing something because images feature an iconic excess that is genuinely visible or phenomenal. If this supposition is correct, then we need an alternative to the approach that has so often been taken when it came to defining images: we need an alternative to the representational approach.

Indeed, images have often been measured by how much they represent other existing things or facts and by how reliable and truthful these representations are. The representational model is partly responsible for the traditional subordination of the image. On the one hand, it reduces being an image to being a copy insofar as pictorial representations only ever represent, after the fact, something that already exists independently of the image. On the other, it subordinates pictorial forms of expression to verbal forms of expression insofar as it takes propositional statements to be the standard of truthful reference (an image is then as truthful as a proposition that reliably conveys a state of affairs).

This book sets out to take a different approach that draws on the methodological resources of phenomenology and deploys the basic category of phenomenality in an alternative analysis of images and their operations. Whereas the representational approach is primarily concerned with the question of what the represented image content consists in, a phenomenological approach begins with the question of how something presents itself in images. This shift of emphasis, of course, has immediate consequences: aspects of referentiality and aboutness are initially bracketed, and priority is given to an analysis of how something appears in a given instance.

A picture is worth a thousand words—this proverb gives expression to a conviction that remains to be justified. What exactly does images' persuasive power consist in? If it is correct to suppose that images produce significance differently from how verbal language does and that, in images, a sense appears that has no propositional equivalent, then an image is not just one phenomenon among many. Since Edmund Husserl, phenomenological analysis has consisted in, first of all, describing things as they show themselves, as phenomena. Yet if the specificity of iconic sense is that sense here shows itself differently (namely, in visual form), then we are evidently dealing here with quite a special phenomenon, with an appearance whose sense constitutively depends on its being an appearance. Whereas a proposition that is uttered can be repeated by another speaker without there being a change in its propositional content, a slight change in just one pictorial parameter (color values, light values, format, mirroring,. . .) already suffices to have us deal with a second, a different image. Put succinctly: images are appearances that in their appearing are crucially concerned with their very appearing. Against this foil, this book advocates a phenomenological approach in the analysis of pictoriality.

There is, moreover, a second characteristic that comes up immediately. Images are not only particularly useful for understanding what it means to appear. Images are also virtuoso presentations of the relationship between appearances and their media. For, strictly speaking, images are not phenomena but rather media in which something else appears; they do not themselves appear but in them show something other than what they are. While the first characteristic of images thus has to do with their constitutive phenomenal suchness, the second characteristic reminds us of their being conditioned by media and thus of the fact that, in this case, visibility is due to our looking through media. Much of this book is concerned with this problem of seeing through but also with the logic of this "through," which it understands to be not only spatial but also operative, that is, generative. The history of pictorial media offers a series of examples that show that we do not just see through visual media without obstacle—as through an open window—but that these media participate in producing the visible in the first place, such that we see not so much despite but thanks to their particular makeup; perception happens on the material, in the patterns, grain, color spots, or pigments; pictorial media refer beyond themselves only by strictly limiting themselves to their immanence. Seeing takes place not beyond the image but in the image, even if we also see more than what is visible in the moment.

Reconstructing the logic of iconic seeing through also means taking an alternative approach to media processes that differs from that of orthodox media theory. From that perspective, this book is also a contribution to reflections on media studies. It is generally taken for granted that, historically, reflection about media is due primarily to the rise of mass media, and the paladins of media studies indeed almost exclusively issue from among theorists of mass communication, from Walter Benjamin and Bertolt Brecht to Marshall McLuhan or Jean Baudrillard. Yet that, of course, also implies granting an outsize role in the definition of media logics to one particular kind of media: to discretizing media, and thus to media whose mode of functioning consists in disassembling, transporting, and reassembling any conceivable content. The medium here is being turned into a channel that transmits the message all the more reliably the less friction there is and the less the final message shows through which channels it reached the end user. This is the foundation of the famous thesis of the transparency of the medium—duly enshrined in the media theory creed. The fact that images, too, are taken apart, stored, and transmitted, that indeed there are such things as digitization techniques for images, does not change anything about this other fact: there are no digital images. Data masses become images only when they are brought into an internally consistent pictorial appearance for receptors capable of perception.

Unlike discrete media, pictorial media are replete media, that is, media in which every phenomenal difference makes a difference. Unlike discrete media, which serve their purpose all the more efficiently the less the alphabet of signs used to encode the content bears any relation to that content, replete media as a matter of principle make it very difficult to draw a line between meaningless sign support and meaningful appearance. There is no change, in principle, in the content of a text message when it is transmitted via a telegram service, via electronic impulses or Morse code rather than in a letter, when it is displayed via LEDs or in ink; at issue here is the message itself, not reproductions of the message. Not at all so for images, where every display feature, such as size, orientation, color hues, distances, gaps, facture, and so on, could in principle be constitutive of meaning and in any case cannot be subjected to any standardized coding procedure applicable to all images.

These short indications, which I will spell out in the last part of the book especially, by no means aim at isolating some kind of iconic essence or anything else of that sort. They rather seek to show how media theory's historical bias toward discrete media has marginalized other media logics. The conceptual couple of transparency and noise that media studies inherited from the beginnings of communication studies in engineering is still being applied to pictorial procedures without considering that images are not more or less transparent tubes but possess a material density of their own that endows them, in the first place, with the visual power of letting something become visible that does not exist behind them but (if it exists at all) somewhere else entirely. Nor do I mean to suggest that there is something like an essence of replete media. Repleteness, rather, is the result of a densification; media setups bring together and condense things that lie apart, displaying them succinctly and concisely. This is not the least of reasons for the often striking character of images.

Yet it is this very strikingness that has prompted sustained epistemological skepticism concerning images in philosophy. Such skepticism cannot be disentangled by a certain distrust toward what can be seen by the "corporeal eyes" as opposed to the "eyes of the mind." Although profoundly visual in its metaphors, the European semantics of knowledge persists in a suspicion toward anything that originates from the bodily senses, which leads to a strange divorce between the logical insight and its subordinate graphical representations. Martin Jay's provocative diagnosis of a "denigration of vision" in twentieth-century philosophy, even among some of the supposedly most "body-friendly" thinkers, is thus to be reassessed against a broader and older metaphysical backdrop.[4] As I show in the first chapter, the very search of philosophy for its own identity cannot be disentangled from a struggle with and against images. In a sense, much of Plato's battle against the Sophists is an attempt to locate the trickeries of the image on the side of sophistry, reserving the sturdiness of the *logos* for true philosophy. The statement that Plato dismissed images hardly fathoms what is happening in this historical moment where philosophy consolidates as an organized and self-conscious discipline: we would be hard pressed to find anyone who grants images a greater (albeit negative) power than Plato himself. His attempts to circumscribe, quarantine, and ultimately expel the dangerous images from the Republic only hint at the outrageous credit he grants them.

The reservation the philosophical tradition has voiced since its beginnings is that images overpower the senses instead of convincing the understanding. Images are fundamentally "a-logon," as Plato's Socrates puts it, that is, they show up without giving their reasons (*logoi*) and therefore lead us down the path of the illogical and the irrational. Over the course of history, this skepticism has sometimes turned into unabashed iconoclasm, from the Byzantine iconoclasm through the image wars of the Reformation. Just as Plato denounced the emptiness of the simulacra, the religious iconoclasts warned against yielding to the powers of the idols. Hence this paradox: those who insist that the idols are nothing but dull, stubborn presences lacking any force of their own are also the ones who seem most convinced that their allure must be warded off. "They have mouths but cannot speak, they have eyes but cannot see"—it is impossible not to detect in the Psalmist's conjuring verses a fear that the supposedly toothless images might have agency after all.[5] From antiquity through the twentieth century, the ban on images was given many reasons, but most of these were proclaimed to accord with reason itself. In the heyday of Enlightenment, Immanuel Kant claimed that "the most sublime of all laws" is the biblical prohibition of images.[6] Such almost religious undertones echo in the critique of the iconic all the way through the twentieth century, for instance in Adorno's demand to uphold the prohibition of representation pronounced in the Jewish scriptures.

Another strong motivation of the criticism of images comes from a tradition deeply rooted in epistemology that trusts only discursive sources of knowledge. In this respect, images have usually been denied the capacity to provide any reliable knowledge at all. "A picture held us captive," we read in Wittgenstein.[7] Although he can hardly be suspected of hostility toward images, even Wittgenstein still gives voice to the philosophical inclination to distrust the obviousness of images and to seek clarity on the side of concepts instead. The logocentrism shaping metaphysics and epistemology well into the twentieth century may serve to explain why philosophy has had such a hard time with images for so long. Moreover, the critique of logocentrism such as it emerged, for example, in the tradition of deconstruction by no means entailed a rehabilitation of iconic knowledge. Quite the contrary: even in Derrida, images are still very much suspected of catering to a metaphysics of presence and thus of immediate and comprehensive intuition.

This book takes a long detour via the history of philosophy, and the first part in particular discusses theories of visuality and mediality from the Presocratics to the Renaissance. This is due to the conviction that it would be naive to present a new theory of pictoriality without thinking about the origin of the conceptual tools employed in such an endeavor. In this regard, materialist, hermeneutic, and finally deconstructive criticisms of phenomenology have made an important point: bracketing questions of causality and provenance must not mean the absence of reflection on the provenance of one's own categories (and on their metaphysical, technical, or metaphorical baggage). The genealogical readings that decipher some of contemporary image theory's basic conceptions through the contexts in which they emerge, however, do not merely bring out the normative framings within which debates are conducted; they also discover neglected resources for alternative narratives. This implies, for example, showing in what sense media theory does not begin only in the twentieth century but in Greek philosophy and begins precisely where the concern is with reflecting on the elementary media of perception; or showing that modern image theory unfolds guided by a conceptual couple—transparency and opacity—that initially did not refer to images at all but was developed in medieval Scholasticism to come to grips with Aristotle's groundbreaking theory of the medium of sight—the diaphanous.

This book aims to trace the rhizomatic ramifications of the philosophical discourse on images in the varied layers of forms of thought, including where thinking in images is not yet called philosophy, for example, in theological textbooks, artists' manifestos, or descriptions of experimental setups. Such an archaeological recovery unearths recurrent patterns that have guided—and, most often surreptitiously, continue to guide—these approaches. Beyond a kind of immutable infrastructuralism, but also beyond an unflappable teleological narrative of progress, a crossing of *archaeology* (which describes the epochal layering of orders of knowledge) and *genealogy* (which traces diachronic lines of development, historical processes of formation, and the conflicts about their interpretation that ensue) brings out a different structuring of the history of ideas, one that resembles less the temporality of "turns" in the humanities than it does the slowness of a geological *longue durée*.

In this sense, then, the history this book seeks to begin to write would be the history of a double and, as a look at the Western view of images reveals, dominant paradigm. Where they are not simply banned from the regime of knowledge, images are put to epistemic use and distributed among the two orders this taxonomy provides for, the order of things and the order of signs. Images are legitimized either when, just like windows, they open up the view onto the meaning behind them (*transparency paradigm*) or when, as opaque, smooth objects, they reflect back onto whomever or whatever stands in front of them (*opacity paradigm*). Yet this double paradigm of "transparency" and "opacity," which Arthur C. Danto developed to describe images in modernity, does not begin there. Rather, it constitutes the double guiding thread that has oriented speculation about images for more than two thousand years now.

The goal of this book is threefold:

(a) More often than not, the process by which modernity claims to have rendered the image autonomous, to have endowed it with a valence of its own, unfolded along the very paths that had once served to disavow iconicity. As we will see, such attempts at autonomizing invoke either the immaterial sense to which images give access or the immanent self-enclosure of things. The book thus reconstructs the *historical trajectories of these paradigms of transparency and opacity as well as their consequences for incorporating the image into the orders of knowledge*. Both, however, avoid the *skandalon* that triggered reflections on images in the first place: the fact that images are, first of all and above all, *appearances*. Where the question of images becomes virulent in Greek thought, it is anything but a regional problem. It is the touchstone for the possibility of philosophy in general. To the extent that in the Greek world the question of images cannot be separated from phenomenality, it points in the direction of phenomenologizing the iconic.

(b) If phenomenality is to be not just an image-theoretical appendix but the starting point of the reflection on images, it is necessary no longer to think phenomenality from the perspective of images but instead to think iconicity from the perspective of what it means for something to appear. To do so, this study takes a detour via philosophies that do not immediately present themselves as philosophies of the image. It begins with those that consider images to be a particular (that is, framed, limited, succinct) kind of appearance. The radical reflection on structures of appearance such as we find in the phenomenological tradition instituted by Edmund Husserl has a precursor in Greek philosophy and in Aristotle's theory of the soul in particular. Such a historical detour follows Hegel's suggestion to reread Aristotle's treatise *On the Soul* on the basis of a modern philosophy of experience, thereby undoing the effects of centuries of scholastic superimpositions.[8] This phenomenologically informed rereading serves to demonstrate the second point I would like to make in this book: *phenomenal and propositional structures are not subject to the same laws and cannot be reduced one to the other*. Moreover, rethinking phenomenality as something that cannot subsumed under the same categories as propositionality also amounts, in the long run, to opening up the perspectives of a different, a phenomenological, theory of images whose potential remains concealed in the constellations of our contemporary thinking of images. In turn, a revaluation of Husserl's phenomenology with respect to what it might contribute to a philosophical theory of images evidently generates new impulses for understanding Husserl's thought as well.

(c) Husserl's phenomenology is marked by an obvious logical primacy of the *constitutum* over the *constituens*, of what is constituted over what constitutes it, even if Husserl's thought itself traces some lines of flight for overcoming this primacy. Crossing Aristotle's aisthetics with Husserl's theory of appearance not only allows us to decipher the former with the help of the latter; the latter, too, can be revised in surprising ways in light of what came earlier. Going back to Aristotle's theory of the *diaphanous* medium, which explains why the addressee of appearances cannot simultaneously be their author, allows for counteracting the egological tendency of Husserlian phenomenology and for transforming it into a "diaphenomenology." Thus reformulated, it not only accounts for the coconstitutive role of media *through* which something can come to appear at all but also brings out the fundamentally *heteronomous* character of mediality. This transformation of phenomenology from an egological-transcendental into a *medial* phenomenology also traces the third dimension this book seeks to unearth: *there is no pure appearance; every appearing appears through something that inevitably shines through in what it brings to appearance.*

The book's triple movement is spelled out in detail in five independent studies, each subdivided into ten sub chapters, that can also be read separately.

(1) *An inquiry into philosophy's iconophobia* (chapter 1). Starting off with Plato, this study deals with philosophy's deeply rooted ambivalence toward images and finds the source of its age-old denigration of the iconic to lie in its distrust of the most sublime of all image-makers, the Sophists. To confront the spectacular, ever-moving nature of images, which are incapable of providing reasons (*logoi*) for their visual claims, Greek philosophy in the fourth century BCE begins to construct a metaphysical watershed of lasting consequence: whatever appears either is in and of itself or is dependent on something else. This inaugurates the ontological alternative of things and signs, an exclusive alternative into which images, given their phenomenal excess, never properly fit.

(2) *A reconstruction of Aristotle's media theory* (chapter 2). This part offers a systematic reconstruction of this first philosophical explanation of what a medium is, in which Aristotle closely associates mediality and phenomenality.

Significantly, the kind of medium Aristotle has in mind is that of perception. According to him, perception takes places within certain surrounding elements (air, water, fire, etc.). These elements function as perceptual media: it is through them that the sensible objects are apprehended. As a result, visibility is not a given but requires mediation through the elements. These perceptual media are far from being transparent windowpanes but have a texture of their own. Aristotle thinks of the perceptual medium (*metaxy*) as something endowed with a certain plasticity, which turns it into a receiver of forms: water or air have the capacity to take on a certain form without taking on its matter and to transmit it to the eye. Whatever appears (*phainesthai*) in sense perception appears through (*dia*) something else that, in turn, does not itself appear but lets something else appear instead, and it is in this context that Aristotle coins the neologism *to diaphanēs*, the diaphanous. The diaphaneity of experience thus harks back to a basic condition of elemental media.

(3) *A history of readings of the diaphanous as a history of forgetting the medium of appearances* (chapter 3). Posterity has rarely appreciated Aristotle's pathbreaking description of the medial process for what it is and neglected it in favor of other aspects of his philosophy. This part of the book is concerned with bringing together the rare occasions in late antiquity and the Middle Ages when his theory is being discussed and also, above all, with asking why so basic an insight had to wait for so long to be taken up in a sustained manner. What Aristotle sees as a problem of media logic is separated out into optical, physiological, and physical laws. Beginning in the High Middle Ages, however, there is also a moralization of the aspects of transparency and intransparency, which indirectly contributes to aesthetic discourse in the Renaissance as well. The chapter brings the media- and image-theoretical discourses together and explains why, polarized around the notions of transparency and opacity, the modern discourse about images increasingly marginalizes the dimension of appearance.

(4) *An analysis of the place of images in phenomenology* (chapter 4). This part articulates the major breakthroughs of classic phenomenology with a view to a phenomenology of pictorial experience for today and asks what it means to think images starting from their appearing. In Husserl's and Jean-Paul Sartre's reflections on image consciousness—as Eugen Fink's or Maurice Merleau-Ponty's objections show—we always already find the trace of the medium. Readers solely interested in the positions and arguments of phenomenology concerning the problem of the image can read this part separately.

(5) The book concludes with a sketch of *a diaphenomenology of images* and an outline of *an iconic symptomatology* (chapter 5). What do I mean by this? If the thesis is correct that replete media are such that their content is relatively

difficult to isolate and decontextualize, then a phenomenology of visual media obviously requires discernment. There can be no general rule to go about detaching the content presented in a given image appearance safely from the support medium. In artifacts in which every mark and every difference counts as a matter of principle, we must look carefully; the art of looking at images is thus always occasional and refuses generalization. When are we dealing with an image? What distinguishes images? The book's final chapter dismisses the thesis according to which there would be a closed ontological class of images that could be determined by necessary and sufficient conditions. Instead, it suggests a methodological alternative. On the model of Nelson Goodman's shift away from the ontological question, *What is art?*, toward asking about its symptoms, this part elaborates a number of characteristic traits of the iconic to be obtained from a phenomenological analysis.

A diaphenomenological approach to images then amounts to taking images' immanent phenomenal qualities seriously and, at the same time, considering the heteronomy of this appearing. Replacing the traditional representational approach with one that stresses the *presentational* aspect of pictorial media also means that pictorial appearances never appear by themselves; that, visible on their surface, there is always already something other than them. Presence then is less synonymous with living presentness than it is the result of a preceding presentation. Always already breaking onto the image surface is something other than what is currently the case, and this expresses the extent to which visual media—like all other media—are fundamentally heteronomous and have always already begun elsewhere. Inversely, however, images are not just transitory moments, not permeable window openings or stainless looking glasses to be passed through unscathed. They are diaphanous things with a pictorial plane through which the medium still shines, and they impress a sometimes more, sometimes less obtrusive watermark on the visibilities they provide for their viewers.

One final remark, on the insertion of images at ten points across the volume. They are intended to function as a form of paratext in the margins. Much like medieval book illuminations, they entertain a relationship with what is being said but resist any attempt at completely incorporating them into the linearity of discourse.

I

Between Thing and Sign

The Hubris of the Image

There is a twofold movement of the mind towards an image: one indeed towards the image itself as a certain thing; another, towards the image in so far as it is the image of something else.

—Thomas Aquinas, *Summa Theologiae*

1. THE ATOPIC CHARACTER OF IMAGES

What philosophy is, a commonplace holds, is apparent less in the content of the answer than in the form of the question. Unlike questions of an instrumental or practical kind, which define the meaning of things with respect to the use we make of them, philosophy's questions, as Socrates relentlessly insists, have to fit the mold of the question, *What is x?* This is also true when we ask about the nature of the image. If we asked someone what an image is, they would probably answer something like *paintings, drawings, photographs, sketches*, perhaps also *diagrams, pictograms*, or *symbols*. Some might also count *mirror images, shadow images*, or *metaphorical images* as members of the image family, if only because of the linguistic proximity. This question, the question of the semantic extent of the concept of the image, is the one the visitor poses to Theaetetus in Plato's *Sophist*, when he asks him to explain "what in the world we mean by image." Theaetetus then lists several examples: "images in water and mirrors, and also images that are drawn and stamped and everything else like that." The visitor, however, playing the role of the inquisitive Socrates, rejects such an answer. Theaetetus, he says, has given examples of images but failed to pinpoint what all of these share.[1] As in Plato's early protreptic dialogs, the interlocutor is supposed to attain the insight that philosophy is characterized less by the specific *content* of its questions than by the form they take, by the *ti esti*, the question, *What is x?*

Yet such a didactic training in dialectics is not what this passage is really concerned with. The *ti esti* does not simply delineate philosophy from everyday opinion. At stake in the question whether such a delineation is possible, in the fight against the Sophists, is philosophy's very right to exist. Theaetetus's examples, the visitor replies, are obviously just different forms of images. The Sophist reveals himself to be a strange creature who, refusing to acknowledge what is evident, will "seem to you to have his eyes shut, or else not have any eyes at all." To deal with the Sophist, it is necessary to leave the terrain of commonplaces and of what meets the eye (*opsis*). The battle can be waged only on the ground of the logos, *ek tōn logōn*. In all the different things Theaetetus has called "by the one name," there must, the interlocutors finally agree, nonetheless be something that is "one," *hōs hen on*.[2] Finding a common term would prove the Sophist to have contradicted himself: where the Sophist purports to defend irreconcilable *logoi*, he is in fact, by virtue of employing the logos, referring to *something specific*.

The Sophist thus for the first time explicitly articulates a principle engrained in Western philosophy since its very beginnings: all saying (*legein*) is always *saying something* (*legein ti*), all speech is speech about "something," about a *tinos*.[3] The transitive something is at first specified in one respect only, namely, insofar as it is *one* something: "a person who says *something* has to be saying some *one* thing."[4] If not at least *one* thing were said (so the conclusion, which Aristotle will repeat), it would not be possible to speak insofar as not saying one thing is tantamount to not saying.[5]

The question of how consistent this concept of unity can be, however, is not settled here. Plato recalls that for Parmenides, all speech refers not only to a specific one thing but to the *only* one, to that Being, that is, beyond which there can be nothing and beyond which, accordingly, nothing can be said. It is therefore entirely "impossible to say, speak, or think *that which is not* itself correctly by itself." Rather, it is "unthinkable, unsayable, unutterable, and unformulable in speech."[6] As the dialog continues, Plato, in his confrontation with the Sophists, finds himself obliged to take recourse to Parmenides's notion of the *One*, which, however, he has to liberate from its equation with Being.

As the exchange goes on, the twofold tactical goal of the dialog becomes evident. Against the background of Eleatic doctrines, with which the visitor's views accord at least in the beginning, the aim is to bring to light two silent prejudgments of the Sophist school: on the one hand, the sophist procedure presupposes, despite all assurances to the contrary, a certain concept of unity; on the other, it silently presupposes, despite—or perhaps because of—the antagonism with the Eleatic school, the latter's basic supposition that the relationship between being and not-being is a relationship of opposition (*enantiōsis*). Protagoras's claim to be able, in all matters, to defend thesis and antithesis alike, however, implicitly presupposes an (at least "focal") unity of the matter at hand that serves as the touchstone of the opposition of thesis and antithesis in the first place.[7] Protagoras's claim thus consists not only in asserting opposites but also in being able to give reasons for why and to what extent something simultaneously "is" and "is not." While this claim, unlike the claims of the Eleatics, integrates not-being into the domain of what can be said, it nonetheless leaves one of the Eleatics' fundamental maxims intact, even elevates it by making it the warrant of successful sophistic proof: the antinomy of being and not-being. If being and not-being make opposing but nonetheless equivalent claims to truth, there is no place left for deception and no concept for images. Plato's daring way of securing the manifold for philosophy while simultaneously salvaging the truth criterion with respect to the One is made possible, as the continuation of the dialog bears out, by his reintegration into philosophy of what Parmenides had banished from it: appearance.

Here, if anywhere in *The Sophist*, we find the bottleneck between Sophist and Eleatic doctrines through which Plato seeks to guide philosophy. The static juxtaposition of being and not-being posited by Parmenides and cashed out in turn by the Sophists is to be softened, their reciprocal dependencies spelled out. *The Sophist* brings to a head the discovery of the early dialogs (the so-called elenchtical, that is, refutational dialogs), namely, that the Sophists pretend there to be an opposition where there is only a difference. There is thus no opposition—to use Plato's example—in Sophroniscus being both father and not-father at the same time since, in relation to his son, Socrates, he is a father, yet in relation to everyone else, he is not.[8] *Not being a father is no mere not-being but simply another kind of being.* This already constitutes a more precise conception of Parmenides's proposition. While it is indeed impossible to "say . . . that which is not itself by itself,"[9] it can be predicated when referred to another entity (*pros alla*), as a negation, for example. As it turns out, the definition of the concept of the image that follows not only is more coherent than has sometimes been alleged;[10] it also, for Plato, has another, articulatory function to avoid that his differential scalar ontology comes unhinged.

Jean-Pierre Vernant, in a famous article, argues that in the Greek world, between the seventh and fourth century BCE, the concept of the image undergoes a shift from a presentification of the invisible to an imitation of appearance.[11] On the view I am about to present, however, what emerges is less a new concept of the image oriented toward appearance than an intellectualized concept of the image that nonetheless can itself be considered a theoretical response to the insight that all images are determined by appearance.

In fact, the new word that gains currency in Plato's day is not *eidōlon*, which has to do with the *appearance* of images, but *eikōn*, which describes an inner essential relationship. *Eikōn*, of which there is no record prior to the fifth century,[12] derives from a different root than *eidos* and *eidōlon*. These latter are formed from the Indo-Germanic paradigm *ϝeid* or *id-*, which indicates an originary indistinction of seeing and knowing. Those who have seen may consider themselves to be in possession of knowledge.[13] In this context, the Greek world develops a rich metaphorics of evidence: from *idein* (to see) via *eidenai* (to distinguish, to know) to *eidos* and *idea* (aspect, shape, form).[14] While seeing, on the one hand, is tied in with a semantics of knowing insight, the root of *idein*, on the other hand, also entails an entire field of meanings that designates semblance, the merely probable, or even the deceptive. The deficient character of the *eidōlon* as image or semblance is already apparent in the negative diminutive suffix, which subordinates the *eid-ōlon* to the *eidos* as a lesser stage.

The *eikōn*, which Plato mobilizes in the course of the *Sophist* and delineates from the *eidōlon*, is distinct from the register of visual externality. It differs, first, in that it is formed from the paradigm *ϝeik* and thereby suggests an inner coherence (for example, in *epieikeia*, moral decorum). The accordance of an *eikōn*, which produces a likeness with its model, lies less in visual similarity than in its possessing the model's essential properties and, in that respect, lies in a similarity of essence. In that it has something of the model, it *is* something of the model, albeit not the model itself but only something similar to it. How, then, can we distinguish between something that only *seems to be* similar and something that actually *is* similar?

In demarcating true philosophy from Sophistic practices and earlier Eleatic doctrines, which each in their way absolutize not-being, Plato elevates the image and the problem of similarity it raises by making it the touchstone of the philosophical question, *What is . . . ?* For unlike Parmenides, Plato in the *Sophist* is not concerned with the question *whether* an image is but *what* it is. Putting the question this way might seem like entering into a circular argument from the outset. For if speech always implies a something spoken *about*, a *kata tinos*, it must necessarily be admitted that this one something already displays a degree of being (however minimal). To ask *what* an image is thus simultaneously postulates that the image "somehow" (*pou*) *is*—a presupposition the Eleatics, of course, cannot accept. Yet Plato cleverly reverses this possible reproach of a fallacious *petitio principii* and aims it at the Eleatics themselves: the very moment that something is said about not-being (and be it only that it is not), this some-thing in a certain respect already *is*. Insofar as any speech is always speech "about something," and insofar as this "something" (*ti*) presupposes that speech is referred to a being-such, speech has meaning only to the extent that it presup-poses something identical, which this being-such turns into an entity. Yet dem-onstrating this ontological thesis at the basis of all predication is aimed not only at the Eleatics. It also aims at ending the Sophistic game of mirrors that was supposed to prove the image to be a nonentity. That the image of a thing is not *the thing itself* remains uncontested: it has merely been "made similar to" the real thing.[15] The image, strictly speaking, is thus a nonentity not *in itself* but with respect to the thing it depicts.

In the attempt to soften the rigid opposition of being and not-being, the example of the image serves as an experimental object and the category of simi-larity as a solvent (*lysis*): what is merely "like" cannot be "identical." Yet this is only one aspect. For while, on the one hand, the image does not coincide with the thing (and, in that respect, is to be considered a "nonentity" [*ouk ontōs*]), on the other hand, it also *is*, namely, insofar as it is *an image* (*eikōn ontōs*). The inter-locutors realize they find themselves in a paradoxical situation, facing the conundrum that the image, on the one hand, is "that which is like" and hence "not really that which is" (*ouk on ontōs*), while, on the other, it is "somehow," if not entirely, an entity.[16] The image thus oscillates between being and not-being; it therefore is, in Plato's words, well and truly *atopon*.[17]

Plato here alludes to the double meaning of *atopos*: something is said to be "atopical" when it cannot be unambiguously located. In its figurative sense, the expression names all ambiguous or "paradoxical" phenomena.[18] The Sophist, the visitor continues, perfectly knows how to exploit the atopical character of images for his ends. A master of semblance, he produces brilliant deceptions that make him appear "many-headed," deceptive images from which he has long with-drawn by the time one tries to pin him down in them.[19] The Sophist's goal, in the visitor's interpretation, is to make what is untrue pass for what really exists by rendering us incapable, through the variety of appearances, of separating the wheat from the chaff. Plato's dialog has thus been correctly interpreted as a jux-taposition of, on the one hand, the Sophists as proponents of plurality and, on the other, the visitor as advocate of the Eleatic doctrine of the unity and homo-geneity of being.[20]

There is much to suggest that Plato saw the Sophists as Protean quick-change artists who pretend to have knowledge and appear to be "many-headed" because they have "woven" images together in such a way as "to force us to agree unwill-ingly that that which is not in a way is."[21] It would be hasty, though, to simply attribute Plato's own view to the words of the visitor, not to mention that it underestimates Plato's sophistication in the register of dramatic dialectics. When we pay close attention to his exact choice of words, we may indeed come to see an interpretation of the Sophist point of view that does not coincide with the Eleatics' view of multiplicity. The term *epallaxis*, which can mean "alternation," "crisscrossing," "dovetailing," or "interlacing,"[22] suggests not that what Plato has in mind here is a constant switching of positions but rather that there are, strictly speaking, only two possible positions that, moreover, stand in a relation of symmetry (*ep-allēlon*). In the early sixteenth century, Stephanus renders the term—which in Homer designates the swinging back and forth of the "cords of mighty strife" or "rope of hard conflict" and thus of the fortunes of war—as *alternatio*.[23] Although, in fact, there are only ever two mutually exclusive positions possible, *epallaxis* displays a dizzying speed.[24]

What is unsettling about the Sophist is that he does not simply move from one position to another but, thanks to his agility, permanently switches between incompossible positions. The hunt for the Sophist turns out to be so difficult only because he does not move, like all other animals, from one pasture to the next but instead is capable of assuming, without effort or movement, it seems, two opposing positions. Whenever it looks as if he has been tracked down, he is no longer where he claims to be. It will not suffice to aim for him where he pretends to take position; if he is to be taken down once and for all, his change of position must be tracked and his exact location on the path between two positions determined. To pin the Sophist down, his "atopic place" or "difficult region" must be found out,[25] and this place, it turns out, consists in none other than the "atopical" images behind which he conceals himself and which he employs. Yet where are images located? In the realm of truth, the Sophist responds, a realm, however, that is no longer based on common ground.[26] In making the image pass for something that is both nonuniform and nondeficient, the Sophist comes to make the peculiar claim that the image belongs simultaneously both to mere not-being and to pure being. This amounts to claiming, in opposition to Eleatic doctrine, that it is possible to stand on both sides of the ontological watershed. The watershed itself, however, is never questioned.

The dialectic juxtaposition of Eleatic and Sophist doctrines not only brings out the argumentative framework they both share; the framework itself begins to sway dangerously. The conflict with the Sophist, as Plato significantly has the visitor say, "force[s] us to agree unwillingly that that which is not in a way is."[27] On the face of it, this sentence expresses the breach the Sophist has opened in the dam of the Eleatic doctrine of the exclusiveness and unity of being. A closer look, however, sees in the "somehow" an indication of Plato's gradational ontology: *the measure of the being of the image is the entity it depicts.* By the measure of the depicted, the image is shown to be *other* without, for all that, already being *the other* of the depicted. The logic of the "somehow" calls for a more precise definition of this otherness, which does not go as far as opposition (*enantiōsis*) but must rather be a kind of *difference* (*heteroiōsis*) such as it is introduced in Theaetetus's first definition.

2. MIMESIS AND METHEXIS: DESCENDING AND ASCENDING ONTOLOGICAL DEPENDENCE

In Theaetetus's first definition, where each word is significant, the image is "something that's made similar [*aphomoiōmenon*] to a true thing [*pros talēthinón*] and is another thing [*heteron toiouton*] that's like it."[28] The visitor, in repeating this definition—"You're saying it's another true thing like it?"[29]—significantly leaves out *aphomoiōmenon*, "made similar," for which there can be no place in an antithetic logic. Theaetetus, however, does not let the visitor get away with this abbreviation and insists on the characteristic similarity (*eoikós*) of the image.[30] Now, the *aphomoiōmenon* concept Theaetetus employs contains two opposing movements: while the negative prefix *ap-* indicates the image moving away from what it depicts (drawing always implies drawing away, as it were), the *homoiōmenon* indicates a moving toward the depicted in the mode of becoming similar (*homoiōsis*). While the image is similar to what is, it is necessarily already other (*heteron*) *without* already being *the other of the depicted* (*to heteron*) and thereby merely not being.

Such passages not only make G. W. F. Hegel's condemnation of Platonic logic seem odd, they practically anticipate Hegel's own logic: the negativity of the image proves that there is nothing "which is not itself . . . by itself"[31]—that is, in Hegelian parlance, "in and for itself"—but only ever a *specific* not-being that refers to something that is. This also resolves the apparent aporia the visitor claims to discern in speaking about images. The fact that it is not possible to speak of images in and for themselves because they are different from what is does not mean that they are in themselves "unthinkable, unsayable, unutterable, and unformulable." What is true of speech is true of images as well: their reference to an object is constitutively inscribed in them. Just as all speech is always speech *about* something that is (however minimal the definition of this entity may be), so images stand in a specific relation to the depicted object, a relation that presupposes both a separating distance and a shared relationship. When we speak of images as "somehow" being, then, we do not contradict ourselves, as the visitor thinks.[32] But we must be able to say *in what respect* images "somehow" are. The proof that this not-being *is* does not suffice; we must show *how* exactly it is. In other words, we must disentangle the interlocking (*symplokē*) of being and not-being. Images thus turn out to be not a marginal topic in Plato's gradational ontology but literally its fulcrum. The constitutive deficit of the iconic allows us to see another, a differential kind of being that will ultimately lead directly to the famous "parricide" of Parmenides.[33] The fact that something that is not at all can nonetheless in a certain respect be something that is presupposes, against all Eleatic principles, a *koinōnia* or shared essence of being and not-being that must now be spelled out.[34] That which depicts is evidently not that which is depicted; yet in being something similar to what it depicts, it nonetheless shares some of its properties and to that extent has a *share*—that is, participates—in its being.

The question raised here seems to beg for the solution Plato offers elsewhere, the theory of *methexis* or "participation." Rejecting at the same time both Parmenides's monolithic concept of Being and the Sophists' ontology of incompossibility, the *methexis* doctrine represents an attempt at preserving the unity of being without neglecting gradational internal differences. The image of a thing is then not simply to be equated with the thing but rather "participates" in it. Whereas the category of *mimēsis* or "similarity" stands for the downward move from what is presented to that which presents, the category of *methexis* stands for the upward move from the depicted entity to the entity itself.

This double definition provides the conceptual tools for charting the interval between the terms of the opposition of being and not-being.

With respect to all appearances, an image cannot have "true being" (*alēthinon ontos*), yet for all that, it is by far no nonbeing: its being, rather, lies in "being an image" (*eikōn on*). This being an image differs from being Socrates or being a tree insofar as it is referred to a being or entity such as "Socrates" or "tree" whose image it is. In declaring the negativity of the image to be no longer an external but an internal difference of being, Plato operates a *division of the realm of being* within the closed Parmenidean sphere of being, and this division was to be of great consequence in European metaphysics.

3. BETWEEN ONENESS AND TWONESS

Once Theaetetus and the visitor have acquired insight into the *gradation* of being, they further subdivide the field of being according to five operative principal concepts: being itself / that which is, rest, motion / change, same, other / different.[35] Yet these principal ontological concepts, it turns out, can be translated back into two fundamental kinds of being, a point made in the following, fateful sentence: we must admit, the visitor objects, that "among the things that are, some are in themselves [*autò kath'autò*], and some are always said with respect to others [*pros alla*]."[36] There is much more at stake in this proposition than the rest of the dialog suggests, as commentators have pointed out since antiquity. Plato only touches on the difference between "in and for itself" and "in relation to other things" here, and its implications remain unclear and therefore controversial. Some modern interpreters, influenced by the linguistic turn, have even seen in this juxtaposition quite simply the foundation of Plato's theory of language and interpreted the sentence to mean that a proposition *X is* (*is* understood as *autò kath'autò*, being *in and for itself*) amounts to an existential thesis (*X is* in the sense of *there is X* or *X exists*), while as a proposition *pros alla* (where *is* means being *in relation to other things*) names a process of predication (*X is white* in the sense of *the property of being white is predicated of X*).[37] Even if only implicitly, such an interpretation is based on Aristotle's doctrine of the categories: Plato, in that case, would simply anticipate Aristotle's insight that we must distinguish between substantial being (being Socrates, being a tree, etc.) and accidental being (being white, being larger, being warmer, etc.).

It is nonetheless worthwhile to dwell at the point where Plato reaches the consequential thesis of the bipartite nature of being. A closer look shows that it arises in the first place from the question of the extent to which an image can at the same time be something that is and something that is not. Dividing the question of being, wherever its referentiality is concerned, into two aspects resolves the aporia: *as itself* (*kath'autò*), an image is strictly speaking not what it presents, yet *in relation to other things* (*pros alla*), an image is always already an image *of something*. When we look at Socrates in an image, we do not see a nonbeing, we see a being that is presented.

The thesis at 255c allows Plato to show that the claim that images are and at the same time are not does not necessarily constitute a Sophistic absurdity: while *as themselves*, images are not really what they present, they are, *with respect to their presentation function*, nothing but what they present. Put differently, images *are*, but only at the price that this being is not founded on itself but on something different. As paradoxical as it may sound, images can be acknowledged ontologically only to the extent that they reveal their nonautonomy and noncompletion.

This noncompletion must not, however, be confused with a failure on the part of the image-maker, as the dialog *Cratylus* makes clear.[38] Images are always imperfect because they are similar to their models only ever in a certain respect. If they were similar to the model in each and every respect—for example, because they were produced by a divine demiurge—they would not be better images but no longer images at all. The moment the representation becomes a perfect copy (in this case, the moment the copy of Cratylus takes on all features of the real Cratylus), it loses its image character since one is now simply dealing with "two Crayluses."[39] When two things resemble each other completely and no difference can be found between them, it becomes quite simply absurd to speak of one as the image of the other. Augustine later puts this fact in succinct form: an egg is not an image of another egg but is quite simply another egg.[40] The idea of a pictorial difference, articulated before Augustine by Gregory of Nyssa, resurfaces in modernity when Husserl laconically notes: "The similarity between two objects, however large it may be, does not make one the image of the other."[41] Inversely, the moment an image in a *restitutio ad integrum* becomes a second thing and fully acquires a thing-like, physical character, its image-relation lapses.

We thus have two boundary markers of being-an-image: as long as images are considered under the aspect of their thingness, they remain underneath the threshold of iconicity and are only canvas, wood panel, or stone. For images to count *as images* and thus perform their presentation function, they must be images *of something* and be directed at a *pros alla*. When, however, they go over to the side of this "other" and adopt all of its properties, they again—albeit differently— become things and lose their iconic features. "An image," we read in the *Cratylus*, therefore "cannot remain an image if it presents all the details of what it represents."[42] The branching-off of the image and its being into a being *kath'autò* and a being *pros alla* thus does not stand for two ways of approaching the image, between which we could freely choose. Instead, it reveals itself as the double condition of Plato's scalar ontology: only if an image is considered simultaneously "in and for itself" and "with respect to another thing" can we exclude that it either degenerates into a "mere thing" (and thus becomes open to attacks by Eleatic and Sophist rhetoric of not-being) or attains the level of a "second thing" (and thus, as its simulacrum, contests the position of "what truly is"). What is inevitably lost in both cases is the very category Plato had introduced against the Eleatic and Sophist schools: the category of *difference* (*to heteron*). In the first case, we hypostasize *autò kath'autò* and lose sight of the *pros alla*; in the second, we absolutize the assimilation to the other in such a way as to get caught in a new logic of identity, in which the difference from the other loses all validity. The question thus remains open: How are we to conceive of the "difference" of the image, and how are we to define the *pros alla* to avoid that the image becomes another *autos*?

In his *Lives of Eminent Philosophers*, Diogenes Laertius offers an interpretation of Plato's alternative kinds of Being that was to prove influential. In his presentation of Platonic doctrine, Diogenes discusses the distinction between "for itself" and "for another," which he considers to be one of its fundamental discoveries:

> Of existing things some are absolute [*kath'eauta*] and some are called relative [*pros ti*]. Things said to exist absolutely are those which need nothing else to explain them, as man, horse, and all other animals. For none of these gains by explanation. To those which are called relative belong all which stand in need of some explanation, as that which is greater than something or quicker than something, or more beautiful and the like.[43]

This recapitulation of the ontological bipartition operates a significant conceptual shift when it replaces Plato's *pros alla* with an Aristotelian term from the theory of the categories, namely, the "that toward which" (*pros ti*). Aristotle turns the term "category," taken from the rules governing forensic investigation, where it designates the different forms of questions employed by legal institutions in establishing facts (*When* did it happen? *Who* did it?), into a guiding speculative concept. Yet even in its philosophical deployment, it continues to name possible forms of *questions* and *propositions* about beings. The category of "toward what?" or *pros ti* encompasses all propositions about relations, and it would make no sense to say something is similar without adding what it is similar to. Whereas qualitative or quantitative properties are contained *in* things ("the wall is white" or "the table has four legs"), relational properties are situated between things and result from attributions of properties.

The influence of Aristotle's doctrine of the categories on Diogenes Laertius's Plato interpretation is evident already in the fact that he interprets the "relation to another" as a linguistic problem of relational terms that "stand in need of some explanation."[44] Aristotle himself suggests such a "deontologizing" interpretation of the *pros ti* when he associates the category of relation with the lowest kind of being.[45] This reinterpretation of the *pros alla*, which depends on being, as a *pros ti*, which pertains to a theory of attribution, has of course grave consequences for the question from which the reflection about the *autò kath'autò* and the *pros alla* emerged in the first place, namely, the question of images. What does it mean when images are not similar per se, when they are not "what has been made to resemble another," when it is instead a third who institutes a relationship of similarity between the image and the depicted? It means nothing short of this: the question of the being of an image recedes in favor of the question of *what* it is an image of, *who* it is an image of, in favor, that is, of the question of how it depicts and why it counts as a depiction for someone. If iconicity is founded neither in the image nor in what it depicts but in their relation, the original question must be reformulated. It would no longer be, *What* is an image?, but, *To what extent* is x an image of y? What this shows is that iconicity cannot be a unary predicate but must be described as a binary property. In a formal logical notation: not *image (x)* but *image (x,y)*. Put differently: iconicity must always be a transitive concept; as an intransitive concept, it remains empty.

In one blow, this would get rid of a series of apparent aporias in which Plato has Theaetetus and the visitor trapped. Sophism, as we know from Plato's early refutational dialogs, operates precisely by blurring the distinction between unary and binary propositions, in the popular father sophism, for example.[46] That now Sophroniscus is a father and now he is not is a rhetorical sleight of hand: as needed, "father" is used now as unary predicate ("*x* is a father") and now as binary predicate ("*x* is the father of *y*"). In the first version, Sophroniscus is a father without restrictions; in the second, he is a father only to his son.[47] Things shift when we think the language-theoretical articulation of the image relation all the way through, when we think it only as a binary predicate. The question of the image moves from an immanent ground of being to the question *when* and *in what respect*, in short, to the question *in relation toward what* a thing can become an image. This conjures the danger of reification that arises from the exaggerated focus on either the depicting thing or the thing depicted since being an image shifts from being an inherent essence to an externally attributed relationship. What counts now is less *what* an image is in itself than *how* it refers for someone to another.

If we follow this train of thought, image theory becomes a subdivision of a general "semiotics" or theory of signs that investigates all the ways in which a thing can point *to another* or stand *for another*. The sign relation is generally described as the epitome of relation as such, since the nature of the sign does not depend on the things that are being put into relation: thanks to the constitutive arbitrariness of the sign, just about anything can be declared a sign of something else. Taken by itself, *autò kath'autò*, the sign is nothing. It becomes meaningful only in relation to something else, *pros ti*. The makeup of the sign is a matter of indifference; indeed, the sign must even draw attention away from its own material properties to be able to refer to what it designates. Integrating the image into the class of signs, its incomplete being-such transforms from an ontological flaw into a semiotic identifying feature. Insofar as it does not *participate in* what it designates but merely *represents* it, the sign must, precisely, not be like what it designates. The disjunction Aquinas describes as *motus duplex* is already on the horizon.

4. *MOTUS DUPLEX*: THE TWO PARADIGMATIC WAYS OF LOOKING AT IMAGES

If our hypothesis is correct that philosophy historically demarcated its identity by confronting the Sophists and hence took on the issue of images that lies at the core of this confrontation, it allows for a better grasp of the ambivalence with which philosophy as an established discipline has treated the problem of the image in the course of its history. Caught between strategies of inclusion and of exclusion, the image never became a field of inquiry of its own, and no subdiscipline emerged to study such a field: the question of the image flares up at the beginning of classical ontology, then for a long time counts as an object of epistemology, sometimes serves as a model in the philosophy of language, and, by way of experiment, is integrated in the comprehensive project of a philosophical semiotics without ever fully being absorbed in it. All attempts at settling the question of the status of the image once and for all only seem to affirm its nonclassifiability.

The nomadic existence to which images seem to be condemned within the historical formations of knowledge is due not least to the new kind of structuring Augustine operates in his immensely influential theory of science. At the core of this semiotic theory, with which he prefaces the four books of his *On Christian Doctrine*, Augustine writes unambiguously: "All teaching is either about things or signs."[48] Signs (*signa*), however, are not (yet) immaterial simply because, in the system of categories, they are juxtaposed to things (*res*). Indeed, "every sign is also a thing" because it must have a material foundation in the realm of the senses.[49] Already in *De dialectica*, an early work attributed to Augustine, we read that "a sign is something which is itself sensed [*se ipsum sensui*] and which indicates to the mind something beyond the sign itself [*aliquid animo ostendit*]."[50] This second something is defined more precisely in *On Christian Doctrine*: "A sign, after all, is a thing, which besides the impression it conveys to the senses, also has the effect of making something else [*aliud aliquid*] come to mind." The next sentence explains the sign's referential function with examples: "as when we see a spoor, we think of the animal whose spoor it is; or when we see smoke, we know there is fire underneath; and when we hear the cry of a living creature, we can tell what its mood is; and when the trumpet sounds, soldiers know that they must advance or retreat, or whatever else the battle requires."[51]

Whether spoor, signal, or warning, which must in some way be sensual to be able to attract attention at all, observers never dwell on its materiality. For this very reason, signs should not be considered with respect to what they are (*ne quod sunt*) but with respect to what they are as signs, that is, what they indicate (*quod significant*).[52]

There is no provision for a third discipline between the sciences of things (*doctrinae rerum*) and the sciences of signs (*doctrinae signorum*) that would be dedicated to images and their appearance. This excluded middle legitimates a procedure of selection within this set of "nonauthentic" intermediate phenomena, even renders it necessary to serve, as the case may be, ontological, ethical-moral, or epistemological purposes. It is only against the foil of these two adverse perspectives that the splitting of images into *eikones* and *eidōla*, into transitive icons and intransitive idols, acquires force of law.

Scholasticism applies the Augustinian alternative between *res* and *signa* to the question of the image. The canonic formula, which appears all the more apodictic for its invocation of *the* authority, Aristotle, comes from Aquinas, who writes in the *Summa Theologiae*: "As the Philosopher says . . ., there is a twofold movement of the mind towards an image: one indeed towards the image itself as a certain thing [*res quaedam*]; another, towards the image in so far as it is the image of something else [*imago alterius*]."[53]

The Greek pair of *autò kath'autò* and *pros alla* is thus dressed in Latin robes. More than that: Aquinas goes on to justify the difference between the two, writing that "between these movements there is this difference; that the former, by which one is moved towards an image as a certain thing, is different from the movement towards the thing [presented in the image]: whereas the latter movement, which is towards the image as an image, is one and the same as that which is towards the thing [presented in the image]."[54] What is behind this formulation? Aquinas evidently suggests that looking at an image for the sake of its mere materiality interrupts its reference, while looking at an image in terms of its iconicity—and this will have important consequences—amounts to looking at the depicted. In abbreviated form: *it is not possible to look at the appearance of the image as something autonomous and distinct from the referent.* When we look at Christ in an image, we do not look at Christ appearing this way or another—as Christ on the cross, as Christ *pantokrator*, or as a Christ on golden ground, for example—we are looking at the person of Christ *himself.*

This indifference or nondistinction is particularly significant in the context of the discussion of worship (*latreia* in Greek, *latria* in Latin) and specifically of the worship of images (*idolatria*). While idolatry should be condemned in general, Aquinas states, matters are significantly different if the images are considered not for their own sake but as transitional signs. The idol is the perfect case of a phenomenon lacking the transitional character of a sign: it does not refer to any other, transcendent reality, and it is nothing but a brute, material thing venerated by the idolatrous. Yet Aquinas wants to save images for devotional purposes and therefore distinguishes the icon from the idol. Unlike idols, icons refer to something that exceeds them, in this case, to a divine reality. No one will contest that Christ deserves adoration, Aquinas explains. Now, given that true believers do not look at the icon as a material thing (*qua re*) and that they do not stop at the level of appearances but look at it as a sign (*qua signo*), it is perfectly acceptable to adore an icon of Christ. "The same reverence should be shown to Christ's image as to Christ Himself. Since, therefore, Christ is adored with the adoration of '*latria*,' it follows that His image should be adored with the adoration of '*latria*.'"[55] The old debate about idolatry is thus solved by a simple semiotic distinction that locates the idol on the side of brute things and the icon on the side of signs and dismisses the question of the phenomenality of images.

A further element is, strangely, left out in this controversy, namely, what it means to refer to something absent. After all, this type of reference is never at stake, since we either talk about idols that are nothing but what they are or we talk about the true icons that imply a specific form of reference, reference as presentification. Aquinas's argument that there is no difference between Christ in the icon and Christ as a person hinges on the implicit assumption that Christ is as *present* in the image as he is everywhere else and that the icon merely *presentifies* this presence. But what does it mean for images to refer to something absent? On this issue, it is worth returning to Aristotle himself.

5. REFERRING TO SOMETHING ABSENT

In Aristotle, the concept of absence is of a different hue than in later Christian Aristotelianism, for he tackles the question of how we can refer to something absent at all, specifically in the treatise *On Memory*. Aristotle starts with assigning a specific source of knowledge to each mode of time: we refer to something *future* by making *suppositions* (for example in the "mantic" arts), and we know of what is *present* thanks to perception; but to what is *past*, we refer to via our *memory*, which comes in whenever something is no longer present.[56] Accordingly, we can neither perceive what has not yet happened nor remember what is happening before our eyes only now.[57]

Yet what exactly does memory consist in? We can evidently remember only what has been the case at an earlier point in time and affected us in such a way as to leave a pictorial impression. But we wonder whether, in remembering a past event, we call up the event itself or only its memory-image.[58] Should it turn out that we relive merely a presentified affective image, we would find ourselves back in the mode of the present. And should it turn out that we have a sensation of the event itself, the question arises how it is possible that we perceive presently something that is past.

Aristotle later resolves this aporia by showing that we must not conceive of memory-images on the model of perception-images. They constitute a class of their own. When we remember something, we call it up in our memory and see it before us, although this seeing is of a different kind from physical seeing. And yet there remains a case in which we do indeed "perceive what is absent" (*to mē paròn akouein*).[59] What begins as a distinction between two mnemic types, namely, memory-images and recollection-images (*mnēmata* and *phantasmata*), soon upsets the textual economy of *On Memory* and leads to a much larger problem, that is, the *as*-structure of images. Memory-images differ from representational or recollection-images in that they, unlike perception-images, which at all moments become past, are images of what is past *as* past. This distinction is also relevant in other texts collected in the *Parva naturalia*. There, it applies in contexts that are not limited to merely rememorative forms of images. In *On Dreams* and *On Divination*, which Freud saw as forerunners to his *Interpretation of Dreams*, Aristotle holds that in our conscious dreams we can observe dream-images as they unfold, in which case they count for us *as* images and not as reality.[60]

Although we find these views all the way to modernity, our focus here is on Aristotle's brief discussion of viewing images in *On Memory* 2.450b11–451a14 that, beyond introducing the *as*-structure of images, brings up fundamental insights concerning the question of images. The question is quite simply this: In what way can we refer to something that is not present? Such, according to Aristotle, is the case when we look at a painted image: "A picture of a living being painted on a panel is at once a living being and an image."[61] In looking at an image, we thus perceive both the image panel and a living being that is de facto absent but nonetheless present thanks to the image's *presentation*. Separating these two aspects results in the two movements discussed in the *Summa*

Theologiae. For Aristotle, they are at most analytic separations of contemplative thinking, not objective differences.[62] In looking at an image in the mode of perception, both aspects are always copresent because "while one and the same, it is both of these."[63] When we look at images, there is a kind of twofoldness: we are caught up in a logic of *both . . . and*, not of *either . . . or*.

What does it mean, then, that in images something absent appears to us? In what respect do a painted living being (*zōon gegramménon*) and a depiction (*eikōn*) belong to recollection-images, as we read a little later?[64] Aristotle's theory of *memoria*, which provides the context for these reflections on the image, evidently has little connection with the Thomist discussion of adoration. Nor does it have much in common with Plato's theory of the soul's existential anamnesis of eternal forms, even if the title, *On Memory and Recollection*, takes up Plato's couple *mnēmē* and *anamnēsis*. Independently of whether Aristotle explicitly uses a Platonic term to give it new meaning or uses the term without referring to Plato at all, the anamnesis Aristotle aims at here is not meant to presentify anything that lies beyond the realm of the senses. It is concerned neither with the Church Fathers' uncircumscribable God nor with Plato's ideas, which the soul, not yet imprisoned in the body, would have beheld in the heaven of ideas. Rather, the faculty of memory is situated where the faculty of perception (*prōton aisthētikon*) is to be found as well.[65] Recollection-images thus serve the same function as portraits: they presentify what is no longer present. In the image of Coriscus, Coriscus becomes present once more even when he is longer there—when, for example, rather than in Athens, he is in Asia Minor.[66]

Generally speaking, images for Aristotle can count as dependent phenomena because they presuppose a preceding perception now being actualized. Presentification here aims at a past presence. Absence here is a merely relative one that can be located on an arrow of time.[67] Yet images are not always unambiguously temporally indexed. It is not always possible to attribute them to a specific time in the past at which something was present to us. Indeed, sometimes we are not even sure, Aristotle says, whether the representational image was preceded by a perception at all; in short, "we doubt whether the case is or is not one of memory." What is represented is not currently present in perception, but was it ever? It happens that after a certain time we seem to remember when "we heard or saw something formerly." We then go looking what this image was an image of and thus move from looking at the image "in itself" (*hōs auto*) to looking at it "as relative to something else" (*hōs allō*).[68]

Yet what happens when we cannot for the life of us recall at what point in time we experienced something? Some are downright obsessed by the idea that every image must be an image of something precedent and develop fictitious prequels for each image. Aristotle cites a certain "Antipheron of Oreus and others in a state of ecstasy," who were convinced that their "visions" were "facts of their past experience, and as if remember[ed] them."[69] In this early description of déjà-vu experiences, Aristotle aims for something decisive: such a representation arises "whenever one contemplates what is not a likeness as if it were a likeness."[70] Antipheron and his peers cannot think of representational images as anything other than copies, and they see what is present as a sign of something that preceded it—the way we might interpret dream images as signaling something future.[71] Yet in so doing, they precisely do not stay with the image contemplated "in its own right" (*hōs kath'autó*).[72]

The Antipheron episode may be read as Aristotle's criticism of a misconceived concept of absence. *Phantasia*, in the famous definition in *On the Soul*, becomes effective whenever we cannot draw on a present perception.[73] Thanks to this faculty of visualization, humans produce *phantasmata* or representational images that are able to presentify something absent. It is then just as untenable to think that everything absent must formerly have been present as it is to consider every dream image to be an anticipation of what is to come. That an image is always the image of something not present does not mean that the nonpresent is *no longer* or *not yet* present. *Phantasmata* can be reproductive or anticipatory, but they do not have to be either.

6. AN ANTHROPOLOGICAL INTEREST IN IMAGES AS IMAGES

Aristotle thus introduces a whole new aspect. Images are interesting not only because they provide information about a previous (or subsequent) state of affairs; images are interesting in themselves. The *Poetics* turns the empirical statement into an anthropological thesis: human beings differ from other organisms in that they take pleasure in imitations. And "the reason of the delight in seeing the picture [*eikónas*] is that one is at the same time learning—gathering the meaning of things, e.g. that the man there is so-and-so."[74] Here, seeing images is initially a form of seeing-again, a recognizing gaze, but the possibility is not excluded that whatever is seen is totally unknown to the viewer, that it may not even exist in reality (Aristotle speaks of "imitating" centaurs or Cyclopes). Some visualizations through images precisely do not aim at materializing the object itself but represent a way of keeping it at a distance. Here, too, Aristotle cites a well-known argument: "though the objects themselves may be painful to see, we delight to view the most realistic representations of them in art, the forms for example of the lowest animals and of dead bodies."[75] What interests spectators in images, then, is not *what* these represent but *how* they represent something. The theoretical frame thus shifts from a theory of imitation that starts with the object to a theory of the phenomenal attributes proper to the image. The following passage marks the point where an Aristotelian theory of the image sets in, a theory that does not coincide with the classical theory of mimesis elaborated by Xenophon and propagated even long after Aristotle: "For if one has not seen the thing before, one's pleasure will not be in the picture as an imitation [*mimēma*] of it, but will be due to the execution or colouring or some similar cause."[76]

Beyond an epistemological interest, which sees in images merely a means of information, there is, for Aristotle, a uniquely human interest in genuinely pictorial qualities. Such qualities can neither be derived from the motif of the image nor be reduced to the purely material properties of the image support. Interest in images is not an interest in color per se but in the specific configuration of color on the surface of the image support, thanks to which a wooden panel becomes an image of something else. What intrigues people about images is not primarily the motif represented, nor the material support, but first of all the way in which something is represented or in which it appears. In inquiring into the autonomy of the image, in asking about the image "itself," *hōs kath'autó*, Aristotle from the very beginning operates beyond a scalar, Platonic ontology in which the image could at most achieve a deficient or subordinate status.

The problem of the phenomenal value of images, however, arises even before the suspension of the ontological value of images. As a matter of fact, it is inherent to the ontological question itself. As a remainder that cannot be reduced to either being or not-being, the image acts both as a motor that gets the constitution of the theory of being going in the first place and as a wrench in the strict ontological machinery that thereby ultimately threatens to go out of control.

7. WHAT IT IS AND HOW IT APPEARS

In book 9 of the *Republic*, Glaucon distinguishes between productive art (*technē poiētikē*), which produces things that are in fact new, and merely imitative art (*technē mimētikē*), which leaves us with nothing but reproductions of things. Socrates, however, contests Glaucon's opposition and wonders if it is not somewhat too simplistic. There is no denying that even a reproduction is a form of production, since the painter, too, is fabricating something. In response to

Socrates's objection, Glaucon revises his definition and suggests conceptualizing the imitative arts in more precise terms as the production of semblance.[77] Yet of course, this new definition betrays a certain embarrassment and shows how difficult it is to circumscribe a clear ontological position for painted artifacts. Even at the moment that an effort at differentiation seeks to sort it out, the fundamental *hubris of the image* asserts itself. Once again, Plato resorts to irony to address this moving target. After having assigned every single profession a precise function in the organization of the state in the preceding nine books, Plato now parodies the makers of images as extraordinary and peculiar people: "This same craftsman is able to make, not only all kinds of furniture, but all plants that grow from the earth, all animals (including himself), the earth itself, the heavens, the gods, all the things in the heavens and in Hades beneath the earth."[78] The painting "craftsman" is ultimately compared to a Sophist who pretends to have abilities he has never had. For the painter does not really know how to produce a table, which is why he only ever produces the semblance of a table. Imitative art, however, is not an ability reserved exclusively for painters. Everyone has that ability, but, moreover, it is a superfluous ability for humans since nature provides an even more perfect "painter" capable of reproducing the visible much more quickly than any painter could: "You could do it quickly and in lots of places, especially if you were willing to carry a mirror with you, for that's the quickest way of all. With it you can quickly make the sun, the things in the heavens, the earth, yourself, the other animals, manufactured items, plants, and everything else mentioned just now."[79] Of mirrors as of the painters who reproduce all these things, it is possible to say that in a sense they imitate but do not really produce them. Unlike the divine demiurge, painters (like, incidentally, poets) give rise to only a semblance of objecthood. A few pages later, Glaucon, in response to Socrates's question whether painting imitates "that which is as it is or . . . that which appears as it appears," affirms the latter without hesitation.[80]

This blunt separation between being and semblance, however, quickly comes up against its limitations, already in the example of the carpenter. Like all other crafts, carpentry belongs to the mimetic arts, namely, insofar as it produces a sensuous table according to the model of the idea of the table. The carpenter thus "isn't making that which is [*ouk to on*], but something which is like that which is [*hoion to on*]."[81] Not unlike the way the geometers' hand-drawn circles never attain the perfection of the idea of the circle (and in fact are not really circles according to the geometric definition), every material entity is imperfect. Yet if carpenters, just like painters, are indeed limited to the realm of semblance, how is it possible still to distinguish between "good" semblance and deception? The

tripartite hierarchy of being that Plato expresses in the simile of the three beds—
the bed as idea, the bed as sensuous depiction, and the bed as image of the image
in painting—turns out to be too optimistic or, in any case, useless. For if a painter
is skilled enough to capture an object on his panel, some "children and foolish
people" who lack the appropriate sense of distance will take the image for the
object itself.[82]

In invoking the trope of the illusionistic trompe l'oeil, Plato inscribes himself
in a classical tradition that culminates in the legendary grapes painted by Zeuxis
that fooled even birds. What he criticizes in these illusions is not so much that
they are "far removed from the truth."[83] Rather, they are dangerous because they
deny this distance and seek to hide it. In being reduced to the level of appearance,
a univocally vertical hierarchy of being, where the degree of being decreases as
one moves down, becomes a horizontal contest between the sensible object as a
true representation and the painted picture as a simulacrum, which refuses to
acknowledge its deficient being and thereby rejects the entire ontological order. A
distinction between being and semblance therefore no longer suffices: the *agon*
now takes place within the realm of appearances itself, and this realm now needs
new differential criteria. However, while, as we saw, the theory of *methexis* or participation owes its articulation to the principle of the image in the first place, the
image as an applied example now threatens to explode this very theory. It is
worthwhile taking another look at the passage where the distinction is made:
"What does painting do in each case? Does it imitate that which is as it is, or does
it imitate that which appears as it appears? Is it an imitation of appearances or of
truth?"[84] Glaucon's answer seems to leave no room for doubt: painters do not
turn to being, they turn to semblance. That at least is the way this sentence, which
until Nietzsche vouched for Plato's fame as an enemy of art, has usually been
understood, and according to some recent interpretations, the entire history of
aesthetics can even be read as one long footnote to Plato's original dichotomy.[85]
On this reading, aesthetics, in responding to this dichotomy, can either (in
Hegelian fashion) conceive of semblance as a way of accessing being or (in a
vulgarization of Nietzsche) one-sidedly affirm the omnipotence of semblance.
Ultimately, though, both variants would merely, albeit unwittingly, reaffirm the
original opposition of being and semblance.[86]

Yet a closer look at Plato's subtle dialectic shows that it defends itself against
a "Platonist" reduction all by itself: the alternative Plato has Socrates propose is
precisely not a simple alternative between being and semblance. It consists in the
question whether painting is a reproduction of "that which is as it is" or of "that
which appears as it appears" (*to phainomenon hōs phainetai*). Why this duplica-
tion, which is superfluous in a static theory of decreasing ontological content?

Why does painting not simply stand on the side of appearance but rather on the side of the imitative appearance of appearance itself? Obviously, there are also appearances that imitate that which is *such as it is*. What had hitherto served as a criterion of *dependence* to relate the levels of a vertical ladder to one another other now morphs into a criterion of *orientation* that allows for differentiating between several phenomena competing with one another on one and the same level.

Yet if the contest is carried out on the level of appearances, on the level of images, in any case, the differentiation between being and semblance is invalid or at least insufficiently complex.[87] Although they can never leave the realm of semblance, true depictions are oriented toward being and depict it *such as* (*hoion*) it is. In taking this right measure as their guide, the maker of likenesses can claim his products to be valid, whereas the painter, who takes appearances as his guide, cannot. To summarize: the problem raised by the question of how to classify the pictorial artifacts has shifted. The issue has moved away from the ontological status of images within the order of what is, since images, by refusing to defer to it, threaten the vertical architecture of Being. No longer a matter that could be solved according to the logic of derivation and dependency, which deliberately left out how images *appear*, images now have to be addressed differently, according to how their appearance takes into account either what they represent or whom they appear to. This shift is to be observed in moving from the analysis of images in the *Republic* to the analysis of images in the dialog *The Sophist*.

8. *THE SOPHIST*: THE IMAGE IN PERSPECTIVE

But let her dare to seem the thing she is!

—Friedrich Schiller, *Mary Stuart*, act 1, scene 7

The *Republic* already prepared the ground for a "technical" interpretation of the question of the image: Socrates asks whether art "imitates that which is as it is" or "that which appears as it appears" and immediately adds: "Is it an imitation of appearances or of truth?"[88] This last phrase contains the elements of the solution spelled out later in the *Sophist*, which distinguishes between two kinds of imitation or image-making. Plato names the first kind "the art of likeness," *eikastikē*, and says of it that it is the most capable of living up to its potential, thus making it the closest to truth.[89] In imitating, the art of likeness-making "takes" the "true proportions" (*symmetrías*) from what is to be represented to reproduce them in the depiction in their "length, breadth, and depth." Beside the form, the eikastic art also reproduces the "colors appropriate to each part" the way they are in what truly is (*alēthinón*).[90] Arguably, we are witnessing here the historical foundation of the restitution model of painting, a model still echoing in Cézanne's "I owe you the truth and I will tell it."[91] Theaetetus asks whether the reproduction of reality is not the aim of all imitative art. The stranger denies this. Some painters, he adds, only observe the proportions as they *appear*, for "if they reproduced the true proportions of their beautiful subjects, you see, the upper parts would appear smaller than they should, and the lower parts would appear larger, because we see the upper parts from farther away and the lower parts from closer."[92]

As Pierre-Maxime Schuhl has shown in a now-classic study, these are not just speculative games.[93] Plato is taking sides in an aesthetic debate that may be characterized as an Attic prelude to the *querelle des anciens et des modernes*. With their revolutionary refinement of fresco painting, Apollodorus, Zeuxis, and Parrhasius took a step that crossed a threshold in the European history of images, toward the actual reproduction of visible appearances. The true-to-reality presentations of the diaphanous-transparent fruit bowl on a fresco in an Oplontis villa, even if it is of a later date, conveys a sense of what the painted fruit must have looked like that attracted even birds (fig. 1.1).

This kind of reproduction, meanwhile, is not limited to images. It contaminates sculpture and architecture as well. The sculptor Lysippus is reputed to have said that "whereas his predecessors had made men as they really were [*quales essent*], he made them as they appeared to be [*quales viderentur*]."[94] There is much to suggest that the example in the *Sophist* just cited refers to the new technique in sculpture—not to Euphranor and Lysippus, though, as Schuhl still thought, but to Phidias's monumental sculptures. The twelfth-century Byzantine historian Tzetzes tells an anecdote about an artistic contest between Alcamenes and Phidias that, given the historical distance, is unlikely to be authentic but is telling nonetheless. At first, Alcamenes's statue seemed the more "delicate." Phidias, however, had calculated all effects and proportions according to the height from which viewers would look at his own statue, and when it was installed, it surpassed Alcamenes's statue in verisimilitude.[95]

In recent years Lambert Wiesing has once again argued for suspecting Phidias's scandalous works to be behind Plato's criticism, particularly the monumental *Athena Parthenos*, almost forty feet high, erected in the cella of the Parthenon in 438 BCE.[96] Athena's head is drawn out lengthwise, but when it is

FIGURE 1.1 Fruit bowl with transparency effects, fresco, 1st century BCE. Villa Poppaea, Oplontis (Torre Annunziata). Courtesy of Beni Culturali Italiani.

viewed from the temple floor, perspectival distortion gives the statue as a whole a unified aspect. Phidias (if he is the one at whom the criticism is leveled) sacrifices the true proportions of the head and aims for an illusionistic total impression; his presentation only "appears" (*to phainómenon mén*) to be appropriate.[97] Phidias thus acts contrary to the demand articulated in book 4 of the *Republic* to respect the proportions of individual parts, which must not be sacrificed to the whole.[98] There, Plato opposed the hieratic sublimity of Egyptian art to the new illusionistic tendencies of the Greek aesthetics of effect.[99]

The demonstration that the Greek masters of illusion indulge in mere appearance, however, states only part of the truth: the appearance is taken to be true only because it considers the position of the viewer. The atopical, discordant character of the simulacrum can be concealed when it includes the place of the viewer in its staging. Standing in the spot assigned by the artist, viewing the appearance "from the proper location" (*ek kalou théan*), will lead viewers to judge it as lifelike.[100] Yet even the slightest move away from this ideal standpoint allows them to recognize the faults of the illusionistic construction. The correctness of the point of view itself—this is the underlying paradox—depends on one's point of view, on whether we want the illusion to succeed or seek to unmask it.

Acknowledging this paradox also allows for resolving a philological inconsistency that has bothered Plato scholars since Friedrich Schleiermacher. Most of the late-medieval manuscripts on which modern editions of the *Sophist* are based state at 236b that "something . . . appears to be like a beautiful thing, but only because it is seen from a viewpoint that is not [*ouk*] beautiful." For Schleiermacher, the "not" must be a copyist's erroneous interpolation since the appearance can have its illusionistic effect only from the correct perspective. "Thus, the *ouk* is to be deleted," Schleiermacher writes, and he points to manuscripts in which the *ouk* is missing: "We finally have found some manuscripts that do this."[101]

Yet Schleiermacher's philological hypothesis works only on the condition that the correct or "proper" place is referred to the appearance: the enchantment works and remains undetected only in the spot the artist has intended for the viewer. If this place is referred to truth, though, the viewer's standpoint turns out to be the *one* "wrong place" because there, the illusion precisely does not appear. If viewers were "at eye level" with Athena, they would immediately notice the distortion. It is entirely possible, therefore, that some copyists sought to pin down the meaning of this ambiguous passage in one or the other sense: the manuscripts with *ouk* refer the "place" to truth, and the manuscripts without *ouk* refer it to the illusionistic device. Of course it would be futile to ask which manuscript version conforms to the original and which presents interpolations or deletions. The variants, rather, are telling symptoms of the polysemy of Plato's dialogs. What is curious is that Schleiermacher, the founding father of hermeneutics, whose central insight is the plurality of interpretations, falls prey here to the temptation of imposing a single meaning. Although, or perhaps precisely because, it cannot be decided whether it is oriented toward the perspective of truth or that of semblance, the passage thus affirms the unavoidable perspectivism Plato discovers here, a perspectivism Platonism diligently worked for centuries to eradicate. Against the background of this general perspectivism of the phenomenal world, the "correct" perspective becomes merely one perspective among others.

The decisive shift taking place between the *Republic* and the *Sophist*, then, is less to be sought in some kind of "self-criticism" on Plato's part than in a shift of the question of the image from the category of *participation* to the category of *orientation*.[102] While *eikastikē technē* is oriented toward essence, *phantastikē technē* is oriented toward the viewer and governed by the rules of consistent appearances. What an image is cannot be defined *in the image* itself (*kath'autó*)

FIGURE 1.2 View of a city, fresco of the eastern wall, Villa P. Fannius Synistor, 1st century BCE. Boscoreale. Courtesy of Beni Culturali Italiani.

but only with respect to (*pros alla*) that which makes it an image.[103] But—and this is the point—the scene on which the battle between the legitimate and the illegitimate *pros alla*, between *eikōn* and *eidolōn* (and thus also between philosophy and Sophism), is fought is itself nothing but the space of appearing. The separation of the legitimate image (as representation) from deceptive simulacra and the selection of the legitimate pretender from the bevy of illegitimate rivals take place against the backdrop of an irreducible coexistence of claims.

As Gilles Deleuze has argued in a short but compelling essay on the logic of the simulacrum, Plato's later theory of images is based on a situation of *amphisbētēsis* or "rivalry." In confronting the pretenders that claim to be what they are not and lay claim to a position they do not deserve, authentic images must meet these claims and thereby simultaneously the simulacra on their own terrain: "The essence of division does not appear in its breadth, in the determination of the species of a genus, but in its depth, in the selection of the lineage. It is to screen the claims (*pretensions*) and to distinguish the true pretender from the false one."[104] The entire dissecting procedure of selection in the *Sophist*, which, long before Aristotle's *Categories* and Porphyry's aborescent diagrammatics, lays out the hierarchic structure of Western speciated ontology, ultimately derives from the primary mechanism that distinguishes between the legitimate offspring of what truly is and what would be an illegitimate intruder: "It has to do with selecting among the pretenders, distinguishing good and bad copies or, rather, copies (always well-founded) and simulacra (always engulfed in dissimilarity). It is a question of assuring the triumph of the copies over simulacra, of repressing simulacra, keeping them completely submerged, preventing them from climbing to the surface, and 'insinuating themselves' everywhere."[105]

Without further tracing these genealogical lines of flight and their reinterpretations, which Deleuze associates with Nietzsche's formula about the "reversal of Platonism," I would simply like to emphasize a starting point presupposed but never made explicit by Deleuze: the *Sophist* marks the point at which *the question of being can no longer be asked beyond the space of phenomenality*. If the simulacrum indeed *pretends* to be the thing itself while the legitimate likeness openly *displays* its imperfection vis-à-vis what it depicts, then the logic of dependence and the logic of pretense must be distinguished *in* their appearing, within the phenomenal order in which their difference becomes manifest. Put differently, this means that "the question concerning being can never be posed outside the level of semblance" or, abbreviated: all future ontology will have to be a phenomenology.[106]

Constitutively, albeit in different ways, both the *eidolōn*, "this appearing and seeming but not being,"[107] and the *eikōn*, which, unlike the *eidolōn*, indicates not only *itself* but also the distance that separates it from the thing itself, stand in need of appearing to someone.

In the desperate struggle with the Sophist and his simulacra, Plato seems concerned with nothing less than establishing on this "multicolored" (*poikilon*) level of phenomena the possibility of conceptual differences and, on that basis, the possibility of true judgments.[108] In this late dialog, then, something is coming to a head that already occupied Plato in the *Euthydemus*, namely, the question of whether it is possible to engage with the manifold of phenomena and at the same time maintain the distinction between truth and falsehood.

The Sophist presents itself like a belated answer to Protagoras, who, according to the sources, attributed a truth value to every proposition and considered false propositions to be simply unthinkable.[109] A formal dissection of Protagoras's argument becomes possible thanks only to the conceptual differentiation, in *The Sophist*, of not-being as difference: "If it [that is, nonbeing] does not mix with them [belief and discourse], it is necessary for all things to be true, but if it does mix, false belief and discourse can arise."[110] Parmenides and Protagoras are thus diametrically opposed: for Parmenides, false belief or *doxa* is identical to not-being, while for Protagoras, *doxa* cannot be deficient because there is no such thing as not-being. The possibility of the *critique* of images Plato has in mind— the differentiation between truthful and false images—thus depends on establishing the interweaving (*symplokē*) both of being (against Parmenides) and of not-being (against Protagoras) in the domain of *doxa*.

The autonomy of the phenomenal realm inaugurated by the debate around images is revoked at the neuralgic point where it comes to the possibility of making correct statements. A true statement is defined as a statement that is identical to what is; a false statement is one that claims something that is not the case.[111] In thus tying the domain of semblance back to being, Plato conjures the threat of the aporetic end an autonomy of appearances would have led to: the relaxation of the scalar ontology and its being retooled as a purely relational logic threatened to turn images into merely the "different," beyond being and not-being, without any beings from which they could differ.

The free-floating philosophy of difference that announces itself at the end of the confrontation with Parmenides,[112] however, comes to an abrupt end when the visitor responds that ultimately, "not only does the attempt to separate everything from everything sound discord, it also completely lacks the Muse and is unphilosophic. . . . To dissociate each thing from everything else is to destroy totally everything there is to say" as well as all philosophy since both essentially rest on a "conceptual interweaving."[113] While the Sophist has severed all links and retreated to a domain where "all things" are "full of images and likenesses and appearances,"[114] the philosopher's task is to conceptually map and logically determine this savage and allegedly undifferentiated field as well. Only when the Sophistic illusions are shown to have no foundation, only when the foundational relationship between logos and things has been restored, will the hunt for the Sophist come to an end and the "strange animal" be captured.

While Plato, in confronting Parmenides, actively renders the *doxai* autonomous as something purely "different" and thus increasingly as something true per se, he reverses himself already in confronting the Sophists in order to maintain the possibility to refer to truth. In the concluding part of the dialog, Plato intertwines appearance and being more closely again, thanks to a mediation via the *logos*. Yet while the introduction of the logos into doxa separates likenesses from illusions, the logos, inversely, is not safe from the intrusion of images. Just as, within the domain of images, Plato had tried to distinguish between images that are capable of logos and those that are not, toward the end of the dialog he is concerned with separating illusionary discourse from discourse capable of the truth. *The Sophist*'s seventh and last dissection consists in differentiating two ways of producing illusions: the first class "comes to be by way of instruments, and in the other the maker of the appearance presents himself as the instrument."[115] This refers to situations in which "somebody uses his own body or voice and makes them appear similar to your character or voice." In this kind of verbal deception, images intrude into words and the visible into the sayable.[116]

The Sophist concludes with an outline of a critique of rhetoric that Plato did not develop further.[117] If we follow the classical historians, it was Plato's star student Aristotle who was charged with lecturing on rhetoric at the Academy. To what degree the *Rhetoric* that has come down to us corresponds to these lectures we will never know. In the text we do have, however, Aristotle tears down a number of safety fences Plato had put up to isolate the art of speech from philosophical dialectic.[118] The object of rhetoric, according to Aristotle, is *doxa*—yet *doxa* here no longer means "opinion" or "mere semblance."[119] What stands behind the term now, rather, is the conviction that things appear differently to different people or in different situations: "When people are feeling friendly and placable, they think one sort of thing; when they are feeling angry or hostile, they think either something totally different or the same thing with a different intensity."[120] The goal of the *philosophical* discussion of rhetoric is to inquire into the possibilities of judgments about objects of doxa.[121] The rules governing the doxical formation of judgments differ from those governing the dialectical formation of judgments: while the basis of dialectics is the syllogism, rhetoric employs the so-called enthymeme, which Aristotle also calls the "rhetorical syllogism."[122] The dialectical syllogism refers to what is *true*, the enthymeme to doxa, and thus to what is *likely* to be true. While in the *Rhetoric* Aristotle rehabilitates doxa philosophically—something Husserl was to call for again in the twentieth century, as we shall see later—in the *Metaphysics* he explicitly elaborates on the possibilities and limits of absolutizing doxa.

9. PROTAGORAS'S PROVOCATION OF PHILOSOPHY

In book 11 of the *Metaphysics*, little remains of Plato's caricature of Protagoras. Aristotle confronts the theses of Protagoras's *Aletheia* (*Truth*) as those of an equal whose radical thinking deserves to be assessed in all its speculative consequences. Since the opponent would not play by dialectical rules, such a dialog must take place immanently, as it were, from the inner perspective of the Sophistic view of the world. Having inquired into the shared features of various aspects of Protagoras's theory, Aristotle reaches the conclusion, strange at first, that thanks to Protagoras, "that which appears to each man" becomes "the measure [*metron*] of all things."[123]

This conclusion is all the more curious in that it immediately recalls Plato's characterization of the image of the Sophists who make "that which appears as it appears" the decisive measure.[124] Both Plato and Aristotle thus acknowledge the Sophists' *paradigmatic* effort, which separates appearance out and ties it back to itself as its own measure. With phenomenality as paradigm comes, as Aristotle remarks, an ontic bloodletting: the world escapes us, things melt into a bunch of infinite references, and we confront an empty world because Protagoras has turned all objects into relations.[125] These relations, however—and that is the point—are not infinite. They are preferentially and perspectivally organized toward a *pros hen*, a "that-toward-which": the human being. The dereification of the world silently presupposes the *anthrōpon* as its unquestioned fixed point.[126]

At this point, Aristotle introduces his magisterial argument, which, because of the abbreviated presentation typical of the lecture transcripts collected in the *Metaphysics*, requires spelling out. What happens when humans refer not to some object in the world but to a fellow human being? Necessarily the same thing as for all other objects: the person multiplies into many perspectives, and in this multiplicity its unity escapes. What served as the measure of all things, what counted as solid ground, collapses and offers no more support. The *homo mensura* principle amounts to a contradiction in terms.[127]

The question, though, of what is meant here by *anthrōpon* remains open. In the wake of George Grote, for whom the Sophists were humanists avant la lettre, many interpreters, especially in the late nineteenth century, did not take the term to refer to individuals but read *anthrōpon* as a generic plural.[128] The point of reference of the Sophist's cosmos, accordingly, was not the individual human being but humanity. Half a century earlier, Hegel had put it in even more radical terms: the *homo mensura* principle, he writes, not only does not mean any kind of individualism but marks the birth of absolute idealism.[129] Conceived of as absolute subject, however, the individual *anthrōpon* could of course no longer be played off against another one. For the ancients, this posed the problem of the "third man": for it to be possible to refer the individual and the general-generic human being to each other at all, something shared was required, a third kind of "being human" that could mediate the two. If such a third man were admitted, however, it must also be possible to think of a fourth to correlate the previous three, and so on: the threat of an infinite regress arises.

This argument of the *tritos anthrōpos*, which Aristotle in the *Metaphysics* mentions only in passing,[130] opens up an intellectual space in which the human being figures not so much as the foundation of appearances but as their addressee. There is no appearance that does not appear to someone, or, in Aristotle's protophenomenological formula, "what appears exists for him to whom it appears."[131] That is the core of Protagoras's doctrine—and at the same time what makes it so eminently modern.[132] Aristotle picks up on this when, in *On the Soul*, he speaks of a focal unity in perception that makes it possible for me not to taste sweetness and for someone else in turn to see whiteness.[133]

Yet while every appearance is in fact always an appearance *for someone*, it is at the same constitutively also always an appearance *of something*. This second moment, however, is lost in the Sophists' epistemology, where appearance and that which appears coincide without differentiation, and knowledge becomes tautological. Strictly speaking, then, Protagoras's worldview according to Aristotle means that we never perceive any sensible object but only another perception. Knowledge, accordingly, no longer refers to an object of knowledge but only to other knowledge. What remains, therefore, of Sophism's original starting point, the conflict of appearances, is merely a paltry intellectualism. Aristotle's objection contains what might be the first articulation of the structure of intentionality: "sight is the sight of something, not of that of which it is the sight."[134] In other words, seeing is not exhausted by the truism that, from a structural point of view, the act of seeing (like any other act) must have an object: that which is seen is something that cannot be derived structurally, namely, color or, in more general terms, the visible.

That is why an actual process of perception cannot have itself as its object without ceasing to be a perception and becoming a self-reflective act of thinking (of thinking perception). Without diminishing the importance of the perceiver or, more generally, the knower in the constitution of the appearance, and without excluding the possibility of a self-reflective turning back on oneself, Aristotle insists explicitly that appearance is possible only if, besides the one to *whom* something appears, there is also something *that* appears to him or her.[135] But Aristotle does not leave it at stressing the necessary correlation between the two poles. He even postulates an asymmetrical relationship diametrically opposed to the one Protagoras had posited. While in book 5 of the *Metaphysics* he describes knowledge via the category of relation, relation here, in the context of perception, is a relation whose terms do not mirror each other. The knower, to be sure, is dependent on what can be known, but what can be known does not depend in the same way on the knower.

Aristotle thus assigns the world a primacy the Sophist denies it. In complete opposition to Kant's Copernican turn, what can be known is not set up for the knower; instead, "knowledge is measured by the knowable."[136] To the Protagorean notion of measuring as *metron*, a notion whose very etymology points to its Promethean origin in the human mastery of technology, Aristotle opposes a "limit" or *nemesis* imposed by natural phenomena. When it is said that science or perception is the measure of other things, we must understand that "they are measured rather than measure."[137] We must, of course, not confuse this "objectifying" aspect with Plato's theory that images are oriented toward ideas. Truth and error are not properties of depictions or representation; truth and error pertain exclusively to *judgments*.

The question of whether and, if yes, to what extent error is possible comes up in the context of the debate with the Eleatic and Megarian schools. How can we say that which is not, how can we make illusionary or pseudo-propositions? Aristotle's way out of the aporia consists in distinguishing between two levels, the level of things and the level of thinking. Truth and error, accordingly, are no longer properties of things but merely modalities of thinking.[138] Thinking is now being conceived as the faculty of judgment that attributes or denies properties, that combines (*synthesin*) or separates (*diaresin*) the subject and the object of a proposition.[139]

Truth, then, is not situated *in things*, nor does it amount, in formal logical terms, to a structure that is immanent to propositions. A proposition proves to be true, according to Aristotle, when the combination of object and property in the proposition (or their disjunction in negation) corresponds to a combination (or disjunction) of object and property in reality. In the history of philosophy, this theory of truth, which Aristotle elaborates in *On Interpretation* and refines in *Metaphysics* 8.4 and 9.10, is known as the "correspondence theory." However, the canonical formula coined in the Middle Ages, *adaequatio intellectus et rei*, is misleading in that it could be read as positing a symmetrical equation. Aristotle seeks to prevent such a reading by insisting on the asymmetrical dependency of judgments on the world of phenomena: "It is not because we think that you are white, that you *are* white, but because you are white we who say this have the truth."[140] Here, as elsewhere, he gives voice to the priority of phenomena that, as he puts it in the *Prior Analytics*, will have to be the starting point of any future science.[141] Modern thinkers have considered this simply to prefigure empirical science. Such an equation, however, suffers already by its one-sided definition of the concept of the phenomenon.

10. SAVING THE APPEARANCES

In the sixth century CE, the Neo-Platonist Simplicius wrote an influential commentary on Aristotle's *On the Heavens*. At least as influential as the commentary as a whole, it would turn out, was the claim he makes there that Plato, as a sort of motto for research at the Academy, had exhorted his students to "save the appearances" (*sōzein ta phainómena*).[142] On this rather meager philological basis, neo-Kantianism, especially Paul Natorp in his classic interpretation, wanted to see in Plato the father of modern empirical science.[143] In his book of essays, *Die Rettung der Phänomene* (*The Saving of the Phenomena*), Jürgen Mittelstrass has shown that *sōzein ta phainomena*, translated as *salvare apparentias*, could indeed become the basic program of modern science since Galilei, but only at the price of ignoring that this modern science is indeed "modern," that it marks a new beginning, and that its concepts of both phenomena and empiricism, although they formally take them up, significantly diverge from the Greek concepts *phainomenon* and *empeireia*.

But first, let's go back to Simplicius. In his commentary, he names Eudoxus of Cnidus as the "first Greek" to have collected on Plato's supposed claim to *sōzein ta phainomena*.[144] At this point at the latest, it is clear that the concept of the phenomenon (which Aristotle expands beyond empirical natural science) is narrowly conceived. In Greek, *phainomena* initially designated celestial phenomena, and the many treatises simply called *Phainomena*, of which mostly only fragments remain, are nothing but astronomical texts. Accordingly, Simplicius writes about Eudoxos that he investigated "which uniform and ordered movements must be supposed to preserve the appearances connected with the movements of the planets."[145] So, even if it may be impossible to name the author of the principle, *sōzein ta phainomena*, it is unquestionably an *astronomical* principle meant to aid in demonstrating that the apparently disorderly movement of the "erring stars" in fact corresponds to a uniform movement.[146] The explanation of the appearances must thus be adapted to the appearances in such a way as to harmonize with them.

This goal, however, is difficult to reconcile with Plato's conception of philosophy. While Plato would not disagree with the reduction to "uniform and ordered movements" and thus to a form shared by conflicting appearances, this reduction has little to do with "saving the appearances." For Plato, the lack of harmony between phenomenon and logos could never be imputed to the imperfect phenomenon. The claim that Plato inaugurated the principle *sōzein ta phainomena*—a claim still defended by Cassirer with reference to Simplicius's text, written eight hundred years after Plato—thus must clearly be rejected.[147]

Not at all so for Aristotle, who plays only a marginal role in Mittelstrass's comprehensive analysis and is also largely ignored in the classic anthology *Die Entdeckung der Phänomene* (*The Discovery of the Phenomena*), even though he, as many authors since Mittelstrass have shown, in fact does demand fidelity to the phenomena.[148] There is even much to suggest that Aristotle's criticism of those who come up with astronomical hypotheses "looking for confirmation rather to theory than to the phenomena" contains a hidden sideswipe at his teacher. In the *Timaeus*, Plato makes it very clear that there is no need for us to take the true form of the celestial orbits from their apparent forms because we already know it: their form is the ideas.[149]

In book 5 of the *Republic*, Plato also encourages astronomers to treat the visible celestial bodies the way geometers look at a drawn diagram: it is useful but not indispensable for knowledge properly speaking, which can be attained only via mathematical models.[150] For Aristotle, astronomy is superior to arithmetic and geometry: the latter's abstract objects are eternal, while the objects of astronomy are *both* eternal (*aidion*) *and* perceptible (*aisthēton*).[151] Given this conception—rather uncommon in antiquity (and moreover not consistently maintained in the Aristotelian corpus)[152]—it is worthwhile to ask whether such a definition of astronomy might have implications for a theory of science that go beyond the framework of this particular science. The first thing to note is that, given the choice between mathematical-geometric and descriptive astronomies, Aristotle undoubtedly grants the latter epistemic primacy.

ILLUMINATION 1

The Philosophers Mosaic in Naples

There is in the collections of the Naples National Museum the so-called philosophers mosaic (fig. 1.3), discovered in Torre Annunziata (the ancient Oplontis) in 1879, a square eighteen inches wide, on light background. The left of the image is framed by two columns connected by an architrave, on which four golden vessels are placed. In the middle background, a pillar supporting a sundial juts out. A mountainscape is suggested in the upper right; below it, in the middle ground, is a set of buildings recalling

FIGURE 1.3 Mosaic of philosophers, Oplontis (Torre Annunziata), 1st century BCE. Museo Nazionale, Naples. Courtesy of Beni Culturali Italiani.

(*Continued next page*)

(Continued)

an agora with an amphitheater. The foreground is structured by a semicir-
cular bench resting on lions' feet. Sitting or leaning on the bench are seven
men. Their gaze is directed toward the center, and their attention is
focused on the object in their midst. A golden sphere is mounted on a
pedestal; its strong golden color stands out against the pale yellow and
green of the pedestal. The third man from the left, wearing a bluish robe,
directs the others' gaze toward the sphere with a pointer.

The mosaic presents a discussion about *phainomena*, about the cartogra-
phies of celestial phenomena transmitted by Eudoxus, Aratus, Euclid, Gemi-
nus, and others (this may be indicated by the scroll held up by the figure on
the right, clad in a chiton). The debate is not merely theoretical or about
texts, it is concerned with relating a hypothesis back to what it describes. The
man with the pointer is either reciting one of these writings about *phainomena*, which because of a mnemotechnic principle are usually composed in
verse, or expounding his own explanation. In both cases, the gesture of
pointing is meant to produce a simultaneity of what is heard with what is
seen. At night, one would point directly to the constellations of stars; during
the day, to constructions that depict the different celestial spheres (other
depictions feature nested spheres).[153] The gesture of showing connects what
can be said with what can be seen. It must be possible to reconstruct the evidence of the words by way of that which, thanks to the showing, shows itself.
The deixis reinforces the visibility of what is already visible.

The enduring importance of the idea of visualizing the laws of nature even in
postclassical antiquity is evident in a remark by Theon of Smyrna. He, too, attributes *sōzein ta phainomena* to Plato, but he also makes a connection with didactic visualizations: "For Plato says that we would be engaging in futile labor if we
tried to explain these phenomena without images that speak to the eyes."[154]

Aristotle, meanwhile, is concerned with more than merely pedagogical rec-
ommendations, namely, with positing a principle of research in natural philosophy. The visible is not only a post-facto way of conveying knowledge to
laypeople. Instead, those exploring the heavens are to take the visible itself as
their starting point and then to come up with explanations to reconcile the conflicting appearances. There is, therefore, a correlative relationship between the

phenomenon and its reason (*logos*) insofar as phenomena "confirm" the explanations and vice versa.[155] Aristotle, accordingly, reproaches the Platonists for trying to save their hypotheses (*sōzein tēn hypothesin*) instead of saving the phenomena.[156] And he reproaches the Pythagoreans, in turn, for having been fooled by the beauty of their own intellectual construct when they add an invisible tenth celestial body to the nine visible ones in order to make the decadic series perfectly harmonious.[157]

Already in these purely astronomical examples it is possible to see that Aristotle's concept of *phainomena* is much more than an astronomical *terminus technicus*: it asserts principles of natural science as such. As a mathematical-empirical hybrid science, astronomy, Aristotle explains in the *Prior Analytics*, plays a paradigmatic role: "Consequently it is the business of experience to give the principles which belong to each subject. I mean for example that astronomical experience supplies the principles of astronomical science; for once the phenomena were adequately apprehended, the demonstrations of astronomy were discovered. Similarly with any other art or science."[158] The example of astronomy serves to demonstrate the epistemological primacy of the *that* over the *why*.[159] Only a meticulous description of the advance of the shadow in a lunar eclipse can lead to discovering the cause, namely, that the Earth has moved between the moon and its source of light.

In *On the Parts of Animals*, Aristotle expands the principle asserted for astronomy to the investigation of nature generally. Those investigating nature must "begin," on "the plan adopted by the mathematicians in their astronomical demonstrations," "with the phenomena" and only then proceed to inquiring into their causes.[160] Modern authors have repeatedly cited these passages to turn Aristotle into the founding father of value-neutral empiricism. Yet Mittelstrass was not the first to show that, despite its etymology, the modern concept of empiricity is incongruous with the Greek *empeireia*. Nonetheless, translators of Aristotle have continued to hold on to a neo-Baconian empiricist reading.[161]

The turn came at the beginning of the 1960s with G. E. L. Owen's "Tithenai ta phainomena," which conclusively showed that Aristotle's concept of phenomena encompasses much more than the experimental conception. It aims at positing and securing all modes in which world is given, which means not only empirically observable appearances but generally shared views (*endoxa*) as well. That *phainomena* and *endoxa* do in part intermesh is evident, for example, in the discussion of weakness of the will in the *Nicomachean Ethics*: "We must, as in all other cases, set the phenomena before us and, after first discussing the difficulties, go on to prove, if possible, the truth of all the reputable opinions about these affections or, failing this, of the greater number and the most authoritative; for if we both resolve the difficulties and leave the reputable opinions undisturbed, we shall have proved the case sufficiently."[162]

What follows next is a list of opinions about strong- or weak-willed characters that concludes with the remark that this is what "they sometimes say."[163] Aristotle rejects Socrates's claim that there is no such thing as a weak will, only ignorance (since no one with the right conviction would act against what is best), because "this view contradicts the plain phenomena."[164] As Owen points out, *phenomena* here obviously does not mean any kind of empirical data gathering but something entirely different. What Aristotle wants to "posit" here are not contents of experience but *endoxa* or common views and opinions on this problem.

Important though this indication is, the conclusion Owen draws is odd: Aristotle, he writes, uses an inconsistent concept of phenomena, oscillating between purely observable semblance and the view shared in a community and sedimented in language. In "Saving Aristotle's Appearances," Martha Nussbaum has shown that this impression of indecisiveness can arise only if one imposes a Baconian model of knowledge on Aristotle's biology. Aristotle's science of phenomena, she argues, does not aim at securing "hard facts." As a science of phenomena, it is a science of experience. It is on these grounds, and not beyond experience, that *distinctions* can be made. Aristotle, after all, refers to both the aisthetic and the dianoetic faculties as *kritika*, as capacities for making distinctions. Whether Aristotle is studying shellfish on the beach of Lesbos or describing the ethical varieties of weak wills, making zoological observations or discussing socially accepted views, they equally belong to the purview of *phainomena*.[165]

This expansion of *phainomena*, of course, tends to complicate the "saving" of the phenomena rather than simplify it. Given the multitude of conflicting appearances, criteria must be found for judging the relationships among phenomena without, in judging, sacrificing the variety of phenomena. Aristotle, accordingly, makes a reproach against the Eleatics: although they began with manifold of appearances, their desire to explain their being led them to dismiss the phenomena. From a logical point of view, their arguments are conclusive, he says in *On Generation and Corruption*, but "no lunatic seems to be so far out of his senses as to suppose that fire and ice are one."[166]

Nussbaum cites this and other passages as evidence for seeing in Aristotle a commonsense pragmatist. Chief witness for this view is a passage from book 4 of the *Metaphysics*, where, on the basis of everyday practices, the conflict between optical appearances turns out to be a false problem: "No one, at least, if when he is in Libya he fancies one night that he is in Athens, straightway starts for the

Odeum."[167] We commonly evaluate appearances differently. We are able to judge them or rely on the appropriate external authorities: as Plato already pointed out, when it comes to judging an illness, the opinion of the physician and the opinion of the layperson do not carry the same weight.[168] Now, we cannot in turn evaluate the judgment of the physician; our trust in his judgment is merely of a life-practical kind. The reason for this trust does not lie *behind* but solely *in* our practice.[169]

In his essay "Saving Aristotle from Nussbaum's Phainomena," William Wians objects that, in this elegant (and indeed Wittgensteinian) turn, Nussbaum in a way sacrifices the very thing she claimed to save: phenomenality. Precisely to save the variety of phenomena, Nussbaum must rely on experts who introduce hierarchies into the apparent side-by-side of appearance and thereby make it possible to apply the law of noncontradiction in the realm of appearances as well. However, as Wians reminds us, the role of experts consists not in establishing the phenomena (*tithenai ta phainómena*) but in *making judgments about* phenomena. While Aristotle undoubtedly often takes recourse to reports from experts and even more often deploys familiar expressions and linguistic examples as philosophical arguments, he is fully aware that they need to be used with caution. On the one hand, Wians reproaches Nussbaum for interpreting Aristotle from the vantage point of the linguistic turn and for overemphasizing the verbal dimension, which amounts to collapsing *phainomena* into *endoxa*. On the other hand, Nussbaum's reconstruction and the important role it accords to the judgment of experts runs the risk of relating phenomena back to what she sought to exclude from them: external authorities.[170]

The flaw might be that Nussbaum's inclusive concept of the phenomenon does not start with the appearances of perceptions but from the judgments valid in a community. Yet thinking of *phainomena* from the perspective of judgment fails to recognize that Aristotle's decisive move for "saving the phenomena" consists precisely in describing the level of phenomena and the level of judgments as two initially conflicting modes of access to the world.

2

Aristotle's Foundation of a Media Theory of Appearing

The sun . . . is of the breadth of a human foot.

—Heraclitus

1. APPEARANCE AND JUDGMENT: ARISTOTLE'S PROTOPHENOMENOLOGY

Cicero's treatise *On Ends* (45 BCE) yields, among other things, a scientific argument aimed at settling once and for all a fundamental debate raging for centuries about the actual size of the ball of the sun: "Democritus, being an educated man and well versed in geometry, thinks the sun is of vast size; Epicurus considers it perhaps a foot in diameter, for he pronounces it to be exactly as large as it appears [*quantus videtur*], or a little larger or smaller." For Cicero, the error of the Epicureans' point of view, repeated almost verbatim by Lucretius in book 5 of *De rerum natura*, is that they rely on the testimony of the senses. Had Epicurus only made use of geometry, however, he would never have given credence to such opinions and instead been familiar with the true size of the sun.[1]

What to Cicero's mind can be put to rest as an epistemic fallacy, to Aristotle's mind appears more ambivalent. Everything indicates that, philosophically, Aristotle takes Heraclitus's statement seriously. In any case, he does not consider it to be the result of astronomical calculations since in the work on heavenly bodies, he speaks of plausible "astronomical demonstrations" according to which the sun is larger than the Earth.[2] From this perspective, the idea occasionally voiced in commentaries that the Heraclitus fragment lays the foundation for trigono-metrically calculating the diameter of the sun turns out to be rather absurd. Rather, the fragment anticipates a fundamental insight of Aristotle's philosophy of nature: *we may well know that the sun is larger than the Earth, but it nonetheless only ever appears to us to be a foot wide.*

Accordingly, when he discusses the disjunction between judgment and appearance, Aristotle cites the example of Heraclitus. The *Parva naturalia* treats of several kinds of fallacies and sensory illusions that arise, for example, when an illness or a certain somatic disposition taints our perceptions: "This is the reason too why persons in the delirium of fever sometimes think they see animals on their chamber walls because of the faint resemblance to animals of the markings thereon when put together in patterns."[3] Yet even when we are "in excellent health" and—this is Aristotle's decisive argument—"know the facts of the case perfectly well," the sun still "appears to us to be [*dokei*] only a foot wide."[4]

In the third chapter of the third book of *On the Soul*, the sun example comes in once again at a strategic point, albeit in inverse order: "The sun, for example, appears [*phaínetai*] to be a foot in diameter and yet we are convinced [*pisteúetai*] that it is larger than the inhabited part of the Earth."[5] What are we to make of this inversion, of this shift? *On Dreams* leaves no doubt as to the fact that the sun is significantly larger than the Earth. But what counts as secure knowledge in that work is reduced, in *On the Soul*, to mere conviction (*pistis*). We are convinced that the sun is larger than our planet because we rely on the judgment of specialists or on our own earlier judgments.

The certainty of our generally shared views is to be questioned just as much as the certainty of our sense perception, albeit not for the same reasons. Our conceptions constantly take up views whose content may—and often, in fact, does—turn out to be wrong. We must thus constantly make adjustments. In the case of sense perception, we may be wrong about what we perceive something *as* but not about the fact *that* we perceive something, and perceive it as something determinate. As *On Dreams* already tells us, "Even to see wrongly or to hear wrongly can happen only to one who sees or hears something real [*alēthes*], though not exactly what he supposes [*ho oietai*]."[6] What are we to make of these passages? One possible interpretation is that Aristotle sets out to distinguish two separate domains, judgment and appearing. The sun example postulates an irreducible autonomy of appearing that remains untouched even when we are certain that it is something false that appears. The way things appear to us cannot be fully determined by the judgments we make about them—*knowing that* and *seeing how* are disjunct, or, to put it differently, we do not only see what we deem to be the case—and consequently, the specific phenomenality of appearing things deserves to be studied in its own right.

Jocelyn Benoist has interpreted these passages as indicating an analytical separation on Aristotle's part between two domains that cannot be subsumed under the same law. The distinction between true and false characteristic of the level of judgment cannot immediately be transferred to the level of appearance because appearing does not abide by the alternative between true being and deceitful semblance. Saving the phenomena thus turns out to be possible only if we postulate an autonomy of phenomena that is not reducible to the propositional alternative of either true or false. In his "autonomization of the level of appearing [*plan d'apparaître*]," Benoist writes, Aristotle paves the way for all future phenomenologies.[7] This thesis, however, raises more questions than it answers. If it is meant to be more than plain phenomenism, what can a phenomenology actually be? Can we even talk about this appearing? What logos can be assigned to the phenomenal itself?

As much as he emphasizes the conflict between experiential datum and judgment—"often something else contradicts the appearance that the sun is one foot wide"[8]—as much as in *On the Soul* he delimits *aisthēsis* from the higher faculties, which he describes as faculties of conception or *hypolepsis*,[9] Aristotle also leaves no doubt that the separation between the level of experience and the level of judgment is a methodological separation that does not apply in the lifeworld. For something to be able to appear to us, the world must fan out, something must stand out, be set off from something else. The domain of perceptions is thus not merely a realm of *perceptiones confusae*. Rather, perception itself is a faculty of making distinctions. This culminates in the famous claim that *aisthēsis* already is a *krinein*, a "separating" and "discriminating."[10] Interpreters like Barbara Cassin and Michel Narcy have pointed out that Aristotle also uses the verb *krinein* when he speaks of the act of making judgments. This would indicate a polemical difference between Aristotle and Plato, for whom *krinein* is precisely that which perception is *lacking*.[11] On this reading, perception already intrinsically has something of the logos that secures an authentic epistemic and truth value; every perception, the thesis goes, already contains at its core a propositional content.[12]

Such a rehabilitation of sensible knowledge, for which Aristotle is said to vouch, immediately erases the delicate differences just made. Ultimately, in projecting Aristotle on the Stoics' later views, it even turns out to be counterproductive.[13] Moreover, the propositionalist thesis loses some of its radicalness when we remember that the equation of *krinein* and *judgment* is not an invention of modern philosophy of language but a mainstay of scholasticism. Although the verb *discernere* was common in other contexts, Aristotle's Latin translators, such as William of Moerbeke, consistently use the verb *iudicare* for *krinein*, which sometimes leads to intellectualist fallacies (not least in Aquinas, for example).[14] Hermeneutical prudence demands that we do not rush into conceiving of *krinein* as making *judgments* and, for the moment, render it as making *distinctions. Krinein* would then be less a subsumption of the act of perception under the act of judgment than a guarantee of its independence since a perceptual contrast does not necessarily imply a propositional content. A color may be distinguished from the other colors surrounding it, a white surface from a green or a blue one. Simple animal organisms already possess this "connate discriminatory capacity" (*dynamin symphyton kritikēn*),[15] those faculties Arabic authors, and Avicenna chief among them, call *vis aestimativa* (*al-qûwah al wahmiyyah*).[16] Higher forms of life, however, Aristotle insists, also always *judge* what they perceive (the verb he uses is *doxázein*).[17]

The possibility of falsehood makes its entry into appearances with judgment—and not before then. Insofar as we say something about appearances, we conceive of them *as something* (ὅς) determinate.[18] Now, the space of appearing is not per se alogical. When an object is perceived *as itself*, there is correspondence and hence a correct judgment. When something is perceived in or on something else, that is, when it is perceived accidentally, the possibility of falsehood arises.[19] Finally, there is also the possibility that something be perceived neither as itself nor in something else but as something shared, as something that accompanies all perceptions, movement or magnitude, for example. Such collateral perceptions, Aristotle holds, are particularly prone to error.[20]

As we shall have occasion to return to the various criteria of Aristotle's aisthetics in more detail, the point to be stressed here is that truth or falsehood cannot be measured by the *immediacy* of the appearance. Instead, what appears is particularly vulnerable to error when it is referred to something that exists independently of it. The level of appearances is thus neither purely in conformance with the logos nor perfectly alogical. The sphere of perceptions "cannot easily be classed as either irrational [*álogon*] or rational [*lógon échon*]."[21] The aisthetic, rather, is open toward the logos but not congruent with it. A "logos of the aesthetic world" of the kind Husserl appeals to, meanwhile, can be had only at the price of letting in falsehood along with truth, semblance along with being.[22] If it wants to be what it claims to be in its very name, every phenomen*ology* must unavoidably keep the space of appearances open to semblance as well.

This ambivalence comes out in the role *doxa* plays in Husserl's phenomenology but also already in Aristotle's theory of appearances. Aristotle, unlike Plato in book 5 of the *Republic*, does not oppose true *epistēmē* and false *doxa*. Instead, he constantly returns to the level of valid assumptions, opinions, and views, a return marked, for example, by the commonly used expression *dokei moi*, "it seems to me to be the case that." Yet, just as constantly, he points to the fragility of these assumptions, opinions, and views—not to reject *doxa* as such but to show that a conception commonly held to be valid could just as well and at any point have a *different* content. Aristotle is making a double move here: (1) He stresses that in the context of the lifeworld, we always interpret appearances to be this or that appearance. (2) He underlines that what is valid for us is not definitively taken out of the domain of the phenomenal but, in the reflexive turn back, is itself endowed with the index of phenomenality: to oppose, compare, and vary validities is to treat them as *seeming* certainties, as, more precisely, *phenomena* of validity.

What characterizes Aristotle's thinking in practice, in Husserl becomes the subject of a methodological reflection. Starting from the level of everyday *doxa* and commonly held assumptions, Husserl sets out to bracket the judicative aspect of *doxa* in favor of the phenomenal aspect. In seeking to operate a radical "epochē of any critical position-taking which is interested in their truth or falsity," Husserl's phenomenology initially presents itself as a separation of experience and judgment.[23] Every judgment initially means taking something to be *true*; every perceptual experience initially consists in taking something to be *existent*. Considering existent, however, does not take the form of an existential *thesis* but remains implicit or pre-predicative: "We do not usually speak of considering true—the word *perception* [*Wahrnehmung*, lit. a taking to be true] is an uncomfortable exception—where there is no underlying propositional thought. We say: 'That God is just is true,' yet not: 'God is true' but: 'God is.' In both cases, there is a predication, and at the basis of predication, as such, there are intellectual objectivations. This is out of the question in the case of perception."[24]

The methodological bifurcation of perception and judgment, of course, aims at everything but instituting a new two-world ontology of *aisthēta* and *noēta*. As in Aristotle, the distinction is strictly one of *method* and serves better to prove the irreducible connection between the genesis of appearances and their validity. If what characterizes the phenomenological procedure is indeed "a consistent universal interest in the 'how' of the manners of givenness,"[25] then we must ask what it really means that something is *for me in this way*. "To be sure, that objects in the broadest sense (real physical things, subjective processes, numbers, states of affairs, laws, theories, and the rest) exist for me is a statement that says . . . only that objects are accepted by me."[26] Husserl's answer is unambiguous: beyond a crude split into either authentic intuition or merely alleged opinion, Husserl emphatically points out that validity itself is nothing but the fact that some-thing appears to me as X or Y. The famous "abstention from performing indi-vidual validations" is not simply a purely passive contemplation of essences.[27] It always already presupposes an active modulation of these validities whose phe-nomenality simultaneously brings out their contingency: *something counts as this or that for me, but it* could *also count as something else*. Bracketing validity opens up a space where "alteration[s] of validity" are possible, alterations that modalize that which simply is and allow it to change its mode of being: "being is transformed into illusion or simply into being doubtful, being merely possible, being probable, being after all not completely illusory, etc."[28]

The phenomenological bracketing (*epokhē*) is thus not limited to its role as a tool for a descriptive psychology. In loosening the articulations that hold the world together, it moves closer once more to the site of their genesis. Ultimately, Husserl, not unlike Aristotle, is concerned with a return to the things of the lifeworld, *para ta pragmata*: the systematic observation of all validities in light of their "how" shows the way in which, "throughout the alteration of relative valid-ities, subjective appearances, and opinions, the coherent, universal validity *world—the* world—comes into being for us."[29] Husserl is a far cry from all the theories about excentricities and epicycles, all the hypothetical corrections of the *phainomena* that didn't quite conform to the logos, that were introduced, from Hipparchus to Kepler, to save the phenomena. Nonetheless, he is much closer to an Aristotelian conception of the *sōzein ta phainomena* than is gener-ally thought—including by Husserl himself.

The instigator of phenomenology seems to have excluded the possibility that the twentieth-century phenomenological turn back take place on a ground pre-pared by Aristotle and that Aristotelian philosophy provide, in Rémi Brague's formula, a "path to phenomenology."[30] Husserl makes abundantly clear his per-sonal preference for Plato, whose notion of insight into the idea he considers a model for his own eidetic insight into essences. Aristotle, by contrast, he treats rather condescendingly. "As an objective science among others—with its inca-pacity to do justice to intentionality on the levels of analysis and of method," Husserl writes in *Erste Philosophie* (*First Philosophy*), for example, Aristotle's psychology lacks "the ability to become a rigorous science of subjectivity."[31] This harsh judgment would seem to preclude any closer connection between Aristo-telian and Husserlian philosophy. Like others, Benoist, in his already mentioned essay, nonetheless suggests that there is a more profound connection between the two approaches than Husserl's judgment would lead us to expect.[32] Husserl is notorious for the limited scope of his familiarity with the history of philoso-phy. His knowledge of Aristotle is secondhand (from Brentano's hands, to be precise). That alone should guard us against putting too much store by statements of this kind. Yet there is someone who very early and very clearly recognized the subterraneous links between Aristotle and Husserl. It is none other than Husserl's student and sometime assistant, Martin Heidegger.

To introduce students to phenomenological research, Heidegger, in his early reading seminars in Freiburg and Marburg, chose texts by Aristotle, especially *On the Soul*,[33] a book in which, Heidegger would later say, Aristotle is "really phenomenological."[34] The link is explicitly thematized in the Marburg lecture *Introduction to Phenomenological Research* (1923/24), whose first part is entitled "ΦΑΙΝΟΜΕΝΟΝ and ΛΟΓΟΣ in Aristotle and Husserl's Self-Interpretation of Phenomenology."[35] Before turning to a detailed commentary of Husserl's concept of phenomenology as developed in the *Logical Investigations*, Heidegger embeds the concept in a history of philosophy and asks where the question concerning appearances becomes acute. At the very beginning of his text, Heidegger provides a historical sketch of pre-Husserlian phenomenologies that goes from Lambert via Kant and Hegel to Brentano. Before he enters into how Husserl conceived of his own thinking, Heidegger as it were opens a historical as well as conceptual parenthesis on the origin of *phainomenon* and *phainomai*: "In a concrete text of scientific investigations we seek to establish what facts of the matter are meant by the words. . . . For this purpose we choose Aristotle's De anima, B (II), chapter 7, that deals with perceiving the world by way of seeing. It is necessary to keep every bit of knowledge from physics, physiology at bay since they lack Aristotle's focus." And he immediately adds, laconically: "No explication with this sort of concreteness has ever been attempted again."[36]

2. SPECULAR BEINGS: IMAGES AS MIRRORS OF THE WORLD

Nietzsche famously said that the "Greeks were superficial—*out of profundity!*"[37] Not the least important implication of this assertion is that the Greek world is a world of appearances in which even the gods do not *become* embodied but always already *have* a visible body. In everyday life, the predilection for visibility—apparent in the very name of nature as something visible opening itself (etymologically, *physis* is connected to the verb *phyesthai*, which means opening up, unfolding, blossoming)—is manifest in the fact that when the Greeks refer to what they know, they define it as something they have seen and that they refer to property itself as what is visible and meets the eye. Before it became the basic ontological concept par excellence, *ousia* was a commercial term used to designate possessions, goods, or sinecures that were classified as visible and invisible goods (*ousia phanera* and *ousia aphanēs*), tangible possessions such as landed property, on the one hand, and immaterial property such as loans or money, on the other.

Yet while, in philosophy, *ousia* names the solid, secure, and thereby also invisible core of the external thing, the opposite is the case in the household and in everyday habits. Abstract property like bonds, securities, or loans are considered changeable, whereas visible, accessible land from which the income of a sinecure comes counts as the real, enduring *ousia*.[38] Despite their opposition, both conceptions intersect in assigning a prominent (albeit differently assessed) position to the faculty of seeing. What unfolds in the tension between the empirical and the intelligible is the photocentrism of post-Greek metaphysics, which identifies what has been seen as what is certain and always already defines knowledge literally as a "having seen" (*eidenai*). As we will see, this alliance is rooted in a specific conception of seeing as "reflection."

The notion that the Greek world is characteristically a world of appearances explains why philosophy before and after Socrates largely presents itself as a site where a conflict about the place and importance of visibilities is waged. Even if the image itself turns out to be something inessential, the material support on which the image appears undoubtedly is *something*. The question concerning the genesis of pictorial appearance leads back to the place where this appearance becomes autonomous. Plato seems to want to take this into account when in the *Timaeus* he describes pictorial appearance as *emphasis*, as a formal "entering into appearance" (*em-phanein*): just as an image makes its way onto a mirroring surface, it will make its way into the pupil of the eye, where it will be reflected. In both cases, a smooth reflecting surface (*emphanē*) is needed for the form to become visible.[39]

At least conceptually, Plato's topical theory of the image as *emphasis* joins a theory with a completely different origin. As we know from Gérard Simon's decisive studies on the historiography of visibility, and as Agnès Rouveret has vividly demonstrated with archaeological evidence, classical Greek theories of seeing and theories of the image are inseparably interwoven.[40] Becoming visible and making visible belong together insofar as images are now subject to the same rules of generating visibility as perception itself. If we can trust Vitruvius, the new scientific exploration of what it means to see is due to the rise of a new, perspectival kind of scene painting. In his books on architecture, he claims this new type of painting (*skiagraphia*) to have been invented by Agatharchus for a staging of a play by Aeschylus.[41]

In our context, however, it is less the discussion about the paternity and the dating of this invention that is important than Vitruvius's other remark, namely, that Agatharchus had written a text on scene painting that prompted Democritus and Anaxagoras to turn to questions of optics.[42] And indeed, we may see in the fifth century BCE, in Vasco Ronchi's words, "an unceasing attempt to determine the link between the eye and the object seen," an attempt where joyful experimentation with new pictorial techniques yields insight into how natural perception takes place and vice versa.[43] Whether something is visible or is being made visible, whether something shows itself or someone shows something: in both cases, the problem of reproduction arises, which Vitruvius literally describes as "restoring" or "rendering" (*redditio*).[44] Rather than seeing painting as a reproductive technique that comes after natural, immediate perception, both are ways of "rendering" something, of instituting it as a visible phenomenon. Rather than thinking of mirrors as artificial devices that redouble authentic immediacy, it is vision itself that is often described as a form of mirroring (*anaklasis*).[45] What moderns would strictly dissociate as being either organic or mechanical, as native or artificial, in ancient sources is often entangled.

Although ancient conceptions of vision are never fully captured by modern patterns of explanation, the scientific names of several parts of the eye continue to testify to their archaic-Greek origin to this day. The pupil, for example, which dilates and contracts at the center of the iris, is none other than the Latin *pupilla*, which in turn translates the Greek *korē*—the "girl." A passage from Plato's *Alcibiades* explains how this denomination could come about. "When a man looks into an eye," we are told, he sees a tiny mirror image of himself, "his face appears [*emphaínetai*]" in the face he looks into "like in a mirror."[46]

What is remarkable in this dialog is the way in which Plato closely aligns two modes of the visible, the *appearance in* (*emphasis*) and the refracting mirroring (*anaklasis*). The explanation of the word follows immediately: "We call this the 'pupil,' for it's a sort of miniature [*eidōlon*] of the man who's looking."[47] This is not just a semantic extension of the word *korē*, which in Homer is used exclusively to denote girls and seems to run counter to the semantic shift of the synonymous *glēnē*.[48] This shift testifies once more to the high regard in which the Greek world held the sense of sight: what people consider most valuable and noble is the apple of their eye, their *pupilla*. Plato immediately follows up with a philosophical interpretation: "Then an eye will see itself if it observes an eye and looks at the best part of it, the part with which it can see."[49] In Plato, the *pupilla* becomes the fundamental figure of introspective self-knowledge obtained through a mirroring of the self in the *alter ego*. (The resemblance with modern philosophies of the subject is as striking as it is misleading.) But, in parallel with Plato, a materialist interpretation of the figure emerges that would influence Aristotle's theory of seeing. Whereas, in the *Alcibiades*, the figure of the "girl in

the eye" is just that, a *figure* that serves poetically to guide readers toward a philosophical figure of reflection, the atomists deploy it as the foundation of a theory of bodily processes of seeing. For Democritus, the phenomenon of the "little
image" in the eye yields insight into how the outside world enters the organism.
In seeing my image mirrored in someone else's eyes, that person's eyes become a
stage for my self, and I see how seeing as such takes place. But this, precisely, is
where Aristotle identifies a misunderstanding.

What I see in the eyes of another appears only to *me*: it is not an image
seen but an image mirrored, not *emphasis* but *anaklasis*.[50] It is only I who see
the image, not the other person. My ability to see myself in the other is due
solely to the smooth and level surface of the eye that reflects my own sight.
The reality of the mirror image in no way depends on any faculty of the
psyche: mirroring occurs on all smooth surfaces, also and especially on surfaces without a soul. If the other person were dead, I would still find myself
mirrored in his or her eye.[51] This observation then leads Aristotle, somewhat
perplexed, to note: "It is strange . . . that it never occurred to him [Democri-
tus] to ask why the eye alone sees, while none of the other things in which
images are reflected do so."[52]

Seeing thus cannot be derived solely from the analysis of natural images,
images that occur in the world, or, put differently: a theory of the iconic and
a theory of the aisthetic do not match. Some image theories—Plato's chief
among them—formally emphasize the discrepancy between image and seeing.
Socrates's ironic recommendation to the painter is not to trust his own eyesight but to take the mirror as his teacher, which always (and without being
asked, as it were) captures all the forms of things, irrespective of the eyes for
which they are intended.[53] Such an *anaclastic* or mirror-image model of the
image, which underwent a large number of variations in Western history,
derives its legitimacy precisely from its refusal to submit itself to the rules of a
living eye.

Aristotle takes a different path. His theory rather conforms to an *emphatic*
model of the image, yet also, unlike Plato's, conceives *emphasis* and *anaklasis*
disjunctively: an image always *appears in* a medium, yet this medium, to make
anything visible, must rely on a seeing eye. The necessity of a theory of mediality
is already apparent in the discussion of the "girl in the eye." Democritus is said to
have realized that seeing comes about thanks to the eye being made of water.[54]
Yet because he lacks understanding of the mediality of the natural elements
(water, air, earth, fire), he fails to capture the peculiar dynamics of seeing. For
the element water can actualize in different ways: either as *mirroring* on the

surface of the water, which leads to the tiny image on the pupil, or as *transparency*, which renders the medium translucent.

Both modes refer to two different domains of the optical: on the one hand, to a physics of mirrorings and refractions (the Greek *anaklasis* does not distinguish between the two meanings), in which Aristotle is interested in an entirely different context, namely, meteorology;[55] on the other hand, to a description of the living eye's ability to see. Only when seeing is no longer described exclusively according to merely physical laws and the event of seeing is no longer exclusively understood as a topological movement, only when, therefore, the idea of a material image substance and the conception of mechanic image transmission are dismissed, only then is it possible to understand the originary unity of phenomenality and iconicity. For something to be mirrored on the surface of a thing, it takes certain invariant light conditions; for *anaklasis* to become *emphasis*, however, it takes more than just light: it takes an active, living seeing eye to whom the image appears. This eye, as addressee of the appearing, plays a constitutive role in the process of appearing. This role does not amount to a projection, though.

The seeing eye does not bring forth that which appears from out of itself, and neither does that which appears exist, ready-made, in some outside. Highlighting the mediated act of constitution—the salient characteristic of Aristotle's theory of appearances—serves to counter both the idea that becoming visible is limited to local movement of something already visible and the temptation to see it as purely the result of a self-positing imagination. Aristotle's genetic theory of appearing, which we now have to spell out, is thus subject to two conditions:

(1) The discovery by the natural philosophers that the appearing world goes back to a fundamental elementarity cannot be exhausted by describing the various material amalgamations. The eye contains water. What determines the ability to see is not the eye's watery basis but the fact that the eye, as transparent element, allows for seeing (through).[56] The element's mediality here refers to a potential seeing; yet the potentiality thus instituted is made actual only by an active seeing endowed with soul. *A theory of visibility must therefore begin with a theory of the soul, and a physical determination has to start with a psychological foundation.*

(2) Even if seeing cannot be thought outside the psyche and if it cannot be thought other than as a seeing "of the soul," this amounts to anything but a spiritualization of the optical. Insofar as the psyche in Aristotle serves as the principle of *kinēsis* or movement, the body's seeing—as an *act* of seeing—can

make sense only as a faculty of the soul. The fact that describing this activity as merely a *faculty* of the soul is insufficient, and that the faculty depends on a mediating medium, shows why Aristotle's theory of appearances must necessarily be a media theory. *A theory of the soul must therefore begin with describing that medial element within which and through which a faculty of the soul can actualize.*

These two conditions, which describe two opposing movements, once again, and in a manner completely different from Plato, discover an interspace that would become the site of philosophical conflict: the level of appearances. To the extent that the soul no longer constitutes the visible but in exercising its faculty as passive addressee helps what is potentially visible to become actually visible, the traditional locus of seeing shifts as well, from either the eye or the object to the elementary middle in which *something appears*. Only when seeing is no longer reduced to analogical or metaphorical pictoriality, only when images are no longer constituted by perception alone, when instead—one level down, as it were—the ground shared by both perception and images is discovered (namely, their phenomenal aspect), only then is the path cleared both for a nonreductionist philosophy of images and for a different theory of aisthesis.

3. ANTIPODES OF SEEING

Like Plato, albeit with different connotations, Aristotle distinguishes between *aisthetics* and *phantastics*, that is, between a description of the faculty of perception and a description of the faculty of the image. The analysis I propose in the pages that follow sets out to show that while both faculties are irreducible to each other, they do not for all that oppose each other frontally (as some modern philosophers have claimed)[57] but rather stand in a relationship of asymmetrical *implication*. There are many passages in Aristotle to show that for him, there is a downright "material" continuity between seeing and imagination, between light and media of presentation. These passages raise obstacles for all those commentators who, beginning in antiquity, have sought to categorically separate bodily and mental faculties, physical and noetic processes. Thinking, in Aristotle's famous formula, is never possible without *phantasmata*, yet these *phantasmata* or images of representation in turn obtain their meaning from *phōs*, from light, which is the basis and condition of every bodily, act-like perception.[58]

The essential unity of *phainomenon* and *phantasmata*, *phōs* and *aisthēsis*, of these different ways of orienting oneself in the world is founded—if we follow Aristotle's advice always to pay attention to etymologies—on their reference to a center that opens up always anew, to a never-conclusive phenomenalization of the **a(u)i*, which one might tentatively render as "opening-ness."[59] For something different to arise as the always-identical and for this other to come in *as something else*, as something *different from the identical* in the first place, there must be a constitutive distance, an inherent interspatiality that makes appearing possible and yet opens up at all only in this appearing. Just how radical a gesture on the part of Aristotle it was to begin with neither a purely active projection nor a merely passive reception but with a phenomenalization in the middle voice is evident when we consider the conceptions of the sense of sight current in his time (and often well beyond).

Discussing such theories of seeing also reveals that the old question of whether Aristotle can be read as a historian of philosophy or not ultimately amounts to positing a false alternative.[60] When he summarizes and comments on his predecessors' positions, Aristotle's description can be understood only as a thinking that is itself in movement. It is precisely in speculatively developing its ultimate consequences and discovering its nonthematized premises that Aristotle provides a cartography, as it were, of so-called pre-Socratic philosophy. Accordingly, his discussion of his predecessors' theories of seeing brings out a strong polarization of optical perception into theories of emission and theories of reception. The demonstration that aisthesis is an autonomous faculty of a being with a soul begins with a critique of mechanistic theories of the image.

Among the senses, Aristotle—in keeping with his predecessors—assigns the greatest significance to sight. The orientation in space, the meaning of forward and backward, and therefore an organism's entire ability to move, is determined by where the eyes are located on the body.[61] It would nonetheless be hasty to reduce the famous "nobility of sight" Hans Jonas sees as characteristic of Western views shaped by Greek antiquity solely to a capacity for contemplative distancing.[62] The primacy of sight asserted at the beginning of the *Metaphysics* is due to the eye's greater "evidential power" (*enargestatē*).[63] Such evidence, then, consists in visualizing things as they really are, that is, in making sure that reality truly "meets the eye." Yet precisely because of its frontally "striking" character, sight never loses its violent affective power. The paradoxical consequence is that what we perceive with the eyes touches us the most enduringly, more than all senses of contact.[64] What is true of all the other senses is true par excellence of the sense of sight: every *aisthēsis* is a "being moved" (*kineisthai*), a "being affected" (*paskhein*), and thus means "undergoing alteration" (*alloiōsis*).[65] The relationship between the object of perception and the organ of perception, that is, the basic structure of perception, is to be thought in the mode of movement. It remains to be determined, however, how exactly this being moved is to be understood.

(a) Atomistic Decals

The atomistic theories of perception we find in Aristotle's discussions of Leucippus or Democritus, for example, take this movement literally and conceive of it as, in Aristotelian terms, a local movement.[66] According to such archaic cosmologies, the eye is affected by *eidōla* (simulacra) that convey a "view" or "image" of things to the perceiver. We are to imagine these *eidōla* as thin skins detaching from the surface of things. Lucretius takes up both this tradition and Epicurus's ideas when he introduces the *simulacra* in his didactic poem, "which, like films drawn from the outermost surface of things, flit about hither and thither through the air."[67] These tiny images, which have become detached from the surfaces of things or, as a kind of spawn, come from the inside of things, as it were, are such "thin shapes" (*tenuis figuras*) that they are not visible to the naked eye.[68] Lucretius's notions here recall the whirring films mentioned in Epicurus's *Letter to Herodotus*, "outlines or films, which are of the same shape as solid bodies, but of a thinness far exceeding that of any object that we see."[69] Perception fundamentally is due to an immediate, albeit atomized, microscopic contact, comparable to the salty spray lashing against one's face on the seashore.[70]

What is decisive here is the material, physical tie between the image and the original set up by these delicate detachments of things. Such a theory of simulacra (*eidōla*), tiny images (*deikela*), or effusions (*pórroia*)—which in the photographic nineteenth century has a late follower in Balzac[71]—points to the constitutive physical common ground of the perceived and the perceiver. However, it does not explain their difference, which every process of cognition presupposes. The idea of perception as local transmission of a material epidermis demonstrates its own absurdity when we consider that the eye would rather quickly be filled with skins flooding in. One solution of this aporia consists in supplementing the theory of effusion with something like regulative pores.[72] The relative opening of the organs of perception, conceived of as pores, regulates whether and how something is perceived. Yet even if the tiny images do not gain access to the organ of perception and come to a halt just before it, this is not how seeing comes about; it even becomes impossible. Aristotle's objection on this point is as simple as it is convincing: "If what has colour is placed in immediate contact with the eye, it cannot be seen."[73]

From this reflection, Aristotle derives the structural necessity of a constitutive distance and difference. To describe the process of perception as an emanation of the perceived is to accept as given what arises in this process in the first place. In the terms of *Sense and Sensibilia*, the object of perception is being ascribed a *poiein*, a productive doing, when in fact its effect is limited to putting a faculty of perception in a state of *energeia* or action.[74] The atomistic interpretation, at least on Aristotle's reading, reifies the process of perception as such, and identifying perception with images of perception ultimately turns images into things as well.[75]

(b) Empedocles's Lantern

Diametrically opposed to this objectivizing reception theory of the visible is an activist emission theory of seeing, which also has a long history. Besides the word *opsis*, another term for seeing is attested early on: *aktis*.[76] Literally denoting a "ray of fire," it is associated with the representation of the act of seeing as constituting the visible thanks to a ray of light that, as it were, shoots out from the eye. Such a representation of a fiery arrow testifies to the subsistence within perception theory of the archaic theory of the elements to which, on occasion, even Aristotle pays tribute. Hearing, for instance, is associated with the element air, touch with the element earth, and seeing with the element fire. And Empedocles accounts for cosmogony, for example, in terms of four elements he calls generative "roots" or *rhizōmata* that are kept in motion by love and conflict. Each rhizome is associated with the name of a god: Zeus, for instance, designates the fire of the sun. Visibility depends on the issuing ray of fire. Its reflection, as the parable of the lantern quoted by Aristotle in *Sense and Sensibilia* suggests, lights up the world:

> As when one who purposes going abroad prepares a lantern,
> A gleam of fire blazing through the stormy night,
> Adjusting thereto, to screen it from all sorts of winds, transparent sides,
> Which scatter the breath of the winds as they blow,

> While, out through them leaping, the fire, i.e. all the more subtle part
>   of this,
> Shines along his threshold with incessant beams:
> So the primaeval fire, fenced within the membranes.
> And delicate tissues gave birth to a round-eyed daughter [kourēn]—
> Tissues bored through with wonderful channels—
> And these fended off the deep surrounding flood,
> While letting through the fire, i.e. all its more subtle part.[77]

Like a lantern, the eye is "glowing" from within and lights everything around it. The generative force of seeing refers back to a primary cosmic act. Empedocles's, like other emission theories that survive even in medieval optics (in Robert Grosseteste, for example), manifest a belief in a magical efficacy on the part of the eye that acts on the objects it sees, that can bring them about and change them. The power of sight thus becomes a magical power that can have miraculous but also threatening effects. It crystallizes in the notion of the "evil eye" discussed in the pseudo-Aristotelian *Problemata*.[78] In Aristotle himself we find such strange relics of archaic notions when he declares that menstruating women can turn mirrors bloody simply by looking into them.[79] Yet despite such anecdotal excursuses, Aristotle focuses on the systematic significance of the activist thesis. What does it mean to suppose, as the Pythagoreans do, for example, that the eye is the trigger for anything to appear at all?

Aristotle in his early works seems not to have been unsympathetic to the idea of a ray of sight, for example, in the context of an analysis of optical scattering. If there were a tube between the eye and the object, one would see more clearly because the rays would then not scatter.[80] Yet with few exceptions—notably the discussion of how rainbows come about[81]—the ray of sight hypothesis seems no longer to be an option; indeed, it is described as "idle" (*kenon pantelōs*), "irrational" (*alogon*), and "trifling" (*euethes*).[82] Everything thus seems to indicate that the detailed discussion of the lantern allegory is meant to make an example of Empedocles's theory.

The author of a *Poetics* and a *Rhetoric* will hardly have failed to realize that the Empedoclean poem, which he cites at length, is not an argumentative text. Nonetheless, Aristotle gives a curiously literal reading and distills a theoretical position from it. Empedocles's verses serve Aristotle to develop a massive argument against any kind of theory of seeing that reduces visibility solely to the pole of the one who sees. The objection is that emission theories expunge the coconstitutive role of the space of perception and turn the in-between into a negligible entity. As Aristotle's main argument puts it, "if vision were the result of light issuing from the eye as from a lantern, why should the eye not have had the power of seeing even in the dark?"[83]

As a state of the perceptual field (which later acquires a specific function in Aristotle's theory of media), darkness here initially indicates only that the space of appearance must be conceived as a modal space. The space of appearance can assume various states but must in any case be posited as a conditioning co-cause of the visible. The possibility for this space to light up has nothing to do with an optical *aktis* but with a receptiveness to light. Just as this receptiveness is predicated on a certain plasticity and malleability, so the activity of the perceiving embodied soul must allow for being moved.

Aristotle adopts the pre-Socratic *physiologoi*'s attempts at tracing the process of seeing back to purely material processes and tests them as to their theoretical consequences. If indeed every perception is an "alteration," if indeed every *aisthēsis* implies an *alloiōsis*,[84] then doctrines that exclusively take either the one who sees or that which is seen as their guide evidently fall short. An adequate theory of visibility must instead be able to explain how visibility can come about and how something that was previously not there can emerge. The archaic cosmologies have to be overcome in favor of a more subtle conception of transformative processes.

4. A WAY OUT OF THE APORIA: SEEING AS ALTERATION

"Perception," we read in *On the Soul*, "depends . . . on a process of movement or affection from without, for it is held to be some sort of change of quality."[85] Strikingly, here and elsewhere, Aristotle speaks of a *qualitative* alteration.[86] Everything seems to suggest that this *alloiōsis* is to be marked off from that of the atomists, who confuse change with the substantial movement defined in the *Physics*.[87] What takes place in perceptual *alloiōsis* is not a switch from a previous to a new state; rather, it is an *epidosis eis auto*, a self-increase and self-improvement.[88] The perceptive faculty does not gain anything in the process of perception but instead actualizes its intrinsic capacities. (In the sixteenth century the Padua Aristotelians refer to this as a change that is not destructive but perfective—*alteratio non corruptiva sed perfectiva*.) This shows that the longstanding debate whether perception consists in the effect of the opposite on the opposite or of the same on the same—which Aristotle marginally alludes to repeatedly and which Theophrastus summarizes succinctly—quite simply does not go far enough.[89] And, according to *On the Soul*, this is also the reason why Plato's description of the process of seeing in the *Timaeus* is problematic.

The already more refined version the *Timaeus* offers cannot be reduced either to a theory of emission nor to one of emanation. Rather, it constitutes a synthesis of the two approaches.[90] The "pure fire inside us, cousin to that fire," that is, daylight, "flow[s] through the eyes" "close-textured, smooth and dense" to encounter the ray that in turn is coming from the things: "like makes contact with like and coalesces with it to make up a single homogeneous body alighted with the direction of the eyes. . . . And because this body of fire has become uniform throughout and thus uniformly affected, it transmits the motions of whatever it comes in contact with as well as of whatever comes in contact with it, to and through the whole body until they reach the soul. This brings about the sensation we call 'seeing.' "[91] For something noncorporeal (that is, the ray of light) to densify into something corporeal (that is, the uniform body in the center), an action of the same on the same is required. Or, in Goethe's words: "Were the eye not sun-like, never could it see the sun."[92]

This homology thesis, which undoubtedly covers only part of Plato's theory of seeing, differs from the conception that only opposites could act on opposites, traditionally attributed, for example, to Heraclitus or Anaxagoras.[93] Aristotle, meanwhile, criticizes both conceptions and, in *On the Soul*, refers to his more detailed discussion in *On Generation and Corruption*. As an event that provokes a change, the aisthetic relation can exist neither between entirely identical terms nor between entirely different terms. If both were entirely different, *anómoia*, there would be no being affected (*pathos*); if both were entirely identical, there would be no qualitative change (*alloiōsis*). There must always be a certain commonality that takes the form of a *qualified difference*. Things that are different differ *from each other*. Aristotle also describes this relational opposition as *antikeimena*, being opposite to one another. Only where there is such a relationship can there be action upon and change. Already here, in *On Generation and Corruption*, Aristotle distinguishes between genetic commonality and eidetic difference, between belonging to a species and a formal difference. Only where there is a distance between forms can there be a transfer of forms: "agent and patient must be like (i.e., identical) in kind and yet unlike (i.e., contrary) in species."[94]

These basic rules of Aristotle's theory of affection already point to a specific constitution that characterizes that which affects and that which is being affected, a constitution that can also be described as *positionality*. The perceptive apparatus and its object, *aisthetērion* and *aisthēton*, must be set up and directed toward each other. Only when the perceptive organ is opposite its object of perception can *aisthēsis* in its various forms take place. The *aisthētikon* or faculty of perception actualizes whenever it encounters "its particular" object, the *idion aisthēton.* Accordingly, the *idion aisthēton* that corresponds to hearing is that which can be heard; to tasting, that which can be tasted; to smelling, that which can be smelled; to touch, that which can be touched. The systematic analysis of the individual sense functions, each of which has a chapter in *On the Soul* 2.7–11, begins with a definition of the *aisthēton* of seeing: "The object of sight is the visible, and what is visible is colour."[95] We thus have the external terms of the aisthetic relation.

Up to this point, Aristotle is roughly in agreement with his predecessors. The relationship between the sense organ of perception and the object of perception is a necessary, albeit not yet sufficient, condition for the *alloiōsis* at the basis of every act of perception to take place. Having made clear that what happens in perception cannot be reduced to either of the two terms of the relation alone, Aristotle in these five chapters focuses on the question what happens *between* the two terms, what kind of connection they have. To anticipate: the question is whether *alloiōsis* is to be thought as mediated or not.

5. WHAT LIES IN BETWEEN: ARISTOTLE AND DEMOCRITUS ON THE VOID

According to Aristotle, not all organisms that have a soul also have the faculty of perception. In his theory of life as a continuum, in which species differences are gradual and the higher faculties build on the lower, plants, for example, have a "threptic" or nutritive faculty of the soul, but they do not have perception (*aisthēsis*). The function of the vegetative soul is limited to maintaining the plant's material constitution. Plants are materially acted on, but they lack the ability to mediate, they lack a medium that could intercept and transform this action. In lacking *aisthēsis*, plants lack the ability to detach themselves from matter. The reason, for Aristotle, is that plants "have no mean, and so no principle in them capable of taking on the forms of sensible objects but are affected together with their matter."[96]

This already gives a sense of the direction in which Aristotle is taking his criticism of materialist doctrines. The site of *aisthēsis* must be conceived of as a middle or mean (*mesótēs*), a certain intermediate position, in which the material allows for its own overcoming. Perception must not be reduced either to the perceiving body or to the perceived object; instead, it is "a sort of mean between the opposites that characterize the objects of perception."[97] This shift of attention toward the situation where perceiver and perceived are entangled characterizes

Aristotle's aisthetics. But it needs to be further defined, for it remains open what this kind of distancing from the material leads to.

It may seem obvious to conceive of this noncorporeal interspace, this necessary distancing thanks to which something can stand out, as an *empty* interspace or as a gap. This was the interpretation of Democritus (or at least it is the interpretation his theory of perception suggested to Aristotle).[98] In *On the Soul*, Democritus's ant example becomes the central case study for leading the theory of an empty interspatiality ad absurdum.

> Democritus misrepresents the facts when he expresses the opinion that if the interspace [*to metaxy*] were empty one could distinctly see an ant on the vault of the sky; that is an impossibility. Seeing is due to an affection or change [*paskhen*] of what has the perceptive faculty, and it cannot be affected by the seen colour itself; it remains that it must be affected by what comes between. Hence it is indispensable that there be *something* in between [*anagkaion ti einai metaxý*]—if there were nothing, so far from seeing with greater distinctness, we should see nothing at all.[99]

Democritus's example serves Aristotle as an occasion to repeat the principles of his media theory of appearances: *something appears to a perceiver because the perceiver is affected.* This affecting, however, does not take place immediately; the object of perception (in this case, "the seen color") does not act directly but mediately and at a distance. What operates the affection here is that which lies "between" the organ and the object of perception: the medium. The dimension of pathos, of affection, makes his theory a mediology of appearances. Yet precisely because mediality constitutively depends on the pathic dimension of appearing, the medium cannot be a void. The medium guarantees not only the necessary distance but its bridging as well: it is *moved* by the perceived and transmits this movement. That "there must be *something* in between" (*anagkaion ti einai metaxý*), a medium, a *metaxy,* means at the same time that this medium must have a certain, even if minimal, density, a however slight but nonetheless real resistance such that it can be moved. While an empty interspace, a pure vacuum, would correspond to Aristotle's topological definition of the medium in the *Meteorology*—it "lies between"[100]—it does not correspond to the functional-dynamic definition of the medium in *On the Soul*.

Thus even in rehabilitating the *metaxy*, the in-between, Democritus undermines the medial: he treats what lies in between as a necessary but nonetheless bothersome entity. Only once its inner consistency has been undone, only once the interspace has been entirely depopulated, is it possible that one may "see through" all the way to the most inconspicuous object—the ant. Elsewhere, Aristotle explains that the benchmark for any real knowledge is *akribeia*, rigor and precision.[101] Here, however, the epistemological validity of *akribeia* presents itself in a more ambivalent light, since its pretense of immediacy comes at the price of forgetting the context: associated semantically with *akron* (tip) and *aktis* (ray of sight), *akribeia* may well be "to the point," but it remains blind. Eliminating what lies between does not allow for sharper, more penetrating seeing (*orasthai akribōs*); it allows for no seeing at all. Without a medium, however loosely textured, there can be no resonance and hence no transmission of the visible. Accordingly, an authentically *medial* foundation of appearing cannot but assign to the medium a certain materiality (albeit a minimal and liminal one). Democritus's theory of the empty medium is thus a media theory in name only.

All later attempts at saving Democritus's theory of media have not taken this fundamental objection into account. Instead, there are complaints that the presentation of Democritus's theory of sight in *On the Soul* is deliberately crude, so as to make it conform to Aristotle's argument, and attempts are made, by bringing other sources in, to reconstruct a different Democritean philosophy of nature.[102] The medium would accordingly be able to counter Aristotle's objections against the theory of simulacra: the tiny images (or *apotyposes*, as Democritus calls them) now no longer enter into the eye directly but are slowed down by the medium. Such a theory of a retarding medium, however, has two decisive drawbacks. On the one hand, it reinforces the theory of seeing as pictorial representation, which it mitigates but whose basic impetus remains intact. On the other hand, the function of the medium as retarding medium is a compensatory one and thus remains external.

Yet if there must be a medium—as Aristotle asserts again in *Sense and Sensibilia*[103]—and if this medium is to play a role, if it is to be *effective* at the core of the perceptual process, it is necessary to consider not only its *intermediary position* but its *mediating function*. As the discussion of the vegetative soul showed, the idea of mediality arises where the task is to describe a form of non-immediate efficacy, an effect that is not transmitted "through matter" alone. *Not alone* and *not primarily* through matter, for in a certain respect, the medium is indeed material: only because the in-between is, in a certain respect, impermeable and resistant can it be put into movement and affected by the sense object and transmit this affection to the sense organ.[104] That which separates what lies in between also holds it together (*syn-echein*) and produces a continuity that is neither completely corporeal nor entirely immaterial. In this sense, what lies in between resembles rhythmic-spatial diesis in music: the medium coordinates the terms of the relation and puts them in resonance.[105]

The idea of the medial continuum central for Aristotle may be seen as an early symptom of the *horror vacui*, which was to have a long history and which Aristotelian logic countered with the principle of plenitude.[106] But it must also be seen as allowing Aristotle to meet two conditions, namely, to conceive of perception (1) as an affective being moved and (2) as a distancing from corporeal entities. Being moved points to a physics of the continuum, in which all beings touch each other at their *eschata* or outer limits, while the distancing points to a theoretical logic that proceeds by isolating and distancing its elements. Aristotle contrasts both views, which also represent two attitudes toward what is, in his lectures on physics. The physics of the continuum and the theoretical logic of the disjunctive are each embodied in two examples, the point and the number, geometry and arithmetic. Natural things are characterized by being "at once" (*hama*).

This "at once," however, must not be confused with a temporal "at the same time." Aristotle rather means "being at once in one place," which is why many translators choose simply to translate *hama* as "together." Natural things are together at once in one place insofar as their "extremities" *touch*.[107] Touch (*haptesthai*), as Aristotle explains in earlier chapters of the *Physics*, guarantees the transmissibility of movement. As long as this touch is only external and the boundaries remain, there are successive series but no continuous connection.[108] Continuous structures, complex figures that have a certain extension (*megethos*), are captured particularly well by perception insofar as aisthesis, thanks to its being anchored in the body, is itself embedded in the continuous and moving. The body, for Aristotle, projects into depth; in Merleau-Ponty's terms, we might speak of the "dimensionality" of the body.[109]

Noesis (thinking) proceeds differently from aisthesis. It depends on separating and detaching (*khorizein*), it operates via definition (*horismos*) and, in a procedure called *diairesis*, divides what is phenomenally continuous. Put in such general terms, Aristotle here rejoins Plato. In Plato's ontology, ideas are defined, precisely, as detached, separated by a kind of *khōrismos* or chasm, and as dwelling in a different, namely, a heavenly place, *hyperouranios*. While Aristotle takes up Plato's *khōrismos* notion for all forms of ideality, he nonetheless criticizes Plato for retopologizing what has been separated. As Heidegger remarks in an excursus on Aristotle's concept of mathematics, the question of abstraction is linked with the question of place already on the linguistic level—*khōrizein* is related to *khōra*.[110] What has been separated analytically is not be found in any other place; the separation quite simply renders it placeless. Mathematicians, Aristotle says in the *Physics*, separate or detach by abstracting something from an entity characterized by movement. But that does not mean that they put what they detach somewhere else. "In thought," the detached is instead freed from its topological limitation: "Mathematical objects are nowhere."[111]

While a surface is usually regarded as the *peras* or limit of a body that, as body, always has a certain *topos* or place, mathematicians thus view the structure of a body purely in itself but do "not treat of them [that is, lines, surfaces, points] as the limits of a natural body."[112] Nonetheless, there are several levels of the mathematical effort of abstraction that are at varying distance from the natural body. Aristotle opposes arithmetic—for him, the epitome of the disjunctive approach—to geometry, which operates with objects that are, albeit detached, connected and thus analogical. Geometrical objects, to be sure, do not stand in physical space, they do not have a *topos*. They nonetheless form a certain spatial unity, they are oriented and have dimensions such as top, bottom, left, right, and so on. It is possible, in other words, to *orient* oneself in geometric objects. (Aristotle thus names the preconditions of later mathematical topology.) The definition of this position in ideal space is also called *thesis*.

What holds the *thesis* of the geometrical together is, on the smallest level, the point. Yet it would be wrong to see in the point a kind of elementary grammar: lines never emerge from points and, accordingly, surfaces never emerge from lines and bodies not from lines.[113] Insofar as geometric objects are continuous, it is always possible to insert between two points yet another point. Points are common to all geometric objects because points are undifferentiated (*adiaireton*).[114] Taking a point out of a line changes nothing about the line. Matters are completely different in arithmetic. Numbers do not touch; they do not have a common boundary (*horos*). They are disjunct. The transition from the number 1 to the number 2 is a jump because there is no in-between or *metaxy*.[115] While the geometrical is characterized by *connection* (*synechés*), the arithmetic, as epitome of the discrete, is configured at most as a *series* of individual, independent elements.

Things, then, are connected or continuous "if their extremities are one" and "in succession if there is nothing of their own kind intermediate between them."[116] While geometry, based on a fundamental and elementary commonality, elaborates different forms, arithmetic treats as equivalent what is in itself different.[117] Discrete elements (*stoicheia*) are completely external to each other. There is no interspace between them, or only an empty one. As an individual (*hekaston*), each element remains separate. Continuous structures, in turn, are relational entities connected in space that can infinitely be analyzed into discrete elements.[118] Between two points, there is nothing or, rather, there is nothing *other* than an infinite number of additional possible points. There is nothing that can come between two points.

This brings us back to the question of mediality. Distancing and ability to touch still oppose each other, without mediation. Geometry offers a model in which there is nothing alien; arithmetic, one in which there is nothing common. In neither case does the in-between play a constitutive role. The arithmetic in-between comes down to pure distance, while the attempt to give a purely geometrical definition of the interval always amounts to a post-facto operation on something continuous. In those passages of *On the Soul* concerned with elaborating a philosophy of mediality, Aristotle makes use both of moments of the continuous and of moments of the disparate, such as I have sketched them. At the same time, however, he explodes the alternative. His clever move—to anticipate this right away—consists in conceiving the point of contact necessary for every movement no longer as localized point but *as space itself.*

6. A MEDIA THEORY OF APPEARANCES

Aristotle initially and paradigmatically lays the foundation of his mediology of appearances in discussing the sense of sight. At the beginning of the sequence of chapters that analyze the perceptive faculties individually in *On the Soul* (2.7– 11), he brings up once more the relational nature of *aisthēsis.* Just as each sense of perception refers to an object of perception, the sense of sight refers to the visible. Yet what is their relationship? What status does the necessary in-between have? Is this in-between merely an intellectual construct? Obviously not, since Aristotle includes it from the outset in the sphere of the aisthetic. "What is visible is colour and a certain kind of object which can be described in words but"— this is the strategic apostrophe of the empty space—"which has no name," which literally remains anonymous.[119]

(a) This Nameless Something:
The Invention of the Diaphanous

What are we to make of this peculiar "anonymous," this nameless something that belongs to the visible but is itself without color, that can be named but has not yet given its name? "What we mean," Aristotle adds, "will be abundantly clear as we proceed." And he continues with this explanation: "Whatever is visible is colour and colour is what lies upon [*epí*] what is in itself visible [*kath'autò horatou*]; 'in itself' here means not that visibility is involved in the definition of what thus underlies colour, but that that substratum contains in itself [*en eautō*] the cause of visibility."[120] Insofar as the objects of the world always have sensible properties of their own (a colored surface, for example), they are *visible* objects and carry in themselves the cause of their appearing. And yet their own constitutive visibility is only coconstitutive. Insofar as every visible object depends on appearing to someone *as something visible*, it must step out of itself and show itself to another, animate being. Color, as the object's *own* visibility, must set the medium into motion, and the medium thereby receives the visibility it gives rise to in the perceiver as *something alien*. The medium thus already belongs to the visible but it does not have its visibility in itself (*kath'autò*) but by means of another. This names the fundamental paradox of mediality: what is independently visible is visible independently only on the condition that it dispossesses itself in the coconstitutive force of the alien medium; the medium, inversely, only unfolds its own mediating function once it accepts being defined heteronomously by something else.

That which shows itself thus never shows itself *out of* itself (*en eautō*) alone. It always shows itself in passing *through something else*, "through" (*diá*) an other. Every appearing—and this is the thesis whose radicalness and scope we have yet to fathom—is always an appearing-with or an appearing-through. The fact that the radicalness of the claim went unnoticed is due primarily to Aristotle's using an expression that made it seem self-evident. He fills the conceptual empty spot, which he has so carefully prepared and delimited, with a peculiar, newly minted concept: that through which and in which that which appears does appear is "what shines through," the "diaphanous" (*diaphanēs*). This semantic sleight of hand, which disguises a fundamentally new philosophical orientation in the argumentative use of linguistic self-evidence, is all the more effective in that Aristotle takes an everyday word and merely remints it conceptually.

The word *diaphanēs* is indeed documented going back a long time. It describes a luminous or light-like quality attributed to certain stones or objects and considered in antiquity to be all the more magical for the rudimentary state of glass and mirror technology. The expression can already be found in Homer, where it designates a "pure place" (*en katharō . . . diephaineto chōros*).[121] The diaphanous, however, not only refers to purity, it is also threatening: a forest ablaze "glows terribly" (*diephaineto d'ainōs*). Some centuries later, Herodotus uses *diaphanēs* to describe the "red-hot stones" he says the Scythians employed in a purification ritual. The word becomes poetic when it describes the morning light at dawn (in Herodotus and later in Polybios). Pindar uses it when he seeks to suggest something shining brightly, the flickering flames of a campfire, for example.[122] A decisive example—decisive because it anticipates the heteronomy of the medium Aristotle aims at—is that of the moon. Plutarch, in commenting on Democritus, describes the Earth's satellite as a celestial body that receives its own light from another celestial body, namely, the sun. In the luminous shining of the moon (*phaínesthai*), that to which this shining is due is simultaneously *shining through* (*diaphaínein*).[123] In later centuries, the diaphanous designates so-called selenite, whose origin, according to Pliny, lies in Persia.[124]

The diaphanous, moreover, appears in philosophical contexts already before Aristotle. Xenophon puts it in Socrates's mouth when, in conversation with the painter Parrhasius and the sculptor Cleiton, Socrates wonders how artists might present a person's inner character. What is important, he says, is that the character's essential traits "shine through," *diaphaínei*, in the face and the attitude of the body.[125] In the Socratic conversations recorded by Plato, the term usually has the common meaning of bright clearness, for example, when it refers to the river Ilisos on whose banks Socrates and Phaedrus reflect on the beauty of the soul.[126] In the *Phaedo*, *diaphanēs* refers to a far-off land where, from the mountains to the rocks, everything shines, a perfect shining in which "our highly valued emeralds and cornelians and jaspers and other gems" participate, albeit only imperfectly.[127] There even is, in Plato, a passage that links the diaphanous and the process of seeing. At the point where the *Timaeus* mentions the "body" that materializes midway between the ray of sight and the emanations of things, Plato speaks of the diaphanous as the imperceptible: "Of the particles coming from other bodies which fall upon the sight, some . . . are imperceptible, and we call them diaphanous."[128] The principle of equalization that governs the theory of seeing in the *Timaeus* renders the particles of sight indistinguishable; they are beyond perceiving. Accordingly, not only that which is not in itself visible but also that which is not visible at all is said to be transparent, *diaphanēs*.

In elevating the word as a concept and in substantivizing the adjective, Aristotle does take up the transparency aspect of the diaphanous at play in Plato. But he treats it only as an *aspect*. The diaphanous can at times indeed remain transparent and thus unseen, albeit not because it is invisible per se but because it is currently not visible. Yet how are we to conceive of this translucidity? How does Aristotle justify this substantivization? Anca Vasiliu has argued that Aristotle introduces the substantivized diaphanous abruptly.[129] "Thus there clearly is something diaphanous"—*esti de ti diaphanēs*. In the *Analytics*, Aristotle had announced that he would sometimes proffer definitions to which no name corresponded as yet.[130]

Here, however, we are dealing with a name to which no definition corresponds. Nowhere does Aristotle suggest a definition of the essence of the diaphanous. The apodictic *there is something diaphanous* is even accompanied by a "thus" (δή), as if the demonstration had already been made. Aristotle, to quote the context, writes in book 2 of *On the Soul*: "Every colour has in it the power to set in movement what is actually transparent; that power constitutes its very nature. That is why it is not visible except with the help of light; it is only in light that the colour of a thing is seen. Hence our first task is to explain what light is. Thus there clearly is something diaphanous."[131] Phylogenetic textual criticism (by Jaeger, Nuyens, Dumont, and others) usually stipulates that book 3 of *On the Soul* was written before books 1 and 2. The description in book 3 could thus count as presupposed. But how does Aristotle describe the diaphanous there?

Book 3 features the discussion of the question whether there are specific media to correspond to each individual object of the senses, media in which objects can appear. Now, for some objects, there are obviously several media. For color, for example, there is "water as well as air," and the reason is that "both are diaphanous."[132] Diaphanousness here is evidently still a *property* of different media, and the use of the term here seems to follow common usage. But this adjectival dependence seems to dissolve progressively. The diaphanousness that is to be found in different media seems to become a new, autonomous factor. At the very end of book 3, the concept comes up one more time. Organisms have a sense of sight because they live "in air or water, or generally in the diaphanous [*en diaphanei*]."[133]

If we assume—and there is good reason to do so—that the final chapters of *On the Soul* (3.12 and 3.13) in fact belong in book 2, precisely in the empty spot between 2.4 and 2.5, then the invention of the diaphanous at 2.7 is no longer as abrupt.[134] In this description, the diaphanous—which we also find in other Aristotelian and pseudo-Aristotelian texts, from *Sense and Sensibilia* to the treatise *On Colors*, a text probably to be attributed to Theophrastus—is an autonomous factor.[135] Organisms move in a space that can only be a space of motion because it is a space of appearance in which organisms can orient themselves. Animals thus see because they are embedded in a space of visibility. Because seeing is an immanent structure, its justification must necessarily be circular: the principle of visibility lies neither in the organism nor in some ground, of whatever kind, beyond the world, but in the space in which animals move. Such a space in turn is a space of visibility insofar as, within it, there is seeing taking place. The reason anything appears to the soul in a movable body is that it lives "in the diaphanous."[136] This prepares the transition from an adjectival diaphanous as a property of a given element (air, water, and so on) to a structural definition of the essence of media: what takes form is the space of what the Averroists would later refer to as an anonymous *natura communis*, an as yet nameless shared essential nature of appearing.

We now have to show how a theory of mediated seeing, from a "phenomenological description" of a medium of seeing that cannot be reduced to physics,[137] becomes a general theory of appearing in media. The philosophy of media does not develop all at once. It emerges step by step and discards earlier archaic notions only gradually.

(b) Point Continuum and Space Continuum

Aristotle bends the old theory of the elements, which assigned a specific perceptional sense to each of the elements, toward a theory of mediation: for him, the eye is able to see because it itself contains air and water, that is, something diaphanous. On the other hand, he initially takes up the Empedoclean idea of fire-likeness: the eye sees because the fire stimulates the diaphanous liquids inside it, they are "lit" and become light-like. The limits of these explanations, however, quickly become manifest. The diaphanous can neither be tied back into a cosmological theory of the elements nor grasped by way of hasty reifications: it is "neither fire nor any kind whatsoever of body nor an efflux from any kind of body (if it were, it would again itself be a kind of body)."[138] Where a structural description is needed, both physiological and cosmological models fall short. The medium cannot count as a continuation of the object of the body; it is not an aura, not an emanation, not an efflux. It must have a certain autonomy. And there is another reason for this: as an excitable medium that transmits the movement it has received, it can fully transmit this movement (as the example of the medium of sound shows) only if it is itself uniform.

This is the point where the previously developed idea of the continuous comes in. A medium becomes a medium of transmission only "when it is set in movement as one continuous mass."[139] At the same time, it is ready to receive a certain form only if it is not yet fully defined and only loosely connected. A form can be transmitted (*phorá*) between two bodies only when they are not welded together, that is, when they do not form a physical unity. An appearance—a sound pattern, for example—emerges only where two bodies are juxtaposed as an effective and an affected body. One body is insufficient to produce sound, just as one hand alone cannot clap.[140] What is needed, therefore, is a kind of primary difference or exteriority that here takes the form of a medium.

Unlike the modern concept of space, Aristotle's "exterior" medium is not to be understood as *partes extra partes* but permeates what it separates. The medium is even, as Aristotle writes explicitly, "grown together" (*symphyēs*) with the organ, for example, the air around and inside the ear.[141] In the model of aisthetic mediality, continuity and discreteness, which earlier described different ontological regions, correlatively refer to each other. The medium, accordingly, is that which produces a continuous connection (*synecheia*) between the perceived and the organ of perception.[142] The contact thus produced, however, is mediated, that is, it leaves the distance between the terms of the mediation intact. This is the difference between the aisthetic in-between, or *metaxy*, and the logical *metaxy* Aristotle introduces in his doctrine of syllogisms.[143] Aristotle operates a philosophical rehabilitation of the distance Plato evoked to justify his degradation of appearing images (Plato's ontology of degrees is an ontology of degrees of remoteness): Aristotle turns it into the precondition of all appearing in the world. Only where there is a gap can connections be made across a distance.

We are now able to follow Aristotle's ingenious move: where previously an almost Ockhamian razor separated continuous bodies from discrete *eidē* and a pathic regime of material contact from a rational regime of placeless forms, *aisthesis* represents a third, a new form of configuration. Continual movability, such as it is claimed for the aisthetic, presupposes an identity of the two endpoints, or *eschata*.[144] On the other hand, it was postulated that a form can be perceived only if the perceived remains "external" (*exothen*) for the perceiver, if the *eschata* of the *aisthētikon* and of the *aisthēton* differ from each other.[145] But how is it possible to speak of simultaneous (*hama*) contact where a distance exists? Aristotle fulfills the double condition of, at the same time, identity and differentiability by redefining the *eschata*, from being *points* of contact into being a *space* of contact.[146] The medium, henceforth thought as a space of appearance, becomes that which "delimits" both the organ and the object of perception, yet not thanks to a limit of its own but because it borders on and comprehends the bodies themselves. The diaphanous, which reaches from the *aisthēton* to the *aisthētikon*, furnishes both with a limit while it has its own limit at the surface of things—"we may define colour as the limit of the transparent in [a] determinately bounded body."[147] Through the medium, bodies are endowed with a limit and a surface; only through the medium do they receive a visible shape and can appear—literally—as *interface*.

It would be insufficient, though, to think the medium merely as a space for transmitting something that already exists, identically, elsewhere. The perceiving soul can be moved by the medium because it itself moves in this medium. The space of perception is what it has or, even more literally, "holds" around itself (*peri-echōn*). The space of perception makes a relationship possible. On the one hand, it coconstitutively participates in what sustains the soul; on the other hand, it also makes it possible that it relates to what it sustains. What emerges here is a *transformative* interspace, that is, a space of experience in which material *forms can be transmitted without their matter*; in short, a space of *appearances*. Aisthesis does not condemn the perceiving organism to passivity only on the condition that the affection (*pathē*) itself leaves space for action. Only on the condition that what happens to the organism can be varied and transformed is it possible for an experience I undergo to become an experience I might call my own.

(c) *Meson Kritikon*

A perception is not an internal representation; perceivers do not already carry within themselves that which they perceive. What appears to them in perception is determined by two criteria. First, it is "external" (*exothen*) and already in an actual state outside the soul.[148] Second, the perceived is always attributed to a specific object (*hekaston*).[149] This brings in, once again, the methodological distinction between the level of appearances and the level of judgments. What is perceived is not a pure quality (a pure yellow, for example), nor does it comprehend a whole object (the way concepts do, for example). As a matter of principle, aisthesis always refers to *aspects of an object*: neither to an abstract yellow nor to lemons, but to *something yellow*. Aristotle speaks of "the colorful" (*kechrōsménon*) or "that which has color" (*chrōma echei*). The soul can never be wrong about the fact *that* it perceives something yellow; at most, it can be wrong about that which appears to it really being attributable to a specific object. The level of appearances thus acquires a relative autonomy that situates it beyond true and false and thus beyond attributive thinking. And yet thinking and perceiving are equal in one respect: both are primarily faculties of *making distinctions*.[150] But since, as we saw in section 5, the aisthetic *krinein* cannot be a judgment in the noetic sense of the term, it must be specified differently.

Aristotle does so at the end of his analysis of the individual senses, where he introduces what at first seems an odd definition: perception is a *meson kritikon*, a medium for making distinctions.[151] Unlike thinking, the aisthetic space is a space "in between"—it does not have access to the extremities. If what is perceived in the medium is identical (for example, when we dip our hand in water at body temperature), there is no sensation of the "external"; similarly, an extreme stimulus (a very hot beverage, for example) makes it impossible to perceive the sensual quality in question. That is why perception is "a sort of mean [hoion mesotētos tinos] between the opposites that characterize the objects of perception. It is to this that it owes its power of discerning the objects in that field. What is in the middle is fitted to make distinctions [meson kritikón]." A few lines later, however, the perceiver is also defined as dektikon, or "receptive."[152] To what extent is the aisthētikon a faculty that is activated by something other being impressed on it? Does this not open the floodgates for a return of the theories that describe vision as physical impression (so-called apotyposis)?

To answer this question, we must delimit the aisthētikon more clearly from the aisthetērion. Although it includes more than just a physical dimension—beside a purely material structure of flesh and bones, the sensorial apparatus comprises the medial resonance spaces—the aisthetērion corresponds to a certain bodily apparatus with a certain disposition. The aisthētikon, by contrast, is a capacity for assuming different dispositions. Even if perception remains completely ineffective without a bodily aisthetērion, it is a faculty of perception only insofar as it is an aisthētikon. The aisthētikon can perceive, it can receive the forms of matter because it is materially undetermined itself. Aristotle now introduces the famous thesis that, by itself, would fully suffice to justify all the works written on Aristotle in later centuries: "Generally, about all perception, we can say that a sense is what has the power of receiving into itself [to dektikon] the sensible forms of things without the matter [aneu tēs hylēs], in the way in which a piece of wax takes on the impress [or sign, sēmeion] of a signet-ring without the iron or gold."[153] Aristotle does not detail how the reception of the form aneu tēs hylēs, without the matter, is supposed to work; this taciturnity explains why his successors felt the need to elaborate on this point. Those among them who suspected an ontological dualism of form and matter to be at work here, though, should have been given pause by the very next sentence. Form is always the form of a matter; the eidos thus does not exist in detachment but always only as the eidos of a hekaston, of a corresponding object. If, then, form is received without matter, as in the analogy of the signet ring, it means that although the form of the sign (the image of the signet) is the form of a gold or iron signet, this image is not received "qua bronze or gold" (hē chrysos ē chalkos).[154] Here, too, the adverbial pronoun hē (ῇ), which functions as a modal particle, proves to be the basic operator of Aristotle's metaphysics: just as it was used for outlining what ontology is about (namely, being *qua* being), it is used to specify how the form is received *qua* form, and not inasmuch as it has a specific material quality.

In showing the category of modality to be the basis of aisthesis, the comparison with the signet image also contains propositions that can be expanded to include images in general. The signet image is a specific, extended structure of the surface of matter and in that respect designates the iconicity of the signet. At the same time, the meaning of the signet resides precisely in that the form of the signet detaches from its primary support and reduplicates itself. The signet image, then, is that which appears on the surface of the wax. This ambiguity of the concept of the image may also be described as the difference between the appearance of the image and the support of the image.[155] When we talk about a bronze statue, we do not say that it *is bronze* (or only if we plan to melt it down, like the statue robbers Pliny mentions) but rather that it is *of bronze*. Being an image cannot be reduced to being a material image. In Aristotelian terminology: what presents itself as a *homonymy* is only a *paronymy*; what might sound very similar is actually different. On the pretext that we still call dead or painted eyes "eyes," we reduce what eyes are capable of to what eyes are materially. Yet the fact that dead and wooden eyes are designated as eyes does not make them seeing eyes.[156] Like the sense of sight, the sense of perception generally must be conceived of as a specific capacity for receiving appearances.

Aristotle's choice of wax, among all materials, as his example of this "receptive" mediality suggests, on the one hand, that the medium must feature a certain capacity to condense but also, on the other, that it must be possible to undo this density again—through the presence of fire, for example, which will play a role in the context of the diaphanous, as we shall see. Insofar as the medium can include in itself different forms, it is also a place of making distinctions. In the medium, which as *meson kritikon* differs both from the object of perception and from the perceiver, the forms that appear are distinct from what they are appearances *of* and from whom they are appearances *for*. The medium of appearance is thus a *dia*—an operator "through" which everything has to pass, and which also differentiates, separates, opens up. The medial *dia* also implies a discretizing, a singling out, and as operator of modality it can be associated with the Latin *discretio*, with a capacity for making distinctions that is capable of differentiating aspects from each other without turning them into independent entities.[157] In the lecture on *Physics*, we read in a different context that bodies become distinguishable only once they appear as *aisthēta*.[158] That they become *aisthēta*, we may now add in line with the argument of *On the Soul*, is guaranteed by the media that frame them.

The capacity of the medium for being determined—to sum up the argument so far—is conditioned by its formal indeterminacy, which places it close to the *prima materia*. The capacity of the receptacle (the *dektikon*) to take different forms means that it is not itself fixed by any form but remains elastic and malleable. *Mediality thus names the capacity for taking the shape of something that one is not.* As the space of potential shaping, the medium becomes a figure of the possible as such; its indeterminacy indicates a fundamental potentiality. Put differently: "Only a potentiality that is freed from all relations with the forms is capable of receiving each one of them." If the medium had a form of its own, it would thereby already be limited. Not only could it not receive its own form (if it already had a specific form, it could not receive *this* form in the first place), every further impression of form would amount to a modification of the basic form.[159] As we can see, the relationship with the forms is neither one of property nor one of partial participation. A medium can no more be defined by a specific form than by any other form, it is neither *this* form nor *the other of* form: it is the potentiality of form for appearing, the capacity for taking on any form.

This same move also overcomes another antinomy: on this interpretation, the natural philosophers who described the process of perception as action of the same on the same or of the different on the different would not fundamentally be wrong but ultimately be bound by a static image of the cosmos. Sameness and difference each only describe the two sides of a process that, as process, is to be thought dynamically.

7. AISTHESIS: FROM POTENTIAL TO ACTUAL PERCEPTION AND BACK

At the beginning of *On the Soul* 2.5, Aristotle recapitulates: "Sensation depends, as we have said, on a process of movement or affection from without, for it is held to be some sort of change of quality [*alloiōsis tis*]." This "sort of change of quality," however, is also an alteration "in a quite different sense," since such a being moved does not entail a change of place (*kinēsis kata topon*).[160] What kind of being moved are we dealing with, then? Aristotle helpfully indicates that this alteration is to be understood as a *metabolē*. That which is moved aisthetically does not move anywhere but rather turns in on itself (*metabállein*). Insofar as the same, prompted by what is different from it, thus steps outside itself, the aisthetic process, conceived of as *metabolē*, literally becomes an *ekstatic* process.[161]

How are we to imagine this perceptual ekstasis? To what extent does something that was not there and as such had not been anywhere else step out in this ekstatic process? To what extent is aisthesis a remaining identical within change, an ekstasis at a standstill? Ekstasis, after all, names quite simply a stepping out of one place to assume a new place and thus usually implies a loss.[162] The soul's being moved thus doubly provokes "a departure from its essential nature":[163] on the one hand, because it is embedded in the body, the soul indirectly participates in all of the body's movements in space; on the other, it is a self-moving force. Nonetheless, this departure from itself is not an estrangement but—as we will see—constitutes the possibility of *entelecheia*, or perfection. The movement model of perception thus comes up against its limits as quickly as the qualitative change model earlier. Just as the task here, within the framework of *kinēsis*, is to think a movement that does not lead anywhere else, the task in the context of *alloiōsis* is to conceive of an alteration that does not produce anything "new" that has not been there before.

In this sense, Aristotle in *On the Soul* 2.5 refers to his analysis in *On Generation and Corruption*. Between what is wholly "like" (*homoion*) and what is wholly "unlike" (*anomoion*), there can be no effective relationship: "agent and patient must be like (i.e., identical) in kind and yet unlike (i.e., contrary) in species."[164] In basic terms: a new shape can be received only where it is not already present. Aristotle then goes on to specify the *metabolē* of perception. Insofar as the moved takes on the form of the mover, aisthetic movement is a movement of approximation of form. "Hence it is that in one sense, as has already been stated, what acts and what is acted upon are like, in another unlike; for the unlike is affected, and when it has been affected it is like." And just a few lines later, we find an even more explicit statement: "As we have said, what has the power of perception is potentially like what the perceived object is actually; that is, while at the beginning of the process of its being acted upon the two interacting factors are dissimilar, at the end the one acted upon is assimilated to the other and is identical in quality with it."[165]

The term used here, *homoion* (assimilated), is related to the substantivized verb *homoiōsis*, the very term that was to be a central concept of image theory for centuries and served to combine neo-Platonic and Patristic notions. Here, however, it does not designate any fusion of the depicting and the depicted, no confusion, but rather a clear awareness of nonidentity. The moved is merely "identical in form" (*hoion ekeino*), that is, only in a certain, partial way. What kind of assimilation, then, is at issue here? Aristotle also speaks of *homoiōsis* in the context of the "threptic," the preserving and vegetative function of the soul.[166] In the threptic soul's process of assimilation—nourishment and digestion—the preservation of the soul comes at the price of the destruction of the form of that which nourishes it. In aisthetic assimilation, however, the issue is precisely a double preservation: the preservation of form and the possibility for the receptive perceiver, the *dektikon*, to preserve other forms.

Such a transformative dynamics that turns out not to be assimilating in the earlier sense presupposes that aisthesis is thought as *dynamis*—in every respect. Organisms are said, Aristotle explains, to be perceptive in two respects, namely, insofar as they actually exercise this capacity and insofar as they have this capacity in the first place: "We use the word 'perceive' in two ways, for we say that what has the power to hear or see, 'sees' or 'hears,' even though it is at the moment asleep, and also that what is actually seeing or hearing, 'sees' or 'hears.' "[167] Living beings are perceptive now as a possibility, now as an actuality; now as *dynamis*, now as *energeia*. In the actual, real process of perception, then, nothing new is taking place. The process merely actualizes what is already a property of the soul: its being perceptive. When the faculty of perception, the *aisthētikon*, is affected by something external, it becomes what it really is. And insofar as it potentially already is what it becomes, this development is an externalization.

This nuance is decisive: actualizing the *dynamis* of the perceiving soul consists in its actually taking on all possible forms. It is not the case, as many translations suggest, that the object acting on the perceiver *makes* the perceiver what he actually is; rather, for Aristotle, the perceiver in being affected becomes *like* the object perceived: there is, literally, a process of assimilation. More succinctly: to perceive is to take on. The *homoiōsis* at issue, however, is precisely not a linear process but a dynamic one that manifests itself ever anew. Only in *taking on* (another) form without *becoming* this form can the perceptual capacity truly remain a *capacity*.

If this is indeed the case, we can also shed new light on the difficult passage in which Aristotle presents aisthesis as *epidosis eis auto*, "a development toward the like." In discussing the question of what exactly the capacity for change consists in, he distinguishes between two modes of change, between destructive (*stérēsis*) and preserving change (*sōteria*). He illustrates the difference with the example of knowledge. There is destruction when instruction changes the ignorant into the knowing, who thereby lose their earlier state of not-knowing. There is preservation when knowers apply their knowledge. In this actualization (and thus externalization), knowers do not lose anything but rather preserve their capacity for further actualization. The capacity is not voided by the actualization, it realizes itself, and in that sense it is possible to say that the *entelecheia* of aisthesis as it were lies outside of itself. It is in this context that we must read the definition, which follows immediately afterward, of *alloiōsis* "in a quite different sense,"

one that does not come at the price of destroying earlier actual states but constitutes "a development toward the like or perfection" (*eis autò gar hē epidosis kai
eis entelecheian*).[168]

In his edition of *On the Soul*, Friedrich Adolf Trendelenburg suggests reading
αὐτό as αὐτό, turning the *epidosis eis autò* into an *epidosis eis h(e)auto*, a development into itself, which echoes a Hegelian notion of *becoming-toward-oneself*.[169]
Although both thinking and perceiving are faculties whose capacities increase
in their application, Aristotle stresses that the application of perception always
begins in an outside. Perception thus fulfills itself in its own ekstasis, it always
already begins elsewhere, outside (*exothen*).[170] What appears is always already
the appearance of something (else), and the initiative for this appearance does
not lie with perceivers themselves.[171] Accordingly, the *epidosis eis autò* cannot be
a return to oneself. Instead, it recalls that the *aisthētikon* always remains an
ekstatikon. There is no entering into perception, no initiative for action. The process of perception must always already have begun for there to be perception at
all. This leads to the paradoxical conclusion that every perception is always an
already having perceived: aisthesis means to "always hear and have heard—and,
in general, perceive and have perceived—at the same time."[172]

With this chiasma-like structure, in which a prioric perfect and procedural
becoming, return and ekstasis constantly intertwine, Aristotle once and for all
anchors the perceptive soul in an external corporeal spatiality (the *periéchon*) but
at the same time insists that this situated sensorial space resists the topologies of
the *Physics*. For if perception is indeed procedural, and actual perception must
first reach the perceiver, one might at first think that perception approaches via
several intermediate positions in the interspace.[173] The interspace would in this
case be not only spatial but temporal as well: the *aisthēton* would reach the
aisthētikon step by step across the temporal interval. But this would amount to
thinking the medium once more as one that hinders or delays. This is Empedocles's view, which Aristotle cites here, where the light first arrives in a metaxy, an
in-between, before it reaches the eye. "This might plausibly seem to be the case.
For whatever is moved, is moved from one place to another; hence there must be
a corresponding interval of time also in which it is moved from the one place to
the other."[174] Such a theory of the medium as channel would still suffer from a
confusion of dynamic *alloiōsis* with spatiotemporal transmission (*phorá*).[175] In
this regard, the phenomenon of sound, of which we might think it was a temporal transmission in space, leads us astray when we seek to describe a medial
alloiōsis that does not traverse any interval.[176]

This adds another argument to account for the choice to explain the theory
of appearances by way of the phenomenon of seeing: the visible does not unfold

in time and in space; it is always already there, namely, thanks to light. Light is "not a movement" but, as Aristotle writes in the third chapter of *Sense and Sensibilia*, *parousia*, presence.[177] This presence, however, must not be confused with Platonic *parousia*, nor, as we will see, with the Scholastics' *praesentia*, which allegedly translates it. Light here instead stands for a certain kind of *presentation* of the visible, a coming-into-appearance. Aristotle replaces the corpuscular theory he had explicitly rejected with a mediology of light: things becomes visible only through light (which Aristotle also describes as the presence of fire) yet light itself presupposes the "existence of something in something [*tō einai*]" that lets light come into appearance.[178] Light itself does not take any shape but puts *aisthēta* in a state of actual visibility.[179]

Yet we might wonder: Was this not the role previously assigned to the diaphanous? At first, this introduction of light cannot but be confusing, for it shatters the announced tripartite schema object of perception–medium–organ of perception. Are we now, in the case of seeing, dealing with two competing media? As it turns out, Aristotle instead is thinking of reciprocal inclusion. Light is both a *state* of the diaphanous and its *condition*; it is a modality and at the same time that which allows the medium to be a medium, a second-order medium, as it were. On the one hand, light causes the diaphanous to shift into *energeia*. As a pure act, the diaphanous is then entirely transparent and permeable, colorless and unmoved (because it is purely present). On the other hand, however—and this apparent reversal has confused many commentators—Aristotle writes that "light is as it were the proper color of the diaphanous."[180] If we remember, however, that, for Aristotle, color is synonymous with the visible *aisthēton* and that the *aisthēton* is that which initiates movement,[181] a new meaning emerges: while light does not itself take on any color, it, as it were, lets the diaphanous come to color. Light in this sense is literally *energeia*, actual and effective.[182] It effects the medialization of the diaphanous and thus in a way represents the effective cause of the diaphanous.[183]

Yet if in the state of full light only the colorful is visible, then what about the other states of the diaphanous? Is all there is besides pure visibility mere invisibility, as some passages in which Aristotle opposes light to darkness might suggest?[184] A dynamic conception such as Aristotle's leaves no room for a two-worlds theory on the Anaxagoreic model, which opposes the visible and the invisible things, the *phanera* and the *adēla*. Just like perfect visibility, darkness is to be thought not in substantial but in modal terms: darkness is light in the mode of potentiality.[185] Yet there are many shades between light and darkness.

Aristotle's definition of perception as being directed at the particular, the *hekaston*, concerns only full visibility. Besides the fully visible, Aristotle's phenomenological interest includes all other gradations of the visual. Thus there is the "barely visible" (*tò mólis horōmenon*) but also the "infinitely small" to which the entire sixth chapter of *Sense and Sensibilia* is devoted.[186] Aristotle's reflections aim to show that even that which does not *as such* become visible is already (at least potentially) visible. Only what belongs to the domain of the visible can subsequently become visible explicitly as well. From afar, the rocky ledge just before the mountain pass is not visible as such; it merges with the crestline. Only once we have almost reached it does the ledge stand out independently and become actually visible as *hekaston*.

Yet this approach, too, has its limits. As human beings we can isolate, for example, a grain of millet but not a thousandth part of a grain of millet, "even if we look at it very carefully."[187] Such micrologies become visible only in the context of a greater whole in which they come into their own but in which they can also dissolve "like a drop of sapid moisture poured out into the sea."[188] These observations, which are compelling in their wealth of detail and seem to anticipate Leibniz's meditations on the *petites perceptions*, open a wide spectrum of "small" visibilities, coperceptions, and nonthematized modes of being between objectivized visibility and invisible state of latency. Visibility and invisibility thus are not substantial but dynamic properties; their difference can only be understood as the difference between actuality and potentiality.[189]

Aristotle thereby also revises the schema he had announced at the beginning, according to which seeing aims at the object of perception, namely, the visible. Now, seeing aims at "both what is visible and what is invisible (for darkness is invisible and yet is discriminated by sight; so is, in a different way, what is over-brilliant)."[190] Just as a dazzled eye does see *something*, even if it is not the thing it tries to see, so perception in a dark environment is not simply interrupted, it merely sees something *else*. Some things "which in light are invisible, in darkness stimulate the sense"—phosphorescent objects like scales or fish eyes, for example. There is, however, no single name shared by all these things, Aristotle notes.[191]

The reason for this, Heidegger surmises in his comments on these passages at the beginning of the *Introduction to Phenomenological Research* of 1923/24, is that the Greek language—and hence, *mutatis mutandis*, the language of Western philosophy—is "a language of daylight." This preference, of course, is not being neutralized by simply supplementing the photological categories with categories of the night. Rather, we have to understand in what way darkness, too, is not an *adiaphanēs* but "is something that, in a quite specific way, lets things be seen." Heidegger points out that the letting see of darkness is to be thought together with *sterēsis* (lack) but does not elaborate on this point in the Marburg lecture.[192]

Robert Fludd, or Darkness as *Privatio*

Besides the medieval tradition of the metaphysics of light, which estab-lishes a connection between the *parousia* of the diaphanous and neo-Platonist thought of *parousia* as full presence, there is a second, more subtle tradition that can give Aristotle's theory of the sensible medium an aesthetic turn. In later life, Augustine, who until his conversion had sub-scribed to the dualist beliefs of Manicheism, had to attack time and again the legacy of this theory, which referred to itself as a "religion of light." The conceptual vocabulary he employs to denounce ontological fallacies in the Manichean theodicy is primarily Aristotelian. Evil in the world, he argues, does not come from an opposition between creation and another entity, namely, nothingness. For nothingness is not an entity, not a nega-tive being, but a certain disposition, more precisely, a *sterēsis* or, in Latin, a *privatio*: nothingness quite simply "lacks" being. Augustine refers to this *privatio* also as *tenebrae* or darkness. As part of his effort to rehabilitate darkness in *On Genesis Against the Manicheans*, he cites a number of anal-ogies for *tenebrae*: *nuditas* (nakedness is not a particular kind of body or object), *inanitas* (emptiness is not some thing), and *silentium* (silence is neither word nor object but a *privatio* of the word).[193] These comparisons are part of Augustine's attempt to show how darkness is not external to the order of creation but essentially participates in it. Darkness becomes a *page blanche* in Mallarmé's sense, a blank space of possibilities in which particulars individuate. Martha Colish has pointed out the almost mod-ern characteristics of this aesthetics: the productivity of *privatio*, accord-ing to Augustine, is apparent in musical intervals and in shaded parts in painting where they let the most important elements stand out in the first place such that observers can delight in the order.[194]

This Augustinian tradition of a privative metaphysics of darkness has a prominent revival in the seventeenth century, namely, in Robert Fludd, who erects an emblematic, visible monument to it. Accompanying Fludd's *Utriusque Cosmi Maioris scilicet et Minoris Metaphysica, Physica Atque Technica Historia* (*History of the Two Worlds*, published in 1617) are engravings by Johann Theodor de Bry, who has a talent for succinctly

(*Continued next page*)

illustrating Fludd's often obscure trains of thought. In the section *De ten-
ebris et privatione*, Fludd evokes Augustine's book against the Manicheans
to explain the process of creation. This section is preceded by an engraving
that seems strangely familiar to a modern viewer: a black square on a
white background (fig. 2.1). Ink that would have sufficed for many pages is
condensed on a few square inches, ink that would have sufficed for many
pages that would have been possible, ink for many signs that here remain
in a state of indistinct, pure possibility. And, to be precise—and just like
Kazimir Malevich's revolutionary icon of a modernity that had reached

FIGURE 2.1 Engraving by Johann Theodor de Bry,
too: Robert Fludd, *Utriusque Cosmi Maioris scilicet et
Minoris Metaphysica, Physica Atque Technica Historia*
(Oppenheim, 1617), 26.

point zero—the light frame does not contain a square but a rhombus. Was Fludd concerned with pointing out its literally dynamic character, as Malevich was? The inscription on all four sides would suggest so: *et sic in infinitum*, "and so on to infinity." Viewers are evidently meant to extend all four sides of the black rhombus in their minds until it shatters the boundaries of the lighter frame and thus shoots beyond the space of visibility as such. *Privatio* as lack of specific properties and, more generally, as lack of specificity as such cannot be presented but only be reenacted performatively. Because it is possible in a mental exercise to extend the geometric presentation of *privatio* beyond the boundaries of the frame, it is also possible to deprive it of its specificity. The figure of Fluddean *tenebrae* paradigmatically embodies a dimension in which delimitation and concretization, de-presentation and re-presentation amalgamate inseparably.

8. SEEING IN THE DARK: THE POWER OF NOT ACTUALIZING A POWER

How is it possible to see in the dark? Aristotle maintains that we may speak of an act of seeing only if an eye is affected by a given sensible object. To what extent, then, do we see when there is no longer anything to see? May we still say of someone living in total darkness that he *can* see, the way—to borrow Aristotle's example—it may be said of a boy that he *can* (potentially) become an army general?[195] Evidently, what is at issue in the case of the faculty of perception is a different kind of "can": we do not become perceivers the way one becomes a general. Being perceptive must mean something different for beings that are already sentient, and for beings that never became sentient in the first place.[196] But what does the perceiver still have when all objects are lacking?

Aristotle's solution couldn't be simpler: the perceiver "has" a lack, since *sterēsis*, too, "is in a sense having."[197] The reciprocal structure of the opposites (*aisthēton–aisthētikon*) is thereby preserved, but the object the perceiver has is no longer a specific sense object but, rather, the lack of all objecthood. (In Husserlian terminology, we might refer to this as "empty intention" [*Leerintention*].) Seeing thus refers both to the visible and the invisible because even in darkness, there is still seeing, albeit in the mode of emptiness.[198] Even in the dark, we can still make distinctions: "for even when we are not seeing, it is by sight that we discriminate darkness from light, though not in the same way as we distinguish one colour from another."[199] What is true of all perception—and this claim almost amounts to a provocation—is true even of perception in the dark: like thinking, perception is an art of making distinctions.

Whereas in bright light, the perception of objects is due to the reception of chromatic hues, when it comes to darkness, Aristotle seems to think of something like orientation thanks to light values. If it is permissible to read this notion into his text, then Aristotle anticipated baffling findings of modern physiological optics. Whereas nineteenth-century optics focused on color perception (think of the Young–Helmholtz theory of trichromatic color vision), twentieth-century research added decisive insight into night vision, for example, and so-called scotopic vision, that is, seeing under low light conditions. There are two kinds of photoreceptors to be found on the retina. Concentrated around the fovea centralis are about seven million cones that are responsible for sharp and chromatic vision. Distributed across the entire retina are about 120 million rods with a lower resolution but a better reception of black-and-white shapes, which are activated in low light conditions. Neurophysiology has made it possible to elucidate how exactly rods and cones interact. Depending on how the light falls on specific areas of the retina, so-called OFF/ON cells switch from and to particular kinds of day or night vision. Recent neurophysiology includes further differentiations among cell types, for example, so-called edge detectors that identify the movements of rectilinear shapes on the periphery of the field of vision (they are particularly prominent in the eyes of insects).[200] The perceptional apparatus makes particular use of such detectors in the dark, and movement and form become the preferred parameters for orientation—parameters that Aristotle counts among the *koina aisthēta*, those perceptional qualities, that is, that are experienced thanks to a synesthetic cooperation of the individual senses. Where the capacity of seeing tends toward zero, the alliance of the senses continues to maintain a sensorial activity. Where seeing no longer has an object of its own (in terms of its purely visible properties), that which all senses share—their synesthetic, common property—returns to the foreground.

On the Soul 3.2 raises the question whether perceivers can perceive themselves perceiving. Granted that we do indeed perceive ourselves as seeing,[201] we must suppose that there is another sense with which we perceive the first sense. This, however, would open the floodgates to an infinite regress. Or we suppose that the sense of sight perceives itself seeing. Some have tried linking such a (Platonically inspired) model of reflection to modern philosophies of consciousness and reading it as a precursor of reflexive self-awareness. We must keep in mind, however, that the Ancients hardly ever spoke of consciousness but talked all the more about sensation.[202] The reflexivity of seeing at issue here is not a purely mental or "inner" event but rather refers to heightened attention to the very condition of seeing. Every time seeing becomes a seeing without an object (in the dark, for example), it experiences its own state, namely, as a lack of objecthood. Whenever we are unable to see *something*, we are thrown back onto our capacity of seeing as such, onto the fact that we have an ability of seeing thanks to the operative medium. Where the *quid* is lost, the *quod* comes out all the more prominently: the diaphanous as "the condition, invisible as such, of the appearance."[203]

The self-referentiality of experience should not be confused with a cognitive effort on the part of a consciousness. Rigorously thought through, self-referentiality for Aristotle even leads to a strange notion: "if to perceive by sight is just to see, and what is seen is colour (or the coloured), then if we are to see that which sees, that which sees originally must be coloured."[204] Strange though this may be, we must concede, Aristotle says, that "in a sense that which sees is coloured."[205] What we are to understand by this being colored becomes clear when we look at the analogous passages on the diaphanous. There, too, the light-like medium is said to change, in the state of the pure act, into the color of the diaphanous.[206] Importantly, however, the diaphanous, unlike objects, is not colored in itself but only mediately.[207]

This accidental and mediate aspect must be read as a trace of a media operation. A thought experiment suggested by Myles Burnyeat allows us to grasp what is meant by medial coloration.[208] A glass is filled with water and placed on a table, right in front of the observer. The observer is then asked to hold a red object at short distance behind the glass. The water in the glass now functions as a medium *within* a medium, namely, within the surrounding air. The water appears to be colored red. Yet unlike the redness of a dye mixed into the water, this redness is not visible to other observers looking at the glass from different angles. We might now extend in our minds the limits of the medium (the glass) to reach the eye as well as the object such that a watery media continuum is established. If—to further develop Burnyeat's thought experiment—there were a mirror in the eye, it too would be colored red because it would mirror the seemingly red medium, but it would not lose its capacity to turn blue or green the very next moment.

Fit as it is for demonstrating how both the interspace and the faculty of perception are media processes, Burnyeat's example reaches its limits when it comes to showing the procedurality of the medial. The red coloration of the glass of water does of course point to the medium's capacity for taking on sensual quality or form without taking on the matter of the senses, which Aristotle evokes again in this context.[209] And yet, as the sequel shows, it would be wrong to see the medium merely as a sieve filtering out matter, as Burnyeat suggests in his "spiritualist" interpretation of the process of perception. Because of their inherent plasticity and resistance, media are also factors of remanence: in them, things remain that have already passed elsewhere. It is worthwhile rereading Aristotle's very dense argument in context:

> For even when we are not seeing, it is by sight that we distinguish [krínomen] darkness from light, though not in the same way as we distinguish one colour from another. Further, in a sense even that which sees is coloured; for in each case the sense-organ is capable of receiving the sensible object without its matter. That is why even when the sensible objects are gone the sensings [aisthḗseis] and imaginings [phantasiai] continue to exist in the sense-organs.[210]

As much as the aisthetic forms must always also appear in a material that embodies and instantiates them (this is the point of the *enhyla eide*, the "embodied forms"),[211] perceptibility equally presupposes that they always already stand out from it. The autonomization of the form of appearance to the detriment of the present object of perception is at the same time the guarantee of the object's continued existence in absentia. While it became clear that seeing does not include any delaying, what is seen perdures beyond current perception as image in the *aisthetērion*. Appearances thus obey a nonmechanical procedurality of their own.

Summing up, we may say that we still see even when the object of perception is lacking in two respects. On the one hand, even not seeing some thing does not amount to not seeing. On the other, even the no longer present object can be presentified in another mode than being present to the senses. In contrast to the merely vegetative dimension of the soul, which is subject to a stimulus-reaction, the distancing from matter in the space of perception already points to a virtualization that, for Aristotle, is simply intensified in the higher mental faculties. Although the two differ in their kind of impassibility (*apatheia*),[212] it is not just the noetic soul but already the perceiving soul that takes on and coconstitutes the *pathē* that affect it. Where the affection immediately transitions to a reaction and the movement undergone transitions to movement transmitted, that which happens to the perceiver can be *experienced* by the perceiver and the *kinēsis* can, thanks to the action of the medium, be converted into a *hexis* or attitude. Such an axiology of distancing also leaves its marks on Aristotle's biology, for example, when he chooses the possession or lack of eyelids as a criterion. Animals without eyelids "at once [*eutheōs*] see whatever presents itself in the diaphanous medium" whereas human eyes "have in the eyelids a kind of shelter or envelope, which must be shifted or drawn back in order that we may see."[213]

Since the landmark study by Hintikka, it has been widely assumed that Aristotle's logic and cosmology follow a rule that Lovejoy called *principle of plenitude*: everything that is possible must at some point in time become actual.[214] Within the framework of the principle of plenitude, there would indeed be little sense in not exercising a faculty: "animals do not see in order that they may have sight, but they have sight that they may see."[215] And although, as Hintikka has sufficiently demonstrated, the act for Aristotle is logically prior to potentiality, nonactualization has a decisive role to play. A *dynamis* is characterized not only by being *able to do* something in a concrete situation but also by being *able not to do* it. Nonactualization would then refer not only to an incapacity (*adynaton*) but also to the preservation of the possibility of nonactualization.[216] The possibility of closing one's eyes here marks the site of a stepping back from what stands before one's eyes in order to bring before one's eyes that which is not yet, is no longer, or has never been actual, that is, to presentify that which is present only in the mode of lacking. Themistius, in his commentary on *De anima*, clearly recognized this flipside of the theory of act and potentiality:

> Now if sense-perception did not have a potentiality both for being active and for being inactive but was always active, it would never perceive darkness [*ēsthaneto tou skótous*] (nor hearing perceive silence [*akoē tēs siōpēs*]). Similarly, unless there were also an intellect naturally fitted both for thinking and for non-activity (or better, both for thinking and for non-thinking), it would not think objects that are bad, nor think any object that is without structure [*amorphon*] and form [*aneideon*].[217]

Themistius shifts both perception and thinking in the direction of a primary matrix that is not wholly unrelated to the Platonic *khōra*. In the space of variation of the possible, before forms coagulate, the capacities of the *psychē* assert all their formative force. Perception and thinking are *faculties* of individuation; they allow the soul "to make something out." As capacities of discernment—as *kritika*—they are "means" of the soul because they act as a "sort of middle term." Neither *aisthēsis* nor *noēsis* has a determinate form. Rather, they are *dektika* and can "receive" or take on forms. There is a figure that perfectly embodies what it means to take on the form of some other being, without being this being: it is the figure of the actor. An actor performs an appearance; he presents himself under the guise of someone else's form. He stages another person's way of being, her likeness and fashion, and embodies it in everything from tip to toe, and thus fully presentifies another being. The actor is a medium: he takes on a being's form without being (it).

9. PHANTASIA: THE FORCE OF VISUALIZATION

A phenomenon is something that shows itself. The first meaning of the phenomenon is derived from sense appearances, from "phenomena corresponding to sense perception" (*tōn phainomenón kata tēn aisthēsin*).[218] Perceptual appearances depend on the factual presence of an external object.[219] Yet appearance, which in order to appear at all must stand out from what has caused it, perdures as appearance even if that which evoked it is lacking. The space of phenomenality thus goes beyond the field of what is given in the senses. Aristotle, in *On the Soul*, accounts for this extension when he adds to the analysis of *aisthēsis* a description of *phantasia*. While *phantasia* is rooted in and emerges from *aisthēsis*, it also shatters its limits. The simple textual fact that the characterization of *phantasia* stands between the analysis of perception and the analysis of thinking has led some commentators to see in Aristotle's *phantasia* an anticipation of Kant's productive power of the imagination, capable of mediating between sensibility and the understanding. While such a reading would overcome the Scholastic tradition, which clearly separates *phantasia* from thinking and assigns it to the domain of the sensible,[220] it also, inversely, tends to present *phantasia* as too independent, too separate a faculty. Aristotle clearly insists on its dependence on or secondariness to perception: *phantasia* itself "is held to be a movement and to be impossible without sensation, i.e., to occur in beings that are percipient and to have for its content what can be perceived."[221]

Were we to give a minimal definition of *phantasia*, we might say that what it puts before our eyes is the *appearance of a sense object*. *Phantasia* thus marks "the state or capacity in virtue of which we say we are appeared to."[222] What *shows* itself (through a medium) now shows *itself* (to someone) through the soul's *phantasia*. We might speak here of a visual reconstruction that once again places before its eyes that which places itself before its eyes. In this self-reduplication of *aisthēsis*, a gap opens up that distances the doubled from what characterizes *aisthēsis*, namely, its presence character. While *phantasia*, too, implies a certain affection, its peculiarity is that we have power over this affection.[223] What appears in *phantasia* is something we let appear, for example, by suspending the exercise of other faculties. *Phantasmata* or images of representation "appear to us even when our eyes are shut" (*kai myousin horámata*).[224]

Even when our eyes are shut but—and this is decisive—*not only* then. Aristotle's view on this point differs fundamentally from a centuries-old tradition that saw in imagination a faculty for representing an object in its absence.[225] Aristotle at first seems to join this tradition when he compares *phantasia* to a mnemotechnics, namely, the art of *loci memoriae* said to have been invented by Simonides.[226] This has led some to claim that Aristotle thereby described the faculty for placing something absent before our eyes and thus invented the concept of *phantasia*.[227] Yet even in evoking mnemotechnics in *On the Soul*, Aristotle seems to be thinking less of remembering what has been buried—tradition has it that, after a house had collapsed, the surviving Simonides was able to identify all corpses because he remembered the seating arrangement—than of mnemotechnics as the rhetorical art of configuring images in virtual spaces in a certain retrievable order.[228]

The fact that Aristotle most often speaks of *phantasmata* when the referent is absent but, on occasion, uses the term to designate something factually present, has given commentators headaches.[229] These various uses, however, converge when we acknowledge that the criterion of presence is quite simply not relevant for the definition of *phantasia*. What Aristotle is interested in when he discusses appearances is phenomena in their phenomenality, and all the more so the further off (*porró*) the *phantasma* is from the object.[230] This distance, however, must not be confused with being removed or lacking. Instead, it points to a fundamental, a primary distance. The object is not simply present or absent, it first of all quite simply is at an unspecified distance. Once the question of presence (and with it, the question of absence) is kept at a distance, as it were, *phantasia* is no longer a remedy for perception when the object perceived is lacking, nor is it the faculty that provides conceptual thinking with intuitions. Aristotle's remark that the soul never thinks without *phantasmata* is not to be understood as saying that some kind of imagination is always also active beside thinking, as if an *I see* must be able to accompany every *I think*.[231]

The main difficulty in understanding Aristotle's concept of *phantasia* is probably that it continues to be regarded as an autonomous *faculty*. To define a faculty is to define its reach and its delimitation from other faculties. The history of the reception of Aristotelian psychology is a long history of complex models elaborated to explain how the faculty of *phantasia* evidently intervenes in other faculties, from *aisthēsis* via *orexis*, desire, to *noēsis*. The High Middle Ages witness sometimes violent confrontations between Averroists, Avicennists, Albertists, and Thomists about where exactly to situate *phantasia* within the so-called inner senses. Yet as early as 1935 Wolfson demonstrated how the distinction between inner and outer faculties is a post-facto construction not to be found as such in Aristotle.[232] Even more important, however, the very consolidation of *phantasia* as an autonomous faculty of the soul took place retrospectively. A whole new picture emerges when we loosen this unity once more and understand *phantasia* not so much as a separate faculty but as the characteristic of a movement in which all higher faculties are swept up.

Phantasia would then be linked with *phainesthai*—appearing—as many commentators have suspected, because it describes a process of opening-ness that reaches from the physiological senses to the noetic sense.[233] What is decisive here is not representation but, even earlier, *presentation*.[234] Whatever appears as a *phantasma* does not have any necessary connection with what is the case; what asserts itself here, rather, is once more "Aristotle's basic interest in appearing."[235] That is why the attempt to explain *phantasia* by pointing out that, unlike sense perceptions, *phantasiai*, imaginings, are usually false, turns out to be insufficiently complex.[236] It is true that Aristotle says that *phantasiai* are false in most cases.[237] But it is also true that he makes this claim not about just any *phantasma* but about dream images, images, that is, that play no role in the cognitive process. Dream images *can* be false, they almost always are (this is what *On Divination in Sleep* seeks to demonstrate), but that says little about dreaming itself. Everything seems to indicate that in discussing *phantasmata* in dreams and in all other varieties of *phantasia*, Aristotle aims at a matrix thanks to which the soul detaches *phainomena* from their being factually conditioned. Even where *phantasia* is tied back to practical action, namely, in the necessity for the appetitive or desiring soul to have representations accompany its action, this distancing remains valid: what organisms in desiring are moving toward is not what they are or have but what they "have in mind."

We can now summarize our findings. Aristotle's characterization of the faculty of *phantasia* has "little consistency"[238] for the simple reason that *phantasia* is not a faculty. In what Schofield called a "loose-knit, family concept" we must instead acknowledge *the* basic trait of Aristotle's theory of the soul, something that, as Wedin was able to show, accompanies all higher faculties in the background.[239] If every receptive sense experience is already characterized by a basic contrast, then the higher-level differentiating faculties merely continue this primary virtualization. "Thinking," we might say with Nietzsche, "is highlighting," and insofar as every representational image is a way of eliciting, thinking, too, "is only a selection of representations."[240] The effort of abstraction thus constitutes a gain in empty spaces that simultaneously express an increased leeway. To be precise, we would have to speak less of abstraction than of articulation: what must already be articulated to be cognized at all continues to be articulated.[241] Every rearticulation comes with a dearticulation of what came before. In this process, new possibilities for connections emerge, new similarities become noticeable. "Patients suffering from fever treat walls and wallpaper in this way," Nietzsche writes in this same context, "while the healthy also project the wallpaper."[242] The possibility for variation in the medium of appearances expands to become a variation of the medium of appearance itself.

Here, it is crucial to emphasize once more that in this becoming phantasmatic, leaving the sensually given behind does not take place against but out of a rootedness in *aisthēsis*. *Phantasia* is already contained in perception the way the square is already contained in the triangle.[243] This analogy, which Aristotle uses to explain the relationship between lower and higher faculties, is precisely not a description of an inverse geometrical relationship. The square is not contained in the triangle the way the triangle is contained in the square but rather in the sense of an implication, of a folded virtuality, or of a not yet actualized envelopment.[244] The square is to be thought operatively, as it were, and thus from the perspective of geometrical performativity: as a triangle from one of whose sides the fourth corner is pulled out and that is thus stretched into a quadrangle. A higher faculty thereby actualizes the "dynamic" potential of the more basic faculty the way a corner actualizes the autonomy of a point-like part of a continuous segment. This also makes sense of the remark in *On Dreams* that the part of the soul responsible for imagining (the *phantastikon*) is congruent with the *aisthētikon* while at the same time differing from it.[245]

If, then, Aristotle's faculties of the soul must be thought from the perspective of their foundation in media, media cannot be extensions of the soul. Rather, the *psychē*, inversely, becomes an extension of a medium every time it continues the process of differentiation initiated there. If we take this logic all the way, we will have to get used to the strange idea that every time we visualize something, we become a medium of ourselves.

10. DOES ARISTOTLE HAVE AN IMAGE THEORY AT ALL?

In subsequent parts of this book, the basic structures of Aristotle's mediology of appearing thus described will serve as the grounding for a phenomenology of images. Those chapters will explain how it is possible to practice a phenomenology of images *with and after* Aristotle, but it is legitimate to ask at this point whether there is a theory of images *in* Aristotle. To be sure, it might seem odd to look for a full-fledged image philosophy in Aristotle. Unlike in Plotinus or Peirce, Goodman or Gadamer, Fichte or Fechner, Lucretius or Lacan, there is little explicit discussion of the concept of the image to be found in Aristotle. While his theories of imitation, his thoughts about *phantasia*, or his doctrine of what signs are have had long-lasting historical effects on Western thinking, his concept of the image is generally regarded as underdeveloped. Although there are elements of an image semiotics or an image psychology, of an ontology of the image or a physics of the image support to be found, none of these approaches furnishes by itself the key to Aristotle's concept of the image. Only once the question of the image is founded on the wider ground of a theory of appearing does it become possible to trace a line of flight that from the outset avoids some of the aporias in which other approaches inevitably get bogged down sooner or later.

It seems that Aristotle developed concrete reflections on images and their fabric within the framework of his theory of color.[246] That such questions played a role at the Academy is borne out by a text (though likely not written by Aristotle himself), *On Colors*.[247] There are also embryonic reflections on the medial peculiarity of images, for example, in the remarks on Pauson's *Hermes*, which oscillates oddly between flatness and corporeality.[248] Beyond the framework of individual passages, which so far have only rarely been discussed from the perspective of image theory, Aristotle's thinking of images has usually been correlated with his theory of mimesis. This connection is suggested by Aristotle himself when in the *Topics*, he defines the *eikōn* as something that is produced thanks to *mimēsis*.[249] Yet little is gained if *mimēsis* is conceived of as imitation, as a long tradition going back all the way to Charles Batteux's *Fine Arts Reduced to a Single Principle* in the eighteenth century has done.[250] Stephen Halliwell makes the point succinctly: "The understanding of Aristotelian *mimesis* has suffered almost as much at the hands of its ostensible friends as at those of its avowed opponents."[251] Thanks to the tradition of more detailed exegesis since Auerbach, though, it is generally acknowledged that *mimēsis* is in no way reducible to the modern *imitatio* and rather means something close to "reproduction" or "refashioning." Several other passages also show that Aristotle did not at all associate the art of image making with some kind of slavish imitation of the visible. For instance, he praises "good portrait-painters" for skillfully embellishing individual facial features in order to portray the person all the more realistically.[252]

This aims at anything but a hieratic intellectualism à la Plato. Just as he criticizes an alleged transparent transmission of what is seen, Aristotle critically opposes the notion that the visible is rendered intelligible only by an invisible meaning. Just a few lines after the definition of the image as active imitation in the *Topics*, archaic Greek painting is faulted for taking ideal representations rather than visible things as its guide.[253] In this kind of art, the visible always needs a pretext: without an accompanying title, "it is not evident what it defines."[254]

The concern here is not merely with discovering a pure visibility: precisely because it shows not only what is present, because it presentifies what is absent, the image process is not reducible to the sense of sight but always already appeals to an interplay of all sense faculties and therefore belongs to the *koinē aisthēsis*.[255] Moreover, images generally—and this is the decisive move against any hypostatization of the *idea*—are conceivable only where there is a body capable of affection. The starting point of image theory, therefore, is a theory of sensible pathos that in turn comes out in the fact that looking at images evidently triggers affects: "the sight of the picture [*graphē*] makes the man burst into tears."[256] This efficacy of "external" images allows for inferences about all images (including so-called inner images): the faculty of images is first of all a process of *presentation* that lets something appear where at first there does not seem to be anything. That is what the power of *phantasia* consists in.

Aristotle is thus as far removed from a mere receptivity to penetrating simulacra in perception as he is from a modern conception of *imaginatio* as free spontaneity. As we have seen, *phantasia* instead proves to be a complex correlative structure and designates not so much a separate faculty (hence its strange position in the architecture of *On the Soul*) as the articulation of the various faculties among themselves, whose commonality consists in a basic *presentative* trait. What *shows* itself to an organism is what an organism is able to amplify and *show to itself*. The higher faculties thus presentify (*prospherousi*) things of the kind by which organisms are already affected in perception.[257] As amplification of this initial affection, organisms capable of *phantasia* have a certain leeway insofar as they not only can be affected but also can affect themselves. The fact that there is a somatic reaction to a painted image or even just to an inner representation proves that the organism gives itself something to see that is evidently not factually there. The expression "I shudder to think" must thus be taken literally.[258]

From an Aristotelian perspective, pictoriality never begins with itself; it is always already a rearticulation of the given. This rearticulation always already contains the potential for another articulation that detaches from the facticity of the actual. Those images that are brought into appearance by the *phantasia*, on the one hand, continue a process of appearing that has begun earlier and is founded cosmologically. Only that which could be seen appears in images.

Images, to use Welsch's term once more, become amplifiers of a primordial "opening-ness."[259] On the other hand, images place before the eyes what is precisely not currently before the eyes and thus extend the sphere of intuitiveness beyond current visibility.[260] What becomes visible in the image this way is factually *not there* here and now: it might be present to my mind while not being present in person. This brackets, for the moment, the question whether what appears is *elsewhere* or is simply *not at all*: to appearances taken by themselves, as our analysis has shown, the predicates of truth and falsehood are inapplicable. Prior to any question about *presence* (or absence), the pictorial space is a medial space of *presentation*.

3
Forgetting Media

*Traces of the Diaphanous from
Themistius to Berkeley*

Writing the reception history of the diaphanous—of the first coherent media theory, that is—amounts to writing a ghost story. After Aristotle, the diaphanous becomes a waning, spectral phenomenon that, at best, flares up in eerie hauntings of the history of knowledge. The diaphanous is never granted the status of an autonomous philosophical concept, and where it does remain among the ideas in circulation, it is a marginal terminus technicus, a subsidiary metaphor, or an intellectual figment. The present chapter follows these traces, which resemble spectral appearances that here and there intrude into the well-ordered play of the two paradigms that, as we will see, developed from the reception of the diaphanous in the first place.

The first chapter introduced the fundamental strabismus, the two directions or *motus duplices* that in Western intellectual history have channeled views on the image and, going beyond the question of the image, are intimately tied in with the fate of philosophy itself. Following the reconstruction of the diaphanous in Aristotle in the second chapter, we are now able to specify these two directions and situate them within the history of the reception or transformation of the diaphanous. The first section of this chapter shows how these two guiding threads, the *transparency paradigm* and the *opacity paradigm*, emerged and developed. The eight sections that follow outline the way in which, from the Renaissance to the age of rationalism, this double paradigm goes hand in hand with a systematic overwriting of the process of mediation. In the move from the eye to the image in the Quattrocento and in the inverse move from the image to the eye around 1600, the diaphanous is deprived of any systematic discursive function. Yet as a motif—as *velum*, for example—it continues to haunt discourse all the way to George Berkeley. Paradoxically, in the twentieth century, the modernist rehabilitation of images as an epistemic means sui generis still develops along the very lines along which they have long been disavowed (see section 10). Two movements go hand in hand: a semantization of the image on one side, which is to ennoble images as constituents of meaning (most salient in Erwin Panofsky's *Studies in Iconology*), and a radical reduction of the image to its objecthood on the other, which is to emancipate it once and for all from idealistic projections (most evident in modernism and the agenda of minimal art). While the former insists on what lies *beyond* the image, the latter insists on the thing *before it becomes an image*. Both approaches are less contradictory than it might seem at first and even need each other to legitimate their existence. This also explains why, once again, the supposed rehabilitation of the image's specificity has resulted in the marginalization of the process of production, of the beholder's affection, and phenomenality in general. This is where modernist concepts of meaning and of objecthood hark back to ancient categories: where an ontology of thingness and a transcendentalism of meaning engage in a fateful alliance, no space remains for a procedural, experience-based thinking. In a way, modernism repeats an old, familiar scenario. Once again, eye and hand, sense of sight and sense of touch become polar emblems of two regimes of knowledge that have been opposed so as to make them irreconcilable, as the example of Berkeley's reading of the diaphanous shows. The "forgetting" of the medium, we may surmise, begins with the polarization of the senses, which unavoidably always also produces an axiomatization: the violence of dichotomic logic lies not so much in its dualism; rather, it is violent because, inevitably, the semblance of dialectic opposition always already contains an overlooked hierarchy.

1. THE SENSE OF TOUCH, OR THE LIMITS OF MEDIA THEORY

In *Sense and Sensibilia*, Aristotle summarizes his criticism of pre-Socratic philosophies of nature in the succinct, and blunt, formula, "they represent all objects of sense as objects of touch" (*pánta gar ta aisthēta hapta pouiousin*).[1] From the perspective of a mediology of perception, it must indeed look as if those pre-Socratic "natural philosophers" who think perception along the lines of the haptic reduce all sensing to touching. This discursive sideswipe, however, does not fully manage to divert attention from the fact that the sense of touch puts media-based models of *aisthēsis*—such as Aristotle's—to trouble as well. The fifth sense generally seems to be less specific than the four others. In fact, touching an object also means being touched by it, and just as we do today, the

Greeks sometimes used "touch" in the broader sense to refer to affections, to the fact of "being touched." Aristotle himself on occasion uses the expression *haphē*, "touching" or "feeling," in this transsensoric sense of "affection." Is it even possible at all, then, to say that there is something specific to the sense of touch that differs from what characterizes each of the other senses?

Alexander of Aphrodisias seems to have doubts: "What can be touched differs from the other senses that display a uniform substrate [*hekaston hypokeimenon*] and are called by a proper name [*oikeion onoma*]," thus color for vision, sound for hearing, and so on. What can be touched, on the contrary, does not have "its own proper name" (*hen oikeion onoma*).[2] If Alexander is right, are we to conclude that Aristotle now subscribes to a view that elsewhere he has denounced? He would then align himself with earlier theories of the senses, for example, that of Alcmeon of Croton, who supposes only four senses, as if the fifth were merely the link between the others.[3] Even in Plato's theory of perception in the *Timaeus*, where the sense of touch counts as independent, we do not find the word *haphē* (touch) but only the expression, "those disturbances [*pathēmata*] that affect the whole body in a common way."[4] Is it possible to say that Aristotle neutralizes touch in the same way?

The situation is complicated. Richard Sorabji suspects that in not assigning a perceptive organ specifically to the sense of touch, *On the Soul* takes up the placelessness of touch in Plato.[5] The problem of immediacy, though, is even more likely to be decisive for Aristotle's aisthetics than Sorabji's "nonlocalization criterion." Whereas the description of perception in a medium can be transposed without difficulty from seeing to the finer senses, such as hearing and smelling (hearing always takes place in an auditive space and smelling in an olfactory space), an analysis in terms of media no longer works when it comes to the so-called immediate senses. The sense of touch is activated by direct touching, and accordingly, "taste also must be a sort of touch, because it is the sense for what is tangible and nutritious."[6]

The examples of touching as well of taste (traditionally considered the lower senses) are thus crucial for determining the scope—and thereby also the viability—of the explanation of perception in terms of mediation.[7] The distinction between the sensitive and the merely vegetative soul made at the beginning threatens to be erased as the analyses of individual senses proceed,[8] for even those organisms that do not have *kinēsis*—and therefore do not have a perception space—must be capable of touch, namely, insofar as nutrition is a kind of touching. Aristotle explicitly writes, "Without touch it is impossible for an animal to be."[9] The senses of touch are necessary for life (*zēn*), he explains by way of a distinction taken from Plato's *Philebus*, while the senses of smell, hearing, and sight are necessary for the *good life* (*eu zēn*): "nutriment . . . is . . . tangible body; whereas sound, colour, and odour are not nutritious."[10]

(a) In Itself—Through Another

This amounts to a deep rift running across the senses that separates the lower senses of immediacy, necessary for life, from the higher senses of media—a rift with significant consequences for the reception of media theories of the senses. Aristotle's theory would then merely constitute a more moderate continuation of the intellectualism that, judging by the sources, he still advocated in his early days at the Academy.[11] The famous opening of the *Metaphysics*, according to which humans privilege sight among all other senses,[12] was long seen as expressing an idealism still very much shaped by Plato and, indirectly, counts as a philological criterion for situating the first book of the *Metaphysics* in a time when Aristotle was still at the Academy. The criterion of distance, thought logically as the possibility of coming into appearance, would then indicate its origin in a certain hierarchy of values: the senses of distance, seeing and hearing, would be superior to the three other, supposedly "immediate" senses because they serve to keep that which affects at a distance. The sense of sight and the sense of touch would, accordingly, constitute the two poles that orient the other senses and against which these senses have to measure themselves: like seeing, for example, hearing also presupposes an absence of purposiveness.

In the *History of Animals*, Aristotle develops a theory of meaning grounded in the capacity to distinguish between sounds.[13] The primacy of the distant over the immediate, an epistemological criterion, unexpectedly turns into a moral criterion when it serves to justify the polarization of the two kinds of senses: the two lower senses (touch and taste) assimilate the human to the animal because they are susceptible to excess, while in the case of sight, hearing, and smelling, any exuberant pleasure is supposedly excluded from the start.

The idea, meanwhile, that the touching organ immediately acquires the properties of what is touched (a hand touching a hot object, for example, becomes hot itself) whereas seeing limits itself to mere, nonaffective contemplation (*theoria*) was as consequential as it was misguided, for it fundamentally misses the point of Aristotle's multilayered and complex aisthetics.[14] Shaping the reception of Aristotle's theory of the senses for a long time, this notion not only points to the strong neo-Platonic overtones of the commentaries from late antiquity.[15] It has also provoked diametrically opposed interpretations that replace such a top-down reconstruction with a bottom-up approach inspired by Galen's medical theory, which explains the so-called higher sense faculties, too, in terms of touch. Both the intellectual and the physiological approach either reduce the differentiation of the senses to a monistic explanation or divide it into two opposing sense modalities.

Both approaches are telling in that they systematically elide the very means of articulation that Aristotle's theory of the senses has to offer for this differential organization: the medium. The peculiarities of their respective strategies for marginalizing mediality are particularly apparent in the place they assign to touch. The top-down model quite simply excludes touch from what constitutes knowledge, properly speaking, and from what distinguishes it from merely biological preservation. Intellectualist aisthesis would then be an epistemological aisthesis that must exclude all other forms of perception. The physiological bottom-up explanation, in turn, is able to restore the unity of the senses, albeit at the price of having to describe the higher senses, too, as modifications by matter. All *alloiōsis* through the senses would thus be equivalent to a direct physical touching.

Among the commentators on Aristotle, Themistius is not only the one who allows mediality the most room; he also notes, lucidly, that the possibility of a general media theory of appearing stands and falls with the possibility of thinking touch itself as mediated. At first, of course, the idea seems counterintuitive. That makes it worthwhile to recapitulate the subtle argumentation of *On the Soul*. In book 2, Aristotle asks: "Is then the perception of all things one only, or is it different of different things, just as it is now generally supposed that taste and touch both act by contact [*haptomenon*], but that the other senses act at a distance [*apothen*]?"[16] In this passage, Aristotle seems to consider two alternatives: (1) *All* senses are structured in a similar fashion. According to Aristotle, this was the dominant opinion among the pre-Socratic philosophers. Such unified conception of perception, as it were, means reducing all senses to a kind of touch. (In *Sense and Sensibilia*, Aristotle complains about the fact that all "natural philosophers" have taken touch to be the prototype of all the other senses.)[17] (2) There are *certain* senses that are based on haptic, immediate contact, while *others* occur at distance, in a mediated way. On this view it is necessary to distinguish between senses that operate "by themselves" (*di'autēs*) and senses that operate indirectly, "through something else" (*di'heterou*). Another passage gives further indications:

For without touch it is impossible to have any other sense; for every body that has soul in it must, as we have said, be capable of touch. All the other elements with the exception of earth can constitute organs of sense, but all of them bring about perception only through something else, viz. through the media [*di heterou*]. Touch alone, as it is generally held today [*kathaper nun dokei*], takes place through itself [*di'autēs*], by direct contact with its objects, whence also its name.[18]

The question here is whether Aristotle endorses the opinion "now generally supposed" (*kathaper nun dokei*). Some prominent readers are convinced he does. According to one of the most widely recognized scholars of Aristotelianism, Enrico Berti, "Aristotle demonstrates that some senses require a medium situated between the sensorium and the sensible object, sight and hearing for instance, while others do not require any medium."[19] It needs to be said, however, that if this were the case, Aristotle would only be articulating, in a somewhat modified way, an older idea we find in Plato concerning an internal division of the senses.[20] Medial sense perception takes place *di'heterou*, through another; in this dependence on an outside, the medial senses are *heteronomous*. Unmediated senses, by contrast, are an immediate access; they operate *di'autēs*, through themselves. Moreover, mediate senses receive the forms alone, but immediate senses are in contact with matter as well. This conception not only continues to have an effect in the Scholastic distinction between *immutatio spiritualis* and *immutatio materialis*;[21] it also continues to shape the two main currents in Aristotle research today: the cognitive-mental interpretation (emphatically advocated by Myles Burnyeat) and the physiological one (represented by Richard Sorabji).[22]

Yet it would be hasty and ultimately insufficient to call these conceptions philosophies of, respectively, mediacy and immediacy. Indeed, it seems that, astonishingly, time and again in the history of theory, the two switch positions. Kant, who in his *Anthropology* demotes touch as the lowest sense precisely because it is the most immediate and therefore most prone to affect, just a couple of paragraphs later praises sight for being, thanks to its mediacy, less prone to affect *and therefore* closer to "the immediate representation of the given object."[23] The odd switch from immediacy to mediacy shows that the extremes meet, that these two opposing concepts are more akin than one might think. Rearticulations of the mediacy–immediacy relationship polarize seeing and touching in such a way as to allow for neatly separating knowledge and affect. Theories of sense knowledge that are thus guided by a notion of seeing as being mediated confirm the latent ocularcentrism of the Western tradition. In their reflex-like opposition of seeing and touching, moreover, they obfuscate what the oldest systematically elaborated theory of seeing had discovered: the fundamental mediality of *all* appearances. If appearances can be received not only through the sense of sight but by means of all the senses, then the sense of touch, too, must participate in what has become evident for seeing. Themistius points out that while Aristotle does not make the decisive argumentation explicit (*mē proságetai*), the following conclusion necessarily follows from the premises: "If all perception is through a medium, so too is touch."[24]

(b) The Mediality of the Sense of Touch

The main difficulty of a media theory of touch, according to Themistius, is that touching does not take place in any medium: "But between the object of touch and the capacity for touch, there is no medium other than the body."[25] Under stood in terms of its surface, this body, in turn, is nothing but an organ that stretches across its entirety. First coined by Alexander of Aphrodisias, this formula of the bodywide organ is taken up by almost all later commentators from John Philoponus to Aquinas.[26] If it is correct, however, then the neat distinction between organ and medium collapses. The medium model, furthermore, is threatened from the side of the object as well: not only does there not seem to be a *proper name* for what can be touched (like *color* for what is seen or *sound* for what is heard), organ and object generally are confusingly similar. The basic principle of difference according to which the one perceiving can only receive what it is not (yet) itself becomes inapplicable when the organ (the surface of the body) has the same properties as the sense object that corresponds to it: rough/smooth, cool/hot, dry/wet, and so on.[27]

The sense of touch would thus not only bring the general theory of media up short; Aristotle's theory of hetero-affection would once more be haunted by the specter of auto-affection. Philoponus notes that Aristotle's aisthetics threatens to dissolve completely if there is no distinction between organ and object. "It is impossible for a body to touch itself [*autò to autou tigganein*]," he writes, because "nothing affects itself [*hyph'eatou paskhei*]."[28] Touch, too, must bear out what Gilbert Romeyer-Dherbey succinctly describes as the result of *On the Soul*: *there simply is no such thing as auto-affection.*[29] To avoid the coincidence of the *aisthēton* with the *aisthētikon* and thereby to keep the operation of the medium open in the case of touch as well, Aristotle resorts to a trick, which we will now reconstruct.

It is generally supposed that Aristotle's theory of the senses in *On the Soul* and the *Parva naturalia* builds on the wide-ranging biological studies of his middle period. As in other contexts, questions of systematics appear already in the work on living matter, and *On the Parts of Animals* thus discusses the sense of touch in more detail. At the beginning of book 2, touching is defined solely by the corresponding sense organ, namely, "flesh" (*sarx*).[30] As the analysis progresses, however, a moment of indecision emerges, namely, in the chapter discussing the flesh of a series of animals. Is it not conceivable to think of flesh not as an organ but rather as the medium of an organ? Like sight, touch would then have a medium of its own—"comparable," Aristotle tellingly adds, "to the pupil with the whole transparent medium attached to it."[31] But if the flesh becomes the medium of touch, how can it be distinguished from the organ of touch?

While ancient commentators always consider it to be self-evident that all "higher" senses have their own medium (even introducing names where Aristotle had not given them any: *diekhēs* for the medium of hearing and *diosmōs* for the medium of smelling), opinions diverge on the proximal senses. One could of course ask why proximity would be an argument for mediation. After all, is not smell a sense of proximity, too? But the real puzzle lies somewhere else: How could there be a medium at all between the touching organ and the object touched?

Aristotle at this point resorts to a clever trick: without further ado, he shifts the organ of touch inside the body. The two-part structure of organ and medium is less apparent in the case of touch, he explains, because "the primary organ of this sense is not the flesh or analogous part, but lies internally."[32] This internalization of the organ is reaffirmed in *On the Soul*: "This again shows that what has the power of perceiving the tangible is seated inside." There, too, Aristotle specifies this relocalization: the seat of the inner organ is close to the heart, which brings the sense of touch in close proximity to the *sensus communis*, located, according to ancient conceptions, in the heart. This guarantees, at the same time, that the sense organ itself remains undetermined, that it is not already warm or cold, rough or smooth. The flesh, then, is no longer the organon but rather "the medium of touch." General mediology is thus saved, and for the sense of touch, too, which is in "a complete analogy with all the other senses."[33]

While influential commentators, from Alexander of Aphrodisias to Enrico Berti (or, more recently, Thomas Kjeller Johansen), have maintained that flesh is the organ of touch and that touch is immediate, we should recall that there is also a long parallel tradition that reminds us why Aristotle describes flesh as a medium and not as an organ.[34] Themistius makes that argument, as does Averroes after him, and in the Latin Middle Ages several such positions can be found: in the fourteenth century Nicolas d'Oresme affirms that "the flesh is not the organ of touch but a medium," and even Francisco Suárez in the early seventeenth century still recalls this conception.[35]

What about taste, then? The Aristotelian corpus that has survived is much less explicit on this point than the discussion of flesh and touch. Does Aristotle claim that, among all senses, taste is the only immediate sense? In *On the Soul*, we find the following remark: "But the perception does not arise for us through a medium. . . . Therefore there is no medium" in taste.[36] Although the statement is formulated in an irrevocable way, commentators have sought to explain it away because Aristotle does not seem to have any good arguments here. According to Aquinas, the reason is simply that taste is a kind of touch, and as a "kind of touch, the tasteable is not perceived through any extraneous medium."[37] But what if touch itself is not immediate either? Can there be a medium that would be internal, somehow attached to the body? Aristotle hints at this possibility.

Taste, he says, does not arise through an (external?) medium "but by the flavor's being mixed with moisture, just as in the case of a drink."[38] In his *Long Commentary*, Averroes elaborates on the importance of saliva for taste: "Nothing receives the sensation of flavor, which is called taste, unless the flavor is in a liquid and the liquid is in what is flavorful either in act or in potency, for instance, salt, which is in proximate potency to being wet since it is dissolved quickly and it dissolves liquids which are on the tongue."[39] Avicenna, in turn, who already knew about the nervous system, states that the organ of taste consists in the nerves in the tongue, and he credits the saliva for being the medium. While he wants to take a middle ground between the argument of either the tongue or the heart as the organ of taste, Albertus Magnus sides with Avicenna when he reiterates that the medium of taste is saliva.[40]

There is some ground to the conclusion, then, that while in proximal senses, such as taste or touch, the medium cannot be separated from the organ, this fact does not annul the functional distinction between both. Rather, there seems to be a concrescence between the medium and the organ: they are *sumphuēs*, "grown onto each other," just as the air is to the ear.[41] Among the most notable details of Aristotle's analysis of the perceptual medium is the fact that he does not distinguish between natural and artificial media: he mentions pressure applied to a membrane wrapped around our skin or blows to a shield which the soldier holds in front of him. The transmission of the movement is instantaneous, and the soldier feels the impact "at once" (*hama*).[42] As we can easily see, however, the point here is that *sensation, though instantaneous, is not immediate*: although it would be absurd to consider these accoutrements as part of ourselves, they react just the way our flesh does—or rather: our flesh acts the way such an accoutrement would.

It can thus be argued that Aristotle does not think of touch as an immediate sense but at best as a proximal sense (*eggúthen*). And indeed, proximity is not immediacy, since to show that touch involves a sense of proximity is to show that it involves a sense of distance. Accordingly, it is possible to claim that not only the higher but *all* the senses are means of critical distinctions. Contrary to the common view, there is no immediacy (*eutheōs*) in perception, just as it is not possible categorically to separate senses of distance from senses of touch. Instead, what Aristotle had paradigmatically shown for seeing applies to all senses: "there must be *something* in between."[43]

(c) Forgetting Media as Anesthesia

Despite these explicit articulations of a general theory of media, we may speak of a downright systematic forgetting of the *metaxy*. As we saw, even in the twentieth century well-known experts on Aristotle still assert that some senses, like seeing and hearing, are dependent on a medium while others are not.[44] The history of this forgetting of media is yet to be written; the sections that follow are meant as initial explorations. To avoid possible misunderstandings from the outset: the reasons for the elision of the medial are not only *discursive-historical*, they are *systematic* as well. That is why, paradoxically, even outspokenly affirmative theories of media still participate in the elision. The fact that there is a forgetting of media that is not only discursively constructed but *constitutive* is something Aristotle himself already points out.

To the extent that the space of perception (air or water) cannot be reduced to a material instrument through which we look at the object of perception as if through a magnifying glass but instead constitutes a field in which we are embedded, the constitutive mediation of the medial surrounding usually goes unnoticed; it remains concealed. To characterize this peculiar form of going unnoticed, Aristotle uses the Verb *lanthanō*, like Heraclitus before him: "Men are unaware [*lanthánei*] of all they do when they are awake, just as they forget [*epilanthánontai*] all they do while they are asleep."[45] To translate *lanthanō* with a modern concept of the unconscious, as is sometimes done, is to commit an anachronism: the word has optical connotations and refers to inconspicuousness, to an overlooking.[46] Air thus is hardly ever conspicuous because it is situated at the minimal degree of touchability.[47] In our everyday experience, we forget that it is not only *in* but also *through* the air that we are capable of movement and thus of perception in the first place.

The reasons Aristotle cites are telling: when we forget about the elemental medium, about this thin air we move through and this sensorial atmosphere we evolve in, we do not do so only because of its quasi-immateriality, which makes it so hard to grasp, but because such overlooking is inherent to the logic of the medium. Inconspicuousness not only applies to the atmospheric mediality of vision or sound, it begins with the medium that is simultaneously the most material and the closest: the body. We cannot place our body in front of us, the way we can do with lifeless things, just as we cannot represent it to ourselves in its totality and thereby objectivize it. What is closest to us (*eggúthen*) is always also the most inconspicuous for us and hence—to cite Nietzsche—what is furthest away. Relegating the medium of the body to the margins of our perception is practically a precondition of our capacity to place before us what is given us through the body.

This has consequences for a definition of the medium. Let me emphasize once more that Aristotle's concept of media does not in any way rest on a naturalistic presupposition. Media, rather, transcend the distinction between the living and the lifeless, as the following thought experiment with a sense prosthetic illustrates quite well:

> If the experiment is made of making a sort of membrane [*hymen*] and stretching it tight over the flesh, as soon as this web is touched the sensation is reported in the same manner as before. . . . Yet, to repeat what we said before, if the medium for touch were a membrane separating us from the object without our observing its existence [*lanthánontos*], we should be relatively to it in the same condition as we are now to air or water in which we are immersed; in their case we fancy we can touch objects, nothing coming in between us and them.[48]

Artificial prostheses or technical media of extension do not question the primary model of media aisthetics. They merely allow for understanding the constitutive concealment, which characterizes all media procedures, in the process of transmission. In this case, the artificial membrane, the *hymen*, is at once a vector of perception and an aperture, simultaneously a projection surface and a cause of concealment. In other terms: every hymenology is also always a mediology. The hymen refuses us what it gives us to desire; it unstitches the threads it sews at the same time. The suturing produces a tissue that must be loose enough for something other to inscribe itself there.[49] To put this succinctly: the *metaxy* allows for a form to *come through*, but, inversely, forms only ever come through thanks to the *metaxy*. Aristotle here appears to think the medium as a sensible texture that transmits movement all the better the more its weaving becomes imperceptible and disappears into the very form it carries along. In its subtlety, the *hymen*, interpreted by Aquinas as "skin or delicate web" (*pelliculam aut telam subtilem*), tends toward anesthesia.[50] As medium of visualization, the hymen, as it were, withdraws its own materiality from the scene of appearances and becomes translucid.

Media work behind our back, unbeknown to us, withdrawing from our grasp; they precede the distinction between agent and recipient and stand for a performance that can no longer be subject to any intentional premeditation. Aristotle in his biological writings emphasizes the difference between the eyelid and the *hymen* for a reason. Higher animals, we read in the section of *On the Soul* analyzed earlier, have eyelids and thus have the ability to stop the flow of appearances, whereas lower animals do not: the latter are incessantly subjected to what they experience; they see immediately.[51] We may also cite in this context Aristotle's concept of exposure (*desmós*), which he opposes to the detachment from perception phenomena caused by closing one's eyes.[52] The corresponding chapter in *Parts of Animals* is more precise on this point: animals without eyelids (lizards, birds, and so on) do not see without mediation; there is, rather, a transparent skin on their eye that constantly moistens it. This operation almost goes unnoticed even by an external observer. Since Aristotle, this skin has also been called "hymen."[53]

The analysis thus gradually proceeds from artificial media, which are most easily objectivized, to the media that are particularly inconspicuous because they are ingrown or innate (*symphyēs*), in a way similar to Merleau-Ponty speaking of the body as an "innate complex."[54] Independently of whether they are thin *hymen* or resistant bodies, media work all the better under the conditions of anesthesia. The less media can be objectivized, the less perception takes place *by means* or *through* (*hypó*) but rather *simultaneously with* (*hama*) the medium.[55]

Aristotle gives an illustrative example: a soldier might not receive the blow of a sword immediately but through his shield, yet there is no delay; the shield becomes as if his second skin and he feels the blow, as the expression has it, at a single stroke. What envelops the body, then, increasingly resembles the shirt of Nessus given to Heracles by his servant, Lichas, which grew into the hero's skin such that it could no longer be detached from it. *Media become a second skin*—and yet the skin itself is already a (foreign) medium: in Aristotle's mediology the boundary between inside and outside begins to oscillate dangerously, as does the possibility generally to distinguish between the proper and the prosthetic. The fact that the traditional hierarchies no longer seem to apply in this media aisthetics must not make us forget, though, that these hierarchies arise only from the axiologizations introduced in the course of the history of its reception.

2. TRANSPARENCY AND OPACITY, OR THE PROGRESSIVE
POLARIZATION OF THE DIAPHANOUS

The meandering detours of the reception of Aristotle's theory of the diaphanous seem to indicate that the Western tradition long hesitated between two options that can be described, in Rémi Brague's terms, as *inclusion* and *digestion*.[56] In the former case, a figure of thought is integrated into a tradition but retains its foreignness and thus its disruptive potential; in the latter case, it is assimilated without remainder. Accordingly, the policy that guided translation in the Latin West frequently hesitated between these two options. The Greek *diaphanēs* was variously transliterated as *diaphanum, dyaphanum, dyaphonum, diaffanum*, or *diaffonum* and thus remained clearly recognizable as a foreign word. Although the borrowing from Greek remains in usage far beyond philosophical circles well into the early modern period—in Giovanni del Virgilio's love poem, *Diaffonus*, for example—translators around the middle of the twelfth century begin to adopt a policy of linguistic incorporation. As far as we know, Burgundio of Pisa is the first, in 1165, to introduce the neologism *transparens*, a morphological equivalent of the Greek term.[57]

This Tuscan scholar, however, was not translating the Aristotelian corpus but another text entitled *Peri physeōs* (*On Nature*), which he erroneously attributes to Gregory of Nyssa and which today we know to have been written by Nemesius of Emesa. This Syrian bishop's treatise, translated by Burgundio as *De natura hominis*, may rightly be considered the first attempt at systematically elaborating something like a Christian anthropology.[58] Reworking Aristotle's theory of the soul in neo-Platonic terms, Nemesius correlates human faculties with material qualities. His translator, Burgundio, evidently feels the need to explain the newly minted term, *transparens*, and does so by way of a material comparison: to look through the *transparens* is like looking "into mirror and glass" (*ut in speculis et vitro*).[59] This comparison is more than just a reference to theories of reflection and refraction. And it cannot fully be explained with reference to the Paulinian formula according to which "we see through a glass, darkly" (*per speculum in aenigmate*).[60] The comparison with the opaquely reflecting mirror and the transparent pane that is to facilitate the acclimatization of the loan word instead seems to anticipate the two metaphors that were to guide the progressive reframing of the diaphanous.

The ambivalence of the diaphanous highlighted by both Greek and Latin commentators on Aristotle dissolves into a veritable dualism when Roger Bacon, seeking to settle the debate about the term's translation once and for all, asserts in his *De multiplicatione specierum*: "And 'dyaphanum' means 'double in appearance,' that is, in the surface and in the interior; for 'phano' in Greek has the same meaning as 'appearance' in Latin, and 'dya' means 'two.'"[61]

The following two sections describe two major pathways of interpreting the diaphanous as the *transparency paradigm* and the *opacity paradigm*, reaching from the first commentaries on Aristotle all the way to the eighteenth century. They do not seek to reconstruct a chronology but rather highlight systematic aspects of the two paradigms, by way of succinct insights into the main stations along these interpretative trajectories.

3. CLIMBING THE LADDER: THE TRANSPARENCY SCENARIO

(a) Themistius: The Elevation of the Diaphanous

Around the time Nemesius develops his theory on the essence of man, Themistius is writing his paraphrase of *On the Soul*, which may well be considered, after Alexander of Aphrodisias's, the most influential commentary in the history of early Aristotelianism. Averroes repeatedly cites it, and Aquinas, too, makes significant use of the text in William of Moerbeke's translation from around 1260. Although Themistius's paraphrase is considered to be particularly close to the Aristotelian original and Henry Blumenthal saw in Themistius "the last Peripatetic,"[62] it already shows undeniable signs of neo-Platonist influence. Even if it is still rather restrained in Themistius, a tradition sets in here that, in its attempt at reconciling Aristotelianism and neo-Platonism, grafts the latter onto the former. In a way similar to his paraphrase of book 12 of the Metaphysics, where he goes back to Plotinus's *nous* to explain Aristotle's theology,[63] Themistius's account of *On the Soul*, as Anca Vasiliu has shown, features a series of almost imperceptible but nonetheless decisive shifts in the presentation of the theory of media.[64]

The way the diaphanous is introduced is particularly striking: where Aristotle limits himself to pointing out that the diaphanous can occur in different elements and materials, Themistius quite simply summarizes Aristotle's "many solid bodies" as "stone." The diaphanous, according to him, lies in rocks, glass, horns, and "other types of bodies," but it attains its best and highest form in "the eternal and divine body."[65] The *prōton sōma*, the "primary body" Aristotle speaks of in his theory of the heavens, is thus conceived of as divine and the diaphanous equated with the cosmological ether.[66] The divine body, then, "is transparent in a primary sense, air is so in a secondary sense, and water in a third," and all other matter follows in descending order.[67]

The vertical reorganization of the faculties of the soul already operated earlier thus manifests in the material domain as a sorting of materials according to value.[68] Although Alexander of Aphrodisias already surmised that the presence of *diaphaneia* determines how "transparent" (*diopta*) bodies are,[69] Themistius establishes the premises for spiritualizing the diaphanous, transforming it into an ethereal immateriality that bodily beings might experience only in diminished form. From now on, the diaphanous "embodies" the (unbodily, immaterial) substance of *intermediary beings* (*intelligences* or, more precisely, *angels*) according to their luminosity and purity. As an "interval container," the diaphanous now "serves to transmit light from a higher 'order' to a lower 'order,' progressively diminishing it."[70]

The concern with harmonizing Aristotle and Plato—a project even more salient in John Philoponus—contains the premises of what has since been discussed under the label *metaphysics of light*.[71] The diaphanous is now not just being elaborated starting with supralunar ether; Aristotle's media theory of light degenerates to a mere tautology when Themistius declares that light is not only that which causes the medium to be in a state of actuality, it also is *both* this actuality *and* the result of this actuality.[72] The highest, ethereal body is pure luminosity, pure actuality without lack. While the lower "bodies" are only ever partially or potentially transparent, the "divine body" is transparent throughout.[73] Themistius thus not only suspends Aristotle's media dynamics; in his hierarchical model, the sensual as in a pyramid is oriented toward the light, which, without differentiation, is actualization (*entelechia*), the actualized (*teleiōtēs*), and pure presence (*parousia*). Mediality survives, at best, as a relay function in a crystal construct within which the *perfectio* at the top must be conveyed to the lower levels as well.

(b) Plotinus: Medium vs. *Sympatheia*

With his theory of perception, Plotinus contributes to the post-Aristotelian forgetting of media in his own way as well. He practically inverts the peripatetic theory of the soul: for Plotinus, the question is not whether it is possible to perceive without mediation but whether perception can be anything but immediate at all. Having raised the question at the end of *Ennead* 4.4.23, he discusses it in more detail in 4.5. He first compares several positions before, in section 3, he proffers the decisive argument for revising the *metaxy* theory. If seeing did indeed take place thanks to the participation of the medium, the medium itself would have to be affected.

To explain this affection, Plotinus—in a significant shift—cites Aristotle's signet and wax example. He infers that an affection must necessarily be physical (*sōmatikōs*).[74] His initial hypothesis seems severely to distort his reading of Aristotle: if every perception is always a *sympatheia* that presupposes perceiver and perceived to melt into a continuum, then there is indeed little space left for a medium. Either the medium is so intimately sutured to the organ that both become a new body (then "the apprehension," the move from the organ of perception to the perceived, "would be a violent business," as Plotinus notes ironically), or perception must be explained by something other than a material process: then every in-between can only be an obstacle that hinders the unmediated synchronicity of *sympatheia*. Plotinus writes: "If then the object has the capacity to act, and the recipient of the perception, or in any way the sight, has the capacity to be affected, why does it need another medium to act on what it is capable of acting on? This is to need a hindrance [*empódion*]. For when the light of the sun approaches, it does not have to reach the air first and then us, but it reaches both at the same time [*hama*]."[75]

With his theory of *sympatheia*, Plotinus not only restores the old homology thesis according to which only like can act on like; he also provides a concept of a new kind that renders the theory of the medium obsolete. In Eyjólfur K. Emilsson's terms, "What other philosophers explained in terms of a medium, Plotinus explains in terms of the phenomenon of *sympatheia*."[76] The structure of *sympatheia* explains how Being can unfold and at the same time return to its unity by mediating itself with itself. Even if this unity is traced out in advance in our thinking, "our awareness of that One is not by way of reasoned knowledge or of intellectual perception, as with other intelligible things, but by way of a presence [*parousía*] superior to knowledge."[77] Beyond or, rather, this side of duality, Plotinus's concept of presence seems to furnish the foil against which Themistius and later commentators interpret Aristotle's concept of *parousia*.

(c) *Dum Medium Silentium*: Reinterpreting Presence

Heidegger famously claimed that the Greeks never thought of Being other than in the mode of *parousia*, a concept central to his reading of the metaphysics of presence. Yet, other than the name, Aristotle's concept of *parousia* has little in common with Plato's or Plotinus's. Against both Parmenidean and materialist conceptions, Aristotle mobilizes the thesis that anything becomes visible only when, in the diaphanous, that fire is "present" that makes the medium enter the state of actuality.[78] The word employed here, of course, has a history of its own: it is, after all, *parousia* or "presence" through which, according to Plato, ideas are present in things.[79] There has thus been a misunderstanding whenever Aristotle's concept is explained via Plato's use of *parousia* in the theory of ideas.[80] If we follow a suggestion by Robert Hicks, moreover, Plato's concept of *parousia* is already much less monolithic than it might seem.[81] There is good reason to believe, in any case, that what Aristotle had in mind was the "presence of white" the dialogue *Lysis* talks about rather than Plato's doctrine of ideas.[82] Such a dynamic concept of *parousia*, which implies a process of actualization rather than pure givenness, is also at odds with Heidegger's sweeping statement that Greek ontology always thought Being as presence in the mode of *parousia*.[83] That light is present, then, has as little to do with Platonic *parousia* as it does with its Paulinian variant. The later retroprojection of theological motifs onto Aristotle's thought clearly demonstrates how peripatetic theories were being transcendentalized in retrospect.[84]

Equating Aristotelian and Scholastic *parousia* and partly assimilating it with the neo-Platonically inspired notion of *praesentia* cuts the remaining "physical" ties. As a result, presence becomes a purely spiritual concept, assigning an object an essential position within an intellectual order. This equation is most clearly evident in John Duns Scotus, who, in the context of a new definition of the essence of the image, retools *praesentia* as an inferential representation of the object. While Scotus denies the existence of a physical medium, he nonetheless presupposes a spiritual medium in which the *species intelligibilis* are present.[85] Scotus's contemporary Meister Eckhart even goes one step further. For him, the use of images does not bring the soul closer to knowledge but even takes it a little further away. Insofar as images are always images of external things, the soul through them comes to know things that are mediated—but not itself. When the soul thinks in images, it knows nothing so imperfectly as its own nature. As Olivier Boulnois has shown, Eckhart's criticism of images is thus a criticism of mediation: images turn out to be dispensable because they take being oneself out of reach.[86] Only when nothing foreign blends in with the soul anymore and it reaches its ultimate, unmediated ground can the soul be said to be fully with itself.

In the sermon *Dum medium silentium*, Eckhart makes this point with a play on words: *dum medium silentium* is not to be understood only as a local "in the midst of silence." Rather: "At the bottom of the soul, every *medium* must fall silent."[87] For "when humans give up all activity and silence the active reason within them, then God *must* necessarily accept the task and *must* himself be the workman and birth himself [*sich selber gebern*] into the passive soul." The divine light is present in all creatures "immediately" (*âne alle mittel*) just as the sun pierces the air and penetrates everywhere.[88]

(d) A Speculative Metaphysics of Light

One of the models of Meister Eckhart's hyperbolic philosophy of the One is Dionysius the Areopagite. Writing at the end of the fifth and the beginning of the sixth century CE, the Syrian author behind this pseudonym does not himself use the concept of the diaphanous; he employs similar terms such as *diauges* and *photodosia*, which John Scotus Eriugena translates as *lucidus* and *claritas*.[89] Unlike Eriugena, however, Dionysius does not suppose an instant omnipresence of light but a photological outpouring of sorts whose intensity diminishes in moving from level to level as the objects it traverses become more impenetrable and rough:

> By conducting Its own gift of Light to the most reverend Beings, through them, as first, [the divine power of light] distributes in due order to the subordinate, according to the power of each Division to bear the vision of God; or to speak more strictly, and through familiar illustrations (for if they fall short of the Glory of God, Who is exalted above all, yet they are more illustrating for us), the distribution of the sun's ray passes with easy distribution to first matter, as being more transparent [*dieidestéran*] than all, and, through it with greater clearness, lights up its own splendours; but when it strikes more dense materials, its distributed brilliancy becomes more obscure, from the inaptitude of the materials illuminated for transmission of the gift of Light, and from this it is naturally contracted, so as to almost entirely exclude the passage of Light.[90]

The movement of the light, however, is not one-sidely exhausted in a descent (*parathosis*); it also solicits an opposing ascent (*anagōgia*) of the soul. Dionysius should thus not only be credited for inventing the concept of hierarchy (*hierarcheia* as a sacred order); his conception of hierarchy, moreover, rests fundamentally on the principle of analogy, which allows both for vertical ascents and for strict axiomatic distinctions between component parts.

These and similar motifs exert a defining influence on the development of the Oxford School in the thirteenth century that, until the very end, is unable to decide between physics and metaphysics. Roger Bacon, like Robert Grosseteste before him, considered optics to be the discipline guiding all knowledge because only light guarantees the cognizability of objects. In Bacon's fusion of experimental natural science and theological speculation (again, as in Grosseteste before him), research on the refraction of light can never be separated out from a deductive doctrine of grace.[91] Just as light spreads in all directions and encounters impenetrable bodies, so the effusion of grace encounters obstacles: "For the infusion of grace in perfectly good men is analogous to light incident directly and perpendicular. . . . The infusion of grace in imperfect, but good, men is analogous to refracted light. . . . However, sinners who are in mortal sin reflect and repel God's grace from themselves, and therefore grace in their case is analogous to repelled or reflected light."[92]

Not much later, Bonaventure makes a similar argument when he compares divine being with a "spiritual light" (*lux spiritualis*) in which the thinker and the thought become indistinct. The path there is illuminated by the "corporal light" (*lux corporalis*), which is already more than corporal forms but less than spiritual forms, that is, a "*medium . . . inter formas spirituales et corporales*."[93] This bodily light shines back and points to its supracosmic origin, while all things in general are characterized by a *relucere*, a "shining back," that shows the way upward, as it were, leading to the ultimate principle. Progressively leaving behind the material, we accomplish the ascension to the highest, completely luminous principle.

(e) Aquinas: The Closure of the Diaphanous

Thomas Aquinas outlines a completely different architecture of the levels of being—and hence also a different reinterpretation of the luminous medium. His, the final variant of transparency theory as theory of permeability to be discussed here, also prepares the transition to the opacity scenario.

In his sentences on *Sense and Sensibilia*, Aquinas at first defends Aristotle against Democritus and approvingly repeats the assertion that seeing cannot be thought as a mechanical mirroring: "The eye is a seeing thing not because it is smooth, but because it has the power of sight [*virtus visiva*]." Yet immediately after that, he describes the affection of seeing as a refraction of light: *passio . . .*

est refractio. Despite his criticism of Democritus, he then reintroduces the mirror analogy to explain the effect of the diaphanous: when the diaphanous (*dyaphanum*), moved by a visible body, encounters a nondiaphanous body (*corpus non dyaphanum*), the movement is halted and "is somehow turned back, like a ball thrown at a wall and bounced back." Thanks to this "rebound," the "form of the thing seen" (*forma rei vise*) detaches from the wall and leaves an image. For an image to arise, accordingly, there must be an interplay of permeability and closure, of *pervietas* and *terminatio*.[94]

This polarization ultimately allows Aquinas to outline an architecture of degrees of transparency that conforms to "an order of three levels." Corresponding to the first and highest level is pure luminosity; to the second, that which is receptive to luminosity; and finally, to the third and lowest, the things of this Earth that are so far removed from the sun that they remain opaque and without light.[95]

In establishing this hierarchy, Aquinas concurs with earlier commentators; his notion of levels of luminosity within his own noetic architecture are, at the very least, not far from the Oxfordian metaphysics of light (even if he did not read its authors). And yet Aquinas does not go so far as to explain diaphaneity in terms of the two poles of purely actual transparency and purely actual opacity. Strictly speaking, he says, only the intermediate level, characterized by a potentiality for actualization, can genuinely be called the diaphanous. And such diaphanous bodies—which Thomas designates by means of the various translations then current: *perspicua sive transparencia vel dyaphana*—point to a specific conception of the visible, one he calls "Greek."[96] The fact that this correlation of the diaphanous and the visible, the *phainomenon*, needs explanation at all confirms, ex negativo, that there is hardly any place for the diaphanous on the new value scale that ranges from bright clarity to impenetrable materiality.

Although Aquinas is quite clearly aware of the stakes, he does not opt for an inclusion of the diaphanous as a foreign fragment. Instead, he seems to prefer an assimilatory incorporation into the newly erected intellectual construct, which the diaphanous, under a new name, serves to reinforce. A few centuries later, G. W. F. Hegel cursorily remarks, in his *Lectures on the History of Philosophy*, that invoking Aristotle's name has often enough served to propagate views that are "diametrically opposite to his philosophy."[97] The diaphanous in the state of actuality (the ether) marks a boundary between the visible and the invisible. The modal distinction is replaced with a substantial one: from now on, what is invisible no longer depends on the movement of an embodied viewer; the invisible is invisible as a matter of principle. All that is possible is a mediation via the

ILLUMINATION 3

A Tunnel of Light and a Blind Man's Cane

According to the Aristotelian-Ptolemaic view of the world, the Earth is surrounded by nine concentric celestial spheres. The first eight heavens are populated, respectively, by the moon, Venus, Mercury, the sun, Mars, Jupiter, Saturn, and the fixed stars. The ninth celestial sphere is the so-called Crystalline Heaven and contains the *primum mobile*. This is where Dante's *Convivio* (written 1304–1307) situates the diaphanous (*il diafano*), something that is not visible in itself and sets the preceding spheres into motion: "The ninth is not perceptible to the senses, except in the movement spoken of above; many call this the Crystalline Heaven, that is, the heaven that is diaphanous or completely transparent."[100]

In contrast with the cosmologies of late antiquity, however, Dante introduces another heaven beyond the ninth, a tenth, "Empyrean" heaven that is to set the diaphanous into motion.[101] Yet the "Empyrean Heaven, meaning the heaven of flame or of light" not only stands at the end of Dante's journey across the nine heavens in *Paradiso*, where he has Beatrice declare: "We have emerged now from the largest body to the heaven of pure light."[102] It is also at the center of Flemish-Rhenish mysticism, in Ruysbroeck or Seuse, for example. Later, the ecstatically invoked "flaming" *coelum empyreum* finds a striking artistic representation in Hieronymus Bosch's polyptych *Visions of the Hereafter*. In the panel *Ascent of the Blessed* (fig. 3.1), the souls

FIGURE 3.1 Hieronymus Bosch, *Paradise. Ascent to the Empyreum* (1500/1504), oil on canvas, 86.5 × 39.5 cm. Palazzo Ducale, Venice.

(*Continued next page*)

(Continued)

are carried upward by angels, becoming ever more weightless and already dematerializing, an impression reinforced by the perspectival effect. One after the other, the souls fly through a horizontal light tunnel at whose end they are welcomed by a figure outlined against a dazzling white background.

At the completely opposite end of the spectrum there is an emblematic embodiment of seeing that in its own way, in a new way, continues the tradition of the diaphanous. An edition of Descartes's *Discourse on Method* published in Paris in 1724 not only includes new commentary by the Révérend Père Poisson, it also contains engravings by an artist who has remained anonymous (fig. 3.2). One of these illustrations takes up the motif of the crossed blind person's canes from the *Dioptrics*. Clad in Rococo fashion and blindfolded, it remains

FIGURE 3.2 Copper engraving from René Descartes, *Discours de la méthode suivi de la dioptrique, les météores, la géométrie*, ed. Père Nicolas Poisson, 2 vols. (Paris, 1724).

unclear ultimately whether the figure is really blind; he rather resembles a courtier who momentarily forgoes his eyesight in order to fully abandon himself to "seeing with his hands." This new seeing promised by the *Discourse*, the engraving seems to suggest, replaces the dubitable natural senses with prosthetic equipment.

symbol, as is evident in Ramon Llull's interpretation of the burning bush on Mount Sinai as the dawn of a new age: an age in which meaning, fundamentally, is accessible only symbolically.[98] What Aristotle understood as a purely medial phenomenal space independent of all values is now being invested aesthetically and metaphysically. In the words of Stefan Hoffmann:

The metaphorization of the aisthetic concept of the medium and of the classic diaphanous medium in particular shifts the medium itself ever further away from the earthly sphere of a materiality fully graspable by the senses toward the higher spheres of ethereal spiritual beings and phenomena. . . . The rhetorical deployment transposes what in the aisthetic concept of the *medium diaphanum* had designated a *transparency* aspect into a new—suprasensual—domain and thereby transcends the zone of the visible.[99]

4. WHEN BLIND MEN SEE: THE OPACITY SCENARIO

(a) Stoa: Condensations of *Pneuma*

"That which is seen is seen by contact with the ray of vision."[103] This statement, which the tradition (wrongly) attributed to Aristotle, can serve as the motto of that second scenario taking up the theory of the diaphanous. Everything seems to indicate that the materialist transformation of the diaphanous is of Stoic origin. For the Stoics, an optical *pneuma* flows from the central controlling faculty (the *hēgemonikon*) and links up with the surrounding air, thereby placing the surroundings in a state of tension. The medium, accordingly, transforms into an instrumental extension of the body. Cicero even goes so far as to write that for the Stoics, "the air itself is our partner in seeing" (*aër nobiscum videt*).[104]

Some Stoics, though, seek to emphasize that the coalescence with the air is at best metaphorical. For Chrysippus and Apollodorus, the tip of the cone formed by the air placed in a state of tension is located in the eye while its base is situated with the object. In that sense, the intermediary space does not itself "see"; rather, "the thing seen is reported to us by the medium of the air stretching out towards it, as if by a stick."[105]

(b) The Stick Metaphor in the Commentaries on Aristotle

Very likely, the first commentator to take up the metaphor and summarize such theories as "touch stick" theories is Alexander of Aphrodisias, who writes: "There are some who say that seeing comes about through the tension of the air. For the air which is in contact with the pupil is pierced by the sight and shaped into a cone. When this is as it were stamped at its base by the objects of sight perception comes about, as with contact through a stick."[106] In the sixth century this interpretation becomes canonical when Simplicius grafts it onto Aristotle's theory of media. In doing so, he appears to go back to the Stoic notion, but he may also have been influenced by Plotinus, who voices similar ideas.[107] Another possible influence might be the fourth-century neo-Platonist Calcidius. In his commentary on the *Timaeus*, Calcidius coins the so-called spider metaphor according to which the *hēgemonikon* is situated at the center of the soul like the spider at the center of its web. When an insect is caught in the web, the entire web begins to vibrate and transmits the movement to the center.[108]

In his commentary on *On the Soul*, Simplicius associates the diaphanous with a *mokhlos*, a bar or lever. The *mokhlos* Odysseus rams into Polyphemus's eye in Homer's epos here serves not to blind but on the contrary to make visible. According to Simplicius, seeing must always be mechanically stimulated, "just as a lever does in the manual moving of a rock."[109]

(c) Galen and Ocular Anatomy

The condensation and concretization of *pneuma* in a quasi-tactile prosthesis, however, is only one variant of a theory of vision widely adopted in antiquity that can be summarized as emanationism, the idea that seeing is an activity initiated by the eye.[110] In the progressive transformation of the ray of sight into a solid stick, the visible gradually becomes the object of physical optics. One interesting intermediary in the process is Hunayn ibn Isḥāq, the ninth-century author of *Kitāb al-ašrat maqālāt fī al-ʿayn* (*Ten Treatises on the Eye*), which situate Galenic medicine in the context of Arab knowledge.[111] Although in his optics, this Baghdad scholar, known in the West as Johanitius, takes up Galen's notions practically without exception, he does not adopt the criticism of the stick of vision. Instead he explicitly writes in book 3 that someone walking in the dark can indeed see objects, employing a stick to that end. He then extends and applies this case study to all ways of seeing, writing that sight perceives its object via the movement of the air the way a blind person touches the object via a stick: seeing becomes the event of a "collision." This collision theory, however, cannot be reduced to a physical materialism because it posits a qualitative change of the medium that is, as it were, mentally assimilated to the soul.[112] It would

take several centuries before Descartes would consolidate the subordination of
the visual under the palpable.

(d) Alhazen: The Segmentation of the Visible

Avicenna's and Alhazen's theories had a decisive influence on the subsequent
development of optics. To criticize the model of active seeing and undermine its
plausibility, both use arguments analogous to that model's claims. Hasan ibn
al-Haytham (ca. 965–1040), born in Cairo and working in Baghdad, known in
the West as Alhazen, puts the theory of rays emanating from the eye to rest once
and for all, but he retains an axial structure of seeing. For him, optical rays do
not emanate from the one seeing but from every individual point on the surface
of a thing. While this does partially rehabilitate Aristotle's theory of perception,
namely, insofar as seeing is triggered by the visible object, Alhazen stresses the
insufficiency of the Aristotelian conception of the medium. If the visible object
sets the medium into motion and if the medium takes on the color of the objects,
then how does one explain that the field of vision is not monochrome, that
instead it is possible to distinguish colored objects within it? Or, put differently:
if the medium is to assimilate to the object, *which* of the many objects is it to
assimilate to?[113]

From Alhazen's perspective, Aristotle's theory is too abstract: against the
background of new anatomic findings inspired by Galen and new geometric
tenets inspired by Euclid, the object and the organ of perception can be dissected into individual segments and even into individual points. Taking up al-
Kindi's *De radiis* (*On Rays*), which, however, does not come to any systematic
conclusions,[114] Alhazen in his optics—translated in the Latin West already
around 1200 under the title *Perspectiva* or *De aspectibus*—supposes that vision
rays emanate from every individual point of objects' surfaces, cross the transparent medium, and at a specific angle meet the crystal body (*corpus crystallinum*), which transmits them to the faculty of seeing.[115] It is thus already on the
level of the crystal body that individual points are arranged in contrasting segments that the faculty of vision can distinguish and recognize.[116] Vitello and
Kepler, both of whom refer to the first book of *Perspectiva*, rigorously spell out
Alhazen's program of punctualization and segmentation, once and for all dis-
missing the concept of a diaphanous medium of the senses that Alhazen holds
on to.[117]

(e) Descartes: Seeing with Sticks

Insofar as all of life depends on the senses, Descartes writes in the opening of his *Dioptrique* (1637), and insofar as, among the senses, the sense of sight is "the most comprehensive and the noblest," the task of all lovers of truth must be to hone their gaze.[118] Against medieval conceptions of "intentional species"—"all those small images flitting through the air"—Descartes mobilizes the old simile of the blind person's cane.[119] Bodily seeing does not arise from some kind of spiritual intuition but from a downright tactile scanning. The degree of resistance of objects (trees, rocks, sand, and so on) that are percussed, as it were, by the extensions of the soul that are the senses becomes the measure of (blind) seeing. In a way similar to a ball bouncing off a wall whose rigidity determines the angle and speed with which it rebounds, tactile seeing forms a relief-like image in the eye.[120] Optics thus becomes tactics in the literal sense, and the blind person's stick becomes emblematic of a thinking that once and for all crushes phenomenality between objective extension and intentional content.[121]

In adopting the motif of blind peoples' canes, Descartes does more than take on a traditional trope.[122] The doubling of the cane into two crossed sticks revivifies the discussion going back to Aristotle's day about the exact function of the optic chiasm.[123] As the illustration added to the sixth chapter is meant to demonstrate, the vision pathways (which Descartes describes as bundles of nerves, as "fibers . . . much thinner than those spun by silkworms")[124] cross in the *chiasma opticum* and join the pineal gland, which is reputed to be not only the seat of the soul but also the site where the two halves of vision come together in a single image.

Already in the *Dioptrique*, a suggestion for improvement follows the experimental description. While Descartes, on the one hand, here describes seeing as opaque impenetrability (an image emerges when "in the eye" light hits "the first opaque membrane," *primum opacum, quod est in oculo*),[125] the ideal articulated in the *Principles of Philosophy* of perceiving *clare et distincte*, "clearly and distinctly," suggests a clarification and correction of seeing. All too many people throughout their lives do not see "with sufficient accuracy" (*recte*).[126] Where the seventh discourse of the *Dioptrique* discusses the means to be employed to improve seeing, metaphysics—in a reversal of the movement described above for scholasticism—is being physicalized. Having retraced the process of seeing, Descartes comes to the conclusion that the visible objects and the internal, nervous processes of transmission cannot be influenced, but the "external organs—among which I include all the transparent parts of the eye, as well as all the other bodies that we can place between the eye and the object,"[127] can. The imperfect human apparatus for sight is supplemented by prostheses, by "other organs that are artificial,"[128] such as the already existing lens of the eye or "very transparent liquids," or "through art," thanks to "a piece of glass or of some other transparent body . . . in order to curve the rays falling on them."[129] The transparent glass becomes a corrective that remedies a lack of clarity.

(f) Extensions of the Soul

"The Cartesian concept of vision," Maurice Merleau-Ponty asserts in a famous analysis, "is modeled after the sense of touch."[130] There are traces galore of such a tactilized Cartesianism in later authors. In Nicolas Malebranche's *Recherche de la vérité* (1674/75), the touching stick model serves to guarantee a naturalized geometry: "For just as a blind man could touch a given body with the ends of two straight sticks of unknown length and judge its approximate distance according to a kind of natural geometry by the position of his hands and the distance between them, so might the soul be said to judge the distance of an object by the disposition of its eyes."[131]

The model remains popular for a long time: Diderot refers to it in his *Letter on the Blind*, Condillac bases his perception theory of touch on it, and Rousseau has his Émile see with his fingertips. In art theory, the conception survives in Riegl's "haptic gaze," in Berenson's "tactile values," and in Deleuze's "digital seeing." There are echoes even in Kant, for example, in the transcripts of the *Lectures on Anthropology*: "We find in vision . . . much similarity with touch; for a ray of light that falls from the object into my eye is like a stick that falls in a straight line from the object into my eye and by means of which I touch the surface of the object."[132] The Cartesian model echoed and metaphorized here turns the simile of the blind person's staff—which as late as in Cesare Ripa's *Iconologia* (first illustrated edition 1603) emblematized Error[133]—into the very model of correctness. The seventeenth century thus conceptualizes something that had been initiated experimentally two centuries earlier. As I will show in the next section, the construction of central perspective rests, despite its protestation of pure seeing-through, on a trailblazing alliance between transparency and physicality, a well-structured mechanism that involves at once both opening and closing. Such alliance is particularly palpable in Brunelleschi's perspective experiment, which is able to construct a powerful *dispositif* for legitimatizing images thanks only to a procedural correlation of hole and mirror—a fact hardly ever mentioned in the voluminous literature on this major event in the history of artificial images.

5. THE COMPUTABILITY OF THE IMAGE: BRUNELLESCHI'S EXPERIMENT

The name Filippo Brunelleschi metonymically stands for an experiment that may be seen as the primal scene of a thoroughly new conception of knowledge. Brunelleschi's experiment embodies an inaugural moment for a visual epistemology that blends scientific and artistic, optic and poetic skills. The importance attributed to him already by his contemporaries is confirmed by the honor (never bestowed on the often anonymous medieval artists) of having his biography written. Thanks to Antonino di Tuccio Manetti, we are able at least partially to reconstruct Brunelleschi's procedure.[134]

One day around 1425—the precise date can no longer be ascertained—Brunelleschi takes up position in the shade of the portal of the Florence Duomo (which will be completed some years later by a dome of his design) and paints, probably aided by a mirror, a picture whose sides are half a *braccio* (less than a foot) long. It shows the octagonal baptistery and the rest of the piazza. "And he placed burnished silver where the sky had to be represented," Manetti tells us, "so that the real air and atmosphere were reflected in it, and thus the clouds seen in the silver are carried along by the wind as it blows." The canvas is then turned on its vertical axis and a "hole . . . as tiny as a lentil bean" is drilled into it from behind. For a spectator looking through the hole at mirror held up at half an arm's length in front of it (fig. 3.3), the baptistery "with the aforementioned elements of the burnished silver, the piazza, the viewpoint, etc." looked like the real thing: "the spectator felt he saw the actual scene" (*e pareva che si vedessa 'l propio vero*). For emphasis, Manetti adds: "I have had it in my hands and seen it many times in my days and can testify to it."[135]

While Manetti describes this process of verification, which can be iterated at will, in great detail, he remains completely silent on the way the picture is painted, as has often been pointed out. A considerable share of the extensive research done on Brunelleschi has been concerned with testing possible hypotheses, from the mirror via an anticipation of Alberti's veil (as Vasari already surmised) to the use of a camera obscura.[136] All these approaches, however, miss that what is instructive in Manetti's biography is not what remains unsaid but what is explicitly being said. The fact that Manetti has nothing to say about the

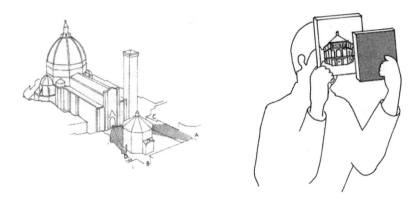

FIGURE 3.3 Brunelleschi's first experiment, in Hubert Damisch, *L'origine de la perspective* (Paris: Flammarion, 1993), 115, 142.

perspectival painting procedure is due not only to temporal distance (the biography is written decades later); taken by itself—and in this, Manetti was quite farsighted—it is meaningless: Brunelleschi's experiment does not represent the inaugural moment of a new pictorial practice but rather the investiture of its normativity. Brunelleschi's disruptive device emblematically embodies the optical instrument for the modern way of finding the truth that comes into its own in the iteration of the identical. The mediation through the mirror image in Brunelleschi's pictorial *dispositif* allows *perspectiva naturalis* and *perspectiva artificialis* to become congruent.

By itself, though, the mirror is insufficient for assimilating the viewing of images to natural seeing. Whereas Plato had suggested always carrying a mirror to let all natural phenomena reflect themselves, Brunelleschi, for his part— "since every point . . . change[s] the appearances to the eye"[137]—calls for arresting the point of the eye, not unlike the focalizing of the burning glass with which Archimedes (also the author of a *Catoptrica*) put fire to the sails of an enemy fleet. Mirror image and image of perception, meanwhile, overlap only once the viewing through the hole is reduced to a single angle. This demands a window-like aperture that separates the roaming gaze from the eye and focuses the eye on the central ray of light that ends in the image's vanishing point. Whereas the Middle Ages thought of the mirror as of a monstrance, the Renaissance, with the help of the window metaphor, reinterprets the mirror as a tool of de-monstration, the *demonstratio picturae* Alberti speaks of later in the context of the metaphorical "open window" that he refers to as miraculous.[138]

The interplay of opening and mirror may be irrelevant for the way the image shows (*mostrare*) itself, but it is indispensable to proving (*dimostrare*) the legitimacy of the image. Brunelleschi first *shows* his artificial perspective in the painting (*nella prima cosa in che e' lo mostro*) and then *proves* how artificial and natural perspective become transparent to each other in the mirror seen through the hole (*per quanto s'aveva a dimostrare del cielo*). The coalition of mirror and window thus presents itself as a pictorial *discourse* that ennobles the image and allows it to become veridical. Even before perspectival painting technique has been perfected, the *dispositif* of its post-facto justification develops, which the normativity of any future image—in the future perfect, as it were—will have had to measure up against. Where painting henceforth has to pass through the needle's eye of transparency, every future image becomes computable.

Now, remarkably, the pictorial *dispositif* establishes a self-referential circle: the fixed point is both the condition and the result of the process of making visible. What the point-like eye sees in the mirror is the vanishing point in the image, which in turn remains invisible insofar as its place is taken by the eye reflected in the mirror (fig. 3.4). The eye point produces the vanishing point in the first place, and the vanishing point, inversely, yields the standpoint of the viewer: Brunelleschi's pictorial *dispositif* thus inaugurates the "mirror stage" of modernity and discovers the fixed point of the eye that both doubles and reinforces itself and which Jean Pélerin Viator in his *De artificiali perspectiva* (1505) would describe, without being able to anticipate the fate of the word, as "subject."[139]

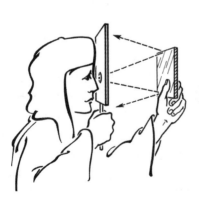

FIGURE 3.4 Brunelleschi's first experiment—the eye behind the image. Drawing by Philippe Comar, in Philippe Comar, *La perspective en jeu: Les dessous de l'image* (Paris: Gallimard, 1992), 33. Courtesy of the author.

Vredeman de Vries: The Obstructed Horizon

In 1604, roughly one century after Viator publishes his textbook on perspective, the Dutch printmaker Hondius prints Hans Vredeman de Vries's treatise *Perspectiva*. The "distance point procedure" it theorizes and illustrates with numerous practical examples seeks to intertwine eye, image surface, and perspective. At issue, Vredeman de Vries remarks, is a generalized "foreshortening" (*vercortinghe*) of spatiality. Among the many projection sketches, plate 30 stands out (fig. 3.5). It shows, from the back, a

FIGURE 3.5 Hans Vredeman de Vries, *Perspectiva*
(Leiden, 1604), plate 30 ("Perspective dat is").

(*Continued next page*)

(*Continued*)

man standing on the lowered floor of a space underneath a vaulted dome who apparently does not take any notice of the figures approaching from the sides. Instead he is fixedly oriented toward the vanishing point that seems to be located at the center of an aedicula piercing the surrounding wall. All the auxiliary lines, too, run toward that point, which is not itself visible because it is blocked from view by the man's head. Pictorial technique and the calculation of gaps introduced in the Quattrocento collaborate when the vanishing point turns out, literally, to be what Brian Rotman and Sybille Krämer call a "zero-point": "The vanishing point structures the picture like a coordinate system, whose zero-point it is," and accordingly, "the organizing principle of all visible objects—which, like the vanishing point itself, is invisible—coincides with the position of the eye of the observer."[140]

Vredeman de Vries's distance point procedure telescopes the eye point and the vanishing point; "in his mind," the viewer is already where he will never be with his body, namely, with the infinite that painting generally (to avoid having to represent it as a point and thereby already to limit it) conceals: in the literal sense, Vredeman de Vries illustrates Pascal's notion of the infinite as always lying "in the back of the mind" (*derrière la tête*).[141] The zero-point is itself an *ineffabile*, blocked by the body of the viewer. What the eye sees can, in this regard, be seen by no other eye. Such seeing, however, remains blind to its own conditions of possibility, namely, to the perspectival configuration of space that only the intersubjective view from outside can bestow.

6. UNVEILINGS (ALBERTI)

The year 1436 sees the publication of *Della pittura*, written in the Tuscan dialect and dedicated to Filippo Brunelleschi. In this work, already published in Latin the year before, Leon Battista Alberti claims to be the inventor of the seeing veil. Giorgio Vasari would later place it on the same level as the cultural-technological revolution of Gutenberg's printing with movable type.[142] It seems he discerned parallels between the book printer's new screen printing technique (which allowed both for a greater mobility of the elements and, thanks to its fixing the composition, greater iterability) and the *velum* whose advantage, according to Alberti, lies in "always present[ing] . . . the same unchanged plane" such that the object "is always the same thing in the process of seeing."[143] The taming of the mobile in the medium of pictorial *circumscriptio* results from the demetaphorization of the visual intersection, namely, in that the *intersegatione* is no longer a virtual cross section of the visual pyramid but materially condensed in the construction veil.

As Alberti emphatically stresses, however, his new pictorial geometry of point, line, and plane is not be conceived of mathematically; the one who is speaking is "the painter," for whom every point always already expands from geometrical extensionlessness to become a *macchia*, a dot; in that sense, he does not follow the nimble, philosophical Minerva but a "fatter" one (a *pinguiore minerva* in Latin or, in Tuscan, a *più grassa minerva*).[144] The *velum* that Alberti "among his friends" calls "intersection" (*intercisio*) is "a thin veil, finely woven, dyed whatever colour pleases you and with larger threads [marking out] as many parallels as you prefer. This veil I place between the eye and the thing seen, so the visual pyramid penetrates through the thinness of the veil."[145] As in a Byzantine sudarium, the visible is to impress itself in the very fabric, get caught in it, and coalesce in a new pictorial plane. The image, accordingly, is precisely not a "transparent glass" but a plane on which the visible things themselves stop to "inscribe and depict" themselves (*rem ipsam . . . in istac planitie veli conscriptam et depictam videas*). The veil-grid is "very useful," moreover, because on this grid, the visible disassembles into parts as it were by itself: "Here in this parallel you will see the forehead, in that the nose, in another the cheeks, in this lower one the chin and all outstanding features in their place. On panels or on walls, divided into similar parallels, you will be able to put everything in its place."[146] With his *intercisio* or *intersegatio*, Alberti anticipates the anatomical experiments of Andreas Vesalius, who was the first to dare disaggregate the *corpus integrum* into individual organs. The parallelograms formed by the threads of the veil, furthermore, are a preliminary stage to Kepler's dissolution of vision into individual points. In employing them, the visual surgeon has no need to get his hands on the bodies themselves: as Dürer's illustration shows, he keeps the objects he studies at a safe distance (fig. 3.6). The cutting (*ritagliare*) also marks the transition from the closed space of the Middle Ages to the unlimited space of modernity, an incorporation of the indefinite, as it were, a cultivation of the pictorial field expressed in the metaphor of the *campo* (field) and the verb *campeggiare* (to depict by filling a field with colors) derived from it. Alberti's conception finds a perfect illustration in a woodcut by Hieronymus Rodler that shows how a painter "squares" reality in order to make it manageable (fig. 3.7). We see a young master squinting through a latticed window, transferring the

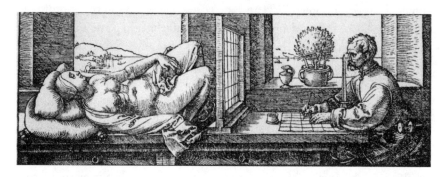

FIGURE 3.6 Albrecht Dürer, *The Draughtsman of a Reclining Woman*, woodcut, 7.5 × 21.5 cm, in *Underweysung der Zeichnung* (Nuremberg, 1538), contained in third edition only, therefore possibly from the workshop.

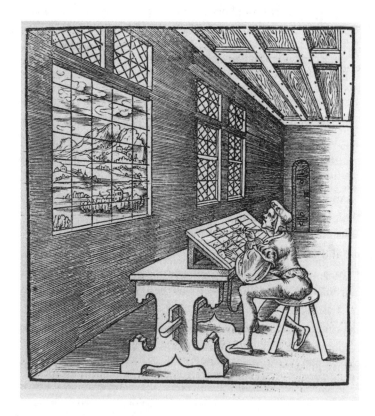

FIGURE 3.7 Woodcut from Hieronymus Rodler, *Eyn schön nützlich büchlin und unterweisung der kunst des messens* (Simmern, 1531).

sections onto his drawing board: the underlying organizing structure of the window must be solid while also allowing for the "visible" to come through. Alberti's medium thus necessarily features only a loose coupling: the *velum* is only "loosely woven" (*rare textum*) and underdetermined ("dyed whatever colour"), yet also structured by "larger threads" (*filis grossioribus*), and it can thus be a great "aid" (*adiumentum*) in fashioning all as yet unknown objects.[147]

Characteristically, this new visualization technique, which Vasari considered to be revolutionary, is hardly even mentioned in the discourse legitimizing perspectival painting. Alberti's *De pictura*, which celebrates the combination of late medieval technical artists' manuals with the lyrical flair of ancient poetics, turns out to play in two different metaphorical registers that seem strangely disconnected. While the procedure of central perspective is explained in operational terms with the medial veil, its claim is legitimized by the negation of any hindering medium and by the triumph of the transparent "open window" (*aperta fenestra*).[148] Procedure and rhetoric are irresolvably asymmetrical, given that the rhetoric is to make the procedure possible in the first place and argumentatively place second what genetically comes first. What we can observe in this foundational text, in which a painter inaugurates the modern regime of images, is the symptomatic marginalization of operative mediality taking place in modernity.

7. THE PICTORIALIZATION OF VISION (KEPLER)

The eye has been made as it is because the mind is as it is,
and not the other way round

—Johannes Kepler, *The Harmony of the World*

While in the Quattrocento, the normalization of central perspective consists in translating the laws of vision into laws of painting, about 150 years later, around 1600, there is an inverse movement of modeling vision on the standards of painting; or, in other terms: a pictorialization of vision takes place. As a matter of fact, the movement is now reversed, and the formation of natural pictures described follows patterns that are directly inspired by artificial pictures. By insisting on the fact that it casts pictures directly onto the retina, nature is conceived of as a painter who has no need of observing the laws of physiological optics. No longer does an inner geometry of seeing impose its laws on the artistic

elaboration of external nature. At a time when the convention of central perspective is increasingly being discredited artistically, there is an inverse artificial-
ization of the visual perspective insofar as the *perspectiva artificialis* is no longer
conceived of as an extension of the *perspectiva communis* but rather as its ground
and precondition.[149] Natural vision thus presents itself as the result of a pictorial
art that circumvents the laws of the eye. A downright inversion of fiction and
fact, of art and nature takes place between 1600 and 1750: natural vision now
presents itself as derived from artificial vision.[150]

Johannes Kepler operates this internalization in his epoch-making *Ad Vitel-
lionem Paralipomena* of 1604. In its own way, his demonstration of the existence
of images on the retina anticipates Kant's inversion of Copernicus. In Kepler's
"revolution of the way of thinking," the eye itself must subordinate itself to the
laws of the inner images. Initially, though, the assistant of Tycho Brahe, imperial
court astronomer in Prague, is concerned with astronomy, not perception.
Thanks to a pinhole camera, he had observed how, during a solar eclipse, the
diameter of the moon shrinks although its distance from the Earth remains
constant. Kepler surmised that the phenomenon could be verified in the hole-
like human eye as well. He adopts the camera obscura model of the eye of
Giovanni Battista della Porta, who writes: "I say that just as light passing
through the narrow opening of a window portrays bodies illuminated by the
sun on paper placed opposite, so also does it, proceeding through the aperture of
the pupil, portray the image of things seen on the crystalline humor."[151] This
model, however, does not explain how the rays of light are bundled again and
focused in the eye; moreover, by restricting itself only to perpendicular rays, it
cannot account for the incoming peripheral rays. Vitello in turn includes these
peripheral rays in his model but faces a new problem: if every point on the retina
were to receive incoming rays from each and every point of the visual field, the
result, in theory, would be total confusion. Kepler finds out that, just like della
Porta, Vitello misconstrues the eye's anatomy. In his response to his predecessor,
Kepler thus introduces two decisive novelties. On the one hand, he defines the
eye lens no longer as merely an opening but as a bundling body; on the other, he
discovers the curved retina on which the rays bundled by the lens reassume their
original configuration (fig. 3.8). Starting with Kepler, it becomes possible to
speak of a full-fledged correspondence theory of vision that is based on so-called
stigmatism (the Greek *stigma* meaning "point"): to every object point corresponds an image point. "And thus, finally, if straight lines were drawn from the
points of the hemisphere through the center of the retina and of the vitreous
humor, those lines will mark [*signabunt*] the points of their own respective picture on the retina opposite."[152]

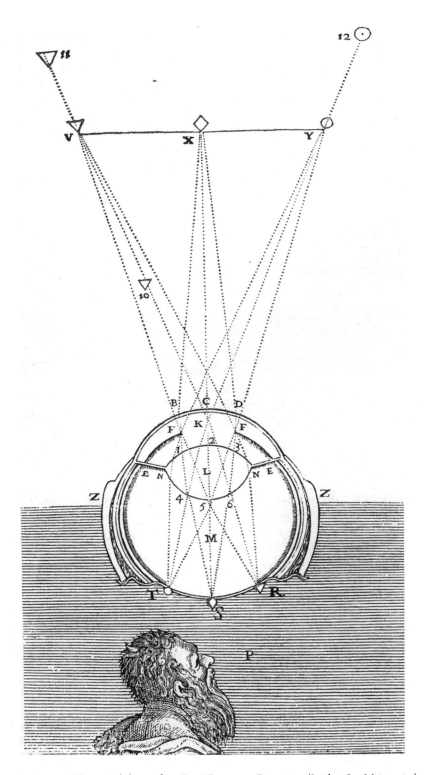

FIGURE 3.8 The retinal theory, from René Descartes, *Dioptrique* (Leiden: Jan Maire, 1637).

Having followed the ray of light from the moon to the eye, Kepler does not stop at the retina since the mechanical model evidently does not suffice to explain how the punctualized image gets from the retina into the "soul." "For the arsenal of the optical writers does not extend beyond this opaque wall" where a *quaestor* "might go forth to meet this image" and carry it into the soul. The rest is to be left to those who have more experience in dissections.[153]

In Kepler's theory, significantly, it does not matter whether there is actually anyone looking, since an inscription takes place in a wholly mechanical way, namely, the inscription of an "image or picture" (*idolum seu picturam*) on "the white wall, tinged with red, of the concave surface of the retina." The internalization of painting we observe here is manifest in Kepler's terminology: he speaks of images that literally inscribe or engrave themselves (*impingitur*) on this "opaque wall" (*opacum parietem*). If he possessed "sufficient keenness of vision," the anatomist would see the image on the retina.[154]

Such a pictorialization of seeing as inaugurated by Kepler, however, turns the investigation of the visual into an art of reading. Just as paintings demand an iconographical interpretation, so the inner images are visible signs demanding to be read. And, as Kepler metaphorically writes, the images at the back of the *crystallinum*, too, contain a chapter of the "book of Nature" as whose "priest" Kepler wants to be seen.[155]

8. THE LITERACY OF THE EYE (DESCARTES)

Even thirty years after Kepler, Descartes, too, speaks of "pictures" (*peintures*) painted into the eye.[156] But, at the same time, he voices his suspicion that such a theory of physical retinal images might accidentally serve to rehabilitate the medieval doctrine of *species* (these "similitudes" of things that the intellect can "see" and that Descartes will deride as empty superstitions). The large woodcut included in the Leyden edition of his *Dioptrique* (1637) seems both to illustrate Kepler's discovery and to question it ironically: the engraving shows a diagram with the crossing of the visual rays inside the eye but also a three-dimensional onlooker (Kepler's *quaestor*?) looking at the formation of the visual image. For the notion of a really existing image that is no longer to be seen—as previously thought—in the diaphanous ocular liquid but henceforth at the back of the eye, on the retina, calls for a further eye, a second-order eye, as it were, capable of seeing this image. This marks the endpoint of transposing pictorial laws onto the process of vision, since the retina images differ from painted images in that they show something without themselves being visible. "Apart from that, it is necessary to beware of assuming that in order to sense, the mind needs to perceive certain images transmitted by the objects to the brain, as our philosophers commonly suppose; or, at least, the nature of these images must be conceived quite otherwise than as they do."[157]

In criticizing two-dimensional perspectival painting for necessarily distorting three-dimensional objects, Kepler had paved the way for Descartes's abandoning the pictorial model in favor of a new conventional grammar of the visual. Complete acceptance of the pictorial model was problematic because, as Kepler's colleague Wilhelm Schickard puts it, "Our vision does not in fact have a plane surface like a tablet [*nullum planum pro tabella habet*]."[158] A resolute break, emphatically pursued by Descartes, henceforth separates the planar regime of the image and the extensionless (that is, intensional) regime of inner representation. Descartes insists on the necessary distance between the two: there must be a dissemblance between the image and the depicted, "for otherwise there would be no distinction between the object and its image."[159] In opposing the criterion of similarity, which had dominated medieval aesthetics for centuries and still served as the basis for the scholastic theory of the *species intentionales*,[160] which he sharply criticizes, Descartes declares the greatest possible dissimilarity to be the ideal of all pictorial representation: "Often, in order to be more perfect as images and to represent the object better, they must not resemble it."[161]

Descartes's example is telling. The dissimilarity thesis is not illustrated by painting but by the technique of *taille-douce*, a certain kind of fine-line engraving also known as intaglio. Descartes thus refers to an activity that is probably the closest to that of the writing thinker. Instead of letters, the artist applies lines of ink to the paper:

> For example, you can see that engravings, being made of nothing but a little ink placed here and there on the paper, represent to us forests, towns, men, and even battles and storms, even though, among an infinity of diverse qualities which they make us conceive in these objects, only in shape is there actually any resemblance. And even this resemblance is a very imperfect one, seeing that, on a completely flat surface, they represent to us bodies which are of different heights and distances, and even that following the rules of perspective, circles are often better represented by ovals rather than by other circles; and squares by diamonds rather than by other squares; and so on for all other shapes.[162]

The fact that we see something in the engraving is not due to any kind of analogy with natural vision but to the pictorial conventions that make the

engraving legible. "Instead, we should consider that there are many other
things besides pictures which can stimulate our thought, such as, for example,
signs and words, which do not in any way resemble the things which they signify."[163] Images thus have their foundation not in perception but in a visual
alphabet of ovals and diamonds. As much as Descartes must be considered the
founder of mental representationalism, which provides the imagination with a
physiological and hence a material foundation, the *Dioptrique* inversely
reduces material images to their representational character. Descartes thereby
confirms, to put it in very succinct terms, the *subordination of the image under
the regime of signs.*

9. THE DIAPHANOUS AS PARTITION (BERKELEY)

Since his *New Theory of Vision* of 1709, Bishop Berkeley has usually been considered a radical critic of a "natural geometry" of seeing associated with the
names Kepler and Descartes. And indeed, Berkeley ardently defends a deper-
spectivization of seeing and, consequently, a liberation of the visible from the
illusion of spatial depth. And yet—as the studies by Margaret Atherton and,
especially, Philippe Hamou suggest—Berkeley's sensualism not only continues
constitutively to depend on the Cartesian paradigm he opposes; paradoxically,
it may be regarded, as Hamou argues, as the historical culmination of the "age
of perspective."[164]

The core thesis of the *New Theory of Vision*, whose implications Berkeley later
spells out in greater detail in *The Theory of Vision Vindicated and Explained*
(1733), consists in supposing that the order of the visible has nothing in common
with the order of extended bodies. This basic supposition supports the criticism
of the pictorial representationalism with which Berkeley—not unlike Descartes
in his criticism of his scholastic contemporaries—reproaches Locke and others.
The images on the retina, Berkeley explains by taking up a criticism of John
Norris's, are misunderstood as a kind of picture gallery that in turn presupposes
an eye lying behind it that not only will have to revert them (the images appear
inverted) but will have to *see* them in the first place. This conception of a second-
order vision ultimately amounts to applying a *homunculus* theory to the visual.
The image on the retina is still being understood as a tactile object on the model
of painting, even though, for Berkeley, the emergence of microscopes has irrefut-
ably demonstrated once and for all the heterogeneity of the order of the visible
and the order of the touchable, since in microscopy, we only see what we cannot

touch. Or, in a formulation from the *Philosophical Commentaries*: "Ignorance of Glasses made men think extension to be in bodies."[165]

Unlike Descartes, however, Berkeley does not associate a hope for a more penetrating vision with the new optical instruments. For him, they confirm the autonomy of visual appearances only retrospectively. In the context of the debates about the tactility of sight and the visuality of touch, Berkeley, against Molyneux, takes the position that tactility and visuality are fundamentally irreconcilable. Seeing, for him, yields no insight into relationships of spatial depth.

It is therefore all the more of a misunderstanding when, in his *Techniques of the Observer*, Jonathan Crary, probably caught in his own periodization, sees in Berkeley a representative of the camera obscura model. He bases his argument on the reference to perspectival apparatuses in section 55 of *The Theory of Vision Vindicated*, although, as Crary acknowledges, the passage does not explicitly mention the camera obscura.[166] What the text does, instead, is reactualize Alberti's veil, which Berkeley now calls "diaphanous plain":

> For the better explication of this point, we may suppose a diaphanous plain erected near the eye, perpendicular to the horizon, and divided into small equal squares. A straight line from the eye to the utmost limit of the horizon, passing through this diaphanous plain, will mark a certain point or height to which the horizontal plain, as projected or represented in the perpendicular plain, would rise. The eye sees all the parts and objects in the horizontal plain, through certain corresponding squares of the perpendicular diaphanous plain....
>
> It is true this diaphanous plain, and the images supposed to be projected thereon, are altogether of a tangible nature: But then there are pictures relative to those images: and those pictures have an order among themselves.[167]

The analogy of the permeable veil does not serve to emblematize the eighteenth-century effort at a "fundamental harmonization of the senses," as Crary claims.[168] On the contrary, it separates the space of tactile appearances from that of visual appearances once and for all. Henceforth, the diaphanous names neither a structural nor a literal medium for producing appearances but serves instead to consolidate separate sense spheres.

———————

What I have pursued up to this point under the general heading of a history of the "forgetting of the medium" has been a tentative reconstruction of a motif that runs all the way from antiquity to early modernity and of the progressive establishment of modern dualism. The Scholastic alternative between the study of things (*doctrina rerum*) and the study of signs (*doctrina signorum*) already foreshadows the division of labor in the Cartesian model between the *res extensa* and the *res cogitans*, between extended things and mental representations. Where the only alternative is between things that stand for themselves and representations that depend on the mind, a subjectless description such as the one of the *metaxy* will find itself at odds. It is therefore hardly surprising that in the reception of Aristotelianism, the radical discovery of the diaphanous medium was marginalized in favor of other concepts in Aristotle's work. The image of Aristotle that later Aristotelianism consolidated obstructed the insight into such a groundbreaking conceptual framework even further. This chapter has attempted to gather some of the metaphysical, theological, and epistemological reasons that account for such an oblivion of the *metaxy*. Trying to write the history of the reception of the diaphanous amounts to writing a ghost story, first because it is to write the history of a nonreception but second also because it increasingly becomes clear that the diaphanous medium, although not recognized as such, continues to haunt the Western order of knowledge. Tellingly, the negation of the medium and the establishment of a bicameral science has repeatedly relied on what Aristotle describes as the diaphanous. By either lifting the translucid in-between toward the higher abodes of spirituality or, on the contrary, grounding it in mechanical or physiological determinations, the diaphanous is cleft into transparency and opacity. As they polarize, transparency and opacity, the two concepts obtained from a specific interpretation of the diaphanous, settle ever more unambiguously in the realm of the *res cogitans* and the realm of the *res extensa*, respectively, where they become, once they are turned into metaphors, the guiding authorities of the dichotomous division of the world.

Where conceptual history is tamed because the concepts it studies enter everyday language and their semantic values become fixed, a historical construction may come to a halt and exploit its findings systematically. And yet the fact that, over time, concepts become banal does not lessen their efficacy. To be sure, transparency and opacity have since the eighteenth century entered the most varied discourses, and particularly moral and political ones. Already one century after Bishop Berkeley's description of the diaphanous, transparency and opacity could be used in a purely metaphorical sense, without any connection to optics and visuality. But the normative use of these two polar concepts (themselves drawn from a discussion of the diaphanous, as we saw) is not restricted to personal and societal morality. What we must now analyze is how they have made their way back into discourses about the visual and about the visual arts. Indeed, discourses about images have arguably been polarized along the duality of transparency and opacity for a long time, which suggests that the domain of images is where the oblivion of the medium can be best studied.

10. WHAT IS A TRANSPARENCY THEORY, WHAT AN OPACITY THEORY OF THE IMAGE?

James Joyce has spoken of the "greekjew" and Jean-Luc Nancy of a "greek-jew alliance."[169] Such an alliance (of sorts) finds expression in a specific relationship to images. A famous series of images by René Magritte illustrates this relationship. In *La condition humaine* (*The Human Condition*, 1933), a canvas set up on an easel in front of a window continues the landscape, which prominently features a tree, stretching behind the windowpane (fig. 3.9).[170] Only the slight angle at which the canvas is set up, thanks to which the nailed white side edge of the canvas is visible and hides a narrow strip of the opened curtain, disturbs the transparency dispositif. Shifted to the correct frontal position, the view no longer allows for distinguishing between picture and depicted. In its iconic indifference, the image multiplies the real by two and, like a total map, depicts it in every respect as a territory. Where no more distinctions can be made, the image sheds its deficiency of being *too little*; where no iconic excess exists, the assertive hubris of the *too much* capitulates. Such an idea is old, and it is expressed already in Plato's *Cratylus*, where the painter is exhorted neither to add anything nor to leave anything out but instead to render everything correctly.[171] In absolute transparency, the image becomes a second thing; to still be an image, to not be a second Cratylus, it must erase its materiality and give up its thingness. To be accepted, the image must become permeable in every respect.

The hubris of images' claim to be where and what they are not points to their irredeemably equivocal character. The symptomatic answer to this equivocal-polysemic character that dominates the history of Western discourses on images is to tame it and confine images to univocation. Be it iconoclastic strategies of reducing images to their materiality or the inverse iconophile strategy of rehabilitating images as merely symbolic means of access to transcendent knowledge: each time, images are reduced to *one* principle.

In what follows, I suggest referring to such strategies of univocal retranscription as *transparency* and *opacity theories of the image*. These labels are taken from

FIGURE 3.9 René Magritte, *La condition humaine* (1933), oil on
canvas, 100 × 73 cm. National Gallery of Art, Washington, D.C.
© ProLitteris.

Arthur C. Danto, who uses them to describe discourses about art, but they are
easily transposed to discourses about images.[172] In general terms, the *transparency thesis* claims that *images are defined by what lies behind them* while the *opacity thesis* states that *images are fully determined by their material objecthood*. This
general definition, of course, acquires substance only once we start differentiating it and put it to the test. The following analysis of different variations of
transparency and opacity shows not only that both instances at times become
entangled but that ultimately, transparency and opacity are less antagonistic
than it may seem at first.

(a) Transparency Theory of the Image

(i)   Material transparency: In the early Renaissance, there is a sharp contrast between the metaphor of the image as open window and the practical manufacturing of images. Whereas the procedure depends on the at least partial material impermeability of the *velum intersegationis* in which the visible is to be intertwined, as it were, Alberti sums it up in the much more successful metaphor of the open window. While initially, *perspectiva* was simply Boethius's Latin translation of Aristotle's *optiká* from the *Posterior Analytics*, in the late Middle Ages, the knowledge of seeing converges in a science of transparency: "*Perspectiva* is a Latin word which means 'seeing through' [*Durchsehung*]."[173]

With transparency comes a certain concept of space that postulates a fundamental continuity between what lies this side and what lies that side of the image support. Accordingly, Panofsky defines central perspective as

> the capacity to represent a number of objects together with a part of the space
> around them in such a way that the conception of the material picture support
> is completely supplanted by the conception of a transparent plane through
> which we believe we are looking into an imaginary space. This space comprises
> the entirety of the objects in apparent recession into depth, and is not bounded
> by the edges of the picture, but rather only cut off.[174]

Masaccio's *Holy Trinity* (ca. 1426) in Santa Maria Novella thus marks a double breakthrough. It is the first implementation of the perspectival view (*veduta*), and it literally breaks through the material: as Vasari writes, with his depiction of the *Trinità*, the painter was able to "break through the wall" (*bucato il muro*).[175]

Such notions of a medium becoming permeable resurface especially in the age of photography, from Henry Fox Talbot via André Bazin to Roland Barthes, who says of photographs that they are "always invisible" for themselves because something else is always being seen through them.[176] For Kendall Walton, the photographic even becomes the paradigm of a general theory of transparency.[177] And Ludwig Wittgenstein succinctly sums up the result of such transparency phantasies: "The impression that the transparent medium makes is that something lies *behind* the medium."[178] The consistent negation of the image support comes, as the example of Masaccio shows, with a reification of what lies behind it, whereas the image in gaining "mimetic transparency" is no longer marked as a medium of presentation.[179]

(ii) Semantic transparency: Besides the negation of the mediating image and the reinterpretation of the operative *per* of *perspective* in terms of a local *through*, there is also a *semantic* variant of transparency theory. The saturation of images, their overdetermination, can be reduced insofar as images can be deciphered as a discourse sui generis. Yet it is possible to speak of a pictorial semantics only on the condition that a pictorial surface contain a finite number of differentiable elements that in turn serve as letters of a legible pictorial language, that is, that the message they contain be transparent to the reader/viewer. That propagators of such a pictorial reductionism, like Otto Neurath with his international picture language Isotype, often saw this reductionism as an extension of iconic potential is paradoxical only at first glance. The history of apologies of the image quite often overlaps with a history of semanticizing the iconic, from Cesare Ripa's *Iconologia* (1593) to Rudolf Modley's glyphs in the 1930s and Otl Aicher's pictograms in the 1970s. Philippe Junod even considers the agenda of art criticism as such largely to overlap with the project of rendering images semantically transparent.[180] What becomes visible is to be visible unequivocally *as something* while the material support of the signs itself must be univocal.

(iii) Syntactic transparency: Syntactic transparency presents itself as a kind of synthesis between material and semantic transparency. In the terms proposed by Colin Rowe and Robert Slutzky, what is at issue is neither a "literal transparency" of the material nor an immediate legibility of figures but instead a "phenomenal transparency." When two systems are superimposed (for example, the representational system and the order of the represented), each and every point on the plane can indiscriminately be assigned to both systems.[181] From an entirely different perspective, John Kulvicki objects that it is hardly ever possible to speak of actual phenomenal transparency since images can differ from what they depict not only in terms of color and wealth of detail but also in their projective scale. And yet it is not an error to think of them as depictions since transparency, according to Kulvicki, is "without reference to perception" and instead follows purely *syntactic* principles. Pictoriality as such is to be understood on the basis of syntactic transparency, which in turn is defined by the fact that in a transparent system every element has the same syntactic value as it does in the system being referenced. For Kulvicki, transparency thought on the model of the "seeing through" of central perspective furnishes the criterion that Nelson Goodman was lacking to define the class of pictorial symbols satisfactorily.[182]

Nonetheless, Kulvicki does not seek to conceal the obvious limits of his grammatical model: image and original do not have to share *all* syntactic properties, only the syntactically *relevant* ones.[183] A discrepancy in color or size, for instance, does not disqualify an image, does not make it a nonimage. Yet what

properties, exactly, are relevant for syntactic identity depends not on intrapicto-
rial determinations but simply on pragmatic use: pictorial syntax becomes the
effect of pictorial pragmatics. It is nonetheless possible for such pragmatic theories, which start from an everyday understanding of images and at first sight
seem to be quite open, to be rather normative, as is the case for some proponents
of a semiotic interpretationism in whose work pure description seamlessly turns
into prescription.[184]

(b) Opacity Theory of the Image

Opacity theories of the image are situated at the completely opposite end of the
theoretical spectrum—or so it seems. While they differ from transparency theories in that they refuse any idea of transitivity, they agree with syntactic transparency theory, at least, in supposing images to be independent of the perspective of
the viewer and in asserting that their definition must happen immanently. Transparency theory remains univocal in that it obtains the sense of the image solely
from a ground external to the image, and opacity theory, too, follows such a uni-
fying principle: it reduces pictoriality to the image's materiality. Where the image
as open window is a *document* yielding insight, the impermeable-opaque image is
a self-contained *monument*.

(i)   Presence without remainder: If the thesis is correct that the earliest
theorizations of images are those of their enemies, then the earliest explicit
image theories undoubtedly fall under the opacity paradigm.[185] On these views,
images can be dismissed because they do not contain anything beyond their
thingness: images are only what they are made of. This criticism of images is
primarily a criticism of *sculptures*, which allows it to link up with a tradition
from the Hebrew Bible. *Manus habent et non palpabunt*, the Psalmist denounces,
"they have hands but they handle not."[186] What is thereby stigmatized is less the
representation of God than the *production* of God, less that God is *shown* than
that he is being *made*.[187]

The opacity paradigm then serves the iconoclasts to prove that the image is
exhausted by its mere being-such and that every transparency is blocked. The
god in the (idolatrous) image is fully exhausted by the immanence of his earthly
existence. In Jean-Luc Nancy's terms: "What is condemned . . . is not that which
is an 'image of' but rather that which asserts its presence only through itself,
a pure presence in a certain sense, a massive presence that amounts to its

being-there."[188] Idols would thus be images of self-sufficient presence without remainder, as it were: they do not lack anything; the godhead fully fills them. Yet they also cannot have any real relation with an outside, as many formulas in Deutero-Isaiah indicate. Those who nonetheless appeal to such idols must themselves be obtuse, like the Byzantine patriarch Germanos, who is excommunicated by the iconoclast council of Hiereia in 754 and denounced as a *xylolatros*, a "wood worshipper."[189]

(ii) Autoinscription: Where theories hostile to images reproach the worshippers of images with mistaking something merely made for effective entities, the answer of many iconophile defenses, from Theodor the Studite to Aquinas, consists in detaching pictoriality from artifactiality and in conceiving of pictoriality as a transitive act of going beyond matter. According to the definition accepted since the Second Nicean Council, whenever a believer venerates the icon, the veneration traverses the artefact and is transferred to the godly prototype. Whether an image is legitimate no longer depends on how it is made but on the attitude of the believer beholding it. Nonetheless, there are also defenders of the image who emphatically seek to shake off such psychologizing and anthropologizing and to restore to the image an immanent legality. For them, legitimate images would be images that minimize the potential for being instrumentalized in that they are not produced for any particular purpose or possibly, even, are not produced at all but generate themselves.

In Byzantine apologetics, the legitimacy of pictorial practices is repeatedly justified by reading the magic images of Christ, the *acheiropoieta* or "images not made by (human) hands," as signs of Christ's will to leave pictorial traces. Holy faces, sudaria, mandylions, or Veronicas are not mere depictions but are thought to have entered into a material exchange with the depicted such that the original, as it were, impressed itself in the material. In a strong sense, then, acheiropoieta are nothing but what they depict. The chronicles of Byzantine devotional literature that tell of believers who scratched the color pigment off icons, dissolved it in water, and drank it testify to the strength of the notion of a real presence. Albeit ironically refracted, of course, Diderot seems to allude to this when in *D'Alembert's Dream*, he describes a process of pulverizing marble statues, dissolving them in water, and mixing them with compost in which to grow vegetables, a process that allows him to feel the matter of artistic force from within.[190] The auratic presence in the *acheiropoieton*, moreover, does not exclude the latter's reproduction: even walled in, the Edessa Mandylion famously leaves an imprint in a tile of the wall and later continuously reproduces itself. Each image equally participates in the archetype, which resolutely undermines any distinction between primary and secondary copies. The acheiropoieton not only inaugurates the age of the technical reproducibility of the image, it also shows itself to invert Benjamin's thesis: the capacity for multiplication is not a loss but what ultimately guarantees the aura.[191]

Even then, the modern discourse of photography is related to the structure of the tactile relic. Nineteenth-century pioneers praise the technology of these images made by light as a revolution that, thanks to photographic chemistry, puts down on paper no longer copies but the things themselves. Nature itself, Henry Fox Talbot writes in *The Pencil of Nature*, inscribes itself in the photograph.[192] For Joseph von Gerlach, the pioneer of scientific photography, this new medium of visualization even transforms the viewer's observing subjectivity into an autopresentation of the object.[193] When Fox Talbot for his part writes that "it is not the artist who makes the picture, but the picture which makes ITSELF,"[194] he is reactivating none other than the old topos of the self-generating image on which the Byzantine *acheiropoieta* were based: image and thing coincide completely. In this indifference, Ernst Cassirer argues, radical materialism and a mythical conception of the world come together: the absence of any distinction between image and thing characterizes mythical consciousness as such. Against classic interpretations of the mythical as an interpretational framework according to which the real meaning of a myth lies in what it conceals, Cassirer asserts the absence in myth of any reference function. In myths, representation and represented coincide undistinguishably.[195]

(iii) Nonmediatedness: A third variant that takes up and aesthetically elevates the two preceding ones is an opacity theory of the image-object that operates via a becoming transparent of the image producer. Pictorial works, resting in themselves, liberated from any signature of the poetic genius, are said to refuse any transcending of sense and to expose their unmediated existence. Such tactics initially take up classic authentication strategies that aim at rendering the painter transparent—from ancient legendary origins (the stories of paintings by Saint Luke for which Mary modeled immediately in person or of Protogenes, who was only able to add authentic foam to the lips of a dog when he stepped back as artist and let the material itself take over) via Baroque stagings of the transparent painter all the way to modernity and the present day where they manifest as strategies of stylelessness and occasionality, of indexicality and anonymity.[196]

American minimal art enshrined such a reduction of the image to its raw immanence in an aesthetic-political agenda. What remains—so the claim of minimalist discourse—are works that refuse any projection of a world and instead, as integral parts of world, already coincide with it (fig. 3.10). Such a programmatically elevated opacity is formulaically captured in a statement by

FIGURE 3.10 Donald Judd, *Untitled* (1972), copper and cadmium
red on aluminium, 91.6 × 155.5 × 178.2 cm. Tate Modern, London.
© ProLitteris.

Frank Stella: "What you see is what you see."[197] What is at stake is the immacu-
lateness of what is given in each case, what Donald Judd also called "whole-
ness."[198] Almost feverishly, Judd erases the traces of the genesis of the work in
favor of a tautological *this*-ness of the material; the point is to set up anti-
illusionistic and antirhetorical artifacts that are meant to be self-contained. The
so-called specific objects—or, rather, the artist's discourse about them—are des-
tined to provide a form of tautologic visibility that denies any role to the
beholder but also to the creation process itself. American minimalism can be
seen as a peculiar form of the opacity scenario where it is the artists themselves
who participate in the downplaying of the processual part.[199]

   In philosophy, such an opacity theory was advocated by Richard Wollheim. Cautiously labeled as merely a "hypothesis," so-called physical object
theory was to reduce the work of art to this physical substrate in order to put an
end to the work's being colonized by exogenous projections.[200] The work is
what it is, and in being such it at the same time reveals the structure of world.
An unblemished mirror of nature would then be a mirror that would be

indistinguishable from what is mirrored in it and would thus sublate itself as mirror. If in its precritical phase, as it were, art was still looking for an *adaequatio imaginis ad naturam*, a correspondence of the image to nature, such a speculative image theory postulates an *equatio imaginis et naturam*, an identity of image and nature.

(c) The Transparency-Opacity Paradigm

When we correlate their variants, the opposition between the transparency and the opacity thesis turns out to be superficial. Their apparent contrariness amounts to a mere shift of perspective. Whether image theorists were looking for a meaning "beyond" the image or, on the contrary, insisted on the fact that images should be defined by their material qualities of objects, the two attitudes, transfiguration and reification, have more in common than would at first appear. They equally participate in one and the same paradigm that becomes effective thanks only to the smooth operation of a double mechanism of fixation and transitivity. From the reduction of the image to its "content" via "a logical invisibility of the medium" to its abbreviation in terms of being given operated by rendering its recipients logically transparent,[201] both procedures are allied in a strategy of univocation that still gives in to the longing for "Apollonian clarity without any foreign admixture whatsoever" castigated by Nietzsche.[202]

Such an unequivocal image theory, in Lyotard's words, "regards the support at once as a transparency that makes visible and an opacity that makes legible."[203] This is particularly salient in the much-praised category of "literality," which is meant to designate artworks' nondiscursive, pure being-such and yet, tellingly, takes the detour via language and its discursive elements.[204] The stage of appearances on which sophism and philosophy once fought is being organized, polarized, and ultimately fixed in two mirroring options: the image ends up either a *pure tautology* (*to autò legein* = to say the same thing) or a *heteronomous allegory* (*allo agōreuein* = to say something else). Be it as transparency or as opacity: images are caught in a process of objectivization that leads to a disjunction between meaning or sense and the material process by which things make their appearance. Faithful to Aquinas's *doctrina rerum* and *doctrina signorum*, such a division into an order of things and an order of signs is able to maintain the traditional repartition of knowledge. In this dichotomy, of course, there is no need for any phenomenological account, that is, for an account that describes images in their appearing.

Window and Mirror: Gerhard Richter's *Eight Grey*

Semblance . . . is the theme of my life. . . . All that is, seems, and is visible to us because we perceive it by the reflected light of semblance. Nothing else is visible.

—Gerhard Richter, "Notes, 1989"

E. T. A. Hoffmann's tale "The Artus Hof" centers on a painter named Berklinger and his endeavor realistically to represent paradise on the canvas. In the first attempt—a representation of paradise lost—the painting had turned into an allegory. On the second try, paradise is not to be to be depicted like an *object* lost but appears on the canvas as a *condition* regained. What he is seeing, the painter declares to a visitor just entering his studio, is " 'Paradise Regained,' and I should pity you if you were to try to discover any hidden allegory in it. It is only weaklings and bunglers who paint allegorical pictures. This picture of mine does not suggest; it *is*!" What this pure, completely nonallegorical image looks like is quickly said, and it horrifies the visitor: it consists of nothing but "a large canvas, all covered with a grey ground-tint."[205]

Where every association is side-stepped and every external reference strictly avoided, no color seems more appropriate than the "noncolor" gray. Its obstinate material suchness, its stubborn lack of expression, leads back to the pure ipseity of the pictorial. Where art is painting gray in gray, dialectics, too, has grown old. As in probably no other work of his, Gerhard Richter has pushed the Western logic of the image to the edge of self-dissolution in his installation *Eight Grey* (2002, fig. 3.11). Installed on each of the two long walls of a tunnel-like room at the Berlin Guggenheim are four monumental gray planes that dominate the room and reflect one another. The visitor moving between them, too, is reflected and modifies the visual action. The gray planes, unlike earlier works of Richter's from the 1970s, are not painted, but neither are they transparent glass planes of the kind used in *4 Panes of Glass* (1967). In the Berlin installation, transparent seeing-through is halted by Richter's having covered the glass panes in enamel, rendering them opaque. Two-dimensional tableaus, as it were grown into the wall, become pictorial objects that can be experienced in their literalness because they are mounted, using only thin steel supports, some twenty inches from the wall and hence appear to be floating. Thus situated between pure planeness and volumetric presence, Richter's layered windows undermine the separation of pictorial and spatial art; their monumentality—a criterion usually associated with artistic uniqueness—here joins with machinic seriality. What you see is what you get.

And yet Gerhard Richter's *Eight Grey* stops short of reification. The impenetrable windows become veritable mirror *dispositifs* that as a matter of principle obtain their visibility thanks only to what reflects itself in them. Unlike Duchamp, who in his *Fresh Widow* stages painted-over, made-opaque window doors that mark the preliminary (ironic) end of the modern paradigm of the transparent window, Richter goes through the paradoxes of representation once more, with an even greater sense of ambiguity, and mirrors them in one another. Monochrome art itself is radically reinterpreted, for it is no longer associated with an experience of color intensity but instead with the loss of any affective efficacy, recalling Jorge Luis Borges, who in "The Wall and the Books" defined the aesthetic as "this imminence of a revelation which does not occur."[206]

FIGURE 3.11 Gerhard Richter, *Eight Grey*, 11.10.2002–05.01.2003, view into the exhibition hall, 2003. Deutsche Guggenheim, Berlin. Photo by Mathias Schormann. Courtesy of Deutsche Guggenheim.

(*Continued next page*)

Not unlike the work of the painter Berklinger in Hoffmann's tale, Richter's gray images are to be open to the fullness of all forms and yet simultaneously reject any external determination. That is why Richter does not see his works as negating traditional illusionism but rather as unearthing its veritable core in that the gray images "are the most rigorously illusionistic of all."[207] Just how sensitive the work is, despite its apparently objectivizing coldness, is evident not least in the fact that the gray plates live on what is mirrored in them. For the duration of the exhibition, the artist had the usually darkened side windows of the exhibition space opened such that the outside always already enters, mirrored, the self-contained white cube architecture. According to time of day and season, artificial or natural light coming in from the street, *Eight Grey* marks out the scale between the clinical paleness of the neon lighting and the atmospheric twilight of late hours. The light effect is calculated with great precision, and the artist explicitly seeks to approximate the spatial effects of Gothic cathedrals.

In the resolute sobriety of *Eight Grey*, Gerhard Richter lets the two dominant paradigms of window and mirror collide, and thereby also the apparent opposites of transparency and opacity, of before and behind. In Richter's playful vexations, however, antinomies revert into impenetrable labyrinths, and certainties revert into their opposites. Transparency and reification, the two historical pictorial paradigms of a "peephole metaphysics," are no longer opposites but rather turn out to be two vectors that, all the while staging their mutual exclusion, ultimately remain solidary.[208] Beyond the "here" of suchness and the "there" of reference, between opacity and reflexivity, between a material that displays its own infrastructure and mirroring surfaces that throw back the beholder unto himself, Richter's disturbing image dispositifs open up yet another experience: in exhibiting their sensitivity to even the slightest variations, they also manifest that iconicity cannot be reduced to one factor alone, that pictoriality always still remains in becoming and is therefore yet to come. Between autarkic immanence and foundational transcendence, they become *gray imminences*, subliminal engines of an appearing as yet to come.

4
A Phenomenology of Images

1. PHENOMENAL THINGS (HUSSERL)

One might be forgiven for thinking that a philosophy devoted to the things themselves can happily do without images. It looks like a foregone conclusion that phenomenology's thrust that aims at regaining direct contact with the concrete comes with a liberation from all the symbols, images, and other mediations with which post-Hegelian and, later, neo-Kantian currents had interspersed philosophy in the late nineteenth century.[1] The sense of Husserlian phenomenology would then, as Max Scheler puts it, consist precisely in its unmediated, symbolless apprehension of reality. And indeed, for Edmund Husserl, the idea that a subject's relationship to the world represents something to be overcome is a relic of a second-order idealism, which presumes that within the subject there are better or worse, congruent or less congruent representations of world: "These images, like all other images, are more or less good images, congruent or not congruent according to the constitution of the subjects."[2] To assume that subjects have representations at their disposal that stand in a certain relationship with a thing to which subjects do not have access would amount to postulating an initial duality that no later mediation could ever undo. This, however, is hardly the point: Husserl's phenomenology never meant to explain how our representations match with the true nature of the things of the external world.[3]

(a) Expansion of the Intuition Zone

From the very start, we must remember that the rebuttal of representationalism Husserl undertakes in the *Logical Investigations* goes hand in hand with a semantic expansion of the concept of *Anschauung*. In the philosophical tradition, *Anschauung* (generally translated as intuition) is opposed to *Begriff* (concept) and is related to the insight provided by sensorial perception. Husserl makes a decisive move that needs to be stressed if we want to understand what happens to the notion of intuition. From Husserl on, intuition is no longer limited to sensorial perception but henceforth comprehends all higher acts of consciousness, from the arithmetic operation of $2 + 2 = 4$ via the presentification of an absent person to the so-called categorial intuition, the intuition, that is, of matters of fact for which there is no equivalent in the sensuous world (such as *number*, *unity*, or *similarity*) and which nonetheless, accordingly to Husserl, are "intuited" (*eingesehen*) with all conceivable clarity.[4] Husserl's new concept of intuitiveness ultimately amounts to self-givenness: what proves to be evident refers not to something else but shows itself by itself, as it were. Such an expanded concept of intuitiveness stakes out the field of inquiry phenomenology is to till. Only what is viewed is admissible is the maxim that the so-called principle of principles articulates in these precise terms: the one and only "legitimizing source of cognition" is "originary presentive intuition," from which follows "that everything originarily (so to speak, in its 'personal' actuality) offered to us in 'intuition' is to be accepted simply as what it is presented as being, but also only within the limits in which it is presented there."[5] It is a short step from such an agenda, which emphatically insists on originary or "personal" self-giving as criterion for the field of inquiry,[6] to an understanding of phenomenology as a philosophy of immediacy, and that step has often been taken. In 1923–1924 Heinrich Rickert publishes an essay, much debated at the time, on "The Method of Philosophy and the Immediate" that critically revises phenomenology from a neo-Kantian vantage point. Paradoxically, Rickert does not take issue with the desire for immediacy itself but only with the path to get there that phenomenology proposes.[7] Husserl, Rickert writes, aims for an immediate access to the things, but his very concept of the phenomenon is already the result of a mediation since appearance can only ever be the appearance of something that itself does not appear. There is thus an inherent duplicity inscribed in every phenomenology, and this duplicity is only verbally bridged by the concept of the phenomenon: "The immediate is being confronted, as an object, with an I that orients itself toward what it apprehends intuitively, and with this construction, the sphere of immediacy is left behind as a matter of principle." An authentic philosophy of immediacy cannot be obtained this way. Even worse, "our contemporary intuitionism has contributed more to obscuring the problem of the immediate than it has to clarifying it" because, according to Rickert, it always already works with "mediations *gone unnoticed*."[8]

(b) To the Things Themselves

Heidegger found it necessary to contradict Rickert's interpretation of phenomenology emphatically and to clarify Husserl's intentions. Against Rickert, he writes in *History of the Concept of Time: Prolegomena*, "it must first be stated generally that phenomenology does not wish to be either a philosophy of intuition or a philosophy of the immediate. It does not want to be a philosophy at all in this sense, but wants the subject matters [*Sachen*] themselves."[9] Heidegger thereby also warns against conceiving of intuition as an intuition immanent to consciousness. What shows itself in intuition is not a *representamen* but *the subject matter itself as that which appears itself.* Thanks to this peculiar characterization, it is evident that Husserl's concept of appearances is not tantamount to some kind of two-world doctrine (as Rickert thinks he can argue). It is remarkable, generally, how sharply Husserl separates originary intuition from any kind of symbolic conception, in which, he suspects, relics of such a two world representationalism survive. The polemic against the concept of the image surfaces almost exactly at all those points at which images are equated with representatives or signs. As perception constitutes the paradigm of originary and personal intuition, he suggests laconically, "a picture-consciousness or a sign-consciousness must not be substituted" for it.[10]

Such iconoclastic impulses may be seen to express a fundamental skepticism concerning any kind of representationalism that topologizes and thereby ultimately naturalizes phenomena. The notion, inspired by Locke, of an inner life populated by representational concepts virtually turns the mind into a camera obscura and consciousness into some sort of box. Significantly, Husserl does at first equate the notion of (mental) pictures with everything he wants to do away with. According to him, representationalism is a kind of picture theory: "the picture theory plainly does not accomplish anything. In it, one envisages the thinking consciousness as in a box. Through some opening, a little picture by chance detaching itself from the thing makes its way in from the outside."[11] In a way, Husserl treats modern representationalism as a resurgence of the archaic

Greek conceptions of the eye as a receptacle for thin pellicles peeling off the things themselves. Such a return of the pellicle theory surreptitiously also introduces another precondition into thinking that Sartre later calls the "illusion of immanence":[12] while it may not be the things themselves that enter into consciousness, there are copies of them that do and whose existence is solely an existence for consciousness. Such a vision of an encapsulated subject or a pigeon loft metaphysics, according to Husserl, covers over the fact that appearance does not lie *in* consciousness; nor does the represented lie outside of it. The decisive aspect of the concept of appearance is founded on the fact that every appearance is always an appearance *of something*. The "rough way of talking about inner likenesses (as opposed to outer objects)," he writes in the appendix to the fifth of the *Logical Investigations*, is generally to be avoided.[13] After all, we do not see chromatic sense data but colored objects; we do not hear pitches but a singer's song. Thanks to this intentional reference, the restriction of the legitimate domain of cognition to appearances for consciousness thus already means that in the move toward the things of the world, one has left behind the field of psychology.

Husserl's critique of psychologism thus initially consists in a liberation of the concept of the phenomenon from a purely internalist conception. "It is a serious error," he writes, "to draw a real [*reell*] distinction between 'merely immanent' or 'intentional' objects on the one hand, and 'transcendental,' 'actual' objects, which may correspond to them on the other."[14] This tearing of the intentional fabric—elsewhere Husserl speaks of a "bundle" and of "interweaving"[15]—leads to a dualism in which appearance is either an imperfect representative ("sign or image") of what is absent or, inversely, endows the unattainable, transcendent object with a new, preliminary sense in absentia.[16]

The passages quoted from texts close to the fifth *Logical Investigation* of 1901 indicate that the "image's entry onto the scene" (Iris Därmann) takes place according to an astonishingly classic script. There is nothing in this mounting the stage to suggest that the iconic might be given any other role within phenomenology than that of ushering out. Here as elsewhere, the concept of the image remains beholden to unmistakably traditional conceptions of depiction.[17] What is more: compared to originary intuition, image and sign both equally belong to the order of the secondary and belated. If they are so radically separated from originary phenomenality, can images ever be more than parasitic marginal effects of a philosophy of appearance thus conceived? The programmatic expulsion of images from the rigorous science of the categorial apprehension of essences, however, relativizes itself—as I will show—whenever Husserl finds himself constrained to determine his own agenda starting from its limits. What the "itself" of "subject matter itself" means, it turns out, is only ever discovered at the blurry edges, the gray zones of the inauthentic.

(c) Act

Husserl's effort in the fifth of the *Logical Investigations* consists in outlining more precisely what is to be understood by intuitive intention. He compares it to pictorial or signitive intentions that he also calls symbolic or transitive (*transeunter*). Now, transitive signs are not merely nonintuitive idealities. To become intentions in the first place, they must already belong to the domain of that which appears. "The sign as object is constituted for us in an act of appearing. This act is not significant yet"; only in the appearing being conceived of *as a sign* does the sign obtain its specific meaning. "The likeness similarly, e.g., the marble bust, is as much a thing as anything else: the new way of regarding it first makes it a *likeness*. Not merely a thing of marble appears before us, but we have, based on this appearance, a reference to a person through a likeness."[18] Images and signs, treated in the *Crisis* as symptoms of the historical supplementation of the originary and counted among the "surrogates" of immanent experience,[19] fulfill here, in the fifth (as already in the first) *Investigation*, a fundamentally demonstrative function: they serve to explicate the scope of the phenomenological concept of the act.

In summary terms, "act" means that meaning generally does not lie in the things but is instituted by a performance of consciousness. Now, act-productivities are not merely chained together successively but build on each other and step by step form act-complexions. In mathematical concept formation, $(5^3)^4$ already presents itself as a complex concept that results from the lower act of $5^3 \times 5^3 \times 5^3 \times 5^3$, which itself is based on the operation $5 \times 5 \times 5$, and 5 rests on $5 = 4 + 1$, 4 on $4 = 3 + 1$, 3 on $3 = 2 + 1$, and 2 on the operation $1 + 1 = 2$.[20] To illustrate this interlocking of levels of acts, Husserl goes back to the comparison with metapictorial interlocking: "we represent a matter to ourselves through images (pictures) of images (pictures)." Characteristically, these mediate representations are "presentations built upon other presentations," in short, "presentations which present their objects *as objects of other presentations*."[21] In the *Ideas*, this recursive interlocking is exemplified by a pictorial *mise en abyme*:

> A name reminds us, namingly, of the Dresden Gallery and of our last visit there: we walk through the halls and stand before a picture by Teniers which represents a picture gallery. If, let us say, we allow that pictures in the latter would represent again pictures which, for their part, represent legible inscriptions, and so forth, then we can estimate which inclusion of objectivations and which mediacies are actually produceable with respect to objectivities which can be seized upon.[22]

The chasm opening up between physical sign carrier and meaning in the common conception of images and signs is indeed quite welcome here. The example of the iconic and the signitive (at this point, both are still conceived of as binary—in the shift from this binary to a ternary concept, Husserl's image theory will later prove its originality vis-à-vis all semiotics) can serve like no other to spell out the synthetic achievement of the phenomenological I as an "interconnecting unity" (*Verknüpfungseinheit*).[23] What something is is not determined by its material characteristics but by the way in which it is conceived of in the act that endows it with or fulfills a meaning. In a game of chess, for example, the particular material constitution of the knight is irrelevant; the only thing that counts is that, on the board, it is seen as a knight. In the fifth of the *Logical Investigations*, Husserl exemplifies the indifference of the carrier via an intermedial recursivity: "A photograph of the sign A is immediately taken to be a picture of the sign. But when we use the sign A as sign of the sign A, as when we write 'A is a letter of the Latin written alphabet,' we treat A, despite its representational similarity, as a sign, and not as a likeness."[24] As much as Husserl initially emphasizes the difference between meaningless carrier and intended meaning, he also insists that the signitive synthesis becomes understandable only as a "transitional unity" (*Durchgangseinheit*). For Husserl, the fact that signs (and beyond them all images understood as bivalent predicaments) refer to something other ultimately means that we do not dwell with them. In the first of the *Investigations*, he already discusses how equivocal it is to consider signs in their "surrogative function."[25] Signs, Husserl says, are more than merely signifiers; whenever we use signs, we are not dealing with stand-ins but reach out to the signified itself. When mathematicians sketch the schema of a straight line, they do not for a moment think about the line drawn in fact not being a straight line: the line drawn is thought as a straight line.[26] Mathematicians nonetheless operate with sensuous media, like Aristotle's geometer who, always aware of the insufficient character of his drawing, works with visual sketches.[27]

Husserl's approach to the things themselves—as the *Philosophy of Arithmetic* as well as the first and sixth of the *Logical Investigations* show—takes slip roads. Time and again, the issue of mediation resurfaces, complexifying what was meant to be a direct take. Yet the question remains where to start when describing processes of object constitution. Does the uncovering of pure validities inevitably need to pass through inauthentic, mediating levels of acts? We might ask whether such a path could not also be taken in the other direction. In that case, from a focus on the *self* in the self-giving, attention then shifts to the *giving* of the self, to the processes, that is, that allow for this givenness in the first place. It may be this suspicion of a possible reversal that Natorp has in mind when he writes about the *Logical Investigations* that Husserl in that work has already gone so far as "to replace the being-present of the content with an act of presenting."[28] Husserl seems to draw the consequences from this observation, at least indirectly, when, after the *Logical Investigations*, he restricts or relativizes the concept of the act.[29] The entire "stream of mental processes can never consist of just actionalities," we read in *Ideas* 1; rather, it is "continually surrounded by a medium of non-actionality."[30] The introduction of the concept of an "arousal of an act" is to take into account moments of "non-effected acts" or "acts which 'have fallen out of effectuation,'" in short, acts that lack the character of actionality. In this sense, Husserl can write in *Ideas* that the concept of the act has been "broadened."[31] While acts are, as a matter of principle, always marked by the signature of a productive ego, there are intentional experiences (so-called background experiences) that are devoid of any egological act-productivity and refer to passive productivities that will become significant later on. But first, let us go back once more to the *Logical Investigations*.

(d) Adumbration

In section 14 of the fifth of the *Logical Investigations*, Husserl distinguishes between images and signs by noting that in the case of images, the connection between the depicting and the depicted is motivated by a relationship of similarity, whereas in signs, the signifier and the signified "have nothing to do with one another." Whether motivated or arbitrary, constitutive of both modes of referring is binarity, for only the binary institutes the transitive character of the act. Such signitive and pictorial intentions, however, differ from intuitive or "originary" intention. In perception, the latter's paradigmatic actualization, "the object 'itself' appears, and does not merely appear 'in a likeness.'" The self-presentation in perception is a complete act insofar as it "itself requires no further fulfillment." The self-fulfillment of appearance in perception initially remains a "mere pretension."[32] As a precondition for appearing aisthetically at all, the object must appear perspectivally, from a certain vantage point, in profile, as it were. Its being given in profile and thus not completely, however, is not simply a restriction; it initiates the profiling of the object: in perception, the sides of the object are successively inspected without thereby ever being actually visible all at the same time. For any corporeal being, the world inevitably always consists only of fronts.

If there is to be more of the world than mere representations, and if things are to appear as actual perceptions, the actually appearing things must be able to sink back into a state of latency or inactuality. For something to come into view *itself*, other aspects must recede into the background. To name this logical necessity, Husserl introduces the concept of "adumbration." Adumbration refers to the fact that for a certain aspect of a thing to come to the fore, others will be overshadowed. In moving around things and discovering further aspects of them, some thematic aspects will become inconspicuous while those that have remained overshadowed will now come into focus. Yet the fact that sensible things only ever present themselves through partial profiles is not a limitation but the condition for those things to be sensible and irreducible to actual consciousness (some might even say, to be mind-independent). Without this process of progressive profiling, every look at the world would amount to a view of a rigid tableau, for "if percepts were always the actual, genuine self-presentations of objects that they pretend to be, there could be only a single percept for each object, since its peculiar essence would be exhausted in such self-presentation."[33]

While in introducing the core element of his theory of appearing—the theory of adumbration—Husserl categorically excludes pictorial representations, images, albeit under different auspices, make their reentry. With his theory of adumbrated appearing, he enters a territory that is sufficiently mapped neither by the duality of referring nor by the oneness of self-giving. In aspectual phenomenality, "the object, as it is in itself . . . is not wholly different from the object realized . . . in the percept." While the back of the object does not currently appear, it is not simply lacking but rather copresent, albeit in a nonintuitive mode, as the horizon that surrounds the currently appearing side of the object. What is meant along-with, in passing so to speak, the "appresented" (the interior, the back, etc.), is "symbolically suggested" and differs from the originarily intuitive in that it must be referred to as "illustrated in the nuclear content of the percept."[34] This raises the question why Husserl situates the pictorial, which up to now had been exiled along with signs and symbols to the edges of phenomenological investigation, at the core of perception. To what extent does the iconic thus always already corrode the originary perception? The concept of the image that time and again flashes up in Husserl's ekphrases only to be rejected quickly afterward can be interpreted only as indicative of a tension-filled relation at the very core of the concept of the phenomenon.

In perception, according to Husserl, the thing itself shows itself; its *self*, however, shows itself only through the manifold of the thing's adumbrations. But what does it mean when a self shows through a multifarious other and *only* ever through a multifarious other? Here, when the self enters the stage, it always already diffracts itself in time and space. Every self-presentation already comes with a chronotopical self-deferral.[35] To start from showing-itself, then, necessarily means to start from an originary diastasis, from something that always already differs from itself.[36] In intentional actionality, the object always turns out to be imperfectly constituted and points ahead to a perfection that can only ever be conceived of as horizoned.[37]

Phenomenality is neither purely immanent to consciousness nor entirely transcendent or inaccessible to it. Rather, the concept of the phenomenon presents, as the lecture *Natur und Geist* (*Nature and Mind*) has it, a tension between "the object of perception itself and its appearances," a tension that in turn "expresses an unconditional necessity." If both coincided, one would be dealing not with a worldly object but with an idea; if both separated into two disjunctive entities, one would find oneself in the aporia of having to think perceptions "in which they would give themselves personally [*leibhaft*] in their being-other."[38] This is the basis of Husserl's repeated invocation of a "transcendency within immanency."[39] To be able to think such an intrinsically tension-filled concept of appearances, which can be put down neither to an integral being-such nor to a sheer being-other, Husserl repeatedly invokes scenes of an initial diastatic iconicity, in which the presenting has not yet fully detached from the presented. What we also find here are the outlines of an alternative concept of the image that moves away from the semiotic model and is no longer exhausted by deputation, a concept of the image that bears traits generally associated with the aesthetic.

(e) Aesthetic Consciousness

It might be daring to try and derive from Husserl's theory of knowledge a full-fledged aesthetics, let alone a philosophy of art. As has often been noted, Husserl himself never wrote an aesthetics of his own.[40] Although his references to the aesthetic attitude are sparse,[41] and references to art even more so, Husserl's epistemology nonetheless contains, in Jacques Derrida's formulation, a "latent aesthetics."[42] This is what later phenomenologists so productively elaborated, beginning with Fritz Kaufmann, Moritz Geiger, and Wilhelm Schapp, continuing with Eugen Fink, Jean-Paul Sartre, and Roman Ingarden, and all the way to Maurice Merleau-Ponty, Mikel Dufrenne, or Henri Maldiney.[43] It practically seems as if, to cite Emmanuel Levinas, the historical turn of aesthetics toward experience crossed with a becoming-aesthetic of phenomenology as an experiential science.[44] That Husserl himself was not entirely blind to the proximity of his own project to certain contemporary aesthetic projects is apparent from his letter to Hugo von Hofmannsthal.

In the letter Husserl sends to the Viennese writer in 1907, he appeals to the essential relation between the aesthetic and the phenomenological attitude. While in the natural attitude things are posited as really existing, the phenomenological attitude is related to "the aesthetic intuiting in 'pure' art" insofar as existential validities are bracketed and validity itself is considered a phenomenon among others. The way in which things present themselves, their phenomenal quality proper, counts only "under a strict suspension of all existential attitudes."[45] Some years later, Husserl notes under the heading "Aesthetic Consciousness": "We are living in an aesthetic consciousness. In it we ask no questions about the being and non-being of what directly appears or appears in an image."[46] In the aesthetic domain, Husserl seems to want to suspend the distinction on which he had previously so much insisted between direct and pictorially mediated appearance, acknowledging, it seems, the change of attitude that takes place in the aesthetic *epokhē*. Every real performing of an act "aims at an appearing object through the appearance, but the situation is totally different in the case of aesthetic feeling, which does not aim through the appearance but aims at it, and aims at the object only 'for the sake of the appearance.'"[47]

Although only rarely employed by Husserl, the comparisons with art bring out the thrust toward the appearances "for their own sake" that is inherent to his project. The talk of so-called figural moments gradually acquires its own valence when he looks at the logic proper of what in the early writings designates a set of elements amalgamating into specific intuitive "configurations."[48] Only where something is not simply regarded as being *there* but as *something presenting itself* is the mediality of appearing no longer simply passed through and over. No longer the *what* (*quid*) but the *how* (*quomodo*)—traditionally seen as inessential and contingent—represents the material of "phenomenology as a rigorous science."

The elaboration of a no longer just binary but *ternary* concept of the image goes hand in hand with a more precise elaboration of the concept of appearance that now also sheds its dual basic definition. It is preceded, starting in the mid-1890s, by the progressive shift of focus from acts of signification to acts of intuition.

2. FROM ARISTOTLE TO PHENOMENOLOGY: FRANZ BRENTANO'S RECONCEPTUALIZATION OF INTENTIONALITY

It is hard to overestimate the influence that Franz Brentano, who sought to rehabilitate Aristotle's theory of the soul in the sense of a descriptive psychology, exerted on Husserl. Husserl's terminology, unsteady to the end and often falling back onto Brentano's concepts, is a telling symptom. According to Husserl himself, the interest in questions of pictoriality and fantasy that reawakens after the publication of the *Logical Investigations* is a return to first impulses he owes to "Brentano, a teacher of genius," "who already in the mid-eighties at the University of Vienna gave a lecture course I will never forget on 'Selected Psychological and Aesthetic Questions,' which (in two hours a week) was concerned almost exclusively with the analytical clarification of phantasy representations as compared to perceptual representations."

With these words, Husserl opens his Göttingen lectures in the winter semester 1904–1905, apologizing for postponing the previously announced analyses of judgment theory in favor of an investigation of phantasy representation, image representation, memory, in short, an investigation of "inauthentic" representation.[49] The fact that so-called inauthentic representations are no theoretical marginalia is something he highlights already in the *Philosophy of Arithmetic*, where he writes that it is to Brentano that he "owe[s] the deeper understanding of the vast significance of inauthentic representing for our whole psychical life."[50]

And yet while the discovery of inauthentic representation may well be called the catalyst of Husserl's oeuvre,[51] Husserl's critique of Brentano essentially amounts to a critique of the latter's concept of "inauthenticity." Brentano has indeed given the clearest answer to date to the question concerning the "the relationship between perceptual presentation and phantasy presentation" at the center of the Göttingen lecture course, Husserl argues, but this answer must yet be interrogated as to its actual implications.[52] What exactly Husserl heard Brentano say can no longer be reconstructed in detail; Husserl's notes on Brentano's aesthetics lectures have not survived. Brentano's own notes, however, which have since been published, offer at least partial insights. They show that the lectures Husserl heard largely consisted of an analysis of the concept of *phantasia*. For Brentano, the standpoint of nineteenth-century psychology— but also that of English empiricism of a Humean inspiration, according to which the imaginative faculty is characterized by a lesser intensity than perception—can be traced back to Aristotle. In a scholastic tradition, Brentano conceives of *phantasia* as inauthentic, "weak" intuition, lacking in vivacity and intensity when compared to perception.[53] Brentano concludes the history of this inauthenticity, which in the course of his lectures he traces from Aristotle all the way to modernity, with the following preliminary summary: "Fantasy representations are nonintuitive or inauthentic representations that approximate intuitive representations."[54]

Husserl takes up this definition in the Göttingen lectures but highlights that Brentano thereby reduces the *fantasy* aspect to a specific aspect of the content (intensity or vivacity), which leads to irresolvable problems. For, indeed, both fantasy images and perceptions are intensity-bound; they can increase and diminish and thus gain and lose in vividness. Sometimes doubts arise whether we actually perceived something or only fantasized it, "when, for example," as Husserl has it, "late in the evening we await with anxious anticipation the stroke of the tower clock and, misled by our expectation hastening on ahead, believe that we are hearing it and yet again doubt that we are hearing it, and so on."[55] The difference between fantasy and perception, Husserl concludes, thus lies not in their *content* but in their *form*.

Both perception and fantasy refer to the same "appearance," yet perception-consciousness posits this appearance as *present* (*gegenwärtig*) while fantasy-consciousness posits it as *re-presented* or *presentified* (*vergegenwärtigt*).[56] Brentano's psychology, in short, lacks an understanding of "objectivating acts" since his psychology still rests on a hidden ontology. The restriction of the field of evidence to psychic certainty (that is, the merely "authentic") does indeed open up the possibility of a pure analysis of mere intuition. But, Husserl continues, the analysis will again and again necessarily be haunted by objectivating parasitic effects because Brentano failed to operate the methodological *epokhē*. Ultimately, for Husserl, Brentano's reduction to the strictly consciousness-relevant field of inquiry is doomed to fail because the supposition that all contents of judgment exist, and thus the general thesis of a world defined as *real*, is never questioned and remains in force. Purely descriptive psychology does put metaphysical speculations aside for a moment, but because the *epokhē* has never taken place, these speculations always threaten to invade again.

Brentano himself at least does not exclude the possibility (to put it cautiously) that philosophy could become a house with two sections, psychology and metaphysics, when he defines the domain of the "science of the soul" as "the whole of the inner world" from where it would be possible to "achieve . . . the securing of the outer world."[57] Brentano's enterprise must thus be doubly suspected of a naturalized version of objectivism: on the one hand, because the outer world is regarded as something mind-independent of which we merely fail to see the essence; on the other, because it defines psychic phenomena as real components of an "objectively existing world."[58] Far from overcoming a two-world doctrine by means of this continuity thesis, Brentano's psychology ultimately even reinforces the subordination of the phenomenal under the existential concept of being. Inner appearances, accordingly, are supposedly *more real* because their mode of presentation entirely coincides with their being; for

Brentano, phenomenal evidence must be sought out exclusively within the framework of inner appearance.

As early as in the appendix to the *Logical Investigations*, Husserl hints that Brentano's preference for the so-called inner appearances still rests on an unquestioned ontology that illicitly concludes existence from essence. Beside other arguments, Husserl also takes recourse—in order ultimately to refute it—to the master example of pain. While I might doubt that the wind shakes the trees or that the box is square and brown, I cannot doubt "that pain bores into my tooth."[59] At closer inspection, however, this fact of perception is no less inexistent than all external "deceptive" appearances, despite its irrepressible obtrusiveness. What decides existence and inexistence is the act of judgment—which, however, in the *epokhē* precisely brackets facts of appearance.[60] If the phenomenon is not ultimately to be subordinated to some kind of external entity once more, then not only must the separation between inner and outer appearances be suspended on the path to a pure theory of appearances, the dual determination of the concept of appearance must be avoided in general.

After going through the aporias of a descriptive psychology, Husserl concludes that the "equivocations" of the term *appearance* must be cleared up.[61] Renaud Barbaras has managed to show that for Husserl, elaborating a coherent transcendental phenomenology leads through the ternary rearticulation of a concept of appearance that, when put in binary terms, remains insufficient.[62] "The appearing of the thing (the experience) is not the thing which appears," we read as early as 1901 in the fifth of the *Logical Investigations*, but only an exposition of the three moments of phenomenalization suspends the inevitable tendency toward reifying appearance.[63]

There are indications of the three-tier concept of the phenomenon, for example, in the time manuscripts of 1909, which distinguish between (1) appearing as the uninterrupted stream of consciousness; (2) distinct appearances; and (3) the object appearing through the appearances.

The three moments can be correlated with noesis, noema, and real object.[64] In the course of Husserl's transcendental turn, characteristically, the first moment—appearing as the general medium of individual appearances and their objects—is progressively equated with the *ego*. This is particularly evident in the late *Crisis*, where the ternary structure has settled and comes to be typified in Cartesian terms. It has now become possible analytically to distinguish three moments:

(1) the addressee of the appearances, the *whom* (now characterized as *ego*);
(2) the mode of appearing, the *how* (now characterized as *cogitatio*); and
(3) the appearing object, the *what* (now designated as *cogitatum*).[65]

This ternary articulation, according to Husserl, preliminarily provides a satisfactory response to the "shock" he suffered in elaborating the *Logical Investigations*: the discovery of the "universal a priori of correlation between experienced object and manners of givenness."[66]

Appearance content and mode of appearance, what and how—and thus their differences as well—can persist only if there is something that allows them to become appearance. There is, therefore, a need for a third term that relates both to each other and brings them out, ensuring, in other words, that "appearance" is not an empty word and that, instead, every appearing is always an appearing of something for something or someone. Quite early, Husserl's attention turns to this third term that enables the appearance and the appearing and may therefore generally be called "that which lets appear," its medium.

Traces of this attention can be found in Husserl's struggling with the concept of intentionality he adopts from Brentano and which he then shifts. As the "principal theme of phenomenology,"[67] intentionality is capable of guaranteeing the unity but also the difference between object of appearance, mode of appearance, and the subject as the addressee of these appearances. Husserl, meanwhile, does not unambiguously assert which place is to be assigned to intentionality as indicator of an operative process of mediation. Intentionality, he stresses on several occasions, cannot be reduced to a subject's ("intentional") production without transforming the appearance's receptivity into a self-produced projection. Intentionality then merely provides the name for a synthetic process taking place by itself, thereby resembling a "universal medium which ultimately bears in itself all mental processes, even those which are not themselves characterized as intentive."[68] Yet most of the time—and particularly in phenomenology, which explicitly presents itself as transcendental—this "universal medium" that has no place and arises purely from logical necessity does indeed lead back to the transcendental ego. The ternary articulation of the three moments indispensable for the phenomenality of appearing—the referential *what*, the modal *how*, and the datival *to whom*—is thus, as Jan Patočka lucidly points out, tied back to one of these very moments, namely, the third one.[69] The subject of appearances turns from a datival *to whom* into appearances' constitutive *through which*.

Commentators—starting with Heidegger but also in the French reception of phenomenology, especially and concisely Levinas, Ricœur, and Derrida—have stressed this promotion of a new philosophy of constitution that does not hide its sympathies for a *cogito* understood along Cartesian lines. Yet early attempts at interpretation by Fink or Patočka already prove that it is precisely in trying to uncover structural moments of appearing that we find reflections that do not really fit into an egological foundation. The concept of intentionality itself always already refers to something more and something different, assuming with Merleau-Ponty an "operative intentionality" (*intentionnalité opérante*) that can no longer be attributed unambiguously to a single agent. It practically seems as if in the transition from a classic binary to a phenomenological ternary concept of appearance, the problem of mediality imposed itself. The appearance and what appears in it then are capable of showing themselves only because there is something *through* which they become visible. That through which they become visible, Husserl writes in the *Ideas*, is none other than the one *to whom* they become visible. The possibility of a *medial* phenomenology, however, is closed down once more when the third moment is reduced to a constitutive act of the transcendental subject.

The following sections thus examine a twofold hypothesis:

(1) The transformation of the concept of the phenomenon from a binary into a ternary concept has a theoretical prologue in the transformation of the concept of the image in the Göttingen lectures on "Phantasy, Image Consciousness, and Memory" of 1904–1905.

(2) While the concepts of the image and the phenomenon are congruent in two of their moments (the *what* and the *how*), they differ in the status they assign to their third (the material-medial or subjective-constitutive) moment. Returning to Husserl's analysis of the image thus might be able to open up once more a dimension that the transcendental reduction closed down prematurely.

3. FROM BINARY TO TRIAD: THE ENCOUNTER WITH IMAGES

In the *Logical Investigations*, the stakes of the concept of the image remain quite problematic, for it designates—prominently in the appendix to section 21 of the fifth investigation, for example—the naturalist vanishing point common to both reifying and idealizing epistemologies. Evidently, Husserl does not break through to a more nuanced concept of the image until the Göttingen lectures of 1904–1905, which were not published until 1980. For Husserl, images are not something already present. Pictoriality, generally, is not a physical property but an *act* (a point Sartre picks up on in *The Imaginary*). Through a specific gaze, everything can become an image; through the performance of a pictorial act, it counts as an image. This image-act, however, must not be presented as the result of a merely arbitrary positing. Rather, the performing consciousness is co-"excited" by the appearance occurring in an image-carrier.

Nonetheless, Husserl is obviously thinking about the physical image-carrier's coconstitutive role in pictorial appearance in a note of 1898: as "instigator of the re-presenting image," the physical image-thing (*Bildgegenstand*) can be looked at in its own right. We may make our best effort to look at the image-carrier as a mere thing: pictoriality involuntarily thrusts itself upon us; we may pay attention to "the rough surface of the paper (China paper)": the becoming visible of the female figure on it cannot be suppressed. "Not to notice the excited appearance at all is, of course, impossible. If I see the physical image, I also see the excited appearance."[70] Pictoriality thus provokes an irrepressible insistence. At the surface of the image, something emerges and confronts us in a sort of third space that amounts neither to the extrapictorial space to which the depicted object belongs nor to the physical extension of the image-carrier. What appears in the image, as it were, hovers before us.

Accordingly, pictoriality—and this is the paradox Husserl investigates in later texts on the *constitution of time*—would be neither psychological nor physical: "When the image fades, its effect is different or is entirely lost. Purely physical fading and effects starting from the physical . . . has a causal, psychophysical effect." The image is always already more than its psychophysical individuality; it is always already "effective toward the outside" and characterized by a surplus.[71] When the gaze is directed at the physical image-thing, at its aboutness, or at the suchness of the pictorial appearance, respectively, what is designated are not different substances but different attitudes toward the image: "it is one thing to focus specifically on the *excited* image, to be absorbed specifically in the presentation of the subject, and another to focus specifically on the *physical* image."[72] In the Göttingen lecture Husserl once more, and more effectively, stages the transition from a binary to a ternary concept of image, which this note from 1898 prepares *in nuce*. We usually, he says, think of pictoriality as a binary relation: every image is an image of something, for example, a photograph of a child. (Here as elsewhere, Husserl seems to be thinking of a photograph of his daughter Elisabeth.) When we say that the photo of the child is bent or torn, the daughter in the image—its aboutness—remains untouched by this. Yet if the father now judges the photo to be a failure, "we of course do not mean the physical image, the thing lying there on the table or hanging on the wall. The photograph as a thing is an actual object and is accepted as such in perception. That image, however, is an appearing that has never existed and never will exist, that of course never counts for us as actuality."[73]

What appears "in disagreeably grayish-violet coloring," however, is not the image-child but rather the child-image. That is why it does not suffice to distinguish between "subject [*Sache*] and image."[74] Instead, three moments must be differentiated analytically:[75]

(1)   The physical image-carrier made from canvas, wood, marble, and so on, which Husserl also calls *image-thing* (*Bildgegenstand*).

(2)   What the image is about and what it presents, which is also described as *image-subject* (*Bildsujet*).

(3)   The presenting appearance, that is, the way in which the image-subject shows itself, a mere phenomenality "that has never existed and never will exist" and that Husserl (somewhat confoundingly) characterizes as *image-object* (*Bildobjekt*).[76]

In section III of *Ideas: General Introduction to Pure Phenomenology* (1913), Husserl rehearses the iconic triad of *image-thing—image-object—image-subject* using a famous example whose ambiguity has often been overlooked, Albrecht Dürer's engraving *Knight, Death, and the Devil* (1513, fig. 4.1). Looking at the image means first of all an object-perception directed at the engraving, at "this print in the portfolio."[77] The optical arrangement of the lines on the paper lets figures emerge that in turn are recognized as "knight on the horse," "death," and "devil." The gaze goes through the image-appearance to what is presented there, yet in opposition to a merely intended object of sign-comprehension (the word *knight*, for example), image consciousness aims at the knight "in the flesh" presentified in the image.

Husserl, whose image analysis prematurely breaks off at this point, seems to shy away from the consequence of his own ideas: what is true of the knight must equally be true also of death and the devil—the paradox of pictoriality is that in the image, death and the devil appear "incarnate" and thus lay claim to what had been reserved to originarily perceptive or at least reproductive acts. Death and the devil appear in Dürer's engraving "in the flesh," although they do not even for a moment count as actual, as the Göttingen lecture had it. The fact that images yield such an incarnation is a performance of the appearing "image-object" that "is present to us neither as existing nor as not existing, nor in any other positional modality," that simply hovers before us.[78] Its being is "crossed-out," as it were.[79] Yet this operation does not deprive it of anything; it does not effect "any privation, but instead a modification." As the "consciousness of the 'picture' . . . which mediates and makes possible the depicturing," image-consciousness is thus also a *neutrality modification*.[80] These passages suggest themselves as a practical foil to bring out the irreconcilability of Husserl's and Sartre's respective use of "image consciousness."

FIGURE 4.1 Albrecht Dürer, *Knight, Death, and the Devil* (1513), copperplate engraving, 25.08 × 19.37 cm. Los Angeles County Museum of Art. Courtesy of the museum.

4. IMAGES AS PURE ABSENCES (SARTRE)

Of Husserl's image theory, Jean-Paul Sartre knew only the cursory remarks in the *Logical Investigations* and in the *Ideas*, but he suspected Husserl to have "a theory that he has probably elaborated in his courses and his unpublished works."[81] Sartre's thesis, entitled *L'image* and, following a decision by his editor, published in two parts, is among the most nuanced and at the same time most systematic elaborations of a phenomenological image theory. While the first part, published as *The Imagination* in 1936, represents a critical revision of historical positions on the concept of the image, Sartre in the second, much longer part (known as *The Imaginary* and published in 1940) unfolds his own phenomenology of the image with the goal of uncovering an autonomous faculty independent of perception: image-consciousness. The historical disavowal of the pictorial, according to Sartre, follows from two fundamental misunderstandings. (1) The so-called *illusion of immanence* leads to the notion that the thing itself, in the form of its representative, is present in the mind. Yet just as there are no chairs to be found in our heads, we will not find a bunch of images of chairs there. And we have to beware of the second misunderstanding looming, (2) the *confusion of essential and existential identity*. When we imagine a chair, we see a chair and not an image of a chair. Chair and chair-image differ in their mode of existence. Pictoriality thus proves to be not a property but an act-quality with which an object is endowed by a specific act of consciousness.

What, following Sartre, is required to rehabilitate pictoriality as a faculty (that is, as imagination) is a complete emancipation from any physical dependence. Images generally must not be measured by the real if they are not to be subordinate to the real from the start. Pictoriality and physical existence are not in conflict—and this is where Sartre, though not explicitly, moves away from Husserl—they are quite simply incomparable and without relation with each other.

Sartre's rehabilitation of the imaginative faculty takes an idiosyncratic path here that differs fundamentally from similar attempts made before and after. To anticipate the core of this endeavor: *the imagination can claim an autonomous status only if and when it presents itself not as a creative and self-enhancing faculty but as an essentially deficient one*.[82] The reason for this is to be sought in Sartre's polar opposition of the real and the unreal. The real is characterized by an "overflowing," and it is, as a matter of principle, unfathomable—"to exhaust the richness of my current perception would take an infinite time"—while "in the image," the emblematic embodiment of the unreal, "there is a kind of essential poverty."[83] This thesis is spelled out with an example Sartre takes from the philosopher, Alain: when I ask someone to imagine the Pantheon in Paris, he will usually do just that without much difficulty. It becomes much more difficult for him, however, when I ask him to look into his representation and to tell me how many columns there are in the lantern.[84] Sartre concludes from this example that imagination images only ever capture the reduced, essential aspect of the object of perception.

This practically sets up an evaluative scale of imaginative potential, starting from the (unavoidably always lacunary) memory image, via the photo portrait that seems realistic but in which we nonetheless never recognize ourselves, to the caricature that thanks to cutting back on the details is able to bring out the basic traits, that thanks to reducing the facts is able to bring out the essence.[85] The power of the imaginary, which Sartre studies in so disparate phenomena as sketches, dream images, obsessive representations, or the experience of music, thus consists in a distancing from the real he calls "nihilation." What is being imagined is quite simply not being perceived. "A white wall as imaged is a white wall that lacks perception."[86] We can only imagine something where in perception there is, precisely, *nothing*. Whenever I take the imaginative attitude, the structure of perception and the world of real things that belongs to it must therefore be posited as a *nothingness* or be "annihilated." Accordingly, "in order to produce the object 'Charles VIII' as imaged, consciousness must be able to deny the reality of the painting," and this negation cannot stop at the individual image-thing but must comprehend the world as a whole: it must "posit the world as a nothingness."[87]

Sartre explicitly points out that he has taken this idea from Husserl. A closer look, however, shows this idea nowhere to be found in the writings Sartre draws on. The only passage in which Husserl speaks of the "annihilation of the world" is precisely not about a *negation* of the world but rather about proving that "real being" is *not necessary* for intentional reference generally (that is, not only pictorial references).[88] With the progressive narrowing of phenomenology to a dialectic ontology that is already taking shape toward the end of *The Imaginary*, however, the subtle modal nuances still to be found at the beginning of the book are quashed. The way in which Sartre reduces all four variants of *modification* to only one of them, namely, *privation*, can be seen quite well when we contrast the first and the last parts of the *Imaginary*. With all desirable clarity, Sartre at the beginning categorizes Husserl's objectivating consciousness and shows how it can take four (and only four) forms: the objectivating act "can posit the object as nonexistent, or as absent, or as existing elsewhere; it can also 'neutralize' itself, which is to say not posit its object as existent."[89] To the first act would correspond a consciousness of unreality (for example, with reference to objects like mythic deities); to the second and third, retentional and protentional consciousness, respectively; and to the fourth, finally, image consciousness properly speaking (in Husserl's sense) as a neutral abstaining from any assertion.

In the course of the investigation, Sartre interprets each of these four characterizations as negations. The positive characterization already of the fourth act (being-elsewhere) is interpreted as an implicit negation (as a not-being-here) and hence as privation. The reinterpretation of Husserl's neutrality modification, however, is even more consequential: in the course of his study, Sartre rearticulates it from "not posit[ing] its object as existent"—that is, refraining from a thesis, positive or negative—into "posit[ing] its object as non-existent," which allows him to conclude that "the negative act is constitutive of the image."[90] Nihilation is interpreted as indicating the fundamental freedom of a consciousness that experiences itself in the first place in the possibility, which is its own, of positing the world in each case in this and that way.[91] Sartre thus assigns a fundamental systematic position to the imagination like few, if any, before him; yet he is unable to think the distancing from the world in the image in any other way than in the mode of denying the world.

This of course has consequences for the position Sartre assigns to the first moment of Husserl's image-appearance: the image-thing or appearance-carrier. A painting (the structure of frame, canvas, varnish, grain, and so on) is not an image, strictly speaking it paradoxically even makes the image impossible: "So long as we consider the canvas and the frame for themselves, the aesthetic object 'Charles VIII' does not appear. . . . It appears the moment that consciousness, effecting a radical conversion that requires the nihilation of the world, constitutes itself as imaging."[92] The painting might burn to ashes; that will not touch a hair on the head of the sovereign in the image.[93] Sartre, who rehearses the tension-filled relationship between image-object and image-subject in a variety of ways (we say of Charles VIII that he is convincingly represented although we have never seen the historical monarch), dissolves any connection between image-object and image-thing by shifting the two, each to a different world— the image-object to an "image"-world, the image-thing to a "thing"-world. Where all description of medial performance is lacking, image and thing must necessarily be conceived of as antithetical and mutually exclusive.

Paradoxically, Sartre cites as a palpable criterion for distinguishing between these two worlds the very thing that Merleau-Ponty considers the emblematic instance of media's making-visible: illumination. When the cheek of Charles VIII is illuminated, "it is the canvas that is illuminated and not the object of aesthetic appreciation."[94] The illumination of the image-object "has been ruled in the irreal once and for all by the painter."[95] In the image, nothing can be changed, "the world of images is a world where nothing *happens*."[96] This irrevocably evacuates from image-consciousness what Husserl considered fundamental, that is, its *modificatory* character, since modification is now equated with *privation*.

5. PRESENTATION AS SELF-REDUPLICATION (HUSSERL)

While Sartre claimed that he was merely explicating and extending Husserl's phenomenology of images, his very idiosyncratic reorientation of it may shed light, ex negativo, as it were, on what constitutes Husserl's peculiarity. As it turns out, Sartre's approach is at odds with some of Husserl's main tenets. A good entry point to disentangle the differences is the issue of negative judgments, which are analyzed in the third section of the *Ideas* (the work of Husserl's, that is, that Sartre read most intensively and where the basic articulation of noesis and noema opens up the space of infinite series of modal positings). The question of whether there can be negative judgments, which Adolf Reinach had raised anew in his *Theory of the Negative Judgment* (1912) and which was still to occupy the young Heidegger, is solved by Husserl by presenting even the positing of something "as being null" as a gain because a new term is thereby obtained that can in turn be affirmed or negated in so-called reiterated modifications.[97] "Negation, which . . . has its positive effect in the negatum,"[98] can become the ground of a Sartrean philosophy of freedom because it is in the negating act that the discretionary force of the act-character as such is most clearly experienced. A phenomenology of modification that takes negation as its guide is thus back with the question of being (albeit under inversed conditions), which Husserl had put aside in the *epokhē*. Accordingly, Husserl follows up on the analysis of affirmation and negation, in which there is the constant threat that the phenomenal be subsumed under the predicative, with an analysis of *neutralization*. In a modification in the sense of neutralization (the fourth category Sartre identified), the image-object is not posited as not-being but *not posited* at all.[99] Rather, in neutrality-consciousness, which represents neither a cancelation as in the case of negation nor an emphasis as in the case of affirmation, lies an "abstaining-from-producing something, putting-something-out-of-action, 'parenthesizing-' it, 'leaving-something-undecided.' "[100]

In such formulations, to which Husserl research has not paid sufficient attention, there are hints at a path between pure givenness and active representation.

Not thinking the appearing as the result of a *placing-before-oneself* but *leaving-it-undecided* in its being means to open the gap between naked being and its belated representation for an anonymous *presentation*: "If we thus exclude the letting-it-be-undecided pertaining to everything voluntary, but also not under-standing it in the sense of something dubitable or hypothetical, then there remains a certain having-an-'undecided'-something or, better still, a certain having-something-'standing there' which is not 'actually' intended to as standing there" in the constant field of tension of ascriptions, between *presenting-oneself* and *letting-(oneself-)be-presented*.[101] For Husserl, the neutrality modification becomes emblematic of the modifying attitude as such,[102] yet on the other hand, it breaks out of this framework again insofar as in it, the—in principle infinite—variation comes up against its limit: while every propositional judgment can itself in turn become the object of a higher-level (modifying) judgment, the neutrality modification provides something like an appearance that balks at any conversion into the assertory.

At this precise point a tension becomes especially palpable that recurs in Husserl's entire endeavor. Those who in the course of discovering a pure plane of appearances go so far as to declare that "'feigning' ['*Fiktion*'] makes up the vital element of phenomenology" and to suppose it to be "the source from which the cognition of 'eternal truths' is fed" cannot but conceive of fictionalization as a remodeling of the material present in the world, or else they would create a par-allel world whose relationship to the first would have to be justified.[103] Even ostensibly pure appearances to which no entities correspond in the empirical world (like centaurs) already bear interactive traits because in them, the appearance-*hyle* of other worldly objects (bulls, humans, and so on) repeat themselves, albeit in a new combination.[104] Phantasy can thus become the emblematic space of possibility only when the matter of its virtualization is not posited but is already present.

Now, what is paradoxical about modification—as Derrida emphatically points out in his readings of Husserl—is that the process of modification requires a preceding something-to-be-modified when this precedent essentially finds itself only through the modification. "The presence-of-the-present is derived from repetition and not the reverse."[105] The eidetic variation, the free rehearsing of all essential possibilities of a certain object, is based on the matter of the originary, actual perception that it transforms; because of perceptual per-spectivism, however, this originary unity of the object of perception produces the modifying operation in the first place. Derrida was right to speak of a down-right ambivalence of phantasy in Husserl: in separating "the sense of the fact" from "the factuality of the fact," Husserl makes phantasy "a derived and founded reproductive ability on the one hand" and "on the other, the manifestation of a radical theoretical freedom."[106]

The relevant sections of the *Ideas* and the numerous working manuscripts collected in *Husserliana* 23 testify that Husserl is quite aware of this tension between pictoriality as a merely reproductive mode, on the one hand, and pictoriality as an originary access to the essential unity inaccessible in perception, on the other hand, and that he tried, time and again, to resolve it anew. The concept of appearance itself, he also writes, must be thought procedurally: appearance is thus not a *presence* but a presentation, an appearing or, rather, an infinitive whose "universal characteristic" is "to make an object appear."[107] Included among the different kinds of presentation, besides perception, are phantasy and fiction. These, Husserl remarks in a later note, "have two signitive directions: 1) One is directed toward *reproduction* (and *re-presentation of whatever kind*), and in that case every memory is also called a phantasy. . . . 2) The other is directed toward the *mode of performing*, in which case one can speak of perceptual fiction, and then the memory is not a fiction, not a phantasy."[108] Imagination thus oscillates (as it does in Aristotle, whom Husserl mentions at this point) between reproductive presentification and productive depresentification, between the repetition of something past and the replacement of the actually present by something merely possible.

In the course of the Göttingen lectures, Husserl put a preliminary end to such divergent polysemies when he methodically delineated phantasy and image consciousness from each other.[109] In contrast to the *Logical Investigations*, which conceive of phantasy and image-consciousness (alongside memory) as modes of presentification opposed to the pure perception of the present, both phantasy and image consciousness are now each endowed with one, albeit a different one, characteristic of the perceptive. Unlike phantasy, image consciousness has a foundation in a material image-thing. That is why images (in opposition to objects merely imagined) are necessarily always also *perceived* as physical objects. Phantasy, too, lets something appear, but it does so not *through a third* (the medial carrier) but as "self-presenting" of a modified third (the perceived). Phantasy—as the summary in the *Ideas* has it—is "the presentation simpliciter, which, in its own essence, remarkably enough, is given as modification of something else."[110] *Remarkably enough*, Husserl writes, it is the modification and yet, as he puts it in section 43, "it is said to be immediately intuited as 'it itself.'"[111] Phantasy then confronts us with the paradox of a presentation that is devoid of all *re*-presentation and yet begins elsewhere than with itself.

As Ernst Tugendhat already notes, Husserl here comes up against the aporias of presenting-"itself" on which, however, the principle of principles is based.[112]

The concept of "self-presentification" (*Selbstvergegenwärtigung*) deployed in the Göttingen lecture course of 1904–1905 (in the fourth part, which Heidegger edited under the title *The Phenomenology of Internal Time-Consciousness*) turns out to be downright contradictory.[113] How can a faculty consist in presentifying something else and in so doing show "as itself" without thereby already usurping the place of what is absent? The "self" of self-givenness, the last remaining refuge after Husserl's epistemological shakeup, already bears signs of alien contamination. According to Tugendhat, Husserl in the wake of this insight gradually gives up the expression "self" and replaces it with *originary* appearance or appearance "in person." Although Husserl subsequently most often uses both terms synonymously, "originary" strictly speaking names the difference from reproductive modes and "corporeal" the opposition to the mere "hovering before us" of the image.[114] Even if it is neither originary nor corporeal, phantasy for Husserl nonetheless retains a "self"-character insofar as its appearance, just like that of perception, is unmediated. Far from any consciousness of symbols or signs, phantasy can now ascend to the status of a form of intuition on equal footing with perception.[115]

And yet it becomes apparent in the course of volume 23's erratic analyses that phantasy, too, can claim legitimacy only because it produces images that do not compete with the originary object of perception. Their detachment deprives them of the property that explicitly falls to the faculty of *mediate* representation (image-consciousness): *corporeality*. Insofar as every image-object depends on a sensuous appearance-carrier, every image-consciousness always contains (at least partially) a corporeal moment that may practically impose itself but in any case *conflicts* with the very image-appearance it itself produces. The neutrality that phantasy, because of its decontextualization, could still claim for itself, recedes in favor of a merely metastable, constantly reconfiguring modification. Because of the "double objectivity" (*Gegenständlichkeit*)[116] of two incompossible things in one and the same place, there is a *conflict* that no kind of positing arbitration can stop completely. In every negative synthesis, the two poles cannot coincide; they turn out to be contradictory and—in Leibniz's terms—incompossible. "The appearance belonging to the image-object is distinguished in one point from the normal perceptual appearance. This is an essential point that makes it impossible for us to view the appearance belonging to the image-object as a normal perception: It bears within itself the characteristic of *unreality, of conflict with the actual present*."[117]

Unreality, or the character of the "null," as Husserl sometimes writes in this context, is thus—in stark contrast to what it is in Sartre—not the result of a preceding decree but itself represents an enduring field of tension. What announces itself in Husserl's notion of conflict, to which there is a prologue in the *Logical Investigations*,[118] is really an overcoming of the similarity paradigm, namely, insofar as the conflict is not sparked by a comparison (which could be judged now this way, now that) but by a question of reconcilability. Now, the conflict is not an a priori conflict; it, too, is made possible by the correlation in the first place: "conflict and unity do not 'absolutely' [*schlechthin*] exclude one another, but only in a variously determined correlation which changes from case to case." The conflict thus comes out only in the experience of a "resistance."[119]

Although he devotes a few paragraphs of the fifth of the *Logical Investigations* to the concept of "conflict," *Widerstreit*, Husserl as always refuses to engage in any speculation that would go beyond the strict framework of what can be experienced. In this regard another author, who was committed to phenomenology early on even if his later work can hardly be called phenomenological, went further: Jean-François Lyotard. In his opus magnus, *The Differend*, Lyotard distinguishes conflict, the differend (*le différend*), from what is merely distinct, the different (*le différent*), by noting that differends cannot be arbitrated once more by a neutral third (the "judge")[120]—just as Husserl distinguishes between merely "different" colors and "conflicting" ones, the latter being phenomenal qualities or facts that dispute each other's claim to validity. Both are *equally valid* (*gleich gültig*), exist simultaneously in the space of the possible, but in the "space of actuality" they exclude each other and are therefore not *indifferent* (*gleichgültig*).

Now, images can claim more for themselves than being only signs of the natural world of perception. What is fascinating about them is precisely that they demand to be more than representatives of an absence, sometimes even more than the presence of what is present. The incompossibility of image-perception and natural perception does not automatically imply an *isostheneia*, a state of equality of forces. "The image-object *does triumph*, insofar as it comes to appearance," but natural perception persists; it "gives the characteristic of present reality."[121] Images are thus characterized by a simultaneous too little and too much; no proposition can conclusively impose norms on their efficacy. With his conflict thesis, Husserl conceives of the image less as something that would have to be measured against "reality" along the scale from transparency to opacity than as something that demands an autonomous existence that renders the usual standards inadequate.[122] It seems that Husserl seeks to take this autonomization into account when, starting in 1918, he critically revises his own mimetic pattern of description: "Earlier I believed that it belonged to the essence of fine art to present in an image, and I understood this presenting to be depicting. Looked at more closely, however, this is not correct."[123] The place of a theory of the image as depiction is now taken by an expanded theory of pictoriality as presentability, in which the iconic sheds the traditional mimetological subordination. As Bernhard Waldenfels puts it: "In disputing the merely depicting character of perceptual consciousness, Husserl restores to pictoriality its proper function."[124] In this transformation, the example that prompted his rethinking is telling: the *theater*.

> In the case of a theatrical performance, we live in a world of perceptual phantasy; we <have> "images" within the cohesive unity of one image, but we do not for that reason have depictions. . . . We speak of theatrical presentation and perhaps even call it imaging presentation. The actors produce an image, the image of a tragic event, each actor producing the image of a character in the play, and so on. But here "image of" does not signify depiction of.[125]

The example of theatrical presentation prompts the neat repartition between phantasy and image-consciousness to collapse again. Of course the Wallenstein or Orestes on the stage—just like the centaur in phantasy—"is not taken by us for even a moment as something real," and yet he appears only because he comes into appearance in and through the factually present body of the actor. "The actor's presentation is not a presentation in the sense in which we say of an image-object that an image-subject is presented in it."[126] Can the actor be conceived of as mere carrier or "image-thing"? Hardly. The comparison with the actor's staging power brings forth a new dimension in which it becomes difficult to maintain Husserl's disarticulation of the material and the phenomenal. The actor proves to be both image-thing and image-object at the same time; his body does not recede from what it allows to be seen, but it is precisely on the condition of showing his own body that the actor lets something appear corporeally.

The carrier, then, is no longer what Sartre claimed it to be, a mere "analogon" of that which appears; "by means of his real actions, and among these are his movements, his change of expression, his external 'appearance,' which is his production," the actor produces something new that yet is none other than this specific "appearance" (the specific "style" of the appearing).[127] By thus emphasizing the appearance of the image as the "production" of the living actor, Husserl stresses the not just physical but medial aspect of the image-body. Far from Sartre's reduction of the image-thing to an obstacle of full-fledged image-consciousness, the question of the image once more announces Husserl's later philosophy of constitution in *Ideas* 2.

6. THRESHOLDS: ON THE MARGINS OF IMAGES

(a) Carriers

Among the first articulations of the ternary theory of the image is a manuscript from 1898. Husserl exemplifies the relationship between the three moments or "layers" (image-thing—image-object—image-subject) via Raphael's *Theology* from the Stanza della Segnatura in the Vatican, of which he had a reproduction hanging above his writing desk:

> For example, I am just now contemplating the engraving of Raphael's *Theology* that hangs on the wall here. First I contemplate it as this physical thing. I then change my way of considering it; I focus my attention not on what hangs on the wall but on the subject of the picture: an exalted figure of a woman, enthroned on a cloud, with two robust and youthful angels fluttering around her, and so on. I again change my way of considering it and turn from the presented image-object to the image that presents it, in the sense of the representing image-object. It is a rather small woman-doll with two considerably smaller angel-dolls, objectively colored in mere shades of gray.[128]

Characteristically, Husserl's phenomenology of images does not set in with a description of the *original* but contemplates Raphael's work already in the medium of technical reproduction. It can thus hardly be true to claim that Husserl pays attention to modern image techniques only according to the standards of painting.[129] Indeed, the opposite is the case.[130] Husserl employs the medially refracted engraving of the fresco in order to stress didactically the difference between the image-subject presented and the image-object (the "angel-dolls, objectively colored in mere shades of gray"). This does not mean that Husserl suddenly developed technophile tendencies: for Husserl, media dispositifs remain, as ever, supplements to a lacking perception of the original. For him, black-and-white reproductions of the *Theology* are but compensatory measures. While in the case of the Raphael *Theology* he had never seen the original himself (his trip to Italy dates to 1907, and he does not get further than Florence), most other examples he mentions have to do with paintings he had seen in museums, such as in the Dresden Gemäldegalerie, of which the reproductions thus serve as memoranda of a past perception of one's own.

"The Stuttgart publishing house recently started issuing volumes containing complete series of works by Dürer, Raphael, and so on, in the most minute reproductions." These images, however, do not count for themselves, they are "repertories of memory," "illustrative keywords,"[131] as it were, that one might call (adopting a felicitous invention of Aby Warburg's) "striking images" (*Schlagbilder*). Images become signals that reignite old memories and then act no differently from the name we hear that "reminds us, namingly, of the Dresden Gallery and of our last visit there" and effects the "mise-en-abyme of one in another" (*Ineinanderschachtelungen*) of the images in consciousness.[132] There is no denying that Husserl's theory of images ultimately does not weaken the primacy of "originarily presentive" perception, that it indeed anchors it more securely.[133] But there is another Husserl, too, who time and again involuntarily undermines this primacy of the immediate. The black-and-white print does not refer to any originarily pure perception but to another mediation: to an image, the way metapictoriality had already dizzyingly multiplied in the memory of David Teniers's image of a gallery of paintings, and the boundaries between presentation proper and merely mediating presentation had threatened to blur.[134]

Facing the threatening prospect of these blurred boundaries, Husserl again and again makes new attempts at distinguishing image-consciousness from signitive but also from originarily perceptive modes of consciousness. To what extent, he asks, is presentifying through an image different from presentifying through a symbolic sign? Seeing something *through* an image, for Husserl, means first of all *looking through it*:

> In mediate intuition, in the consciousness we usually simply call "looking at images," the ray of attention at first goes in through the image-object as through a medium—and specially through the presenting moments. In pictorial-symbolic objectivation, in understanding an advertisement image, the ray of attention at first goes into the image-object only promptly to be deflected and to penetrate an empty objectification woven into.[135]

When images are comprehended signitively-symbolically, their deficiency all the more quickly steers us toward what is really meant. However, deficiency here does not yet stand for defectiveness. Defects might generally exist only in an identifying nexus of meaning based on an unambiguous fulfilment of an intention. A typographical error "inhibits" the identification and yet negatively refers back to it. In aesthetic contemplation, images can never be "defective" because they do not possess any unambiguously intended content to which they would refer. Nonetheless, we feel uneasy with certain images; an image "displeases us (even before we know what about it displeases us)." The "deficient image does not represent to us a perfect one," it too points beyond itself: "we easily think that it ought to have been different in this or that sense, and thus our thoughts are directed at something more perfect as their goal. But this goal is not determined."[136] Very much the opposite of the intentional telos of fulfilling opinion, another telos, as if subliminally, announces itself in Husserl here, a telos of the aesthetic image as horizoned nonascertainedness, as the indeterminacy that modernity enthroned as the basic trait of the iconic.[137] Unlike phantasy, meanwhile, the image obtains its indeterminacy not from its proteiformity but rather because it is not determined *within the boundaries* of its being presented.

(b) Frames

Unlike phantasy, image-consciousness always has a material foundation. It is simultaneously more and less than this material continuum in which it is anchored. *More* because it gestures beyond itself (without for that reason already referring to an *elsewhere*); *less* because every image becomes an image only when it delineates itself as something separate against the background of a spatial continuum. The "visual field . . . extends further than the field of the image," and it does so because of pictorial *framing*.[138] Now, framed appearance is subject to a strange paradox that has a detrimental effect on the linear temporal hierarchy: the frame, the enclosure of the image, as that which makes the image an image in the first place, is what is perceived *first*. In Husserl's conception, this of course does not mean any chronological primacy but a logical priority in the succession of combinations of acts. The frame encloses the image, lets it step out, and mutatis mutandis turns itself into "what is incidentally noticed" with the perceptual surroundings.[139] This does not, for all that, suspend the perceptive continuum; materiality "runs" on from the wall via the frame to the surface of the image. The conception of the materiality of the image's surface, however, the apprehension of the carrier of the canvas or of paper, is, then, at most a "nongenuine [*uneigentlich*] presentation," and as a matter of fact, we "do not see" this parergonal carriership—this appendix—"in the proper [*eigentlich*] sense."[140] The only thing *seen in the proper sense* is the image-appearance.

    The phenomenon of the image thus destabilizes the primacy of originary perception because in images, the perception of the image-thing dips back into the sphere of what is seen nongenuinely, whereas the unreal but phenomenal image-object now advances to the status of what is seen "in the proper sense." When the image enters the stage, an answer to the question of genuineness is only ever possible within the frame of a constantly fluctuating economy of attention.

What *counts* as primary in a given instant is determined by movements of focusing that are shaped by directions of the gaze as much as by the material preconditions. Evoking an aisthetic *at the same time* instead of Sartre's *either–or* means that the determination of the status of the image is no longer possible categorically but only in interplay of shifting gazes.

In this respect, Husserl leaves no room for misunderstandings: physical image and image-object do not have different but the exact same apprehension-contents: "The same visual sensations are interpreted as points and lines on paper *and* as appearing plastic form."[141] Nonetheless, the space of appearances does not merely consist of parataxis; rather, in a situation of generalized conflict, the institutions and articulations of sense result from continual process of sub- and superordination. For Husserl, unlike for Sartre in *The Imaginary*, the appearance of pictoriality does not follow from precedent subjective positings; instead, positing claims themselves are subject to the generalized conflict. While the cognitive interest might be directed at the image-subject, "the framing . . . forces itself through to momentary notice." Put differently: because of the intrinsic interweaving of image-object and materiality, the limit "between reality and pictoriality" is not posited once and for all but must permanently be renegotiated.[142] Rather than at its expense, individuations take place on the basis of a continuum, the way the melody of an individual instrument becomes evident only against the background of the basso continuo on which it is based.

Now, the fringe of appearance—"the surroundings of the picture" that make the image particular—is always fluid; differential framing phenomena now take the place of a primordial positing. For Husserl, the frame is neither an independent *thing* (in the sense of something that shows itself) nor a representational sign (deferring to something else). He writes: "The frame exercises no representational function." Rather, it appears *along-with*, as a visible addition or "appendix," and it produces that of which it turns out to be the appendix. Rather than as a "border," the frame would thus have to be defined as a *threshold* that belongs to both orders, that joins them and allows for a transition between them. Not only is the wandering gaze being steered into the image by fading out the perceptual fringes; the image, too, in stepping out like a relief, "leaps" out of the frame.[143]

If what we are looking for in Husserl's manuscripts is a fully articulated descriptive theory of images, then Husserl's account of images must be unsatisfying. But if we recognize them to be a cautious circular movement around changing phenomena, we are able to focus on the theory of thresholds that announces itself here and that others pursued further.

(c) Windows

One of the earliest attempts at making Husserl's image theory phenomenologically productive is Eugen Fink's dissertation (1929), published a year later under
the title *Vergegenwärtigung und Bild: Zur Phänomenologie der Unwirklichkeit*
(Presentification and image: On the phenomenology of nonactuality) in Husserl's series *Jahrbuch für Philosophie und phänomenologische Forschung*.[144] Fink's
question is how, in the first place, we assign the image-carrier and what appears
on it to different orders ("actuality" and "nonactuality," say) and yet conceive of
both as a unity. While Husserl's analyses do not conceal an underlying identificatory telos, which has a correlate in the transcendental synthesis, Fink, on the
contrary, suspects the image to be a site for testing ligatures other than that of
transcendental egology.

Through what, Fink asks initially, does image consciousness arise in the first
place? Evidently not solely through an arbitrary change of attitude. The physical
carrier always constitutively participates in producing a new attitude; it is copresent yet not—and this is decisive—in the mode of an aesthetic nonactuality (as
would be the case of the back of the object, for example) but as coappearance.
The carrier's "cohaving" cannot be inverted into a cohaving of the image: in
shifting the gaze to the paper, the image disappears as well. Fink's solution now
consists in making the carrier that *through* which the image is being seen. The
pictorial attitude, which belongs to the "medial acts," institutes the unity of the
fact of the image in which the space of perception itself becomes the horizon of
the image-object. The image-appearance lies neither *in* the image-thing nor
behind it; thanks to a medial act, both become "transparent" not because but
despite their incompossibility. In that sense, "the whole image is only a small
'window' out into the world of the image."[145]

In this context, Leon Battista Alberti's trope of the *aperta fenestra*, the "open
window," is being updated, and not in an innocent way. Husserl had brought up
the window motif already in his Göttingen lecture: "We look through the
frame, as if through a window, into the space of the image, into the image's
reality."[146] The Husserl-Fink window implies less a seeing-into than a seeing-
through, since "the world in the image is no more in the plane than the landscape
seen outside is in the actual window."[147] In presenting his research project, Fink
even hinted, explicitly referring to Hegel, at seeking to open a "window onto the
absolute."[148] But Fink's way of thinking is characterized precisely by an aversion
against any kind of Hegelian sublation, as it were. As a "pure image phenomenon," the window is to be understood literally as a medium of "transparency."

Fink's windows meanwhile do not only, as they did in the Renaissance, present the opening of the modern subject to the outside. Through them, rather, the outside permeates the inside as well. "Every image-world in its essence opens into the actual world. The site of the opening-itself is the image." The image-object on the carrier is not identical with the image-subject in the world of the image, but it shares its properties: "'one and the same' red color is, first, the red paint on the piece of canvas, and it also is the red color of the evening sky of the world of the image."[149] In Husserl's terms, this may be called an identity of apprehension-contents; in Nelson Goodman's terms, an exemplificatory identity of properties shared by the object and the sample.

7. FROM PICTORIAL MEDIUM TO GENETIC PHENOMENOLOGY

If, in keeping with its founder's wishes, phenomenology is first of all an *investigation of correlations*, it is necessary—notwithstanding the demotion of the terms related in favor of the relation—to define the content and scope of the moments being correlated.[150] Yet in turn, the articulation of the appearing, appearance, and addressee of the appearance, which was shown to be the yield of the shift from a binary to a ternary concept of appearance, now reveals itself to be underdetermined.[151] While the appearing presents itself as referential *what* and the addressee as datival *for whom*, the scope and modalities of the *how* of the appearance still remain unspecified. This now is the point where a distinction between a static and a genetic phenomenology sets in. This distinction, which Husserl makes quite early without for all that already developing its full critical potential, concerns two different conceptions of the *how*.[152] While the static *how* describes mode, coloring, profile, and variation of the appearing, the genetic *how* inquires into the site of its genesis; while the object of static description is a present *phainomenon*, genetic analysis aims for the process of the *phainesthai*.

The aim to trace the appearing in its appearing—that is, according to Husserl, the basic question of phenomenological analysis as such—can no longer be met with a generic reference to the modal *how* because, with the becoming-genetic of the description, the grammar of the phenomenon multiplies as well. Aristotle already had pushed in this direction when he differentiated the *phainesthai* into a *for whom*, a *when*, an *in the sense in which*, and an *in the way in which*.[153] Yet such a loan from Aristotle would not suffice since these characterizations in his *Metaphysics* remain within the framework of a static description. The becoming-genetic of the question concerning the *how* of the appearance must instead take the fact into account that a *doubling of appearance* into an *eidetic "how"* and a *medial "through"* has taken place.

In Husserl, characteristically, the discovery of a genetic dimension of phenomenology that could have opened up the field of mediality results in this field being closed down. In the terms of Paul Ricœur's on-target diagnosis, what can be observed in the transcendental turn is that a phenomenology of appearing "for me" turns into a phenomenology of the constitution of appearances "from out of me."[154] The third moment, the subject as the *what for* of appearances, turns into a subject as a productive constituens. Patočka for his part highlights this ultimate reduction that turns the appearance as a performative event into a performance of the subject, which thereby mutates from a mere addressee into an exclusive agent.[155] It is in fact even possible to speak of a "hidden voluntarism" on the part of Husserl, who in the *epokhē* returns to a constitutive subject on the Cartesian model.[156]

The criticism of the egological turn to be found in practically all post-Husserlian phenomenologies is usually joined to an attempt to once more and differently undertake the "inquiry back" into the genetic *how*. The following three sections study just three among the many ventures in that vein. Each in its own way, these three approaches—by Eugen Fink, the early Jacques Derrida, and the late Maurice Merleau-Ponty—clearly convey how this renewed inquiry opens up the perspective of a different phenomenology that reconsiders mediality.

8. THE RELUCENCE OF THE MEDIUM (FINK)

Even where his thinking still moves along entirely Husserlian lines,[157] Eugen Fink, remarkably, does not begin with the emblematic case of giving-itself (the immediate evidence of the present sense object) but with a "consciousness of nonactuality" that, unlike phantasy, is nonetheless embedded in a corporeal-spatial structure of the present. What is to be seen *hic et nunc* in *this* image does not show itself and does not *give* itself by itself. But that giving-itself does not take place does not mean that no giving takes place. What the image gives to see is in a certain way inevasibly given; the nonpresentness is not a lack of consciousness but a certain fullness yet to be determined more precisely. Instead of starting, like Husserl, from the "consciousness of what is not present" alone,[158] an analysis of the peculiar temporal structure of what appears in the image is called for. Fink's thesis here, which he develops via the example of Ferdinand Hodler's *The Woodcutter*, is that what reigns in the image (without ever being present in the strict sense) is always the present.[159] Picking up on Fink, Roman Ingarden in his phenomenological ontology of the image thus also speaks of the "actuality" of the image-appearance.[160] Where no horizon for variations is available, temporality must inevitably take different paths. Succession, while not excluded, remains subjected to the principle of a simultaneous presentation—before and after compress, as it were, in a synoptic presentation.

However, the simultaneous compression of what is incompossible on a plane surface, according to Fink, requires other concealments. The image-thing leads to the intuition of the image-object (the woodcutter appearing, for example) by curtailing, as it were, its own objectness. Such curtailing must not be taken for transparency; rather, the concealment of the medium also always designates the limits of the medium and lets it shine through as what is covered over. Fink goes back to the example of natural media here: "For example, a mirror image in the water 'conceals' the water in a peculiar covering over. This concealing covering-over, however, is such that through it, the reality of the carrier can shine." Fink thus operates a radical reversal of the transparency paradigm. The "transparency" he speaks of here is not a becoming-invisible of the carrier. The gaze is brought to bear on the water as the medium of making-visible in the first place by the precarious image appearing in the water. This inverse movement, of course, requires an "anomality" of the direction of the gaze that not only inhibits the synthetic consciousness of identity but inquires, from a description of eidetic givenness, back to the site of its genesis.[164]

For Fink, the irreconcilability of image-carrier and image-appearance—in covering each other, the two can never coincide—expresses, once more, the lack of a specific space granted to images within a traditional ontology of objects. What appears in the image *is* not in the full sense, yet neither is it *nothing*. The "unreality" of the image cannot be compared to that of the ideal object, indeed, not even to the "ideal singularity of a work of art" like that of a "symphony that is the same in manifold repetitions."[165] Images are singular because of their intrinsic tension between facticity and unreality, which does not resolve in a unity and always already veers from a classical logic of identity. It points to a "meontics" or nonontology that cannot be characterized other than merely negatively: the transparency of what is objective lets being appear in its being withdrawn.[166]

The themes of Fink's late philosophy that ultimately result in a negative ontology of the medial are prepared in the early work when Fink juxtaposes Husserl's intentional presentification in the image with its flipside, ontological depresentification.[167] From Husserl's perspective, of course, the coining of the term—influenced, as the unpublished work from the period shows, by the recent discovery

Impacts of Time (Hodler, Bellechose)

The axe brandished by the woodcutter is forever frozen and ever an arm's length above his head. The man's tensed muscles, the left leg extended, the entire bearing of the body whose effect is amplified further by the perspectival top view, comes together in the completion of a movement that in the image has been accomplished only proleptically but has long been concluded by the eye. The extreme gestural tension Ferdinand Hodler offers in *The Woodcutter* (fig. 4.2) demands an optical discharge that can actualize in the viewer's imagination alone. In the chronotopical imaginary, the blade has long plunged down into the block of wood, has deepened the cleft a little further, and perhaps is already brandished again, shooting up at the end of the long shaft. The moment recorded by Hodler, however, is not a snapshot but a gesture conjured on the canvas that compresses the entire cycle of movement. Classicist discourse about art would have mobilized the old expression *kairos*, that moment of extreme tension, emblematically embodied for Johann Joachim Winckelmann by the scrambling bodies of the Laocoon Group.

While in Hodler the gestural symbolizes the wiry-steely mountain farmer's perfect domination of the anorganic, it acquires an entirely different significance in a different context. In his Burgundy altarpiece of 1416, Henri Bellechose stages the martyrdom of Saint Denis, from the last communion, which he receives in the dungeon from Christ's own hands, to his beheading alongside his companions Eleutherius and Rusticus (fig. 4.3). The entire pictorial temporal structure—familiar to a fifteenth-century viewer but somewhat challenging for a modern viewer trained in the principle of incompossibility—comes to a head in the scenic presentation of the decapitation in the picture's right half. The topography, ascending toward the right edge of the painting and meant to suggest the hill of Montmartre, is countered by the figures' downward movement. Unlike Voltaire, who drastically shortens the account of the execution,[161] the painter staggers the thrice-repeating event across an open temporal stack. On the right, standing upright, is Eleutherius, clad like the other two martyrs in a gold-embroidered blue cope; on the left, having rolled to the side of his bleeding trunk, lies the head of the already beheaded Rusticus.

FIGURE 4.2 Ferdinand Hodler, *The Woodcutter* (1910), lithograph. Sheet dimensions: 40.01 × 31.12 cm. Framed dimensions: 62.55 × 50.17 × 4.13 cm. Dallas Museum of Art. Courtesy of the museum.

FIGURE 4.3 Henri Bellechose, *The Martyrdom of St. Dionysius* (detail) (c. 1416), tempera on wood, 162 × 211 cm. Louvre, Paris.

(Continued next page)

(*Continued*)

The connection between the protension of Eleutherius and the future perfect of Rusticus is established by Denis, his body leaning over the block. While the executioner, dressed in white linen and green sleeves, is brandishing the axe above his head, the martyr's naked neck already bears the blemish of an impact that recalls the cleft in Hodler's *Woodcutter*. In dramatic slow motion, Bellechose presents the last deferment, a neither–nor between the time before and the time after. A daring interpretation might consider the judgment yet to come and see in the wound on Denis's neck the fateful anticipation, as it were, of the assimilation to Christ. While the axe, raised high, is touched by the rays of the divine *nimbus*, the saint, even before actually being touched, receives the stigmata, portents on the path to a perfected *imitatio Christi*.

These, like other examples, may absolve Fink's surprising thesis, according to which, in the world of the image, it is always a present that reigns, from the suspicion of Laocoon-like abridgements. It is a present that reigns, not because the world of the image would represent, as it does in Sartre, a world "in which nothing *happens*," but because even what offers itself as past or futural, in offering itself, presentifies.[162] Far from being any kind of presence, "presentative-impressional intuitiveness" is instead a presentifying positing-as-present.[163]

---

of the Heidegger of *Being and Time*[168]—represents a misunderstanding: the image-appearance is not so much a "depresentification" as it is a "dedonation."[169] If we push Fink's definition of "medial acts" beyond what he himself writes about them,[170] the following situation arises: what gives itself in the image does not *itself* give *itself* but gives itself because of the constitutive performance of the medium that makes the "appearing and being-able-to-show-oneself" possible in the first place. The figure of "relucence," which goes back to Heidegger and which Fink endows with new accents, must accordingly be read in two directions.[171]

In the terms of a media aesthetics, *relucence* or "shining back" means that in images, the watermark of that which produced them remains recognizable in a particular way: the backside of the medium, as it were, comes through the concealment. On the other hand, relucence for Fink also contains a cosmological thesis: shining back is the way in which the world, as that which cannot be viewed as a whole, can appear at all. Thought radically from a perspective of finitude, "the whole, which is never visible as a whole, appears in a field within itself."[172] World thus appears through a part of itself. According to Fink, two techniques repeat and amplify this process, techniques by means of which a finite subject gives its finitude a positive turn: image and play. Despite certain differences, both represent modes of dealing with limitedness.[173] Both underline their restricted closure and thereby simultaneously let something appear in the inner space that is not factually there.[174] Image and play are not windows onto the world but rather certain "refraction angles" of the totality (totality is given as refracted; only as refracted can it be given at all).[175]

Now, Eugen Fink is of interest not only for reconstructing a history of phenomenological theories of the image; he also had a decisive influence on the way a certain kind of phenomenology was transferred to and grafted onto French thought. The lecture "Operative Concepts in Husserl's Phenomenology," given in French at the historic Husserl conference in Royaumont in 1957, is serious about interpreting phenomenology as a philosophy of finitude and derives methodological consequences from this interpretation. In analogy with perception, a finite subject's thinking, too, is always only ever partial, aspectual, or, more precisely, "shadowed": "The presence of a shadow [*Verschattung*] is an essential feature of finite philosophizing. . . . Only God knows without shadows."[176] Insofar as Husserl hopes to obtain the possibilizing principles from the description itself and denies himself any metaphysical speculation, it is precisely the central operative concepts that remain in the dark in the process of thinking:

> Conceptualization in philosophy aims intentionally at those concepts in which thought fixes and preserves what is being thought. We call these concepts "thematic concepts." . . .
>
> But in the formation of thematic concepts, creative thinkers *use* other concepts and patterns of thought, they *operate* with intellectual schemata which they do not fix objectively. They think *through* certain cognitive presentations toward the basic concepts which are essentially their themes. Their understanding moves in a *conceptual field*, in a *conceptual medium* that they are not at all able to see. They expend medial lines of thought to set up that which they are thinking about. We call that which in this way is readily *expended* and *thought through* in philosophical thinking, but not *considered* in its own right, operative concepts. They form, metaphorically speaking, the *shadow of a philosophy*.[177]

According to Fink, Husserl was unable to clarify the constitution of phenomenality because he takes his conceptual means for doing so from the very sphere he seeks to break through, namely, the naive use of language.[178] Only a radical inquiry back into the operatively shadowed linguistic medium of Husserl's reduction and its overcoming by means of a language no longer contaminated by the everyday could really discover the transcendental constitution.

Fink's lecture influenced not least of all two thinkers in the audience who were to provide significant stimuli for the reception of Husserl in France. The first is Maurice Merleau-Ponty, who maintained a close personal connection with Fink, from their first meeting in Leuven in 1939 to their late letters, and who always ascribed special significance to the "shadows" of Husserl's phenomenology. The second is Jacques Derrida, for whom Fink's notion that a thinking is unable to include the central moments of its own process practically became a personal signature. Although Derrida presented his own reading of Husserl as a turn away not only from Sartre's but from Merleau-Ponty's as well, texts published since relativize this generational contrast.[179] At least between Merleau-Ponty's and Derrida's readings of Husserl's *Origin of Geometry*, there are strong analogies as both seek to rearticulate Fink's constitution problem via the vector of material-historical institutions of meaning.

9. MEDIALITY AS DEFERRAL OF PRESENCE (DERRIDA)

In the long introduction to his translation of *The Origin of Geometry* published in 1962, Jacques Derrida refers explicitly to Fink with respect to the genetic turn of phenomenology, but he doubts that a transcendental language will ever be able to rid itself of the facticity of natural language.[180] Separating the empirical and the transcendental, he argues, would require a site from which such a distinction could be made. Where doubts about such a general's perspective arise, the dimension of historicity suggests itself. In the lecture "Genèse et structure et la phénoménologie," given in 1959 and subsequently reworked several times, Derrida shows how the analysis of the passive synthesis necessarily results in an inclusion of historicity.[181]

If the passive synthesis consists in consciousness not constituting but merely revealing its objects, then this implies that the objects already constitute themselves genetically elsewhere. Seen this way, Husserl, who so sharply criticized psychologism and historicism as reconstructions of "de facto geneses," is forced to describe idealities as anchored temporally and historically after all. Beside a genetic inquiry, which Derrida, taking up Fink, characterizes as an "archaeology" already in the early thesis *The Problem of Genesis in Husserl's Philosophy*, there would thus be an opposite movement, a dynamic that pushes ahead.[182]

The question of genesis (for Derrida, phenomenology's emblematic blind spot) shows the irresolvable interlocking of archeology and dynamology, of the question of the origin and that of becoming. The origin does not lie in what has become and yet—if one accepts no metaphysical horizon—does not lie beyond it. What remains to be thought is the paradox of a genesis that is always simultaneously the transcendental condition of the historical appearance and, as an event de facto taking place, is already empirically contaminated.[183] Derrida analyzes this entanglement in a text that previously only existed on the margins, an appendix to the *Crisis* on the origin of geometry.[184] He was prompted to do so, among other things, by Trần Đức Thảo's *Phenomenology and Dialectical Materialism*. For the Vietnamese Marxist phenomenologist, to whom Derrida acknowledged he was indebted in pursuing his own interest in the historicity of idealities, *The Origin of Geometry* proves that "*sensible life* for man does not consist in immediate interactions with the environment but is mediated by the *production* of the conditions of his existence."[185]

The problem of mediation poses itself for Husserl every time it comes to clarifying how ideality is able to objectivate in the lifeworld. The question of the constitution of ideal entities that was already at the basis of the *Philosophy of Arithmetic* is thus embedded within the horizon of possibilities for historical emergence. Husserl focuses the problem via the example of geometry: "How does geometrical ideality (just like that of all sciences) proceed from its primary intrapersonal origin, where it is a structure within the conscious space of the first inventor's soul, to its ideal objectivity?"[186]

Where the philosophy of arithmetic described the constitution in consciousness of ideal mathematical objects, the late Husserl of the *Crisis* asks how something that has been constituted in pure evidence can "remain objectively knowable and available without requiring that the formulation of their meaning be repeatedly and explicitly renewed."[187] Although its beginnings can be dated historically, Euclidean geometry has an ideal validity that, independently of its empirical reconstructions and applications, always remains identical with itself and is thus iterable.

Ideality can, for instance, be handed on "by means of language, through which it receives, so to speak, its linguistic living body [*Sprachleib*]."[188] "In the contact of reciprocal linguistic understanding, the original production and the product of one subject can be actively understood by the others." Yet "even during periods in which the inventor and his fellows are no longer wakefully so related or even are no longer alive," ideality persists, namely, in the medium of writing. "The important function of written, documenting linguistic expression is that it makes communications possible without immediate or mediate personal address; it is, so to speak, communication become virtual. Through this, the communalization of man is lifted to a new level."[189]

With the medium of writing, language steps out of a context of simultaneity and enters into the context of an extended communicative situation that no longer knows of fixed addressees and whose writing "original founder" becomes anonymous.[190] Writing would then turn out to be both the precondition of tradition and a threat to tradition. "By emancipating sense from its *actually present* evidence for a real subject and from its present circulation within a determined community . . . [b]y absolutely virtualizing dialogue, writing creates a kind of autonomous transcendental field from which every present subject can be absent."[191] This pinpoints the basic tension that inhabits the phenomenological project: only through repeatability does Husserl's discovery of the identical approach its goal and *telos*; yet with every iteration, it becomes clearer that the current intuition cannot but be approximative:

> He never directly defined its type of evidence within phenomenology, whose "*principle of all principles*" and archetypal form of evidence is the immediate presence of the thing itself "in person." Implicitly that means: of the phenomenally defined or definable thing, therefore the *finite* thing. (The motif of finitude has perhaps more affinity with the latter implication than it first seems to have with phenomenology's principle of principles. Phenomenology would thus be *stretched* between the *finitizing* consciousness of its *principle* and the *infinitizing* consciousness of its final *institution*, the *Endstiftung* indefinitely deferred [*différée*] in its content but always evident in its regulative value.)[192]

This passage is worth citing not least because the very context in which Derrida attempts a minute description of the Husserlian "zigzag" movement of *institution*—that "vital movement of the coexistence and the interweaving of original formations and sedimentations of meaning"[193]—features the earliest appearance of the verb *différer* and thus of *différance*.[194] The necessity of the de facto "reconstruction" (*Nach-Vollzug*) of the institution as well as the renewed presentifying of its event is not opposed to a virtualization, an extended deferral; it practically provokes it. Far from the rash judgment that Husserl rejects mediality, Derrida's reading brings out the tense dependence of Husserl's agenda on media: evident self-giving is possible only in the living present, yet in the living present all giving is always incomplete and hence dependent on being continued: "truth is not fully objective, i.e. ideal, intelligible for everyone and indefinitely perdurable, as long as it cannot be said *and* written." In the enduring of the present as the *possibility of reactivation*, the phenomenological concept of the living present always points to the horizon of survival.[195] Here too, once again, we see that what some readers of Derrida considered a dismantling of Husserl's thinking initially consists in nothing but a minute exposition of its most intimate principle. Caught between the claim of apodictic self-giving and the infinite task of reason, Husserlian phenomenology, obviously, must inevitably result in a revaluation of the medial. Complete evidence presupposes mediality but is at the same time rendered impossible by it: "The medium is thus to be conceived of as the condition of ideality that is at the same time the condition of the crisis."[196]

Derrida's early readings of Husserl thus continue the archeological turn toward the life-world genesis of appearances initiated by Fink,[197] but they also situate Derrida in proximity to a thinker of the generation that preceded him from whom he falsely believed to be delimiting himself by focusing on *The Origin of Geometry*: Maurice Merleau-Ponty.

10. THE ONTOLOGICAL MILIEU OF VISIBILITY (MERLEAU-PONTY)

Two years before Derrida's translation of and commentary on *The Origin of Geometry* appears in print, Merleau-Ponty devotes the main part of his lecture course on "Husserl at the Limits of Phenomenology" at the Collège de France to this text. The lecture notes from the years 1959 and 1960 yield insight into the astonishing proximity between the two thinkers' attempts at accounting for the materializations and sedimentations of ideality in the life-world. On the traces of Fink, who uses "embodiment" (*incorporation*) and "localization" to characterize language generally, writing in Derrida becomes emblematic of the "ability to be embodied" (*incorporabilité*) and of "temporalization," whereas Merleau-Ponty suspects in writing the condition of becoming-sensory and becoming-public.[198] Under the conditions of communalization, of the publicly appearing, however, the perspective of an individually operated intentional institution of sense perfecting itself in the fulfillment of sense shatters as well. Not only can no adequate fulfillment ever be attained; the originary institution (*Urstiftung*) itself becomes anonymous and its authorship uncertain.

For Merleau-Ponty, though, this is not a shortcoming but the sign of a cultural process of transmission he also describes as "infinite mediation" (*médiation infinie*).[199] The topos that relieving individual consciousness inevitably leads to a loss of living knowledge is endlessly repeated by the philosophy of technology from Plato's *Phaedrus* to Husserl's *Crisis*, but this loss, as Merleau-Ponty stresses, is practically indispensable for an ideality to be thought through in actual consciousness. Forgetting the empirical conditions of its occurrence is necessary for what is past not to fall back into "something which was past" and for it to continue effectively to accompany the "open community." "This forgetfulness of origins by means of what survives in the present is traditionality, *Tradierung*, the handing over of ... to."[200] The communalized coconstruction, the cultural reconstruction, aided by what elsewhere he also calls "apparatuses of knowledge (words, books, works)," does, however, increasingly bear the traits of reactivating something that has never been actual and "has never been given in evidence" (*n'a jamais été dans l'évidence*).[201] In thus breaking through the telos of meaning that conceives of temporality only ever as a confirming future perfect and of every event of sense as doubling something already present, Merleau-Ponty opens the path for a different concept of history on which he worked in his later years. The broad space he allows for aesthetic phenomena in this endeavor is due less to a desire also to account for art in its historicity than it is to his attempt at thinking historicity on the very model of art.

Art allows for a particularly insightful approach to the double movement of *Fundierung* (founding) and *Stiftung*, Husserl's "fine word," which Merleau-Ponty renders in French as *institution*. Artistic events of institution

> continue to have a value after their historical appearance and open a field of
> work beyond and the same as their own. It is thus that the world as soon as he
> has seen it, his first attempts at painting, and the whole past of painting create
> for the painter a tradition, that is, Husserl says, the power to forget origins, the
> duty to start over again and to give the past, not survival, which is the hypo-
> critical form of forgetfulness, but the efficacy of renewal or "repetition," which
> is the noble form of memory.[202]

In Fink's terms, we might speak in this context of a "secondary *Verweltlichung*" or of a *production* of world that does not bring about a different world but repeats the same world, the only world, once more in its becoming-visible. Every production of images, for Merleau-Ponty, is due to a process continually taking place in perception, a process it repeats and amplifies: "The painter follows the course of perception" because he voluntarily intensifies a process of expression that is already taking place in the perceiving living body as a passive synthesis.[203] Just like the painting hand, the perceiving living body always already comes too late; it merely reactivates something already present, albeit present not in the mode of a readily given (and not even of a sense datum) but only ever as something prestructured yet to be actualized by the living body. Only because the frame of the perceptual field is horizonal and thus mobile, only because the process of perception cannot as a matter of principle be brought to an end is there perception as a *possibility* at all. The relationship of institution is thus one of reciprocal dependence, of *intertwinement*, as Husserl says, or of *chiasm*, as the late Merleau-Ponty puts it. Something appears only because it appears to someone seeing, yet the one seeing is seeing only because his seeing is founded in a living body that itself is subject to the condition of visibility.

In the living body, the paradoxical nature of appearing as such shows: the living body is constitutively visible and yet never *completely* visible; it lies before our eyes, and yet the one seeing cannot walk around it to get a full view of it. The living body is able to become visible only because it is not yet completely visible. The visibility of the living body is a visibility always yet to come, a visibility in the potential. Announcing itself in the voluntary or involuntary turn of the gaze to one's own body is the reflexivity of the appearing: the living body is visible through the same living body that allows it to become visible; the reflexive turn back recalls that seer and the seen share a single body. The split that nonetheless never makes the living body fall apart must instead be grasped both as material indifference and as continual differentiation of aspects.

From his early work to the late unpublished notes, Merleau-Ponty thus seeks to think the appearing of objects neither as mechanical causality nor as idealist projection but rather as continual, splaying genesis that precedes the distinction between subject of appearance and object of appearance, indeed, produces the distinction in the first place. The progressive formation of a figure on a ground against which it stands out constitutes the differential contrasting process for Merleau-Ponty's thinking all the way to the ontology of his final years.[204] "To see," he writes in *Phenomenology of Perception*, "is to enter into a universe of beings that *show themselves*,"[205] yet being itself, around which the unfinished late book *The Visible and the Invisible* revolves, must be described on the model of the process of figurative seeing.

Such a vertical phenomenology, which allows for gradations and levels but not for a fundamental caesura between the perceptive and the linguistic, between the individual and the cultural, will not suppose a higher manifestation of culture—art—to be the final stage of a crystallization but instead consider it an intensified visualization of an articulatory process that already begins in perception.[206] Images thus play a central role in Merleau-Ponty's oeuvre. Not because it would be possible to quarry a handy concept of the image from his writings, never mind a distilled image theory. Generally, it seems that for

Merleau-Ponty, no images exist beyond imaging and becoming-image. For an objectivated image would simply no longer be an image; it would be an idea.

Creative geneses of sense, which Merleau-Ponty tracks in bodily gestures, in linguistic propositions, in the discovery of mathematical formulas, or in the articulation of new visibilities in images, all indicate that meaning cannot be something readily present but must always already be performed. Every advent of sense (*avènement du sens*) announces further events of sense (*événements du sens*). In the creative expression, "a system of definite powers suddenly decenters . . . breaks apart, and is reorganized."[211] Sense thus always rests on material foundings that imprint it with their particular "coefficient of facticity."[212] Every expressive gesture plays on the "keyboard of acquired significations"; the new modulations it produces thus begin earlier than with themselves and always point beyond themselves.[213]

Expression does not externalize a sense already present within, in a convolution of the brain, or without, in the things; it "accomplishes" sense in the first place.[214] As a performative process, expression is neither pure creation nor mere repetition; only in this intermediate area is it possible at all: creative speech without all preconditions would amount to saying without anything to be said, a mere repetition would amount to something being said without saying anything. Or, to rephrase one more time: speech that is creative through and through would have *nothing* to say; speech that only confirms has nothing *to say*.[215] A phenomenology trying to follow the process of expression would thus from the outset begin this side of the readymade object, with sense *in statu nascendi*. The task would be to understand how "the structure of the world is such that all the possibilities of language are already given in it" without these possibilities already being actually articulated in the world.[216]

Insofar as every giving of sense takes place in a dimension that is simultaneously opening up and necessarily anchored somewhere, it must be centrifugal and centripetal at the same time.[217] In this "phenomenology of genesis,"[218] Merleau-Ponty assigns a special role to painting, for it conveys even more insightfully than speaking why there is no "pictorial language" beyond images, why its means cannot be inventoried but emerge in the implementation in the first place. "Cézanne's doubt," around which the early homonymous essay revolves, would then really consist in that the painter is never assured of his vectors of visualization, that he cannot make use of a preexisting keyboard of visual signs that would precede the event of the image's becoming: visibility could only be had potentially. The painter must involve himself; he puts himself at stake with his living body: *le peintre apporte son corps*—the painter, in Valéry's formulation, appropriated by Merleau-Ponty, brings in his living body.[219] And yet, what is

Intuitive Arithmetic (Gauss)

Although ideas cannot be derived from perception—Merleau-Ponty insists on this difference—both share the property of creative intuitiveness.[207] What kind of creative intuitiveness is at issue may be seen in examining the origin of Carl Friedrich Gauss's series sum formula. In the history of mathematics, images are usually assigned the role of external additions without significance in the articulation of proofs except perhaps as post-facto visualizations. As noted earlier, Aristotle, for example, ascribed no epistemic function to geometrical drawings.[208] The historical derivation of the series sum formula, however, yields an entirely different picture:

$$\sum_{i=1}^{n} i = \frac{n(n+1)}{2}$$

To calculate the sum of n successive natural numbers ($1 + 2 + 3 + \ldots + n$), Gauss arranged the numbers progressively in pairs from the outside to the inside. He noticed that the sum of each pair of numbers yields precisely n + 1. To obtain the final result, however, it is still necessary—in order not to double-count any of the paired-up elements—for the result obtained for each pairing to be multiplied with the sum of all numbers (n) and divided by 2. With reference to Max Wertheimer, who considers it a classic example of "productive thinking," Merleau-Ponty conceives of the arithmetical operation as a thinking taking place in the image.

$$(10+1)\left(\frac{10}{2}\right) = 55$$

The graphic and the arithmetical formalizations are semantically equivalent and lead to the same result (= 55). The mere formula, however, does not bring about any evidence: "We would not *see* the evidence."[209] Intuitiveness thus not only plays a constitutive role in obtaining pure validity; the reconstruction of the laws in place in turn unfolds along the same paths as those of the "originary institution." The arithmetical operations themselves, insofar as they must be reconstructed by a human subject, thus contain pictorial moments that make arithmetic a creative process.[210]

being expressed through him does not lie in any kind of inaccessible interiority. Rather, through the living body, the imaging continues a becoming-visible that has already begun between the viewer and the things.

This completes the decentering that sets in in the 1950s and leads to the late ontology of visibility: "Between the alleged colors and visibles, we would find anew the tissue that lines them, sustains them, nourishes them, and which for its part is not a thing, but a possibility, a latency, and a *flesh* of things."[220] This stuff the world is made of, Merleau-Ponty explicitly notes, is to be thought neither as matter nor as mind nor as substance but as an element.[221] As a finite element of my living body, it is eminently my own; simultaneously, as infinite fullness of the world, it is irretrievably anonymous. Flesh is *doublure* in every sense of the term: as doubling, as shadow-like double, but also as material lining of the reverse, as nourishing stuffing. The concept of flesh, *chair*, allows Merleau-Ponty to erase the remainders of the philosophy of consciousness that characterize his early work without having to sacrifice corporeality. Quite the contrary: whereas previously it was the privileged mode of access to the world of a consciousness, corporeality now, in the radical form of subjectless flesh, is understood as the principle of world itself.

Only against the background of this "new ontology" of the flesh is it possible to grasp why Merleau-Ponty, despite his harsh criticism of ocularcentrism, develops his late thought guided by painting and thus by seeing. Seeing now is no longer the "noblest sense" because through spatial distance it would operate a "dynamic neutralization" on the visible such that it becomes theorizable; rather, it brings out the one who is seeing as someone who is himself pervaded by the visible: "the visible ceases to be an inaccessible if I conceive it, not according to the proximal thought, but as an encompassing, lateral investment, *flesh*."[222] Or, put differently: the one seeing and the visible do not confront each other head-on but stand in a relationship of reciprocal, chiasmatic intertwinement.

The one who sees is seeing only because he belongs to the visible himself without being fully reducible to it—and vice versa: "Yet this flesh that one sees and touches is not all there is to flesh, nor this massive corporeity all there is to the body."[223] Just as in the realm of the visible there are invisible reverse sides, so my seeing is shot through with blind spots, with zones of invisibility that open up a seeing not already directed at what is merely seen. In Merleau-Ponty's own words: "One has to understand that it is the visibility itself that involves a non-visibility."[224] This nonvisibility, meanwhile, is neither a negation of visibility nor a currently merely absent (and thus restitutable) visibility; rather, it is a *punctum caecum* in seeing itself that presentifies the visible as a "certain absence."[225]

To avoid the suspicion of both negation and deficiency, Merleau-Ponty, instead of a nonvisible speaks of an "in-visible," though it should have become clear from the discussion so far that this is anything but a mystical turn. The visible *and* the invisible are always to be thought together; they condition each other and yet cannot be made congruent. As the principle of visibility, the blind spot is not invisible *as a matter of principle*; it can, according to a universal reversibility, itself become visible. In striving to break out of thinking in oppositions and at the same time to hold on to reflexivity as what drives philosophy, Merleau-Ponty assumes an originary "coiling over of the visible upon the seeing body," that is, a seeing that unfolds from the heart of the visible and folds back into it, a movement he also characterizes as "mirror phenomenon."[226] The mirror paradigm is thus transformed: instead of an infinite, frontal reversibility of the identical, it reveals both the nonidentity and the reciprocal belonging of the seeing and the seen. Reversibility—that other fundamental term of the later Merleau-Ponty—then means that I as the one who sees can only ever stand on one side of the threshold while my own invisibility always already shifts into what is visible, that I become aware of myself when I perceive myself as another.

In *On the Soul*, Aristotle, as we have seen, discusses the difficulty of a perception of perceptions themselves.[227] Merleau-Ponty describes this paradox via an example he returns to repeatedly: every time I touch my right hand with my left, I alternately experience myself as someone who touches and as someone who is being touched. But if I want to alleviate this self-doubling and experience this touching being-touched by in turn touching my left hand with my right, the experiment shifts at the very last moment. Where the greatest proximity exists, the greatest distance gapes as well; the living body is the site of a constant *déhiscence*, a gaping-open, a relationship to the self that is at the same time a splitting of the self. Derrida's insinuation that the autoaffective "structure 'touching–touched'" in "a certain phenomenology" is the basic figure of the Western metaphysics of presence thus turns out to be indefensible. Rather, Merleau-Ponty's phenomenology seeks to account not for the transparent relationship of self to self but for the divergent forces. Hence the quasi-programmatic tone of a late note: "the originating breaks up, and philosophy must accompany this break-up, this non-coincidence, this differentiation."[228]

The becoming-genetic of phenomenology Merleau-Ponty announces already in the preface to the *Phenomenology of Perception* and that in the late writings advances to a dynamic ontology, to a "perpetual pregnancy, perpetual parturition, generativity," takes place guided by images.[229] Yet images here must not be conceived of as typical essences but as phenomena that exhibit the conditions of their provenance—the locus of their "becoming."[230] The task of "learning to see anew" (*réapprendre à voir*) that Merleau-Ponty speaks of always begins already when we stand before an image.[231] Insofar as we do not look at images the way we look at things but rather look "according to" images, as he puts it, there is a kind of visual thinking at work already in the images: "a figured philosophy vision—its iconography" unfolds in them. What is figured does not lie anywhere else, in some kind of sacred text or crypt, and no insider knowledge is required to read its artifacts. Merleau-Ponty asserts that "painting celebrates no other enigma but that of visibility." This enigma, though, has nothing of a cryptic riddle. Its enigmatic nature is due to the challenge that all things pose that come too close to us. Philosophy has invited us so often to look behind the veil, but the real difficulty is in learning to see what is in plain sight. That is why Merleau-Ponty, borrowing an expression from the surrealist poet Henri Michaux, thinks of painting as the production of a thing that breaks the "skin of things."[232]

The art of painting, in other words, makes use of a power intrinsic to all images: the power to make visible what was not sufficiently visible; the power to let the inconspicuous appear. Images show us things as we have never seen them. For Merleau-Ponty, rather than objects to be seen in and of themselves, images are media *through which* we see: "Rather than seeing it, I see according to, or with it." Even more explicitly, he writes in an unpublished note: "What is an image? Obviously we do not look at an image the way we look at a thing. We look according to the image."[233] As a medium that orients and generates perception, the image opens onto something else, something inconspicuous that remained outside the frame. To see in images means to see more than what meets the eye.

5
Media Phenomenology

1. THEORY OF BLIND SPOTS, BLIND SPOTS OF THEORY

How can we see how we see? Or, put differently: Where is the visible before it becomes visible? Can we catch a glimpse of the visible in the moment of its emerging visibility? If existence, as George Spencer Brown's famous formula has it, "is a selective blindness,"[1] then, from a phenomenological perspective, this cannot mean an act of distinguishing but a rhythmic process of rising and ebbing saliences in which some figures emerge and others are submerged. For *something* to be seen, something else must necessarily remain unseen, or: every *per-cipere* is an *ex-cipere*.[2] As Jean-François Lyotard rightly remarked, however, this asymmetry contains the basic contradiction of Husserlian phenomenology:[3] although assuming an asymmetrical field of object and horizon—and thus *depth*—allows phenomenology to advance to a concept of experience that intellectualism and empiricism struggle in vain to achieve, both object and horizon remain within a smooth projection of the world, as it were, to which all relief must be added artificially. Moreover, by insisting on the asymmetry, phenomenology in turn becomes ensnared in hierarchizations that it escapes only with great effort.

If the object appearing and its conditions of possibility are no longer simply assigned to the orders of visibility and invisibility, if the relationship between figure and ground is thus thought as a dynamic relationship that can in principle be reversed, the question arises: What makes the figure a figure and the ground a ground? Such a desubstantialized and liquified world calls for something different, something that is capable of generating identifiable objects in the magma of appearances. Confronting this ongoing phenomenalization is a mobile eye capable of orienting itself within it and of recognizing eidetic invariants in the manifold of adumbrations. To note the iterated in the empirical stream, to capture the identical, that is, to cognize *something as something* at all, the singularity of its appearance must be disregarded. That is why, if phenomeno*logy* is to be pursued and the *sense* of phenomena to be saved, Husserl must think of the adumbrations starting from the identical object shining through them, not the other way around.

Time and again, therefore, Husserl's genetic phenomenology has to struggle with its own hidden teleology, which unravels the unfolding phenomenon from its ideal end or from an adequately focused center. This unabashed Cartesianism of insight thereby still participates in a central perspective paradigm that has governed thinking since early modernity. The asymmetry of the retina, with its foveal sharp-sightedness and marginal indeterminacy, gives rise—figuratively—to an ideal of *clare et distincte* vision that spreads even to those intellectual traditions that seek to account for the halo surrounding appearances, their indeterminate potentiality. Caught in such efforts at centralization, phenomenological eidetics, according to Lyotard, necessarily remains dependent on starting from the fully constituted object: the adumbration is then conceived of as presumptive anticipation of the complete object, and the object is conceived of as the complete synthesis of all adumbrations. What risks getting lost here is the fact that what shows itself does not initially show itself as something seen foveally focused but always already as an ongoing *event* of seeing: "In the thing's entrance into the field, the sketch is merely what will remain as element of the seen object; on the contrary, the event is what is excluded from the field."[4]

A phenomenology that conceives of mediality not as inauthentic but as constitutive must therefore begin elsewhere than with the constituted noema. The reflections that follow are searching for possible points of entry into such an a-teleological, medial phenomenology, a phenomenology, that is, that does not—similar to Henri Bergson's "retrograde movement of the true"—predate what is to be obtained and retroproject it into a precedent realm of *eidē*. Such a search necessarily takes place on unsecured terrain because, at least partially, it goes beyond the framework of a mature, internally communicating tradition. It nonetheless remains dedicated to the intuition that, hidden on the margins of the "phenomenological movement" (Herbert Spiegelberg), there are still unexploited potentials. In what follows, I begin such tentative explorations guided by the physiological-optical concept of *laterality* to point to a path that leads from the so-called *eidetic* via *transcendental* to a *medial* phenomenology taking shape on the horizon and yet to be elaborated.

Phenomenology does not have to come down to a teleology of coincidental syntheses, as the work of acknowledged phenomenological authors such as Maurice Merleau-Ponty or Aron Gurwitsch attests, who privilege the marginalia of identifying intuition. As they both stress, the visible *takes place* on the margins of the frontal gaze, in an as yet prethematic field of perception, on what William James called the "fringes" of seeing. As the potentiality of individual appearances, the field itself is not merely invisible; rather it is—nonthematically—always copresent. Everything that successively comes into the focus of attention assembles and consolidates there. To be sure, the peripheral cannot be focused on *as peripheral*, and any attempt to do so will inevitably lose sight of it since there is no perception of lateral emergence, only a lateral emergence of perception. Lateral seeing would thus be not a diminished form of focal seeing but, inversely, its precondition, and every figure would be a manifestation, pushing its way to the center, of a figural matrix indicating itself as the undetermined, shimmering margin of the figures. Beside a *genetic phenomenology* that seeks its origin in a more fundamental *ground*, there would thus be a *generative phenomenology* that situates the origin of the potentiality of appearances in a perceptive *laterality*.

It is not without reason that such a lateral phenomenology is not fundamentally hostile to the empirical sciences. Both Merleau-Ponty and Lyotard repeatedly take recourse to physiological facts to support the lateralization thesis: while the human eye has an opening angle of about 150° vertically and 170° laterally and binocular vision can extend to 210°, only 2° may be considered foveal vision.[5] Nonetheless, these and similar references hardly constitute a return to any kind of biological determinism: Lyotard instead recalls Anton Ehrenzweig's analysis of patients with hemianopsia. In this example, where a lesion of the optical nerve causes the loss of use of one half of the retina, the eye adapts to the new conditions, plastically, as it were, and reconstitutes the same field organization of sharp center and unsharp periphery on the remaining rods. For Ehrenzweig, this is proof that there is not only a phylogenetic but also an ontogenetic need for the larger part of the field of vision remaining indeterminate. Ehrenzweig, Lyotard, but already Merleau-Ponty, too, connect such physiological findings with other developments unfolding in parallel. The lateralization operated by a certain kind of phenomenology corresponds to a movement that takes place not only in Saussurean linguistics but in modern painting as well.[6]

Judged by the metrics of central perspective, Cézanne's visions must count as incompossible and thus as downright wrong. If, however, we follow Ehrenzweig in supposing that Paul Cézanne was interested in the marginal constitutive processes of becoming-visible and that his paintings stage peripheral vision, a new picture emerges.[7] The viewer's experience of seeing a Cézanne is then one of an impossible centering. Every part of the image (the edge of the table, the pot of ginger, the corner of the wallpaper, the apple) constitutes the starting point of continually reforming configurations that thwart any final objectification. There is no face-to-face relationship, no direct take on things, but rather the rendering visible of the "mute germination" Cézanne, and with him so many others, from Georges Seurat to Paul Klee, speaks of. *What* is to be seen steps back in favor of *how* it is seen, or, in the words of Klee's famous statement in his "Creative Confession": "Art does not reproduce the visible; rather, it makes visible."[8]

The path of lateralization along which linguistics and art precede philosophy has immediate ethical implications. As Merleau-Ponty notes, it marks a clear critique of focalizing thinking whose regulative idea, despite its constant awareness of its imperfection, is an infinite "approximation." Instead of representing perception as a progressive circling around and review of the object, visibility must be conceived as "an encompassing, lateral investment."[13] What I am unable to bring into view is not just the back of the object, which I could actualize at any moment by walking around the object; it is something unforeseeable that already encircles me and can break into my field of vision at any moment. The intentional orientation toward the world can at any moment be disrupted by the occurrence of something unexpected; the *projective* attitude that derives from the orientedness of the body schema can itself be thwarted by *introjective* events.

Yet it would be throwing out the baby with the bathwater to give up all of phenomenology as a project because of its historically conditioned focus on intentionality. If indeed, as Paul Ricœur writes, phenomenology consists of nothing but a long series of heretical deviations,[14] then there is hope that a systematic suggestion founded on a revision of one of its core ideas does not as such have to be disloyal and might develop one of its potentials previously concealed by other realizations.

2. FROM LATERAL TO MEDIAL PHENOMENOLOGY

Emmanuel Levinas was not only one of the earliest advocates of Edmund Husserl, he was also one of his earliest critics. What follows does not seek to discuss his multilayered and complex oeuvre that goes far beyond the phenomenological project but merely to draw on aspects of his interpretation of phenomenology

Newman's Lateralities

This is how Barnett Newman introduces his 1964 series of lithographs, *18 Cantos*:

> I should say that it was the margins made in printing a lithographic stone that magnetized the challenge that lithography has had for me from the very beginning. No matter what one does, no matter how completely one works the stone...the stone, as soon as it is printed, makes an imprint that is surrounded by inevitable white margins.[9]

In Newman, the contamination of the figure by the ground shining through, the autonomous life of the margins the artist describes here in the example of the lithographic process (fig. 5.1), refers back to a caesura in

FIGURE 5.1 Barnett Newman, *Canto VII from 18 Cantos* (1963/64), lithograph, composition 37 × 32.9 cm, paper 41 × 40.3 cm. © Barnett Newman Foundation / ProLitteris.

(Continued next page)

(*Continued*)

his work that may be described as the discovery of laterality. Since 1946, as Yve-Alain Bois reminds us, there is an increasing interest on Newman's part in symmetrical pictorial constructions. Works such as *Moment* (1946), for example, are composed of two halves separated by a vertical sallow-yellow central strip. Here, the painter later critically notes, he still presumes that the canvas is first of all "a void" the artist must populate with forms. The breakthrough occurs two years later, by his own account on January 29, 1948.

Newman has primed a canvas with brown paint and applied protective adhesive tape vertically across the canvas to test an orange blend. The result is disturbing: nothing can be added to what was supposed to be an intermediary step; the work has irreversibly reached its end. For months, Newman is brooding, convinced that he is allowed to continue painting only once he has understood the enigma of the work later to be called *Onement I*. At first sight, *Moment* and *Onement I* obey an analogous structure. A vertical stripe divides two halves situated symmetrically to each other. On closer inspection, however, speaking of image "halves" does not hold up in the case of *Onement*. Whereas in *Moment* the untreated ground articulates the two form-pregnant halves, *Onement*'s orange meandering vertical—Newman's famous "zip"—inversely welds the pictorial space together and lets the vibrating brown ground itself come to the fore. The centered zip of *Onement I*, which the painter immediately afterward brings out on a larger scale in *Onement II*, functions as an indexical usher for the body of the viewer who is assigned a place from which the space is to be opened up. The zip, which continues the vertical-symmetrical axis of the human body, as it were, allows the painted canvas to become an appearance for a spectator—in short: an image.

The discovery of the vertical as the visual organizing principle of all bipeds, however, immediately comes with its decentering. In the productive creative phase that follows the eureka moment of *Onement* (in 1949 alone, he produces eighteen works), Newman is working through the focalizing-centering mode of vision that, with some exceptions, characterizes Western pictorial conventions all the way to modernity. What was significant about the discovery of bilateral symmetry was, in Yve-Alain Bois's formulation, "less the central axis and the self-duplication—the *bi*—than the *laterality*, the lateral extension."[10] The dividing function of the zip assigns a place to viewers and, if they seek to view the entire surface, appeals to their marginal perceptive capacities by forcing them into a sideways movement. The zips, with whose exact arrangement on the canvas Newman experiments again and again over the years, develop a magnetizing attraction that ties the viewers' eyes to the image but at the same time makes it impossible for them to continue contemplating the image as a phenomenon of framing. As Newman drily remarks on a typed note tacked to the wall at a solo exhibition at the Betty Parsons Gallery in 1951, "There is a tendency to look at large pictures from a distance. The large pictures in this exhibition are intended to be seen from a short distance."[11] Photos of viewers whom Newman evidently placed with precise instructions, mostly in frontal and lateral views, seem to stage the incompossibility of viewpoints, the impossibility of a total view (fig. 5.2). Unlike the axis lines of the quattrocento, the zips are not guides providing rapid orientation in the image, nor are they to be understood on the model of Heinrich Wölfflin's baroque diagonals that internally endow the image with a dynamic. They are eminently visible; they are even themselves, as Newman

FIGURE 5.2 *Barnett Newman and an Unidentified Spectator in Front of Cathedra in the Studio of the Artist, 1958.* Photo by Peter A. Juley (detail). Peter A. Juley & Son Collection. Courtesy of Smithsonian American Art Museum.

(*Continued next page*)

(*Continued*)

himself stresses repeatedly, "surfaces and not lines." In *Untitled I* (1949), for example, the blue zip in the middle of the image is as wide as the ochre ground situated at the extreme left, separated by the second, yellow zip. The zips in themselves reveal the event of becoming-space and thereby simultaneously provoke an overtaxing of frontal vision, leading, in Gottfried Boehm's terms, to a "calculated failure in confronting the image."[12]

Thanks to this strategy of overtaxing, which cannot but drive the mechanism of identification insane, a space opens up, inversely, for another self-reflective process: where the constitution of something visible cannot be brought to an end, this very process itself becomes noticeable. Between a formalist reading interested only in the material properties of Newman's paintings (such as Donald Judd's exemplary description of *Vir heroicus sublimis*) and a cabbalistic interpretation à la Thomas Hess, which suspects an arcanum hidden in every pictorial element, we must acknowledge that Newman was interested in the event of becoming-visible in general.

and to complete it with those moments of his later thinking that promise a fruitful, intraphenomenological correction.

In his dissertation on *The Theory of Intuition in Husserl's Phenomenology* (1930), Levinas debates to what extent, for Husserl, there must necessarily always also be a representation at the basis of every intentionality. Although Husserl claims, in the fifth of the *Logical Investigations*, that not only so-called objectifying acts but *all* acts have intentional character, Levinas aims to demonstrate that only objectifying acts participate in the constitution of an identical (noematic) core and that all other acts, acts of evaluation or practical dealings, for example, are "grafted" onto this originary objective pole constituted in representational *phantasy*.[15] The objectifying act thus forms the backbone, as it were, of all phenomenological analysis; because of this basic structure, intentionality must be conceived of as unity-forming phantasy.

This is not the place to assess whether this criticism does justice to Husserl.[16] Undoubtedly, however, it inaugurates a tradition of criticizing intentionality that was successful in French phenomenology in particular.[17] Encouraged by Heidegger's diagnosis of the modern paradigm of re-presentation, this tradition objects to the subliminal telos of identification in phenomenology. Levinas himself in his later works discusses the objectivating impulse in Husserl under the heading "thematization": thematization always only concerns phenomena that are not conspicuous enough and need to be clarified, ultimately treating what is not thematic as a thematic object yet to come. Levinas here joins Eugen Fink, who considers Husserl's conceptual reduction of the horizon to that which the horizon makes accessible to be fundamentally mistaken: "Horizons," Fink writes, "are primarily 'withdrawings,' the making-accessible of the 'withdrawings' is really only a 'penetrating' into the horizons of withdrawing. . . . Husserl's approach to the constitutive problem of the horizons is an attempt at grasping the 'abstents' ['*Enthalte*'] through the 'contents' ['*Inhalte*'], the horizons through the intrahorizonal."[18] Insofar as eidetic variation can be operated only on the condition that there exist an identical that is maintained through all variations, insofar as the manifold maintains itself only by being conceived of as the variation of one and the same thing, there is, according to Levinas, a moment of violence that inheres in every intentional act. Although the object immanent to consciousness still has to be brought into evidence through a reduction, consciousness nonetheless always already *has* the object, as it were.

For Levinas, the necessary intentional *anticipation* (in referring to a cup in perception, I do not refer to one side of the cup but always already to the *whole* cup) is always a *violation*. When Husserl says that "at any moment, this something meant [*dieses Vermeinte*] is more—something meant with something more—than what is meant [*Gemeintes*] at that moment 'explicitly,'" this excess, which goes beyond *what* is meant, still remains *something* already meant.[19] Within the framework of the Husserlian telos of fulfillment, that which goes beyond the current experience would be merely something *not yet* experienced that nonetheless already exists within the boundaries of consciousness in the form of latent possibility.[20] Levinas famously opposes such an analogizing conception of thinking, which via appresentation is able to integrate what is unavailable to it, with an ethics of radical alterity that is no longer capable of reducing the excess in the face of the other to any kind of epistemological fact. According to Levinas, the other can never be "thematized" because she only ever appears in the past tense, as something irrecoverable or as "trace."

While there is perceptive commentary on the diachronous dimension of time—as opposed to being "present" in consciousness—it is less regularly pointed out that Levinas explicitly aims for a spatial displacement to avoid the reproach that his concept of the encountered "face" could still be subject to the law of frontal re-presentation. There is a lateral shift from the subjective *ipse* to the anonymous *ille*, whereby the Husserlian ideal of the adequation of sense becomes problematic: "The relation between signified and signification is, in the trace, not a correlation but *irrectitude* itself. . . . The significance of the trace puts us in a 'lateral' relation, inconvertible into rectitude (which is inconceivable in the order of unveiling and being) and responding to an irreversible past."[21]

While the idea of a lateral excess is indeed a link between Levinas and other phenomenologists, his completely diverging concept of transcendence separates him from them. For him, the motif of a "transcendency within immanency" to be found in Husserl and used extensively by Merleau-Ponty is a relic of a Cartesian philosophy of the subject.[22] Where every transgression is always bent back into a field of immanence (for Merleau-Ponty, the field of vision is "the model of every transcendence"),[23] all exteriority cannot but remain merely an "exteriority in immanence."[24] A real transcendence, such as Levinas favors, one that breaks through, is unthinkable within this framework.

Without bringing up in this context the entire debate about phenomenology's "theological turn" that Dominique Janicaud has identified via such symptomatic passages,[25] the following paragraphs seek to highlight several moments in Levinas's critique of Husserl that prepare a transcendentalism of a different kind, one that nonetheless remains strictly within the framework of immanent experience—and thus within the framework of a phenomenological project. Despite the ontological primacy of objectivity he ascribes to Husserl, Levinas grants his philosophy the achievement of having uncovered on the margins of its primary focus aspects that can lead to overcoming this very focusing. Despite all his criticism of Husserl's concept of the horizon, Levinas acknowledges that the horizonedness of existence not only traces the framework of possible cognition but, first of all, addresses the *situatedness* of a subject. The horizon implied in intentionality in each case represents not only an as yet confused, diffuse nexus of meaning but rather the place of the living body's existence. The fact of being embedded in a sensible world, which Levinas, like Merleau-Ponty, stresses, cannot be adequately grasped by any noetic-noematic structure but should rather be described as "proximity."

By "proximity," Levinas means all those constellations that cannot be objectified without thereby rendering them incomprehensible. Just as the living body cannot be *represented* because it cannot be *self-present*, so everything that surrounds a living body is not distant simply because it cannot be objectified. At least in those reflections on the "proximate" that lies outside the thematic field, Levinas, too, circles around those margins of Husserl's phenomenology I have called "lateral phenomenology." Thanks to Merleau-Ponty and Lyotard, a visible comes to bear that cannot be "surveyed from above" but rather insinuates itself into the gaze or, in Friedrich Nietzsche's expression, "come[s] on the feet of doves."[26] Even if the unforeseeable is not always extraordinary as well, it still

remains singular. Between a closedness of immanence within consciousness as
the field of projection of objects that appear, on the one hand, and the unattain-
ability of the absolutely transcendent, on the other, lies a fluctuating margin of
imminence. What is imminent is not thematically before our eyes but imposes
itself from the outside (Raphaël Gély in this context speaks of "marginal
transcendence").[27]

The revision of a restricted concept of intentionality manifests not only in a
certain kind of post-Husserlian phenomenology. Wolfgang Hogrebe's criticism
of a reductionist practice of semantics represents a structurally similar enterprise.[28] Under the heading "mantics" and the tradition connected with it,
Hogrebe is concerned with prepropositional forms of cognition, *gnoseologiae
inferiores*, as it were, that are called on whenever the outlines of the object of
cognition are not yet fixed. Unfamiliar situations, a dark room one is entering
into, for example, demand attention for every detail that might yield information on the situation as a whole. In situations of "not-knowing" that simultaneously contain a higher risk, every event must initially, as a matter of principle, be
interpreted to be significant. A certain, entirely undirected type of attention is
called for. Hogrebe himself understands "mantics" to be an "extension of semantics downward,"[29] yet his characterization of "mantic attention" could just as
easily be recast to apply to an aesthetic attention. It is generally said of the aesthetic attitude that it brackets the recognizing-identifying gaze and that its
floating attention makes a particular sensibility toward situatedness possible.
Moments of risk and structures of aesthetic experience resemble each other in
that in them, the marginal field of attention is in particular demand. Where the
everyday orientation toward the *what* retreats, fields of possibility open up for
something new and unforeseeable. Those who step out of goal-oriented action, it
is said, can let themselves be surprised.

The formulation *let oneself be surprised* already indicates that what is at issue
here is neither mere activity nor a something we would be passively subjected to
but rather a dimension in which the grammatical "medium" of early Indo-
Germanic languages lives on: in the aesthetic attitude, what can come to
attention—provided one *lets it happen to* oneself—is what usually remains
unnoticed. This letting is not a subservient submission, but neither is it a violent
transgression from the outside. This might be the very place where the narrow
line between *passivity* and *mediality* runs. Pure pathos always represents an
intrusion into the present order, it is extraordinary and always bears traumatic
traits. Medial processes, by contrast, let singularities step forward within the
existent order. Pure happenings-to immediately penetrate the flesh; they refuse
any kind of phenomenality. Medial events, by contrast, let something become

visible. *What* becomes visible this way is not already determined, only *that* it can become visible.

As Martin Seel stresses, such a *letting* (*lassen*) can be assigned exclusively neither to activity nor to passivity. To *permit* something (*etwas zulassen*) is to allow for things to happen of which one is not the author. To *get oneself involved* in something (*sich auf etwas einlassen*) is to "permit not knowing with full determinedness what will happen to oneself in the course of one's action." Every getting oneself involved thus also contains "an affirmation of the undeterminable in the determinedness of thinking and acting."[30] To describe what Seel situates between active and passive, I would like, in what follows, to rehabilitate the grammatical form of the *middle voice*. Beside the two *genera verbi* active and passive, ancient Greek—like other Indo-Germanic languages—has the so-called middle voice for activities the subject is neither wholly uninvolved in nor the sole author of but in which it participates "coconstitutively," as it were (classical examples include being born and sacrificing oneself).

The Greek grammarian Dionysius Thrax (c. 170–90 BCE) distinguishes between these three *genera* as follows: beside *energeia* indicating activity and *pathos* indicating a happening-to, there is an intermediate form that he tentatively calls *mesotēs*.[31] Similar to the name *Metaphysics*, which was invented in embarrassment by the editor Andronicus of Rhodes and yet, as that which comes "after the physics," fits the subject matter, Dionysius's word *mesotēs* names, beyond the intermediate position between active and passive, something of the medial character. With Dionysus, grammar shifts over against earlier models that distinguished only between an active and a medial-reflective form.[32] Linguistic archaeology has shown that such reflections on the *diatheseis* or "positions" of the verb developed from music: descriptions by Greek grammarians like Dionysius almost seamlessly adopt a typology in music of aesthetic attitudes or *diatheseis* between *energeia* and *pathos*.[33] As a genus of the verb, the middle voice nonetheless had only a short history: already in Latin, it is considered to be a *passivum* that has "shed" its passivity, as it were (*modus deponens*), and in other languages, too, it lives on only in marginal forms, for example, in the factitive case of "letting do."[34] The *triton genos* of the middle voice was forgotten not just in linguistics; philosophers usually grant it no more than a cursory remark. In historical studies on the concept of the phenomenon, the morphological particularity of *phainesthai*—the fact that the verb's form is the middle voice—is not mentioned at all.[35]

Yet what does it mean that Greek thought characterizes appearing with a verb form that is neither passive nor active but precisely "medial"? Following the first anticipation in chapter 2.5, we can now bring together the threads of our analysis of Aristotle (chap. 2) and the chapter on phenomenology (chap. 4). The first step consists in recapitulating the guidelines of "phenomenological technique" to bring out its blind spots.

3. APPEARING IS APPEARING-THROUGH: EIDETIC, TRANSCENDENTAL, AND MEDIAL ASPECTS

What appears can be questioned in a number of ways. *Whether* something is and *what* something is, this basic Aristotelian distinction is translated by Thomist scholasticism into the categories of the *an sit* and the *quid sit*.[36] *Whether* something is designates its *existence*; *what* something is in turn designates its *essence*. The existential *an sit* thus represents something merely accidental, just an *addition*.[37] In Kantian terms: for Thomism, existence is not a real predicate; it always remains external to essence and does not touch upon it.[38] Husserl both moves away and continues Thomist scholasticism by other means when he claims, on the one hand, that every essence can always only be read off something actually occurring and, on the other hand, that for the essence, each occurrence is contingent. Husserl reformulates the classic pair *existence* and *essence* as *matter of fact* and *essence*.[39] The difference between essence and fact is that essence "designate[s] what is to be found in the very own being of an individuum as the What of an individuum," while factual being-such is accidental: "in respect of its essence it could be otherwise."[40] Identifying a What, of course, does not remain a privilege of philosophical cognition; it takes place in our everyday orientation in the world, every time we recognize a note as a high C, name a geometrical figure, or identify a type of tree.[41] What the *Logical Investigations* call "ideative abstraction" and what the *Ideas* name "seeing of essences" thus methodologically concludes a process that is continually practiced in the everyday attitude as well. The phenomenological highlighting of a *what* or *eidos* thus simply consists in something *showing* itself as what it is *itself*.

What something is in itself, of course, points back to the Aristotelian *autò kath'autò*, the formula of ontological self-identity. Yet what relationship is there between a phenomenology that rests on a *tautophenomeny* (the task is to let see what shows itself by itself) and traditional ontology, which is supported by an *ontotautology* (being as being-itself)? While Husserl consistently refuses any kind of definite ontological statement, his students in the Göttingen circle (Adolf Reinach, Hedwig Conrad-Martius, Moritz Geiger, Roman Ingarden, and others) propagated phenomenological eidetics as a rejection of any kind of idealism and the foundation of a realism of ideas. The being-in-itself of the phenomenon showing itself "lies beyond all the historical philosophical differences between mere appearance and metaphysical in-itself. It would therefore be better ... to call it, for example, theory of essence." According to Conrad-Martius, essence must first be understood as something *given* and thereby *positive* and second as something distinct from factual data, a merely *eidetic datum*, as it were: "There are empirical data but there are essential data as well."[42]

But what ontological consequences result from the separation of fact and essence, facticity and validity? How is Husserl's proposition to be understood that "the essence (Eidos) is a new sort of object?"[43] Are we dealing, to stick to scholastic terminology, with a *distinctio realis* or merely a *distinctio rationis*? This question famously sparked the controversy between, on the one side, the Göttingen circle, which would argue for the first interpretation and considers Husserl's transcendental turn after the *Logical Investigations* to be a betrayal of the basic distinction of essence and matter of fact, and, on the other side, later phenomenologies that take up the *Ideas* and consider it indispensable to bring this distinction back to its shared transcendental ground.

Besides the *eidetic reduction*, whose ontological implications he summarizes in the *Ideas'* first, methodological chapter ("Matter of Fact and Essence"), Husserl develops the procedure of *transcendental reduction*. The question is: What makes the capturing of essence possible in the first place? If the eidos is not to turn into a Platonist hypostasis, it must be clear how the essence can become the essence of a specific matter of fact and, inversely, how the essence, in eidetic variation, can be obtained from matters of fact. According to Husserl, this connecting act is performed by transcendental consciousness. While eidetic reduction cannot fully secure itself against the potential suspicion of psychologism, a clarification of the medium of consciousness "*in* which this and all being present— for 'us'—'makes' itself through certain apperceptions" is tasked with finding safe ground.[44]

Over against the mathematical ideal of objectivity, there is the example of perception, which must from the outset conceive of identity differently. Identity here does not stand at the end of an eidetic *anabasis* but is initially given in every adumbration; invariant selfness can be experienced only where altering variation is possible. The method of going through varieties of an object's properties, of course, leads to a limit at which the object modified in phantasy is no longer what it is. Without this specific set of properties, however, the object is not simply *nothing* but merely some other thing. As Merleau-Ponty rightly remarks, eidetic variation thus reveals "the *Sosein* and not the *Sein*," being-such, not being, not the *what*, as Husserl thought, but the *how*.[45]

Yet how is this to be reconciled with Husserl's claim that in perception, it is not simply a depiction of the things (which might look *like* the thing itself) that appears to us? Is there not a risk of falling back into the doctrine of images the *Logical Investigations* were supposed to overcome? At this point—and to open up the path to a different concept of mediality—we have to go back to the problem of "self-giving" once more. How are we to understand the assertion that what is given in empirical intuition is not a mediating representative but *the thing itself*? In his still-unsurpassed study on the relationship between time and perception in Husserl, Gérard Granel has shown how selfsameness (the *tauton*) can be *given* only on the condition that it always remain inadequate because different. The fact that the table always appears as *such and such* is the condition for it not to appear as *wholly different*. The table is thus *given* and it *itself* is given— these are not two different matters of fact but "one and the same," *unum et idem*.[46] The table's self-identity does not lie concealed behind the phenomena as an inaccessible essence but lies nowhere else but in the temporal structuring of the procedural phenomenon *table* itself. Despite the filiation Husserl himself choses, his phenomenology turns out to be inspired not so much by a Platonic-Kantian *horismos* as by an Aristotelian-Hegelian *Also*. In other words: *kath'autò* and *pros hēmas* must always be thought together.[47]

Referred back to the theory of adumbration, this means that that which appears always appears *different* than what it *is* but never as *something different*. What *shows* itself as an invariant self-identity (and what can neither be had as detached entity nor be produced in any way) shows itself only through that which it itself, in a pure state, *is not*, through a contingent facticity that cannot be derived from its *eidos*. To the extent that the thing, insofar as it appears, depends on a horizon of appearance, each new partial capturing opens up a new horizonal structure that refers to the fundamental inadequacy and nonconcludedness of every experience. Intuition as such is conceivable only in temporal syntheses of the manifold; as a matter of principle, an object appears "only through the medium of an appearance relief [*Erscheinungsrelief*]," and not even the hypothetical intuition of God could, according to Husserl, escape this law.[48] In that sense, phenomenology could indeed be called what Rickert called it, a "philosophy of immediacy," provided that immediacy is always conditioned by operative mediacy. Accordingly, phenomenology represents—to adapt a formula of Helmuth Plessner's—a philosophy of "mediated immediacy." Self-giving, we might summarize this reading of Husserl's theory of adumbration, constitutively depends on taking place *through something different* or, in a word: *phenomenality is transphenomenality, every appearing is an appearing-through*.

These observations open up the field of a phenomenology that *that no longer starts with intentionality but with mediality*. Media in that sense would first of all be that "something different" that lets something *itself* appear. The research domain of *medial phenomenology* would thus concern above all the *medial difference* between *that which* appears and that *through which* it appears. This, however, leaves unanswered how this medial difference is distinct from the transcendental difference discussed earlier. Does not the analysis of the theory of adumbration merely discover the laws of what is required as the condition of possibility of appearance? There are, scattered across Husserl's transcendental philosophy, possible starting points for a medial phenomenology that seeks not only to describe preconditions and their laws but possibilizations as they take place, yet these do not suffice for a full and consistent elaboration. The path there might lead via a rereading of Aristotle's media theory, which we can now use as the corrective of a phenomenology that sees in intentionality the "universal medium" as such.[49]

4. ELEMENTARY VISUALITY

A philosophy of appearances remains short-sighted as long as it does not consider the horizon of its own possibility; a philosophy of the conditions of possibility remains formalistic as long as it cannot explain why this and not that concrete becoming-visible is taking place. Both, as it were, mistake the moment of the instantiation of visibility, the former because it conceives of appearances as instant-like and immediate, the latter because it subordinates the process of *instantiation* to that which they instantiate in. But how is this medium of visibility to be conceived of? According to Kant, space and time as the a priori forms of intuition cannot be perceived "in themselves."[50] Yet is this addition "in themselves" not superfluous? If space and time are the condition for anything to appear, it would seem plausible to state that they never appear at all. Husserl's advances toward a material a priori open a breach to a different, not just formal conception of the medium.[51] Kant's addition, "in themselves," on this reading, is to be interpreted to suggest that the forms of intuition are to be perceivable if not in themselves then at least *differently*, that they can be derived not just from reason but from aisthesis.[52] Space and time would accordingly be not just conditions but possibilizations of singular appearances that take place not only *within* their limits but also *through* these restrictions.

When he seeks to describe time not as form but as "element," Goethe famously takes up an ancient notion of perception media with whose help things are being aisthetized. But he is not the only one. Heidegger too does so in seeking to keep Husserl's concept of the phenomenon clear of neo-Kantian misunderstandings. "*Phainomenon*," he says in the Marburg *Introduction to Phenomenological Research*, "means something that shows itself. *Phainomai* is the same as 'to show itself,' *phainō* the same as 'to bring something to the light of day.'"[53] "*Phainomai* or *phainesthai*," we then read in the methodological section 7 of *Being and Time*, "is a middle-voiced form which comes from *phainō*—to bring to the light of day, to put in the light," and this "light" is being defined as "that wherein something can become manifest, visible in itself," or, in the Marburg lecture, as "something of the sort that lets something else be seen through it . . . *diaphanes*."[54]

Although elsewhere he does indeed turn the grammatical middle voice into a figure of thought,[55] Heidegger draws surprisingly little profit from these observations: he neither appropriates the middle voice of the verb theoretically nor comments on the element of seeing in detail. In the economy of the text, Heidegger's "in the light" rather has a strategic function and serves as a shifter, as it were, between Aristotle and Kant. In a first step, he equates the diaphanous (*diaphanēs*) and light (*phōs*) and translates them indiscriminately with *Helle*, "clarity" or "light"; in a second step, he identifies Aristotle's remark that the object of perception appears *en phōti*, in the light, with the forms of intuition *in which* something appears; in a third step, finally, he replaces these forms of intuition with the formula of the "the Being of beings" at the basis of every appearing, which anticipates the core of the *Kant* book's ontological argumentation.[56]

Such ontological alignments drew sharp criticism, not least from Emmanuel Levinas. To avoid them, the Lithuanian-French philosopher in *Totality and Infinity* develops a different concept of the phenomenal element that neither lives up to a formal theory of transcendentals nor requires ontological categories. Between infinity and finite beings, there is "the elemental" that as an unlimited but for all that not yet immaterial medium amounts to a thinned-out "content without form." Intentional directedness, instrumental use, and, finally, technical operationality, according to Levinas, do not at all consist in action on the elemental environment; all means and instruments themselves, rather, are taken from that primary medium that makes them all possible in the first place. The elemental milieu, moreover, "has its own density," although it can never be condensed into a graspable objectivity.[57]

Levinas's thinking of elementarity, in turn, can be related to Merleau-Ponty's phenomenology of mediality. Merleau-Ponty develops Husserl's notion of the living body as the point zero or transcendental originary pole, elaborated in *Ideas 2*, in the sense that he does not merely elevate the living body to the status of a material-logical necessity but sees in it the only possibility of holding together the two diverging parts of phenomenology: its intuitionism and its life-world teleology. To overcome subjectivism, however—as Renaud Barbaras has shown—it does not suffice to liberate corporeality from being a mere condition of our existence and declare it to be its essential determination (or even its *existential*).[58] It can be shown that Merleau-Ponty in the *Phenomenology of Perception* still thinks corporeality in terms of the *own-ness* of one's own living body but not in terms of *becoming a living body* that would precede any separation of subject and object.[59] The book nonetheless contains the beginnings of a thinking of corporeality as mediality, which moves to the foreground in the late oeuvre.[60]

In the *Phenomenology of Perception* already, the living body, despite an undeniable primacy of *ownness*, is not exhausted by the factual-physical body in space; it is always already a "virtual body" that produces and modifies an environment.[61] The living body institutes a spatial structure that "is not the milieu (real or logical) in which things are laid out, but rather the means by which the position of things becomes possible."[62] The unfinished late work, *The Visible and the Invisible*, radicalizes this insight ontologically: a living body is capable of ordering objects, giving them validity, and letting them become visible only because there is already a bond that exists between it and the objects. All the problems of the subject–object dichotomy that, according to a very self-critical Merleau-Ponty, still underlie the *Phenomenology of Perception* derive from a subject (however embodied) still being thought as *standing over against* the world. With Hans Blumenberg we might say that we do not look *onto the world* like onto a panorama built for a one-eyed Polyphemus. Rather, because of our constitutive two-eyedness, joined by the mobility of our living body, we always look *into the world*.[63]

If all seeing is always already an approximation, then this approximation is due to a stepping back that lets some aspects step forward and others step back into the depth. This simultaneous approximation through distancing, meanwhile, can be thought only if that which is visible and that which sees "are made of the same stuff," a stuff that pervades them. Seeing is always a seeing *of* the visible, not only as *genitivus obiectivus* but as *genitivus subiectivus* as well. Using the term with a positive connotation, every perception for Merleau-Ponty is "narcissistic" in that it is necessarily always thrown back onto itself. He names this common stuff "flesh" (*chair*), to be understood as "the formative medium of the object and the subject."[64] We are beings in the flesh not because we have a living body; there can be living bodies in the world because it is the nature of the world to be flesh.[65] With the expression *chair*, which he opposes to the *corps propre*,

Merleau-Ponty accordingly seeks to indicate a dimension that escapes any kind of substantiality or essentiality, any kind of "property." *La chair* does not found anything, it merely articulates; it is not contained in a body but rather, as inter-corporeality, structures bodies. For Merleau-Ponty, it must be thought on the model of the pre-Socratics' "element" in which we move.[66] This elementality, which using Saussurean terminology he also characterizes as "diacritical," lies neither in the things nor outside them; in Merleau-Ponty's late ontology, it shows how the fundamental mode of being of all things must be understood as an *être-parmi*: on the one hand, as a topological "being-among"; on the other, as an almost causal "being-through(-something)."[67]

Merleau-Ponty, who described himself as "no great Aristotelian,"[68] does not establish an explicit link with Aristotle's medium of perception. The proximity, however, is hard to ignore. In writing "Eye and Mind," Merleau-Ponty solidifies his point that the elementary medium of perception must be thought neither corporally nor immaterially by describing the functioning of the diaphanous aqueous element: "When through the water's thickness I see the tiling at the bottom of a pool, I do not see it despite the water and the reflections there; I see it through them and because of them. If there were no distortions, no ripples of sunlight, if it were without this flesh that I saw the geometry of the tiles, then I would cease to see it as it is and where it is—which is to say, beyond any identical, specific place."[69]

The mediality of perception thus produces an unstoppable atopy: what appears always appears differently and in a different place than it should. This experienced elsewhere, however, is not a second, merely representational place of mirroring; it questions the very possibility of an elsewhere existing in itself.[70] Against Husserl's notion of the positivity of essence, taken up by the Göttingen Circle in particular, Merleau-Ponty thinks that "there is no positive vision that would definitively give me the essentiality of the essence." Inversely, this also puts an end to a certain view, of a Kantian inspiration, that sees in essence merely a regulative, ultimately unattainable ideal. When identical structures form in intuition and in the concept, they do not do so as preliminary surrogates of a total grasp accessible to an unlimited subject. The distinction between matter of fact and essence, between genesis and validity ultimately remains artificial and thereby still beholden to the "dream of a variation of the thing that would elimi-nate from it all that is not authentically itself and would make it appear all naked."[71]

God's intuition itself, as Husserl repeatedly says, depends on going through all the perspectives. The notion of a total intuition would thus be like that of a wooden iron. There are, therefore, no essences without time and space that would come unmoored, like icebergs made of indivisible entities. With "Being no longer being before me, but surrounding me and in a sense traversing me, and my vision of Being not forming itself from elsewhere, but from the midst of Being," matter of fact and essence are no longer distinguishable.[72] "Defining philosophy as the search for the essences" or "as the fusion with the things" means resolving philosophy in pure transparency or in materialized opacity. Rationalist positivism and materialist mysticism are much closer to each other than might be supposed: at the basis of both is a metaphysics of coincidence that remains blind to the geneses of meaning that are continually taking place.[73] Merleau-Ponty's indirect ontology must thus be understood as a medial ontology: "The sensible is precisely that medium in which there can be being without it having to be posited; the sensible appearance of the sensible . . . is Being's unique way of manifesting itself without becoming positivity, without ceasing to be ambiguous and transcendent."[74]

The Aristotelian ontology of substance that Merleau-Ponty is working through critically to develop a medial process ontology nonetheless undeniably points back to a different Aristotle who would be much closer to a modern complementarity theory. The Aristotelian–Merleau-Pontyan condition of possibilization sketched here leads to a redefinition of the classical concept of the a priori. The a priori morphs from being a *that in which* as the form of all possible contents of intuition to being a *that through which* that manifests as instantiating concrete forms. Be it mediated by the apparatus of perception or by technical dispositifs, every visibility is at first due to apparatuses of visibilization or, to put in a formula, *everything appearing is always already apparative.*[75]

5. TRANSPARENCY AND INTERFERENCE

Merleau-Ponty's intuition that beings are only ever given mediately and that every appearing is always already a shining through would not seem strange to a thinker whom contemporary media theory has rightly enthroned as one of its forerunners: Fritz Heider.[76] In his essay "Ding und Medium" (Thing and Medium, 1926), Heider pursues the question of what it means that something is presentified for us through signs, that we hear the sound of the bell through the air or that, as the proverb has it, we are looking through the eyes into another man's soul.[77] Here, too, Heider's prime example for the notion of an "external conditionality" (*Außenbedingheit*) of all medial events—what, using Sybille Krämer's terms, might be termed the *heteronomy* of media—is transparent air:

in looking at a house, what there is "before my eye" is "the transparent air. Of it, I am not perceiving anything, I am looking through it."[78]

Heider's main goal is to criticize what we may call the objectifying bias: we attribute to things what in fact pertains to the environment in which they appear. The environing perceptual medium escapes traditional knowledge, by virtue of the law according to which we do not know that which we are immersed in. Heider's ideas anticipate what Marshall McLuhan often liked to illustrate with the example of life under water: the only thing that fish know absolutely nothing about is water because, for them, there is no counterenvironment that would allow them to perceive the element they live in. One explanation for this ignorance is that the way we conceive of knowledge: for something to be the object of knowledge, it must be able to present itself as an "ob-ject," that is, it must be in a position of frontal opposition, in the mode of the *Gegen-Stand*, as the German has it, of that which "stands against" us. But the point, precisely, is that we are never in front of a medium: most of the time, we pay no attention to the medium's efficacy. And because that is so, the same thing can end up appearing, in a different light, as something else.

Take the example of lighting effects. Under the effect of yellow light, a white wall may appear yellow. This raises the question, so often repeated by skeptical philosophers, of what allows us to argue that in reality the wall is not yellow but white. If already a simple light variation fundamentally changes the perceptual nature of the thing, then maybe the perceptual quality is not an objectual quality inherent to the thing. The reasons for this "obliviousness" of the medium should be remembered every time the trope of the transparency of the medium is invoked, every time, that is, someone repeats the commonplace in media theory that media function all the better the more they merge with their use, the more they distract from themselves and do not impede the bridging of distances. For Heider, a transparent medium is far from being immaterial. Rather, it receives imprints, with which, thanks to its inner structure, it resonates without dissonance: it is "in tune." When, on the contrary, the medium's "own laws," the way it is self-organized or resists the imprint, gain the upper hand, "turbidities" and "perturbations" arise.[79]

Just as Heidegger's analyses of equipment had to wait to be applied in media theory, Heider's thinking of media remained relatively unnoticed until Niklas Luhmann took it up in his systems theory.[80] The conceptual pair *transparency* and *perturbation* received a theoretical foundation proper, some twenty years after Heider's essay, in information theory. In 1948 Claude Elwood Shannon published "A Mathematical Theory of Communication" in the Bell Laboratories' in-house journal, and one year later, expanded by an essay by Warren

Weaver, the text appeared in book form. For Shannon, "The fundamental problem of communication is that of reproducing at one point either exactly or approximately a message selected at another point."[81] According to this conception, the process of communication is preceded by the message it is based on, while the process of communication itself is merely limited to transmitting the integral message as transparently as possible.

The decisive point of this often criticized but rarely read channel theory of communication is that the degree of transparency and the degree of perturbation always correlate. Pure transparency for Shannon is identical to being fully known, in which case there is no transmission. For there to be any exchange, a minimum of nonidentity or uncertainty must be presupposed, which manifests itself in perturbations. Where no perturbation is possible and the information content is already known, the information value, too, tends toward zero: in Shannon's definition, information is the degree of uncertainty in a transmission of messages that, as a matter of principle, takes place "in the presence of noise."[82] At the other end of the spectrum, however—and this rule became the cardinal principle of later cryptography—pure perturbation is indistinguishable from pure information. If everything dissolves in noise, everything is equally significant—and equally insignificant.

This is where the paradox of Shannon's thesis lies. On the one hand, he explicitly excludes the dimension of meaning from his theory of communication: "Frequently the messages have *meaning*. . . . These semantic aspects of communication are irrelevant to the engineering problem."[83] On the other hand, it is precisely this emphatic claim that becomes a conjuration, as if it were a matter of immunizing a purely technical theory of communication against contamination by the problem of meaning. Of course it is irrelevant for a theory of information whether units of information refer to objects outside of the communication process, whether the language used is formal or natural. Yet for the information content, the perturbation factor that allows the transferred dataset to be meaningful in the first place is anything but irrelevant. While the repetition of the message, understood as redundancy, is a means for reducing noise insofar as it allows the correctness of the transmission to become measurable, every repetition of the message in turn corrodes the information value of the message. What today counts as a sensation tomorrow disgraces the newspaper that prints it too late. For Shannon, the entropic tendency toward an increase in information can be traced all the way to what would be pure redundancy or white noise: what's being twittered from every tree is no longer information, only noise.

Whether an information is informative thus does not depend on any kind of transparency between the message at the beginning and the message at the end but rather on its relationship with the diffuse background from which it stands out. Using Gregory Bateson's succinct example, we may say that the degree of information something has is measured by what it negates: in that sense, a Chinese character would be more informative than a letter in the Greek alphabet because it excludes not twenty-five but thousands of other possibilities.[84] Unlike later theories of communication—and also unlike Norbert Wiener's cybernetics—information is thus not a category that would be superordinate to and capable of structuring noise. Instead, information and perturbation are symmetrically dependent on each other. When cognitive processes endow moments of perturbation with value, they do so not against but on the basis of Shannon's mathematical theory of communication.

In 1966 Michel Foucault, in "Message or Noise?," returned to this symmetry to shed light on the historical contingency of medical symptoms.[85] Against the notion advanced by the psychiatrist Michael Balint, according to which the body emits signals the physician simply has to decode, Foucault asserts that this presupposes a specific epistemic frame to determine in the first place where messages can arise and where they cannot. Some parts of the body make noise, as it were, and are thus potentially significant; others remain completely mute within such a frame and are thus left out. Whether as an asemantic "nonsilence of the organs" or as an eloquent symptom, the language of the body awaiting its interpretation is in any event already caught in the webs of relevance. That is why noise merely seems to oppose the order of meaning: only against the backdrop of expectations of meaningfulness can noise be perceived at all. Michel Serres, too, in his essay on the figure of the parasite, skillfully presents the subterranean solidarity of transparency and perturbation: "The counternorm is never a noise of the norm but the same norm reversed, that is to say, its twin. If you make a motor turn in reverse, you do not break it: you build a refrigerator."[86]

The reason why transparency and perturbation still remain, despite all criticism, the basic operators of media theory lies in a de facto preference that characterizes all twentieth-century media theories: the *digital a priori*, which can be derived both historically and methodologically.

(1) *Historically*, the digital a priori is due to the fact that the question of mediality made it onto the agenda only in the wake of the introduction of mass media—digital mass media in particular. It was the radical change digitalization, and thereby the progressive detachment of the medial content from its

medial form, marked in the history of media that made mediality an acute problem for theory and demanded, on the model of a general theory of signs, a general theory of media.[87] The fact that the historical condition of a change of media brought about a general reflection about mediality that included all media (and thus not just digital, not even just technical media) does not annul the preferential perspective that makes media that operate by discretizing the model of mediality as such.

(2) *Methodologically*, the digital a priori is founded on the kinship between computing digital apparatuses and a certain rational logic of thinking. A media philosophy in that case is all the easier to elaborate because it leaves the premises of its own economy of thought untouched: digitality is the property not of an object but of a procedure.[88] This procedure is that of reducing complexity. The basic cultural operation, which consists in reducing a complex state of affairs to its "essentials," remains resource-intensive as long as a given reduction procedure is made to depend on that which is to be reduced. The digitalizing procedure inverses this order and applies the same method of discretizing independently of how a given field is configured. The digitalizing procedure thus obtains a solution not only via detaching (*ana-lysis*) individual subproblems from each other but also by treating all the subelements produced by the standardized parsing the same way. In a way similar to the formation in philosophy of a concept of a *calculus universalis* thanks to Descartes and Leibniz, the universal Turing machines of the twentieth century, on a technological level, provide processors that make complexities calculable.[89] The separation between semantic structure and medial substrate allows for decisive cultural achievements (for example through the autonomization of processes of transmission and reception, of storage and interpretation) but promotes a concept of media that is far from neutral.

The fundamental opposition between transparency in the process and the self-thematization of media in perturbations—this much should be clear—can be developed only via the example of those media in which the medial support does not influence the meaning of which they are the vehicle. Such a digital a priori turns mediality into the "accursed share" that intervenes in processes of meaning at most as a "haunting" or as the negative counterfigure to the semantic. In fact, the basic definition of the medial that holds that media operate all the better "the more transparent they remain, the more inconspicuously they linger below the threshold of our attention," undoubtedly works better for digital modes of presentation than it does for analog ones.[90] In presentative media in which, as a matter of principle, every difference counts (as the most basic definition of the analog has it), there can be no question of separating the what from the how, the content of presentation from the medium of presentation.[91] Now, the analog and the digital do not relate to each other like mirror-images: while what is analog can, as a matter of principle, be digitalized or discretized ever further, a retranslation is only ever possible partially and with losses. The analog-continuous and the digital-disjunctive thus confront each other asymmetrically. Because of this asymmetry, a system of explanation reduced to a finite alphabet of meaning supports can only partly do justice to forms of presentation where, as a matter of principle, there is always yet another element to be found between any two elements or, put differently, where interstices do not function as an outside but always already intrinsically belong to the very texture.

There are thus good reasons not to explain analog forms of presentation (which, beside all nuanced phenomena such as gestures, dance, or voice, also and eminently include images) according to the schema of transparency and perturbation. In what follows, the question is not just to what extent the description of medial processes in analog processes might demand specific new concepts but moreover to what extent a media theory in the spirit of the analog—and, within the frame of this book, of the *iconic* in particular—might furnish perspectives for a general concept of media that would closely interlock with the concept of the phenomenon.

6. THE EXEMPLARITY OF THE IMAGE: AGAINST PURE VISIBILITY

Although images are able to make their materiality step back in order to allow for the view onto what allegedly lies behind them, it must be asserted, against a long (and not just Albertian) tradition of window metaphors, that precisely what distinguishes images from other forms of presentation—citing Gottfried Boehm, we might speak of "strong," citing Hans-Georg Gadamer, of "eminent" pictoriality[92]—lies in the inseparable copresence of shape and makeup, of the plasticity that makes visible and the objectness that becomes visible. Acknowledging that the material obeys its own laws is not a provisional transitory stage for obtaining an iconic *as*, one that would allow for detaching the signified from its sign support. Rather, the material ground and the figure that stands out oscillate continuously; the visible is, as it were, steeped in the materiality in which it appears. Brushstroke, impasto and paint application, shine, shading, and support—materiality is not a dispensable parergon of the image but, as type or style, constitutively participates in the visible.

It is a subtle but ultimately decisive nuance that separates the concept of materiality deployed by such image-theoretical approaches from the one used in Shannon-inspired media theories. Of course a project devoted to "exorcizing the human spirit from the humanities" presents itself above all as rehabilitating the materiality of culture.[93] Yet, as Sybille Krämer has noted, remnants of such a spirit survive even where it was allegedly chased out long ago. As ghost in the machine, the fundamentalism of apparatuses participates in a grand gesture of unavoidability that the philosophical *esprit* disavowed by media theory indulged in all too often.[94] Such technicist media fundamentalism not only dresses transcendental a prioris in new garb, it also—and this is more serious— repeats the two-world doctrine such a priories are based on. The unspoken, because fantasmatic, goal of such a media theory is uncovering a pure medium: only by leaving the empirical aside, such a view holds, only by bracketing the practical implementation, as it were, can the medium come into appearance. What in static phenomenology was performed by the methodological procedure of the *epokhē* is now left to the anonymous, material-bound perturbation, where the medium no longer shows anything but itself.

At least where pictorial phenomena are concerned, such oppositions remain dubitable. There are no pure self-images, just as there are no images of pure alterity. The reflexivity of the iconic thus names less a reference back to the pure presence of the image support than one to an always already preceding self-reduplication of the deictic function: images do not only show something, they also always show *how* they show. The extent to which images make visible what appears on and in them can be seen in them. Images thus prove to be exemplary cases for spelling out the phenomenological rearticulation of the transcendental-philosophical question that marks modernity. The ground of possibility of the aisthetic is always inscribed in the aisthetic as a visible watermark; as such, this ground can by definition not only be thought but be experienced as well. We see, in Merleau-Ponty's terms, not *despite* but *through* and *by means of* the medium of the visible. What is needed, then, is a thinking along or according to (*selon*) the images.[95] The result of this shift is that iconic phenomena no longer are regional applications of a general media theory but instead constitute the guiding thread for a different thinking of the medial that would open new paths besides the ones already taken.

In a number of texts, Lambert Wiesing, who explicitly conceives of his agenda as a phenomenological one, makes a similar suggestion. For him, what is to be observed in Husserl's analyses of the image is the difference between genesis and validity. A real hat and a hat presented in an image are similar in that they are both *visible*. The visibility of the image hat, however, differs from the visibility of the real hat in that the pictured hat is "no longer subject to the laws of physics."[96] The decisive point of Husserl theory of the image is not what is being *signified* in the image (the image-subject) but only what becomes *visible* there. And, according to Wiesing, the only thing that becomes visible is the image-object. The visibility of the image-object can hardly be confused with the visibility of a physical-material object, since the image-object "does not grow older; it cannot have light shed on it; it cannot be touched; it cannot be examined under a microscope; it cannot move; it cannot trigger any physical effects; and it cannot be looked at from the side."[97] In short, the visible image-objects are, as Wiesing, drawing on Hans Jonas, writes, "removed from the causal commerce of things."[98]

Nonetheless, for Wiesing, such an interruption of causality is not yet to be equated with a logic of perturbation. Rather, on his reading, the image functions as a medium of isolation that replaces physical visibility (and the laws of alterability that come with it) with *pure* visibility. The historical tradition of formal aesthetics associated with the names Zimmermann, Riegl, Wölfflin, and above all Fiedler to which Wiesing dedicated his *The Visibility of the Image* would thus be continued by Husserl and Merleau-Ponty, who are thereby included in a Kantian scenario.[99] According to Wiesing, the project of uncovering a pure visibility released from the "present dictates of the physical world" and "cleansed of mundane traffic in causes and effects"[100]—a project he identifies with Fiedler and with phenomenology—is to be understood as countering the Hegelian figure of the "Also" the *Phenomenology of Spirit* speaks of: "The typically Kantian concept 'pure' here names the exact opposite of Hegel's 'also': the image-object—the object we see in the image—consists exclusively, and not among other things, of visibility. The image thus appears as a technique for being able to produce a certain kind of visible things—namely things that are only-visible."[101] Wiesing correlates the notion of the "only-visible," which he borrows from Robert Musil, with Husserl's "validity." Just as Husserl in the *Prolegomena* makes a distinction between the specific, always causally determined making of the judgment $2 \times 2 = 4$ and the established truth that $2 \times 2 = 4$, so the visible image-object is to be conceived of as a pure validity completely freed from its factual genesis.[102]

Yet introducing the problem of validity via the mathematical example is misleading, if only because, as Wiesing himself points out, it suggests that validity is identical with truth. For Husserl, however, validity is no more to be equated with transtemporal truth than it is to be immediately derived from the empirical. The expression *validity* instead indicates that something is in a certain way *binding*.[103] Because validity is binding, it connects and assembles the different ways in which it is being referred to. The precondition for agreeing about correctness or falseness is that the participants refer not only to the *same* but to the *selfsame* thing.[104] The image would thus find its deeper significance in the image-object because the image-object has conclusively operated the detachment from the causal genesis; all that is left is "visible validity." In short: "What Husserl calls image-object is only a form of appearance of visible validity specific to the medium of the image." Building on this definition of the image-object, Wiesing can follow up with a general definition of medial processes: "media are those tools that make it possible to separate genesis from validity." In medial contexts, "validity is artificial selfsameness [*Selbigkeit*], and media are the means for the production of artificial selfsameness."[105]

Such a media theory has the advantage that, unlike many others, it offers a very handy definition. Such clarity at first glance, however, comes with other adumbrations at a second glance. For what does it mean that beside "artificial" selfsameness, there is also a "natural" one? This distinction presupposes that there is a relationship in the first place between the object becoming visible in the natural attitude and the object made visible in the image. The intentionally restrictive media concept of *Artificial Presence*, however, does not leave space for such a relationship. According to Wiesing, media *exclusively* make visible things that without media cannot be visible at all because they are without physics. Making an object standing in the dark visible by means of a ray of light, for Wiesing, is not a medial process because the light illuminates only that (selfsame) thing that already exists physically.[106] What kind of selfsameness, then, exists between the object visible in the light and the object photographed? Merely a conventional one? Such a position can certainly be defended, but it does not have much in common with Husserl.

Moreover, despite his trenchant criticism of meaning-based image theories, there is a second reason why Wiesing robs himself of the very contribution the phenomenological tradition could make to a general theory of images. For what does it mean that images show "artificial selfsameness"? To insist that images give to see not only the *same* but the *selfsame* thing is to undo the medial difference, the difference, that is, between the showing and its how, by which the phenomenology of images puts such store. What is decisive about validity, of course, is precisely not its singular circumstance (its *quomodo*) but the fact that, through all its repetitions, it counts as *the selfsame*. Yet over against Lotze and a certain kind of Platonism, the late Husserl in particular insists on validities' being anchored in the life-world, their necessary taking-place. We might surmise that Husserl's entire work—from the *Philosophy of Arithmetic* to the late texts on the life-world—consists in practically nothing but the attempt to find the genetic place of Lotze's validities. In the terms of the *Crisis* this means that the objective-logical a priori must not be confused with the a priori of the life-world.[107] The question *as what* images are valid, what they count as, already comes in too late; we ought to begin with where and to whom they appear as images.

That, phenomenologically, validity must always be thought together with its genesis is a point made not least of all by Husserl's theory of images. The image-object is not already visible; it wants to be made visible in the first place, both through the "image-constituting consciousness" (the gaze of the viewer that lets a piece of canvas become a landscape) and through the material makeup of the image support itself that (unlike pure imagination) offers only certain views. The definition of images as "dematerializations that transform things into pure visibility"[108] cannot be applied to Husserl because for him, images (unlike fantasies) essentially depend on a supporting and coconstitutive materiality. Moreover, the visibility of the image-object is never fully independent of what it shows (the image-subject).

In *Thing and Space*, Husserl speaks of the depicted shining through in images; he is evidently thinking of an "at the same time," an "also" of what appears and the appearance. Unlike writing, or even my own body, which usually does not enter my field of vision, "in image consciousness, I see the image and through the image" (*Im Bildbewusstsein sehe ich das Bild und durch das Bild hindurch*).[109] This does not, however, necessarily imply a representationalist conception of the image, as the Polish phenomenologist Roman Ingarden lays out in his reflections on "So-called Abstract Painting." In viewing a Kandinsky or a Mondrian, the image-subject transforms into a presented that does not exist anywhere beyond the materially presenting image and that yet is always seen *in it*.[110]

To sum up, the following points in Wiesing's reconstruction of Husserl turn out to be problematic:

(1)   The emphasis on validity razes the difference between the *what* (the image-subject presented) and the *how* (the image appearance/image-object).

(2)   The constitutive productivity of making-visible tends to be marginalized as physically conditioned; the reciprocal interpenetration of the material substrate and the object appearing is negated as a matter of principle.

(3)   The question of how the separation between validity and genesis arises in the image remains unresolved, as does the question of how the connection between artificial visibility (the hat in the image) and natural visibility (the hat on the table) becomes possible.

Beside the one-sidedly static-eidetic reading of Husserl, Wiesing's account of Fiedler, who as the inventor of the expression "pure visibility" is a second major reference, is very partial as well. It might not be superfluous to recall that for Fiedler, visibility is never a completed entity. Rather, like a kaleidoscope, the world restructures itself in new "visibility constructs" (*Sichtbarkeitsgebilde*). Pic-torialization does not whisk us off into a *different* world but lets the physical world (the only world there is) appear *differently*. Time and again, Fiedler insists (for example, by stressing the reciprocal relationship between eye and hand) that image making consists in a processual fashioning of materiality and that intu-ition therefore is "a seeing implemented by the acting human being as a whole."[111]

Ludger Schwarte judges Wiesing's image theory even more harshly. With his static separation of physicality and visible form, he writes, Wiesing indirectly propagates the reintroduction of a two-worlds metaphysics. The reason for this is not only a reductive conception of matter, which does not take into account that every becoming-image consists in an embodiment. For Schwarte, Wiesing's theory of visibility is focused on the "definable" and does not sufficiently con-sider the "nonvisible" and "opaque."[112] Images, we might summarize this criti-cism, are said by Wiesing to end where the undefined begins, to be fully exhausted by their *formed* visibility. An explicit confirmation of this supposition can be found in Wiesing's essay on monochrome painting, where he writes: "An image without forms is like a square without corners."[113] This does distinguish Wiesing's approach from a semiotic one in that the basic visible form is not already a *signifying* form—yet it remains a theory of form.

The following section sketches how the tools provided by phenomenology are not necessarily limited to eidetics, how they can serve to describe images not just as artificial, formal presences that bracket validities off from their geneses, but instead yield insight into how "presentation (of itself or of something else) and thus the possibility of appearing" can be thought at all.[114] To do so, it is necessary to show—against Theodor W. Adorno, who reduces Husserl's philosophy to the isolation of validity from its genesis and saw in this isolation the "schema of reifi-cation" as such[115]—that Husserl's *epokhē* does not consist in detaching validity from its genesis but, first of all, in a bracketing operated to highlight its genesis.

7. *MINIMA VISIBILIA*: SYMPTOMATOLOGY, OR THE OUTLINE OF A NEW APPROACH IN IMAGE THEORY

Phenomenological philosophy, we might say, citing Adorno's apt formula in his *Metacritique of Epistemology*, subsists on the congenital paradox of being a "theory-free theory."[116] It claims to refrain from any prior conceptual judgment concerning the *quod erat demonstrandum* (or *quod erat describendum*) and to obtain characteristics and structures only from a patient description. That is why it has always been suspicious of *what is* questions. At this point, at least, it intersects with Nelson Goodman's theory of symbols, reformulating *what is* questions into, preferably, *when is* questions. In a succinct article from 1977, Goodman suggests, on the basis of his diagnosis that the arts have gone beyond all boundaries and that this process is irreversible, replacing the old question of what the essence of art consists in with a new question, a symptomatological one, as it were: *When* or *under which circumstances is art?*[117] In exchanging the question of essence for a symptomatology of elements, the following sections, which conclude this book, trace this shift.

What, then, is an image? The matter proves to be highly mercurial. When we just take a look at what everyday language provides us with, there seem to be images everywhere: there are artistic images (paintings, photographs, drawings, woodcuts, statues), communication images (billboards, ads, press images), operative images (charts, diagrams, models, maps, graphs), mental images (memories, dreams, ideas, representations, fantasies), natural images (mirror images, silhouettes, constellations of stars), linguistic images (metaphors, metonymies, allegories), political images (self-images, enemy images, stereotypes, myths or symbols)—the list goes on and on. Hans Belting laconically comments on such overboarding catalogs that "everything that comes into view or before the inner eye can thus be declared to be an image or be turned into an image."[118] The difficulties that arise when in principle anything and everything can be declared to be an image are obvious. If everything is an image, nothing is an image anymore—the concept of the image loses its shape.

This threat of a complete dissolution of the concept has been met with a whole series of efforts at imposing a narrow definition on the resplendent phenomenon of iconicity. Vilém Flusser, for example, advances the thesis that images are "a surface covered in symbols," which explicitly seeks to exclude all three-dimensional objects, such as "statues and stage sets."[119] Like all methodologically motivated definitions, this raises the question of what ultimately drives such a restriction that, at the least, objects to a certain kind of linguistic practice and how it can defend against the accusation of being arbitrary. Klaus Sachs-Hombach, too, advocates a narrow concept of the image and suggests a more comprehensive definition: objects may count as images "if they fulfill three phenomenal criteria," namely, if they are "artificial, flat, and relatively permanent."[120] This, however, excludes not just mental and linguistic images, as Sachs-Hombach thinks, but many others as well. The criterion of *artificiality* excludes all phenomena like mirror images, silhouettes, or star constellations. The criterion of *flatness* excludes all three-dimensional depictions, such as statues, busts, or masks (and thus also what in the Roman world was called *imago*). The criterion of *permanence*, finally, excludes all fleeting images, such as images from video, performance, or process art but also and especially images used in communication contexts (think of Snapchat photos that disappear after ten seconds at the most).

Lambert Wiesing attempts an equally trenchant outlining of the concept of the image when, following Konrad Fiedler, he advances the thesis that images are to be deciphered based on their mere visibility and concludes that *images are objects that can show only what is visible*.[121] This conceals that images do not only reproduce what is already visible but also make visible what is not yet visible. What is more, it confines images to a monosensualist channel that hardly coincides with a good number of iconic practices. Not only does such a theory find itself constrained to isolate in all audiovisual works a level of pure visibility; one also has to wonder whether this imposes counterintuitive partitions, for example, when type (*Schriftbild*) may count as an image because it is visible, but the tactile image (*Tastbild*) of Braille does not. It is very difficult not to get the impression of a certain arbitrariness when, in a different approach, modern works of painting for reasons of theoretical coherence lose their status as images at some point, namely, when they become monochrome. Because, according to Wiesing, an image must always have a content other than itself, works by Yves Klein may still pass for art but no longer for images. This seems similarly arbitrary as Umberto Eco's definition of the image as sign. If images are images only if—like all other signs—they can also always be used to lie, and if mirror images cannot lie because they only ever show exactly what is standing before them, then mirror images are not signs and thus are not images.[122]

Such preclusive definitions not only point back to Platonic domestication strategies, they also forestall from the beginning any possibility of gaining insight into the family likeness of different pictorial phenomena based on natural language. Just as there is, beyond the limits of a given *politics*, a field of the *political* whose outlines are always in flux and that is the very basis for various politics to emerge in the first place, so we must suppose that *images* in the strict sense of being framed, planiform visualities are embedded in a much vaster field of the *iconic*. If we want to describe image processes as they emerge, we must therefore not content ourselves with completed objects but take the fact into account that there is something like a precedent and, as it were, "pervasive iconicity" that is no more exhausted by individual images than the political is by politics or the technical by technology.[123] A phenomenology of the iconic must therefore set in earlier than with "pure visibility"; it cannot stop at what is as yet barely visible or at what is hardly visible anymore. This would explain the shift, which Goodman does not justify in detail, from questions of essence to questions of time. In a short but influential essay entitled "When Is Art?" Goodman, in a radical gesture, dismisses wide swaths of philosophical aesthetics: the question is no longer *ti esti*, *what* is art, but *when* is it? As a result, iconicity is to be conceived of as a temporal process. This, however, has another consequence: as a temporal process, iconicity is not an *extensive* but an *intensive* category.

Once we accept that among all the iconic phenomena listed earlier there is something like a family likeness, the focus shifts from an ontology that sorts out specific differences to an ontology of degrees of intensity. How far does "family" reach? Whether one counts a third cousin as part of one's own family depends on the circumstances. This is what Jean-Paul Sartre is getting at when he says that images are to be considered as one big "family." Whether something counts as an image is less a question of belonging than one of effect, less a question of the pedigree than one of the degree of intensity.[124] This is not, however, a defense of some sort of contextualism. There are indeed characteristics that suggest we are dealing with images; only, these characteristics are not necessary and certainly not sufficient. We find ourselves, as it were, in the situation of the physicians of antiquity who had to learn the see the bodily symptoms properly in order to know what disease they were dealing with.

A symptomatological approach is thus neither ontological nor contextualistic but always case-sensitive and situation-bound. It thus follows the suggestion by Nelson Goodman—the second source of inspiration, beside Freud, for this symptomatological project—to rearticulate the question of the essence of art. Since modernism, specifying art independently of context has become a precarious enterprise: at the latest since Duchamp or the conceptualist approach of the artists of the *Art&Object* group, whether a chair is an object for use or an art object is conditioned by artistic positings and functional framings: "Whether an object is art—or a chair—depends upon intent or upon whether it sometimes or usually or always or exclusively functions as such."[125]

Accordingly, it is not possible to give a conclusive definition of the artistic, Goodman argues, but at best to describe symptoms suggesting that with a certain degree of probability one is dealing with a work of art or an aesthetic experience: "These symptoms provide no definition, much less a full-blooded description. . . . Presence or absence of one or more of them does not qualify or disqualify anything as aesthetic; nor does the extent to which these features are present measure the extent to which an object or experience is aesthetic."[126]

Picking up on Goodman, the argument developed in what follows is that beside the "symptoms of the aesthetic" there is also something like "symptoms of

the iconic." If taken *individually*, the presence of such symptoms is not a sufficient criterion to infer the presence of an image and the experience thereof. If
taken *together*, however, their presence—not unlike bodily symptoms—does
indeed suggest that one is dealing with pictorial phenomena. Mobilizing the
categories of formal logic, we might say that in many cases it is true that the
symptoms are *disjunctively* necessary and *conjunctively* sufficient to define
images. But that is precisely true only in *many* and not in *all* cases, which is why
a symptomatological approach is always conditioned by a context and dependent on a situation and cannot easily be generalized. It is dealing with pragmatic
indications, not with logical inferences.

How many symptoms of the iconic are there? In *Languages of Art*, Nelson
Goodman lists four symptoms of the aesthetics, five in *Ways of Worldmaking*.[127]
The advantages of so succinct a symptomatology are readily apparent; its disad-
vantages are pointed out by Goodman himself: it is difficult to address all the
variety and complexity of aesthetic formations with it.[128] An additional difficulty in the case of iconic phenomena is that there are significant differences
between the various natural languages concerning what the concept "image"
covers. It is this kind of difficulty that a symptomatological approach seeks to
address by moving from a logic of categories to a logic of intensities. This also
means that the number of symptoms of the iconic is finite but does not belong
to a countable set. The following is a preliminary list of symptoms: (a) ellipsis,
(b) synopticity, (c) framing, (d) presentativity, (e) figurality, (f) deixis, (g) ostensivity, (h) case sensitivity, (i) the chiasm of gazes, and (j) seeing-with.

(a) Ellipsis

The first symptom to be cited is the *elliptic* character of images. Images show
something by placing it before our eyes and thereby making it intuitive and succinct. This succinctness—"an image is worth a thousand words"—and the
potential evidentiary power of images often have something to do with images
making things or states of affairs visible *in a certain regard*. While three-
dimensional structures such as sculptures want to be walked around to be
grasped, images usually do not have a backside. Images thus are always *aspectual*,
and this implies two things: they are intuitive insofar as they can be looked at
(*ad-spectus, ad-spicere*) and they always show something *only* with reference to a
certain aspect, and no more than that. Because of their necessary intuitiveness,
images never show anything *in general* but always in a specific regard. This is

particularly clear in photographic images: the person who appears in the photo always appears in a respective way, and to that extent, the photographic image is very much situation-bound and occasional. This characteristic can be used when the aim is to put the focus on that respective regard. In a biography, for example, a photo can serve to present someone at a specific time or in a specific function, "Winston Churchill at the Age of Ten" (with the instantly recognizable bowler hat), for instance (fig. 5.3).

What has also been called the image's *as*-structure points to an important connection: iconic visualization is due to a preceding selection. A person, a thing, or a state of affairs being shown *as something specific* means at the same time that it does not appear in all regards, which would be absurd (only where not everything is visible at once can something become visible at all: focal visibility presupposes the relative invisibility of the background). The precondition of becoming visible is thus a withdrawal of general visibility: succinct evidence is necessarily always partial. In photography, this means that there is an excess of reality that cannot be captured within the boundaries of the image. Siegfried

FIGURE 5.3 Anonymous, *Winston Churchill at the Age of Ten* (Brighton), photograph, 1884. Odhams Press Archive.

Kracauer describes this as follows: "A genuine photograph precludes the notion of completeness. Its frame marks a provisional limit; its content points beyond that frame, referring to a multitude of real-life phenomena which cannot possibly be encompassed in their entirety."[129] It is, however, just this capacity for reduction that endows photography with its succinctness, a focusing that at the same time stabilizes a certain *aperçu*. Something similar can be shown for other forms of images as well. Images' power to leave something out is particularly salient in the medium of drawing, both in mimetic and in fictional subjects. The best example here might even be caricature. The progressive removal of likeness that Charles Philipon presents in his famous *Les poires* (1831) and the gradual regression of the king into a pear (fig. 5.4) are an excellent example of ellipsis (from the Greek *elleipsis*, falling short). Caricatures thus are often much more revealing and much more to the point than any proposition, although they precisely cannot claim to depict people correctly. Through deformations, well-aimed exaggerations, and selective omissions, something comes to light that is definitely not the case and yet claims for itself the ability to be true.

Images' ellipticism is intimately connected with their tendency toward intuitiveness. To highlight something specific, something else must step back. This can be verified not only in visual communication or the images of art but in the imaging procedures of science as well: whether through the reduction of complex masses of data to two-dimensional diagrams in the social sciences, through rendering organic matter transparent in medical X-ray images, or through staining techniques in biological specimens, visualization has a lot to do with selectivity. Every illustration is of necessity partial, and images accordingly exemplify ever only *some* but never all the properties of what they depict.

This was already an insight of Plato's image theory. His comment that images are deficient might not have to be seen as an expression of an inveterate enmity toward images. On a charitable reading, one might suspect it to indicate an insight into iconic ellipticism. Images then would always be imperfect because they can always only resemble their models in a specific regard, yet if they resembled the model in every regard—because a divine demiurge produced them, say—they would not be a better image but no image at all: they would be the thing itself. The moment the depiction becomes a perfect copy, it loses its iconic character.[130] When two things perfectly resemble each other and no difference between them can be established, it becomes downright absurd to speak of one of them as an image. Augustine would later put the matter succinctly: an egg is not an image of another egg, it is simply another egg.[131]

The partial aspectuality of images immediately points to a second symptom, that of synopticity.

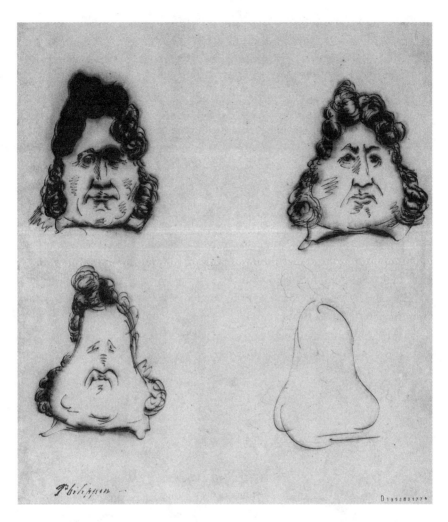

FIGURE 5.4 Charles Philipon, *The Metamorphosis of King Louis-Philippe Into a Pear*. 1831.
Drawing with pen and brown ink, 24.7 × 21.7 mm (sheet). Bibliothèque nationale de France,
Paris, Prints and Photography, Res. B-16-Box (public domain).

(b) Synopticity

Pictures of pipes, landscape views, caricatures, MRI scans, or city maps, despite
all their differences, do share one thing: they are synoptic, that is, their appearance is framed or limited. This property is particularly palpable in epistemic
visualizations such as scientific tableaux, from the *phainomena* tablets of

antiquity via Euler's *Seven Bridges of Königsberg* (1736, fig. 5.5), Quesnay's *Tableau économique* (1759), and Buffon and Cuvier's *Tabulae affinitatum animalium*, all the way to contemporary stock market graphics: complex states of affairs here are illustrated through the simultaneous presentation of their components. Generalizing these observations, we may say that images give states of affairs a *synoptic presentation.*

Ludwig Wittgenstein, who introduces the expression "synoptic presentation" (*übersichtliche Darstellung*), essentially sees in it a reduction of complexity. If in choosing our means of presentation we are guided by forms of presentation that through their limitation allow for basic references to come to the foreground, then the reason is first of all that such a form of presentation corresponds to the way we always already "look at things" as well.[132] Synoptic presentation, which Wittgenstein first discusses in 1931 in the context of ethnographic experiences of the other via the example of Frazer's *The Golden Bough*, not only becomes the methodological guiding thread of all his late work—for Wittgenstein, the idea of seeing things together, or *synopsis* in an almost typographic sense, also contains the basis of aesthetics as such.[133]

That the limiting perspective is the basis of aesthetics may also be considered the basic idea of Clement Greenberg's theory of art.[134] While according to

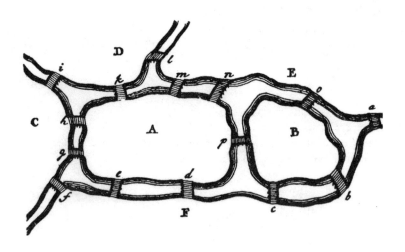

FIGURE 5.5   Leonhard Euler, *Solutio problematis ad geometriam situs pertinentis*, in *Commentarii Academia Scientiarum Petropolitanae* 8 (1736), 128–40, fig. 3.

Greenberg, the pictorial arts share the characteristic of "enclosure" with other arts (such as theater), the specifically *iconic enclosure* refers back to the flatness of the image-thing, "for flatness alone was unique and exclusive to pictorial art."[135] For painting to reach maturity, Greenberg famously explains, it must cleanse itself of everything extrapictorial and return to this two-dimensional flatness. Should the painter feel that the limited depth of the image surface is too constraining, there is only one remedy, according to Greenberg: "let him become a sculptor."[136] Thus, on Greenberg's reading, Courbet's comment that his painter colleague Manet's *Olympia* is no more realistic than the queen on a playing card confirms that with Manet, the modernist telos becomes manifest for the first time. Flatness is no longer something to be overcome by an illusionist pictorial art feigning spatial depth. Instead, mimetic perspectival presentation becomes a parenthesis in the history of a genre that prior to the Renaissance and after the subsiding of its presentational paradigm returns to what it essentially consists in: its depthless extension. In breaking with the "rage for description" and "rage for allegorizing," it is able to reach the state of medial self-reflection that Kant effected for thinking.[137]

There are, of course, precursors to this thesis, which Greenberg defends with particular ardor in "Towards a Newer Laocoon."[138] The painter Maurice Denis, for example, declared that images—long before they become "naked women" or other kinds of depictions—are "essentially a plane surface covered by colors in a specific arrangement." Greenberg's hypothesis that eradicating the mimetic and achieving a "pure opticality" is to take place via an exclusion of the tactile and the sculptural is of course problematic insofar as one quickly runs the danger—as Rosalind Krauss critically objects—of ending up with an entirely disembodied theory of art that will hardly be able to affirm anything like medium specificity.[139] Reducing images to extensions without depth not only means expelling all types of images that constitutively work with image layers, such as collages; if one denies images any kind of objectness and treats them as "*incorporeal*, weightless" matter, there might be no images left at all.[140] Greenberg's thesis is nonetheless useful if we think of the image not in terms of a literal but in terms of a *phenomenal* two-dimensionality. What is important in that case is no longer that the image lacks all material depth but that it *appears flat*. In opposition to sculpture, the thickness of the image support has iconic significance only in exceptional cases; looking at images in turn precisely demands abstracting from this material "depth."

What is also implied besides the material depth of the image-thing is a *presentative* depth of the image-object that does not necessarily coincide with the presented depth of the image-subject. Greenberg, too, seems to want to save such a depth on the part of appearing image by introducing the concept of virtual depth. The geometrical pictorial compositions of someone like Piet Mondrian, for example, institute a spatiality in which the eye can move freely; unlike the merely suggested accessibility of the perspectival *veduta*, however, this spatiality remains strictly restrained architectonically by its own means of composition. Any place the eye can reach within the construct of bars is already visible from the beginning and does not have to be imagined.

Spatiotemporal orientation within the image thus rests on a fundamental synopticity. In Max Imdahl's terms, the image is characterized by a planimetric "frontality" that consists in everything visible in the image being available "once and for all" and "in its entirety."[141] What is not yet visible in the image is not yet visible not because it has yet to enter the stage belatedly but at most because it remains latent and unnoticed within the pictorial field. Not only can *representation* be thought on the basis of an always preceding *presentation* alone; iconic presentations are *finite presentations* that bring the event of their "framing" itself into play.

(c) Framing

The moment an image is posited, a twofold *closing off from the outside* and *enclosing on the inside* takes place, a "two-sided mediation," in Gadamer's terms. The image simultaneously draws all attention to itself, absorbing the gaze of the viewer, and always also points beyond itself and to an unlimited surrounding space. The liberation of a specific time of viewing images, accordingly, is preceded by an iconic isolation: one phenomenal aspect is selected from the continuum of the world and presented as framed.

"Framing" of course does not necessarily mean a physical enclosure made of brass or wood. Framing, rather, is always a process of inclusion and exclusion that organizes, individuates, and differentiates material configurations. In this regard, phenomena of framing comprehend both material restrictions and social delimitations. According to Erving Goffman, the individual frame is both the result and the producer of continually new framings. The frame is thus a "border guard"; it is the place where the image does not yet count, as it were—and yet, at the same time, it marks the lines of potential transgression, it structures the framing and indicates where the limit can become a boundary.[142]

Images again and again push beyond their frames, explode their delimitations, and seek space. *La imagen debe salir del cuadro*—a successful picture, to cite Velázquez's teacher Pacheco, must step out of its frame. Other images in turn are haunted by their edges, such as Paul Klee's *Ad marginem*, a presentation of a brightly glowing red sun on a yellow, parchment-like ground that from the edges is attacked by nightmarish creatures slowly making their way to the center of the image (fig. 5.6).

As Jacques Derrida has so emphatically shown, the frame can thus be neither externalized nor fully incorporated; it marks the lack of the *ergon* that attains itself only through its inessential addition, its *parergon*: "neither work nor outside the work, neither inside nor outside, neither above nor below, it disconcerts any opposition but does not remain indeterminate and it gives rise to the work."[143] Frames are thus merely attachments and additions applied from the outside; nonetheless, it is they that let the work appear as work in the first place: "the frame is a necessary *parergon*, a constitutive supplement. It autonomizes the work within the visible space; it puts the representation in a state of exclusive presence; it gives the appropriate definition of the conditions for the visual reception and contemplation of the representation as such."[144] Every image requires a relative self-enclosure, which is probably what Alberti is getting at when he demands a certain *concinnitas*, a harmony or congruity, from the painter. The frame guides the attention, separates the visible from the invisible, and restricts the potentially infinite field of the visual.

If we accept "framing" as a criterion for saying with a certain degree of probability when and where we are dealing with *iconic* appearances, we suppose that framings always also effect localizations, anchorings, and territorializations. Although images as a matter of principle can become visible everywhere, they cannot do so everywhere at the same time and thus require a spatiotemporal restriction. The image, to use Goethe's definition in the *Color Theory*, is "what is seen with limitations" (*das begrenzt Gesehene*).[145] Iconic processes thus always operate on the border of the undefined; more precisely, they are finite ways of dealing with what remains inherently undefined.

This cultural technique is presented in a particularly impressive way by the Greek *Tomb of the Diver* (fifth century BCE) in Paestum, on whose red-framed sarcophagus cover the diver (that is, the one dying) is jumping off the Pillars of Hercules, the boundary of the known world, into the void in the middle of the image, into the *apeiron* (fig. 5.7). Death and the image are inseparably intertwined insofar as they represent, to pick up on Maurice Blanchot, lines that

FIGURE 5.6 Paul Klee, *Ad marginem* (1930), watercolor and ink on cardboard and canvas, 46 × 36 cm. Kunstmuseum, Basel. Courtesy of the museum.

FIGURE 5.7 *Tomba del Tuffatore* (Tomb of the Diver), tomb slab, ca. 480 BCE. Museo municipale, Paestum. Courtesy of Beni culturali italiani.

separate off the impossible. By marking from the inside a boundary that cannot be crossed, they draw it in the first place. An image is thus always "a limit alongside [*auprès*] the indefinite."[146]

(d) Presentativity

What images give us to see does not always exist independently of the iconic act of showing. Of course many images subsist on their (real or alleged) documentary value—autopsy photos in forensic medicine, courtroom drawings, blueprints in architecture, or cellphone photos documenting a summer vacation—insofar as they present themselves as testimony of a reality archived and thus authenticated on their surface. All these iconic genres claim to reproduce reality. Yet many images also show states of affairs that do not or not yet exist beyond the image. Images can function as visions of the future, projects for utopian cities or artificial worlds; they indicate *how* it would be *if* it were to be. Many iconic modes are thus not in the indicative but in the irrealis mood. It is for that reason that it does not make much sense to tie iconicity to the concept of representation if the prefix *re-* is to indicate a repetition. It seems to make more sense here to exchange the concept of representativity for that of *presentativity*.

Whether for documentary purposes or as aesthetic statements, whether as references back to what exists or as illustrations of what is possible—images are always granted a qualitative primacy in their way of letting appear what is at stake. Images thus not only allow for referring to states of affairs; iconic reference obviously takes place according to principles that diverge from discursive reference. Susanne K. Langer has suggested including images in the series of those systems of symbols she calls *presentational* systems.[147] Langer's distinction between *discursive* and *presentational* forms represents, as it were, the media-philosophical rearticulation of another, classic distinction, namely, Immanuel Kant's distinction, in his theory of faculties, between *discursive* and *intuitive* forms of cognition. Unlike *intuitive* knowledge, in which insight into an entire state of affairs takes place all at once, finite knowledge ineluctably depends on a gradual grasping Kant also calls discursive (that is, literally, going step by step). The human faculty, which is incapable of any simultaneous view of the whole ("intuition"), must thus of necessity grasp its object successively, in time. In Langer, the decisive step now consists in no longer justifying the difference between intuitiveness and discursivity in terms of a theory of faculties and capacities (that is, for example, via the difference between God and human being) but in terms of a theory of media. Discursive forms of symbolization are forms that in order to be significant must be formed into series linearly, successively, while presentational forms of symbolization can be grasped in one glance. To refer to what presents itself in presentational forms, verbal language, for example, must *explicate* or unfold what is implied there little by little, that is, discursively: the *explicative* (interpreting) potential of discursive forms—for example, the explanation of a painting through art historical commentary—supplements the *densifying* potential of presentational forms. The denser images are, the more complex is their interpretation: it is not by chance that Sigmund Freud applies the art of psychoanalysis in the *interpretation* of dreams, and much could be said in the same vein about the need for commentary that characterizes many works of modern art that, in rejecting the claim to *representation*, assert their presentational autonomy. Presentational forms nonetheless are not necessarily abstract or self-referential; they may very well illustrate something other than themselves. *Presenting* then means letting something other than what is currently visible be seen, letting something absent enter into appearance, in short: *presentifying* something that is not present (either at the current moment or generally). Presentativity thus occasions an *effect* of presence all its own that may very well also entail an *affect* of presence. Photographs, for example, can have a downright uncanny effect on the viewer if in them people who have already died appear to be alive again.

This commonplace is an old one: painting, Alberti says in 1435, contains a "divine force" through which "the dead seem almost alive ... even after many centuries." In this, painting is related to friendship, of which it is said that it "makes absent men present."[148] Images thus have a strange effect: they let the past come alive and what is distant seem close, as if temporal and spatial removal had lost their efficacy, while they also render the leaps in presence evident, for example, when a self-portrait shows us differently from how we see ourselves or when the old faded photograph of a beloved person painfully reminds us that the time it captured by chance is forever gone. This paradox is also palpable in the images of rulers or religious cultic images: strangely, they purposely seek to stage unapproachability in the closest possible proximity.

(e) Figurality

Figura nihil probat, "a figure proves nothing at all," Martin Luther proclaimed in the iconographic controversy of the Reformation. Yet there is plenty of evidence in the history of knowledge that the figural can have evidentiary force, indeed, that *demonstration* is essentially reliant on visual *monstration* and that, as we might say with Leibniz and Kant, there is indeed such a thing as "figural cognition" (*figürliche Erkenntnis*).

In fact, a number of major breakthroughs are due to such visualizations in figural arrangements. The benzene molecule had been known since 1800, but decades of research had brought no certainty about the exact structure linking its components (six hydrogen and six carbon atoms). In 1865 the solution finally comes to the chemist August Kekulé in his sleep: he sees a ring structure against the foil of an old alchemist symbol, a snake seizing its own tail, and the next day the inspiration of the dream proves to be correct: overnight, Kekulé has discovered the benzene ring. In mathematics, the view since David Hilbert has been that mathematical principles largely escape intuition. But that was not always the case. In the eighteenth century Leonhard Euler had the idea of presenting syllogistic inferences through closed (overlapping or concentrically nested) circles to immediately make their result plausible (fig. 5.8). Take the following syllogistic inference: *If* (premise 1) *all A are B and* (premise 2) *all C are A, then* (conclusion) *all C are B*. In the diagrammatic visualization, testing the validity of such a derivation turns into child's play. The set theoretical explanation why, if A is contained in B and C in A, all C are B is immediately apparent.

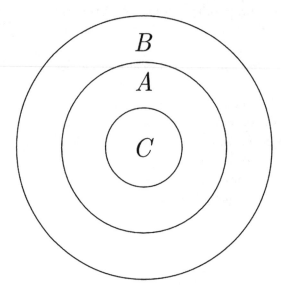

FIGURE 5.8 Euler's
syllogistic circles (E. Alloa).

There is thus a form of evidence particular to figural presentation that is lacking in discursive succession although, strictly speaking, no further element has been added. Through the rearrangement of the elements alone, something comes forward that previously was not recognizable there; the rearrangement effects a redesign that lets a new shape step forward. Or, to put it in yet another set of terms: the graphic sum presents more than the totality of its individual analytic parts. What remains, we may summarize, is an evidence that does in fact result solely from what is there to be seen: *e-videntia*, from out of the visible.

Today, knowledge transfer is unthinkable without the graphic processing of data. There is practically no proof that can do without diagrams or charts. Unlike the logical *sequence*, figural *evidence* allows for immediate grasp. As early as the 1930s the Vienna social scientist and pedagogue Otto Neurath, for example, was working on a method of scientific iconic statistics meant to deploy images as media of cognition. Neurath was not only working on the project of a largely language-free visual Esperanto, which in 1935 he baptized ISOTYPE (International System of Picture Education) and which many of today's internationally used pictograms derive from (such as the symbols for emergency exits and fire extinguishers). For Neurath, a language of images used as international lingua franca also offers "a certain neutrality" because it relies on figures and not on words.

The distinction here is between *figurality as a graphic repertoire of forms*, which nonetheless and like any other symbolic alphabet remains restricted and enumerable, and *figurality as a principle of aesthetic design*, where what counts in each case is the form of the image-signs. Thanks to such aesthetic figurality, a certain meaning takes shape in constellations on the surface of images, a meaning that would dissolve immediately if the figures were reduced to a standardized and translatable vocabulary of forms. Through their figural arrangement, images express something *in themselves*; they represent something by showing it on and in themselves.

(f) Deixis

What does it mean to say that images represent something? What exactly does *depiction* consist in? To conceive of depiction as a kind of referring is to already make a decision that is by no means harmless. Before we look at the inadmissible restriction it entails, however, let us follow this perspective for a moment. After all, *many* images undeniably are used as instruments of reference. As aesthetic statement, as documenting a family vacation, or as evidence in a trial—in all these instances, images are granted a qualitative primacy in the way they refer to what is at stake. Images thus serve not only to refer to states of affairs; iconic reference obviously takes place according to principles that differ from those of verbal reference, or at least those of largely context-independent verbal reference. After all, it is the branch of linguistics that studies the context-dependent aspects of language that provided a rubric under which iconic dimensions of reference are by preference categorized: the category of *deixis*.

In his *Theory of Language* of 1934, Karl Bühler puts the deictic character of language already emphasized by the second-century grammarian Apollonius Dyscolus back at the center of linguistic attention. According to Bühler, language is essentially structured by functional blanks such as *I, you, here, now, there*, indexical linguistic signs whose meaning is fulfilled only when they instantiate in a "deictic field" and the *demonstratio ad oculus* that comes with this instantiation.[149] That which intrinsically remains occasional stands in need of a spatiotemporal *origo* in the coordinate system of expression. Such *I–here–now* points of the event of expression on the one hand are defined by a specific position as emitter in a communication environment; on the other hand, they name a concrete bodily anchoring. What is all too quickly staged as a dichotomy of saying and showing comes together in the expressive verbal gesture. After all, as Bühler reminds us, the Latin *dicere* derives from the Greek *deiknymi*, a literal pointing or showing.

Louis Marin's studies on the concept of representation, too, converge in deixis as articulating something undefined. The *Port Royal Logic* (first published in 1662), which for Michel Foucault inaugurated the classical episteme,[150] circles around the mystery of the Eucharist that it seeks to capture semiotically. What meaning is to be assigned the *hoc* in *hoc est corpus meum*, "This is my body"? The relationship that the neutral deictic term *hoc* establishes between the piece of bread and the body of Christ, according to the Port Royal Jansenists, is not a relationship of substantial identity but is produced in the speech act in the first place. The incommensurable gap between the two is both bridged and, by making the distance visible in the gesture, affirmed at the same time.[151]

Those meaning-instituting gestures of showing (which, for example, assign identity through personal pronouns like *I* and *you*) are not only often operated *via* images; not infrequently, they also already take place *in* images. In those cases, we are dealing with an *internalized deixis*, as it were. The indicating gesture becomes an internal figure in an image that tends toward autonomous unity. Alberti thematizes the gesture in the figure of the *admonitor*, "someone who admonishes," who "beckons with his hands to see" and guides the attention in the image.[152] The meaning of the deictic gesture crystallizes in the stagings, remarkably numerous in Western art, of the gesture of showing, for example, in Plato's raised index finger in Raphael's *The School of Athens* or the youth oscillating between John the Baptist and Bacchus painted by Leonardo.[153] The deictic function is even intensified when the deictic gesture is no longer limited to the hand and the whole body becomes a stage, as it were, as in the case of the skinned Marsyas in a Bologna manual from 1521.[154] A gentle smile on his lips, he seems to lift up the delicately dissected strips of skin as if for one of Vesalius's anatomical sessions—*Marsyas, c'est moi* (fig. 5.9).

For Louis Marin, the deictic logic of representation culminates in the portrait of the king, in which the Eucharistic provenance of performativity crystallizes. The portrait of the king does not depict anything that would already be there: Louis XIV becomes the sovereign in the image in the first place, in the image in which iconic and phatic proposition coincide ("the state is me"). The power of the state thus "resides neither in the king (or the royal dignity) nor in Louis XIV, but it *is* none other than the proper name ('me') of the 'I' that utters, 'The state is me.'" The consecration of the king takes place in the Eucharistic becoming-image: *"Louis suddenly becomes king as the portrait of the king."*[155] Insofar as there is no longer anything represented to be sought before or behind

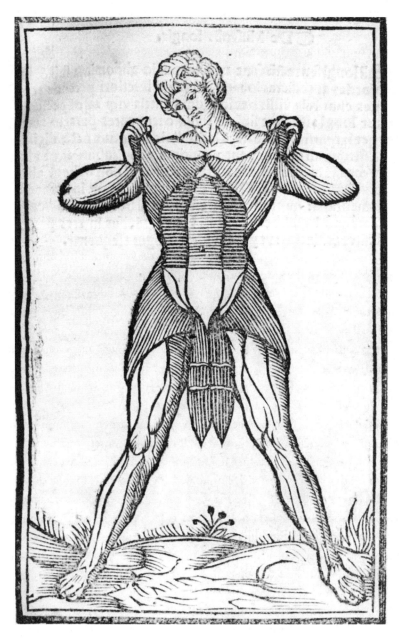

FIGURE 5.9 Jacopo Berengario da Carpi, *Commentaria* (Bologna, 1521), f. 85.

the representation and insofar as the image in giving itself to be seen produces something it can refer to in the first place, we are talking, in the case of the portrait of the king, no longer about deixis but about *autodeixis*.[156] However—and this is the point of Marin's variations on iconic power—autodeixis can no longer be grasped as a subcategory of deixis; the distance-creating theory of the sign, rather, turns out itself to depend on a precedent showing-itself. Representation can become effective only when something present in the mode of presence self-reflexively duplicates and enters into a relationship of representation with itself. Only the interplay of referential positing and phenomenal instantiation secures the power of *repraesentatio*. Or, put succinctly: no deixis without autodeixis.

If that is so, however, then it is no longer possible to say that images are signs that in showing also show themselves. While referring to something else, every sign must show itself since if there were nothing *showing* (itself), nothing could be *shown* either. In the case of most signs, however, we must not dwell on the *autò* of deixis: staring at the pointing finger or the physical makeup of the road sign notoriously leads to missing the meaning of the act of showing. In images (and in all systems of meaning that do not operate merely by denotation), in turn, the "self" of what is showing remains relevant throughout the observation; the mode of being of what shows that is *exposed* in the iconic events, their specific form, is of downright constitutive significance. For, in Henri Focillon's terms, *the sign shows something, the form shows itself*.[157]

The question rightly arises whether such exposition can meaningfully still be categorized as reference (and be it of the self-referential variety) without leading to the absurd conclusion that images are signs of themselves. What can it mean, then, to say that images do not refer to something absent but "to something that is visible on their surface"?[158] Theories of the image that conceive of iconicity as reference to something other on the basis of a precedent self-reference are always on the brink of understanding the reflexivity of the image all too subjectively and, by contrast, no longer understanding its generativity at all. For how is it possible at all to account for something becoming "visible on their surface"? It might turn out that the descriptive relationship must be inversed and that making-visible in the iconic medium must be considered no longer as a collateral effect but as the precondition of any and all reference. Deixis would then prove to be an act of showing that is always preceded by the *phainesthai* as the event of showing, this precedence no longer being a temporal but a logical one.

Still, it remains an open question how an image showing itself differs from any given intuitive object. The following section therefore seeks to describe the singularity of the iconic *phainesthai* via the symptom of ostensivity and its three degrees of intensity, namely, exemplification, ostension, and bareness.

(g) Ostensivity

EXEMPLIFICATION

Yves Klein's blue monochromes *are* not simply blue objects, just as they do not denote any blue object. On the basis of his general theory of symbols, which provides precise concepts for grasping iconic properties, Nelson Goodman would say that Klein's monochromes, too, can be explained in terms of references—not as denotations but as *exemplifications* of a certain kind of blue, more precisely, the registered trademark *IKB*. According to Goodman, those signs are exemplifications that exhibit the material properties of the signified.[159] There is "literal" exemplification every time the image sign does in fact possess the properties it exemplifies. When I want to paint my house, I first compare different *samples* in a catalog of colors. The peculiarity of samples is that they do not list or describe the properties they exemplify but simply illustrate them in themselves. In short: an exemplary sign "possesses" what it signifies, and what is indicated this way can only be thus and not otherwise.[160] Sharing the properties exemplified does not for all that mean that the signifying and the signified share all properties. In *Ways of Worldmaking*, Goodman uses the ironic anecdote about Mrs. Mary Tricias's "samples" and her "single huge cake" to emphasize how samples can at the most only ever share *some* properties with what they exemplify.[161] In short: the meaningful use of samples for Goodman still depends on the context of the symbolization since, as a matter of principle, every object has infinitely many properties and because only the symbolic putting-in-relation with an exemplified lets the property in question stand out.

Yet we may suspect that with this communicational embedding Goodman squanders some of what he has gained with the concept of exemplification. The properties attested by samples and examples are not arbitrary properties of a conventional kind, they are *phenomenal* properties. And this is where an alternative begins to emerge between physical opacity, which possesses without symbolizing, and semantic transparency, which symbolizes without possessing.[162] Exemplification does not consist merely in the solidarity of opacity and transparency, in both possessing and symbolizing, but contains a phenomenal excess that cannot be completely absorbed by either the logic of possession or the logic of meaning.

Yet this third dimension, of course, plays no role for a thinker who, despite an early work entitled *The Structure of Appearance*, is not particularly interested in appearance but only ever in the gamut of predicate logic at its basis. For Goodman, fullness or density are not phenomenal but purely structural properties that could also be calculated by beings (computers, say) that have no sense for appearances.[163] Goodman conceives of exemplification only ever as transitive and thus as transitory: the process of showing quite simply merges with what it shows. Here, too, we see the traditional narrowing-down of showing to showing something in the sense of showing-as. Cognition takes place only where the *einai* is defined as *einai ti* and a predicate can be referred to a subject.[164] Goodman still participates in this telos of definition, but he does point out that exemplification cannot fully be reduced to it: the *as* of exemplification (its "aboutness") remains undefined as long as it is viewed only in its particular materiality. For that very reason, there is always the need for a "label" that accompanies the both over- and underdetermined sample by explaining and defining it.[165] At this point of indeterminacy, however, a phenomenological description of self-exposition could come in that would conceive of showing-oneself as an initially intransitive process that is always at the back of a phenomenal event.

OSTENSION

Gerhard Richter's *Color Charts* (fig. 5.10), which the artist has been producing in ever new arrangements since 1966, are easily confused with the paint sample cards commonly available at hardware stores. And yet they no more serve to guide a buyer's decision than Yves Klein's works serve to delimit patent number IKB CI 77007 from other ultramarines. Just as in Klein's blue a certain experience of perception is at issue, so the decisive point of Richter's color charts is their effect as a whole. Such works consciously contravene the transitivity that is generally projected onto images and bring images back to their intrinsic qualities.

Augustine distinguishes the classic act of signification from a kind of signifying that he calls *ostensio* and in which the signs show in themselves, as it were, what they signify. According to Augustine, words are incapable of *ostensio* because it is simply impossible to show and not signify without in so doing leaving language behind.[166] There is a fundamental *ostensio* without *significatio*, however, where things show themselves by themselves. Is there no mediation,

FIGURE 5.10 Gerhard Richter, *Color Chart*, 1966/1978, oil on canvas, 70 cm × 65 cm (CR 139-3). Courtesy of Gerhard Richter Studio.

then, between the denoting signs that point away from themselves, on the one hand, and the sign-free showing-themselves of the things, on the other? Augustine in *De magistro* does not think so and, via the example of bird hunting, which can be learned only through the visible repetition of gestures, elaborates a space of deictic didactics that was still to impress Wittgenstein.[167] Every *docere* is founded on an *ostendere*, every teaching on a showing, for where something is to be repeated and learned, it must be visibly performed before our eyes.

Images—and this is what, later, the treatises of the Counterreformation make such extensive use of—are thus particularly suited for teaching because they always already perform in themselves what they communicate. This is palpable once more, in a self-reflective intensification, in the Christological *Man of Sorrows*, who pulls the wound in his side apart with his fingers and presents it to the viewer in the gesture of the *ostentatio vulnerum* (fig. 5.11). While on the one hand the principle *noli me tangere* withdraws the body of Christ from touch, on the other hand his corporeality in the visual *exhibitio* could not impose itself more powerfully. Such images of ostension guide the eye in not one but two ways: they draw the gaze into themselves and give us to see that only those acts of showing succeed that attention is being paid to. Every indicating thus needs a preceding turning-toward, every deixis takes place on the basis of a protodeictic orienting-oneself.

When images no longer indicate what they point to, when they thus seem to refuse their own fulfillment, a new stage has been reached that may be described as bared phenomenality.

BARENESS

Where, without a "label," it becomes illegible, exemplification inevitably comes up against its limits. Here, all the image has left is an excessive number of phenomenal properties that only show themselves but can no longer be correlated with any extrinsic reference. Where the image is just bare appearance, it stands out in its bareness. Where images thus externalize themselves, they let their materiality come to the fore, their being made up of oil, turpentine, and resin, of wood, paper, and wire. In that same movement, however, they also highlight that they are not fully reducible to their material components, for images emerge in the first place only via an initial positing (in Husserl's terms: iconicity is the result of an *act*).[168] Pointing out that Robert Rauschenberg's Combine paintings are assembled from tires, sheets of metal, socks, and shoestrings is saying little about the mysteriousness of the iconic act. It is as if crossing out the production of reference and baring their own physicality does not lead to any kind of new perspicacity: in their medial externalization, images exhibit nothing but the paradox of their specific opacity. As an image-phenomenological symptom, bareness thus lies beyond thingness and transparency; in letting materiality come through, the always operative iconic excess shows itself ex negativo.

The baring also points us to another circumstance: the *vulnerability* of images. Because of their exposure, images are also always left open to physical attacks, a point made with particular emphasis in works like Lucio Fontana's *Concetti spaziale* (fig. 5.12). In opposition to exemplification, which can still be inserted into the grid of a type–token relationship, the event of lacerating the canvas also exposes an irreducible specificity, the *thisness* of the picture. Through

FIGURE 5.11 Master Francke, *Man of Sorrows* (ca. 1435), oil (tempera) on oak, 92.5 × 67 cm. Kunsthalle, Hamburg. Courtesy of Kunsthalle.

FIGURE 5.12 Lucio Fontana, *Concetto spaziale: Attese* (1961), 74 × 54 cm. Museum Ludwig, Cologne. © ProLitteris.

a closeness evoked by seeing that is always also a haptic closeness, the image proves to be exposed to potential transgression. This physical sensitivity evoked in the act of image reception can be outlined—from a structural point of view—in terms of a phenomenal *variation sensitivity*.

(h) Variation Sensitivity

The expressiveness of the iconic differs from systems of expression based on an alphabet of finite enumerable semantic units in that every intermediate space of the expressive texture can in itself be significant and serves not just to differentiate the individual semantic units. The supports of the process of expression are not individual instances of a general language; in their singularity they initially speak only for themselves. The variation sensitivity that points to an individual *haecceitas* does not mean that images, as a matter of principle, exist only in the singular (we can very well conceive of several copies of a work), but it means that at issue throughout their iterations is a suchness that already a minimal deviation can void of its meaning.

Operating with distances, be it through leaving something out or adding further differentiations, produces an effect on the phenomenal level that can be outlined in terms of an iconic densification. Images achieve such a concentration effect not only through framing or limiting the image appearance but also by virtue of their intrinsic surface structure. Taking up Nelson Goodman, we can also call this structure *density*. Goodman distinguishes between syntactic and semantic density, but only *syntactic* density can serve as a symptom of the iconic, for every semantics presupposes that there is something it signifies, which is the case only for some images. "A scheme is syntactically dense if it provides for infinitely many characters so ordered that between each two there is a third."[169] This distinguishes it from syntactically loose systems, in which the distance between the signs serves only to distinguish and thus to individuate the elements of meaning.

Syntactically loose systems such as written languages are thus based on the principle of *disjunction* and of *finite differentiability*: all elements are enumerable and are (the occasional mode of being of their token notwithstanding) to be recognized unambiguously. In syntactically dense systems such as music, dance, or images, it is practically impossible to identify elements or, more precisely, marks (as in the Latin *macula*) as exemplars of specific signs. Where between two elements, as a matter of principle, another one can always be discerned and further distinctions can always be made, no detail, no nuance can per se be declared irrelevant. Brushwork, color, shape, choice of material— all these are differences that make a difference. And they all are peculiarities that in disjunctive systems must precisely be neglected in order to guarantee that the process runs in a smooth and standardized way.

A system's degree of density can be measured by the number of its dimensions. Goodman here also speaks of "repleteness," namely, when "comparatively many aspects of a symbol are significant."[170] While in our alphabet the only thing required is being assigned to one of the twenty-six letters, thermometers or diagrams already display a relative density insofar as one or two dimensions, respectively, of their presentation obey analogical principles. While in the mercury thermometer only one dimension is relevant (the position on the temperature scale) and in diagrams two (the position in relation to the abscissa and the ordinate), in images no dimension can be excluded from the outset: height, the extension of the width of the format, the dimension of depth (from the thickness of the paint application to the imperfections of the image support), and even the fourth dimension of time, namely, insofar as traces of aging can be relevant for the significance of the image. The aesthetic all-over principle on which Jackson Pollock's *Drippings* are based can even be translated into an epistemological all-over: there is no moment of the image that is not as significant as all the others around it.

The more multidimensional an object's syntactic density is, the more difficult it becomes to take the object apart into elements and sort them, to discretize it (for the purposes, for instance, of storage, processing, or transmission). In syntactically dense systems, transitions are usually smooth and any drawing of boundaries will be suspected of arbitrariness. In reanalogizing what has previously been digitized, the intermediate spaces that have been inserted are shortened again, depriving the object of its in principle infinite differentiation. The concept of density thus also allows for venturing an answer to the haunting question of the power of images: images are more refractory to complexity-reducing procedures because their peculiarity is not due to any singular trait; they possibly derive their proverbial power precisely from intertwining and densifying different functional strands.[171] In Wittgenstein's words, "the strength of the thread does not reside in the fact that some one fibre runs through its whole length, but in the overlapping of many fibres."[172]

Gorgias, the Sophist, is likely one of the earliest to describe this intertwining effect. He compares the painter with a skilled patcher who is able to "perfectly depict a single body and form on the basis of many colors and bodies." He adds that through this procedure artists become hunters for gazes because their painted patched-together beings "carry away" (*terpousi*) the viewer's gaze.[173]

ILLUMINATION 9

Hokusai and the Dow Jones

At first sight, the two graphic presentations (fig. 5.13) are indistinguishable—and yet each presents something entirely different. The figure on the left shows Japan's "eternal mountain," Mount Fuji, after an ink drawing by Katsushika Hokusai (1760–1849). The presentation is stylized, the sides rise harmonically, and the top is manneristically elevated. Hokusai's Fuji images count as unsurpassed not just because of their form; what makes his works unique is his incomparable brushwork, in which the gesture of their creation is still visible. Every aspect, every hatching, every line drawn is significant here. The figure on the right is a business diagram and documents the ups and downs of the U.S. Dow Jones stock market index in 2008. This presentation purposely leaves out smaller fluctuations to illustrate a general trend. Even if the curve bears remarkable similarities to one of the famous views of Mount Fuji produced by Hokusai in the eighteenth century, it is unlikely that there is anyone interested, from an aesthetic perspective, in the specific color, width, and line design of the stock market graph. It is just the inverse for the work of the Japanese painter: it is less important how exactly the angles of the sides of the mountain are reproduced; the gaze is directed at the artful making of the drawing. And unlike the paper ballot, where any kind of graphic marking (line, dot, cross) counts as a valid vote as long as it is placed within one of the circles next to candidates' names, it is in no way irrelevant where and in what form Cy Twombly has applied the crayon on one of his large-format paintings.

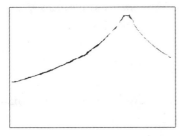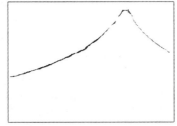

FIGURE 5.13 Hokusai's Mount Fuji and the Dow Jones (E. Alloa).

(i) A Chiasm of Gazes

"The things I see see me as much as I see them," writes Paul Valéry.[174] Things often literally impose themselves on us and unexpectedly seize us; this event of transgression is verbally manifest in the "blink of an eye" or the Augustinian *raptim* (being captured). What in Valéry refers merely to things in dream images can be generalized. As offers of visibility, images simultaneously stage themselves as commandments of visibility that are able to draw in the gaze by virtue of an intrinsic power of attraction. The magical power emanating from the objects depicted irresistibly casts a spell on the gaze as well. Such "traction," which, citing Jean-Luc Nancy, we may consider a basic trait of the iconic,[175] disturbs the circles of routine circumspection and takes the gaze off its habitual track. Where something leaps out, it demands attention for itself. As an always singular appeal, this demand originating from the image can be compared to the request originating in the other person: both call on the viewer and command attention. As in the case of the face that turns to me demandingly and urges me to pay attention, we might speak, in Gilles Deleuze and Félix Guattari's expression, of a "faciality" of the image, a *visagéité* that does not fall silent until it is met by a countergaze.[176]

The topos of being looked at by images is by no means new: from the myth of Pygmalion via the bold gazes directed at the viewer in Lorenzo Lotto's portraits or Edouard Manet's *Olympia* (fig. 5.14), it goes all the way to the *objet petit a* on Lacan's screen. Hegel writes that "art makes every one of its productions into a thousand-eyed Argus, whereby the inner soul and spirit is seen at every point."[177] The most famous and most succinct philosophical articulation of the topos, though, may be found in Cusanus's letter *De visione dei sive De icona*, which he sent to the Benedictines at Tegernsee Abbey in 1453, accompanied by an icon of the "all-seeing God" (*figura cuncta videntis*). Cusanus encourages the monks to form a semicircle in front of the icon of Christ such that each of them will be able to have the experience of being looked at by the gaze from the image. In the ensuing circular movement, in which the monks are to assume various positions along the circle, the gaze follows them; the image, although immobile, moves with each individual. This experimental aesthetics allows for practically experiencing Cusanus's speculative theory of coincidence: seeing and being seen turn out to be one and the same, *videre et videri unum sunt*. "O Lord, when You look upon me with an eye of graciousness, what is Your seeing, other than Your being seen by me?"[178]

In the double and inverse movement of what is looking and what is looked at, which can be observed in many non-Western cultures as well,[179] a cruciform

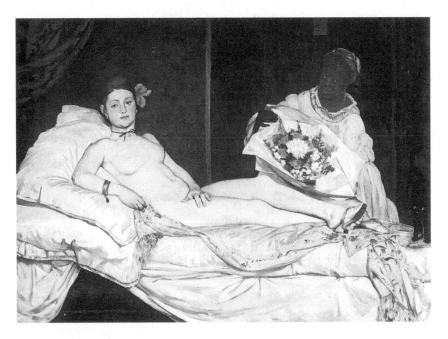

FIGURE 5.14 Edouard Manet, *Olympia* (1863), oil on canvas, 130.5 × 190 cm.
Musée d'Orsay, Paris.

structure emerges that in Merleau-Ponty's terms we may characterize as a chiasm
of gazes. Merleau-Ponty adopts the figure from Valéry, whom he cites as follows:

> As soon as glances meet, we are no longer wholly two, and it is hard to remain
> alone. This exchange (the term is exact) realizes in a very short time a transposi-
> tion or metathesis—a chiasma of two "destinies," two points of view. Thereby a
> sort of simultaneous reciprocal limitation occurs. You capture my image, my
> appearance; I capture yours. You are not *me*, since you see me and I do not see
> myself. What I lack is this me that you see. And what you lack is the you I see.
> And no matter how far we advance in our mutual understanding, as much as
> we reflect, so much will we be different.[180]

This makes clear that the crossing of gazes leads to anything but an undifferentiated amalgamation, that it consists, rather, in a reciprocal dependence based on
a shared lack. Where view and counterview cross, neither one can be taken to a
higher order; both indicate a shift of themselves that manifests as chronological
belatedness. In the anthropologizing expression "gaze of the image," the *genitivus subiectivus* reveals, as a synthetic metonymy, the efficacy of the gaze. The

power of images is due then to the fact that what set in with the response to the image's appeal is being transferred back onto the image itself. Images thus are to be attributed an *iconic appeal character* that is even more fundamental than the appeal of the text Wolfgang Iser (picking up on Roman Ingarden) postulated. Taking up James Elkins, we may say that "the object stares back,"[181] yet this projection of a countergaze is only the post-facto acknowledgment of a visual *punctum* that piqued our attention in the first place. In Georges Didi-Huberman's formula, what we see (*ce que l'on regarde*) always already concerns us (*cela nous regarde*).[182] Benjamin's aura thereby presents itself as the effect of a recursive reappropriation of what preceded: objects that are attributed aura are, as it were, capable of giving a look.[183]

Images thus can render something conspicuous. But then we will have to distinguish between the effect images have in guiding attention and that to which we pay attention thanks to them. In Bernhard Waldenfels's words, we distinguish an effect *by* images from a medial effect *through* images, which always already renders conspicuous more and different things than itself.[184] As pathic media, images are e-motive, they set into motion and, in once more allowing insight into the inseparable ties that link *aisthēsis* and *kinesis* already stressed by Aristotle, restore kinesthesia to literal application. In Merleau-Ponty's terms: "Images appear from the outset to a mobile living body that is the key to the world."[185] Such motoric effects can of course take very different forms, ranging from concentration to ecstasy. The gaze from the image always oscillates between attraction and repulsion, two processes emblematically presented in the mirrorings of Narcissus and depictions of Medusa. The symptom of the unsettled gaze opens up a new range of tensions beyond the mere difference between *what* appears and the *way in which* it appears. The question then becomes that of the difference between the effect of a power *acting on someone* and the effect of a force *effecting something*, the difference between what seeing is affected *by* and what it cannot not respond *to*.[186]

Important though they are for defining images, the relations between gazes are by no means sufficient, as the next, the tenth, symptom makes clear.

(j) Seeing-with

Many newer image theories work with a criterion that goes back to the American theorist of art Richard Wollheim: *seeing-in*. According to Wollheim, images demand a particular way of seeing that differs from the perception of a physical object. Unlike the everyday gaze that recognizes in the thing on the wall a Persian rug and thereby sees *x as y*, iconic (representational) seeing is not exhausted by the structure of *seeing-as*: iconic seeing then means being able to recognize the thing on the wall as a photograph and furthermore to recognize *in it* the person depicted. Images, in this view, are images (and not just mere things) only if they are conceived of as representing something else. In formal terms: *we see images as* x *(the representing) of* y *(the represented)*.

The aporias in which such an undertaking becomes entangled have been discussed at length in analytic aesthetics.[187] This discussion, restricted to aesthetics, is an impressive demonstration of the limitations of a purely propositional theory and of the fallacy of identifying intentionality and propositionality. Such a fallacy is still at the basis of John Searle's theory of intentionality, which infers *seeing something* from *seeing that*: "From the point of view of Intentionality, all seeing is seeing *that*: whenever it is true to say that *x* sees *y* it must be true that *x* sees that such and such is the case."[188] This position amounts to claiming that every *seeing something (p)* must be conceived of as a *seeing that p*: every time I see a red ball I also simultaneously see that the ball is red. Every perception, accordingly, has a propositional content that can be put into language as an assignment of identity or a predication. It may well be correct that this propositional type of seeing (seeing-as) is the most common in everyday life. Nonetheless, such a description ignores that (1) there are intentional forms of seeing that cannot immediately be rearticulated into an assignment of identity, and that (2) there are forms of seeing that are not directed at any intentional content.

(1)   The dimension of an intentional but nonpropositional seeing becomes understandable when we take the situation of *looking like* into consideration. In history paintings, portraits, or photographs whose image-subject cannot be identified with certainty, there is nonetheless an intentional structure. What or who is represented then *recalls* something or someone or "looks *like* x." Such an expedient, a lateral comparison, however, corresponds no more to the classic structure of *apophantic* speech than it does to an *apophatic* absence of content. The analogy thus escapes the alternative between assigning and denying; looking like, we might answer Searle, shows that every seeing something does not necessarily already imply a seeing something as something.

(2)   There is also, distinct from this intentional but nonpropositional *analogizing seeing*, a *seeing of qualia* that operates, for example, in nonrepresentative (rather than "abstract") painting. American Color Field painting, for instance, allows moments of seeing to come to the fore in which the only thing that counts

is the specific color, light, and formal quality of the visible. Such a seeing that entirely depends on the particular act of seeing (its performance) aims solely at the particular *how* of the appearance. In Eva Schürmann's words: "Seeing how something looks cannot in all cases be transposed into utterances capable of being subjected to truth criteria and is therefore neither intentional nor propositional."[189]

Nonetheless, such seeing *per analogiam* or a seeing of *qualia* is no magmatic hallucination; it simply corresponds to possible distinctions insufficiently captured by attributive conceptual logics. Such critical capacities for distinction are in particular demand in saturated or complex contexts—in looking at art, for example. Yet they are deployed not only by trained art critics and *connoisseurs*, as experiments with pigeons have shown. Through targeted training, behavioral biologist Shigeru Watanabe and his team taught birds to distinguish pictures by Picasso from Monets and, generally, Cubist from Impressionist works. Yet few will assign to pigeons a concept of "Cubism" or "Impressionism." How then is their virtually error-free classification to be understood? Evidently, the birds perceive specific visual structures and recognize rule-like patterns. Quite certainly, they do not recognize in the surface structure of Picasso's *Les Demoiselles d'Avignon* either women or sheets or fruit and therefore do not see either that their presentation is distorted. Nonetheless, with almost somnambulistic certainty, they identify a uniform style in the manner of what is seen that can be transformed into instructions for action.[190]

The inductive method suggested by Watanabe's experiment differs from, say, a language-mediated training in recognizing seeing, in that it can only ever be performed *on the object*, in that it always presupposes a *seeing-in*.

SEEING-IN

The Swiss psychiatrist Hermann Rorschach used the ink blots later named after him to stimulate his patients' power of association. In a process of selection, the one administering the test sorts out those formations that patients are likely to designate all too quickly as *image of y*, which would bring the process of association to a halt. The test is considered to have succeeded when a viewing that recognizes gives way to a viewing that "sees in." Such a seeing-in does not exclude seeing-as (after all, an image is useless if nothing at all is seen in the ink blot), but every assignment of identity presupposes a preceding seeing-in.

The relevance of such a seeing-in for image theory is suggested by Leonardo da Vinci's recommendation that aspiring painters practice seeing rivers, valleys, battles, costumes, and gestures in spots that have formed on walls.[191] As much as this kind of seeing-in has been considered the very signature of creative seeing, it is not exhausted by it and in some cases inversely even turns out to be a variant of recognizing seeing. It is possible to speak of constellations of stars as images because within the starry night sky, some stars are literally put into a constellation and constituted as a group of stars. If I am able to project the shape of the homonymous tool onto the Big Dipper, it will be easier for me to find the constellation.

Similar arguments allowed Michael Polanyi to object to Ernst Gombrich's principle of noncontradiction that seeing the *what* and seeing the *what in* do not correspond to the same logic, the first being a "focal," the second a "subsidiary" seeing.[192] In any event, Wollheim's "seeing-in" uncontestably contains a number of difficulties, as several critics have pointed out.[193] To cite but three of them:

(1)   With the concept of "seeing-in," Wollheim seeks to account for the creative potential seeing has. Yet as the example of astronomic constellations shows, not every seeing-in constitutes a creation.

(2)   Wollheim grasps seeing-in as a way of seeing specific to looking at images. Yet when we think that we see a whale in a cloud or that we recognize a face in the spots on a wall, that does not yet mean (as Martin Seel has highlighted) that they are *depicted* there.[194] Jasper Johns's so-called Flag paintings do not depict flags, and it would be just as absurd to say that we see them *as flags*.

(3)   Wollheim's appreciation of the gaze comes with a depreciation of the material process of constitution. His concept of seeing-in grants the *what in* an even smaller role in coconstituting *what* is seen than does Plato's concept of "appearing in."

Such insufficiencies are essentially due to Wollheim's still being beholden to a certain dichotomy: where his theory of objects remains subject to a conception of images' materiality that is too static, he here tries to derive a theory of images from one way of seeing alone. Even more succinctly: *a theory of gazes does not for all that yield a theory of images.*

SEEING-WITH

When we look at images, we do not simply look into something but through them come to see something other than what they are. In Jasper Johns's canvases covered in stripes of color, we might see flags but not—as Sartre would claim—to the detriment of attention to the material but precisely thanks to the material, *with it*. What becomes visible in images is due not only to the free play of the imagination; images, rather, are material objects that preshape the process of becoming visible by their specific constitution. Their matter, in that sense, is always a *materia signata* not because it is exclusively that of an individual (as the Scholastic definition would have it) but because, as structured matter, it lets something individual come forward. Perception is always already formatted by a prepredicative order that precedes evaluative intending. All too often the emphasis on the gaze and the idea, derived from a certain modern tradition of the imagination's freedom, still comes with a neglect or even reduction of the *constitutive* productivity of the material. As Husserl's analysis shows, it is not just phantasy objects that reshape the available sensuous material. Images do so all the more because they cannot do without the support of the image-thing. The material object not only has appearances projected into it, the appearances, rather, come out in the object. The "aboutness" of images is not representational alone but generates a new kind of visibility. Quite often, when seeing "through" images, things come to the fore that could never be seen otherwise. As emerging events, appearances never confront us conceptually naked, they always bear the traces of their provenance.

We thus see not only *in* images, rather rarely *as* images, never *despite* them, but most of the time *with them*, through them and along them. In Bernhard Waldenfels's terms, this generative process can also be described as *medial* iconicity[195]—provided we do not conceive of the medium as the invisible infra-structure of what is generated but as a matrix in which the generating and the generated always mesh and every moment can in principle be significant. Where does the iconic medium end, where does what is presented there begin? Here, too, any kind of identificatory topology is unavoidably undermined: "The ani-mals painted on the walls of Lascaux are not there in the same way as the fissures and limestone formations. Nor are they *elsewhere*. . . . I would be hard pressed to say *where* the painting is I am looking at."[196] Images have an irreducibly atopic character.

———

So much for ten symptoms of iconicity. These symptoms do not always occur in *all* images; most of the time, only some occur, connected in different ways. Indeed, it is possible even to think of images that display only one single symptom. What is decisive is that the domain of images is structured along the lines of family resem-blances. If it no longer constitutes a category mistake to compare natural images, art images, photographs, advertisements, operative images, drawings, graphs, and diagrams with respect to their iconicity, then neither can the proof of burden rest on a single ontological characteristic (which so many image theorists have tried in vain to establish) nor can the comparison be seen to result from the arbitrary conventions of language. Taking the plurality of iconic phenomena into account thus must initially mean describing the interplay of different nonexclusive and yet structurally defining traits. Compared to a classic ontology based on sortal identification, of course, such a symptomatological approach is doubly inappropriate: it always simultaneously offers too little and too much—too little, if the task is to offer robust general categories; too much, if all that is sought are purely conceptual definitions. A symptomatology always provides only an exemplifying phenomenology.

8. ANACHRONISM (TIME-IMAGE 1)

Images, in Hans Belting's terms, open up a gulf. They lie in an intermediate space and accordingly cannot be "situated either 'there' alone, on canvas or photograph, or 'here' in the viewer's head." Rather, they lie in the "interval between 'here' and 'there.'"[197] The question of what an image is transforms into the question of where we are when we look at an image. Obviously, this much is clear, we are no longer entirely where we were just now but not quite yet entirely in the space the image gives us to see. The immersion effect that images prompt in viewers creates a "proximity through distance" (Merleau-Ponty), a gaze that, through them, is steered elsewhere. Images thus prove to be "shifters" of a special kind: they always effect a change of place and time. Where the here becomes telepresence and the distant comes into closest proximity, not just the Euclidian logic of place is unsettled, our very conceptions of time enter into new constellations. The chiastic relationship points to a fundamental iconic nonsimultaneity. When images presentify something that has been, they not so much restore what is past as they attest to its irreversible having-been. For something that has been to become experienceable as having been there at all—*ça a été*, as Roland Barthes would say—it must always already have withdrawn from the surface that makes visible. The experience of images is thus always the experience of a chronological incongruence: the terms of the iconic relation belong to different temporal regions. Simultaneous copresence is replaced by what linguistic sociology calls "distended communication situations": what thus enters into connection lies temporally (and thus also spatially) apart; only an intermediary term institutes an at best secondary, because medial, copresence.

Konrad Ehlich introduced the formula of the "distended communication situation" to describe processes of meaning in writing. As opposed to the face-to-face interaction characteristic of oral cultures, writing—and thus literality in general—opens up another form of communication situation that Ehlich suggests defining as "distended," that is, extended across space and time, in an only virtual copresence. The limited situation of an unambiguously identifiable sender and a corresponding recipient is thus broken up, which simultaneously infinitely expands the possible addressees. Transposing the category of the distended situation to images, as Jan Assmann has suggested, presupposes correlating to the event of speech and its reception the generation of images and their reception with their respective sites.[198] In keeping with the paradigm of communication studies, the imagineering process is then a procedure of compressing time, time that is stored in the image, while the reception of images is the reperformance of the time contained in the image.

The time of reception, however, stands in an inverse proportional relationship with the time of production: confronted with a stratified, necessarily palimpsestic work, whose uppermost layers open up the view on the ones below them in the first place, the constitution of the image in reception amounts to an archeological labor that can find its way back to what stood at the beginning for the producer of the image only by temporally moving away from this originary event. Every attempt at getting at the *origo* of the image's initial positing, every asymptotic approximation to the originary event cannot but push it back further into the past. Speaking of the time being stopped in the image from the outset comprises two things: first, the persistence of the image-object, and second, the temporally indexed positing of the generation of the image. Nonetheless, both of these stoppings acquire their meaning in the first place only by demarcating sites within a temporal continuum. Put succinctly: even what has been stopped is still being stopped *in time*. This state of affairs is confirmed, for instance, in Oscar Wilde's *The Portrait of Dorian Gray* and the mirror-image inversion the novel stages: Dorian succeeds in having not himself but the portrait painted by Basil age, yet here, too, the presenting and the presented inexorably diverge. Depending on one's point of reference, the relationship might change, but the irreversible temporal deferment will not.

The time of the image is thus marked by a peculiar countertemporality or heterochrony. The process of divergence, the distension or diastasis, however, is just one side of the coin; the image relation also consists in a coinciding of the nonsimultaneous, a downright *coincidentia differentiarum*. In Walter Benjamin's terms, images thus represent sudden constellations of the heterogenous, "secret agreements" between what is past and what is present; this constitutes their historicality in the first place. Freely adapting the famous description by Lautréamont, what behaves like a "chance meeting of an umbrella with a sewing machine on a dissecting table" is proven ex post to have been necessary by what is there to be seen. This also means that there is no correct point of view from which appropriately to look at an image, no right moment that would belong to the image *ab ovo*. Why, after all, should the time of the image's emergence be more appropriate for the image than every other later point in time if images, like every appearance, are always appearances for something or someone? Why should images be deciphered in the context of their age, their social and cultural horizon of emergence, if it is part of their destiny that, as a matter of principle, they are open to every future addressee?[199]

The fundamental historicism with which the discipline that long considered itself exclusively to be responsible for images—art history—approached them testifies to its striking blindness to the fact of the originarily distended situation.[200] Benjamin's definition of the dialectical image may serve to repeat the point succinctly: "It's not that what is past casts its light on what is present, or what is present its light on what is past; rather, image is that wherein what has been comes together in a flash with the now to form a constellation. In other words, image is dialectics at a standstill."[201]

The time of the image extends between the appropriate *chronos*, to which we may add Barthes's embedding *studium*, and the *kairos* of the image suddenly imposing itself, the inciting *punctum* that already breaks through any linear epistemic order. In this sense every experience of images contains an anachronistic moment, and every anachronism proves to be both a threat to knowledge and the only level on which knowledge is possible. Iconic epistemes and their "differentials of time" bring out something that is true of historicality as such: the unavoidability of anachronism. Anachronism—to use Georges Didi-Huberman's terms—thus proves to be the "*pharmakon* of history" in the best sense, at once its poison and its remedy.[202] Didi-Huberman's own example points to what an image theory under the auspices of anachronism might entail.

9. IMAGE POTENTIAL, IMAGE ACT (TIME-IMAGE 2)

The fresco of the *Madonna delle Ombre* (ca. 1440–1450) in the eastern corridor of San Marco convent in Florence is characterized by Fra Angelico's habitual quiet sublimity. It shows a Madonna with the child surrounded by various saints recognizable by their attributes. The figures are unambiguously distinguishable, they can be organized into an iconic semantics, and they are thus, as a matter of principle, *legible*. It is a concrete pictorial confirmation of the *istoria* Alberti enthroned as the definition of iconic composition. While iconic research has focused on the iconographic significance of the individual figures, the lower half (fig. 5.15) has been dismissed with the remark that it is just another *finto marmo*, one among many fake marbles painted in the late Middle Ages in Tuscany. This view, however, ignores that this magnificent ornamentation is applied in a convent otherwise striking for its impeccably ascetic purity. Nor is there any indication that the painter sought realistically to imitate marble veins. On the contrary, everything suggests that Beato Angelico has "projected, from a distance, a splattering of blotches, multicolored blotches that produce on the surface . . . a completely irregular splattering."[203]

Such visual deflagrations cannot be attributed to any canonical knowledge; they cannot be deduced from any *Iconologia*, Cesare Ripa's or anyone else's: their illegibility through the iconographic lens quite simply condemned them to invisibility. The chromatic shower of spots disguised as *finto marmo* had to remain ignored until viewed by an eye that, trained in Jackson Pollock's *Drippings*, had learned to see the nonidentical. Yet how is it possible to think something that lies at the center of the field of visibility without for all that counting as something individually visible? This section attempts, in the footsteps of Merleau-Ponty, Lyotard, and Didi-Huberman, to get closer to the difficulty of grasping this thing that belongs to the visual domain while escaping our current vision, this "visual" that is not yet part of what is "visible" right now.

In *Discourse, Figure*, Lyotard distinguishes between *the visual* and *the visible*.[204] The visual, as he writes in later texts, is "not so much seen than it lets see" (*plutôt que vu, il fait voir*) and thus "would include, if not invisibility, then at least actually non-seen givens, some unseen, un-given givens."[205] For Didi-Huberman, who picks up on Lyotard without naming him, the visual therefore always already refers to something virtual, a *virtus*, a potency. The potential, the virtual-visual "never gives a direction for the eye to follow, or a univocal sense of reading." It is not for all that without meaning but instead "draws from its kind of negativity the strength of a multiple deployment; it makes possible . . . entire constellations of meaning, of which we must accept never to know the totality and the closure."[206]

Such sites of indeterminacy in the image—for example, the space gaping between the angel and Mary in Fra Angelico's *Annunciations*—are not meaningless blanks but, instead, matrices of meaning in which a figurative force rests in a state of latency. That is why it is clearly insufficient to define images merely

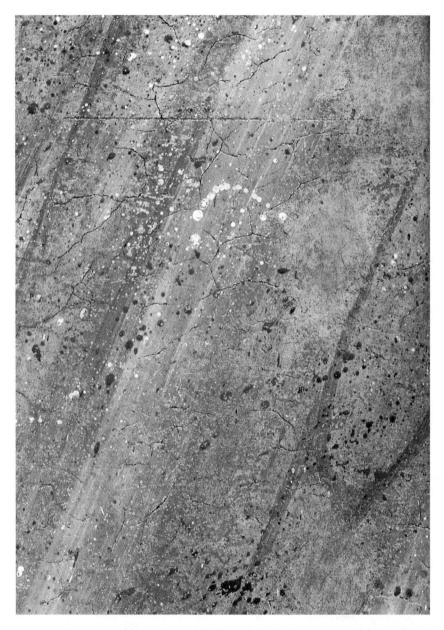

FIGURE 5.15 Beato Angelico, *Madonna delle Ombre* (detail) (ca. 1450), fresco and tempera. Convento di San Marco, Florence.

via the symptom of their synopticity or simultaneity. What needs explanation, rather, is how it is that images do not keep anything from the eye and yet in them, not everything is given visibly from the outset. It is evidently not enough—as we now see—to define images as *plane givens*; they are also inhabited by a specific efficacy of their own: they *allow for time*. It thus turns out that visual efficacy, that ominous figural *virtus*, can be detected simply in its primary effect, namely, the temporality it institutes.

Images, we might say, often require time to fully unfold their content. But in another sense, they also generate a time of their own; they make space for time, as it were. For sure, we can hardly nail down such an "image time" in merely chronological terms, in terms of "clock time." We might then further distinguish a duration or a segment of time documented by an image (a historical event depicted in a history painting or a process archived by a photograph with a long exposure time) and the time it takes for the image to present all its content. In such a case, we would differentiate the *shown time* from the *time of showing*. In that respect, an instantaneous photograph developed in a large-scale format might contain elements the onlookers only discover after an extended scrutiny.[207] In other words, while some images may take an excruciating long time for the beholder to understand their content, others strike us out of the blue. Many images, especially the artistic ones, invite us to dwell, that is, to discover their repleteness by gradually letting them have their effect on us. Yet images can, on the contrary, just act as powerful eye-catchers that summarize a complex state of affairs and turn it into a remarkably simple arrangement. And yet such "striking images" (to cite Warburg again), too, develop a temporality that goes beyond their instantaneous grasp: seeing—as Gorgias has it in the passage from the *Encomium of Helena* cited earlier—irrevocably inscribes images in thinking; images continue to have an effect for a long time. In both cases, iconicity is never given; rather, it wants always to be sought out and earned. In that sense, we may say that images are, literally, "time-workers" that sediment not only the time of their own genesis (something the avant-gardes intensify in the form of self-reflexivity, in Pollock, for example, or in informalist paintings, where the time of production becomes the time of the work); even their genesis depends on being re- and therefore cogenerated in a viewer as the addressee of this image event. If indeed there is a genuine "performativity" of the image, then it is one in which the positing of the image is not opposed to the reiteration of this positing. That something is posited in images is never without preconditions: something already existing is taken up, something present reworked; nonetheless, positing an image is never a mere continuation, it also always coposits its own beginning.[208] Such a theory of positing, however, is not restricted to the initial setting up of visibility; the *creatio continua* that is the chiasm of gazes, too, bears performative traits. Like Sybille Krämer, we might surmise that the performativity of the image is to be located less in the production of images than in the exchange of gazes.[209] In other words: every image process always already starts long before the beholder sets her sight on things.[210]

This has three consequences:

(1)   Images are not limited to real presences; generally, iconicity cannot be thought purely in the terms of the present tense. To quote Gilles Deleuze, "The image is not in the present. . . . The image itself is a bunch of temporal relations from which the present unfolds, either as a common multiplier or as a common denominator."[211] The instantaneous present moment, since Lessing's *Laocoon* the only form of time granted the image, expands and shifts to become duration, a duration, however, that differs from Bergson's (and thus Deleuze's) *durée* in that it is never immediately given but, in Gaston Bachelard's terms, only ever to be constructed.[212]

(2)   It is impossible to draw a line separating temporal genesis and timeless validity once and for all. Rather, in images, genesis and validity amalgamate in a new conjunction. As such, they remain transitory as a matter of principle and are thus, from the outset, beyond the reach of univocal ontological definitions. To cite Aristotle once more, "As becoming [*genesis*] is between being and not being, so that which is becoming is always between that which is and that which is not."[213] What takes shape here is a different concept of time that sees time no longer as a synthesis but as a continuing process of splitting, a sort of *creatio continua* of the discontinuous.

(3)   Such a performative phenomenology of time nonetheless differs from an anorganic process taking place by itself in the dark because its performance itself manifests only in the reperformance. The necessity of the reperformance shows that image acts are actualizations that do not translate potency into acts without remainder; we are dealing with what Aristotle calls *sōtēria*, "preserving potency."[214]

It is well worth keeping this basic theoretical constellation derived from Aristotelianism in mind when we approach the iconic logic of indeterminacy. Figures of ambivalence of the kind embodied in anamorphoses or ambiguous images that, following Dario Gamboni, we may call "potential images" point us to a fundamental *potentiality* on the part of images.[215] "Potentiality" here means the *capacity of taking a visible form without once and for all becoming that form* (and thereby excluding taking other forms later). A philosophy under the auspices of such a potentiality differs from the Wolffian definition of philosophy as "science of the possible *insofar as* it can be" because here, *dynamis* points to the possible independently of whether this possible can *be*. In this regard, Bergson's interpretation of potentiality (which Deleuze takes up) as a structure coming into its own in the actualization does not seem to go far enough. At least in its aisthetic variant, Aristotle's *dynamis* has advantages that are analogous to what Bergson calls (in contrast to the potential) the virtual: the potential does not differ from the real but from the actual, from the indicative *here and now*.

Generally, the possibility of thinking the specificity of images is still weighed down by the historical narrowing of iconicity to iconicity in the indicative mode. Conceiving of iconicity as a process instead means opening the view onto all the iconic practices that allow for images in the conjunctive mood. Charles Baudelaire evidently had this in mind when he described image appearances as "conjectures."[216] At least as often as they serve to point to what is given (to *indicate*), images serve to explore possible situations and to articulate visual hypotheses. Such tentative experimental setups in the image show *how* it would be *if* it were. They then resemble the *Konjekturalbiographie* by the nineteenth-century writer Jean Paul. In this conjectural biography, written in the future anterior, this German Romantic author looks back, although what he describes will perhaps never have taken place.

What is being tested in these experimental setups is nothing arbitrary; it is the intrinsic necessity of relations that, although they are not actual, are not for all that undefined. Examples include Yves Klein's patented "air curtain" project, Henry James's virtual "Madonna of the Future," or the iconic tennis game without a ball in Michelangelo Antonioni's *Blowup*. Such conjunctions develop a different kind of coherence, but they are not for all that arbitrary, by no means. Beyond actual being-such and pure possibility, images approach what Cusanus sought to express when he contracted *posse* (to be able) and *esse* (to be) into the word *possest*.

Insofar as such possibilizations themselves deal with the indeterminate, they show themselves to be rooted in the sensuous space; iconic potentiality in particular depends on a corporeal medium from which the resources for variation are taken. This is what the reperformance of an accident with miniature dolls during a Paris court trial reminds us of, which inspired Wittgenstein's image theory of propositions. The indispensability of the somatic dimension is even more apparent, for example, in Tintoretto's pictorial practice of hanging the painted figures of a pictorial composition up around the studio to test their relations among one another and the effect on the viewer.[217] Along with many others, these examples prove that where something appears, this appearing depends on embodying performances (independently of the existence or nonexistence of that which appears).

10. WHEN THE MEDIUM SHINES THROUGH

From time to time, the way modern exhibitions work still confirms Lessing's and Winckelmann's reduction of the time of the image to an eternally enduring *nunc stans*. The reduction of the image value to its exhibition value comes with a downright detemporalization that manifests, not least of all, in the glass pane that withdraws the image lying behind it, remaining identical with itself, from occasional access. The transparency dispositif of the glass pane not only separates the tactile from the optical, it also takes what lies behind out of the course of things in the world: the more fragile, the more vulnerable to time the materiality of the image is, the more massive is the vitrification operated on it.

Among the works subjected to such a process are the paintings of the Norwegian painter Edvard Munch. Almost all his paintings hang behind laminated antireflection glass to reduce ultraviolet rays: what is to be seen behind it is to remain in the same state for centuries. The artist himself did not take the same kind of care of his works. Visitors report having on occasion to free of snow paintings stored outside in the deep of winter. The works exposed to the seasons were by no means discarded pieces. Munch thought that the becoming-image can take place only under the influence of sun, rain, and snow. The assimilation of corroded substrate and anemic subject is particularly striking in *The Sick Child* (fig. 5.16). The Norwegian painter thus not only offers a prelude to the inclusion of chance that was to become a slogan in twentieth-century material art, his "drastic cure" moreover sets up the decay of the material. The only varnish Munch would accept, the only patina he would allow, was, in his own account, the patina of time.[218]

Especially the products of Munch's late period unmistakably bear the traces of external influences, from damage done by the artist himself, such as carvings on the

FIGURE 5.16   Edvard Munch, *The Sick Child* (1906), oil on canvas, 118 × 121 cm.
Tate Gallery, London.

edges and scratches, to the involuntary traces left by the weather. In the painting of
the *Bathers* (ca. 1913), for example, birds participated: the white splatters in the
upper half have been identified as bird excrement. In short, painting as marking, as
the art of the mark, of the *macchia* or *macula*, here returns to its beginning and
exposes itself, unprotected, to its own temporality. In Merleau-Ponty's terms: "The
objects in a modern painting 'bleed,' their substance spreads under our eyes."[219]
    Such an aesthetics of being conditioned is by no means opposed to a poetics
of possibilization; at most, it opposes an ideology of transparency that conceives
of image worlds as glass cultures in which—in Benjamin's and Paul Scheerbart's
terms—no trace can be left.[220] Munch himself already protested when his works

were put at a standstill by the application of the golden gallery varnish so popular around 1900 because what is at issue for him is that what is painted mixes
again and again with the stuff of the world. The image's temporal condition not
only implies that temporality has constitutively inscribed itself there, it also
means that the process through which something comes into appearance in the
image still shines through in the image itself. Mediality shines through where
every validity is thrown back onto its own genesis. Or, to put it in Mikel
Dufrenne's terms: images are objects that a posteriori exhibit in themselves their
own a priori basic conditions, in the paper left blank in Paul Cézanne's watercol-
ors, in the particularities of the jute fabric shining through in Paul Klee's paintings, in the ground coming to the fore in Frank Stella's *Stripe Paintings*.[221]

Beyond the easel, the South African artist William Kentridge develops a concept
of the image of its own that is made possible only by the interplay of different
media. The screen of a video installation shows, mounted into a sequence, photographs of charcoal drawings in which objects at various stages of a trajectory
can be seen. In contrast to illusionistic animations, the image repetition is significantly less than the frequency of 24 Hz; just a few sketches per second are
mounted together. The bold drawings, sketched in rough charcoal and developing in jumps, are indeed narrative. Short narrative episodes develop, but they
quickly flip and metamorphose into material for new sequences. Kentridge does
not develop a preceding script; rather, the sceneries unfold from the process of
drawing, resembling oneiric visions rather than a common narrative film.

The process in which the shadow images emerge, which calls on drawing,
photography, and film equally, takes place extremely slowly: for eight minutes of
film, Kentridge needs about six months. One particular signature of his drawings is that it is always the selfsame piece of paper that generates an always-new
image: erasing, smudging, and overwriting open up the possibility of differentiation and further development. Early on, the artist still tried to delete the traces
of such preceding shapes completely, but he came to allow the pentimenti ever
more space; now in each actual state the preceding states shine through as on a
palimpsest (fig. 5.17). The procedure comes in to address the question the South
African artist's work incessantly turns around: memory. Events from colonial
history, experiences from Apartheid, but intimate scenes as well, quotidian
phantasies and utopian visions of the future run into each other and yield ever
new time-image layers. Almost like dream sequences whose linearity, too, only
ever lasts for a few seconds, Kentridge's individual image scenes obey a certain

FIGURE 5.17 William Kentridge, *Felix Listens to the World*, coal on paper, in *Sobriety, Obesity & Growing Old* (filmstill). Marian Goodman Gallery, New York. Courtesy of Kentridge Studio.

coherence but melt already the moment they seem to come together in a narrative. What Kentridge mounts together are fragments that resist being tied down into a closed (hi)story.

We may correlate the image appearance in Kentridge, which only ever emerges through the charcoal drawing setting in anew, being deleted anew, with Husserl's analyses of time. More than that: in this correlation, the medial constitution of Kentridge's iconic geneses that various commentators have remarked on sheds new light on the mediality of time in Husserl, who also characterizes time as diaphany or shining-through.[222] At the decisive point where he is concerned with reconciling the primacy of actuality with an ever progressing arrow of time, Husserl introduces the idea of the diaphany of the past, its "shining through." In time, he writes, impressions continually shuffle, shift, overlap, and relocate, such that something identical is only ever to be had in the "mediacy of shining-through" (*Mittelbarkeit des Durchscheinens*). In the continuum of time, what has just been experienced falls back, is concealed by something else, and thus becomes undifferentiated and unintuitive but inversely also comes through and thus makes it possible in the first place that we recognize something *as something*: "The concealed 'shines through,' and what is shining through is itself something that conceals and has its something shining through etc."[223] In their own way, we might surmise, Kentridge's time images perform Edmund Husserl's eidetic variation, which itself constitutively depends on its own temporalization.

———

The temporalization of the image also comes with a corrosion of the very possibility of objectifying images. Where images can no longer be thought as things but henceforth only as processes, their fixity decays and the gaze is steered back onto those constitutive processes that can no longer be the sole result of a positing subjectivity. All the currents and vortices of air, the "moving accessories" at the figure's edge that since the Florentine Renaissance have been pointing to a mobilization of the appearances, are transitory moments.[224] Such medial conditions of becoming visible are not simply invisible; their visuality is itself peripheral and marginal, it literally lies *fra 'l vedi e il non vedi*, between seeing and not seeing. From the edges they set the visible in motion and permeate it at the same time, like those clouds that since Brunelleschi's experiment pervade the order of representation without ever being able to obtain a place of their own within it.[225]

Can the mediality of the medium of perception be rendered visible at all? In everyday perception at least, that mostly happens marginally, on the edges, as it were. While we see things next to and behind each other in space, we see the media of perception as the space that makes them possible only ever in exceptional cases, as in a situation, for instance, that Wilhelm Schapp in his phenomenology of perception describes as follows: "Thus we see the quivering above the hot lamp directly, tearing itself away from the surrounding air; here we see the peculiar elasticity, tenacity of the air. The air then almost appears like a thick liquid."[226] Images, in contrast, are media of presentation that are capable like no others of rendering visible the making-visible of the medium of perception.

When the marginality of the medial is relativized, as in modernism, such conditions of possibility of images become the topic of the images themselves, from Ferdinand Hodler's mountain pictures in which the atmospheric space that lets a mountain chain come forward is illustrated by striata of clouds and other meteorological formations via Victor Hugo's material evocations of the elements in his Guernsey drawings to Jules-Etienne Marey's photographic visualization of currents of air. What, in terms of everyday visibility, is hardly visible—the medial atmosphere, that which surrounds our embodied perception—becomes the very issue at stake: that which conditions experience becomes experienceable in its own right. In Olafur Eliasson's installations, it practically becomes the soundboard of a new poetry of apparatuses.

Olafur Eliasson: Atmospheres of Light

In *The Weather Project,* installed in Tate Modern's turbine hall in 2003, Olafur Eliasson denies the viewer any possibility of focusing on an object of perception. There just isn't anything to see or, more precisely, there is not Something; the viewer is instead practically drawn into the immense space and literally immersed in the golden light emanating from the "sun" installed at the end wall (fig. 5.18). This shining light systematically filters out all colors of the spectrum, and only shades of yellow and black are maintained. What remains is impressive: the more than three thousand square meters of the old turbine hall transform into a unique color space in which visitors can move around freely, sit down, lie down. The spherical "sun" assembled from two hundred monofrequency lights is reflected in the huge mirror affixed to the ceiling at a 40-meter height, and the atmospheric effect is furthermore amplified by a delicate fog being pushed into the room at regular intervals from laterally mounted openings, a fog through which the color condenses in the space itself and, as it were, becomes an infinity of traversable chromatic particles.

Unlike Californian light artists such as James Turrell, Eliasson is not concerned with prompting a magical experience of being overpowered that is produced by skillfully hiding the apparatus. Instead, he consciously exhibits the construction that makes visible (the cables behind the monofrequency lamps are clearly visible). Nor is the artificially produced light supposed to evoke any experience of natural light. Eliasson may indeed serve as prime example for the idea that technically produced mediality and phenomenality do not exclude each other but converge in letting something appear. Thus, although he certainly continues their intellectual heritage, Eliasson takes a path that differs from the radical autonomization of the space of light that Turrell and the California light artists have pursued since the 1960s. While they are concerned with the pure reflexivity of the act of perception, Eliasson exhibits the constitutive dependence of photoform appearance on the apparatuses that make it possible. Mediation—Eliasson's core concept—then means saying goodbye to the notion of a "'natural' state of things, being unaware of the constructions lying behind the situation. The challenge of orienting ourselves

FIGURE 5.18 Olafur Eliasson, *The Weather Project* (2003/2004). Turbine Hall, Tate Modern, London. Artwork courtesy of Olafur Eliasson Studio. Photo by Nathan Williams.

in a mediated realm is therefore to see through and know when, to what extent and by whom a situation has been mediated; to be aware of a situation's relationship with time."[227]

(Continued next page)

(*Continued*)

   This disclosure, however, has nothing of a grand gesture of revelation; the experience of perception takes place despite the simultaneous acknowledgment of its conditions of possibility. Even more than in *360° room for all colours*, Eliasson in *The Weather Project* appeals beyond the sense of sight to synesthetic dimensions in which the media of appearance, such as light and color, are to be felt in one's body. The atmospheric space here is anything but static: in the course of the day, densifications emerge when the fog forms clouds that waft slowly through the space. In Denis Diderot's formula, the artist here endows the air itself with a corporeality that has a weight of its own. There is, however, a principle to counter this densification: as the fog circulates, the air absorbs the water particles. The Icelandic-Danish artist—who in other, earlier interventions in urban as well as landscape settings has worked with water, weather, and wind—here brings the atmospheric weather conditions back to their most basic definition. What becomes experienceable is that which lets experience; the visitor—to cite a formula going back to Alexander of Aphrodisias—is immersed in a literal *phainesthai dia*, a shining through.[228]

   In its own way, such an aesthetics of the atmosphere repeats the disjunction of the level of appearance and the level of judgment. While on the level of judgment, works of art expose themselves to art *criticism*, whose task is to define the genuine value of a work, phenomenal atmospheres initially escape evaluation. When we enter a new space, we try first of all to become aware of the peculiar quality of the space surrounding us. We do not encounter an atmosphere the way we encounter an artistic object-like artifact. We never face an atmosphere: we immerse ourselves in it. That is why it is so difficult to judge it with a detached gaze, the standard stance tasked with judging the merit or demerit of a specific artwork's qualities. Atmospheric qualities are qualities that go under our skin. They derive their specific texture from a certain tuning of the medial surroundings, a certain organization of the intervals in which the surrounding space, like dieses in music, produces a particular mood. The "allure" of things becomes inseparable from the surrounding air, as when a walker is suddenly surrounded by a thick mist.

As these examples show, discussions about the medium in art should not be restricted to an artwork's materiality and its "medium specificity." Media are not only carriers; they are immersive spaces as well. Beyond framed and encircled objects and their specific materiality, there is a mediality of what surrounds the object, its immersive or ambient quality. Hence the need for an expanded and yet all the more phenomenal conception of the medium: its nature corresponds less to an objective feature than to an atmospheric tone. The medium can take the form of an ambience: as something that is neither psychological, arising from within, nor objective, imposed by things from the outside, "ambience" names the atmosphere that colors experience and gives it a particular tone. We do not perceive an atmosphere as we do an object: it lacks the familiar outline of things; we perceive it indirectly, indeed, we breathe it more than we grasp it.

What is opened up here is a dimension that lies this side of rather than beyond the framed image, a dimension of pervasive iconicity that reminds us that images can be explained only if we suppose that the reality from which they derive already bears iconic traits and that in this reality an emergent iconic potential accrues. Iconicity thus begins earlier than with the current image; in all potential, imagined, and future image constellations, it always also exceeds them; it is a matrix of possibilities properly speaking, a *metaxy* of appearances. Between unarity and binarity, between the self-enclosure of things and the referentiality of the sign, the figure of the image shining through names the transitivity of that which precedes duality, a tense, distended identity that has not yet fallen apart into two elements and yet always already has begun elsewhere than with itself.

What thus takes shape is, in Merleau-Ponty's expression, a "thought by divergence" (*pensée d'écart*),[229] a thinking, that is, that begins with the potencies and differences already sensuously organizing themselves and that articulates the very question of what factors define appearance on the basis of the singular factors of appearance. What gives itself to see—this is the intuition slowly outlining itself—is never given immediately but turns out to be the epiphenomenon of an appearing-through-another. A thinking that begins with the primordial budding of the visible and satisfies itself that images are intensifications of such an elementary appearing can never be but a thinking that diverges.

Conclusion

Seeing Through Images—for an Alternative Theory of Media

In Tommaso Campanella's ideal utopian *City of the Sun*, with which this book began, there is no space for libraries: images replace writing. Conspicuously, in fact, the Renaissance, so intimately tied in with the age of Gutenberg in the European subconscious, dreams not of texts but of images. A search for libraries in the era's classic utopias will come up empty: every project of an ideal state resembles an *orbis pictus*, a world full of images. What does this pictorial dream stand for? Might our late modernity have actualized it? Or does our contemporary hypervisualized society instead resemble a Platonic nightmare, in which the Sophists and their play of spectacularly dancing sleeves have taken over? Against the background of the long intellectual history, the current situation acquires an entirely new depth of focus that brings out the oppositions even more sharply. There is, on the one hand, the promise of a new immediacy that pervades already Campanella's Renaissance utopia, the promise of a visual literacy that does not require any antecedent alphabetization and is accessible to all citizens equally; the image as an efficient tool of emancipation that puts everyone on the same level. Yet, on the other hand, there are the warnings against the power of simulacra, the Cassandra calls against the seductive power of semblance. Whereas the ones praise the image surface as a window to the world that clears the view onto the things themselves, the others sound the alarm about the obstructive character of the screen that blocks an authentic grasp of reality. It is little surprise, then, that our concept of the image continues to move between two alternatives, between a conception of the image as transparent seeing through and a conception of the image as an opaque, self-contained artifact.

The goal of this book has been to clarify what patterns still guide our thinking about images today and how these transparency and opacity theories of the image developed historically. The genealogical analysis of premodern discourses about images reveals that the tracks along which today's controversies largely move go back a long way and are closely tied in with antecedent ontological decisions. The lip service paid to postmetaphysical thinking, in any case, will hardly suffice to free ourselves from the grip of metaphysical categories. Those theories especially that consciously stay away from ontological questions along the lines of "what is an image?" are burdened all the more by this epistemic heritage. Newly founded disciplines such as visual studies, too, de facto go back to a conceptual vocabulary that was elaborated centuries earlier and in entirely different contexts and which, in that regard, cannot help but prejudice current reflections. To speak today of images' immateriality, their virtuality, or their efficacy is, for better or for worse, to employ concepts with a long prior history that cannot be separated from a particular history of metaphysics. Quite remarkably, images today are primarily grasped either via their referentiality or via their material thingness. These conceptual crutches allow for avoiding the embarrassments of dealing with images' phenomenality: images, on these interpretations, are artifacts that are either present or representational and thus correspond to either single-digit (image $[x]$) or two-digit predicates (image $[x,y]$). Such categorial place assignments of course also constitute strategies to remedy the unsettling effects of images being appearances. For where something enters appearance in images and through images, both proximity and distance are always involved. Something becomes intuitable and graspable here and now, and yet it is also exceeds this particular given insofar as it is not exhausted by this perspective. Images always already convey something more and something else than what they are themselves; this, precisely, is what makes them media.

One general characteristic of media is that they are never autonomous: heteronomy is their perpetual condition. That is why media theorists should stop trying to hide the link that connects them to the figure of the medium in occultism. The spiritist medium, in fact, illustrates a decisive connection: the medium yields to something else, as a surrogate body, as it were, for messages presented in a stranger's voice. Yet that mediums receive their orders from elsewhere, which they discharge now better, now worse, and that they give expression to a voice that is not theirs does not mean that they do not add something of their own to this process of embodiment. From the perspective of Aristotle's theory of media, we might say that wherever media are at work, they take on a form to whose shaping they have contributed: they "in-form" the information they convey. Although, accordingly, mediums never act on their own initiative, they endow what they allow to become visible and audible with an unavoidable turn of their own. This spin, this specific sense, this particular style can never be expunged completely, and it is responsible for the bad reputation mediums have.

Not just spiritist mediums: messengers, mediators, and translators generally are suspected of pursuing their own agendas in the game of transmission and of sullying the conveyed content with foreign additions. This smoldering suspicion is instructive, for it exposes two things: on the one hand, it continues the dream of a transparent media channel through which bundles of messages produced elsewhere reliably reach their destination. On the other hand, it betrays a suspicion toward all medial processes, namely, the suspicion that these processes are never fully transparent to the observer. Where media are on the move and medial performance takes place, the performance itself, at least to a certain extent, refuses to be retraced precisely because media always allow something other than themselves to appear. Nonetheless, their effect often remains noticeable, like watermarks that shine through what appears in them.

This result of this book's diaphenomenological analysis points us to why traditional media theories fail to capture the specificity of visual media or why they might even pass over a decisive aspect of media generally: the aspect of phenomenality. Based on the general suspicion against all kinds of processes of mediation, it has classically been supposed that media best conduct their business in the dark, that they act covertly and behind the scenes. This history of suspicion, moreover, accords well with the traditional bias of a media theory primarily developed in response to digital media, which rely on a standardized code that is active in the background and need not appear in the transmitted content: both reinforce the conception that media processes fundamentally unfold in a dual manner, that there is a level of appearances to be separated from a background activity, a front end from a back end. Yet such doubling does not take place in the case of media that precisely do not operate behind our backs but in the light of day, before our eyes. We might call them presentative media. Presentative media present something in and via themselves by taking a specific form that has nothing to do with their being. This, put simply, was Aristotle's basic intuition concerning elementary media of perception: media adopt the form without adopting the being and therefore preserve the capacity for further metamorphoses, that is, for further transformations toward (*meta*) other forms (*morphosis*).

Looking at images more carefully, engaging them with the necessary discernment, letting them have an effect on us then means letting ourselves be drawn into a generation of sense that unfolds according to rules that differ from the syntax of finite systems of signs. Images belong to presentative media in that they show something that does not lie elsewhere but is made present in this and not in any other way by their medial embodiment in the first place. Attempts at translation, in this regard, are the best touchstone: while, in principle, digitally coded messages can change supports without problems, the way premodern envoys changed horses at relay stations, presentative media tend to recoil from

such translation. The way images are designed, their proportions, color contrasts, and lines of force, their edges, gaps, and omissions, are no additions that
for the sake of better portability could safely be dispensed with in a formatting
process. Rather, presentative media such as images owe their succinctness to the
fact that in their phenomenality, every aspect tends to count. Images—and this
is the thesis of this book—must therefore be investigated starting primarily
from their phenomenality.

In addition, images (and presentative media generally) allow for bringing out
something that digitizing procedures precisely exclude, namely, what it means
for something to appear. If phenomena generally are defined as finite appearances, then pictorial phenomena are appearances that specifically operate with
and reflectively deploy their finitude. They must generate attention and produce
meaning within the frame of the image plane, within a delineated visual field.
Producers of images are phenomenologists in that they must first find out the
laws of phenomenality in order to then, hopefully, be able to use them as a phe-
nomenotechnique for their specific purposes. (Once more, the laws that govern
appearing cannot be set off against the laws that govern propositions, nor can
they be derived from them.) Such thematizing of superficiality is a downright art
that, picking up on Hans Jonas, we might also call the "frugality" of the image.
Budgeting limited means of presentation and going back to the specificity of the
medium here points less to autonomy than to an economy all its own: what keeps
visual pleasure going is the oscillation between offering and withholding visibility, between opening and closure.

The power of appearing that unfolds in images therefore enjoins us to think
anew the connections between meaning and phenomenality and between medium
and force. Insofar as that through which images appear cannot be detached from
their mode of appearing (insofar, that is, as the content cannot be separated from
the *how* of the work), images always also tell us something about their conditions
of appearing; this constitutes their reflective moment. Conversely, they also force
us to acknowledge that what appears is never given immediately but always ever
only appears through something else. Whether such medial processes take place
behind our backs or right before our eyes, what Hegel says about epistemic concepts also applies to media: that through which thinking takes place is precisely
something that is not being thought *about.* Media are not just largely invisible
because they act behind the scenes: in many ways, they also act directly before our
eyes and yet are often overlooked, like the windowpane our gaze passes through.
Yet if all cognition is refracted by the mediacy of media through which it takes
place, then—as Hegel already stressed—knowing the laws of refraction is of little
use: to subtract the medium of refraction is also to lose the ray of light.[1]

Afterword

Seeing Not Riddling

ANDREW BENJAMIN

The subtitle of Emmanuel Alloa's book defines its task. What is at stake is indeed a phenomenology. While there can be a hermeneutics of art that would be informed by a conception of seeing linked to processes of understanding, *Looking Through Images* advances a radically different project. Its undertaking is clear at the outset. Alloa writes that the "iconic sense cannot be translated into other dialects of sense." While this would seem to be no more than a proclaimed insistence on the irreducibility of the iconic, there is a decisive addition that should be understood as grounding the entirety of his project. He then writes that the effect of such a translation, were it to occur, would be a loss. This loss opens up that which is proper to the image. His founding claim is that "images feature an iconic excess that is genuinely visual or phenomenal." It should be noted that this excess is not a claim concerning horizons of interpretation. The "translation" would efface the "excess" precisely because that excess has to remain what it is, namely, visual. This it is not a claim about the ontology of the object in any direct sense: such a claim concerns the realm of appearances. The entire project of Alloa's aesthetic theory—and it is fundamentally an aesthetic theory—involves maintaining the link between this "excess" and that which is visual or phenomenal.

It is essential to underscore the importance of this move. On the one hand, it is an argument against the reduction of either a visual artifact or the work of art to pure immediacy. In other words, it is to hold to a phenomenological account of both experience and its object and thus avoid the traps of empiricism that remain regrettably endemic within analytic aesthetics. There is, however, more involved. There is another moment of differentiation. While empiricism is easy to ignore, the arguments against its very possibility that Hegel advanced in the opening section of the *Phenomenology of Spirit* have yet to be adequately countered. As significant is Alloa's recourse to a form of phenomenology that is also pitted against a philosophy of art grounded in what can be called the logic of the riddle. While never losing sight of the image's complex materiality, Alloa rejects both the idea of the image as a transparent window as well as that of an opaque riddle that would require the spectator to "read" it as a decipherable text.

The riddle is not a term that is used by chance. It is the one that Martin Heidegger deploys to describe art in the context of his *The Origin of the Work of Art*. Note the opening to the *Nachwort* that Heidegger added to *The Origin of the Work of Art*. He describes the work he has just written and the task to which it gives rise in the following terms: "The foregoing reflections are concerned with the riddle of art [*das Rätsel der Kunst*] that riddle that art itself is. They are far from claiming to solve the riddle. The task is to see the riddle [*Zur Aufgabe steht, das Rätsel zu sehen*]."[1] Note the move to the apparently visual. Seeing emerges. And yet the question must be asked: What is it to see a "riddle"? Answering this question for Heidegger abandons the project of seeing were the latter both to identify and to delimit the philosophical. The abandoning is specific. It occurs to bring into focus the relationship between experience and what art allows to be staged, namely, "the essence of truth." It is this externality that Alloa is constrained to reject in the name of what he refers to as art's "laterality" and by extension its opening to "medial phenomenology." Before pursuing what is meant by "laterality," it is vital to note that what is at stake here for Heidegger is an experience. There are remnants, perhaps even harbingers, of the phenomenological.

In the *Letter on Humanism*, Heidegger writes that in order to understand what is actually at stake in the term *humanism*, a specific requirement needs to be met, namely, "that we first experience the essence of the human being more primordially."[2] He then moves away from experience as understood phenomenologically to reposition it within the project of fundamental ontology. Hence, while Heidegger might have used the language of phenomenology—though only to the extent that the latter can be identified with the evocation of experience—the structure of thought that accompanies it is not. For Heidegger, in such a context, experience is connected to what is not experienced within everydayness and yet which occasions such experiences in the first place; an occasioning that cannot be equated with Kantian conditions of possibility. (Kant will insist on experience's own possibility that is a pure form of occasioning, while Heidegger has to argue that appearing is coterminous with concealing.) The move away from a phenomenological account of experience is marked in the *Letter on Humanism* by the move from the everydayness of existence to what Heidegger identifies there and elsewhere as *eksistence*, the stance made or taken in relation to the truth of Being. An openness to this possibility—a preparedness for a radical transformation within the structure of experience itself—marks the advent of the "primordial." And yet Heidegger's insistence on the logic of the riddle becomes in the end a failed account. The singularity of the work of art is effaced in the precise sense that particularity—the individuated and singular object—is subordinated to what it stages. Here it can be argued that what is staged—namely, art as the "setting-into-work of truth"—is in excess of the work. This excess, however, is not part of work as such. This excess cannot be seen; it remains inapparent. Without ever naming it, such a Heideggerian position and his subsequent existential hermeneutics is what Alloa departs from. It is equally the opening to the singularity of his own enterprise. In refusing the logic of the riddle, and that of a truth that would be inherently invisible, Alloa then has to sustain an excess within the visible itself.

Alloa's pathbreaking book begins with a detailed engagement with accounts of the image within the history of philosophy. He shows that, from Plato on, the "scandal" of the images is that they refuse to be identified either as things or as signs for other signs, inasmuch as they imply an ontological excess: they are appearances that exceed their material ground and the thing to which they refer. Images stage questions. The most significant concern the origin of appearing, thus demanding that an account be given of what it means for something to appear in an image, that is, in a foreign medium. Of decisive importance here is Alloa's interpretation of Aristotle; an interpretation that concentrates for the most part on the *De Anima*. Fundamental to his account of visual appearing in Aristotle is the emergence of an account of perceptual media with two consequences. First, it can be argued that Aristotle is an early advocate of a position demonstrating the myth of the given. Second, it is also the case that Aristotle's account of the presentational medium allows it to be understood as containing a constitutive heteronomy. If we never see things immediately but through a diaphanous medium, this means that the medium is determined by something else while also determining by its own texture the appearance it conveys. This has consequences for a phenomenology of perception (there is no immediacy of perception) but also for artificial media of presentation, such as material pictures. What this means is that the immediacy of givenness cedes its place to a conception of the image that resists either an intended or posited *reductio ad unum*. Again, this has to be the position if both immediacy and the logic of the riddle have been rendered inoperative. Neither accords with the reality of a physiological account of seeing, let alone a phenomenological account. Alloa is keen to demonstrate the important moments of complementarity between "being-embodied" and "becoming-visible."

Crucial here is the incorporation of what might be understood as an ontology of becoming. (Though it should be added that this is a formulation that Alloa himself would not have used.) Once horizons of meaning are put to one side and the primacy of a certain conception of the hermeneutic dispensed with, then what has to be allowed is a different set of arguments concerning the image's irreducibility. The trap of *Verstehen* needs to be prized open. The reconfiguring of the image entails that what is seen continues to allow itself to be seen (what something is, in a field of appearances, is always codetermined by the others to whom and through whom it appears, recalling the link between this "itself" and heteronomy). This is an allowing that breaks with the exigencies of immediacy in the sense that what is seen cannot be either equated with or reduced to all that can be seen. (The shattering of the Cartesian project of "clear and distinct perception" and its afterlife within positivism occurs at this precise point.) What we are left with is an excess. The potentiality of a medium exceeds its single actualizations: taking up a certain form—this lesson is drawn from Aristotle's interpretation of the plasticity of the elemental medium (water, air, etc.)—doesn't preclude it from taking up other forms at a later stage. Mediality is a power of transformation, of ephemerally taking up the appearance of a being and thus transmitting its form, while retaining the capacity of morphing into something else.

Every time this position is made, however, it has to be remembered that this is a phenomenological claim, not a hermeneutical one. Claims about the continuity of singularities, the continuity of that which is in its coming to be seen, are not varying modalities of the logic of the riddle. Hence the image is that which occurs—any determinant image—within the continuity of its coming to be seen, a continuity in which discontinuous moments are the individuated singularities. (Hence the suggestion that underscoring this position might be an unannounced commitment to an ontology of becoming.) The incomplete nature of the image is not a constitutive lack. It is that which occurs once both immediacy and the hermeneutic are put to one side. In the recalibration of images in which they have to be attributed a certain malleability or plasticity, insofar as they have a capacity for transformation, these qualities are an intrinsic part of the image itself. Hence the claim that Alloa locates initially in Aristotle of an intrinsic heteronomy. Inasmuch as it is grounded in a medium, the content of an image is never autonomous; moreover, it constitutively depends on a spectator granting it its visibility. This is part of what gives rise to one of Alloa's summary accounts of the image, namely, as "that which appears for a spectator." This position, however, has to be supplemented by the further claim that an image is what is seen while allowing for the indistinct and marginal presence of that which will come to be seen. What this means is that what appears is not exhausted in its appearing. This is the key moment.

While the details of Alloa's reworking of phenomenology await the careful reader, the final point that needs to be pursued here is how the centrality of the excessive and the marginal are themselves sustained. Again, once this is understood to be a phenomenological question and not an interpretive one, then the stakes change importantly. The last parts of the book open up in terms of the move to what is called "medial phenomenology." Part of the critique of immediacy, transparency, and varying forms of opacity is a repositioning of the concept of the medium. Again, the question of mediality has to be linked to how any medium has the power of letting something appear on its very surface. In the context of the book, arising from an analysis of decisive aspects of the work of both Edmund Husserl and Maurice Merleau-Ponty, is an account of a conception of appearing that allows for specific determinations that still maintain what can be called the complete within the incomplete. This movement is given the description of "lateral seeing." In an important passage, "lateral seeing" is positioned as a central moment in the development of a medial phenomenology. Alloa writes in chapter 5.1 that "lateral seeing" is

> not a diminished form of focal seeing but, inversely, its precondition, and every figure would be a manifestation, pushing its way to the center, of a figural matrix indicating itself as the undetermined, shimmering margin of the figures. Beside a *genetic phenomenology* that seeks its origin in a more fundamental *ground*, there would thus be a *generative phenomenology* that situates the origin of the potentiality of appearances in a perceptive *laterality*.

In this dense passage, the conceptual richness that will allow for an account of excess is being staged. Beyond the traditional focus on the figures and the objects at the center of the field of attention, there is the "shimmering" that occurs at the margin. It worth noting in passing that Alloa's use of "shimmering" and thus the allusion to light almost singlehandedly undoes the role of "light" (*luce*) (while retaining a reworking of light) that figures in Marsilio Ficino's Christianized aesthetics arising from the latter's translation of and commentary on Plato's *Phaedrus*.[3]

The careful development in chapter 5, without doubt a remarkable and significant undertaking in its own right, opens new avenues both for image theory (from an ontology to a symptomatology of images) as well as for phenomenology (from transcendental to medial phenomenology). Leaving to others to assess what this implies in these respective contexts, the focus shall be what this means for a philosophy of art. As a further elucidation of what is meant by laterality, Alloa offers an analysis of some paintings by Barnett Newman. Without repeating the detail of the analysis about the lateralizing effect of Newman's zips that pushes the visual field to its peripheral limits, the point that Alloa argues is that Newman "was interested in the event of becoming-visible in general." What this means is that with works of art there is, in Alloa's terms, "something unforeseeable that already encircles me and can break into my field of vision at any moment."

While this is a claim that is linked to artistic images, it is equally a claim that pertains to the image in general, whether art or not. One of the challenges arising from this book is that the traditional attempt to separate philosophy of art from aesthetics has been undone. Rather than an autonomy of the artwork, Alloa sees the artistic image as an intensification of the logic already at work in any image-like appearance. While all images are delimited appearances that make use of their finitude in order to convey that which exceeds them, artistic images are presentations that expose and play with this always already present excess within the finite borders of appearances. The result is a form of what for Alloa would be a reflexive tension. Artworks are still things that appear and which show in their very appearance why appearances matter. If anything, such a diaphenomenology of art parts with any hermeneutical approach: the artwork is no longer understood as a riddle to be deciphered or decrypted; the meaning is not hidden in any crypt but lies in plain sight. The quality of that site would allow for another consideration of the work of art to then be promulgated.

The opening quotation in Alloa's book is taken from Ludwig Wittgenstein. "We find certain things about seeing puzzling, because we do not find the whole business of seeing puzzling enough." The English translation conceals the fact that in the German original, Wittgenstein uses the word *rätselhaft*, or mysterious.[4] The *Rätsel* returns, although in an altogether different form from that of the hermeneutical riddle. If what is seen puzzles and this puzzle is accompanied by the belief that a solution to the riddle can be found, thus the puzzled simplified, both by uncovering the invisible truth hidden within, then the visible is taken to be the obvious. For Alloa, the contrary is the case. There is nothing transparent about what is in plain sight. Refusing the logic of the riddle while simultaneously resisting immediacy, the book opens up a new chapter in the history of aesthetics. Its challenges are considerable.

Notes

INTRODUCTION

1. Tommaso Campanella, *La città del sole: Dialogo poetico / The City of the Sun: A Poetical Dialogue*, trans. Daniel John Donno (Berkeley: University of California Press, 1981), 31–37. Written in Italian in 1602, Campanella's Latin version of 1613–1614 was first published in Frankfurt in 1623.

2. Augustine, *Confessions*, trans. Maria Boulding, in *The Works of Saint Augustine: A Translation for the 21st Century*, ed. John E. Rotelle, vol. 1/1 (New York: New City, 1997), 11.14.17:295.

3. See their correspondence in Gottfried Boehm and W. J. T. Mitchell, "Pictorial Versus Iconic Turn: Two Letters," *Culture-Theory-Critique* 50, no. 2–3 (2009): 103–21. For an overview of these debates, and for comparing the specifics of the Anglo-American *visual studies* and the German approaches to image sciences (*Bildwissenschaft*), see Emmanuel Alloa, "Iconic Turn: A Plea for Three Turns of the Screw," *Culture—Theory—Critique* 53, no. 3 (2015): 1–24.

4. Martin Jay, *Downcast Eyes: The Denigration of Vision in Twentieth-Century French Thought* (Berkeley: University of California Press, 1999).

5. Psalm 115:5. On the history of iconoclasm more generally, see the still unrivaled David Freedberg, *The Power of Images: Studies in the History and Theory of Response* (Chicago: University of Chicago Press, 1989).

6. See Immanuel Kant, *Critique of the Power of Judgment*, in *The Cambridge Edition of the Works of Immanuel Kant*, trans. Paul Guyer and Eric Matthews, ed. Paul Guyer (Cambridge: Cambridge University Press, 2000), 156: "Perhaps there is no more sublime passage in the Jewish Book of the Law than the commandment: Thou shalt not make unto thyself any graven image." On this passage and its aftermath, see Emmanuel Alloa, "The Most Sublime of All Laws: The Strange Resurgence of a Kantian Motif in Contemporary Image Politics" *Critical Inquiry* 41, no. 2 (Winter 2015): 367–89. In Adorno, the theme of the *Bilderverbot*, the "ban on images," stands for a dialectical reinterpretation of negative theology. It runs through his entire work and is most fully developed in *Negative Dialectics* (1967), trans. E. B. Ashton (New York: Continuum, 1993), esp. 207, 402.

7. Ludwig Wittgenstein, *Philosophical Investigations*, trans. G. E. M. Anscombe, P. M. S. Hacker, and Joachim Schulte, ed. P. M. S. Hacker and Joachim Schulte, 4th ed. (Chichester: Wiley, 2009), 1.115:53ᵉ.

8. See G. W. F. Hegel, *Philosophy of Mind, Being Part Three of the Encyclopedia of the Philosophical Sciences*, trans. William Wallace and Arnold V. Miller (Oxford: Clarendon, 1971), §378:3.

1. BETWEEN THING AND SIGN

The epigraph, "Duplex est motus animae in imaginem, unus quidem in imaginem ipsam secundum quod est res quaedam; alio modo, in imaginem inquantum est imago alterius," is from Thomas Aquinas, *Summa Theologiae*, trans. English Dominican Fathers (New York: Benziger, 1947–1948), 3ᵃ q25 a3co.

1.   Plato, *Sophist* 239d–240a. Translations of Plato are adapted from Benjamin Jowett's *The Dialogues of Plato*, 4th ed. (Oxford: Clarendon, 1953).

2.   Plato, *Sophist* 239e–240a.

3.   Plato, *Sophist* 237d, 262e; cf. Aristotle, *Metaphysics* 4.4.1006a18–25. Translations of Aristotle are taken from *The Complete Works of Aristotle: The Revised Oxford Translation*, ed. Jonathan Barnes (Princeton, N.J.: Princeton University Press, 1984).

4.   Plato, *Sophist* 237d.

5.   This conception is reflected in the Latin negation *non* (= *ne unum*) and the German *nein* (=*n[icht] ein*). For Aristotle, see *Metaphysics* 4.4.1006b7–11.

6.   Plato, *Sophist* 238c.

7.   Diogenes Laertius, *Lives of Eminent Philosophers*, trans. R. D. Hicks (Cambridge, Mass.: Harvard University Press, 2006), 9.51:462–65.

8.   Plato, *Euthydemos* 298b–c, and Aristotle, *De sophisticis elenchis* 4.166b21–23. This well-known sophism, presented in more succinct form in *Euthydemus* (298b–c), may count as example par excellence of Aristotle's second fallacy in the *Sophistical Refutations*. It arises from "the use of an expression without qualification or not without qualification but with some qualification of respect, or place, or time, or relation" (4.166b21–23) and entered the medieval dialectics textbooks under the name *fallacia secundum quid et simpliciter*.

9.   Plato, *Sophist* 238c.

10. Francis Macdonald Cornford, *Plato's Theory of Knowledge: The "Theaetetus" and the "Sophist" of Plato* (London: Routledge and Kegan Paul, 1957), 321–31.

11. Jean-Pierre Vernant, "From the 'Presentification' of the Invisible to the Imitation of Appearance," in *Mortals and Immortals: Collected Essays*, ed. and trans. Froma I. Zeitlin (Princeton, N.J.: Princeton University Press, 1991), 151–63.

12. Vernant, "From the 'Presentification' of the Invisible," 152.

13. Compare the Sanskrit term *vidyā*, which means both sight and knowledge, as well as *veda* (I have seen), from which the Vedas derive their name as well. The traces of this amalgamation can be found in all Indo-Germanic languages: Avestan *waeda* (I know); Greek *oīda* (I know); Latin *video* (I see); Middle High German *wizzan*, Dutch *weten*, Old Russian w*edat'*, and Armenian *gitem* (to know); as well as Lithuanian *véizdmi*, Old Irish *fís*, and Modern Russian *wídet'* (to see). There is an interlocking of visuality and intellectuality to the point of indistinguishability in examples like the ancient Greek *histor* (the historian as eyewitness), the English *wit* (from which the witness derives his knowledge), or the German *Einsicht* (insight).

14. See Charles Mugler, *Dictionnaire historique de la terminologie optique des grecs: Douze siècles de dialogues avec la lumière* (Paris: Klincksieck, 1964); Wilhelm Luther, "Wahrheit, Licht und Erkenntnis in der griechischen Philosophie bis Demokrit: Ein Beitrag zur Erforschung des Zusammenhangs von Sprache und philosophischem Denken," *Archiv für Begriffsgeschichte* 10 (1966): 1–240; and Michail Maiatsky, *Platon penseur du visuel* (Paris: L'Harmattan, 2005).

15. Plato, *Sophist* 240a.

16. Plato, *Sophist* 240b.

17. Plato, *Sophist* 240c2.

18. Socrates himself is called *atopon* by the Athenians (Plato, *Symposium* 175a).

19. Plato, *Sophist* 240c4.

20. Martin Heidegger, *Introduction to Phenomenological Research*, trans. Daniel O. Dahlstrom (Bloomington: Indiana University Press, 2005); Stanley Rosen, *Plato's* Sophist: *The Drama of Original and Image* (New Haven, Conn.: Yale University Press, 1983); Heinrich Niehues-Pröbsting, *Überredung zur Einsicht: Der Zusammenhang von Philosophie und Rhetorik bei Platon und in der Phänomenologie* (Frankfurt: Klostermann, 1987); and, more recently, David Ambuel, *Image and Paradigm in Plato's* Sophist (Las Vegas: Parmenides, 2007).

21. Plato, *Sophist* 240c4–6.

22. Plato, *Sophist* 240c4. The renderings are taken from translations by H. N. Fowler (1922), Nicholas P. White (1993), and David Ambuel (2007).

23. Homer, *Iliad*, 13, 359. The quotations are from translations by A. T. Murray (1924) and Martin Hammond (1981), respectively. Also Stephanus (Henri Estienne), s.v. "Ἐπαλλάξις, Alternatio," *Thesaurus Graecae linguae* (Geneva: Stephanus, 1572), 1:353–54.

24. This is apparent also in the game *daktylon epallaxis* (popular among Romans as well, who called it *micare digitis*), which consists in using one's fingers to form numbers so quickly that the opponent cannot keep up.

25. Plato, *Sophist* 239c6–7.

26. Plato, *Sophist* 239d.

27. Plato, *Sophist* 240c4–6.

28. Plato, *Sophist* 240a7–8.

29. Plato, *Sophist* 240a9.

30. Plato, *Sophist* 240b3.

31. Plato, *Sophist* 238c10.

32. Plato, *Sophist* 238d7.

33. Plato, *Sophist* 241d3.

34. Plato, *Sophist* 240e1–2.

35. Plato, *Sophist* 254c–255e.

36. Plato, *Sophist* 255c.

37. Compare Michael Frede's essay on predications and existential propositions, *Prädikation und Existenzaussage: Platons Gebrauch von 'ist' und 'ist nicht' im Sophistes* (Göttingen: Vandenhoeck und Ruprecht, 1967), and, on the newer developments in the debates, Russell M. Dancy, "The Categories of Being in Plato's 'Sophist' 255c-e," *Ancient Philosophy* 19, no. 1 (1999): 45–72.

38. Plato, *Cratylus* 432b–d.

39. Plato, *Cratylus* 432c5–6.

40. Augustine, *De diversis quaestionibus octoginta*, question 74 (*Patrologia Latina* 40, 80), quoted and translated in Gerald P. Boersma, *Augustine's Early Theology of Image: A Study in the Development of Pro-Nicene Theology* (Oxford: Oxford University Press, 2016), 200.

41. Gregory of Nyssa, *De hominis opificio*, ed. Morel, 1638, in *Patrologia Graecae* 44, 123–256, here chap. 16, 180C; Edmund Husserl, "Beilage zu den Paragraphen 11 und 20: Zur Kritik der 'Bildertheorie' und der Lehre von den 'immanenten' Gegenstände der Akte," *Logische Untersuchungen*, *Husserliana* 19/1, 436–40. [This supplement was not included in John F. Finlay's translation of *Logical Investigations*, ed. Dermot Moran (London: Routledge, 2008).—Trans.]

42. Plato, *Cratylus* 432b2–4.

43. Diogenes Laertius, *Lives* 3.108–9:371.

44. Diogenes Laertius, *Lives* 3.109:371.

45. Aristotle, *Metaphysics* 14.1.1088a26, 29–30.

46. The concepts "unary" and "binary" predicates are unknown in ancient logic and introduced only by modern formal logic. But while ancient logic may not have had the *concept*, it was very much aware of the *fact*.

47. Plato, *Euthydemos* 298b–c.

48. Augustine, *Teaching Christianity*, trans. Edmund Hill, *The Works of Saint Augustine: A Translation for the 21st Century*, ed. John E. Rotelle, vol. 1/11 (New York: New City, 1996), 1.2.2:106.

49. Augustine, *Teaching Christianity* 1.2.2:107.

50. Augustine, *De dialectica*, trans. Belford Darrell Jackson, ed. Jan Pinborg (Dordrecht: Reidel, 1975), 5:86/87.

51. Augustine, *Teaching Christianity* 2.1.1:29.

52. Augustine, *Teaching Christianity* 2.1.1:29.

53. Aquinas, *Summa Theologiae* 3ᵃ q25 a3co.

54. Aquinas, *Summa Theologiae* 3ᵃ q25 a3co [my emendations].

55. Aquinas, *Summa Theologiae* 3ᵃ q25 a3co [modified].

56. On the mantic arts, see two books by Wolfram Hogrebe: *Metaphysik und Mantik: Die Deutungsnatur des Menschen* (Frankfurt: Suhrkamp, 1992); and *Echo des Nichtwissens* (Berlin: Akademie, 2006).

57. Aristotle, *On Memory* 1.449b15.

58. Aristotle, *On Memory* 1.450b11[–451a2].

59. Aristotle, *On Memory* 1.450b19–20 [modified].

60. Aristotle, *On Dreams* 3.462a2–8. We know that Sigmund Freud followed Franz Brentano's lectures and seminars on Aristotle's psychology at the University of Vienna in 1874–1876. Thanks to his marriage with Martha Bernays, Freud was also the nephew of Jacob Bernays, whose work on Aristotle's concept of catharsis, too, anticipated themes of Freud's thought.

61. Aristotle, *On Memory* 2.450b20–22 [modified].

62. Aristotle, *On Memory* 2.450b18.

63. Aristotle, *On Memory* 2.450b22.

64. Aristotle, *On Memory* 2.451a1.

65. Aristotle, *On Memory* 2.451a17.

66. Aristotle, *On Memory* 2.450b31. Coriscus of Scepsis was a student of Plato's who was familiar to Aristotle's listeners, serving as an example in a number of other texts as well. He left Athens and became an advisor of Hermias of Atarneus, at whose court in Asia Minor Aristotle, too, found shelter for a while. The passage may thus be an allusion to the absent friend.

67. See the classic diagram in W. D. Ross's commentary in his edition of *Parva naturalia* (Oxford: Clarendon, 1955), 250. This recalls Husserl's schema in the *Phenomenology of the Inner Consciousness of Time*.

68. Aristotle, *On Memory* 2.451a5–8.

69. Aristotle, *On Memory* 2.451a10 [modified]. According to Michael of Ephesus, this is the same pathological case already mentioned Aristotle, *Meteorology* 3.4.373b4–10.

70. Aristotle, *On Memory* 2.451a11–12.

71. See especially the case studies in the first part of *On Divination in Sleep* in the *Parva naturalia*.

72. Aristotle, *On Memory* 2.451a14.

73. Aristotle, *On the Soul* 3.3.427b15–16.

74. Aristotle, *Poetics* 4.1448b15–17.

75. Aristotle, *Poetics* 4.1448b10. Against this backdrop, Pascal's critical exclamation—"How vain is painting, which attracts admiration by its similarity to originals we do not admire!"—acquires a whole new meaning; see Blaise Pascal, *Pensées*, ed. and trans. Roger Ariew (Indianapolis: Hackett, 2005), S74/L40:12.

76. Aristotle, *Poetics* 4.1448b17–19.

77. Plato, *Republic* 10.596e.

78. Plato, *Republic* 10.596c4–9.

79. Plato, *Republic* 10.596d9–e3.

80. Plato, *Republic* 10.598b2–3.

81. Plato, *Republic* 10.597a4–5.

82. Plato, *Republic* 10.598c.

83. Plato, *Republic* 10.598b.

84. Plato, *Republic* 10.598b2–4.

85. Cf. Martin Seel, "Vor dem Schein kommt das Erscheinen: Bemerkungen zu einer Ästhetik der Medien," in *Ethisch-ästhetische Studien* (Frankfurt: Suhrkamp, 1996), 104–25.

86. Seel, "Vor dem Schein," 104–6.

87. In that sense, it could be asserted (albeit very cautiously) that Seel's "anti-Platonist" thesis, according to which every distinction between what truly is and what merely seems to be can be made only if there is a level of appearances, may be attributed already to Plato himself.

88. Plato, *Republic* 10.598b.

89. Plato, *Sophist* 235d7.

90. Plato, *Sophist* 235e1, 235e6–7.

91. On the implications of reproduction or regiving, which go well beyond image theory, see Jacques Derrida's *The Truth in Painting*, trans. Geoff Bennington and Ian McLeod (Chicago: University of Chicago Press, 1987). In an essay on the artist Salvatore Puglia, Derrida connects the "saving" (*sōzein*) and "giving back" (*apodidonai*) of phenomena; see "Sauver les phénomènes: Pour Salvatore Puglia," *Contretemps* 1 (1995): 14–25. On the relationship between iconic reproduction and an an-economy of the gift, see Katrin Busch's judicious study on "gifted giving," *Geschicktes Geben: Aporien der Gabe bei Jacques Derrida* (Munich: Fink, 2004), esp. 185–282.

92. Plato, *Sophist* 235e6–236a2.

93. Pierre-Maxime Schuhl, *Platon et l'art de son temps* (Paris: Alcan, 1933).

94. Pliny the Elder, *Natural History*, trans. H. Rackam et al., 10 vols. (Cambridge, Mass.: Harvard University Press, 1968–80), 34, 65.176–77.

95. John Tzetzes, "Concerning Alcamenes," trans. Vasiliki Dogani, in *Chiliades or Book of Histories*, 8.38 (story 193), ll. 340–69, https://archive.org/details/TzetzesCHILIADES.

96. Lambert Wiesing, *Artificial Presence: Philosophical Studies in Image Theory*, trans. Nils F. Schott (Stanford, Calif.: Stanford University Press, 2010), 102–21.

97. Plato, *Sophist* 236b4.

98. Plato, *Republic* 4.420c–d.

99. Plato, *Laws* 2.656d.

100. Plato, *Sophist* 236b4.

101. Friedrich Schleiermacher, *Platons Werke*, part 2, vol. 2 (Berlin: Reimer, 1824), 501. Wiesing mentions these same passages and "completely agree[s]" with Schleiermacher (*Artificial Presence*, 119).

102. Cf. Wilhelm Kamlah's study, *Platons Selbstkritik im Sophistes* (Munich: Beck, 1963).

103. "No appearance is *kath'auto*. Appearances are what they are, and to the degree that they are, not in themselves, but in and through something else," as David Ambuel writes in the commentary of his remarkable translation of the *Sophist* (*Image and Paradigm in Plato's Sophist*, 151).

104. Gilles Deleuze, *The Logic of Sense*, trans. Mark Lester with Charles Stivale (New York: Columbia University Press, 1990), 254. This argument is further supported by the fact, not mentioned by Deleuze, that in Attic law (e.g., in Lysias and Isaeus), *amphisbētēsis* refers specifically to claims to an inheritance.

105. Deleuze, *The Logic of Sense*, 257.

106. Iris Därmann, *Tod und Bild: Eine phänomenologische Mediengeschichte* (Munich: Fink, 1995), 107.

107. Plato, *Sophist* 236e1–2.

108. Plato, *Republic* 8.557c.

109. This is what Dionysodorus reports; see Plato, *Euthydemus* 286c–e.

110. Plato, *Sophist* 260b13–c2.

111. Plato, *Sophist* 263b.

112.   Plato, *Sophist* 258c–259d.

113.   Plato, *Sophist* 259d9–e2, 259e3–4, 260a7, 259e6.

114.   Plato, *Sophist* 260c7–8.

115.   Plato, *Sophist* 267a3–4.

116.   Därmann, *Tod und Bild*, 115–19.

117.   See Niehues-Pröbsting, *Überredung zur Einsicht*.

118.   To give but one example: at Gorgias 465c we read that rhetoric has as much to do with justice as pastry baking with medicine.

119.   Aristotle, *Rhetoric* 1404a.

120.   Aristotle, *Rhetoric* 1377b30–1378a2.

121.   Aristotle, *Rhetoric* 1391b.

122.   Aristotle, *Rhetoric* 1356b6 [modified]. Christof Rapp, in his commentary, presents an overview of the debate concerning the status of the enthymeme, which Aristotle also refers to as a "kind of syllogism" (1355a3); see chapter 7.6 in *Rhetorik*, vol. 4 of Aristotle, *Werke in deutscher Übersetzung* (Berlin: Akademie, 2002).

123.   Aristotle, *Metaphysics* 11.6.1062b19.

124.   Plato, *Republic* 10.598b3.

125.   Aristotle, *Metaphysics* 4.6.1011a21.

126.   See the more detailed discussion, including a comparison with Husserl's engagement with Protagoras, in Emmanuel Alloa, "La phénoménologie comme science de l'homme sans l'homme," *Tijdschrift voor filosofie* 72, no. 1 (2010): 79–100.

127.   Aristotle, *Metaphysics* 4.6.1011b10–13.

128.   For an overview of authors favoring this reading, see Mi-Kyoung Lee, *Epistemology After Protagoras: Responses to Relativism in Plato, Aristotle, and Democritus* (Oxford: Clarendon, 2008), 13n13.

129.   Georg Wilhelm Friedrich Hegel, *Lectures on the History of Philosophy*, trans. Elizabeth Sanderson Haldane, 2 vols. (London: Paul, Trench, Trübner, 1892–1894), 1.2.A.1.372–78.

130.   Aristotle, *Metaphysics* 7.13, 1039a2–3, and 1.9, 990b15–17; see also *Sophistical Refutations* 22.178b36–179a10. The argument itself goes back to Plato (*Parmenides* 132a–b). Aristotle apparently gave a complete proof in an early text, *On Ideas*, of which only fragments survive; see Joan Kung, "Aristotle on Thises, Suches and the Third Man Argument," *Phronesis* 26, no. 3 (1981): 207–47.

131.   Aristotle, *Metaphysics* 4.6.1011a11.

132.   "Nothing could appear, the word 'appearance' would make no sense, if recipients of appearances did not exist—living creatures able to acknowledge, recognize, and react to—in flight or desire, approval or disapproval, blame or praise—what is not merely there but appears to them and is meant for their perception." Hannah Arendt, *The Life of the Mind* (San Diego, Calif.: Harcourt, 1981), 19.

133.   Aristotle, *On the Soul* 3.2.426b17–23.

134.   Aristotle, *Metaphysics* 5.15.1021b1.

135.   Aristotle, *On the Soul* 3.2.425b12–26; *On Sleep and Dreams* 1.455a12–23; *Nicomachean Ethics* 9.9.1170a25–b1.

136.   Aristotle, *Metaphysics* 10.6.1057a12.

137.   Aristotle, *Metaphysics* 10.1.1053a33.

138.   Aristotle, *Metaphysics* 6.4.1028a1.

139.   Aristotle, *De Interpretatione* 1.16a12.

140.   Aristotle, *Metaphysics* 9.10.1051b6–9.

141.   Aristotle, *Prior Analytics* 1.30.46a18–23.

142.   Simplicius, *In Aristotelis de Caelo commentaria*, ed. J. L. Heiberg (Berlin: Reimer, 1894), 488, ll. 16–24.

143. See Paul Natorp, *Plato's Theory of Ideas: An Introduction to Idealism*, ed. Vasilis Politis, trans. Vasilis Politis and John Connolly (Sankt Augustin, Ger.: Academia, 2004). On this thesis and its traces in Cohen and the Marburg school generally, see the detailed discussion in Jürgen Mittelstrass, *Die Rettung der Phänomene: Ursprung und Geschichte eines antiken Forschungsprinzips* (Berlin: de Gruyter, 1962), 11–28.

144. Simplicius, *In Aristotelis de Caelo commentaria*, 488, ll. 18–20. The note itself, it seems, comes from Eudemus's history of astronomy. Mittelstrass, *Die Rettung der Phänomene*, 133.

145. Simplicius, *In Aristotelis de Caelo commentaria*, 488, ll. 18–20. The fragments of Eudoxus's *Phainomena* have been edited by François Lasserre, in *Die Fragmente des Eudoxos von Knidos* (Berlin: de Gruyter, 1966), 39–67.

146. Against Walther Kranz, who attributes the phrase to Heraclides Ponticus, Mittelstrass claims to show "with certainty" that it was coined by Eudoxus (*Die Rettung der Phänomene*, 152). Citing Joseph B. Skemp, John J. Cleary remarks that the exact paternity of the principle is of lesser importance than the undoubtable fact that it emerged from an astronomical context; see "Phainomena in Aristotle's Methodology," *International Journal of Philosophical Studies* 2, no. 1 (1994): 89n3. On discussions of *sōzein ta phainomena* from the perspective of the history of astronomy, see Pierre Duhem, *To Save the Phenomena: An Essay on the Idea of Physical Theory from Plato to Galileo*, trans. Edmund Dolan and Chaninah Maschler (Chicago: University of Chicago Press, 2015); and G. E. R. Lloyd, "Saving the Appearances," *Classical Quarterly* 28, no. 1 (1978): 202–22.

147. Ernst Cassirer, *The Individual and the Cosmos in Renaissance Philosophy*, trans. Mario Domandi (Mineola, N.Y.: Dover, 2000), 172.

148. In their anthology, Hans Rudolf Schweizer and Armin Wildermuth seek to document the philosophical genesis of the interest in the pure "appearing of things" from ancient materialism and skepticism to Heinrich Barth; see Schweizer and Wildermuth, eds., *Die Entdeckung der Phänomene: Dokumente einer Philosophie der sinnlichen Erkenntnis* (Basel, Switz.: Schwabe, 1981). In the expansive literature, two classic essays (in addition to Cleary's already mentioned "Phainomena in Aristotle's Methodology") are worth highlighting, namely, Gwilym E. L. Owen, "Tithenai ta phainomena," in *Logic, Science and Dialectic: Collected Papers in Greek Philosophy*, ed. Martha C. Nussbaum (London: Duckworth, 1986), 239–51; and Martha Nussbaum, "Saving Aristotle's Appearances," in *The Fragility of Goodness: Luck and Ethics in Greek Tragedy and Philosophy* (Cambridge: Cambridge University Press, 1986), 240–63; the 1982 article of the same name is a shorter version. Cf. also William Wians, "Saving Aristotle from Nussbaum's Phainomena," in *Essays in Ancient Greek Philosophy*, vol. 5: *Aristotle's Ontology*, ed. Anthony Preus and John P. Anton (Albany: State University of New York Press, 1992), 133–49; and Christopher P. Long, "Saving *ta legomena*: Aristotle and the History of Philosophy," *Review of Metaphysics* 60, no. 2 (238) (December 2006): 247–67.

149. Plato, *Timaeus* 39a–40d.

150. Plato, *Republic* 7.528e–530b.

151. Aristotle, *Metaphysics* 12.8.1073b5–8.

152. In *Posterior Analytics* 1.27, for example, astronomy is once more subordinate to geometry.

153. This is the case, for example, in the depiction in the Casa dei Vettii in Pompeii or in the Roman mosaic found on the Isle of Wight. These are reproduced in Otto J. Brendel's *Symbolism of the Sphere* (Leiden: Brill, 1977), which offers an interpretation of the Oplontis mosaic that is as erudite as it is ambitious. While his theses partly diverge from the traditional interpretation, Brendel agrees with the opinion already put forward in the classic interpretation by Winckelmann, in the eighteenth century, "that the topic under discussion was phenomena in the heavens" (15–16).

154. Theon of Smyrna, *Liber de Astronomia*, chap. 16, quoted in Duhem, *To Save the Phenomena*, 15. Duhem cites, respectively, *Theonis smyrnaei Platonici Liber de Astronomia*, ed. H. Martin (Paris:

e Reipublicae typographeo, 1849), 203, and *Exposition des connaissances mathématiques utiles pour la lecture de Platon*, trans. J. Dupuis (Paris: Hachette, 1892), 239.

155.　Aristotle, *On the Heavens* 1.3.270b5–6.

156.　Aristotle, *On the Heavens* 3.7.306a26–30: "While they, in their anxiety to save their hypothesis, cannot even admit this of every perceptible thing."

157.　Aristotle, *Metaphysics* 1.5.986a11.

158.　Aristotle, *Prior Analytics* 1.30.46a18–23.

159.　Aristotle, *Posterior Analytics* 2.1–2.

160.　Aristotle, *On the Parts of Animals* 1.1.639b7–11, 640a14–15.

161.　In his classic Oxford translation, for example, W. D. Ross renders *phainomena* as "observed facts."

162.　Aristotle, *Nicomachean Ethics* 7.1.1145b2–17.

163.　Aristotle, *Nicomachean Ethics* 7.1.1145b20.

164.　Aristotle, *Nicomachean Ethics* 7.1.1145b27.

165.　Nussbaum, "Saving Aristotle's Appearances," 244, 245.

166.　Aristotle, *On Generation and Corruption* 1.8.325a18–22.

167.　Aristotle, *Metaphysics* 4.5.1010b10–11.

168.　Aristotle, *Metaphysics* 4.5.1010b12.

169.　Nussbaum, "Saving Aristotle's Appearances," 248.

170.　Wians, "Saving Aristotle," 136, 140. Nussbaum herself is aware of this danger. Nussbaum, "Saving Aristotle's Appearances," 479n19.

2. ARISTOTLE'S FOUNDATION OF A MEDIA THEORY OF APPEARING

The epigraph is from André Laks and Glenn W. Most, eds. and trans., *Early Greek Philosophy*, vol. 3: *Early Ionian Thinkers* (Cambridge, Mass.: Harvard University Press, 2016), part 2, 171, D89 (Diels-Kranz B3).

1.　Cicero, *De Finibus Bonorum et Malorum / On Ends* 1.20:23.

2.　Aristotle, *Meteorology* 1.8.345b1–2.

3.　Aristotle, *On Dreams* 2.460b11–14.

4.　Aristotle, *On Dreams* 1.458b28–29.

5.　Aristotle, *On the Soul* 3.3.428b3–5. The sun example seems to have been common among the members of the Academy; see the mention in the pseudo-Platonic dialog *Epinomis*: the real size of celestial bodies is unrelated to their apparent size. Plato, *Epinomis* 983a.

6.　Aristotle, *On Dreams* 1.458b32–34 [modified].

7.　Jocelyn Benoist, "L'idée de phénoménologie," in *L'idée de phénoménologie* (Paris: Beauchesne, 2001), 146.

8.　Aristotle, *On Dreams* 2.460b19–20 [modified].

9.　Aristotle, *On the Soul* 2.3.427b25–28. Aristotle further elaborates the complex concept of hypolepsis, which we cannot analyze in detail here, at *Metaphysics* 1.1.981a5–12; *Nicomachean Ethics* 6.3.1139b15; *Posterior Analytics* 1.33.88b36–89a2; *On the Soul* 3.3.427b15–16; *Topics* 6.11.149a10–11.

10.　See Aristotle, *On the Soul* 3.2.426b10.

11.　The passage most commonly cited to make this point is *Theaetetus* 186b9. See Michel Narcy, "Κρίσις et αἴσθησις (*De anima* 3, 2)," and Barbara Cassin, "Enquête sur le logos dans le *De anima*," both in *Corps et âme: Sur le* De anima *d'Aristote*, ed. Gilbert Romeyer-Dherbey and Cristina Viano (Paris: Vrin, 1996), 239–56 and 257–93, respectively.

12. Thus Cassin, for example, concludes that "sensation is none other but a logos that brings with it the possibility to continue logifying [*logifier*]." Cassin, "Enquête," 292.

13. Jeffrey Barnouw, who in *Propositional Perception* is concerned with showing *phantasia* to be a perception that is already structured propositionally, does not find this conception to be realized until the Stoa. Even if, in his criticism of Plato, Aristotle prepares this shift, his work, for Barnouw, is primarily an "effort to disengage *phantasia* from its entanglement with judgment." Jeffrey Barnouw, *Propositional Perception: Phantasia, Predication and Sign in Plato, Aristotle and the Stoics* (Lanham, Md.: University Press of America, 2002), 5.

14. See the section on "Making Judgments vs. Making Distinctions" in Jörg Alejandro Tellkamp, *Sinne, Gegenstände und Sensibilia: Zur Wahrnehmungslehre des Thomas von Aquin* (Leiden: Brill, 1999), 141–44.

15. Aristotle, *Posterior Analytics* 2.19.99b35–36.

16. See Harry Austryn Wolfson, "The Internal Senses in Latin, Arabic, and Hebrew Philosophic Texts," *Harvard Theological Review* 28, no. 2 (April 1935): 69–133. On the reception of Aristotle's doctrine of the faculties in the Arab world generally, see Helmut Gätje, *Studien zur Überlieferung der aristotelischen Psychologie im Islam* (Heidelberg: Winter, 1971).

17. Aristotle, *On the Soul* 3.3.428b1–2.

18. Aristotle, *On the Soul* 3.3.426b22–23.

19. Aristotle, *On the Soul* 3.3.428b20–21.

20. Aristotle, *On the Soul* 3.3.428b25–26.

21. Aristotle, *On the Soul* 3.9.432a30–432b1.

22. Edmund Husserl, *Formal and Transcendental Logic*, trans. Dorion Cairns, *Husserliana* 17 (The Hague: Nijhoff, 1969), 292.

23. Edmund Husserl, *The Crisis of European Sciences and Transcendental Phenomenology: An Introduction to Phenomenological Philosophy*, trans. David Carr (Evanston, Ill.: Northwestern University Press, 2000), §35:135.

24. Husserl, "Abhandlung über Wahrnehmung von 1898," first supplement to *Wahrnehmung und Aufmerksamkeit* in *Wahrnehmung und Aufmerksamkeit: Texte aus dem Nachlass (1893–1912)*, ed. Thomas Vongehr and Regula Giuliani, *Husserliana* 38, 123–58 (New York: Springer, 2005), §1:124.

25. Husserl, *Crisis*, §38:144.

26. Husserl, *Cartesian Meditations: An Introduction to Phenomenology*, trans. Dorion Cairns (The Hague: Nijhoff, 1960), §26:59.

27. Husserl, *Crisis*, §40:150 [modified].

28. Husserl, *Crisis*, §47:162.

29. Husserl, *Crisis*, §38:144.

30. See Rémi Brague, "La phénoménologie comme voie d'accès au monde grec," in *Phénomène et métaphysique*, ed. Jean-Luc Marion and Guy Planty-Bonjour (Paris: Presses universitaires de France, 1984), 247–73.

31. See Ludwig Landgrebe's summary of Husserl's lectures in the first supplement to Edmund Husserl, *Erste Philosophie (1923/24): Zweiter Teil*, ed. Rudolf Boehm, *Husserliana* 7 (The Hague: Nijhoff, 1959), 300.

32. A wealth of studies exist on the Aristotelian-scholastic background of Brentano's and Husserl's theory of intentionality, from Herbert Spiegelberg's classic essay "Der Begriff der Intentionalität in der Scholastik, bei Brentano und bei Husserl," *Philosophische Hefte* 5, no. 1/2 (1936): 75–91, to Dominik Perler's great synthesis, *Theorien der Intentionalität im Mittelalter* (Frankfurt: Klostermann, 2002). Some, more targeted studies are on possible bridges in Petrus Aureoli, such as Sofia Vanni Rovighi, "Una fonte remota della teoria husserliana dell'intenzionalità," in *Studi di filosofia medioevale*, vol. 2: *Secoli XIII e XIV* (Milano: Vita e pensiero, 1978), 283–98, or Avicenna

(Nader El-Bizri, "Avicenna's *De Anima* Between Aristotle and Husserl," in *The Passions of the Soul in the Metamorphosis of Becoming*, ed. Anna-Teresa Tymieniecka [Dordrecht: Springer, 2003], 67–89). A few scholars have attempted direct comparisons: see John J. Drummond, "On the Nature of Perceptual Appearances, or Is Husserl an Aristotelian?" *New Scholasticism* 52, no. 1 (1978): 1–22; Victor Caston, "Aristotle and the Problem of Intentionality," *Philosophy and Phenomenological Research* 58, no. 2 (June 1998): 249–98; Richard Cobb-Stevens, "'Aristotelian' Themes in Husserl's *Logical Investigations*," in *One Hundred Years of Phenomenology: Husserl's "Logical Investigations" Revisited*, ed. Dan Zahavi and Frederik Stjernfelt (Dordrecht: Springer, 2002), 79–92; and above all Maurizio Di Bartolo, Einsicht: *La costruzione del noetico in Edmund Husserl* (Padua, Italy: Il Poligrafo, 2006), esp. 33ff. As early as 1936, Jan Patočka remarked that in his synthesis of the ideal and the real, Aristotle had implemented the *sōzein ta phainomena* program; see Jan Patočka, *Aristote, ses devanciers, ses successeurs*, trans. Erika Abrams (Paris: Vrin, 2011).

33.   See, for example, at Freiburg in the summer semester 1921: Martin Heidegger, "Phänomenologische Übungen für Anfänger im Anschluss an Aristoteles, de anima [Phenomenological Exercises for Beginners, After Aristotle, *On the Soul*]," in *Heidegger und Aristoteles*, ed. Alfred Denker, Günter Figal, Franco Volpi, and Holger Zaborowski, *Heidegger-Jahrbuch* 3 (Freiburg, Ger.: Alber, 2007), 9–22.

34.   William Ralph Boyce Gibson, "From Husserl to Heidegger: Excerpts from a 1928 Freiburg Diary [Edited by Herbert Spiegelberg]," *Journal of the British Society for Phenomenology* 2, no. 1 (1971): 73.

35.   Martin Heidegger, *Introduction to Phenomenological Research*, trans. Daniel O. Dahlstrom (Bloomington: Indiana University Press, 2005), 3–77.

36.   Heidegger, *Introduction to Phenomenological Research*, 4 [modified].

37.   Friedrich Wilhelm Nietzsche, *The Gay Science: With a Prelude in German Rhymes and an Appendix of Songs*, ed. Bernard Williams, trans. Josefine Nauckhoff (Cambridge: Cambridge University Press, 2001), 9.

38.   See in more detail Louis Gernet, "Things Visible and Things Invisible," in *The Anthropology of Ancient Greece*, trans. John Hamilton and Blaise Nagy (Baltimore, Md.: Johns Hopkins University Press, 1981), 343–51.

39.   Plato, *Timaeus* 46a2–c6.

40.   Gérard Simon, *Le regard, l'être et l'apparence dans l'optique de l'Antiquité* (Paris: Seuil, 1988); and Agnès Rouveret, *Histoire et imaginaire de la peinture ancienne, Ve siècle av. J.-C.–1e siècle ap. J.-C.* (Rome: École française de Rome, 1989), esp. chap. 2, "Scaenographia," 65–127.

41.   Aristotle thinks that *skiagraphia* was first used to stage a tragedy by Sophocles (*Poetics* 4.1449a). Yet a comparison of the various sources shows that the invention must have been made between 468 and 456 BCE.

42.   Vitruvius, *On Architecture*, trans. Frank Granger, 2 vols. (Cambridge, Mass.: Harvard University Press, 1998), 7, pref. 11:71.

43.   Vasco Ronchi, *The Nature of Light: An Historical Survey*, trans. V. Barocas (Cambridge, Mass.: Harvard University Press, 1970), 4.

44.   Vitruvius, *On Architecture* 7, pref. 11:71.

45.   See Rouveret, *Histoire et imaginaire de la peinture ancienne*, 92, who cites both archaeological evidence and the atomist tradition until Lucretius.

46.   Plato, *Alcibiades* 132e7–133a1.

47.   Plato, *Alcibiades* 133a3.

48.   In Homer, *glēnē* designates the eyeball, and later also a doll (*Iliad* 8.164, 14.494; *Odyssey* 9.390). The fragment from Empedocles on the cosmological basis of seeing, which speaks of "the ancient fire, confined in membranes and delicate linens" that "lay in wait for the round-eyed maiden,"

calls for a separate interpretation; see Empedocles, *Testimonia, Part 2: Doctrine (D)*, in *Early Greek Philosophy*, vol. 5: *Western Greek Thinkers*, ed. and trans. André Laks and Glenn W. Most (Cambridge, Mass.: Harvard University Press, 2016), part 2, 547 (Diels-Kranz 31 B84).

49. Plato, *Alcibiades* 133a5–6.

50. Aristotle, *Sense and Sensibilia* 2.438a9–10.

51. This seems to be the thrust of Theophrastus's insistence, too, that mirroring occurs even on "lifeless" objects. Theophrastus, *De sensibus*, ed. and trans. George Malcolm Stratton (London: Allen & Unwin, 1917), 1.36.99. On this as well as many other aspects of the problem posed by the *korē*, see Thomas Kjeller Johansen, *Aristotle on the Sense-Organs* (Cambridge: Cambridge University Press, 1998), 44–49.

52. Aristotle, *Sense and Sensibilia* 2.438a10–14.

53. Plato, *Republic* 10.596d8–e3.

54. Aristotle, *Sense and Sensibilia* 2.438a5–6.

55. Aristotle, *Meteorology* 3.2–5. Cf. Anne Merker's detailed analysis in "Aristote et l'Arc-en-Ciel: Enjeux Philosophiques et Etude Scientifique," *Archive for History of Exact Sciences* 56, no. 3 (2002): 183–238.

56. "True, then, the visual organ proper is composed of water, yet vision appertains to it not because it is water, but because it is transparent." Aristotle, *Sense and Sensibilia* 2.438a13–15.

57. Sartre, for example, with his theory of the imaginary. See chap. 4.4.

58. Aristotle, *On the Soul* 3.7.431a16–17, 3.3.429a3–4.

59. See Wolfgang Welsch, *Aisthesis: Grundzüge und Perspektiven der aristotelischen Sinneslehre* (Stuttgart: Klett-Cotta, 1987), 81, 81n7, which takes up a suggestion of Heidegger's. On the semantic field of **a(u)i* in the Indo-Germanic languages, see Alois Walde, *Vergleichendes Wörterbuch der indogermanischen Sprachen*, ed. Julius Pokorny, 3 vols. (Berlin: de Gruyter, 1927–32), 1:17.

60. The provocative assertion of Harold Cherniss's *Aristotle's Criticism of Presocratic Philosophy* (Baltimore, Md.: Johns Hopkins University Press, 1935) that Aristotle's quotations of his predecessors have no historical value continues to stir debate among scholars to this day.

61. Aristotle, *Progression of Animals* 712b17–19.

62. See Hans Jonas, "The Nobility of Sight," *Philosophy and Phenomenological Research* 14, no. 4 (June 1954): 507–19.

63. Aristotle, *Metaphysics* 1.980a24; *Problems* 7.886b36 [modified].

64. Aristotle, *Problems* 7.886b10–887a1. Starting with Horace, this idea becomes a commonplace; see Rensselaer Wright Lee, *Ut pictura poesis: The Humanistic Theory of Painting* (New York: Norton, 1967).

65. Aristotle, *Physics* 7.2.244b2–245a11; *On the Soul* 2.4.415b24 [modified].

66. Aristotle, *On the Soul* 2.10.422a14–15; *Sense and Sensibilia* 3.440a15–20; but also *On Divination in Sleep* 2.464a5–11.

67. Lucretius, *De rerum natura* 4.30–33:279 [modified].

68. Lucretius, *De rerum natura* 4.42:279.

69. See Epicurus's letter to Herodotus, quoted in Diogenes Laertius, *Lives of Eminent Philosophers*, trans. R. D. Hicks, vol. 2 (Cambridge, Mass.: Harvard University Press, 2006), 565–613, here 10.46.575.

70. Lucretius, *De rerum natura* 4.220–23:295.

71. According to Nadar, the photographer, the difference is that the membranes no longer detach by themselves but must be caught by the daguerrotype. "Thus, according to Balzac, each body in nature finds itself composed of series of specters, infinitely superimposed in layers, sheafed in membranes [*foliacées en pellicules*]. . . . Each daguerrotypic operation thus came and surprised, detached and retained by applying to itself one of the layers of the objected body [*corps objecté*]."

Nadar [i.e., Gaspard-Félix Tournachon], *Nadar*, vol. 2: *Dessins et écrits*, ed. Jean-François Bory (Paris: Hubschmid, 1979), 978.

72. Such speculations were revived, for example, under Theoprastus's successor as head of the Aristotelian *peripatos*, Strato of Lampsacus.

73. Aristotle, *On the Soul* 2.7.419a11–13.

74. Aristotle, *Sense and Sensibilia* 2.438b22–23.

75. There are other possible interpretations of the naturalist philosophers. A particularly striking example is Gilles Deleuze's essay "Lucrèce et le naturalisme" (1961), included as an appendix in *Logic of Sense* under the title "Lucretius and the Simulacrum," in which the theory of simulacra sparks an entire philosophy of difference and of the event. Gilles Deleuze, *The Logic of Sense*, trans. Mark Lester with Charles Stivale (New York: Columbia University Press, 1990), 266–79.

76. For a source study on the history of the concept, see Wilhelm Luther, "Wahrheit, Licht und Erkenntnis in der griechischen Philosophie bis Demokrit: Ein Beitrag zur Erforschung des Zusammenhangs von Sprache und philosophischem Denken," *Archiv für Begriffsgeschichte* 10 (1966): 1–240.

77. Aristotle, *Sense and Sensibilia* 2.437b26–438a2. See also Laks and Most, *Early Greek Philosophy*, vol. 5, D215, 547 (Diels-Kranz 31 B84).

78. (Pseudo-)Aristotle, *Problems* 20.34.926b21–31.

79. Aristotle, *On Dreams* 459b23–460a26. This strange assertion has been interpreted in a number of ways; see Françoise Frontisi-Ducroux's cultural-historical interpretation in her chapter on "Aristote et les règles [Aristotle and Rules]," in *Dans l'oeil du miroir* (Paris: Odile Jacob, 1997), 147–54; and Raphael Woolf, "The Coloration of Aristotelian Eye-Jelly: A Note on *On Dreams* 459b–460a," *Journal of the History of Philosophy* 37, no. 3 (July 1999): 385–91, who mobilizes the passage to argue against Burnyeat's intellectualist interpretation. The idea itself, however, seems not to have been an invention of Aristotle's; it is voiced later by Pliny in his *Natural History*, trans. H. Rackam et al. (Cambridge, Mass.: Harvard University Press, 1968–1980), 28.82;58–59.

80. Aristotle, *Generation of Animals* 5.780b. This passage has sometimes been claimed as evidence that the telescope was invented on the coast of Asia Minor.

81. Aristotle, *Meteorology* 3.2–5; see also Merker, "Aristote et l'Arc-en-Ciel."

82. Aristotle, *Sense and Sensibilia* 2.437b15, 438a25, 438a29.

83. Aristotle, *Sense and Sensibilia* 2.437b12–14.

84. Aristotle, *On the Soul* 2.4.415b24.

85. Aristotle, *On the Soul* 2.5.416b33–34 [modified].

86. See Aristotle, *On Dreams* 459b4–5.

87. Aristotle, *Physics* 3.1.

88. Aristotle, *On the Soul* 2.5.417b6.

89. "The various opinions concerning sense perception, when regarded broadly, fall into two groups. By some investigators it is ascribed to similarity, while by others it is ascribed to contrast." Theophrastus, *De sensibus* 1.1.67.

90. This is how Theophrastus conceives of the Platonic description; see *De sensibus* 1.5–6.69–71; cf. also David C. Lindberg, *Theories of Vision from Al-Kindi to Kepler* (Chicago: University of Chicago Press, 1976), 5.

91. Plato, *Timaeus* 45c2–d2.

92. Johann Wolfgang Goethe, "Zahme Xenien," ll. 724–27, in vol. 1/2 of *Sämtliche Werke, Briefe, Tagebücher und Gespräche*, ed. Karl Eibl (Frankfurt: Deutscher Klassiker Verlag, 1985–). On Goethe's theory of visibility in the context of neo-Platonic metaphors, see Chol Han, *Ästhetik der Oberfläche: Die Medialitätskonzeption Goethes* (Würzburg, Ger.: Königshausen & Neumann, 2007), 49–58.

93.   See Theophrastus, *De sensibus* 1.1:67; 1.27:91. At least some commentators contest these attributions (e.g., Cherniss, *Aristotle's Criticism*, esp. 298n30, 301n40). For an analysis of Plato's theory of seeing in the context of his thinking overall, see Anne Merker, *La vision chez Platon et Aristote* (Sankt Augustin, Ger.: Academia, 2003), 5–124. On metaphors of light, gaze, and image in the Platonic oeuvre, see Michail Maiatsky, *Platon penseur du visuel* (Paris: L'Harmattan, 2005).

94.   Aristotle, *On Generation and Corruption* 1.7.323b33.

95.   Aristotle, *On the Soul* 418a27–28.

96.   Aristotle, *On the Soul* 2.12.424b1–4. This passage draws the conclusion from the analysis of 2.3–4.

97.   Aristotle, *On the Soul* 2.11.424a4–6.

98.   On a number of instances of one-sidedness in Aristotle's interpretation of Democritus, as well as on possible other interpretations of the atomists' notion of the interspace, see Pierre-Marie Morel, *Démocrite et la recherche des causes* (Paris: Klincksieck, 1996), 177–245, and "Démocrite dans les *Parva naturalia* d'Aristote," in *Qu'est-ce que la philosophie présocratique?*, ed. André Laks and Claire Louguet (Villeneuve-d'Ascq, Fr.: Presses universitaires du Septentrion, 2002), 449–64.

99.   Aristotle, *On the Soul* 2.7.419a16–22, emphasis in original.

100. Aristotle, *Meteorology* 1.3.339b13, b31.

101. See, for example, Aristotle, *Posterior Analytics* 1.27.87a31–37.

102. John I. Beare, *Greek Theories of Elementary Cognition from Alcmaeon to Aristotle* (Oxford: Clarendon, 1906), 26–30.

103. Aristotle, *Sense and Sensibilia* 2.438b3–15.

104. Aristotle, *On the Soul* 2.7.419a14–15.

105. Eliane Escoubas, *Imago mundi: Topologie de l'art* (Paris: Galilee, 1986), 165–66. A page later, Escoubas discusses the diaphanous.

106. On the history of the principle of plenitude generally, see Arthur O. Lovejoy, *The Great Chain of Being: A Study of the History of an Idea* (Cambridge, Mass.: Harvard University Press, 1964). Jaakko Hintikka's study, *Time and Necessity: Studies in Aristotle's Theory of Modality* (Oxford: Clarendon, 1975), tailored specifically to Aristotle, builds on Lovejoy but reaches the opposite conclusion. On the various forms taken by the *horror vacui*, which has not wholly subsided even after the domestication of the vacuum in natural science, see Hartmut Böhme, "Das Volle und das Leere: Zur Geschichte des Vakuums," in *Luft: Elemente des Naturhaushalts 4*, ed. Kunst- und Ausstellungshalle der Bundesrepublik Deutschland and Bernd Busch (Cologne: Wienand, 2003), 42–66.

107. Aristotle, *Physics* 5.3.226b23.

108. Aristotle, *Physics* 5.3.227a20–27.

109. Aristotle, *On the Soul* 2.12.423a23.

110. See Martin Heidegger, "Excursus: General Orientation Regarding the Essence of Mathematics According to Aristotle," in his *Plato's* Sophist, trans. Richard Rojcewicz and André Schuwer (Bloomington: Indiana University Press, 2003), §15:69–82.

111. Aristotle, *Physics* 2.2.193b31–34; *Metaphysics* 14.5.1092a19.

112. Aristotle, *Physics* 2.2.193b32.

113. Aristotle, *Physics* 6.1.231a24–25.

114. Aristotle, *Metaphysics* 5.6.1016b24[–30].

115. Aristotle, *Physics* 5.3.227a32.

116. Aristotle, *Physics* 6.1.231a23.

117. Aristotle, *Categories* 6.4b32ff.

118. Aristotle, too, repeats that divisibility is a criterion of all continuous things, in *Nicomachean Ethics* 2.6.1106a26.

119. Aristotle, *On the Soul* 2.7.418a27–28 [modified].

120. Aristotle, *On the Soul* 2.7.418a28–30.

121. Homer, *Iliad* 8.491. This and the following example are taken from Charles Mugler's dictionary, whose entries on the Greek metaphorics of light demonstrate the semantic richness of the field. See Mugler, *Dictionnaire historique de la terminologie optique des grecs: Douze siècles de dialogues avec la lumière* (Paris: Klincksieck, 1964), 96–100, as well as Anca Vasiliu, *Du Diaphane: Image, milieu, lumière dans la pensée antique et médiévale* (Paris: Vrin, 1997), 42–43. For Herodotus, see *Herodotus*, trans. A. D. Godley, vol. 2 (Cambridge, Mass.: Harvard University Press, 1982), 4.73:273.

122. In line 44 of the third Pythian Ode; see Pindar, *Olympian Odes/Pythian Odes*, ed. and trans. William H. Race (Cambridge, Mass.: Harvard University Press, 2012), 255; and Mugler, *Dictionnaire historique*, 96.

123. Plutarch, "Concerning the Face Which Appears in the Orb of the Moon," *Moralia in Sixteen Volumes*, vol. 12, trans. Harold Cherniss and William C. Helmbold, 920b–945d:34–223 (Cambridge, Mass.: Harvard University Press, 1984), 929c:102–3; see also Mugler, *Dictionnaire historique*, 96.

124. Pliny, *Natural History* 3.30, 9.113, 36.160–62. Selenite was inserted into window frames as partition and protection from the cold until the late Middle Ages, before being replaced by cast glass. In Latin, the mineral's telling name is *lapis specularis* (specular stone). The English word selenite derives its name from the Moon goddess Selene.

125. Xenophon, *Memorabilia*, in *Memorabilia. Oeconomicus. Symposium. Apology*, trans. E. C. Marchant, rev. Jeffrey Henderson (Cambridge, Mass.: Harvard University Press, 2013), 3.10.5:246–47 [modified].

126. Plato, *Phaedrus* 229b.

127. Plato, *Phaedo* 110d.

128. Plato, *Timaeus* 67d2–6 [modified].

129. Vasiliu, *Du Diaphane*, chap. 1, "Il y a donc du diaphane," 39–75.

130. Aristotle, *Prior Analytics* 1.35.48a30.

131. Aristotle, *On the Soul* 2.7.418b3–4 [modified].

132. Aristotle, *On the Soul* 3.13.425a1–2 [modified].

133. Aristotle, *On the Soul* 3.13.435b22–23 [modified].

134. See D. S. Hutchinson's rigorous demonstration in "Restoring the Order of Aristotle's De anima," *Classical Quarterly* 37, no. 2 (1987): 373–81.

135. Aristotle, *On Colors*. On the question of the text's authorship, see the remarks of the translator of the German edition, Georg Wöhrle, in Aristotle, *De coloribus*, in *Werke in deutscher Übersetzung*, vol. 18/5 (Berlin: Akademie, 1999), 31–52.

136. Aristotle, *On the Soul* 3.13.435b23 [modified].

137. Rémi Brague, *Aristote et la question du monde: Essai sur le contexte cosmologique et anthropologique de l'ontologie* (Paris: Presses universitaires de France, 1988), 354.

138. Aristotle, *On the Soul* 2.7.418b14–16.

139. Aristotle, *On the Soul* 2.8.419b35.

140. Aristotle, *On the Soul* 2.8.419b11–12.

141. Aristotle, *On the Soul* 2.8.420a4–5.

142. Aristotle, *On the Soul* 2.8.420a3–4.

143. For more detailed discussion of the logical medium, see Emmanuel Alloa, "Metaxy: Aristotle on Mediacy," in *Classics and Media Theory*, ed. Pantelis Michelakis (Oxford: Oxford University Press, 2020), 147–65. Whereas the logical medium, which establishes the connection between the *propositio maior* and the *propositio minor*, disappears in the *conclusio* as soon as subject and predicate are connected, the aisthetic medium would be a medium that preserves the distance (and thus itself).

144. Aristotle, *Physics* 5.3.227a15.

145. Aristotle, *On the Soul* 2.5.417b27.

146. Annette Hilt has previously pointed out this topological transformation in *Ousia, Psyche, Nous: Aristoteles' Philosophie der Lebendigkeit* (Munich: Alber, 2005), 220. Cf. Emmanuel Alloa, review in *Allgemeine Zeitschrift für Philosophie* 33, no. 1 (July 2008): 85–89. This radical expansion of the concept of place necessitated by Aristotle's theory of perception is reversed in the sixteenth century. In his study of Hobbes's *De corpore*, Cees Leijenhorst has impressively shown how Hobbes's theory of perception is a paradigmatic example of a new theory of space that presents itself explicitly as anti-Aristotelian and returns to defining perception as local movement. See Cees Leijenhorst, *The Mechanisation of Aristotelianism: The Late Aristotelian Setting of Thomas Hobbes' Natural Philosophy* (Leiden: Brill, 2002).

147. Aristotle, *Sense and Sensibilia* 5.439b.

148. The Scholastics speak of an *actu extra animam*, an "act outside the soul"; see, for example, Aquinas, *Summa Theologiae*, trans. English Dominican Fathers (New York: Benziger, 1947–48), 1 q79 a1 ad1.

149. Aristotle, *On the Soul* 2.5.417b27, 417b26.

150. Aristotle, *On the Soul* 3.8.432a16.

151. Aristotle, *On the Soul* 2.11.424a6

152. Aristotle, *On the Soul* 2.11.424a4–6, 2.12.424a19 [modified].

153. Aristotle, *On the Soul* 2.12.424a18–21.

154. Aristotle, *On the Soul* 2.12.424a22.

155. Cf. Brague, *Aristote et la question du monde*, 345.

156. Aristotle, *On the Soul* 2.1.412b19–23; *On the Generation of Animals* 2.1.735b24–27. This is a homonymy (*aequivocatio* in Latin): two things are of a different essence and therefore not semantically coextensive, but they nonetheless are called by the same name (Aristotle, *Categories* 1.1a1–6).

157. Vasiliu, *Du Diaphane*, 131n207.

158. Aristotle, *Physics* 7.2.244b5–8.

159. Emanuele Coccia, *La trasparenza delle immagini: Averroè e l'averroismo* (Milan: Mondadori, 2005), 114.

160. Aristotle, *On the Soul* 2.5.416b33–35, 417b6–7.

161. Cf. Aristotle, *Physics* 4.13.222b16: "It is the nature of all change [*metabolē*] to alter things from [*ekstatikon*] their former condition."

162. Cf. *existhesi*, from *existēmi*, to displace, dislodge, remove, in *Physics* 4.12.221a32–221b3.

163. Aristotle, *On the Soul* 1.3.406b14.

164. Aristotle, *On Generation and Corruption* 1.7.323b33–34.

165. Aristotle, *On the Soul* 2.5.417a19–21, 418a4–6 [modified].

166. Aristotle, *On Generation and Corruption* 1.7.324a11.

167. Aristotle, *On the Soul* 2.5.417a11–12.

168. Aristotle, *On the Soul* 2.5.417b2–9 [modified].

169. See *Aristotelis De anima libri tres*, ed. Friedrich Adolf Trendelenburg (Berlin: Weber, 1877), 299. This is taken up by J. A. Smith, who translates as "a development into its true self."

170. Aristotle, *On the Soul* 2.5.417b27.

171. Aristotle, *On the Soul* 2.5.417b25.

172. Aristotle, *Sense and Sensibilia* 5.446b2–3 [modified].

173. Aristotle, *Sense and Sensibilia* 5.446a22–24.

174. Aristotle, *Sense and Sensibilia* 5.446a28–31.

175. Aristotle, *Sense and Sensibilia* 5.446b29.

176. Aristotle, *Sense and Sensibilia* 5.446b29–447a2.

177. Aristotle, *Sense and Sensibilia* 5.446b28, 3.439a21.

178.   Aristotle, *On the Soul* 2.7.418b17; *Sense and Sensibilia* 6.446b27–28 [modified].

179.   Aristotle, *On the Soul* 2.7.418b26–27.

180.   Aristotle, *On the Soul* 2.7.418b11–12 [modified].

181.   Aristotle, *On the Soul* 2.7.419a10–11.

182.   Aristotle, *On the Soul* 2.7.418b10.

183.   Aristotle speaks of *parousia* as efficient cause elsewhere, too; see, for example, *Physics*, 2.3.195a11–14; *Metaphysics* 5.2.1013b15–16.

184.   See, for example, Aristotle, *On the Soul* 2.7.418b18.

185.   Aristotle, *On the Soul* 2.7.418b10–11

186.   Aristotle, *On the Soul* 2.7.418b28; *Sense and Sensibilia* 6.445b4–447a10 [modified].

187.   Aristotle, *Sense and Sensibilia* 6.446a1–2.

188.   Aristotle, *Sense and Sensibilia* 6.446a10.

189.   Aristotle, *Sense and Sensibilia* 6.445b30–31.

190.   Aristotle, *On the Soul* 2.10.422a20–24.

191.   Aristotle, *On the Soul* 2.7.419a2–5.

192.   Heidegger, *Introduction to Phenomenological Research*, 7–8 [modified].

193.   Augustine, "On Genesis: A Refutation of the Manichees," in *On Genesis*, trans. Edmund Hill, in *The Works of Saint Augustine: A Translation for the 21st Century*, ed. John E. Rotelle (New York: New City, 2002), 1.4.7:43; see Marcia L. Colish, "Carolingian Debates Over *Nihil* and *Tenebrae*: A Study in Theological Method," *Speculum* 59, no. 4 (1984): 772.

194.   "In pictures, the shadows mark out the more striking features, and satisfy by the rightness not of form but of order and arrangement." Augustine, "Unfinished Literal Commentary on Genesis," in *On Genesis* 5.25:127; cf. Marcia L. Colish, "St. Augustine's *Rhetoric of Silence* Revisited," *Augustinian Studies* 9 (1978): 15–24.

195.   Aristotle, *On the Soul* 2.5.417b30–31.

196.   Aristotle, *Sense and Sensibilia* 6.446b3–13.

197.   Aristotle, *Metaphysics* 5.12.1019b7.

198.   Aristotle, *On the Soul* 2.10.422a20–21.

199.   Aristotle, *On the Soul* 3.2.425b21–23.

200.   This research was initiated in the 1950s and 1960s by David Hubel and Torsten Wiesel, who received the Nobel Prize for their work in 1981. For an overview, see Robert F. Hess, Lindsay T. Sharpe, and Knut Nordby, eds., *Night Vision: Basic, Clinical and Applied Aspects* (Cambridge: Cambridge University Press, 1991), especially the chapter by Maureen K. Powers and Daniel G. Green, "Physiological Mechanisms of Visual Adaptation at Low Light Levels," 125–45. On the demonstration that this distinction can be found on the ganglion level as well, see Dennis Dacey, "Origins of Perception: Retinal Ganglion Cell Diversity and the Creation of Parallel Visual Pathways," in *The Cognitive Neurosciences*, ed. Michael S. Gazzaniga (Cambridge, Mass.: MIT Press, 2004), 281–301.

201.   Aristotle, *On the Soul* 3.2.425b12.

202.   Daniel Heller-Roazen has magnificently highlighted this point in *The Inner Touch: Archaeology of a Sensation* (New York: Zone, 2007), chap. 3. On Plato's anthropologizing the concept of reflection in the *Cratylus* (399c-d) and on *intueor intueri* (seeing oneself seeing) within the framework of a history of "the mind's eye," see Emmanuel Alloa, "The Madness of Sight," in *Seeing Perception*, ed. Silke Horstkotte and Karin Leonhard (Newcastle: Cambridge Scholars, 2007), 40–59.

203.   Georges Didi-Huberman, "Eloge du diaphane," in *Phasmes: Essais sur l'apparition*, 99–110 (Paris: Minuit, 1998), 107.

204.   Aristotle, *On the Soul* 3.2.425b17–20.

205.   Aristotle, *On the Soul* 3.2.425b23.

206.   Aristotle, *On the Soul* 2.6.418b11.

207. See *Sense and Sensibilia* 3.439a19–21.

208. See Myles F. Burnyeat, "How Much Happens When Aristotle Sees Red and Hears Middle C? Remarks on *De anima* 2, 7–8," in *Essays on Aristotle's* De anima, ed. Martha C. Nussbaum and Amélie Oksenberg Rorty (Oxford: Clarendon, 1992), 425–26.

209. Aristotle, *On the Soul* 3.2.425b24.

210. Aristotle, *On the Soul* 3.2.425b21–26 [modified].

211. Aristotle, *On the Soul* 2.12.424a22. This is their difference from the *ahylon eidos*, which was later read as the basic definition of Aristotle's theology. Such interpretations rely on Aristotle, *Physics* 2.2.194b9–15; 1.9.192a3–b2.

212. Aristotle, *On the Soul* 3.4.429a30.

213. Aristotle, *On the Soul*, 2.9.421b31, 421b28–30.

214. Lovejoy, it is important to note, contests the idea that Aristotle abided by the principle (*The Great Chain of Being*, 55). Hintikka argues the opposite in his study on modal logic, *Time and Necessity*.

215. Aristotle, *Metaphysics* 9.8.1050a10–11.

216. Giorgio Agamben has pointed this out in his "On Potentiality," in *Potentialities: Collected Essays in Philosophy*, trans. Daniel Heller-Roazen (Stanford, Calif.: Stanford University Press, 1999), 177–84.

217. Themistius, *On Aristotle's On the Soul*, trans. Robert B. Todd (Ithaca, N.Y.: Cornell University Press, 1996), 111:26–31:137, interpolation Todd's. See also Agamben, "On Potentiality."

218. Aristotle, *On the Heavens* 3.4.303a22–23.

219. Aristotle, *On the Soul* 2.5.417b27.

220. See, for example, Thomas Aquinas, *Commentary on Aristotle's De Anima*, trans. Kenelm Foster and Silvester Humphries (Notre Dame, Ind.: Dumb Ox, 1994), 3.6:655–70; see also lib. 2, cap. 30, *Sancti Thomae de Aquino opera omnia*, ed. Commissio Leonina, vol. 45/1 (Rome/Paris: Commissio Leonina/Vrin, 1883/1906–1992), 197–200.

221. Aristotle, *On the Soul* 3.3.428b12–14; cf. 427b. Husserl similarly argues that *Phantasie* is only ever a combination of contents of the senses. Even the centaur is a new composite of preexisting perceptive elements. See chap. 4.5.

222. Kimon Lycos, "Aristotle and Plato on 'Appearing,' " *Mind* 73 (new series), no. 292 (October 1964): 497.

223. Aristotle, *On the Soul* 3.3.427b17–19.

224. Aristotle, *On the Soul* 3.3.428a17.

225. For Aquinas, the *imaginatio* is an *apprehensio de re absente*, it "apprehends a sensible species when the thing is absent." Thomas Aquinas, *The Disputed Questions on Truth*, trans. Robert William Mulligan, vol. 1 (Chicago: Regnery, 1952), qu. 1, art. 11:49. For Baumgarten, "imaginations" (*imaginationes*) are nothing but "perceptions that were formerly present . . . they are perceptions of the senses that, while I imagine, are absent." Alexander Gottlieb Baumgarten, *Metaphysics: A Critical Translation with Kant's Elucidations, Selected Notes, and Related Materials*, ed. and trans. Courtney D. Fugate and John Hymers (London: Bloomsbury, 2014), §558:211. Kant is able to build on this conception when he defines the imagination as "the faculty for representing an object *even without its presence* in intuition." Immanuel Kant, *Critique of Practical Reason*, in *Practical Philosophy*, trans. Mary J. Gregor (Cambridge: Cambridge University Press, 1996), §24, B 151, Kant's emphasis. The view that the imagination sets in only when its object is not sensually present is defended, in different ways, by Wittgenstein—"While I am looking at an object I cannot imagine it"—and, with particular emphasis, by Sartre. Ludwig Wittgenstein, *Zettel*, ed. G. E. M. Anscombe and Georg Henrik von Wright, trans. G. E. M. Anscombe, 2nd ed. (Oxford: Blackwell, 1981), no. 621:108. On Sartre and the long tradition of stressing the aspect of absence in theories of the imagination, see Emmanuel Alloa, "Imagination zwischen Nichtung und Fülle: Jean-Paul Sartres negative Theorie der Einbildungskraft auf dem Prüfstein von Tintorettos Malerei," in *Imagination und Invention*, ed. Toni Bernhardt and Philipp Mehne, supp. 2 of *Paragrana* (2006): 13–27.

226. Aristotle, *On the Soul* 3.3.427b20.

227. This thesis has most recently been defended by René Lefebvre, "La crise de la *phantasia*: original-ité des interprétations, originalité d'Aristote," in *De la phantasia à l'imagination*, ed. Danielle Lories and Laura Rizzerio (Leuven, Belgium: Peeters, 2003), 31–47. The thesis that all the various meanings of *phantasia* can be traced back to a presentification of what is absent, however, not only turns out to be a historical retrospective projection but also completely misses what is special about Aristotle's *phantasia* concept.

228. See Aristotle, *Topics* 8.14.163b28–30.

229. See the appearance of the sun as only "a foot in diameter" in Aristotle, *On the Soul* 3.3.428b3–4.

230. Aristotle, *On the Soul* 3.3.428b29.

231. Aristotle, *On the Soul* 3.7.431a16–17.

232. See Wolfson, "The Internal Senses."

233. Martha C. Nussbaum, *Aristotle's De Motu Animalium* (Princeton, N.J.: Princeton University Press, 1978), 222; Malcolm Schofield, "Aristotle on the Imagination," in *Essays on Aristotle's De anima*, ed. Martha C. Nussbaum and Amélie Oksenberg Rorty (Oxford: Clarendon, 1992), 249; and Richard Sorabji, *The Philosophy of the Commentators 200–600 A.D.: A Sourcebook*, vol. 1: *Psychology* (Ithaca, N.Y.: Cornell University Press, 2005), 61.

234. This aspect is emphasized already by Beare, *Greek Theories of Elementary Cognition*, 290.

235. Nussbaum, *Aristotle's De Motu Animalium*, 222.

236. Malcolm Schofield, "Aristotle on the Imagination," thinks this conclusion is warranted by an analysis of the relevant passages.

237. Aristotle, *On the Soul* 3.3.428a1–18.

238. This verdict on the concept of *phantasia* is Hamlyn's, in his translation of *On the Soul, De anima, Books II and III (with Passages from Book I)*, ed. and trans. David W. Hamlyn, rev. Christopher Shields (Oxford: Clarendon, 1993), 131.

239. Schofield, "Aristotle on the Imagination," 256; and Michael V. Wedin, *Mind and Imagination in Aristotle* (New Haven, Conn.: Yale University Press, 1988), 57.

240. Friedrich Wilhelm Nietzsche, *Writings from the Early Notebooks*, ed. Raymond Geuss and Alexander Nehamas, trans. Ladislaus Löb (Cambridge: Cambridge University Press, 2009), frag. 19 [78], 117.

241. On "the Principle of Articulativity," see Welsch, *Aisthesis*, 230–32.

242. Nietzsche, *Early Notebooks*, frag. 19 [78], 117.

243. Aristotle, *On the Soul* 2.3.414b29–32.

244. Welsch, *Aisthesis*, 62.

245. Aristotle, *On Dreams* 1.459a15–17.

246. This theory of color seems to be a direct engagement with Democritus, according to whom color as such simply does not exist and only emerges from the juxtaposition of atoms. For Aristotle, on the contrary, there are two basic colors, black and white, which in turn are the materializations of light and darkness. In addition to juxtaposing these two colors, which Aristotle discusses as an option (*Sense and Sensibilia* 3.439b20), there are then two more possible ways for color to emerge: mixing the basic colors (440b15) as well as overlaying them to produce a diaphanous image. In the latter case, the colors appear literally *one through the other, phainesthai di'allēlon* (440a7–8). We get an idea of such diaphanous layers of color from the Oplontis frescoes (fig. 1.1) or the Macedonian royal mausoleums, which Aristotle may theoretically have seen in person (think of the hair of the figure of Hades in the so-called Tomb of Persephone discovered in Aigai in 1977).

247. (Pseudo-)Aristotle, *On Colors*. Of particular interest for a theory of the diaphanous is the analysis of light effects at the end of the third chapter, which anticipates modern findings concerning diffraction grating. Cf. the commentary in *Werke in deutscher Übersetzung*, 18/5.

248. Aristotle, *Metaphysics* 9.8.1050a19–21. According to Ross, we must presume that this painting oscillates between a framed, closed image surface and an effect of depth; see *Aristotle's Metaphysics*, vol. 2, 3rd ed. (Oxford: Clarendon, 1953), 263ff. Wolfgang Welsch sees this as pointing to what seems at first sight rather un-Aristotelian conception, namely, that the *hylē* is already capable of articulation itself. Welsch, *Aisthesis*, 231.

249. Aristotle, *Topics* 6.3.140a14–15.

250. Charles Batteux, *The Fine Arts Reduced to a Single Principle*, trans. James O. Young (Oxford: Oxford University Press, 2015).

251. Stephen Halliwell, *The Aesthetics of Mimesis: Ancient Texts and Modern Problems* (Princeton, N.J.: Princeton University Press, 2002), 151.

252. Aristotle, *Poetics* 15.1454b9–10.

253. Aristotle, *Topics* 6.3.140a21–22. This reading of it as referring to archaic art (and not to some kind of writing) is suggested not only by the context, in which the term appears, but also by the criticism of archaic art current in the Academy; see Pseudo-Aristotle, *Problems* 10.45.895b (in Aristotle, *Complete Works*, 2), as well as Thomas Pekáry, *Imago res mortua est: Untersuchungen zur Ablehnung der bildenden Künste in der Antike* (Stuttgart: Steiner, 2002), 170.

254. Aristotle, *Topics* 6.3.140a21–22.

255. Aristotle, *On Memory* 1.450a13.

256. Aristotle, *Poetics* 16.1455a2.

257. Aristotle, *Movement of Animals* 11.703b18–20.

258. Aristotle, *Movement of Animals* 7.701b17–22 [modified].

259. Cf. Welsch, *Aisthesis*, esp. chap. 7.

260. Caston, "Aristotle and the Problem of Intentionality," 292.

3. FORGETTING MEDIA

1. Aristotle, *Sense and Sensibilia* 4.442b1.

2. Alexander of Aphrodisias, *De liber de anima cum mantissa*, in *Commentaria in Aristotelem Graeca, Supplementum Aristotelicum 2.1: Alexandri Aphrodisiensis praeter commentaria scripta minora*, ed. Ivo Bruns (Berlin: Reimer, 1887), 56, 4–11. In his essay on the sense of touch in the history of philosophy, Jean-Louis Chrétien, too, points to this passage; see "Body and Touch," in *The Call and the Response*, trans. Anne A. Davenport (New York: Fordham University Press, 2004), 91.

3. See Giancarlo Movia, "Tatto e pensiero in un passo del 'De anima,'" in *Due studi sul "De Anima" di Aristotele* (Padua: Antenore, 1974), 74.

4. Plato, *Timaeus* 65b4.

5. See the classic essay by Richard Sorabji, "Aristotle on Demarcating the Five Senses," in *Articles on Aristotle*, vol. 4: *Psychology and Aesthetics*, ed. Jonathan Barnes, Malcolm Schofield, and Richard Sorabji (London: Duckworth, 1979), 76–92, esp. 88–92.

6. Aristotle, *On the Soul* 3.12.434b22.

7. See Plato, *Philebus* 51a–52a.

8. Aristotle, *On the Soul* 2.4.

9. Aristotle, *On the Soul* 3.12. 434b24.

10. Aristotle, *On the Soul* 3.12.434b19–20.

11. See Ingemar Düring, *Aristotle's Protrepticus: An Attempt at Reconstruction* (Stockholm: Almqvist & Wiksell, 1961), esp. frag. B 24: 56/57.

12. Aristotle, *Metaphysics* 1.1.980a23–29.

13.   Aristotle, *History of Animals* 9.1.608a16–20. This idea also plays a role in the first book of the *Metaphysics*, where higher animals are said to differ from lower animals in that they possess the sense of hearing (*Metaphysics* 1.1.980b25).

14.   Richard Sorabji, "From Aristotle to Brentano: The Development of the Concept of Intentionality," in *Aristotle and the Later Tradition*, ed. Henry Blumenthal and Howard Robinson (Oxford: Clarendon, 1991), 231–32. See also Thomas Kjeller Johansen, *Aristotle on the Sense-Organs* (Cambridge: Cambridge University Press, 1998), 178–225.

15.   See Henry Blumenthal, "Neoplatonic Elements in the *De Anima* Commentaries," in *Aristotle Transformed: The Ancient Commentators and Their Influence*, ed. Richard Sorabji (Ithaca, N.Y.: Cornell University Press, 1990), 305–24.

16.   Aristotle, *On the Soul* 2.11.423b2–4 [modified].

17.   Aristotle, *Sense and Sensibilia* 4.442b1.

18.   Aristotle, *On the Soul* 3.13.435a13–20 [modified].

19.   Enrico Berti, *Aristotele, dalla dialettica alla filosofia prima: con saggi integrativi*, rev. and augm. ed. (Milan: Bompiani, 2004), 452.

20.   Sorabji, "Aristotle on Demarcating the Five Senses."

21.   "Now, immutation is of two kinds, one natural, the other spiritual." Thomas Aquinas, *Summa Theologiae*, trans. English Dominican Fathers (New York: Benziger, 1947–1948), 1 q78 a3co.

22.   On *immutatio spiritualis* in Aquinas, whom Burnyeat sees as anticipating some of his own arguments, see Miles Burnyeat, "How Much Happens When Aristotle Sees Red and Hears Middle C? Remarks on *De anima* 2, 7–8," in *Essays on Aristotle's* De anima, ed. Martha C. Nussbaum and Amélie Oksenberg Rorty (Oxford: Clarendon, 1992), 421–34. A succinct summary of the debate can be found in Stephen Everson, *Aristotle on Perception* (Oxford: Oxford University Press, 1997), 56–60.

23.   Immanuel Kant, *Anthropology from a Pragmatic Point of View*, trans. Robert B. Louden, in *Anthropology, History, and Education*, ed. Günter Zöller and Robert B. Louden (Cambridge: Cambridge University Press, 2007), §§15:265, 19:267. Cf. also Chrétien, "Body and Touch," 105.

24.   Themistius, *On Aristotle's On the Soul* 73.27:94.

25.   Themistius, *On Aristotle's On the Soul* 73.28:94.

26.   Alexander of Aphrodisias, *De anima liber cum mantissa* 52, 4–5; Philoponus (John of Alexandria), *Ioannis Philoponi in Aristotelis De anima libros commentaria*, in *Commentaria in Aristotelem Graeca*, vol. 15, ed. Michael Hayduck (Berlin: Reimer, 1897), 221.37; and Thomas Aquinas, *Commentary on Aristotle's De Anima*, trans. Kenelm Foster and Silvester Humphries (Notre Dame, Ind.: Dumb Ox, 1994), 2.22:163–64 (*Opera* 45 / 1:161). On similar formulations in Augustine and Plotinus, see Chrétien, "Body and Touch," 113.

27.   Cf. the list of all the properties of what can be touched in Aristotle, *On Generation and Corruption* 2.2.329b18–19.

28.   Philoponus, *In Aristotelis de Anima* 292.14, 30.

29.   Gilbert Romeyer-Dherbey, *Les choses mêmes: La pensée du réel chez Aristote* (Lausanne, Switz.: L'Age d'homme, 1983), 162.

30.   Aristotle, *Parts of Animals* 2.1.647a19, 2.6.651b4–5. Cf. also Aristotle, *History of Animals* 1.4.489a24.

31.   Aristotle, *Parts of Animals* 2.8.653b25–27.

32.   Aristotle, *Parts of Animals* 2.10.656b35.

33.   Aristotle, *On the Soul* 2.11.423b22–23, 3.2.426b15, 2.11.423b26, 2.11.423b24.

34.   In his analysis, remarkable in many respects, Johansen concludes that in the case of both taste and touch the sense-organ is flesh (Johansen, *Aristotle on the Sense-Organs*, 193).

35.   See Averroes, *Long Commentary on the* De anima *by Aristotle*, trans. Richard C. Taylor (New Haven, Conn.: Yale University Press, 2009), 230; Nicolas d'Oresme, *Expositio et questiones in*

Aristotelis De anima, ed. Benoît Patar (Leuven, Belg.: Peeters, 1995), 58; and Francisco Suárez, *Commentaria una cum quaestionibus in libros Aristotelis DE ANIMA*, ed. Salvador Castellote, vol. 2 (Madrid: Labor, 1981), disp. 7°: 550. See also Chrétien, "Body and Touch."

36. Aristotle, *On the Soul* 2.10.422a13–16 (trans. Hett).

37. Aquinas, *Commentary on Aristotle's* De anima, 158.

38. Aristotle, *On the Soul* 2.10.422a14 (trans. Hett).

39. Averroes, *Long Commentary*, 221.

40. Albertus Magnus, *De homine*, ed. Henryk Anzulewicz and J. R. Söder (Hamburg: Meiner, 2004), q. 32, a. 3 and 4, 278b–280b.

41. Aristotle, *On the Soul* 2.11.420a4–5. In the twentieth century Merleau-Ponty will speak of the fleshly body as "innate complex [*complexe inné*]."

42. Aristotle, *On the Soul* 2.11.423b8–15 (trans. Hett).

43. Aristotle, *On the Soul* 2.11.423a1; 2.7, 419a21.

44. See, for example, Berti, *Aristotele*, 452; and Johansen, *Aristotle on the Sense-Organs*, 193.

45. Heraclitus, *Testimonia*, in *Early Greek Philosophy*, ed. and trans. André Laks and Glenn W. Most, vol. 3 (Cambridge, Mass.: Harvard University Press, 2016–), 139, Diels-Kranz 22 B 1.

46. The problems Aristotle in *Metaphysics* / refers to as *lanthanet* are not "unconscious." They have remained underexposed and have been "overlooked" (*Metaphysics* 7.17.1041a33).

47. Aristotle, *On the Soul* 2.11.424a14.

48. Aristotle, *On the Soul* 2.11.423a2–4, b8–13.

49. Jacques Derrida, in "The Double Session," stretches Mallarmé's *hymen* poetologically and pushes it to its conceptual limits: "At the edge of being, the medium of the hymen never becomes a mere mediation or work of the negative; it outwits and undoes all ontologies, all philosophemes, all manner of dialectics." Jacques Derrida, *Dissemination*, trans. Barbara Johnson (London: Athlone, 2000), 215.

50. Aquinas, *Opera* 45 / 1.161, *Commentary on Aristotle's* De Anima 2.22.163 [modified].

51. Aristotle, *On the Soul* 2.8.421b31.

52. Aristotle, *On Sleep* 1.454a32, b10–11, b25–27. See also Rémi Brague, *Aristote et la question du monde: Essai sur le contexte cosmologique et anthropologique de l'ontologie* (Paris: Presses universitaires de France, 1988), 373.

53. Aristotle, *Parts of Animals* 2.13.657a.

54. Maurice Merleau-Ponty, *Phenomenology of Perception*, trans. Donald A. Landes (London: Routledge, 2012), 85–91.

55. Aristotle, *On the Soul* 2.11.423b14–15.

56. See Rémi Brague, "Inclusion and Digestion: Two Models of Cultural Appropriation in Response to a Question of Hans-Georg Gadamer (Tübingen, September 3, 1996)," in *The Legend of the Middle Ages: Philosophical Explorations of Medieval Christianity, Judaism, and Islam*, trans. L.G. Cochrane, 145–58 (Chicago: University of Chicago Press, 2009).

57. Anca Vasiliu, *Du Diaphane: Image, milieu, lumière dans la pensée antique et médiévale* (Paris: Vrin, 1997), 90n138.

58. See the introduction, "L'anthropologie de Némésius," by Gérard Verbeke and José Rafael Moncho-Pascual, to their edition of *De natura hominis* (Leiden: Brill, 1975), ix–lxxxv. There are several translations of the text into English, most recently *On the Nature of Man*, trans. Philip van der Eijk and R. W. Sharples (Liverpool: Liverpool University Press, 2008).

59. Nemesius, *De natura hominis* 79, l. 20.

60. 1 Corinthians 13:12.

61. "Dyaphanum idem est quod duplicis apparitionis, scilicet in superficie et in profundo; nam phano Grece idem est quod apparitio Latine, et dya idem est quod duo." Roger Bacon, *Roger Bacon's Philosophy of Nature: A Critical Edition, with English Translation, Introduction, and Notes, of De*

multiplicatione specierum and De speculis comburentibus, ed. and trans. David C. Lindberg (Oxford: Clarendon, 1983), II.2:96/97. See also Vasiliu, *Du Diaphane*, 74.

62. See Henry Blumenthal, "Themistius, the Last Peripatetic Commentator on Aristotle?," in Sorabji, *Aristotle Transformed*, 113–23.

63. As Brague points out in his introduction to the French translation; see Themistius, *Paraphrase de la métaphysique d'Aristote, livre Lambda*, ed. Rémi Brague (Paris: Vrin, 1999), 37–39.

64. Vasiliu, *Du Diaphane*, 81–85.

65. Themistius, *On Aristotle's On the Soul* 59.14:79; cf. Aristotle, *On the Soul* 2.7.418b.

66. Aristotle, *On the Heavens* 270b.

67. Themistius, *On Aristotle's On the Soul* 59.14–18:79.

68. Themistius, *On Aristotle's On the Soul* 100.28–32:125: "Thus what it is to be me comes from soul, yet from it not in totality—not, that is, from the capacity for perception, which is matter for the imagination, nor again from the capacity for imagination, which is matter for potential intellect, nor from the potential intellect, which is matter for the productive intellect. What it is to be me therefore comes from the productive intellect alone."

69. Alexander of Aphrodisias, *Supplement to "On the Soul,"* ed. and trans. R. W. Sharples (Ithaca, N.Y.: Cornell University Press, 2004), §16, 150,6:148.

70. Vasiliu, *Du Diaphane*, 88.

71. Bremer's collection of material on light as "universal medium of representation" provides a bibliography on this rich topos; see Dieter Bremer, "Licht als universales Darstellungsmedium: Materialien und Bibliographie," *Archiv für Begriffsgeschichte* 18 (1974): 185–206.

72. Aristotle, *On the Soul* 2.7.419a11.

73. Themistius, *On Aristotle's On the Soul* 59.28–30:79.

74. Plotinus, *Enneads*, in *Plotinus*, trans. Arthur Hilary Armstrong (Cambridge, Mass.: Harvard University Press, 1966–88), 4.5.4:293.

75. Plotinus, *Enneads* 4.5.4:297.

76. Eyjólfur K. Emilsson, *Plotinus on Sense-Perception: A Philosophical Study* (Cambridge: Cambridge University Press, 1988), 6. On the negation of the medium in the context of Plotinus's theory of sensibility, see also Hubert Benz, *"Materie" und Wahrnehmung in der Philosophie Plotins* (Würzburg: Königshausen & Neumann, 1990), esp. 200–211.

77. Plotinus, *Enneads* 6.9.4:315.

78. Aristotle, *On the Soul* 2.7.418b20; *Sense and Sensibilia* 3.439a20. See also Johansen, *Aristotle on the Sense-Organs*, 65.

79. See, for example, *Phaedo* 100d.

80. On these misunderstandings, see Anne Merker, *La vision chez Platon et Aristote* (Sankt Augustin, Ger.: Academia, 2003), 168–73.

81. See the commentary in Aristotle, *De anima*, trans. R. D. Hicks (Cambridge: Cambridge University Press, 1907), 369–70.

82. Plato, *Lysis* 217c–e. The thesis put forward by scholars such as Taylor and Glaser, who interpret *parousia* and *paireinai* in the terms of a theory of ideas, seems less likely.

83. Martin Heidegger, *Being and Time*, trans. John Macquarrie and Edward Robinson (New York: Harper, 1962), ¶6.47.

84. Vasiliu, *Du Diaphane*, 140–45. On the history of the concept of *praesentia* within Scholastic epistemology, see Stephan Meier-Oeser, *Die Spur des Zeichens: Das Zeichen und seine Funktion in der Philosophie des Mittelalters und der frühen Neuzeit* (Berlin: de Gruyter, 1997), 86–103.

85. John Duns Scotus, *On Being and Cognition: Ordinatio 1.3*, ed. and trans. John van den Bercken (New York: Fordham University Press, 2016), 1.3.3.1:168.

86. See Georg Steer, "Predigt 101: 'Dum medium silentium tenerent omnia,'" in *Lectura Eckhardi: Predigten Meister Eckharts von Fachgelehrten gelesen und gedeutet*, vol. 1, ed. Georg Steer, Loris

Sturlese, and Dagmar Gottschall (Stuttgart: Kohlhammer, 1998), 247–88; and Olivier Boulnois, *Être et représentation: Une généalogie de la métaphysique moderne à l'époque de Duns Scot (XIIIe–XIVe siècle)* (Paris: Presses universitaires de France, 1999), 308–14.

87. Eckhart, "Predigt 101," in *Die deutschen Werke*, vol. 4/1, ed. Georg Steer (Stuttgart: Kohlhammer, 1997), 345.

88. Eckhart, "Predigt 104," quoted in Steer, "Predigt 101," 270.

89. On the vocabulary of transparency in Dionysius, see Anca Vasiliu, "Le mot et le verre: Une définition médiévale du *diaphane*," *Journal des savants*, no. 1994/1 (1994): 149–51.

90. Dionysius, *The Heavenly Hierarchy*, trans. John Parker, in *The Works of Dionysius the Areopagite*, part 2, 1–66 (London: Parker, 1899), 13.iii:47. For a detailed analysis of these motifs, mainly in the context of the *Celestial Hierarchy*, see Wiebke-Marie Stock, *Theurgisches Denken: Zur kirchlichen Hierarchie des Dionysius Areopagita* (Berlin: de Gruyter, 2008).

91. For a view on the oscillation between physics and metaphysics in the Oxford philosophy of light through the prism of Grosseteste's *De Luce*, see Andreas Speer, "Physics or Metaphysics? Some Remarks on Theory of Science and Light in Robert Grosseteste," in *Aristotle in Britain During the Middle Ages*, ed. John Marenbon (Turnhout, Belg.: Brepols, 1996), 73–90.

92. Roger Bacon, *Opus maius*, ed. John Henry Bridges, vol. 1 (Oxford: Clarendon, 1897), 4:216–17, quoted and trans. in David C. Lindberg, *Theories of Vision from Al-Kindi to Kepler* (Chicago: University of Chicago Press, 1976), 99.

93. Bonaventure of Santoregio, *Commentary on the Second Book of Lombard's Sentences*, 14, 1, 3, 2 concl. (2, 348), quoted in Klaus Hedwig, *Sphaera lucis: Studien zur Intelligibilität des Seienden im Kontext der mittelalterlichen Lichtspekulation* (Münster: Aschendorff, 1980), 162.

94. Thomas Aquinas, *Commentaries on Aristotle's "On Sense and What Is Sensed" and "On Memory and Recollection,"* trans. E. M. Macierowski and Kevin White (Washington, D.C.: Catholic University of America Press, 2005), 3:40 (*Opera* 45 / 2.22–23).

95. Aquinas, *Commentaries on Aristotle's "On Sense and What Is Sensed,"* 5:57 (*Opera* 45 / 2.35).

96. Aquinas, *Commentaries on Aristotle's "On Sense and What Is Sensed,"* 5:57 (*Opera* 45 / 2:36).

97. Georg Wilhelm Friedrich Hegel, *Lectures on the History of Philosophy*, trans. Elizabeth Sanderson Haldane, 2 vols. (London: Paul, Trench, Trübner, 1892–1994), 2.3.B:118.

98. Ramon Lull, *The Book of the Lover and the Beloved*, trans. E. Allison Peers (New York and Toronto: Macmillan, 1923), para. 18:49; see also Vasiliu, *Du Diaphane*, 113.

99. Stefan Hoffmann, *Geschichte des Medienbegriffs* (Hamburg: Meiner, 2002), 44. Hoffmann's conceptual history is instructive, not least for its discussion of the *medium dyphanum*'s posterity in the eighteenth and nineteenth centuries.

100. Dante Alighieri, *The Banquet*, trans. Christopher Ryan (Saratoga, Calif.: Anma Libri, 1989), 2.iii.8:47.

101. Ironically, he does so by invoking Aristotle even though the Greek philosopher had ridiculed the Pythagoreans who, in their excessive desire for harmony, had introduced a tenth heaven as well (see *Metaphysics* 1.5.986a11).

102. Dante, *Banquet*, 2.iii.8–12:47–48, and *The Divine Comedy*, trans. C. H. Sisson (Oxford: Oxford University Press, 1998), 30.38–39:482 [modified].

103. (Pseudo-)Aristotle, *Problems* 3.10.872b8 [modified].

104. Cicero, *On the Nature of the Gods / Academics*, trans. H. Rackham (Cambridge, Mass.: Harvard University Press, 1933), 2.83:203/202.

105. Diogenes Laertius, *Lives of Eminent Philosophers*, trans. R. D. Hicks (Cambridge, Mass.: Harvard University Press, 2006), 7.157:261.

106. Alexander of Aphrodisias, *Supplement*, §10, 130, 14–17:99; cf. Diogenes Laertius, *Lives* 7.157:261.

107. Plotinus, *Enneads* 4.5.4:295.

108. Chalcidius, "Ad Timaeum cp. 220," in *Stoicorum veterum fragmenta*, vol. 2, ed. Hans Friedrich August von Arnim (Stuttgart: Teubner, 1964), no. 879:235, translated in Samuel Sambursky, *Physics of the Stoics* (London: Routledge and Kegan Paul, 1959), 124. According to Sambursky, the metaphor was used previously by Chrysippus and, even earlier, Heraclitus (24).

109. Homer, *Odyssey*, 9.332, and Simplicius, *On Aristotle On the Soul 2.5–12*, trans. Carlos Steel in collab. with J. O. Urmson, in *Priscian On Theophrastus' "On Sense-Perception" with 'Simplicius' On Aristotle's "On the Soul" 2.5–12* (Ithaca, N.Y.: Cornell University Press, 1997), 136, l. 15:167.

110. Galen, for example, vehemently criticizes it although he himself advocates emanationism; see *On the Doctrines of Hippocrates and Plato*, ed. and trans. Phillip De Lacy, 3 vols., 2nd ed. (Berlin: Akademie, 2005), 7.7:475; see also Lindberg, *Theories of Vision*, 10–11.

111. Hunayn ibn Ishaq, *The Book of the Ten Treatises on the Eye, Ascribed to Hunain ibn Is-Hâq (809–877 A.D.): The Earliest Existing Systematic Text-Book of Ophthalmology*, ed. and trans. Max Meyerhof (Cairo: Government, 1928).

112. Abdelhamid I. Sabra, *Theories of Light from Descartes to Newton*, new ed. (Cambridge: Cambridge University Press, 1981), 55n34; see ibn Ishaq, *Ten Treatises on the Eye*, 36–37.

113. See Cherniss, *Aristotle's Criticism*, 320.

114. See Lindberg, *Theories of Vision*, 28–30.

115. See Abdelhamid I. Sabra, "Sensation and Inference in Alhazen's Theory of Visual Perception," in *Studies in Perception: Interrelations in the History of Philosophy and Science*, ed. Peter K. Machamer and Robert G. Turnbull (Columbus: Ohio State University Press, 1978), 160–85.

116. Ibn al-Haytam (Alhazen), *The Optics of Ibn al-Haytham: Books I–III on Direct Vision*, trans. Abd al-Hamid Sabrah (London: Warburg Institute, 1989), 2.3–4:126–224. See also *A Critical Edition with English translation of the First Three Books of Alhazen's De aspectibus, the Medieval Latin Version of Ibn al-Haytham's Kitāb al-Manāzir*, ed. A. M. Smith, 2 vols. (Philadelphia: American Philosophical Society, 2001, 2006).

117. Lindberg, *Theories of Vision*, chap. 9 (178–208); Alistair Cameron Crombie, "Expectation, Modelling and Assent in the History of Optics, i: Alhazen and the Medieval Tradition, ii: Kepler and Descartes," in *Science, Art and Nature in Medieval and Modern Thought* (London: Hambledon, 1996), 301–56; A. Mark Smith, "Ptolemy, Alhazen and Kepler on the Problem of Optical Images," *Arabic Sciences and Philosophy* 8, no. 1 (March 1998): 9–44; and Hans Belting, *Florence and Baghdad: Renaissance Art and Arab Science*, trans. Deborah Lucas Schneider (Cambridge, Mass.: Belknap Press of Harvard University Press, 2011), 139–43.

118. René Descartes, *Dioptrique* 1, AT 6.81 / *Optics* 65. References are to the volumes standard edition by Adam and Tannery (*AT*) and to *Optics*, in *Discourse on Method, Optics, Geometry, and Meteorology*, ed. and trans. Paul J. Olscamp (Indianapolis: Hackett, 2001), 63–173.

119. Descartes, *Dioptrique* 1, AT 6:85 / *Optics* 68.

120. Descartes, *Dioptrique* 1, AT 6:89–90 / *Optics* 75–77.

121. To be precise, we would have to speak of sticks, for the singular of the first chapter doubles in the sixth and is condensed in the illustration of the two crossed sticks that turn the blind person into a perceptive dowser.

122. Leibniz, who used the metaphor himself, is even convinced that Descartes took it directly from Simplicius; see Gottfried Wilhelm Leibniz to Queen Sophie-Charlotte of Prussia, 1702, in *Die Philosophischen Schriften von Gottfried Wilhelm Leibniz*, vol. 6, ed. Carl Immanuel Gerhardt (Berlin: Weidmann, 1875–), 499, and undated letter to Molanus (?), *Die Philosophischen Schriften*, 4:305.

123. The first traces of this debate can be found in (Pseudo-)Aristotle, *Problems* 31.§§4, 7.

124. Descartes, *Dioptrique* 4, AT 6:111 / *Optics* 89.

125. René Descartes, *Rules*, Rule Twelve, AT 10:412 / *The Philosophical Writings of Descartes [PW]*, vol. 1, trans. John Cottingham, Robert Stoothoff, Dugald Murdoch, and Anthony Kenny (Cambridge: Cambridge University Press, 1985–1991), 40. The same idea can be found in Alberti's *De*

pictura 1.5; see Leon Battista Alberti, *Das Standbild—Die Malkunst—Grundlagen der Malerei*, ed. Oskar Bätschmann, trans. Christoph Schäublin (Darmstadt, Ger.: Wissenschaftliche Buchgesellschaft, 2012), 201; and *On Painting*, trans. John R. Spencer, rev. ed. (New Haven, Conn.: Yale University Press, 1966), 45–46. References to *De pictura* are to the Latin text first (book and chapter number, then page number), followed by the page numbers of the English translation, which does not include chapter numbers.

126.   Descartes, *Principiorum Philosophiae*, 1.43 and 1.45, *AT* 8:21 / *PW* 1:207.

127.   Descartes, *Dioptrique 6*, *AT* 6:148 / *Optics* 114.

128.   Descartes, *Dioptrique 8*, *AT* 6:165 / *Optics* 126.

129.   Descartes, *Dioptrique 7*, *AT* 6:149, 150–51 / *Optics* 115, 116.

130.   Maurice Merleau-Ponty, "Eye and Mind," in *The Primacy of Perception*, ed. James M. Edie, trans. Carlton Dallery (Evanston, Ill.: Northwestern University Press, 1964), 170.

131.   Nicolas Malebranche, *The Search After Truth*, trans. Thomas M. Lennon and Paul J. Olscamp (Columbus: Ohio State University Press, 1980), 1.9:41.

132.   Immanuel Kant, *Menschenkunde oder philosophische Anthropologie*, based on Johann Adam Bergk's notes, ed. Friedrich Christian Starke (Leipzig: Expedition des europäischen Aufsehers, 1831), 67. [The passage is not included in the excerpts from the *Menschenkunde* translated by Robert B. Louden in *Lectures on Anthropology*, ed. Allen W. Wood and Robert B. Louden (Cambridge: Cambridge University Press, 2012), 281–333.—Trans.]

133.   As Peter Bexte reminds us in *Blinde Seher: Wahrnehmung von Wahrnehmung in der Kunst des 17. Jahrhunderts* (Amsterdam: Verlag der Kunst, 1999), 91–96.

134.   Antonio Manetti, *The Life of Brunelleschi*, ed. Howard Saalman, trans. Catherine Enggass (University Park: Pennsylvania State University Press, 1970). Cf., among others, Samuel Y. Edgerton, *The Renaissance Rediscovery of Linear Perspective* (New York: Basic Books, 1975), who repeated the experiment 450 years later (by photographical means this time); and Hubert Damisch, *The Origin of Perspective*, trans. John Goodman (Cambridge, Mass.: MIT Press, 2000).

135.   Manetti, *Life of Brunelleschi*, 44. For reasons of space, we unfortunately cannot discuss the so-called second experiment here.

136.   Decio Gioseffi (*Perspectiva artificialis: Per la storia della prospettiva, spigolature e appunti* [Trieste: Università di Trieste, 1957]) proffered the hypothesis that Brunelleschi painted directly onto a mirror (Rudolf Arnheim and others followed, but the hypothesis has since been refuted). For Edgerton, the mirror was merely a tool (*The Renaissance Rediscovery*, chap. 10, 143–52). Others again trace the principle of construction back to medieval optics (Alessandro Parronchi, "Le due tavole prospettiche del Brunelleschi," in *Studi su la dolce prospettiva* [Milano: Martello, 1964], 229–95) or, somewhat more convincingly, to planimetric procedures (Martin Kemp, "Science, Non-Science and Nonsense: The Interpretation of Brunelleschi's Perspective," *Art History* 1, no. 2 [June 1978]: 134–61.). Shigeru Tsuji even claims that for his experiment, Brunelleschi constructed a camera obscura, a claim taken up by Friedrich Kittler ("Man as a Drunken Town-Musician," trans. Jocelyn Holland, *MLN* 118, no. 3 [April 2003]: 637–52). For an overview of research on the question, see Johannes Grave, "Brunelleschi's Perspective Panels: Rupture and Continuity in the History of the Image," in *Renaissance? Perceptions of Continuity and Discontinuity in Europe, c.1300–c.1550*, ed. Alexander Lee, Pit Péporté, and Harry Schnitker (Leiden: Brill, 2010), 161–80. Given the paucity of detail on dimensions and the technology employed, however, it seems unlikely that the question will ever be settled.

137.   Manetti, *Life of Brunelleschi*, 44 [modified].

138.   "My demonstrations which were called miracles by my friends" (Alberti, *De pictura* 1.19:228/57).

139.   Viator quoted in Damisch, *Origin of Perspective*, 121n11.

140.   Sybille Krämer, "The Productivity of Blanks: On the Mathematical Zero and the Vanishing Point in Central Perspective: Remarks on the Convergences Between Science and Art in the Early

Modern Period," in *Instruments in Art and Science: On the Architectonics of Cultural Boundaries in the 17th Century*, ed. Helmar Schramm, Ludger Schwarte, and Jan Lazardzig (Berlin: de Gruyter, 2008), 475.

141. See Louis Marin's reading of Pascal in "On the Interpretation of Ordinary Language: A Parable of Pascal," in *Textual Strategies: Perspectives in Post-Structuralist Criticism,* ed. Josué V. Harari (Ithaca, N.Y.: Cornell University Press, 1979), esp. 252–56.

142. Giorgio Vasari, *The Lives of the Artists*, trans. Julia Conaway Bondanella and Peter E. Bondanella (Oxford: Oxford University Press, 2008), 180. Vasari assigns Brunelleschi paternity of the *intersegatione* or "intersecting lines" (113).

143. Alberti, *De pictura* 2.31:249/69.

144. Alberti, *De pictura* 2.31:249/68, 43; cf. 100n7.

145. Alberti, *De pictura* 2.31:249/68–69, Spencer's interpolation modified.

146. Alberti, *De pictura* 2.31:249/69.

147. Alberti, *De pictura* 2.31:249–50/68–69.

148. Alberti, *De pictura* 2.19:224/56.

149. See Philippe Hamou, *Voir et connaître à l'âge classique* (Paris: Presses universitaires de France, 2002), 72–99. On the complex history of perspective between its pictorial variants in Piero della Francesca, Leonardo, and Dürer and their *mise en discours* two hundred years later, see Laurent Vinciguerra, *Archéologie de la perspective: Sur Piero della Francesca, Vinci et Dürer* (Paris: Presses universitaires de France, 2007), which argues that the history of perspective can be written only as a history of epistemic and practical discontinuities.

150. As Philippe Hamou argues in his anthology of texts on perspective from 1435 to 1740; see his "Introduction," in *La vision perspective (1435–1740): L'art et la science du regard, de la Renaissance à l'âge classique* (Paris: Payot et Rivages, 1995), 37.

151. Giovanni Battista della Porta, *Magia naturalis*, quoted in Lindberg, *Theories of Vision*, 185, Lindberg's interpolations. Earlier articulations of the camera obscura can be found, for example, in Alhazen (see Belting, *Florence and Bagdad*, 104–14).

152. Johannes Kepler, *Optics: Paralipomena to Witelo & Optical Part of Astronomy*, trans. William H. Donahue (Santa Fe, N.M: Green Lion, 2001), 184.

153. Kepler, *Optics*, 180, 171.

154. Kepler, *Optics*, 180, 181.

155. Kepler to Herwart von Hohenburg, March 26, 1598, in *Gesammelte Werke*, vol. 13, ed. Max Caspar (Munich: Beck, 1945), 193.

156. Descartes, *Dioptrique* 6, *AT* 6:140 / *Optics* 107.

157. Descartes, *Dioptrique* 4, *AT* 6:112 / *Optics* 89).

158. Wilhelm Schickard quoted in Kepler, "Appendix Hyperaspitis seu spicileium ex trutinatore Galilaei," in *Gesammelte Werke* 8, 413–25, here no. 19:425; see also Erwin Panofsky, *Perspective as Symbolic Form*, trans. Christopher S. Wood (New York: Zone, 1991), 84–85n11.

159. Descartes, *Dioptrique* 4, *AT* 6:113 / *Optics* 90.

160. The *species* are defined *inquantum similitudo rerum* "in proportion to the existence of their likeness in the senses." Aquinas, *Summa Theologiae*, 1 q17 a2co.

161. Descartes, *Dioptrique* 4, *AT* 6:113 / *Optics* 90.

162. Descartes, *Optics* 90.

163. Descartes, *Optics* 89.

164. Hamou, *La vision perspective*, 464n10.

165. George Berkeley, *Essay Towards a New Theory of Vision*, secs. 85–87, and *Philosophical Commentaries*, no. 63, both texts in *The Works of George Berkeley, Bishop of Cloyne*, vol. 1, ed. A. A. Luce and T. E. Jessop (London: Nelson, 1979), 206–7 and 13, respectively.

166. Jonathan Crary, *Techniques of the Observer: On Vision and Modernity in the Nineteenth Century* (Cambridge, Mass.: MIT Press, 1990), 55; see also Margaret Atherton, "How to Write the History of Vision: Understanding the Relationship Between Berkeley and Descartes," in *Sites of Vision: The Discursive Construction of Sight in the History of Philosophy*, ed. David Michael Kleinberg-Levin (Cambridge, Mass.: MIT Press, 1999).

167. Berkeley, *Theory of Vision Vindicated*, §§55, 57, in *Works* 1, 270, 271.

168. Crary, *Techniques*, 57–58.

169. Jean-Luc Nancy, *The Ground of the Image*, trans. Jeff Fort (New York: Fordham University Press, 2005), 146n18.

170. Magritte paints a number of versions of *La condition humaine* in 1935 and, taking up Plato's cave motif, in 1948. He rearticulates the metaphor of the window with reference to the logic of inside and outside in *Éloge de la dialectique* (*In Praise of Dialectics*, 1937).

171. Plato, *Cratylus* 431c.

172. Arthur C. Danto speaks of "transparency theory" and "Opaque Theory" in *The Transfiguration of the Commonplace: A Philosophy of Art* (Cambridge, Mass.: Harvard University Press, 1981), 159.

173. Dürer, *Underweysung der Messung* (1538), quoted in Panofsky, *Perspective*, 27.

174. Panofsky, *Perspective*, 77n5.

175. Vasari, *Lives*, 104. Although Masaccio obviously implements the new principles of central perspective, he also inserts elements into his fresco that refuse incorporation into a unified perspective; see Emmanuel Alloa, "Ist die Perspektive eine symbolische Form?," in *Perspektive—Die Spaltung der Standpunkte: Zur Perspektive in Philosophie, Kunst und Recht*, ed. Gertrud Koch (Munich: Fink, 2010), 13–27.

176. Roland Barthes, *Camera Lucida: Reflections on Photography*, trans. Richard Howard (New York: Hill and Wang, 1981), 6: "Whatever it grants to vision and whatever its manner, a photograph is always invisible: it is not it that we see."

177. See Kendall L. Walton, "Transparent Pictures: On the Nature of Photographic Realism," *Critical Inquiry* 11, no. 2 (December 1984): 246–77: "Photographs are *transparent*. We see the world *through* them" (251, Walton's emphases).

178. Ludwig Wittgenstein, *Remarks on Colour*, ed. Gertrude Elizabeth Margaret Anscombe, trans. Linda L. McAlister and Margarete Schättle (Oxford: Blackwell, 1978), §19:5, Wittgenstein's emphasis.

179. Louis Marin, *On Representation*, trans. Catherine Porter (Stanford, Calif.: Stanford University Press, 2001), e.g., 167.

180. See Philippe Junod's vast *Transparence et opacité: Essai sur les fondements théoriques de l'art moderne* [Transparency and opacity: An essay on the theoretical foundations of modern art] (Lausanne, Switz.: L'Age d'homme, 1976).

181. See Colin Rowe and Robert Slutzky, "Transparency: Literal and Phenomenal," *Perspecta* 8 (1963): 45–54, and *Transparency*, ed. Bernhard Hoesli (Basel, Switz.: Birkhäuser, 1997), as well as Hoesli's "Commentary" in the latter volume, 57–83, esp. 61.

182. John Kulvicki, "Image Structure," *Journal of Aesthetics and Art Criticism* 61, no. 4 (Fall 2003): 330, 324.

183. Kulvicki, "Image Structure," 332.

184. For Günter Abel, for example, the image, to be an image(-sign) at all, must, among other things, "be understood directly, without interference," and "without needing other epistemic mediators" and be "sufficiently clear [*deutlich*] with regard to a goal pursued by means of or it" or be "reliable with a view to action [*handlungs-verlässlich*]" in the sense that "one relies on the image-sign understood directly and without interpretation to such a degree that one acts on it." The six aspects Abel lists are, on his own account, not necessary and sufficient criteria that come to bear at

all times and in all contexts. Yet what are we to make of the fact, then, that Abel describes these aspects in terms of a necessity: "The image-sign must …"? Günter Abel, "Zeichen und Interpretationsphilosophie der Bilder," in *Zeichen der Wirklichkeit* (Frankfurt: Suhrkamp, 2004), 368. In this context, compare this book's chapter 5.7, which explores the possibility of a nonnormative *characteristica imaginalis* in terms of a symptomatology of images.

185.   See Emmanuel Alloa, "Visual Studies in Byzantium: A Pictorial Turn 'avant la lettre,'" *Journal of Visual Culture* 12, no. 1 (2013): 3–29.

186.   Psalm 113:15 Vulgate / 115:7 KJV.

187.   The Septuagint indiscriminately uses the word *eidōlon* to translate Hebrew terms, including *pessel*, *massekah*, *gillulim*, and *semel*, that largely belong to a haptic rather than a visual semantics; see José Faur, "The Biblical Idea of Idolatry," *Jewish Quarterly Review* 69, no. 1 (1978): 1–15.

188.   Nancy, *Ground of the Image*, 30–31.

189.   See Giovanni Domenico Mansi et al., eds., *Sacrorum conciliorum nova et amplissima collectio [etc.]*, vol. 13 (Paris: Welter, 1901–1927), 356A.

190.   Denis Diderot, *Rameau's Nephew and D'Alembert's Dream*, trans. Leonard Tancock (Harmondsworth: Penguin, 1966), 151–52.

191.   For a more detailed discussion, see my "Bildwissenschaft in Byzanz."

192.   William Henry Fox Talbot, *The Pencil of Nature* (London: Longman, Brown, Green & Longmans, 1844–1846).

193.   Joseph Gerlach, *Die Photographie als Hülfsmittel mikroskopischer Forschung* (Leipzig: Engelmann, 1863), cited in Horst Bredekamp and Franziska Brons, "Fotografie als Medium der Wissenschaft—Kunstgeschichte, Biologie und das Elend der Illustration," in *Iconic Turn: Die neue Macht der Bilder*, ed. Christa Maar and Herbert Burda (Cologne: Dumont, 2005), 370.

194.   William Henry Fox Talbot, "Photogenic Drawing: To the Editor of the Literary Gazette," in *The Literary Gazette; and Journal of Belles Lettres, Arts, Sciences, &c. for the Year 1839* [etc.], no. 1150 (February 2, 1839) (London: Literary Gazette, 1839), 73.

195.   Ernst Cassirer, *The Philosophy of Symbolic Forms*, trans. Ralph Manheim, vol. 2 (New Haven, Conn.: Yale University Press, 1953–57), 36–38.

196.   See Pliny, *Natural History*, trans. H. Rackam et al. (Cambridge, Mass.: Harvard University Press, 1968–1980), 35.36.103–4:336–37.

197.   Quoted in Harold Rosenberg, *The Re-Definition of Art* (Chicago: University of Chicago Press, 1972), 125.

198.   See, for example, Donald Judd, *Complete Writings, 1959–1975* (Halifax: Press of the Nova Scotia College of Art and Design, 2005), 66, or *Complete Writings, 1975–1986* (Eindhoven: Van Abbemuseum, 1987), 39, 42.

199.   On this symptomatic repression in the artist's discourse that mirrors Clement Greenberg's "opticality," see Sebastian Egenhofer, *Abstraktion—Kapitalismus—Subjektivität: Die Wahrheitsfunktion des Werks in der Moderne* (Munich: Fink, 2008).

200.   Richard Wollheim tries to defend this physical object hypothesis at least for pictorial works, although in *Art and Its Objects* (Cambridge: Cambridge University Press, 1980), he is quite aware of its problems and addresses possible objections.

201.   Danto, *Transfiguration*, 151.

202.   Friedrich Nietzsche, "Sokrates und die Tragödie," in *Sämtliche Werke: Kritische Studienausgabe*, ed. Giorigo Colli and Mazzino Montinari, vol. 1, 2nd rev. ed. (Munich: dtv, 1999), 544.

203.   Jean-François Lyotard, *Discourse, Figure*, trans. Antony Hudek and Mary Lydon (Minneapolis: University of Minnesota Press, 2011), 196.

204.   See Rainer Metzger, *Buchstäblichkeit: Bild und Kunst in der Moderne* (Cologne: König, 2004).

205.   E. T. A. Hoffmann, "The Artus Hof," in *The Serapion Brethren*, trans. Alexander Ewing, vol. 1 (London: Bell, 1908), 165.

206. Jorge Luis Borges, "The Wall and the Books," trans. James E. Irby, in *Labyrinths: Selected Stories & Other Writings*, ed. Donald A. Yates and James E. Irby, augm. ed. (New York: New Directions, 1964), 188.

207. Gerhard Richter, "Interview with Amine Haase, 1977," in *Text: Writings, Interviews and Letters 1961–2007*, ed. Dietmar Elger and Hans Ulrich Obrist (London: Thames & Hudson, 2009), 97.

208. Theodor W. Adorno, *Negative Dialectics*, trans. E. B. Ashton (New York: Continuum, 1993), 137–38.

4. A PHENOMENOLOGY OF IMAGES

1. The effort to regain a pure viewing, regain things such as they immediately show themselves is by no means limited to phenomenology but may indeed serve to describe an epochal turn that also characterizes other philosophical enterprises (thus Henri Bergson, for example, defines his metaphysics as a liberation from the symbolic). It may also be connected to the artistic avant gardists of the turn of the century. On the historical situation, see Ferdinand Fellmann, *Phänomenologie als ästhetische Theorie* (Freiburg, Ger.: Alber, 1989); on the second aspect, Hans Rainer Sepp's essay on phenomenology and painting, "Annäherungen an die Wirklichkeit: Phänomenologie und Malerei nach 1900," in *Edmund Husserl und die phänomenologische Bewegung: Zeugnisse in Text und Bild* (Freiburg, Ger.: Alber, 1988), 77–94.

2. Edmund Husserl, *Natur und Geist: Vorlesungen Sommersemester 1919*, ed. M. Weiler, *Husserliana* Materialien 4 (Dordrecht: Springer, 2002), 46.

3. Edmund Husserl, *Ding und Raum: Vorlesungen 1907*, ed. Ulrich Claesges, *Husserliana* 16 (The Hague: Nijhoff, 1973), 139.

4. On categorial intuition, see the sixth chapter of the sixth *Logical Investigation*, trans. John F. Finlay, ed. Dermot Moran (London: Routledge, 2008), 2:271–94. From the voluminous literature on the possibilities and limits of categorial intuition, let me cite only Ernst Tugendhat, *Der Wahrheitsbegriff bei Husserl und Heidegger* (Berlin: de Gruyter, 1967), 111–36; Thomas M. Seebohm, "Kategoriale Anschauung," *Phänomenologische Forschungen* 23 (1990): 9–47; and Dieter Lohmar, "Husserl's Concept of Categorial Intuition," in *One Hundred Years of Phenomenology: Husserl's "Logical Investigations" Revisited*, ed. Dan Zahavi and Frederik Stjernfelt (Dordrecht: Springer, 2002), 125–45. Again, Husserl is not the only one to expand the concept of intuition; such demands are practically part of the signature of the late nineteenth century. On the basis of non-Euclidean discoveries in geometry, Helmholtz, for example, advocates extending intuitiveness to all processes of epistemic insightfulness. Hermann Helmholtz, "The Facts in Perception," trans. Malcolm F. Lowe, in *Epistemological Writings: The Paul Hertz/Moritz Schlick Centenary Edition of 1921 with Notes and Commentary by the Editors,* ed. Paul Hertz, Moritz Schlick, R. S. Cohen, and Yehuda Elkana (Dordrecht: Reidel, 1977), 162–63. For Husserl that also means a revaluation of the often overlooked but operatively central concept of insight, *Einsicht*. On this point, see Maurizio Di Bartolo's detailed reconstruction in *Einsicht: La costruzione del noetico in Edmund Husserl* (Padua, Italy: Il Poligrafo, 2006).

5. Edmund Husserl, *Ideas Pertaining to a Pure Phenomenology and to a Phenomenological Philosophy, First Book*, trans. Fred Kersten (The Hague: Nijhoff, 1983), §24:44.

6. Husserl often correlates originarity and "givenness in person [*Leibhaftigkeit*]," and the terms may be considered to be largely congruent. Originarity designates the originarily "giving" or "presentive" (*gebend*) character of intuition; intuition is "personal" insofar as it is not an impression in a Humean sense; the intuitive, rather, is as it were viewed "in person." Around 1911–1912 Husserl

notes that the concept of "givenness in person" introduced in the 1904–1905 lecture "has since entered the literature" (*Wahrnehmung und Aufmerksamkeit*, 344).

7. See Heinrich Rickert, "Die Methode der Philosophie und das Unmittelbare: Eine Problemstellung," in *Philosophische Aufsätze*, ed. Rainer A. Bast (Tübingen, Ger.: Mohr Siebeck, 1999), 107–52.

8. Rickert, "Die Methode der Philosophie," 118; cf. 115.

9. Martin Heidegger, *History of the Concept of Time: Prolegomena*, trans. Theodore Kisiel (Bloomington: Indiana University Press, 2010), §9c:88.

10. Husserl, *Ideas* 1, §43:92–93.

11. Edmund Husserl, *Introduction to Logic and Theory of Knowledge: Lectures 1906/07*, trans. Claire Ortiz Hill (Dordrecht: Springer, 2008), §30d:149. See also *Logical Investigations*, 1:275.

12. Jean-Paul Sartre, *The Imaginary: A Phenomenological Psychology of the Imagination*, ed. Arlette Elkaïm-Sartre, trans. Jonathan Webber (London: Routledge, 2004), 5–6.

13. Husserl, *Logical Investigations*, 2:125 [modified].

14. Husserl, *Logical Investigations*, 2:126.

15. Husserl, *Logical Investigations*, 2:101, 2:81.

16. Husserl, *Logical Investigations*, 2:126.

17. Iris Därmann, *Tod und Bild: Eine phänomenologische Mediengeschichte* (Munich: Fink, 1995), 194.

18. Husserl, *Logical Investigations*, 2:219 [modified].

19. Edmund Husserl, *Die Krisis der europäischen Wissenschaften und die transzendentale Phänomenologie: Ergänzungsband: Texte aus dem Nachlass 1934–1937*, ed. Reinhold N. Smid, *Husserliana* 29 (The Hague: Kluwer, 1992), 35.

20. Husserl, *Logical Investigations*, 2:229. As mentioned, "unity" for Husserl belongs to the "categorial intuitions."

21. Husserl, *Logical Investigations*, 2:230, Husserl's emphasis.

22. Husserl, *Ideas* 1, §100:246–47.

23. Husserl, *Logical Investigations*, 2:86 [modified].

24. Husserl, *Logical Investigations*, 2:219.

25. Husserl, *Logical Investigations*, 1:210.

26. Husserl, *Logical Investigations*, 1:208.

27. Aristotle, *Posterior Analytics*, 76b40–77a2.

28. Paul Natorp, *Allgemeine Psychologie nach kritischer Methode*, 290, quoted in Ferdinand Fellmann, *Phänomenologie zur Einführung* (Hamburg: Junius, 2006), 31.

29. On this revision, see Eduard Marbach, *Das Problem des Ich in der Phänomenologie Husserls* (The Hague: Nijhoff, 1974), §27:193–203.

30. Husserl, *Ideas* 1, §35:72–73.

31. Husserl, *Ideas* 1, §115:272–75.

32. Husserl, *Logical Investigations*, 2:220.

33. Husserl, *Logical Investigations*, 2:220–21.

34. Husserl, *Logical Investigations*, 2:221, 220.

35. See Bernhard Rang's detailed description of the tension between self-giving and representation in Husserl's early theory of perception, "Repräsentation und Selbstgegebenheit: Die Aporie der Phänomenologie der Wahrnehmung in den Frühschriften Husserls," *Phänomenologische Forschungen* 1 (1975): 105–37.

36. The concept of "diastasis" here picks up on Bernhard Waldenfels; see *Bruchlinien der Erfahrung: Phänomenologie, Psychoanalyse, Phänomenotechnik* (Frankfurt am Main: Suhrkamp, 2002), 173–175; and *Phenomenology of the Alien: Basic Concepts*, trans. Alexander Kozin and Tanja Stähler (Evanston, Ill.: Northwestern University Press, 2011), 30–32.

37. Arno Schubbach has shown how Derrida's own critical philosophy sets in at this point; see his *Subjekt im Verzug: Zur Rekonzeption von Subjektivität mit Jacques Derrida* (Zurich: Chronos, 2007), 67–84.

38. Husserl, *Natur und Geist*, 43, 33.

39. Husserl, *Ideas* 1, §57:133, as well as *Ding und Raum*, 20, 337. Cf. the idea of a "transcendence belonging to nature" (*Transzendenz der materiellen Natur*) (*Ideas* 1, §53:125).

40. See, for example, Martin Seel, "Vor dem Schein kommt das Erscheinen: Bemerkungen zu einer Ästhetik der Medien," in *Ethisch-ästhetische Studien* (Frankfurt: Suhrkamp, 1996), 104–25. Seel thereby also seems to exclude any possibility that phenomenology contribute to an "aesthetics of appearing."

41. Despite repeated sporadic references to painting, sculpture, poetry, or theater, the number of texts explicitly devoted to aesthetics is small. The relatively few pages that do exist are essentially assembled in the convolute A VI 1, in which Husserl collected manuscripts written between 1906 and 1918 under the heading "Aesthetics and Phenomenology." Besides the letter to Hoffmansthal (Husserl to Hoffmannsthal, January 12, 1907, trans. Sven-Olov Wallenstein, *Site Magazine* 26/27 [2009], 2, http://www.sitemagazine.net/content/01-issues/19-26-27_2009/26-27_2009.pdf) and the pages "On the Theory of Art" (ca. 1918; in *Phantasy, Image Consciousness, and Memory (1898 1925)*, trans. John Brough [Dordrecht: Springer, 2005], 651–54) that refer to Fontane and Schnitzler, there is also the draft "Aesthetics" (ca. 1906). Gabriele Scaramuzza and Karl Schuhmann have edited excerpts from this draft under the title "Ein Husserlmanuskript über Ästhetik" in *Husserl Studies* 7/3 (1990): 165–77. Symptomatically, here as elsewhere, Husserl starts thinking about the relationship between phenomenology and aesthetics only when prompted by questions from others (in this case, Johannes Daubert and Aloys Fischer).

42. Jacques Derrida, *Margins of Philosophy*, trans. Alan Bass (Chicago: University of Chicago Press, 1982), 162n10.

43. On the history of phenomenological aesthetics, see Georg Bensch, *Vom Kunstwerk zum ästhetischen Objekt: zur Geschichte der phänomenologischen Ästhetik* (Munich: Fink, 1994).

44. As Emmanuel Levinas puts it in an early review of Valentin Feldman's *L'esthétique française contemporaine*, in *Recherches philosophiques* 6 (1936–1937): 409. See also Bensch, *Vom Kunstwerk zum ästhetischen Objekt*, 103.

45. Husserl to Hoffmannsthal, January 12, 1907.

46. Note dated to 1912, *Phantasy, Image Consciousness, and Memory*, 459.

47. Husserl, *Phantasy, Image Consciousness, and Memory*, 464.

48. See, for example, Edmund Husserl, *Philosophy of Arithmetic: Psychological and Logical Investigations—with Supplementary Texts from 1887–1901*, trans. Dallas Willard (Dordrecht: Springer, 2003), 215–22.

49. Ms. F I 9/4a-b; Rudolf Boehm, in his introduction to *Phenomenology of the Consciousness of Internal Time*, quotes the entire text; see *Zur Phänomenologie des inneren Zeitbewusstseins (1893–1917)*, ed. Rudolf Boehm (The Hague: Nijhoff, 1969), xv–xvii.

50. Husserl, *Philosophy of Arithmetic*, 205n1.

51. As Bernhard Rang, in "Repräsentation und Selbstgegebenheit," rightly remarks, this concept allows for explaining Husserl's successive engagement in the 1890s with otherwise disparate fields such as logical calculus, the theory of objectless representations, and the problem of representation; see his introduction to Edmund Husserl, *Aufsätze und Rezensionen (1890–1910)*, ed. Berhard Rang, *Husserliana* 22 (The Hague: Nijhoff, 1979), xxxvn2.

52. Husserl, *Phantasy, Image Consciousness, and Memory*, 6–7.

53. Franz Brentano, *Grundzüge der Ästhetik*, ed. Franziska Mayer-Hillebrand, 2nd ed. (Hamburg: Meiner, 1988), 47. On Brentano's interpretation of Aristotle generally, see Franco Volpi, "War Franz Brentano ein Aristoteliker? Zu Brentanos und Aristoteles' Auffassung der Psychologie als

Wissenschaft," *Brentano Studien* 2 (1989): 13–29; and Dominik Perler, *Theorien der Intentional-ität im Mittelalter* (Frankfurt: Klostermann, 2002), §§1, 35. On the concept of intentionality between Brentano and Husserl, see Peter Prechtl, "Die Struktur der Intentionalität bei Brentano und Husserl," *Brentano Studien* 2 (1989): 117–30; and Dieter Münch, *Intention und Zeichen: Untersuchungen zu Franz Brentano und zu Edmund Husserls Frühwerk* (Frankfurt: Suhrkamp, 1993). Karl Schuhmann has persuasively shown how Husserl's concept of intentionality is not an immediate elaboration and development of Brentano's but emerged in reaction to Kazimierz Twardowski's book *Zur Lehre vom Inhalt und Gegenstand der Vorstellung* [On the doctrine of the content and object of representation] (1894). See Karl Schuhmann, "Intentionalität und intentio-naler Gegenstand beim frühen Husserl," *Phänomenologische Forschungen* 24/25 (1991): 46–75, esp. 49–54.

54.   Brentano, *Grundzüge*, 86.

55.   Husserl, *Phantasy, Image Consciousness, and Memory*, 100.

56.   Husserl, *Phantasy, Image Consciousness, and Memory*, 107–8.

57.   Franz Brentano, *Descriptive Psychology*, trans. and ed. Benito Müller (London: Routledge, 1995), 163. On Husserl's critique of Brentano's concept of the phenomenon, see also Klaus Wüstenberg's study, *Die Konsequenze des Phänomenalismus: Erkenntnistheoretische Untersuchungen in kri-tischer Auseinandersetzung mit Hume, Brentano und Husserl* (Würzburg, Ger.: Königshausen & Neumann, 2004), esp. 133–56.

58.   Edmund Husserl, *The Crisis of European Sciences and Transcendental Phenomenology: An Intro-duction to Phenomenological Philosophy*, trans. David Carr (Evanston, Ill.: Northwestern Univer-sity Press, 2000), §§68:233, 69:240.

59.   Husserl, *Logical Investigations*, 2:341.

60.   Recall that Husserl uses two different notions of reality: to distinguish the phenomenological approach from a standard understanding of reality as empirical physical existence, he calls the former *reell* and the latter *real*.

61.   Husserl, *Logical Investigations*, 2:341–43.

62.   Renaud Barbaras, "The Three Moments of Appearance," in *Desire and Distance: Introduction to a Phenomenology of Perception*, trans. Paul B. Milan (Stanford, Calif.: Stanford University Press, 2006).

63.   Husserl, *Logical Investigations*, 2:83.

64.   See Husserl, *Zur Phänomenologie des inneren Zeitbewusstseins*, 358, 371.

65.   Husserl, *Crisis*, 170–72.

66.   "The first breakthrough of this universal a priori of correlation between experienced object and manners of givenness (which occurred during work on my *Logical Investigations* around 1898) shocked me so deeply that my whole subsequent life-work has been dominated by the task of sys-tematically elaborating on this a priori of correlation" (Husserl, *Crisis*, 162n [modified]).

67.   Husserl, *Ideas* 1, §84:199–201.

68.   Husserl, *Ideas* 1, §85:203.

69.   In the unpublished manuscript "Phänomenologie als Lehre vom Erscheinen als solchem [Phe-nomenology as the theory of appearing as such]," which the editors date to 1973; see Jan Patočka, *Vom Erscheinen als solchem: Texte aus dem Nachlass,* ed. Helga Blaschek-Hahn and Karel Novotný (Freiburg, Ger.: Alber, 2000), 123.

70.   Husserl, *Phantasy, Image Consciousness, and Memory*, 153.

71.   Edmund Husserl, *Späte Texte über Zeitkonstitution (1929–1934): Die C-Manuskripte*, ed. Dieter Lohmar, *Husserliana* Materialien 8 (Dordrecht: Springer, 2002), 378–79.

72.   Husserl, *Phantasy, Image Consciousness, and Memory*, 153, my emphasis.

73.   Husserl, *Phantasy, Image Consciousness, and Memory*, 20–21.

74.   Husserl, *Phantasy, Image Consciousness, and Memory*, 20.

75. On the ternary structure of image-consciousness, as opposed to *phantasia*, see also Emmanuel Alloa, "Bildbewusstsein," in Hans-Helmuth Gander, *Husserl-Lexikon* (Darmstadt: Wissenschaftliche Buchgesellschaft, 2009), 49–50.

76. Husserl, *Phantasy, Image Consciousness, and Memory*, 21.

77. Husserl, *Ideas* I, §111:261.

78. Hua Husserl, *Ideas* I, §111:262.

79. Husserl, *Ideas* I, §106:254 [modified].

80. Husserl, *Ideas* I, §111:262.

81. Jean-Paul Sartre, *The Imagination*, trans. Kenneth Williford and trans. David Rudrauf (Abingdon: Routledge, 2012), 134.

82. For a detailed exposition of Sartre's special approach, which I can only sketch summarily here, see Emmanuel Alloa, "Imagination zwischen Nichtung und Fülle: Jean-Paul Sartres negative Theorie der Einbildungskraft auf dem Prüfstein von Tintorettos Malerei," *Paragrana: Internationale Zeitschrift für historische Anthropologie*, Supplement 2 (2006): 13–27.

83. Sartre, *The Imaginary*, 9.

84. Sartre, *The Imaginary*, 86–88.

85. Sartre, *The Imaginary*, 17–20.

86. Sartre, *The Imaginary*, 126, Sartre's emphasis.

87. Sartre, *The Imaginary*, 183–84 [modified].

88. Husserl, *Ideas* I, §49:110.

89. Sartre, *The Imaginary*, 12.

90. Sartre, *The Imaginary*, 12, 48, 183.

91. Sartre, *The Imaginary*, 185.

92. Sartre, *The Imaginary*, 189.

93. Sartre, *The Imaginary*, 183.

94. Sartre, *The Imaginary*, 189.

95. Sartre, *The Imaginary*, 183.

96. Sartre, *The Imaginary*, 11, Sartre's emphasis.

97. Husserl, *Ideas* I, §§106, 107:253–57.

98. Husserl, *Ideas* I, §109:257–58.

99. Paolo Volonté, *Husserls Phänomenologie der Imagination: Zur Funktion der Phantasie bei der Konstitution von Erkenntnis* (Freiburg, Ger.: Alber, 1997), 203.

100. Husserl, *Ideas* I, §109:258.

101. Husserl, *Ideas* I, §109:258.

102. On this point, see in more detail Eliane Escoubas, "*Bild, Fiktum* et esprit de la communauté chez Husserl," *Alter: Revue de phénoménologie*, no. 4 (1996): 281–300.

103. Husserl, *Ideas* I, §70:160 [interpolation Kersten].

104. On iteration, see Husserl, *Ideas* I, §112:252–53.

105. Jacques Derrida, *Speech and Phenomena and Other Essays on Husserl's Theory of Signs*, trans. David B. Allison (Evanston, Ill.: Northwestern University Press, 1989), 52.

106. Jacques Derrida, *Edmund Husserl's Origin of Geometry: An Introduction*, trans. John P. Leavey (Lincoln: University of Nebraska Press, 1989), 135n141.

107. In a manuscript dated 1898 (Husserl, *Phantasy, Image Consciousness, and Memory*, 139).

108. In a manuscript dated 1921/1924 (Husserl, *Phantasy, Image Consciousness, and Memory*, 693).

109. More precisely: starting at §21 of the lecture; see *The Phenomenology of Internal Time-Consciousness*, ed. Martin Heidegger, trans. James Spencer Churchill (The Hague: Nijhoff, 1964), 47.

110. Husserl, *Ideas* I, §99:244.

111. Husserl, *Ideas* I, §43:93.

112. Tugendhat, "Der Wahrheitsbegriff," 66–68. See also Rang, "Repräsentation und Selbstgegebenheit"; and Därmann, *Tod und Bild*, 216–20.

113. Husserl, *The Phenomenology of Internal Time-Consciousness*, §28:83.

114. Tugendhat, "Der Wahrheitsbegriff," 67.

115. This is Samuel Dubosson's thesis: in the texts on images, phantasy is "legitimized" as a means of knowledge; see his *L'imagination légitimée: La conscience imaginative dans la phénoménologie proto-transcendantale de Husserl* (Paris: L'Harmattan, 2004). The present book differs from this thesis, according to which this very legitimacy of phantasy is possible only by demoting image-consciousness.

116. Husserl, *Phantasy, Image Consciousness, and Memory*, 121.

117. Husserl, *Phantasy, Image Consciousness, and Memory*, 51, Husserl's emphasis.

118. Husserl, *Logical Investigations*, 2:252–58.

119. Husserl, *Logical Investigations*, 2:255, 2:253.

120. Jean-François Lyotard, *The Differend: Phrases in Dispute*, trans. Georges Van Den Abbeele (Minneapolis: University of Minnesota Press, 1988). This is the philosophical *opus magnus* of an author whose first book, published in 1954, was an introduction to phenomenology; see *Phenomenology*, trans. Brian Beakley (New York: State University of New York Press, 1991).

121. Husserl, *Phantasy, Image Consciousness, and Memory*, 50, Husserl's emphasis.

122. Lambert Wiesing emphasizes this point in "Phänomenologie des Bildes nach Edmund Husserl und Jean-Paul Sartre," in *Phänomene im Bild*, 43–59 (Munich: Fink, 2000), 50–51.

123. Husserl, *Phantasy, Image Consciousness, and Memory*, 616.

124. Bernhard Waldenfels, "Das Rätsel der Sichtbarkeit: Kunstphänomenologische Betrachtungen im Hinblick auf den Status der modernen Malerei," in *Der Stachel des Fremden* (Frankfurt: Suhrkamp, 1998), 209.

125. Husserl, *Phantasy, Image Consciousness, and Memory*, 616.

126. Husserl, *Phantasy, Image Consciousness, and Memory*, 21, 616.

127. Sartre, *The Imaginary*, 184; and Husserl, *Phantasy, Image Consciousness, and Memory*, 617. On theater in the context of the regularity of the fictitious, see Edmund Husserl, *Erfahrung und Urteil: Untersuchungen zur Genealogie der Logik*, ed. Ludwig Landgrebe (Hamburg, Ger.: Meiner, 1999), 361–62.

128. Husserl, *Phantasy, Image Consciousness, and Memory*, 132 [modified].

129. Daniel Tyradellis, *Untiefen: Husserls Begriffsebene zwischen Formalismus und Lebenswelt* (Würzburg, Ger.: Königshausen & Neumann, 2006), 123.

130. Husserl's observations are symptomatic of an age in which original works of art were no longer known exclusively through ekphrastic eyewitness-ship (as in Diderot's *salons*, for example) but in which the democratized access to the works via photomechanic printing techniques nonetheless also highlighted the discrepancy between the original work in color and its monochrome reproduction.

131. Husserl, *Phantasy, Image Consciousness, and Memory*, 38 [modified].

132. Husserl, *Ideas 1*, §100:246 [modified].

133. As Detlef Thiel shows in his media-archaeological re- and deconstruction of Husserl's relationship with painting; see his "Der Phänomenologe in der Galerie: Husserl und die Malerei," *Phänomenologische Forschungen, Neue Folge* 2, no. 1 (1997): 61–103.

134. Husserl, *Ideas 1*, §100:246.

135. Husserl, *Wahrnehmung und Aufmerksamkeit*, 352–53.

136. Husserl, *Wahrnehmung und Aufmerksamkeit*, 188.

137. On the logic of indeterminacy that reigns in images, see Gottfried Boehm, "Indeterminacy: On the Logic of the Image," in *Dynamics and Performativity of Imagination: The Image Between the Visible and the Invisible*, ed. Bernd Hüppauf and Christoph Wulf (New York: Routledge, 2009), 219–29.

138. Husserl, *Phantasy, Image Consciousness, and Memory*, 50.

139. Husserl, *Phantasy, Image Consciousness, and Memory*, 133.

140. Husserl, *Phantasy, Image Consciousness, and Memory*, 51

141. Husserl, *Phantasy, Image Consciousness, and Memory*, 48, Husserl's emphasis.

142. Husserl, *Phantasy, Image Consciousness, and Memory*, 133–34.

143. Husserl, *Phantasy, Image Consciousness, and Memory*, 49, 133–34, 51.

144. Eugen Fink, "Vergegenwärtigung und Bild: Beiträge zu einer Phänomenologie der Unwirklichkeit," in *Studien zur Phänomenologie 1930–1939* (The Hague: Nijhoff, 1966), 1–78.

145. Fink, "Vergegenwärtigung," 72, 77–78.

146. Husserl, *Phantasy, Image Consciousness, and Memory*, 50; see also 611–12.

147. Fink, "Vergegenwärtigung," 77.

148. Fink, "Vergegenwärtigung," 18. On Fink's reference to Hegel, see László Tengelyi, "Finks 'Fenster ins Absolute,'" *Phänomenologische Forschungen* 30: Die Freiburger Phänomenologie (1996): 65–87. On his window theory of images more generally, see Gabriella Baptist, "Le finestre di Eugen Fink," *Kainós: Rivista telematica di filosofia*, no. 1 (2001), http://www.kainos.it/Pages/Artdisvela04.html.

149. Fink, "Vergegenwärtigung," 76–78.

150. "Not the 'members' of the correlation, but the correlation is the prior thing." Eugen Fink, *Sixth Cartesian Meditation: The Idea of a Transcendental Theory of Method*, trans. Ronald Bruzina (Bloomington: Indiana University Press, 1995), 45.

151. Husserl, *Crisis*, 167–70.

152. For a fairly recent presentation of the "genetic" Husserl that takes into account the considerable literature on the question, see Donn Welton, *The Other Husserl: The Horizons of Transcendental Phenomenology* (Bloomington: Indiana University Press, 2002).

153. Aristotle, *Metaphysics* 4.6, 1011a23–24.

154. Paul Ricœur, "Phénoménologie et herméneutique," *Phänomenologische Forschungen* 1 (1975): 68. [The passage does not figure in the English version, "Phenomenology and Hermeneutics," trans. R. Bradley DeFord, *Noûs* 9, no. 1 (1975): 85–102.—Trans.]

155. Patočka, *Vom Erscheinen als solchem*, 97. In opposition, Patočka develops his "asubjective phenomenology," in which the subject is as much a "result" of the correlation as the appearing is.

156. See Klaus Held, "Husserls Rückgang auf das phainomenon und die geschichtliche Stellung der Phänomenologie," in *Dialektik und Genesis in der Phänomenologie*, ed. Ernst Wolfgang Orth (Freiburg, Ger.: Alber, 1980), 89–145.

157. Husserl even writes in the preface to Fink's *Vergegenwärtigung und Bild* that the study contains not a single sentence he would "not appropriate in its entirety" (Fink, "Vergegenwärtigung," viii).

158. Husserl, *Phantasy, Image Consciousness, and Memory*, 63.

159. Fink, "Vergegenwärtigung," 75.

160. Roman Ingarden, *Ontology of the Work of Art: The Musical Work, the Picture, the Architectural Work, the Film*, trans. Raymond Meyer (Athens: Ohio University Press, 1989), 139–50.

161. "They imprisoned him with his companions Rusticus and Eleutherus. He there [*sic*] said mass; St. Rusticus performing the part of deacon, and Eleutherus that of sub-deacon. Finally, they were all three carried to Montmartre, where their heads were cut off, after which they no longer said mass." Voltaire, s.v. "Dionysius, St. (The Areopagite), and the Famous Eclipse," in *A Philosophical Dictionary*, trans. Abner Kneeland, vol. 1 (Boston: Mendum, 1865), 266.

162. Sartre, *The Imaginary*, 11, Sartre's emphasis.

163. Fink, "Vergegenwärtigung," 75.

164. Fink, "Vergegenwärtigung," 76, 74.

165. Fink, "Vergegenwärtigung," 73.

166. On the relationship between mediality and meontics, see Hans Rainer Sepp, "Medialität und Meontik: Eugen Finks spekulativer Entwurf," *Internationale Zeitschrift für Philosophie*, no. 1 (1998): 85–93.

167. See in particular Fink's essay "Das Erscheinen als das absolute Medium [Appearing as the absolute medium]," in *Sein, Wahrheit, Welt: Vor-Fragen zum Problem des Phänomen-Begriffs* (The Hague: Nijhoff, 1958), 118–30.

168. Eugen-Fink-Archiv Z-I 89a. Cf. Ronald Bruzina's notes on the sixth of the *Cartesian Meditation*: "Translator's Introduction," in Fink, *Sixth Cartesian Meditation*, lxxxix.

169. As Paolo Volonté points out (*Husserls Phänomenologie der Imagination*, 118n29).

170. Fink, "Vergegenwärtigung," 72.

171. Martin Heidegger, *Phenomenological Interpretations of Aristotle: Initiation Into Phenomenological Research*, trans. Richard Rojcewicz (Bloomington: Indiana University Press, 2010), 87–97. Heidegger nonetheless barely discusses the genuinely *phainomeno*-logical potential of the concept of relucence and conceives of it in its tension with *praestruction*.

172. Eugen Fink, *Play as Symbol of the World and Other Writings*, trans. Ian Alexander Moore and Christopher Turner (Bloomington: Indiana University Press, 2016), 123.

173. "The image is essentially a product, the play essentially the act of producing" (Fink, *Play as Symbol of the World*, 114).

174. See Hans Rainer Sepp, "Totalhorizont—Zeitspielraum: Übergänge in Husserls und Finks Bestimmung von Welt," in *Eugen Fink: Sozialphilosophie—Anthropologie—Kosmologie— Pädagogik—Methodik*, ed. Anselm Böhmer (Würzburg, Ger.: Königshausen & Neumann, 2006), 154–72.

175. Fink uses the expression "refraction angle [*Brechungswinkel*]" in *Das Erscheinen als absolutes Medium* when he criticizes the conception of cognition a "crystal-clear medium," while, according to him, all cognition is already colored by a certain refraction angle (Fink, *Sein, Wahrheit, Welt*, 97–98). This is not far from Ernst Cassirer, whose theory of culture assumes that, as a matter of principle, symbolic forms are "refracting media" that each have a specific "index of refraction." Cassirer, *The Philosophy of Symbolic Forms*, vol. 3, trans. Ralph Manheim (New Haven, Conn.: Yale University Press, 1953–57), 1.

176. Eugen Fink, "Operative Concepts in Husserl's Phenomenology," in *Apriori and World: European Contributions to Husserlian Phenomenology*, ed. W. McKenna, R. M. Harlan, and L. E. Winters, trans. W. McKenna (The Hague: Nijhoff, 1981), 69.

177. Fink, "Operative Concepts in Husserl's Phenomenology," 59, Fink's emphases [modified].

178. Fink, "Operative Concepts in Husserl's Phenomenology," 67.

179. Jacques Derrida, "Punctuations: The Time of a Thesis," in *Eyes of the University: Right to Philosophy 2*, trans. Kathleen McLaughlin, 113–28 (Stanford, Calif.: Stanford University Press, 2004), 117.

180. Derrida, *Origin of Geometry*, 69–71n66.

181. Jacques Derrida, "'Genesis and Structure' and Phenomenology," in *Writing and Difference, trans. Alan Bass* (London: Routledge, 1978), 207.

182. Jacques Derrida, *The Problem of Genesis in Husserls Philosophy*, trans. Marian Hobson (Chicago: University of Chicago Press, 2003), 182n3.

183. On the paradoxical nature of the genesis Derrida, following Fink, stresses, see Leonard Lawlor, *Derrida and Husserl: The Basic Problem of Phenomenology* (Bloomington: Indiana University Press, 2002), 11–23.

184. The text was published by Fink under the title *Die Frage nach dem Ursprung der Geometrie als intentionalhistorisches Problem* in the *Revue internationale de philosophie* in 1939. In 1954 Walter Biemel included it in the edition of the *Krisis* as appendix 3 (Husserl, *Crisis*, 353–78, as "The

Origin of Geometry"). Derrida's translation came out in 1962, with an introduction that had grown into an autonomous text.

185. Derrida, "Punctuations," 117; Trần Đức Thảo, *Phenomenology and Dialectical Materialism*, ed. Robert S. Cohen, trans. Daniel J. Herman and Donald V. Morano (Dordrecht: Reidel, 1986), 125, Thảo's emphases.

186. Husserl, *Crisis*, 357–58.

187. Husserl, *Crisis*, 26.

188. Husserl, *Crisis*, 358.

189. Husserl, *Crisis*, 360–61.

190. Husserl, *Crisis*, 375.

191. Derrida, *Origin of Geometry*, 87–88, Derrida's emphasis.

192. Derrida, *Origin of Geometry*, 137–38, Derrida's emphases.

193. Husserl, *Crisis*, 371.

194. As Leonard Lawlor has pointed out; see "The Legacy of Husserl's 'Ursprung der Geometrie': The Limits of Phenomenology in Merleau-Ponty and Derrida," in *Merleau-Ponty's Reading of Husserl*, ed. Ted Toadvine and Lester E. Embree (Dordrecht: Kluwer Academic, 2002), 205.

195. "Husserl, and we may put it in such summary terms, does not like media," as a volume on Husserl written from a history of science perspective has it (Tyradellis, *Untiefen*, 13); Derrida, *Origin of Geometry*, 90, Derrida's emphasis.

196. As Derrida put it in a roundtable discussion in Vienna; see "Fragen an die Phänomenologie— Abschied vom Prinzipiellen? [Transkription einer Podiumsdiskussion in Wien 1985]," in *Die Krise der Phänomenologie und die Pragmatik des Wissenschaftsfortschritts*, ed. Michael Benedikt and Rudolf Burger (Vienna: Verlag der österreichischen Staatsdruckerei, 1986), 169–79; see also Detlef Thiel, "Husserls Phänomenographie," *Recherches husserliennes*, no. 19 (2003): 67–108.

197. Without drawing all the consequences from his insight, Fink notes lucidly as early as 1939 that in Husserl, the tendency toward "originarity" and the wish to reestablish immediacy is "essentially a movement away from the *mediateness* of beings." Eugen Fink, "The Problem of the Phenomenology of Edmund Husserl," in *Apriori and World: European Contributions to Husserlian Phenomenology*, ed. William McKenna, Robert M. Harlan, and Laurence E. Winters (The Hague: Nijhoff, 1981), 31 [modified].

198. Derrida, *Origin of Geometry*, 89–90; and Maurice Merleau-Ponty, *Husserl at the Limits of Phenomenology, Including Texts by Edmund Husserl*, ed. Leonard Lawlor and Bettina Bergo (Evanston, Ill.: Northwestern University Press, 2002), 64.

199. Maurice Merleau-Ponty, *Merleau-Ponty à la Sorbonne: Résumés de cours 1949–1952* (Grenoble, Fr.: Cynara, 1988), 402.

200. Merleau-Ponty, *Husserl at the Limits*, 28.

201. Merleau-Ponty, *Husserl at the Limits*, 58, 57.

202. Maurice Merleau-Ponty, *The Prose of the World*, ed. Claude Lefort, trans. John O'Neill (Evanston, Ill.: Northwestern University Press, 1973), 68, Merleau-Ponty's emphasis.

203. Merleau-Ponty, *Prose of the World*, 81, 81n.

204. Maurice Merleau-Ponty, *The Visible and the Invisible, followed by Working Notes*, ed. Claude Lefort, trans. Alphonso Lingis (Evanston, Ill.: Northwestern University Press, 1968), 208–9.

205. Maurice Merleau-Ponty, *Phenomenology of Perception*, trans. Donald A. Landes (London: Routledge, 2012), 70, Merleau-Ponty's emphasis.

206. Here, of course, it is no longer possible to find a common denominator for Derrida and Merleau-Ponty.

207. Merleau-Ponty, *Prose of the World*, 125–29.

208. Aristotle, *Posterior Analytics*, 76b40–77a2.

4. A PHENOMENOLOGY OF IMAGES

340

209. Maurice Merleau-Ponty, *Institution and Passivity: Course Notes from the Collège de France (1954–1955)*, ed. Claude Lefort, Stéphanie Ménasé, and Dominique Darmaillacq, trans. Leonard Lawlor and Heath Massey (Evanston, Ill.: Northwestern University Press, 2010), 56 [amended: Merleau-Ponty's emphasis]. See also Merleau-Ponty, *Prose of the World*, 119. The example is taken from Max Wertheimer, *Productive Thinking* (New York: Harper, 1945), 104–6.

210. Derrida's claim that the phenomenology of Sartre and Merleau-Ponty is hostile to science thus turns out to be indefensible at least in the latter's case. On Merleau-Ponty's relationship with mathematics, see Pierre Cassou-Noguès, "Le problème des mathématiques dans la philosophie de Merleau-Ponty," in Maurice Merleau-Ponty, *Notes de cours sur 'L'origine de la géométrie' de Husserl, suivi de Recherches sur la phénoménologie de Merleau-Ponty*, ed. Renaud Barbaras (Paris: Presses universitaires de France, 1998), 369–404. The reference to Gauss completes a circle: in the early Husserl, the mathematician is the guarantor of geometry's need to become intuitive and sensory, just as Gauss claimed that he had "sensified complex numbers." Edmund Husserl, *Studien zur Arithmetik und Geometrie: Texte aus dem Nachlass (1886–1901)*, ed. Ingeborg Strohmeyer, Husserliana 21 (The Hague: Nijhoff, 1983), 312–47.

211. Merleau-Ponty, *Phenomenology of Perception*, 199.

212. Merleau-Ponty, *Phenomenology of Perception*, 414. By stressing the "coefficient of facticity [*coefficient d'adversité*]," Merleau-Ponty evidently takes into account Gaston Bachelard's reproach that phenomenology failed adequately to consider the resistance or adversity of things. For more detail, see Emmanuel Alloa, *Resistance of the Sensible World: An Introduction to Merleau-Ponty*, trans. Jane Marie Todd (New York: Fordham University Press, 2017), 4–9.

213. Merleau-Ponty, *Phenomenology of Perception*, 192.

214. Merleau-Ponty, *Phenomenology of Perception*, 183.

215. On this paradox of expression, see also Bernhard Waldenfels, "Das Paradox des Ausdrucks," in *Deutsch-französische Gedankengänge* (Frankfurt: Suhrkamp, 1995), 105–23.

216. Merleau-Ponty, *The Visible and the Invisible*, 155.

217. Merleau-Ponty, *Phenomenology of Perception*, 464.

218. Merleau-Ponty, *Phenomenology of Perception*, lxxxii.

219. Maurice Merleau-Ponty, "Eye and Mind," in *The Merleau-Ponty Aesthetics Reader: Philosophy and Painting*, trans. Michael B. Smith, 121–50 (Evanston, Ill.: Northwestern University Press, 1993), 123.

220. Merleau-Ponty, *The Visible and the Invisible*, 132–33, Merleau-Ponty's emphasis.

221. Merleau-Ponty, *The Visible and the Invisible*, 139.

222. Hans Jonas, "The Nobility of Sight," *Philosophy and Phenomenological Research* 14, no. 4 (June 1954): 514–17; Merleau-Ponty, *The Visible and the Invisible*, 217, Merleau-Ponty's emphasis.

223. Merleau-Ponty, *The Visible and the Invisible*, 144.

224. Merleau-Ponty, *The Visible and the Invisible*, 247.

225. Merleau-Ponty, *The Visible and the Invisible*, 246–48; and "Eye and Mind," 147.

226. Merleau-Ponty, *The Visible and the Invisible*, respectively, 146 and 255.

227. Aristotle, *On the Soul* 2.5, 417a3–4.

228. Merleau-Ponty, *The Visible and the Invisible*, 124.

229. Merleau-Ponty, *Phenomenology of Perception*, 7; *The Visible and the Invisible*, 115.

230. See the section on the "becoming of a painting" in Maurice Merleau-Ponty, *Nature: Course Notes from the Collège de France*, ed. Dominique Séglard, trans. Robert Vallier (Evanston, Ill.: Northwestern University Press, 2003), 154.

231. Merleau-Ponty, *Phenomenology of Perception*, lxxxv. The expression "learning to see anew" originally comes from Albert Camus. For a more detailed discussion of this topos as a path toward a philosophy beyond the alternative of *praxis* and *theoria*, see Eran Dorfman, *Réapprendre à voir le monde: Merleau-Ponty face au miroir lacanien* (Dordrecht: Springer, 2007).

232.   The quotes are from Merleau-Ponty, "Eye and Mind," 126, 129, 127, 141.

233.   Merleau-Ponty, "Eye and Mind," 126, and "Qu'est-ce qu'un *Bild*?": "Il est manifeste ici que le *Bild* ne se regarde pas comme on regarde un objet. On regarde selon le *Bild*." Undated note for *The Visible and the Invisible*, Fonds Merleau-Ponty, Bibliothèque nationale de France, Paris, vol. 8, f. 346.

5. MEDIA PHENOMENOLOGY

1.   George Spencer Brown, *Laws of Form/Gesetze der Form*, trans. Thomas Wolf (Lübeck, Ger.: Bohmeier, 1997), 192. [This passage appears only in appendix 6 of this bilingual English and German edition, not in the English edition of 1969.—Trans.]

2.   As Aron Gurwitsch's description of the field of perception has it; see *The Field of Consciousness*, in *The Field of Consciousness: Phenomenology of Theme, Thematic Field, and Marginal Consciousness*, ed. Richard M. Zaner and Lester Embree, *The Collected Works of Aron Gurwitsch (1901–1973)*, vol. 3 (Dordrecht: Springer, 2010), 312.

3.   Compare the section "Laterality" in Jean-François Lyotard, *Discourse, Figure*, trans. Antony Hudek and Mary Lydon (Minneapolis: University of Minnesota Press, 2011), 152–56.

4.   Lyotard, *Discourse, Figure*, 154.

5.   Lyotard, *Discourse, Figure*, 427n43; see also André Barre and Albert Flogon, *Curvilinear Perspective: From Visual Space to the Constructed Image*, trans. Robert Hansen (Berkeley: University of California Press, 1987), 82.

6.   For a more detailed discussion of linguistic laterality, see Emmanuel Alloa, *Resistance of the Sensible World: An Introduction to Merleau-Ponty*, trans. Jane Marie Todd (New York: Fordham University Press, 2017), 54–57.

7.   See Anton Ehrenzweig, *The Psycho-Analysis of Artistic Vision and Hearing: An Introduction to a Theory of Unconscious Perception* (London: Routledge & Kegan Paul, 1953).

8.   Paul Klee, *Creative Confession and Other Writings*, ed. Matthew Gale (London: Tate, 2013), 7. On making visible in Merleau-Ponty, see Mauro Carbone, "Sichtbar machen: Merleau-Ponty und Paul Klee," in *Phänomenalität des Kunstwerks*, ed. Hans Rainer Sepp and Jürgen Trinks (Vienna: Turia + Kant, 2006), 55–70.

9.   Barnett Newman, "Preface to *18 Cantos*," 1964, in *Barnett Newman: Selected Writings and Interviews*, ed. John P. O'Neill (Berkeley: University of California Press, 1992), 183.

10. Yve-Alain Bois, "Newman's Laterality," in *Reconsidering Barnett Newman*, ed. Melissa Ho (New Haven, Conn.: Yale University Press, 2005), 34.

11. Newman, "Statement," April 1951, *Selected Writings*, 178.

12. Gottfried Boehm, "Die Epiphanie der Leere: Barnett Newmans *Vir heroicus sublimis*," in *Bilderverbot: Die Sichtbarkeit des Unsichtbaren*, ed. Eckhard Nordhofen (Paderborn, Ger.: Schöningh, 2001), 52.

13. Maurice Merleau-Ponty, *The Visible and the Invisible, Followed by Working Notes*, ed. Claude Lefort, trans. Alphonso Lingis (Evanston, Ill.: Northwestern University Press, 1968), 217.

14. Paul Ricœur, *A l'école de la phénoménologie* (Paris: Vrin, 1986), 9.

15. Emmanuel Levinas, *The Theory of Intuition in Husserl's Phenomenology*, trans. André Orianne, 2nd ed. (Evanston, Ill.: Northwestern University Press, 1995), 94–95.

16. Husserl explicitly calls the identification of objectifying act and its representation an "equivocation." Edmund Husserl, *Logical Investigations*, trans. John F. Finlay, ed. Dermot Moran (London: Routledge, 2008), 5.44:171 [modified]). The fact that Levinas was not able to take into account the many manuscripts in which Husserl's research on, for example, the passive synthesis is recorded may well explain the one-sidedness of some of his criticism. In later texts, Levinas

himself takes back his harsh judgment of Husserl's thinking at least in part; see the various reflections in *En decouvrant l'existence avec Husserl et Heidegger*, 3rd corr. ed. (Paris: Vrin, 2001).

17. For an overview of the various arguments and stages of this critique of intentionality, see Michael Staudigl, *Die Grenzen der Intentionalität: Zur Kritik der Phänomenalität nach Husserl* (Würzburg, Ger.: Königshausen & Neumann, 2003).

18. Staudigl, *Grenzen der Intentionalität*, 62, citing Fink, Eugen-Fink-Archiv Z-VII XVII/15a.

19. Edmund Husserl, *Cartesian Meditations: An Introduction to Phenomenology*, trans. Dorion Cairns (The Hague: Nijhoff, 1960), 2.20:46.

20. See Husserl's essay "Intentionnalité et métaphysique" (*En découvrant l'existence*, 189–200).

21. Emmanuel Levinas, "Signification and Sense," in *Humanism of the Other*, trans. Nidra Poller, 9–44 (Urbana: University of Illinois Press, 2003), 40, Levinas's emphasis.

22. Edmund Husserl, *Ideas Pertaining to a Pure Phenomenology and to a Phenomenological Philosophy, First Book*, trans. Fred Kersten (The Hague: Nijhoff, 1983), §57:133. In a different context, Husserl also uses the nice formula of a "transcendence through appearance [*Transzendenz durch Erscheinung*]." Husserl, *Ideen zu einer reinen Phänomenologie und phänomenologischen Philosophie. Erstes Buch: Allgemeine Einführung in die reine Phänomenologie, 2. Halbband: Ergänzende Texte (1912–1929)*, ed. Karl Schuhmann, *Husserliana* 3/2 (The Hague: Nijhoff, 1988), 563.

23. Merleau-Ponty, *The Visible and the Invisible*, 231.

24. Emmanuel Levinas, "Notes on Meaning," in *Of God Who Comes to Mind*, trans. Bettina Bergo (Stanford, Calif.: Stanford University Press, 1998), 159.

25. See Dominique Janicaud et al., *Phenomenology and the "Theological Turn": The French Debate*, trans. Bernard G. Prusak et al. (New York: Fordham University Press, 2000), as well as the continuation in Janicaud, *Phenomenology "Wide Open": After the French Debate*, trans. Charles N. Cabral (New York: Fordham University Press, 2010).

26. Merleau-Ponty, *The Visible and the Invisible*, 246; Friedrich Nietzsche, *Thus Spoke Zarathustra: A Book for All and None*, ed. Adrian del Caro and Robert Pippin, trans. Adrian del Caro (Cambridge: Cambridge University Press, 2006), part 2, "The Stillest Hour," 117.

27. See Raphaël Gély, *Les usages de la perception: Réflexions merleau-pontiennes (*Leuven, Belg.: Peeters, 2005), 90–98.

28. See Wolfram Hogrebe, *Metaphysik und Mantik: Die Deutungsnatur des Menschen* (Frankfurt: Suhrkamp, 1992); *Echo des Nichtwissens* (Berlin: Akademie Verlag, 2006); and "Orientierungstechniken: Mantik," in *Spur: Spurenlesen als Orientierungstechnik und Wissenskunst*, ed. Sybille Krämer, Werner Kogge, and Gernot Grube (Frankfurt: Suhrkamp, 2007), 281–92.

29. Hogrebe, *Echo des Nichtwissens*, 92.

30. Martin Seel, "Kleine Phänomenologie des Lassens," in *Sich bestimmen lassen: Studien zur theoretischen und praktischen Philosophie* (Frankfurt: Suhrkamp, 2002), 275.

31. Paul Kent Andersen, *Empirical Studies in Diathesis* (Münster, Ger.: Nodus, 1994), 154–62.

32. Pānini, the fourth-century-BCE father of Sanskrit grammar, distinguishes only between verbs that refer to something other (*parasmaipada*) and verbs that refer to themselves (*ātmanepada*). In the first case, the subject performs an action that does not concern it immediately; in the second, the subject itself is at stake. The classic textbook example is the sacrifice ritual: the verb form *yajati* indicates the act of someone—the priest, for example—performing the sacrifice for others, while *yajate* indicates that someone performs a sacrifice for himself. Émile Benveniste, who in a famous essay refers to just this example, considers it to confirm the thesis that the fundamental distinction in the Indo-Germanic languages is not the difference between active and passive but between active and self-reflective/medial; he also speaks of "internal" and "external" diathesis. Benveniste, "Active and Middle Voice in the Verb," in *Problems in General Linguistics*, trans. Mary Elizabeth Meek (Coral Gables, Fla.: University of Miami Press, 1971), 150. Benveniste's thesis, itself building on earlier remarks by linguists such as Antoine Meillet ("Sur les caractères du verbe," in

Linguistique historique et linguistique générale [Geneva: Slatkine, 1982], 175–98), prompted a still-ongoing debate in comparative linguistics. To this day, the status of the medial seems to fluctuate between semantic, morphological, and functional definitions, as Suzanne Kemmer notes in summarizing the situation: "At present, there is no generally accepted definition of the middle voice." Kemmer, *The Middle Voice* (Amsterdam: Benjamins, 1993), 1.

33. As the classicist Hermann Koller explains in "Die Anfänge der griechischen Grammatik," *Glotta* 37, no. 1/2 (1958): 5–40. For one possible reinterpretation of Koller's discoveries within the frame of a performative theory of language, see Sybille Krämer, "Sprache—Stimme—Schrift: Sieben Gedanken über Performativität als Medialität," in *Performanz: Zwischen Sprachphilosophie und Kulturwissenschaften*, ed. Uwe Wirth (Frankfurt: Suhrkamp, 2003), 338–39.

34. See Meillet, "Sur les caractères du verbe," 197.

35. Thus, for example, the otherwise well-informed study by Niels Bokhove on the history of the word *phenomeno-logy* from antiquity to the twentieth century, *Phänomenologie: Ursprung und Entwicklung des Terminus im 18. Jahrhundert* (Aalen, Ger.: Scientia, 1991).

36. Aristotle, *Posterior Analytics* 2.1.

37. "The being which pertains to the question 'Is it?' is an accident." Thomas Aquinas, *Quodlibetal Questions 1 and 2*, trans. Sandra Edwards (Toronto: Pontifical Institute of Mediaeval Studies, 1983), 2, q2 a1:79.

38. "Dico quod accidens dicitur large omne quod non est pars essentiae; et sic est esse [= existere—EA] in rebus creatis." Thomas Aquinas, *Quaestiones de quolibet*, vol. 25 of *Sancti Thomae de Aquino opera omnia*, ed. Commissio Leonina (Paris: Vrin, 1906–1992), 12, q5 a1. John Duns Scotus reduces the difference between *essentia* and *existentia*, which Aquinas merely states but does not discuss in detail, to a *modal* difference. In the fifteenth century Francisco Suárez in turn reduces this modal difference to a merely *conceptual* difference and thus anticipates Kant's assertion that existence "does not add anything" to essence. While for Jean-François Courtine this means that the Western reduction of metaphysics to an onto(theo)logy is to be understood essentially in terms of Suárez's *distinctio rationalis*, Olivier Boulnois defends the originality of Scotus's *distinctio modalis*, of which, he claims, Suárez merely offers a later variation. See Jean-François Courtine, *Suarez et le système de la métaphysique* (Paris: Presses universitaires de France, 2014); and Olivier Boulnois, *Être et représentation: Une généalogie de la métaphysique moderne à l'époque de Duns Scot (XIIIe–XIVe siècles)* (Paris: Presses universitaires de France, 1999).

39. Husserl, *Ideas* 1, §§8:18, 4:11–12.

40. Husserl, *Ideas* 1, §§3:8, 2:7. This, of course, is where Husserl's and Heidegger's concepts take opposite directions: while for Husserl, facticity is contingent, factical Being-such in Heidegger cannot be circumvented.

41. Bernhard Waldenfels, *Einführung in die Phänomenologie* (Munich: Fink, 1992), 31.

42. Hedwig Conrad-Martius, "Vorwort," in Adolf Reinach, *Was ist Phänomenologie?* (Munich: Kösel, 1951), 6, 11.

43. Husserl, *Ideas* 1, §3:9.

44. Edmund Husserl, *Phänomenologische Psychologie*, ed. Walter Biemel, *Husserliana* 9 (The Hague: Nijhoff, 1962), 292. The quote is taken from the fourth and final version of the article "Phenomenology," which Husserl wrote for the *Encyclopædia Britannica*. The passage did not make it into published version, "Phenomenology," *Encyclopædia Britannica*, 14th ed., vol. 17 (New York: Encyclopædia Britannica, 1929), 699–702.

45. Merleau-Ponty, *The Visible and the Invisible*, 109.

46. Gérard Granel, *Le Sens du temps et de la perception chez E. Husserl* (Paris: Gallimard, 1968), 144–48.

47. Hegel conceptualizes the mediality of the object as the mediation between the mode of appearing-for-another and being-in-itself. He calls this mediation the "true Also." See the chapter on

perception and the thing in the *Phenomenology of Spirit*, ed. John Niemeyer Findlay, trans. Arnold V. Miller (Oxford: Clarendon, 1977), ¶¶111–31:67–79.

48. Husserl, *Ding und Raum: Vorlesungen 1907*, ed. Ulrich Claesges, *Husserliana* 16 (The Hague: Nijhoff, 1973), 51. See Husserl's unambiguous statements on this point in *Ideas* 1, §44:94–98.

49. Husserl, *Ideas* 1, §85:203.

50. On time, see Immanuel Kant, *Critique of Pure Reason*, ed. and trans. Paul Guyer and Allen W. Wood (Cambridge: Cambridge University Press, 1998), A183/B226:300–1, A176/B219:296, and A200/B245:310–11; on space, A431n:473n.

51. Husserl's notion of a "material a priori" amounts to obtaining a priori structures strictly from within the limits of experience. For Kant, whose a priori is independent of all specific "material," a material a priori must be a *contradictio in adiecto*. Iso Kern treats this difference in his great study, in section 9 in particular; see *Husserl und Kant: Eine Untersuchung über Husserls Verhältnis zu Kant und zum Neukantianismus* (The Hague: Nijhoff, 1964), 55–68.

52. For Heidegger's revaluation of the transcendental aesthetics in his reading of Kant, often highlighted in the literature, see Martin Heidegger, *Kant and the Problem of Metaphysics*, trans. Richard Taft, 5th enl. ed. (Bloomington: Indiana University Press, 1997), §§9–10:31–36.

53. Martin Heidegger, *Introduction to Phenomenological Research*, trans. Daniel O. Dahlstrom (Bloomington: Indiana University Press, 2005), §1:4.

54. Martin Heidegger, *Being and Time, Being and Time*, trans. John Macquarrie and Edward Robinson (New York: Harper, 1962), ¶7.A:51; and *Introduction to Phenomenological Research*, supplement 2:223.

55. On the middle voice in Heidegger, see John Llewelyn, "Heidegger's Kant and the Middle Voice," in *Time and Metaphysics: A Collection of Original Papers*, ed. David Wood and Robert Bernasconi (Coventry, UK: Parousia, 1982), 87–120; and, through a Gadamerian lens, Philippe Eberhard, *The Middle Voice in Gadamer's Hermeneutics: A Basic Interpretation with Some Theological Implications* (Tübingen, Ger.: Mohr Siebeck, 2004), esp. 20–30.

56. See especially *Being and Time*, ¶¶7.A:54, 7.C:59.

57. Emmanuel Levinas, *Totality and Infinity: An Essay on Exteriority*, trans. Alphonso Lingis (The Hague: Nijhoff, 1969), 130–31.

58. Renaud Barbaras, *Introduction à une phénoménologie de la vie* (Paris: Vrin, 2008), 66–73.

59. See Emmanuel Alloa, "La chair comme diacritique incarné," *Chiasmi International: Trilingual Studies Concerning the Thought of Merleau-Ponty* 11 (2009): 249–61. In "What Is Diacritical Hermeneutics?," *Journal of Applied Hermeneutics* 1 (2011): 1–14, Richard Kearney develops the idea of diacritical flesh in the direction of a general embodied hermeneutics of diacriticality.

60. Christian Bermes has uncovered in Merleau-Ponty a thinking of mediality between the anthropological and the ontological principle; see Christian Bermes, "Medialität—anthropologisches Radikal oder ontologisches Prinzip? Merleau-Pontys Ausführung der Phänomenologie," in *Die Stellung des Menschen in der Kultur: Festschrift für Ernst Wolfgang Orth zum 65. Geburtstag*, ed. Karl-Heinz Lembeck, Julia Jonas, and Christian Bermes (Würzburg, Ger.: Königshausen & Neumann, 2002), 41–58. For an attempt at a transversal reading of Merleau-Ponty's oeuvre based on mediality, see Alloa, *Resistance of the Sensible World*, esp. the final chapter.

61. Maurice Merleau-Ponty, *Phenomenology of Perception*, trans. Donald A. Landes (London: Routledge, 2012), 260–61.

62. Merleau-Ponty, *Phenomenology of Perception*, 253–54. On this topology of the living body, see Stephan Günzel, *Maurice Merleau-Ponty—Werk und Wirkung: Eine Einführung* (Vienna: Turia + Kant, 2007), 67–80.

63. Hans Blumenberg, *Zu den Sachen und zurück*, ed. Manfred Sommer (Frankfurt: Suhrkamp, 2002), 55.

64. Merleau-Ponty, *The Visible and the Invisible*, 147.

65. Barbaras, *Introduction à une phénoménologie de la vie*, 76.

66. Merleau-Ponty, *The Visible and the Invisible*, 139–40.

67. Recall that *parmi* derives from the Latin *per medio*; see Leo Spitzer's now classic essay in semantic history, "Milieu and Ambiance: An Essay in Historical Semantics," *Philosophy and Phenomenological Research* 3, no. 1 and 2 (September and December 1942): 1–42 and 169–218, respectively.

68. "Je ne suis pas un grand aristotélicien" is his answer to R. P. Dubarle's invitation, following Merleau-Ponty's lecture "L'homme et l'adversité" (1951), to discuss Aristotle's theory of the soul. Maurice Merleau-Ponty, *Parcours deux, 1951–1961*, ed. Jacques Prunair (Lagrasse, Fr.: Verdier, 2000), 328.

69. Merleau-Ponty, "Eye and Mind," 142.

70. Merleau-Ponty, *The Visible and the Invisible*, 254–55.

71. Merleau-Ponty, *The Visible and the Invisible*, 112.

72. Merleau-Ponty, *The Visible and the Invisible*, 114.

73. Merleau-Ponty, *The Visible and the Invisible*, 127.

74. Merleau-Ponty, *The Visible and the Invisible*, 214.

75. For more on this thesis, see Emmanuel Alloa, "L'apparaître appareillé," in *Appareil et intermédialité*, ed. Jean-Louis Déotte, Marion Froger, and Silvestra Mariniello (Paris: L'Harmattan, 2007), 17–29.

76. The following reflections are partly identical to those I develop in "Transparenz und Störung: Vom zweifelhaften Nutzen eines kommunikationswissenschaftlichen Paradigmas für die Bildtheorie," in *Hide and Seek: Das Spiel von Transparenz und Opazität*, ed. Markus Rautzenberg and Andreas Wolfsteiner (Munich: Fink, 2010), 21–31.

77. Fritz Heider, *Ding und Medium*, ed. Dirk Baecker (Berlin: Kadmos, 2005). [A partial translation of this text into English does not include the passages cited. See "Thing and Medium," in *On Perception, Event Structure, and Psychological Environment: Selected Papers* (New York: International University Press, 1959), 1–34.—Trans.]

78. Heider, *Ding und Medium*, 32. On heteronomy, developed from a reflection on the figure of the messenger, see Sybille Krämer, "Über die Heteronomie der Medien: Grundlinien einer Metaphysik der Medialität im Ausgang einer Reflexion des Boten," *Journal Phänomenologie*, no. 22 (2004): 18–38, and *Medium, Messenger, Transmission: An Approach to Media Philosophy*, trans. Anthony Enns (Amsterdam: Amsterdam University Press, 2015), 212–16.

79. Heider, *Ding und Medium*, 35, 84–85, 70, and 72.

80. On Heidegger in media theory, see Markus Rautzenberg, *Die Gegenwendigkeit der Störung: Aspekte einer postmetaphysischen Präsenztheorie* (Zurich: Diaphanes, 2009). On Heider's distinction between form and medium as well as its employment by Niklas Luhmann, see Sybille Krämer, "Form als Vollzug oder: Was gewinnen wir mit Niklas Luhmanns Unterscheidung von Medium und Form?," *Rechtshistorisches Journal* 17 (1998): 558–73.

81. Claude Elwood Shannon, "A Mathematical Theory of Communication," in *Collected Papers*, ed. N. J. A. Sloane and A. D. Wyner (New York: IEEE, 1993), 5.

82. Claude Elwood Shannon, "Communication in the Presence of Noise," in *Collected Papers*, 160–72.

83. Shannon, "A Mathematical Theory," 5, Shannon's emphasis.

84. Gregory Bateson, *Steps to an Ecology of Mind: Collected Essays in Anthropology, Psychiatry, Evolution, and Epistemology* (Frogmore, UK: Paladin, 1973), 378.

85. Michel Foucault, "Message ou bruit?" in *Dits et écrits*, ed. Daniel Defert and François Ewald, vol. 1 (Paris: Gallimard, 1994), 557–60.

86. Michel Serres, *The Parasite*, trans. Lawrence R. Schehr (Baltimore, Md.: Johns Hopkins University Press, 1982), 68.

87. One typical response is the suggestion by Stefan Münker to define the subject matter of media philosophy as "the reflection on conceptual problems that arise from the processing and use of

electronic and digital media." Münker, "After the Medial Turn: Sieben Thesen zur Medienphilosophie," in *Medienphilosophie: Beiträge zur Klärung eines Begriffs*, ed. Stefan Münker, Alexander Roesler, and Mike Sandbothe (Frankfurt: Fischer, 2003), 20.

88. That is why, strictly speaking, there are no digital or analog media. Where these terms are used for ease of expression, what is at issue are, respectively, "media operations proceeding by discretizing" and "media operations proceeding by analogizing."

89. Sybille Krämer, "Die Rationalisierung der Visualität und die Visualisierung der Ratio," in *Bühnen des Wissens: Interferenzen zwischen Wissenschaft und Kunst*, ed. Helmar Schramm (Berlin: Dahlem University Press, 2003), 50–67.

90. Thus, for example, Krämer, "Form als Vollzug," 35; or Ludwig Jäger, "Störung und Transparenz: Skizze zur performativen Logik des Medialen," in *Performativität und Medialität*, ed. Sybille Krämer (Paderborn, Ger.: Fink, 2004), 35–73.

91. For a more detailed exposition of the distinction between analog and digital media, see Simone Mahrenholz, "Analogisches Denken: Aspekte nicht-diskursiver Rationalität," in *Die Medien der Künste: Beiträge zur Theorie des Darstellens*, ed. Dieter Mersch (Munich: Fink, 2003), 75–91.

92. On this distinction, see, for example, Boehm, *Wie Bilder Sinn erzeugen*, 245–48.

93. The quote is from the title of a volume edited by Friedrich Kittler, *Austreibung des Geistes aus den Geisteswissenschaften: Programme des Poststrukturalismus* (Paderborn, Ger.: Schöningh, 1980).

94. Krämer, *Medium, Messenger, Transmission*, 222n10.

95. Unpublished manuscript note for *Le visible et l'invisible*, Bibliothèque nationale de France, Fonds Merleau-Ponty, 8:346.

96. Lambert Wiesing, *Artificial Presence: Philosophical Studies in Image Theory*, trans. Nils F. Schott (Stanford, Calif.: Stanford University Press, 2010), 132.

97. Wiesing, *Artificial Presence*, 132; the last thesis in particular will be discussed in detail later.

98. Hans Jonas, "Homo Pictor and the Differentia of Man," *Social Research* 29, no. 2 (Summer 1962): 207.

99. Lambert Wiesing, *The Visibility of the Image: History and Perspectives of Formal Aesthetics*, trans. Nancy Ann Roth (London: Bloomsbury, 2016), 8–12.

100. Wiesing, *Artificial Presence*, 132, and *The Visibility of the Image*, xiv.

101. Lambert Wiesing, "Bilder—Collage—Videoclips: Das Materialkonzept von Kurt Schwitters," in *Stoffe: Zur Geschichte der Materialität in Künsten und Wissenschaften*, ed. Barbara Naumann, Thomas Strässle, and Caroline Torra-Mattenklott (Zurich: vdf, 2006), 249. Compare Hegel, *Phenomenology of Spirit*, ¶121:74: "The Thing is in this way raised to the level of a genuine Also, since it becomes a collection of 'matters' and instead of being a One, becomes merely an enclosing surface."

102. Husserl, *Logical Investigations*, §36:80.

103. On the concept of validity, and especially on the extension of Lotzsche's concept of validity beyond the limits of mathematics to include "cultural validities," see Emmanuel Alloa, "Geltung/-sanspruch/-shorizont," in *Husserl-Lexikon*, ed. Hans-Helmuth Gander (Darmstadt, Ger.: Wissenschaftliche Buchgesellschaft, 2009), 116–17.

104. Wiesing, *Artificial Presence*, 129, 146n12.

105. Wiesing, *Artificial Presence*, 132, 126, 129.

106. Wiesing, *Artificial Presence*, 131.

107. Husserl, *Crisis*, §36:140.

108. Wiesing, *Visibility of the Image*, 6.

109. Edmund Husserl, *Zur Phänomenologie der Intersubjektivität: Texte aus dem Nachlass. Zweiter Teil. 1921–28*, ed. Iso Kern, *Husserliana* 14 (The Hague: Nijhoff, 1973), 487.

110. Roman Ingarden, "Über die sogenannte 'abstrakte' Malerei," in *Erlebnis, Kunstwerk und Wert: Vorträge zur Ästhetik 1937–1967* (Tübingen: Niemeyer, 1969), 51–76.

111. Konrad Fiedler, *Über den Ursprung der künstlerischen Tätigkeit*, ed. Gottfried Boehm, in *Schriften zur Kunst*, 2nd corr. and enl. ed., vol. 1 (Munich: Fink, 1991), 140, 193–94.

112. Ludger Schwarte, "Die Wahrheitsfähigkeit des Bildes," *Zeitschrift für Ästhetik und allgemeine Kunstwissenschaft* 53, no. 1 (June 2008): 112–13.

113. Wiesing, *Phänomene im Bild* (Munich: Fink, 2000), 146.

114. Schwarte, "Wahrheitsfähigkeit des Bildes," 117.

115. Theodor W. Adorno, *Against Epistemology: A Metacritique: Studies in Husserl and the Phenomenological Antinomies*, trans. Willis Domingo (Oxford: Blackwell, 1982), 75.

116. Adorno, *Against Epistemology*, 125.

117. Nelson Goodman, "When Is Art?" in *Ways of Worldmaking* (Indianapolis: Hackett, 1978), 57–70.

118. Hans Belting, *Bild-Anthropologie: Entwürfe für eine Bildwissenschaft* (Munich: Fink, 2001), 11. [This sentence is not included in the English translation, *An Anthropology of Images: Picture, Medium, Body*, trans. Thomas Dunlap (Princeton, N.J.: Princeton University Press, 2011).—Trans.]

119. Vilém Flusser, *Kommunikologie*, ed. Stefan Bollman and Edith Flusser, *Schriften* 4 (Mannheim, Ger.: Bollmann, 1996), 111.

120. Klaus Sachs-Hombach, *Das Bild als kommunikatives Medium: Elemente einer allgemeinen Bildwissenschaft* (Cologne, Ger.: Halem, 2003), 77.

121. For the thesis, see in particular Wiesing, *Visibility of the Image* and *Artificial Presence*; for the conclusion, see Wiesing's discussion of Tim Ullrich's *Blau* series (*Phänomene im Bild*, 139–48, esp. 146): in monochrome art, genesis and validity are equated, but since images are based on their separation, monochrome works cannot be images.

122. Umberto Eco, "Sugli specchi," in *Sugli specchi e altri saggi: Il segno, la rappresentazione, l'illusione, l'immagine* (Milan: Bompiani, 1995), 9–37. Belonging to the class of signs, images must be capable of lying. Because mirrors cannot lie but always show what is currently mirrored in them, mirrors cannot be signs.

123. Bernhard Waldenfels, "Verkörperung im Bild," in *Phänomenologie der Aufmerksamkeit* (Frankfurt: Suhrkamp, 2004), 206.

124. More on this in Emmanuel Alloa, "Visual Studies: A Surrealist Moment," in *Farewell to Visual Studies*, vol. 5, ed. James Elkins, Gustav Frank, and Sunil Manghani (Chicago: University of Chicago Press, 2015), 170–73.

125. Goodman, "When Is Art?," 70.

126. Goodman, "When Is Art?," 68.

127. Nelson Goodman, *Languages of Art: An Approach to a Theory of Symbols* (Indianapolis: Bobbs-Merrill, 1968), 252–55, and "When Is Art?," 67–68.

128. See the discussion of various objections to Goodman in Nelson Goodman and Catherin Z. Elgin, *Reconceptions in Philosophy and Other Arts and Sciences* (Indianapolis: Hackett, 1988).

129. Siegfried Kracauer, *History: The Last Things Before the Last* (Princeton, N.J.: Wiener, 1995), 58–59.

130. Plato, *Cratylus*, 432c5–6.

131. Augustine, *Miscellany of Eighty-Three Questions*, in *The Works of Saint Augustine: A Translation for the 21st Century*, vol. 1/12: *Responses to Miscellaneous Questions*, ed. Raymond Canning, trans. Boniface Ramsey (New York: New City, 2008), 137.

132. Ludwig Wittgenstein, *Philosophical Investigations*, trans. G. E. M. Anscombe, P. M. S. Hacker, and Joachim Schulte, ed. P. M. S. Hacker and Joachim Schulte, 4th ed. (Chichester, UK: Wiley, 2009), §122:49.

133. As Wittgenstein explains in a lecture, "all that aesthetics does is . . . to 'place things side by side'"; see G. E. Moore, "Wittgenstein's Lectures in 1930–33," part 3, *Mind* 64, no. 253 (January 1955):

1–27, esp. 19. As for the typographical nature of his conception, Wittgenstein is said to have remarked to Henrik von Wright that he would like to have the *Philosophical Investigations* printed "like the Bible." This probably suggests a synoptic edition in which textual cross-references become clear. See also Alois Pichler, *Wittgensteins Philosophische Untersuchungen: Vom Buch zum Album* (Amsterdam: Rodopi, 2004), 183.

134.   Even if the origin of Greenberg's theory is more likely to be found in Lessing or in Kant.

135.   Clement Greenberg, "Modernist Painting," 1960, in *The Collected Essays and Criticism*, vol. 4 (Chicago: University of Chicago Press, 1986–93), 87.

136.   See Clement Greenberg, "Abstract Art," 1944, in *Collected Essays*, 1:203. The example Greenberg cites is Hans Arp, who in his view moved on to object collages because of this dissatisfaction.

137.   Gotthold Ephraim Lessing, "Laocoön," in *Laocoön, Nathan the Wise, and Minna von Barnhelm*, ed. William A. Steel (New York: Dutton, 1930), 4.

138.   Clement Greenberg, "*Towards a Newer Laocoon*," 1940, in *Collected Essays* 1:23–38.

139.   To modernism's "disembodied opticality," Rosalind Krauss famously opposes the "optical unconscious" in *The Optical Unconscious* (Cambridge, Mass.: MIT Press, 1993).

140.   Clement Greenberg, "Sculpture in Our Time," 1958, in *Collected Essays*, 4:60.

141.   Max Imdahl, "Ikonik: Bilder und ihre Anschauung," in *Was ist ein Bild?*, ed. Gottfried Boehm (Munich: Fink, 1995), 319.

142.   For these motifs, see the still highly relevant essay by Georg Simmel, "The Picture Frame: An Aesthetic Study," trans. Mark Ritter, *Theory, Culture & Society* 11, no. 1 (February 1994): 11–17.

143.   Jacques Derrida, *The Truth in Painting*, trans. Geoff Bennington and Ian McLeod (Chicago: University of Chicago Press, 1987), 9.

144.   Louis Marin, *On Representation*, trans. Catherine Porter (Stanford, Calif.: Stanford University Press, 2001), 356.

145.   Johann Wolfgang Goethe, *Farbenlehre*, ed. M. Wetzel, Abt. I, Bd. 23/1 of *Sämtliche Werke, Didaktischer Teil*, §191:85; *Goethe's Color Theory*, ed. Rupprecht Matthaei and Herb Aach (New York: Van Nostrand Reinhold, 1971), 226 [modified].

146.   Maurice Blanchot, *The Space of Literature*, trans. Anne Smock (Lincoln: University of Nebraska Press, 1982), 254.

147.   Susanne K. Langer, *Philosophy in a New Key: A Study in the Symbolism of Reason, Rite, and Art* (Cambridge, Mass.: Harvard University Press, 1979), esp. chap. 4, "Discursive Forms and Presentational Forms," 79–102.

148.   Alberti, *De Pictura* 2.25/63.

149.   Karl Bühler, *Theory of Language: The Representational Function of Language*, trans. Donald Fraser Goodwin with Achim Eschbach (Amsterdam: Benjamins, 2011), esp. part 2.

150.   Michel Foucault, *The Order of Things: An Archaeology of the Human Sciences* (New York: Vintage, 1994).

151.   Louis Marin, *La critique du discours: Sur la 'Logique de Port-Royal' et les 'Pensées' de Pascal* (Paris: Minuit, 1975), 181–90.

152.   Alberti, *De pictura* 2.42:270/78.

153.   See the work of André Chastel in *Le geste dans l'art* (Paris: Liana Levi, 2001), especially the essay "Sémantique de l'index" (1980), 49–64.

154.   On this and many other aspects of relevance here, see the analysis by Steffen Siegel, "Die Kunst der Ostentatio: Zur frühneuzeitlichen Bildgeschichte des Selbstverweises," in *Deixis: Vom Denken mit dem Zeigefinger*, ed. Heike Gfrereis and Marcel Lepper (Göttingen, Ger.: Wallstein, 2007), 38–61.

155.   Louis Marin, *Portrait of the King*, trans. Martha Houle (Minneapolis: University of Minnesota Press, 1988), 9, 13, Marin's emphases.

156. Louis Marin, *Food for Thought*, trans. Mette Hjort (Baltimore, Md.: Johns Hopkins University Press, 1997), 193.

157. Henri Focillon, *The Life of Forms in Art*, trans. Charles Beecher Hogan and George Alexander Kubler (New Haven, Conn.: Yale University Press, 1942), 1–2.

158. Martin Seel, *Ästhetik des Erscheinens* (Munich: Hanser, 2000), 258.

159. Goodman, *Languages of Art*, 53–57.

160. Goodman, *Languages of Art*, 53.

161. Goodman, "When Is Art?," 63–64. The name *Mary Tricias*, *meretricious*, puts the *meretrix* in new garb.

162. Goodman, *Languages of Art*, 53.

163. Dieter Mersch has pointed out this forgetting of appearing on Goodman's part, in *Was sich zeigt: Materialität, Präsenz, Ereignis* (Munich: Fink, 2002), 266.

164. On the teleology of determinability, see Aristotle, *Metaphysics* 4.4.1007b19–1008a7. On predicative logic as the only framework for propositions capable of truth, see Plato, *Sophist* 262e, as well as Aristotle, *De Interpretatione* 5.17a21. For a history of philosophy that takes a critique of the logic of determinability as its guide, see Gerhard Gamm, *Flucht aus der Kategorie: Die Positivierung des Unbestimmten als Ausgang der Moderne* (Frankfurt: Suhrkamp, 1994); also see Mersch, *Was sich zeigt*, 270–76.

165. On the necessary "label," see Goodman, *Languages of Art*, 57–67.

166. Augustine, *The Teacher*, in *The Greatness of the Soul / The Teacher*, trans. Joseph M. Colleran, no. 9 (Westminster, Md.: Newman, 1950), 3.6:136–38.

167. Augustine, *The Teacher*, 10.32:171–72. Recall that *deixis* has always been linked with didactics. The modern *to teach*, too, derives from the Indo-Germanic *dik (Sanskrit *diśáti*), and the *epideixis* Aristotle defines in the *Rhetoric* has no other goal than pedagogically to guide students toward the values shared in the *polis*.

168. On the "bareness of the material," see Mersch, *Was sich zeigt*, 275–76. On the possible place of bareness in philosophical aesthetics (related to the categories of beauty, sublimity, and aura), see Dieter Mersch, *Ereignis und Aura: Untersuchungen zu einer Ästhetik des Performativen* (Frankfurt: Suhrkamp, 2002), 115–56.

169. Goodman, *Languages of Art*, 136. The definition applies for all types of density, semantic density as well.

170. Goodman, "When Is Art?," 68.

171. This is attested to, for example, by the fact that iconic competence has in our day become the new Turing test and is employed to differentiate between humans and machines. This is manifest in the increasing iconocization of encryption systems, such as the so-called CAPTCHA procedure (Completely Automated Public Turing test to tell Computers and Humans Apart) that presents numbers and letters in a distorted form that computers are by definition less able to process.

172. Wittgenstein, *Philosophical Investigations*, §67:32.

173. Gorgias, *Encomium of Helen*, in Laks/Most, *Early Greek Philosophy*, vol. 8.1: *Philosophy* (Cambridge, Mass.: Harvard University Press, 2016–), 167–85, ¶18:183.

174. "Les choses que je vois me voient tout autant que je les vois," §67 of the "Analecta" in Paul Valéry, *Tel Quel*, *Œuvres*, ed. Jean Hytier, vol. 2 (Paris: Gallimard, 1957–1960), 729.

175. Jean-Luc Nancy, *The Ground of the Image*, trans. Jeff Fort (New York: Fordham University Press, 2005), 64.

176. See Gilles Deleuze and Félix Guattari, *A Thousand Plateaus: Capitalism and Schizophrenia 2*, trans. Brian Massumi (Minneapolis: University of Minnesota Press, 1987), chap. 6.

177. Georg Wilhelm Friedrich Hegel, *Aesthetics: Lectures on Fine Art*, trans. T. M. Knox (Oxford: Clarendon, 1975), 1.3.A.1:153–54.

178. Nicolas of Cusa, *Nicholas of Cusa's Dialectical Mysticism: Text, Translation and Interpretive Study of De visione dei*, trans. Jasper Hopkins (Minneapolis: Banning, 1988), 5:131.

179. Think of the statues in Jain temples, where small glass mirrors sometimes take the place of the eyes such that the viewer's gaze can be reflected there. Similar techniques are used by the Fang in central Africa and applied in the *nkisi* fetishes from the Congo basin.

180. Valéry, *Œuvres* 2:491–92, quoted in Maurice Merleau-Ponty, *Signs*, trans. Richard C. McLeary (Evanston, Ill.: Northwestern University Press, 1964), 231–32.

181. As the title of James Elkins's book has it; see Elkins, *The Object Stares Back: On the Nature of Seeing* (San Diego, Calif.: Harcourt, 1996).

182. Georges Didi-Huberman, *Ce que nous voyons, ce qui nous regarde* (Paris: Minuit, 1992).

183. Walter Benjamin, "On Some Motifs in Baudelaire," trans. Harry Zohn, in *Walter Benjamin: Selected Writings*, ed. Michael William Jennings, Howard Eiland, and Gary Smith, vol. 4 (Cambridge, Mass.: Harvard University Press, 2005), 337.

184. Bernhard Waldenfels, "Von der Wirkmacht und Wirkkraft der Bilder," in *Movens Bild: Zwischen Evidenz und Affekt*, ed. Gottfried Boehm, Birgit Mersmann, and Christian Spies (Munich: Fink, 2008), 54.

185. Bibliothèque nationale de France, Merleau-Ponty Papers, vol. 11, 4/8, preparatory notes for the Collège de France lectures on *Le monde sensible et le monde de l'expression*. Now also published in *Le monde sensible et le monde de l'expression: Cours au Collège de France, notes 1953*, ed. Stefan Kristensen and Emmanuel de Saint-Aubert (Geneva: MetisPresses 2011), 82.

186. Waldenfels, "Wirkmacht und Wirkkraft der Bilder," 60.

187. See, for example, Richard Wollheim himself, who in a late self-criticism revises his view that the vision appropriate to images consists essentially in a *seeing-in*. On this self-criticism as well as the counterproposal of introducing for the seeing of pictures a place-specific seeing-in, see his essay, "Seeing-as, Seeing-in and Pictorial Representation," which he added to the second edition of *Art and Its Objects* (Cambridge: Cambridge University Press, 1980), 205–26. Robert Hopkins has put forward some important arguments in *Picture, Image and Experience* (Cambridge: Cambridge University Press, 1998), chap. 2. See also John Hyman, *The Objective Eye: Color, Form, and Reality in the Theory of Art* (Chicago: University of Chicago Press, 2006), chap. 7.

188. John R. Searle, *Intentionality: An Essay in the Philosophy of Mind* (Cambridge: Cambridge University Press, 1983), 40. See also Eva Schürmann's criticism, *Seeing as Practice: Philosophical Investigations Into the Relation Between Sight and Insight* (Cham, Switz.: Palgrave-Macmillan, 2019), 31–32.

189. Schürmann, *Seeing as Practice*, 32.

190. This is the direction Markus Wild takes these empirical studies in his discussion of the "mind of animals"; see "Begrifflicher und nichtbegrifflicher Gehalt der Wahrnehmung," in *Poetiken der Materie*, ed. Thomas Strässle and Caroline Torra-Mattenklott (Freiburg, Ger.: Rombach, 2005), 245–62.

191. See Leonardo da Vinci, *Libro di pittura*, ed. Carlo Pedretti, transcr. Carlo Vecce (Florence: Giunti, 1995), 222.

192. Michael Polanyi, "What Is a Painting?," *American Scholar* 39, no. 4 (Autumn 1970): 659.

193. For a comprehensive discussion of Wollheim's thesis and its difficulties, see Flint Schier, *Deeper Into Pictures: An Essay on Pictorial Representation* (Cambridge: Cambridge University Press, 1986); Dominic Lopes, *Understanding Pictures* (Oxford: Clarendon Press, 2006), 43–47; and Oliver Scholz, *Bild, Darstellung, Zeichen: Philosophische Theorien bildlicher Darstellung* (Frankfurt: Klostermann 2004), 66–72.

194. Seel, *Ästhetik des Erscheinens*, 286.

195. Waldenfels, "Wirkmacht und Wirkkraft der Bilder," 54.

196. Merleau-Ponty, "Eye and Mind," 126. I have presented a more detailed elaboration of these arguments in my "Seeing-as, Seeing-in, Seeing-with: Looking Through Pictures," in *The Palgrave Handbook of Image Studies*, ed. Krešimir Purgar (Basingstoke, UK: Palgrave Macmillan, 2021 (forthcoming).

197. Hans Belting, "Blickwechsel mit Bildern: Die Bildfrage als Körperfrage," in *Bilderfragen: Die Bildwissenschaften im Aufbruch*, ed. Hans Belting (Munich: Fink, 2007), 59.

198. See Jan Assmann, "Schrift und Bild: Die 'zerdehnte Situation,'" in *Ägyptische Geheimnisse* (Munich: Fink, 2004), 102–5.

199. This of course does not mean that all images are always already *intended* for a viewer. On "images without a viewer," see Matthias Bruhns, Horst Bredekamp, and Gabriele Werner-Felmayer, eds., *Bilder ohne Betrachter*, vol. 4,2 of *Bildwelten des Wissens: Kunsthistorisches Jahrbuch für Bildkritik* (Berlin: Akademie, 2006).

200. This motto runs through like a *basso continuo* through the work of Georges Didi-Huberman, who, taking up Benjamin, sketches a critique of historicism. On this and on Didi-Huberman's method more broadly, see Emmanuel Alloa, "Phasmid Thinking. On Georges Didi-Huberman's Method," *Angelaki: Journal of the Theoretical Humanities* 23, no. 4 (2018): 103–12.

201. Walter Benjamin, *The Arcades Project*, ed. Rolf Tiedemann, trans. Howard Eiland and Kevin McLaughlin (Cambridge, Mass.: Harvard University Press, 2003), N2a, 3:462.

202. Georges Didi-Huberman, *Devant le temps: Histoire de l'art et anachronisme des images* (Paris: Minuit, 2000), 17, 32.

203. Georges Didi-Huberman, *Fra Angelico: Dissemblance and Figuration*, trans. Jane Marie Todd (Chicago: University of Chicago Press, 1995), 30, Didi-Huberman's emphasis.

204. See Lyotard, *Discourse, Figure*, 244, where the visual "is no longer anything visible" but something that "haunt[s]" legibility.

205. Jean-François Lyotard, "La peinture, anamnèse du visible," in *Misère de la philosophie* (Paris: Galilée, 2000), 110; and *Que peindre? Adami, Arakawa, Buren = What to Paint? Adami, Arakawa, Buren*, ed. Herman Parret, trans. Antony Hudek, Vlad Ionescou, and Peter W. Milne (Leuven, Belg.: Leuven University Press, 2012), 347.

206. Georges Didi-Huberman, *Confronting Images: Questioning the Ends of a Certain History of Art*, trans. John Goodman (University Park: Pennsylvania State University Press, 2005), 18.

207. On the various understandings of *shown time* and *time of showing* (which can both be summarized as "showtime") and of (medial) *exposure time*, see Emmanuel Alloa, "Showtime and Exposure Time: The Contradictions of Social Photography and the Critical Role of *Sensitive Plates* for Rethinking the Temporality of Artworks," in *Time in the History of Art: Temporality, Chronology and Anachrony*, ed. Dan Karlholm and Keith Moxey (London: Routledge, 2018), 223–39.

208. For such a more complex conception of positing, see also Dieter Mersch, "Das Ereignis der Setzung," in *Performativität und Ereignis*, ed. Erika Fischer-Lichte et al. (Tübingen, Ger.: Francke, 2003), 41–56.

209. As Sybille Krämer puts it in "Gibt es eine Performanz des Bildlichen? Reflexionen über 'Blickakte,'" in *Bild-Performanz: Die Kraft des Visuellen*, ed. Ludger Schwarte (Munich: Fink, 2011), 63–89, where she takes up an idea of Hans Belting's.

210. Theodor Adorno articulates the shift from an aesthetic of *imitatio* to an aesthetics of reperformance in the formula: "If artworks do not make themselves like something else but only like themselves, then only those who imitate them understand them." Adorno, *Aesthetic Theory*, ed. Gretel Adorno, Rolf Tiedemann, and Robert Hullot-Kentor, trans. Robert Hullot-Kentor (London: Continuum, 2002), 125.

211. Gilles Deleuze and Félix Guattari, "The Brain Is the Screen," trans. Ames Hodges and Michael Taormina, in *Two Regimes of Madness: Texts and Interviews 1975–1995*, ed. David Lapoujade (Los Angeles: Semiotext(e), 2006), 290.

212. On Gaston Bachelard's criticism of Bergson, see his *The Dialectic of Duration*, trans. Mary McAllester Jones (London: Rowman & Littlefield, 2016).
213. Aristotle, *Metaphysics* 2.2.994a27–29.
214. Aristotle, *On the Soul* 2.5.417b2–5.
215. See Dario Gamboni's counterreading of the history of art via the example of such "potential images" in *Potential Images: Ambiguity and Indeterminacy in Modern Art*, trans. Mark Treharne (London: Reaktion, 2002); he defines these images on 18–20.
216. On this point, see the thirteenth and final chapter, "La conjecture," of Rémy Brague's *Image vagabonde: Essai sur l'imaginaire baudelairien* (Chatou, Fr.: Transparence, 2008), 127–33.
217. I discuss this example in more detail in Emmanuel Alloa, "Suspension et gravité: L'imaginaire sartrien face au Tintoret," *Alter: Revue de phénoménologie*, no. 5 (2007): 123–42, esp. 139–41.
218. Jan Thurmann-Moe, *Munchs "Roßkur": Experimente mit Technik und Material* (Hamburg, Ger.: Dölling und Galitz, 1994), 28–29.
219. Maurice Merleau-Ponty, *The Prose of the World*, ed. Claude Lefort, trans. John O'Neill (Evanston, Ill.: Northwestern University Press, 1973), 152.
220. For more on glass architecture and the ideal of tracelessness in the context of Benjamin's reading of modernity, see Emmanuel Alloa, "Architectures of Transparency," *Res: Anthropology and Aesthetics* 53/54 (2008): 322–30.
221. Mikel Dufrenne, *Phenomenology of Aesthetic Experience*, vol. 1 (Evanston, Ill.: Northwestern University Press, 1973), 391; and, on the material-aesthetic a priori generally, *L'inventaire des a priori: Recherche de l'originaire* (Paris: Bourgois, 1981). For a more elaborate analysis of the ground shining through in Paul Cézanne, Frank Stella, and Simon Hantaï, see Emmanuel Alloa, "Das Medium scheint durch: Talbot—Stella—Hantaï," in *Materialität und Bildlichkeit: Visuelle Artefakte zwischen Aisthesis und Semiosis*, ed. Marcel Finke and Mark A. Halawa (Berlin: Kadmos, 2012), 68–85.
222. For recent commentary on Kentridge, see Schürmann, *Seeing as Practice*.
223. Edmund Husserl, *Späte Texte über Zeitkonstitution (1929–1934): Die C-Manuskripte*, ed. Dieter Lohmar, *Husserliana* Materialien 8 (Dordrecht: Springer, 2002), 81, 87.
224. Aby Warburg, "Sandro Botticellis 'Geburt der Venus' und 'Frühling,'" 1893, in *Werke in einem Band*, ed. Martin Treml, Sigrid Weigel, and Perdita Ladwig (Berlin: Suhrkamp, 2010), 54.
225. See chap. 3.5 as well as Hubert Damisch's magnificent *A Theory of Cloud: Toward a History of Painting*, trans. Janet Lloyd (Stanford, Calif.: Stanford University Press, 2008), which is a meditation on the provocation of the cloud as that which is simultaneously the most real and the most ephemeral that can never find a place in the categories of iconographical knowledge.
226. Wilhelm Schapp, *Beiträge zur Phänomenologie der Wahrnehmung*, reprint (Wiesbaden: Heymann, 1976), 16n.
227. Olafur Eliasson, "Museums Are Radical," in *Olafur Eliasson: The Weather Project,* ed. Susan May (London: Tate, 2003), 135.
228. Alexander of Aphrodisias, *Alexandri in librum De sensu commentarium*, ed. Paul Wendland, in *Commentaria in Aristotelem Graeca* 3.1 (Berlin: Reimer, 1901), 95.11–12:45.
229. Merleau-Ponty, *The Visible and the Invisible*, 198.

CONCLUSION

1. Hegel, *Phenomenology of Spirit*, ed. John Niemeyer Findlay, trans. Arnold V. Miller (Oxford: Clarendon, 1977), §73:47.

AFTERWORD

1. Martin Heidegger, *Der Ursprung des Kunstwerks*, in *Holzwege*, Gesamtausgabe vol. 5 (Frankfurt: Klostermann 1977), 67.

2. Martin Heidegger, *Letter on Humanism*, in *Basic Writings*, ed. David Farrell Krell (San Francisco: HarperCollins, 1993), 248.

3. Marsilio Ficino, *Commentaries on Plato: Phaedrus and Ion*, ed. Michael A. Allen (Cambridge, Mass.: Harvard University Press, 2008).

4. "Gewisses am Sehen kommt uns rätselhaft vor, weil uns das ganze Sehen nicht rätselhaft genug vorkommt." Ludwig Wittgenstein, *Philosophical Investigations / Philosophische Untersuchungen*, ed. G. E. M. Anscombe (Oxford: Blackwell, 1999), 212.

Bibliography

Abel, Günter. "Zeichen und Interpretationsphilosophie der Bilder." In *Zeichen der Wirklichkeit*, 349–69. Frankfurt: Suhrkamp, 2004.

Adorno, Theodor W. *Aesthetic Theory*. Ed. Gretel Adorno, Rolf Tiedemann, and Robert Hullot-Kentor, trans. Robert Hullot-Kentor. London: Continuum, 2002.

——. *Against Epistemology: A Metacritique: Studies in Husserl and the Phenomenological Antinomies*. Trans. Willis Domingo. Oxford: Blackwell, 1982.

——. *Negative Dialectics*. Trans. E. B. Ashton. New York: Continuum, 1993.

Agamben, Giorgio. "On Potentiality." In *Potentialities: Collected Essays in Philosophy*, trans. Daniel Heller-Roazen, 177–84. Stanford, Calif.: Stanford University Press, 1999.

Alberti, Leon Battista. *Das Standbild—Die Malkunst—Grundlagen der Malerei*. Ed. Oskar Bätschmann, trans. Christoph Schäublin. Darmstadt, Ger.: Wissenschaftliche Buchgesellschaft, 2012.

——. *On Painting*. Trans. John R. Spencer. Rev. ed. New Haven, Conn.: Yale University Press, 1966.

Albertus Magnus. *De homine*. Ed. Henryk Anzulewicz and J. R. Söder. Hamburg: Meiner, 2004.

Alexander of Aphrodisias. *Alexandri in librum De sensu commentarium*. Ed. Paul Wendland. In *Commentaria in Aristotelem Graeca* 3.1. Berlin: Reimer, 1901.

——. *De liber de anima cum mantissa*. In *Commentaria in Aristotelem Graeca, Supplementum Aristotelicum 2.1: Alexandri Aphrodisiensis praeter commentaria scripta minora*, ed. Ivo Bruns. Berlin: Reimer, 1887.

——. *Supplement to "On the Soul."* Ed. and trans. R. W. Sharples. Ithaca, N.Y.: Cornell University Press, 2004.

Alloa, Emmanuel. "Architectures of Transparency." *Res: Anthropology and Aesthetics* 53/54 (2008): 322–30.

——. "Bildbewusstsein." In *Husserl-Lexikon*, ed. Hans-Helmuth Gander, 49–50. Darmstadt, Ger.: Wissenschaftliche Buchgesellschaft, 2009.

——. "Could Perspective Ever Be a Symbolic Form? Revisiting Panofsky with Cassirer." *Journal of Aesthetics and Phenomenology* 2, no. 1 (2015): 51–71.

——. "Geltung/-sanspruch/horizont." In *Husserl-Lexikon*, ed. Hans-Helmuth Gander, 116–17. Darmstadt, Ger.: Wissenschaftliche Buchgesellschaft, 2009.

——. "Getting in Touch: Aristotelian Diagnostics." In *Carnal Hermeneutics*, ed. Richard Kearney and Brian Treanor, 195–213. New York: Fordham University Press, 2015.

——. "Iconic Turn: A Plea for Three Turns of the Screw." *Culture—Theory—Critique* 53, no. 3 (2015): 1–24.

——. "La chair comme diacritique incarné." *Chiasmi International: Trilingual Studies Concerning the Thought of Merleau-Ponty* 11 (2009): 249–61.

——. "La phénoménologie comme science de l'homme sans l'homme." *Tijdschrift voor filosofie* 72, no. 1 (2010): 79–100.

——. "L'apparaître appareillé." In *Appareil et intermédialité*, ed. Jean-Louis Déotte, Marion Froger, and Silvestra Mariniello, 17–29. Paris: L'Harmattan, 2007.

——. "The Madness of Sight." In *Seeing Perception*, ed. Silke Horstkotte and Karin Leonhard, 40–59. Newcastle: Cambridge Scholars, 2007.

——. "Metaxy: Aristotle on Mediacy." In *Classics and Media Theory*, ed. Pantelis Michelakis, 147–65. Oxford: Oxford University Press, 2020.

——. "The Most Sublime of All Laws: The Strange Resurgence of a Kantian Motif in Contemporary Image Politics." *Critical Inquiry* 41, no. 2 (Winter 2015): 367–89.

—— "Phasmid Thinking: On Georges Didi-Huberman's Method." *Angelaki: Journal of the Theoretical Humanities* 23, no. 4 (2018): 103–12.

——. *Resistance of the Sensible World: An Introduction to Merleau-Ponty*. Trans. Jane Marie Todd. New York: Fordham University Press, 2017.

——. Review of Annette Hilt, *Ousia, Psyche, Nous. Allgemeine Zeitschrift für Philosophie* 33, no. 1 (July 2008): 85–89.

——. "Seeing-as, Seeing-in, Seeing-with: Looking Through Pictures." In *The Palgrave Handbook of Image Studies*, ed. Krešimir Purgar. Basingstoke: Palgrave Macmillan 2021 (forthcoming).

—— "Showtime and Exposure Time: The Contradictions of Social Photography and the Critical Role of Sensitive Plates for Rethinking the Temporality of Artworks." In *Time in the History of Art: Temporality, Chronology and Anachrony*, ed. Dan Karlholm and Keith Moxey, 223–39. London: Routledge, 2018.

——. "Suspension et gravité: L'imaginaire sartrien face au Tintoret." *Alter: Revue de Phénoménologie* 15 (2007): 123–41.

——. "Transparenz und Störung: Vom zweifelhaften Nutzen eines kommunikationswissenschaftlichen Paradigmas für die Bildtheorie." In *Hide and Seek: Das Spiel von Transparenz und Opazität*, ed. Markus Rautzenberg and Andreas Wolfsteiner, 21–31. Munich: Fink, 2010.

——. "Visual Studies: A Surrealist Moment." In *Farewell to Visual Studies*, vol. 5, ed. James Elkins, Gustav Frank, and Sunil Manghani, 170–73. Chicago: University of Chicago Press 2015.

——. "Visual Studies in Byzantium: A 'Pictorial Turn' *avant la lettre*." *Journal of Visual Culture* 12, no. 1 (2013): 3–29.

——. "What Is Diaphenomenology? A Sketch." In *Phenomenology and Experience*, ed. Antonio Cimino and Cees Leijenhorst, 12–27. Leiden: Brill, 2019.

—— "Writing, Embodiment, Deferral: Merleau-Ponty and Derrida on *The Origin of Geometry*." *Philosophy Today* 20, no. 10 (2014): 219–29.

Alloa, Emmanuel, and Chiara Cappelletto, eds. *Dynamis of the Image: Moving Images in a Global World*. Berlin: de Gruyter, 2020.

Ambuel, David. *Image and Paradigm in Plato's Sophist*. Las Vegas: Parmenides, 2007.

Andersen, Paul Kent. *Empirical Studies in Diathesis*. Münster, Ger.: Nodus, 1994.

Aquinas, Thomas. *Commentaries on Aristotle's "On Sense and What Is Sensed" and "On Memory and Recollection."* Trans. E. M. Macierowski and Kevin White. Washington, D.C.: Catholic University of America Press, 2005.

——. *Commentary on Aristotle's* De Anima. Trans. Kenelm Foster and Silvester Humphries. Notre Dame, Ind.: Dumb Ox, 1994.

——. *The Disputed Questions on Truth*. Vol. 1. Trans. Robert William Mulligan. Chicago: Regnery, 1952.

——. *Sancti Thomae de Aquino opera omnia.* Ed. Commissio Leonina. Paris: Vrin, 1906–1992.

——. *Summa Theologiae.* Trans. English Dominican Fathers. New York: Benziger, 1947–1948.

Arendt, Hannah. *The Life of the Mind.* San Diego: Harcourt, 1981.

Aristotle. *The Complete Works of Aristotle: The Revised Oxford Translation.* Ed. Jonathan Barnes. Princeton, N.J.: Princeton University Press, 1984.

——. *Parva naturalia.* Ed. W. D. Ross. Oxford: Clarendon, 1955.

——. *Werke in deutscher Übersetzung.* Berlin: Akademie, 1956–.

Assmann, Jan. *Ägyptische Geheimnisse.* Munich: Fink, 2004.

Atherton, Margaret. "How to Write the History of Vision: Understanding the Relationship between Berkeley and Descartes." In *Sites of Vision: The Discursive Construction of Sight in the History of Philosophy*, ed. David Michael Kleinberg-Levin. Cambridge, Mass.: MIT Press, 1999.

Augustine. *De dialectica.* Ed. Jan Pinborg, trans. Belford Darrell Jackson. Dordrecht: Reidel, 1975.

——. *The Teacher*, in *The Greatness of the Soul / The Teacher.* Trans. Joseph M. Colleran. Ancient Christian Writers, no. 9, 113–86 (Westminster, Md.: Newman, 1950).

——. *The Works of Saint Augustine: A Translation for the 21st Century.* Ed. John E. Rotelle. New York: New City, 1990–2001.

Averroes. *Long Commentary on the* De anima *by Aristotle.* Trans. Richard C. Taylor. New Haven, Conn.: Yale University Press, 2009.

Bachelard, Gaston. *The Dialectic of Duration.* Trans. Mary McAllester Jones. London: Rowman & Littlefield, 2016.

Bacon, Roger. *Opus maius.* Ed. John Henry Bridges. Vol. 1. Oxford: Clarendon, 1897.

——. *Roger Bacon's Philosophy of Nature: A Critical Edition, with English Translation, Introduction, and Notes, of De multiplicatione specierum and De speculis comburentibus.* Ed. and trans. David C. Lindberg. Oxford: Clarendon, 1983.

Baptist, Gabriella. "Le finestre di Eugen Fink." *Kainós: Rivista telematica di filosofia*, no. 1 (2001). http://www.kainos.it/Pages/Artdisvela04.html.

Barbaras, Renaud. *Desire and Distance: Introduction to a Phenomenology of Perception.* Trans. Paul B. Milan. Stanford, Calif.: Stanford University Press, 2006.

——. *Introduction à une phénoménologie de la vie.* Paris: Vrin, 2008.

Barnouw, Jeffrey. *Propositional Perception: Phantasia, Predication and Sign in Plato, Aristotle and the Stoics.* Lanham, Md.: University Press of America, 2002.

Barre, André, and Albert Flogon. *Curvilinear Perspective: From Visual Space to the Constructed Image.* Trans. Robert Hansen. Berkeley: University of California Press, 1987.

Barthes, Roland. *Camera Lucida: Reflections on Photography.* Trans. Richard Howard. New York: Hill and Wang, 1981.

Bateson, Gregory. *Steps to an Ecology of Mind: Collected Essays in Anthropology, Psychiatry, Evolution, and Epistemology.* Frogmore: Paladin, 1973.

Batteux, Charles. *The Fine Arts Reduced to a Single Principle.* Trans. James O. Young. Oxford: Oxford University Press, 2015.

Baumgarten, Alexander Gottlieb. *Metaphysics: A Critical Translation with Kant's Elucidations, Selected Notes, and Related Materials.* Ed. and trans. Courtney D. Fugate and John Hymers. London: Bloomsbury, 2014.

Beare, John I. *Greek Theories of Elementary Cognition from Alcmaeon to Aristotle.* Oxford: Clarendon, 1906.

Belting, Hans. *An Anthropology of Images: Picture, Medium, Body.* Trans. Thomas Dunlap. Princeton, N.J.: Princeton University Press, 2011.

——. *Bild-Anthropologie: Entwürfe für eine Bildwissenschaft.* Munich: Fink, 2001.

——. "Blickwechsel mit Bildern: Die Bildfrage als Körperfrage." In *Bilderfragen: Die Bildwissenschaften im Aufbruch*, ed. Hans Belting, 49–75. Munich: Fink, 2007.

——. *Florence and Baghdad: Renaissance Art and Arab Science*. Trans. Deborah Lucas Schneider. Cambridge, Mass.: Belknap Press of Harvard University Press, 2011.

Benjamin, Walter. *The Arcades Project*. Ed. Rolf Tiedemann, trans. Howard Eiland and Kevin McLaughlin. Cambridge, Mass.: Harvard University Press, 2003.

——. "On Some Motifs in Baudelaire." Trans. Harry Zohn. In *Walter Benjamin: Selected Writings*, ed. Michael William Jennings, Howard Eiland, and Gary Smith, vol. 4, 313–55. Cambridge, Mass.: Harvard University Press, 2005.

Benoist, Jocelyn. "L'idée de phénoménologie." In *L'idée de phénoménologie*, 123–57. Paris: Beauchesne, 2001.

Bensch, Georg. *Vom Kunstwerk zum ästhetischen Objekt: zur Geschichte der phänomenologischen Ästhetik*. Munich: Fink, 1994.

Benveniste, Émile. "Active and Middle Voice in the Verb." In *Problems in General Linguistics*, trans. Mary Elizabeth Meek. Coral Gables, Fla.: University of Miami Press, 1971).

Benz, Hubert. *"Materie" und Wahrnehmung in der Philosophie Plotins*. Würzburg, Ger.: Königshausen & Neumann, 1990.

Berkeley, George. *The Works of George Berkeley, Bishop of Cloyne*. Ed. A. A. Luce and T. E. Jessop. London: Nelson, 1979.

Bermes, Christian. "Medialität—anthropologisches Radikal oder ontologisches Prinzip? Merleau-Pontys Ausführung der Phänomenologie." In *Die Stellung des Menschen in der Kultur: Festschrift für Ernst Wolfgang Orth zum 65. Geburtstag*, ed. Karl-Heinz Lembeck, Julia Jonas, and Christian Bermes, 41–58. Würzburg, Ger.: Königshausen & Neumann, 2002.

Berti, Enrico. *Aristotele, dalla dialettica alla filosofia prima: con saggi integrativi*. Rev. and augm. ed. Milan: Bompiani, 2004.

Bexte, Peter. *Blinde Seher: Wahrnehmung von Wahrnehmung in der Kunst des 17. Jahrhunderts*. Amsterdam: Verlag der Kunst, 1999.

Blanchot, Maurice. *The Space of Literature*. Trans. Anne Smock. Lincoln: University of Nebraska Press, 1982.

Blumenberg, Hans. *Zu den Sachen und zurück*. Ed. Manfred Sommer. Frankfurt: Suhrkamp, 2002.

Blumenthal, Henry. "Neoplatonic Elements in the *De Anima* Commentaries." In *Aristotle Transformed: The Ancient Commentators and Their Influence*, ed. Richard Sorabji, 305–24. Ithaca, N.Y.: Cornell University Press, 1990.

——. "Themistius, the Last Peripatetic Commentator on Aristotle?" in *Aristotle Transformed: The Ancient Commentators and Their Influence*, ed. Richard Sorabji, 113–23. Ithaca, N.Y.: Cornell University Press, 1990.

Boehm, Gottfried. "Die Epiphanie der Leere: Barnett Newmans *Vir heroicus sublimis*." In *Bilderverbot: Die Sichtbarkeit des Unsichtbaren*, ed. Eckhard Nordhofen, 39–57. Paderborn, Ger.: Schöningh, 2001.

——. "Indeterminacy: On the Logic of the Image." In *Dynamics and Performativity of Imagination: The Image Between the Visible and the Invisible*, ed. Bernd Hüppauf and Christoph Wulf, 219–29. New York: Routledge, 2009.

Boehm, Gottfried, and W. J. T. Mitchell. "Pictorial Versus Iconic Turn: Two Letters." *Culture-Theory-Critique* 50, no. 2–3 (2009): 103–21.

Boersma, Gerald P. *Augustine's Early Theology of Image: A Study in the Development of Pro-Nicene Theology*. Oxford: Oxford University Press, 2016.

Böhme, Hartmut. "Das Volle und das Leere: Zur Geschichte des Vakuums." In *Luft: Elemente des Naturhaushalts 4*, ed. Kunst- und Ausstellungshalle der Bundesrepublik Deutschland and Bernd Busch, 42–66. Cologne, Ger.: Wienand, 2003.

Bois, Yve-Alain. "Newman's Laterality." In *Reconsidering Barnett Newman*, ed. Melissa Ho, 29–45. New Haven, Conn.: Yale University Press, 2005.

Bokhove, Niels. *Phänomenologie: Ursprung und Entwicklung des Terminus im 18. Jahrhundert*. Aalen, Ger.: Scientia, 1991.

Borges, Jorge Luis. "The Wall and the Books." Trans. James E. Irby. In *Labyrinths: Selected Stories & Other Writings*, ed. Donald A. Yates and James E. Irby, 186–88. Augm. ed. New York: New Directions, 1964.

Boulnois, Olivier. *Être et représentation: Une généalogie de la métaphysique moderne à l'époque de Duns Scot (XIIIe–XIVe siècle)*. Paris: Presses universitaires de France, 1999.

Brague, Rémi. *Aristote et la question du monde: Essai sur le contexte cosmologique et anthropologique de l'ontologie*. Paris: Presses universitaires de France, 1988.

——. *Image vagabonde: Essai sur l'imaginaire baudelairien*. Chatou, Fr.: Transparence, 2008.

——. "Inclusion and Digestion: Two Models of Cultural Appropriation in Response to a Question of Hans-Georg Gadamer (Tübingen, September 3, 1996)." In *The Legend of the Middle Ages: Philosophical Explorations of Medieval Christianity, Judaism, and Islam*, trans. L.G. Cochrane, 145–58. Chicago: University of Chicago Press, 2009.

——. "La phénoménologie comme voie d'accès au monde grec." In *Phénomène et métaphysique*, ed. Jean-Luc Marion and Guy Planty-Bonjour, 247–73. Paris: Presses universitaires de France, 1984.

Bredekamp, Horst, and Franziska Brons. "Fotografie als Medium der Wissenschaft—Kunstgeschichte, Biologie und das Elend der Illustration." In *Iconic Turn: Die neue Macht der Bilder*, ed. Christa Maar and Herbert Burda, 365–81. Cologne, Ger.: Dumont, 2005.

Bremer, Dieter. "Licht als universales Darstellungsmedium: Materialien und Bibliographie." *Archiv für Begriffsgeschichte* 18 (1974): 185–206.

Brendel, Otto J. *Symbolism of the Sphere*. Leiden: Brill, 1977.

Brentano, Franz. *Descriptive Psychology*. Trans. and ed. Benito Müller. London: Routledge, 1995.

——. *Grundzüge der Ästhetik*. Ed. Franziska Mayer-Hillebrand. 2nd ed. Hamburg, Ger.: Meiner, 1988.

Bruhns, Matthias, Horst Bredekamp, and Gabriele Werner-Felmayer, eds. *Bilder ohne Betrachter*. Vol. 4,2 of *Bildwelten des Wissens: Kunsthistorisches Jahrbuch für Bildkritik*. Berlin: Akademie, 2006.

Bruzina, Ronald. "Translator's Introduction." In Eugen Fink, *Sixth Cartesian Meditation: The Idea of a Transcendental Theory of Method*. Trans. Ronald Bruzina. Bloomington: Indiana University Press, 1995.

Bühler, Karl. *Theory of Language: The Representational Function of Language*. Trans. Donald Fraser Goodwin with Achim Eschbach. Amsterdam: Benjamins, 2011.

Burnyeat, Myles F. "How Much Happens When Aristotle Sees Red and Hears Middle C? Remarks on *De anima* 2, 7–8." In *Essays on Aristotle's* De anima, ed. Martha C. Nussbaum and Amélie Oksenberg Rorty, 421–34. Oxford: Clarendon, 1992.

Busch, Katrin. *Geschicktes Geben: Aporien der Gabe bei Jacques Derrida*. Munich: Fink, 2004.

Campanella, Tommaso. *La città del sole: Dialogo poetico / The City of the Sun: A Poetical Dialogue*. Trans. Daniel John Donno. Berkeley: University of California Press, 1981.

Carbone, Mauro. "Sichtbar machen: Merleau-Ponty und Paul Klee." In *Phänomenalität des Kunstwerks*. Ed. Hans Rainer Sepp and Jürgen Trinks, 55–70. Vienna: Turia + Kant, 2006.

Cassin, Barbara. "Enquête sur le logos dans le *De anima*." In *Corps et âme: Sur le* De anima *d'Aristote*, ed. Gilbert Romeyer-Dherbey and Cristina Viano, 257–93. Paris: Vrin, 1996.

Cassirer, Ernst. *The Individual and the Cosmos in Renaissance Philosophy*. Trans. Mario Domandi. Mineola, N.Y.: Dover, 2000.

——. *The Philosophy of Symbolic Forms*. Trans. Ralph Manheim. 3 vols. New Haven, Conn.: Yale University Press, 1953–57.

Cassou-Noguès, Pierre. "Le problème des mathématiques dans la philosophie de Merleau-Ponty." In Maurice Merleau-Ponty, *Notes de cours sur 'L'origine de la géométrie' de Husserl, suivi de Recherches sur la phénoménologie de Merleau-Ponty*, ed. Renaud Barbaras, 369–404. Paris: Presses universitaires de France, 1998.

Caston, Victor. "Aristotle and the Problem of Intentionality." *Philosophy and Phenomenological Research* 58, no. 2 (June 1998): 249–98.

Chalcidius. "Ad Timaeum cp. 220." In *Stoicorum veterum fragmenta*, ed. Hans Friedrich August von Arnim. Vol. 2, 235–36. Stuttgart, Ger.: Teubner, 1964.

Chastel, André *Le geste dans l'art*. Paris: Liana Levi, 2001.

Cherniss, Harold. *Aristotle's Criticism of Presocratic Philosophy*. Baltimore, Md.: Johns Hopkins University Press, 1935.

Chrétien, Jean-Louis. "Body and Touch." In *The Call and the Response*, trans. Anne A. Davenport, 83–131. New York: Fordham University Press, 2004.

Cicero. *De Finibus Bonorum et Malorum / On Ends*. Trans. Harris Rackham. In *Cicero in Twenty-Eight Volumes*, vol. 17. 2nd ed. Cambridge, Mass.: Harvard University Press, 1931.

——. *On the Nature of the Gods / Academics*. Trans. H. Rackham. Cambridge, Mass.: Harvard University Press, 1933.

Cleary, John J. "Phainomena in Aristotle's Methodology." *International Journal of Philosophical Studies* 2, no. 1 (1994): 61–97.

Cobb-Stevens, Richard. "'Aristotelian' Themes in Husserl's *Logical Investigations*." In *One Hundred Years of Phenomenology: Husserl's "Logical Investigations" Revisited*, ed. Dan Zahavi and Frederik Stjernfelt, 79–92. Dordrecht: Springer, 2002.

Coccia, Emanuele. *La trasparenza delle immagini: Averroè e l'averroismo*. Milan: Mondadori, 2005.

Colish, Marcia L. "Carolingian Debates Over *Nihil* and *Tenebrae*: A Study in Theological Method." *Speculum* 59, no. 4 (1984): 757–95.

——. "St. Augustine's *Rhetoric of Silence* Revisited." *Augustinian Studies* 9 (1978): 15–24.

Conrad-Martius, Hedwig. "Vorwort." In Adolf Reinach, *Was ist Phänomenologie?*, 5–17. Munich: Kösel, 1951.

Cornford, Francis Macdonald. *Plato's Theory of Knowledge: The "Theaetetus" and the "Sophist" of Plato*. London: Routledge and Kegan Paul, 1957.

Courtine, Jean-François. *Suarez et le système de la métaphysique*. Paris: Presses universitaires de France, 2014.

Crary, Jonathan. *Techniques of the Observer: On Vision and Modernity in the Nineteenth Century*. Cambridge, Mass.: MIT Press, 1990).

Crombie, Alistair Cameron. "Expectation, Modelling and Assent in the History of Optics, i: Alhazen and the Medieval Tradition, ii: Kepler and Descartes." In *Science, Art and Nature in Medieval and Modern Thought*, 301–56. London: Hambledon, 1996.

Dacey, Dennis. "Origins of Perception: Retinal Ganglion Cell Diversity and the Creation of Parallel Visual Pathways." In *The Cognitive Neurosciences*, ed. Michael S. Gazzaniga, 281–301. Cambridge, Mass.: MIT Press, 2004.

Damisch, Hubert. *The Origin of Perspective*. Trans. John Goodman. Cambridge, Mass.: MIT Press, 2000.

——. *A Theory of Cloud: Toward a History of Painting*. Trans. Janet Lloyd. Stanford, Calif.: Stanford University Press, 2008.

Dancy, Russell M. "The Categories of Being in Plato's 'Sophist' 255c-e." *Ancient Philosophy* 19, no. 1 (1999): 45–72.

Dante Alighieri. *The Banquet*. Trans. Christopher Ryan. Saratoga, Calif.: Anma Libri, 1989.

——. *The Divine Comedy*. Trans. C. H. Sisson. Oxford: Oxford University Press, 1998.

Danto, Arthur C. *The Transfiguration of the Commonplace: A Philosophy of Art*. Cambridge, Mass.: Harvard University Press, 1981.

Därmann, Iris. *Tod und Bild: Eine phänomenologische Mediengeschichte*. Munich: Fink, 1995.

da Vinci, Leonardo. *Libro di pittura*. Ed. Carlo Pedretti. Transcr. Carlo Vecce. Florence: Giunti, 1995.

Deleuze, Gilles. *The Logic of Sense*. Trans. Mark Lester with Charles Stivale. New York: Columbia University Press, 1990.

Deleuze, Gilles, and Félix Guattari. "The Brain Is the Screen." Trans. Ames Hodges and Michael Taormina. In *Two Regimes of Madness: Texts and Interviews 1975–1995*, ed. David Lapoujade, 282–92. Los Angeles: Semiotext(e), 2006.

——. *A Thousand Plateaus: Capitalism and Schizophrenia 2*. Trans. Brian Massumi. Minneapolis: University of Minnesota Press, 1987.

Derrida, Jacques. *Dissemination*. Trans. Barbara Johnson. London: Athlone, 2000.

——. *Edmund Husserl's Origin of Geometry: An Introduction*. Trans. John P. Leavey. Lincoln: University of Nebraska Press, 1989.

——. "Fragen an die Phänomenologie—Abschied vom Prinzipiellen? [Transkription einer Podiumsdiskussion in Wien 1985]." In *Die Krise der Phänomenologie und die Pragmatik des Wissenschaftsfortschritts*, ed. Michael Benedikt and Rudolf Burger, 169–79. Vienna: Verlag der österreichischen Staatsdruckerei, 1986.

——. "'Genesis and Structure' and Phenomenology." In *Writing and Difference,* trans. Alan Bass, 193–211. London: Routledge, 1978.

——. *Margins of Philosophy*. Trans. Alan Bass. Chicago: University of Chicago Press, 1982.

——. *The Problem of Genesis in Husserls Philosophy*. Trans. Marian Hobson. Chicago: University of Chicago Press, 2003.

——. "Punctuations: The Time of a Thesis." In *Eyes of the University: Right to Philosophy 2*. Trans. Kathleen McLaughlin, 113–28. Stanford, Calif.: Stanford University Press, 2004.

——. "Sauver les phénomènes: Pour Salvatore Puglia." *Contretemps* 1 (1995): 14–25.

——. *Speech and Phenomena and Other Essays on Husserl's Theory of Signs*. Trans. David B. Allison. Evanston, Ill.: Northwestern University Press, 1989.

——. *The Truth in Painting*. Trans. Geoff Bennington and Ian McLeod. Chicago: University of Chicago Press, 1987.

Descartes, René. *Optics*. In *Discourse on Method, Optics, Geometry, and Meteorology*. Ed. and trans. Paul J. Olscamp, 63–173. Indianapolis: Hackett, 2001.

——. *The Philosophical Writings of Descartes*. Trans. John Cottingham, Robert Stoothoff, Dugald Murdoch, and Anthony Kenny. Cambridge: Cambridge University Press, 1985–1991.

Di Bartolo, Maurizio. Einsicht*: La costruzione del noetico in Edmund Husserl*. Padua, Italy: Il Poligrafo, 2006.

Diderot, Denis. *Rameau's Nephew and D'Alembert's Dream*. Trans. Leonard Tancock. Harmondsworth: Penguin, 1966.

Didi-Huberman, Georges. *Ce que nous voyons, ce qui nous regarde*. Paris: Minuit, 1992.

——. *Confronting Images: Questioning the Ends of a Certain History of Art*. Trans. John Goodman. University Park: Pennsylvania State University Press, 2005.

——. *Devant le temps: Histoire de l'art et anachronisme des images*. Paris: Minuit, 2000.

——. "Eloge du diaphane." In *Phasmes: Essais sur l'apparition*, 99–110. Paris: Minuit, 1998.

——. *Fra Angelico: Dissemblance and Figuration*. Trans. Jane Marie Todd. Chicago: University of Chicago Press, 1995.

Diogenes Laertius. *Lives of Eminent Philosophers*. Trans. R. D. Hicks. Cambridge, Mass.: Harvard University Press, 2006.

Dionysius the Areopagite. *The Heavenly Hierarchy*. Trans. John Parker. In *The Works of Dionysius the Areopagite*, part 2, 1–66. London: Parker, 1899.

Drummond, John J. "On the Nature of Perceptual Appearances, or Is Husserl an Aristotelian?" *New Scholasticism* 52, no. 1 (1978): 1–22.

Dubosson, Samuel. *L'imagination légitimée: La conscience imaginative dans la phénoménologie prototranscendantale de Husserl*. Paris: L'Harmattan, 2004.

Dufrenne, Mikel. *Phenomenology of Aesthetic Experience*. Vol. 1. Evanston, Ill.: Northwestern University Press, 1973.

——. "Suspension et gravité: L'imaginaire sartrien face au Tintoret." *Alter: Revue de phénoménologie*, no. 5 (2007): 123–42.

Duhem, Pierre. *To Save the Phenomena: An Essay on the Idea of Physical Theory from Plato to Galileo*. Trans. Edmund Dolan and Chaninah Maschler. Chicago: University of Chicago Press, 2015.

Duns Scotus, John. *On Being and Cognition: Ordinatio 1.3.* Ed. and trans. John van den Bercken. New York: Fordham University Press, 2016.

Düring, Ingemar. *Aristotle's Protrepticus: An Attempt at Reconstruction.* Stockholm: Almqvist & Wiksell, 1961.

Eberhard, Philippe. *The Middle Voice in Gadamer's Hermeneutics: A Basic Interpretation with Some Theological Implications.* Tübingen, Ger.: Mohr Siebeck, 2004.

Eckhart. "Predigt 101." In *Die deutschen Werke,* ed. Georg Steer. Vol. 4/1. Stuttgart, Ger.: Kohlhammer, 1997.

Eco, Umberto. "Sugli specchi." In *Sugli specchi e altri saggi: Il segno, la rappresentazione, l'illusione, l'immagine,* 9–37. Milan: Bompiani, 1995.

Edgerton, Samuel Y. *The Renaissance Rediscovery of Linear Perspective.* New York: Basic Books, 1975.

Egenhofer, Sebastian. *Abstraktion—Kapitalismus—Subjektivität: Die Wahrheitsfunktion des Werks in der Moderne.* Munich: Fink, 2008.

Ehrenzweig, Anton. *The Psycho-Analysis of Artistic Vision and Hearing: An Introduction to a Theory of Unconscious Perception.* London: Routledge & Kegan Paul, 1953.

El-Bizri, Nader. "Avicenna's *De Anima* Between Aristotle and Husserl." In *The Passions of the Soul in the Metamorphosis of Becoming,* ed. Anna-Teresa Tymieniecka, 67–89. Dordrecht: Springer, 2003.

Eliasson, Olafur. "Museums are Radical." In *Olafur Eliasson: The Weather Project,* ed. Susan May, 129–38. London: Tate, 2003.

Elkins, James. *The Object Stares Back: On the Nature of Seeing.* San Diego, Calif.: Harcourt, 1996.

Emilsson, Eyjólfur K. *Plotinus on Sense-Perception: A Philosophical Study.* Cambridge: Cambridge University Press, 1988.

Escoubas, Eliane. "*Bild, Fiktum* et esprit de la communauté chez Husserl." *Alter: Revue de phénoménologie,* no. 4 (1996): 281–300.

——. *Imago mundi: Topologie de l'art.* Paris: Galilee, 1986.

Eudoxus of Cnidus. *Die Fragmente des Eudoxos von Knidos.* Ed. François Lasserre. Berlin: de Gruyter, 1966.

Everson, Stephen. *Aristotle on Perception.* Oxford: Oxford University Press, 1997.

Faur, José. "The Biblical Idea of Idolatry." *Jewish Quarterly Review* 69, no. 1 (1978): 1–15.

Fellmann, Ferdinand. *Phänomenologie als ästhetische Theorie.* Freiburg, Ger.: Alber, 1989.

——. *Phänomenologie zur Einführung.* Hamburg, Ger.: Junius, 2006.

Fiedler, Konrad. *Über den Ursprung der künstlerischen Tätigkeit.* Ed. Gottfried Boehm. In *Schriften zur Kunst,* vol. 1, 111–220. 2nd corr. and enl. ed. Munich: Fink, 1991.

Fink, Eugen. "Das Erscheinen als das absolute Medium." In *Sein, Wahrheit, Welt: Vor-Fragen zum Problem des Phänomen-Begriffs,* 118–30. The Hague: Nijhoff, 1958.

——. "Operative Concepts in Husserl's Phenomenology." Trans. William McKenna. In *Apriori and World: European Contributions to Husserlian Phenomenology,* ed. William McKenna, Robert M. Harlan, and Laurence E. Winters, 56–70. The Hague: Nijhoff, 1981.

——. *Play as Symbol of the World and Other Writings.* Trans. Ian Alexander Moore and Christopher Turner. Bloomington: Indiana University Press, 2016.

——. "The Problem of the Phenomenology of Edmund Husserl." In *Apriori and World: European Contributions to Husserlian Phenomenology,* ed. William McKenna, Robert M. Harlan, and Laurence E. Winters, 21–55. The Hague: Nijhoff, 1981.

——. *Sixth Cartesian Meditation: The Idea of a Transcendental Theory of Method.* Trans. Ronald Bruzina. Bloomington: Indiana University Press, 1995.

——. *Studien zur Phänomenologie 1930–1939.* The Hague: Nijhoff, 1966.

Flusser, Vilém. *Kommunikologie.* Ed. Stefan Bollman and Edith Flusser. *Schriften* 4. Mannheim, Ger.: Bollmann, 1996.

Focillon, Henri. *The Life of Forms in Art.* Trans. Charles Beecher Hogan and George Alexander Kubler. New Haven, Conn.: Yale University Press, 1942.

Foucault, Michel. "Message ou bruit?" In *Dits et écrits*, ed. Daniel Defert and François Ewald, vol. 1, 557–60. Paris: Gallimard, 1994.

——. *The Order of Things: An Archaeology of the Human Sciences*. New York: Vintage, 1994.

Fox Talbot, William Henry. *The Pencil of Nature*. London: Longman, Brown, Green & Longmans, 1844–1846.

——. "Photogenic Drawing: To the Editor of the Literary Gazette." In *The Literary Gazette; and Journal of Belles Lettres, Arts, Sciences, &c. for the Year 1839* [etc.], no. 1150 (February 2, 1839), 73–74. London: Literary Gazette, 1839.

Frede, Michael. *Prädikation und Existenzaussage: Platons Gebrauch von 'ist' und 'ist nicht' im Sophistes*. Göttingen: Vandenhoeck und Ruprecht, 1967.

Freedberg, David. *The Power of Images: Studies in the History and Theory of Response*. Chicago: University of Chicago Press, 1989.

Frontisi-Ducroux, Françoise. *Dans l'oeil du miroir*. Paris: Odile Jacob, 1997.

Galen. *On the Doctrines of Hippocrates and Plato*. Ed. and trans. Phillip De Lacy. 3 vols. 2nd ed. Berlin: Akademie, 2005.

Gamboni, Dario. *Potential Images: Ambiguity and Indeterminacy in Modern Art*. Trans. Mark Treharne. London: Reaktion, 2002.

Gamm, Gerhard. *Flucht aus der Kategorie: Die Positivierung des Unbestimmten als Ausgang der Moderne*. Frankfurt: Suhrkamp, 1994.

Gander, Hans-Helmuth, ed. *Husserl-Lexikon*. Darmstadt: Wissenschaftliche Buchgesellschaft, 2009.

Gätje, Helmut. *Studien zur Überlieferung der aristotelischen Psychologie im Islam*. Heidelberg, Ger.: 1971.

Gély, Raphaël. *Les usages de la perception: Réflexions merleau-pontiennes*. Leuven, Belg.: Peeters, 2005.

Gernet, Louis. "Things Visible and Things Invisible." In *The Anthropology of Ancient Greece*, trans. John Hamilton and Blaise Nagy, 343–51. Baltimore. Md.: Johns Hopkins University Press, 1981.

Gibson, William Ralph Boyce. "From Husserl to Heidegger: Excerpts from a 1928 Freiburg Diary [Edited by Herbert Spiegelberg]." *Journal of the British Society for Phenomenology* 2, no. 1 (1971): 58–83.

Gioseffi, Decio. *Perspectiva artificialis: Per la storia della prospettiva, spigolature e appunti*. Trieste: Università di Trieste, 1957.

Goethe, Johann Wolfgang. *Goethe's Color Theory*. Ed. Rupprecht Matthaei and Herb Aach. New York: Van Nostrand Reinhold, 1971.

——. *Sämtliche Werke, Briefe, Tagebücher und Gespräche*. Ed. Karl Eibl. 40 vols. Frankfurt: Deutscher Klassiker Verlag, 1985–.

Goodman, Nelson. *Languages of Art: An Approach to a Theory of Symbols*. Indianapolis: Bobbs-Merrill, 1968.

——. "When Is Art?" In *Ways of Worldmaking*, 57–70. Indianapolis: Hackett, 1978.

Goodman, Nelson, and Catherine Z. Elgin. *Reconceptions in Philosophy and Other Arts and Sciences*. Indianapolis: Hackett, 1988.

Granel, Gérard. *Le Sens du temps et de la perception chez E. Husserl*. Paris: Gallimard, 1968.

Grave, Johannes. "Brunelleschi's Perspective Panels: Rupture and Continuity in the History of the Image." In *Renaissance? Perceptions of Continuity and Discontinuity in Europe, c.1300–c.1550*, ed. Alexander Lee, Pit Péporté, and Harry Schnitker, 161–80. Leiden: Brill, 2010.

Greenberg, Clement. *The Collected Essays and Criticism*. Chicago: University of Chicago Press, 1986–1993.

Günzel, Stephan. *Maurice Merleau-Ponty—Werk und Wirkung: Eine Einführung*. Vienna: Turia + Kant, 2007.

Gurwitsch, Aron. *The Field of Consciousness*. In *The Field of Consciousness: Phenomenology of Theme, Thematic Field, and Marginal Consciousness*, ed. Richard M. Zaner and Lester Embree, *The Collected Works of Aron Gurwitsch (1901–1973)* 3, 1–409. Dordrecht: Springer, 2010.

Halliwell, Stephen. *The Aesthetics of Mimesis: Ancient Texts and Modern Problems*. Princeton, N.J.: Princeton University Press, 2002.

Hamlyn, David W., ed. and trans. *De anima, Books II and III (with Passages from Book I)* by Aristotle. Rev. Christopher Shields. Oxford: Clarendon, 1993.

Hamou, Philippe. "Introduction." In *La vision perspective (1435–1740): L'art et la science du regard, de la Renaissance à l'âge classique*, 7–51. Paris: Payot et Rivages, 1995.

——. *Voir et connaître à l'âge classique*. Paris: Presses universitaires de France, 2002.

Han, Chol. *Ästhetik der Oberfläche: Die Medialitätskonzeption Goethes*. Würzburg, Ger.: Königshausen & Neumann, 2007.

Hedwig, Klaus. *Sphaera lucis: Studien zur Intelligibilität des Seienden im Kontext der mittelalterlichen Lichtspekulation*. Münster: Aschendorff, 1980.

Hegel, Georg Wilhelm Friedrich. *Aesthetics: Lectures on Fine Art*. Trans. T. M. Knox. 2 vols. Oxford: Clarendon, 1975.

——. *Lectures on the History of Philosophy*. Trans. Elizabeth Sanderson Haldane. 2 vols. London: Paul, Trench, Trübner, 1892–1894.

——. *Phenomenology of Spirit*. Ed. John Niemeyer Findlay, trans. Arnold V. Miller. Oxford: Clarendon, 1977.

——. *Philosophy of Mind, Being Part Three of the Encyclopedia of the Philosophical Sciences*. Trans. William Wallace and Arnold V. Miller. Oxford: Clarendon, 1971.

Heidegger, Martin. *Being and Time*. Trans. John Macquarrie and Edward Robinson. New York: Harper, 1962.

——. "Excursus: General Orientation Regarding the essence of Mathematics According to Aristotle." In *Plato's Sophist*, trans. Richard Rojcewicz and André Schuwer. Bloomington: Indiana University Press, 2003.

——. *History of the Concept of Time: Prolegomena*. Trans. Theodore Kisiel. Bloomington: Indiana University Press, 2010.

——. *Introduction to Phenomenological Research*. Trans. Daniel O. Dahlstrom. Bloomington: Indiana University Press, 2005.

——. *Kant and the Problem of Metaphysics*. Trans. Richard Taft. 5th enl. ed. Bloomington: Indiana University Press, 1997.

——. "Phänomenologische Übungen für Anfänger im Anschluss an Aristoteles, de anima." In *Heidegger und Aristoteles. Heidegger-Jahrbuch* 3, ed. Alfred Denker, Günter Figal, Franco Volpi, and Holger Zaborowski, 9–22. Freiburg, Ger.: Alber, 2007.

——. *Phenomenological Interpretations of Aristotle: Initiation Into Phenomenological Research*. Trans. Richard Rojcewicz. Bloomington: Indiana University Press, 2010.

Heider, Fritz. *Ding und Medium*. Ed. Dirk Baecker. Berlin: Kadmos, 2005.

——. "Thing and Medium." In *On Perception, Event Structure, and Psychological Environment: Selected Papers*, 1–34. New York: International University Press, 1959.

Held, Klaus. "Husserls Rückgang auf das phainomenon und die geschichtliche Stellung der Phänomenologie." In *Dialektik und Genesis in der Phänomenologie*, ed. Ernst Wolfgang Orth, 89–145. Freiburg, Ger.: Alber, 1980.

Heller-Roazen, Daniel. *The Inner Touch: Archaeology of a Sensation*. New York: Zone, 2007.

Helmholtz, Hermann. "The Facts in Perception." Trans. Malcolm F. Lowe. In *Epistemological Writings: The Paul Hertz/Moritz Schlick Centenary Edition of 1921 with Notes and Commentary by the Editors*, ed. Paul Hertz, Moritz Schlick, R. S. Cohen, and Yehuda Elkana, 115–85. Dordrecht: Reidel, 1977.

Herodotus, *Herodotus*. Trans. A. D. Godley. Vol. 2. Cambridge: Harvard University Press, 1982.

Hess, Robert F., Lindsay T. Sharpe, and Knut Nordby, eds. *Night Vision: Basic, Clinical and Applied Aspects*. Cambridge: Cambridge University Press, 1991.

Hilt, Annette. *Ousia, Psyche, Nous: Aristoteles' Philosophie der Lebendigkeit*. Munich: Alber, 2005.

Hintikka, Jaakko. *Time and Necessity: Studies in Aristotle's Theory of Modality*. Oxford: Clarendon, 1975.

Hoffmann, E. T. A. "The Artus Hof." In *The Serapion Brethren*. Vol. 1. Trans. Alexander Ewing, 152–82. London: Bell, 1908.

Hoffmann, Stefan. *Geschichte des Medienbegriffs*. Hamburg: Meiner, 2002.

Hogrebe, Wolfram. *Echo des Nichtwissens*. Berlin: Akademie, 2006.

——. *Metaphysik und Mantik: Die Deutungsnatur des Menschen*. Frankfurt: Suhrkamp, 1992.

——. "Orientierungstechniken: Mantik." In *Spur: Spurenlesen als Orientierungstechnik und Wissenskunst*, ed. Sybille Krämer, Werner Kogge, and Gernot Grube, 281–92. Frankfurt: Suhrkamp, 2007.

Hopkins, Robert: *Picture, Image and Experience*. Cambridge: Cambridge University Press, 1998.

Husserl, Edmund. "Abhandlung über Wahrnehmung von 1898." First supplement to *Wahrnehmung und Aufmerksamkeit* in *Wahrnehmung und Aufmerksamkeit: Texte aus dem Nachlass (1893–1912)*, ed. Thomas Vongehr and Regula Giuliani. *Husserliana* 38, 123–58. New York: Springer, 2005.

——. *Aufsätze und Rezensionen (1890–1910)*. Ed. Berhard Rang. *Husserliana* 22. The Hague: Nijhoff, 1979.

——. "Beilage zu den Paragraphen 11 und 20: Zur Kritik der 'Bildertheorie' und der Lehre von den 'immanenten' Gegenstände der Akte." *Logische Untersuchungen*. *Husserliana* 19/1: 436–40.

——. *Cartesian Meditations: An Introduction to Phenomenology*. Trans. Dorion Cairns. The Hague: Nijhoff, 1960.

——. *The Crisis of European Sciences and Transcendental Phenomenology: An Introduction to Phenomenological Philosophy*. Trans. David Carr. Evanston, Ill.: Northwestern University Press, 2000.

——. *Die Krisis der europäischen Wissenschaften und die transzendentale Phänomenologie: Ergänzungsband: Texte aus dem Nachlass 1934–1937*. Ed. Reinhold N. Smid. *Husserliana* 29. The Hague: Kluwer, 1992.

——. *Ding und Raum: Vorlesungen 1907*. Ed. Ulrich Claesges. *Husserliana* 16. The Hague: Nijhoff, 1973.

——. "Ein Husserlmanuskript über Ästhetik." Ed. Gabriele Scaramuzza and Karl Schuhmann. *Husserl Studies* 7/3 (1990): 165–77.

——. *Erfahrung und Urteil: Untersuchungen zur Genealogie der Logik*. Ed. Ludwig Landgrebe. Hamburg, Ger.: Meiner, 1999.

——. *Erste Philosophie (1923/24): Zweiter Teil*. Ed. Rudolf Boehm. *Husserliana* 7:298–305. The Hague: Nijhoff, 1959.

——. *Formal and Transcendental Logic*. Trans. Dorion Cairns. *Husserliana* 17. The Hague: Nijhoff, 1969.

——. *Ideas Pertaining to a Pure Phenomenology and to a Phenomenological Philosophy, First Book*. Trans. Fred Kersten. The Hague: Nijhoff, 1983.

——. *Ideen zu einer reinen Phänomenologie und phänomenologischen Philosophie. Erstes Buch: Allgemeine Einführung in die reine Phänomenologie, 2. Halbband: Ergänzende Texte (1912–1929)*. Ed. Karl Schuhmann. *Husserliana* 3/2. The Hague: Nijhoff, 1988.

——. *Introduction to Logic and Theory of Knowledge: Lectures 1906/07*. Trans. Claire Ortiz Hill. Dordrecht: Springer, 2008.

——. Letter to Hugo von Hoffmannsthal, January 12, 1907. Trans. Sven-Olov Wallenstein. *Site Magazine* 26/27 (2009), 2. http://www.sitemagazine.net/content/01-issues/19-26-27_2009/26-27_2009.pdf.

——. *Logical Investigations*. Ed. Dermot Moran, trans. John F. Finlay. London: Routledge, 2008.

——. *Natur und Geist: Vorlesungen Sommersemester 1919*. Ed. M. Weiler. *Husserliana* Materialien 4. Dordrecht: Springer, 2002.

——. *Phänomenologische Psychologie*. Ed. Walter Biemel. *Husserliana* 9. The Hague: Nijhoff, 1962.

——. *Phantasy, Image Consciousness, and Memory (1898–1925)*. Trans. John Brough. Dordrecht: Springer, 2005.

——. "Phenomenology." In *Encyclopædia Britannica*, 14th ed., vol. 17, 699–702. New York: Encyclopædia Britannica, 1929.

——. *The Phenomenology of Internal Time-Consciousness*. Ed. Martin Heidegger. Trans. James Spencer Churchill. The Hague: Nijhoff, 1964.

——. *Philosophy of Arithmetic: Psychological and Logical Investigations—with Supplementary Texts from 1887–1901*. Trans. Dallas Willard. Dordrecht: Springer, 2003.

——. *Späte Texte über Zeitkonstitution (1929–1934): Die C-Manuskripte*. Ed. Dieter Lohmar. *Husserliana* Materialien 8. Dordrecht: Springer, 2002.

——. *Studien zur Arithmetik und Geometrie: Texte aus dem Nachlass (1886–1901)*. Ed. Ingeborg Strohmeyer, Husserliana 21. The Hague: Nijhoff, 1983.

——. *Wahrnehmung und Aufmerksamkeit: Texte aus dem Nachlass (1893–1912)*. Ed. Regula Giuliani and Thomas Vongehr. Dordrecht: Springer, 2007.

——. *Zur Phänomenologie des inneren Zeitbewusstseins (1893–1917)*. Ed. Rudolf Boehm. The Hague: Nijhoff, 1969.

——. *Zur Phänomenologie der Intersubjektivität: Texte aus dem Nachlass. Zweiter Teil. 1921–28*. Ed. Iso Kern. *Husserliana* 14. The Hague: Nijhoff, 1973.

Hutchinson, D. S. "Restoring the Order of Aristotle's De anima." *Classical Quarterly* 37, no. 2 (1987): 373–81.

Hyman, John. *The Objective Eye: Color, Form, and Reality in the Theory of Art*, Chicago: University of Chicago Press, 2006.

Ibn al-Haytam (Alhazen). *A Critical Edition with English Translation of the First Three Books of Alhazen's De aspectibus, the Medieval Latin Version of Ibn al-Haytham's Kitāb al-Manāzir*. Ed. A. M. Smith. 2 vols. Philadelphia: American Philosophical Society, 2001 and 2006.

——. *The Optics of Ibn al-Haytham: Books I–III on Direct Vision*. Trans. Abd al-Hamid Sabrah. 2 vols. London: Warburg Institute, 1989.

Ibn Ishaq, Hunayn. *The Book of the Ten Treatises on the Eye, Ascribed to Hunain ibn Is-Hâq (809–877 A.D.): The Earliest Existing Systematic Text-Book of Ophthalmology*. Ed. and trans. Max Meyerhof. Cairo: Government, 1928.

Imdahl, Max. "Ikonik: Bilder und ihre Anschauung." In *Was ist ein Bild?*, ed. Gottfried Boehm, 300–324. 2nd ed. Munich: Fink, 1995.

Ingarden, Roman. *Ontology of the Work of Art: The Musical Work, the Picture, the Architectural Work, the Film*. Trans. Raymond Meyer. Athens: Ohio University Press, 1989.

——. "Über die sogenannte 'abstrakte' Malerei." In *Erlebnis, Kunstwerk und Wert: Vorträge zur Ästhetik 1937–1967*, 51–76. Tübingen, Ger.: Niemeyer, 1969.

Jäger, Ludwig. "Störung und Transparenz: Skizze zur performativen Logik des Medialen." In *Performativität und Medialität*, ed. Sybille Krämer, 35–73. Paderborn, Ger.: Fink, 2004.

Janicaud, Dominique. *Phenomenology "Wide Open": After the French Debate*. Trans. Charles N. Cabral. New York: Fordham University Press, 2010.

Janicaud, Dominique, et al. *Phenomenology and the "Theological Turn": The French Debate*. Trans. Bernard G. Prusak et al. New York: Fordham University Press, 2000.

Jay, Martin. *Downcast Eyes: The Denigration of Vision in Twentieth-Century French Thought*. Berkeley: University of California Press, 1999.

Johansen, Thomas Kjeller. *Aristotle on the Sense-Organs*. Cambridge: Cambridge University Press, 1998.

Jonas, Hans. "Homo Pictor and the Differentia of Man," *Social Research* 29, no. 2 (Summer 1962): 201–20.

——. "The Nobility of Sight," *Philosophy and Phenomenological Research* 14, no. 4 (June 1954): 507–19.

Joyce, James. *Ulysses*. London: Penguin, 2000.

Judd, Donald. *Complete Writings, 1959–1975*. Halifax, N.S.: Press of the Nova Scotia College of Art and Design, 2005.

——. *Complete Writings, 1975–1986*. Eindhoven: Van Abbemuseum, 1987.

Junod, Philippe. *Transparence et opacité: Réflexions autour de l'esthétique de Konrad Fiedler*. Lausanne, Switz.: L'Age d'homme, 1976.

Kamlah, Wilhelm. *Platons Selbstkritik im Sophistes*. Munich: Beck, 1963.

Kant, Immanuel. *Anthropology from a Pragmatic Point of View*. Trans. Robert B. Louden. In *Anthropology, History, and Education*, ed. Günter Zöller and Robert B. Louden. Cambridge: Cambridge University Press, 2007.

——. *Critique of Practical Reason*. In *Practical Philosophy*, trans. Mary J. Gregor, 133–271. Cambridge: Cambridge University Press, 1996.

——. *Critique of the Power of Judgment*. In *The Cambridge Edition of the Works of Immanuel Kant*, ed. Paul Guyer, trans. Paul Guyer and Eric Matthews. Cambridge: Cambridge University Press, 2000.

——. *Lectures on Anthropology*. Ed. Allen W. Wood and Robert B. Louden. Cambridge: Cambridge University Press, 2012.

——. *Menschenkunde oder philosophische Anthropologie*, based on Johann Adam Bergk's notes. Ed. Friedrich Christian Starke. Leipzig: Expedition des europäischen Aufsehers, 1831.

Kearney, Richard. "What Is Diacritical Hermeneutics?" *Journal of Applied Hermeneutics* 1, no. 1 (2011): 1–14.

Kemmer, Suzanne. *The Middle Voice*. Amsterdam: Benjamins, 1993.

Kemp, Martin. "Science, Non-Science and Nonsense: The Interpretation of Brunelleschi's Perspective." *Art History* 1, no. 2 (June 1978): 134–61.

Kepler, Johannes. *Gesammelte Werke*. Munich: Beck, 1937–.

——. *The Harmony of the World*. Trans. E. J. Aiton, A. M. Duncan, and J. F. Field. Philadelphia: American Philosophical Society, 1997.

——. *Optics: Paralipomena to Witelo & Optical Part of Astronomy*. Trans. William H. Donahue. Santa Fe, N.M.: Green Lion, 2001.

Kern, Iso. *Husserl und Kant: Eine Untersuchung über Husserls Verhältnis zu Kant und zum Neukantianismus*. The Hague: Nijhoff, 1964.

Kittler, Friedrich. "Man as a Drunken Town-Musician." Trans. Jocelyn Holland. *MLN* 118, no. 3 (April 2003): 637–52.

Klee, Paul. *Creative Confession and Other Writings*. Ed. Matthew Gale. London: Tate, 2013.

Koller, Hermann. "Die Anfänge der griechischen Grammatik." *Glotta* 37, no. 1/2 (1958): 5–40.

Kracauer, Siegfried. *History: The Last Things Before the Last*. Princeton, N.J.: Wiener, 1995.

Krämer, Sybille. "Die Rationalisierung der Visualität und die Visualisierung der Ratio." In *Bühnen des Wissens: Interferenzen zwischen Wissenschaft und Kunst*, ed. Helmar Schramm, 50–67. Berlin: Dahlem University Press, 2003.

——. "Form als Vollzug oder: Was gewinnen wir mit Niklas Luhmanns Unterscheidung von Medium und Form?" *Rechtshistorisches Journal* 17 (1998): 558–73.

——. "Gibt es eine Performanz des Bildlichen? Reflexionen über 'Blickakte.'" In *Bild-Performanz: Die Kraft des Visuellen*, ed. Ludger Schwarte, 63–89. Munich: Fink, 2011.

——. *Medium, Messenger. Transmission: An Approach to Media Philosophy*. Trans. Anthony Enns. Amsterdam: Amsterdam University Press, 2015.

——. "The Productivity of Blanks: On the Mathematical Zero and the Vanishing Point in Central Perspective: Remarks on the Convergences Between Science and Art in the Early Modern Period." In *Instruments in Art and Science: On the Architectonics of Cultural Boundaries in the 17th Century*, ed. Helmar Schramm, Ludger Schwarte, and Jan Lazardzig, 457–78. Berlin: de Gruyter, 2008.

——. "Sprache—Stimme—Schrift: Sieben Gedanken über Performativität als Medialität." In *Performanz: Zwischen Sprachphilosophie und Kulturwissenschaften*, ed. Uwe Wirth, 323–46. Frankfurt: Suhrkamp, 2003.

——. "Über die Heteronomie der Medien: Grundlinien einer Metaphysik der Medialität im Ausgang einer Reflexion des Boten." *Journal Phänomenologie*, no. 22 (2004): 18–38.

Krauss, Rosalind. *The Optical Unconscious*. Cambridge, Mass.: MIT Press, 1993.

Kulvicki, John. "Image Structure." *Journal of Aesthetics and Art Criticism* 61, no. 4 (Fall 2003): 323–40.

Kung, Joan. "Aristotle on Thises, Suches and the Third Man Argument." *Phronesis* 26, no. 3 (1981): 207–47.

Laks, André, and Glenn W. Most, eds. and trans. *Early Greek Philosophy*. Cambridge, Mass.: Harvard University Press, 2016–.

Langer, Susanne K. *Philosophy in a New Key: A Study in the Symbolism of Reason, Rite, and Art*. Cambridge, Mass.: Harvard University Press, 1979.

Lawlor, Leonard. *Derrida and Husserl: The Basic Problem of Phenomenology*. Bloomington: Indiana University Press, 2002.

——. "The Legacy of Husserl's 'Ursprung der Geometrie': The Limits of Phenomenology in Merleau-Ponty and Derrida." In *Merleau-Ponty's Reading of Husserl*, ed. Ted Toadvine and Lester E. Embree, 201–26. Dordrecht: Kluwer Academic, 2002.

Lee, Mi-Kyoung. *Epistemology After Protagoras: Responses to Relativism in Plato, Aristotle, and Democritus*. Oxford: Clarendon, 2008.

Lee, Rensselaer Wright. *Ut pictura poesis: The Humanistic Theory of Painting*. New York: Norton, 1967.

Lefebvre, René. "La crise de la *phantasia*: originalité des interprétations, originalité d'Aristote." In *De la phantasia à l'imagination*, ed. Danielle Lories and Laura Rizzerio, 31–47. Leuven, Belg.: Peeters, 2003.

Leibniz, Gottfried Wilhelm. *Die Philosophischen Schriften von Gottfried Wilhelm Leibniz*. Ed. Carl Immanuel Gerhardt. Berlin: Weidmann, 1875–.

Leijenhorst, Cees. *The Mechanisation of Aristotelianism: The Late Aristotelian Setting of Thomas Hobbes' Natural Philosophy*. Leiden: Brill, 2002.

Lessing, Gotthold Ephraim. "Laocoön." In *Laocoön, Nathan the Wise, and Minna von Barnhelm*, ed. William A. Steel, 1–110. New York: Dutton, 1930.

Levinas, Emmanuel. *En decouvrant l'existence avec Husserl et Heidegger*. 3rd corr. Ed. Paris: Vrin, 2001.

——. "Notes on Meaning." In *Of God Who Comes to Mind*, trans. Bettina Bergo, 152–71. Stanford, Calif.: Stanford University Press, 1998.

——. Review of Valentin Feldman, *L'esthétique française contemporaine*. In *Recherches philosophiques* 6 (1936–1937): 408–9.

——. "Signification and Sense." In *Humanism of the Other*, trans. Nidra Poller, 9–44. Urbana: University of Illinois Press, 2003.

——. *The Theory of Intuition in Husserl's Phenomenology*. Trans. André Orianne. 2nd ed. Evanston, Ill.: Northwestern University Press, 1995.

——. *Totality and Infinity: An Essay on Exteriority*. Trans. Alphonso Lingis. The Hague: Nijhoff, 1969.

Lindberg, David C. *Theories of Vision from Al-Kindi to Kepler*. Chicago: University of Chicago Press, 1976.

Llewelyn, John. "Heidegger's Kant and the Middle Voice." In *Time and Metaphysics: A Collection of Original Papers*, ed. David Wood and Robert Bernasconi, 87–120. Coventry, UK: Parousia, 1982.

Lloyd, G. E. R. "Saving the Appearances." *Classical Quarterly* 28, no. 1 (1978): 202–22.

Lohmar, Dieter. "Husserl's Concept of Categorial Intuition." In *One Hundred Years of Phenomenology: Husserl's "Logical Investigations" Revisited*, ed. Dan Zahavi and Frederik Stjernfelt, 125–45. Dordrecht: Springer, 2002.

Long, Christopher P. "Saving *ta legomena*: Aristotle and the History of Philosophy." *Review of Metaphysics* 60, no. 2 (238) (December 2006): 247–67.

Lopes, Dominic. *Understanding Pictures*. Oxford: Clarendon, 2006.

Lovejoy, Arthur O. *The Great Chain of Being: A Study of the History of an Idea*. Cambridge, Mass.: Harvard University Press, 1964.

Lucretius. *On the Nature of Things*. Trans. William Henry Denham Rouse. Rev. Martin Ferguson Smith. Cambridge, Mass.: Harvard University Press, 2002.

Lull, Ramon. *The Book of the Lover and the Beloved*. Trans. E. Allison Peers. New York: Macmillan, 1923.

Luther, Wilhelm. "Wahrheit, Licht und Erkenntnis in der griechischen Philosophie bis Demokrit: Ein Beitrag zur Erforschung des Zusammenhangs von Sprache und philosophischem Denken." *Archiv für Begriffsgeschichte* 10 (1966): 1–240.

Lycos, Kimon. "Aristotle and Plato on 'Appearing.' " *Mind* 73 (new series), no. 292 (October 1964): 496–514.

Lyotard, Jean-François. *The Differend: Phrases in Dispute*. Trans. Georges Van Den Abbeele. Minneapolis: University of Minnesota Press, 1988.

——. *Discourse, Figure*. Trans. Antony Hudek and Mary Lydon. Minneapolis: University of Minnesota Press, 2011.

——. "La peinture, anamnèse du visible." In *Misère de la philosophie*, 97–115. Paris: Galilée, 2000.

——. *Phenomenology*. Trans. Brian Beakley. New York: State University of New York Press, 1991.

——. *Que peindre? Adami, Arakawa, Buren = What to Paint? Adami, Arakawa, Buren*. Ed. Herman Parret. Trans. Antony Hudek, Vlad Ionescou, and Peter W. Milne. Leuven, Belg.: Leuven University Press, 2012.

Mahrenholz, Simone. "Analogisches Denken: Aspekte nicht-diskursiver Rationalität." In *Die Medien der Künste: Beiträge zur Theorie des Darstellens*, ed. Dieter Mersch, 75–91. Munich: Fink, 2003.

Maiatsky, Michail. *Platon penseur du visuel*. Paris: L'Harmattan, 2005.

Malebranche, Nicolas. *The Search After Truth*. Trans. Thomas M. Lennon and Paul J. Olscamp. Columbus: Ohio State University Press, 1980.

Manetti, Antonio. *The Life of Brunelleschi*. Ed. Howard Saalman. Trans. Catherine Enggass. University Park: Pennsylvania State University Press, 1970.

Mansi, Giovanni Domenico, et al., eds. *Sacrorum conciliorum nova et amplissima collectio [etc.]*. 58 vols. Paris: Welter, 1901–1927.

Marbach, Eduard. *Das Problem des Ich in der Phänomenologie Husserls*. The Hague: Nijhoff, 1974.

Marin, Louis. *Food for Thought*. Trans. Mette Hjort. Baltimore, Md.: Johns Hopkins University Press, 1997.

——. *La critique du discours: Sur la 'Logique de Port-Royal' et les 'Pensées' de Pascal*. Paris: Minuit, 1975.

——. *On Representation*. Trans. Catherine Porter. Stanford, Calif.: Stanford University Press, 2001.

——. "On the Interpretation of Ordinary Language: A Parable of Pascal." In *Textual Strategies: Perspectives in Post-Structuralist Criticism*. Ed. Josué V. Harari, 239–59. Ithaca, N.Y.: Cornell University Press, 1979.

——. *Portrait of the King*. Trans. Martha Houle. Minneapolis: University of Minnesota Press, 1988.

Meier-Oeser, Stephan. *Die Spur des Zeichens: Das Zeichen und seine Funktion in der Philosophie des Mittelalters und der frühen Neuzeit*. Berlin: de Gruyter, 1997.

Meillet, Antoine. "Sur les caractères du verbe." In *Linguistique historique et linguistique générale*, 175–98. Geneva: Slatkine, 1982.

Merker, Anne. "Aristote et l'Arc-en-Ciel: Enjeux philosophiques et étude scientifique." *Archive for History of Exact Sciences* 56, no. 3 (2002): 183–238.

——. *La vision chez Platon et Aristote*. Sankt Augustin, Ger.: Academia, 2003.

Merleau-Ponty, Maurice. "Eye and Mind." In *The Merleau-Ponty Aesthetics Reader: Philosophy and Painting*, trans. Michael B. Smith, 121–50. Evanston, Ill: Northwestern University Press, 1993.

——. *Husserl at the Limits of Phenomenology, Including Texts by Edmund Husserl*. Ed. Leonard Lawlor and Bettina Bergo. Evanston, Ill.: Northwestern University Press, 2002.

——. *Institution and Passivity: Course Notes from the Collège de France. 1954–1955*. Ed. Claude Lefort, Stéphanie Ménasé, and Dominique Darmaillacq, trans. Leonard Lawlor and Heath Massey. Evanston, Ill.: Northwestern University Press, 2010.

——. *Le monde sensible et le monde de l'expression: Cours au Collège de France, notes 1953*. Ed. Stefan Kristensen and Emmanuel de Saint-Aubert. Geneva: MetisPresses, 2011.

——. *Merleau-Ponty à la Sorbonne: Résumés de cours 1949–1952*. Grenoble, Fr.: Cynara, 1988.

——. *Nature: Course Notes from the Collège de France.* Ed. Dominique Séglard. Trans. Robert Vallier. Evanston, Ill.: Northwestern University Press, 2003.

——. *Parcours deux, 1951–1961.* Ed. Jacques Prunair. Lagrasse, Fr.: Verdier, 2000.

——. *Phenomenology of Perception.* Trans. Donald A. Landes. London: Routledge, 2012.

——. *The Prose of the World.* Ed. Claude Lefort. Trans. John O'Neill. Evanston, Ill.: Northwestern University Press, 1973.

——. *Signs.* Trans. Richard C. McLeary. Evanston, Ill.: Northwestern University Press, 1964.

——. *The Visible and the Invisible, Followed by Working Notes.* Ed. Claude Lefort, trans. Alphonso Lingis. Evanston, Ill.: Northwestern University Press, 1968.

Mersch, Dieter. "Das Ereignis der Setzung." In *Performativität und Ereignis,* ed. Erika Fischer-Lichte et al., 41–56. Tübingen, Ger.: Francke, 2003.

——. *Ereignis und Aura: Untersuchungen zu einer Ästhetik des Performativen.* Frankfurt: Suhrkamp, 2002.

——. *Was sich zeigt: Materialität, Präsenz, Ereignis.* Munich: Fink, 2002.

Metzger, Rainer. *Buchstäblichkeit: Bild und Kunst in der Moderne.* Cologne: König, 2004.

Mittelstrass, Jürgen. *Die Rettung der Phänomene: Ursprung und Geschichte eines antiken Forschungsprinzips.* Berlin: de Gruyter, 1962.

Moore, G. E. "Wittgenstein's Lectures in 1930–33," part 3. *Mind* 64, no. 253 (January 1955): 1–27.

Morel, Pierre-Marie. "Démocrite dans les *Parva naturalia* d'Aristote." In *Qu'est-ce que la philosophie présocratique?,* ed. André Laks and Claire Louguet, 449–64. Villeneuve-d'Ascq, Fr.: Presses universitaires du Septentrion, 2002.

——. *Démocrite et la recherche des causes.* Paris: Klincksieck, 1996.

Movia, Giancarlo. "Tatto e pensiero in un passo del 'De anima.'" In *Due studi sul "De Anima" di Aristotele,* 61–84. Padua, Italy: Antenore, 1974.

Mugler, Charles. *Dictionnaire historique de la terminologie optique des grecs: Douze siècles de dialogues avec la lumière.* Paris: Klincksieck, 1964.

Münch, Dieter. *Intention und Zeichen: Untersuchungen zu Franz Brentano und zu Edmund Husserls Frühwerk.* Frankfurt: Suhrkamp, 1993.

Münker, Stefan. "After the Medial Turn: Sieben Thesen zur Medienphilosophie." In *Medienphilosophie: Beiträge zur Klärung eines Begriffs,* ed. Stefan Münker, Alexander Roesler, and Mike Sandbothe, 16–23. Frankfurt: Fischer, 2003.

Nadar. *Nadar.* Vol 2: *Dessins et écrits.* Ed. Jean-François Bory. Paris: Hubschmid, 1979.

Nancy, Jean-Luc. *The Ground of the Image.* Trans. Jeff Fort. New York: Fordham University Press, 2005.

Narcy, Michel. "Κρίσις et αἴσθεσις (*De anima* III, 2)." In *Corps et âme: Sur le* De anima *d'Aristote,* ed. Gilbert Romeyer-Dherbey and Cristina Viano, 239–56. Paris: Vrin, 1996.

Natorp, Paul. *Plato's Theory of Ideas: An Introduction to Idealism.* Ed. Vasilis Politis, trans. Vasilis Politis and John Connolly. Sankt Augustin, Ger.: Academia, 2004.

Nemesius. *On the Nature of Man.* Trans. Philip van der Eijk and R. W. Sharples. Liverpool: Liverpool University Press, 2008.

Newman, Barnett. *Barnett Newman: Selected Writings and Interviews.* Ed. John P. O'Neill. Berkeley: University of California Press, 1992.

Nicolas d'Oresme. *Expositio et questiones in Aristotelis De anima.* Ed. Benoît Patar. Leuven, Belg.: Peeters, 1995.

Nicolas of Cusa. *Nicholas of Cusa's Dialectical Mysticism: Text. Translation and Interpretive Study of De visione dei.* Trans. Jasper Hopkins. Minneapolis: Banning, 1988.

Niehues-Pröbsting, Heinrich. *Überredung zur Einsicht: Der Zusammenhang von Philosophie und Rhetorik bei Platon und in der Phänomenologie.* Frankfurt: Klostermann, 1987.

Nietzsche, Friedrich. *The Gay Science: With a Prelude in German Rhymes and an Appendix of Songs.* Ed. Bernard Williams. Trans. Josefine Nauckhoff. Cambridge: Cambridge University Press, 2001.

——. "Sokrates und die Tragödie." In *Sämtliche Werke: Kritische Studienausgabe*, ed. Giorigo Colli and Mazzino Montinari. Vol. 1, 531–49. 2nd rev. ed. Munich: dtv, 1999.

——. *Thus Spoke Zarathustra: A Book for All and None*. Ed. Adrian del Caro and Robert Pippin. Trans. Adrian del Caro. Cambridge: Cambridge University Press, 2006.

——. *Writings from the Early Notebooks*. Ed. Raymond Geuss and Alexander Nehamas. Trans. Ladislaus Löb. Cambridge: Cambridge University Press, 2009.

Nussbaum, Martha C. *Aristotle's De Motu Animalium*. Princeton, N.J.: Princeton University Press, 1978.

——. "Saving Aristotle's Appearances." In *The Fragility of Goodness: Luck and Ethics in Greek Tragedy and Philosophy*, 240–63. Cambridge: Cambridge University Press, 1986.

Nussbaum, Martha C., and Amélie Oksenberg Rorty, eds. *Essays on Aristotle's* De anima. Oxford: Clarendon, 1992.

Owen, Gwilym E. L. "Tithenai ta phainomena." In *Logic, Science and Dialectic: Collected Papers in Greek Philosophy*, ed. Martha C. Nussbaum, 239–51. London: Duckworth, 1986.

Panofsky, Erwin. *Perspective as Symbolic Form*. Trans. Christopher S. Wood. New York: Zone, 1991.

Parronchi, Alessandro. "Le due tavole prospettiche del Brunelleschi." In *Studi su la dolce prospettiva*, 229–95. Milano: Martello, 1964.

Pascal, Blaise. *Pensées*. Ed. and trans. Roger Ariew. Indianapolis: Hackett, 2005.

Patočka, Jan. *Aristote, ses devanciers, ses successeurs*. Trans. Erika Abrams. Paris: Vrin, 2011.

——. *Vom Erscheinen als solchem: Texte aus dem Nachlass*. Ed. Helga Blaschek-Hahn and Karel Novotný. Freiburg, Ger.: Alber, 2000.

Pekáry, Thomas. *Imago res mortua est: Untersuchungen zur Ablehnung der bildenden Künste in der Antike*. Stuttgart: Steiner, 2002.

Perler, Dominik. *Theorien der Intentionalität im Mittelalter*. Frankfurt: Klostermann, 2002.

Philoponus (John of Alexandria). *Ioannis Philoponi in Aristotelis De anima libros commentaria*. In *Commentaria in Aristotelem Graeca*, ed. Michael Hayduck, vol. 15. Berlin: Reimer, 1897.

Pichler, Alois. *Wittgensteins Philosophische Untersuchungen: Vom Buch zum Album*. Amsterdam: Rodopi, 2004.

Pindar. *Olympian Odes/Pythian Odes*. Ed. and trans. William H. Race. Cambridge, Mass.: Harvard University Press, 2012.

Plato. *The Dialogues of Plato*. Ed. and trans. Benjamin Jowett. 4th ed. Oxford: Clarendon, 1953.

Pliny the Elder. *Natural History*. Trans. H. Rackam et al. 10 vols. Cambridge, Mass.: Harvard University Press, 1968–1980.

Plotinus. *Enneads*. In *Plotinus*. Trans. Arthur Hilary Armstrong. Cambridge, Mass.: Harvard University Press, 1966–1988.

Plutarch. "Concerning the Face Which Appears in the Orb of the Moon." In *Moralia in Sixteen Volumes*, vol. 12. Trans. Harold Cherniss and William C. Helmbold, 920b–945d:34–223. Cambridge, Mass.: Harvard University Press, 1984.

Polanyi, Michael. "What Is a Painting?" *American Scholar* 39, no. 4 (Autumn 1970): 655–69.

Powers, Maureen K., and Daniel G. Green. "Physiological Mechanisms of Visual Adaptation at Low Light Levels." In *Night Vision: Basic, Clinical and Applied Aspects*, ed. Robert F. Hess, Lindsay T. Sharpe, and Knut Nordby, 125–45. Cambridge: Cambridge University Press, 1991.

Prechtl, Peter. "Die Struktur der Intentionalität bei Brentano und Husserl." *Brentano Studien* 2 (1989): 117–30.

Rang, Bernhard. "Repräsentation und Selbstgegebenheit: Die Aporie der Phänomenologie der Wahrnehmung in den Frühschriften Husserls." *Phänomenologische Forschungen* 1 (1975): 105–37.

Rapp, Christof, ed. *Rhetorik* by Aristotle. Vol. 4 of *Werke in deutscher Übersetzung*. Berlin: Akademie, 1956–.

Rautzenberg, Markus. *Die Gegenwendigkeit der Störung: Aspekte einer postmetaphysischen Präsenztheorie*. Zurich: Diaphanes, 2009.

Richter, Gerhard. *Text: Writings, Interviews and Letters 1961–2007*. Ed. Dietmar Elger and Hans Ulrich Obrist. London: Thames & Hudson, 2009.

Rickert, Heinrich. "Die Methode der Philosophie und das Unmittelbare: Eine Problemstellung." In *Philosophische Aufsätze*, ed. Rainer A. Bast, 107–52. Tübingen, Ger.: Mohr Siebeck, 1999.

Ricœur, Paul. *A l'école de la phénoménologie*. Paris: Vrin, 1986.

——. "Phénoménologie et herméneutique." *Phänomenologische Forschungen* 1 (1975): 31–77.

——. "Phenomenology and Hermeneutics." Trans. R. Bradley DeFord. *Noûs* 9, no. 1 (1975): 85–102.

Romeyer-Dherbey, Gilbert. *Les choses mêmes: La pensée du réel chez Aristote*. Lausanne, Switz.: L'Age d'homme, 1983.

Romeyer-Dherbey, Gilbert, and Cristina Viano, eds. *Corps et âme: Sur le De anima d'Aristote*. Paris: Vrin, 1996.

Ronchi, Vasco. *The Nature of Light: An Historical Survey*. Trans. V. Barocas. Cambridge, Mass.: Harvard University Press, 1970.

Rosen, Stanley. *Plato's Sophist: The Drama of Original and Image*. New Haven, Conn.: Yale University Press, 1983.

Rosenberg, Harold. *The Re-Definition of Art*. Chicago: University of Chicago Press, 1972.

Ross, W. D., ed. and trans. *Aristotle's Metaphysics* by Aristotle. Vol. 2. 3rd ed. Oxford: Clarendon, 1953.

Rouveret, Agnès. *Histoire et imaginaire de la peinture ancienne, Ve siècle av. J.-C.–1e siècle ap. J.-C*. Rome: École française de Rome, 1989.

Rowe, Colin, and Robert Slutzky. *Transparency*. Ed. Bernhard Hoesli. Basel, Switz.: Birkhäuser, 1997.

——. "Transparency: Literal and Phenomenal." *Perspecta* 8 (1963): 45–54.

Sabra, Abdelhamid I. "Sensation and Inference in Alhazen's Theory of Visual Perception." In *Studies in Perception: Interrelations in the History of Philosophy and Science*, ed. Peter K. Machamer and Robert G. Turnbull, 160–85. Columbus: Ohio State University Press, 1978.

——. *Theories of Light from Descartes to Newton*. New ed. Cambridge: Cambridge University Press, 1981.

Sachs-Hombach, Klaus. *Das Bild als kommunikatives Medium: Elemente einer allgemeinen Bildwissenschaft*. Cologne, Ger.: Halem, 2003.

Sambursky, Samuel. *Physics of the Stoics*. London: Routledge and Kegan Paul, 1959.

Sartre, Jean-Paul. *The Imaginary: A Phenomenological Psychology of the Imagination*. Ed. Arlette Elkaïm-Sartre, trans. Jonathan Webber. London: Routledge, 2004.

Schapp, Wilhelm. *Beiträge zur Phänomenologie der Wahrnehmung*. Reprint. Wiesbaden: Heymann, 1976.

Schier, Flint. *Deeper Into Pictures: An Essay on Pictorial Representation*. Cambridge: Cambridge University Press, 1986.

Schiller, Friedrich. *Mary Stuart*. Trans. Joseph Mellish. https://www.gutenberg.org/ebooks/6791.

Schleiermacher, Friedrich, ed. *Platons Werke*, part 2. Vol. 2. Berlin: Reimer, 1824.

Schofield, Malcolm. "Aristotle on the Imagination." In *Essays on Aristotle's De anima*, ed. Martha C. Nussbaum and Amélie Oksenberg Rorty, 249–77. Oxford: Clarendon, 1992.

Scholz, Oliver. *Bild, Darstellung, Zeichen: Philosophische Theorien bildlicher Darstellung*. Frankfurt: Klostermann 2004.

Schubbach, Arno. *Subjekt im Verzug: Zur Rekonzeption von Subjektivität mit Jacques Derrida*. Zurich: Chronos, 2007.

Schuhl, Pierre-Maxime. *Platon et l'art de son temps*. Paris: Alcan, 1933.

Schuhmann, Karl. "Intentionalität und intentionaler Gegenstand beim frühen Husserl." *Phänomenologische Forschungen* 24/25 (1991): 46–75.

Schürmann, Eva, *Seeing as Practice: Philosophical Investigations Into the Relation Between Sight and Insight*. Cham, Switz.: Palgrave-Macmillan, 2019.

Schwarte, Ludger. "Die Wahrheitsfähigkeit des Bildes." *Zeitschrift für Ästhetik und allgemeine Kunstwissenschaft* 53, no. 1 (June 2008): 107–23.

Schweizer, Hans Rudolf, and Armin Wildermuth, eds. *Die Entdeckung der Phänomene: Dokumente einer Philosophie der sinnlichen Erkenntnis*. Basel, Switz.: Schwabe, 1981.

Searle, John R. *Intentionality: An Essay in the Philosophy of Mind*. Cambridge: Cambridge University Press, 1983.

Seebohm, Thomas M. "Kategoriale Anschauung." *Phänomenologische Forschungen* 23 (1990): 9–47.

Seel, Martin. *Ästhetik des Erscheinens*. Munich: Hanser, 2000.

——. "Kleine Phänomenologie des Lassens." In *Sich bestimmen lassen: Studien zur theoretischen und praktischen Philosophie*, 270–78. Frankfurt: Suhrkamp, 2002.

——. "Vor dem Schein kommt das Erscheinen: Bemerkungen zu einer Ästhetik der Medien." In *Ethisch-ästhetische Studien*, 104–25. Frankfurt: Suhrkamp, 1996.

Sepp, Hans Rainer. "Annäherungen an die Wirklichkeit: Phänomenologie und Malerei nach 1900." In *Edmund Husserl und die phänomenologische Bewegung: Zeugnisse in Text und Bild*, 77–94. Freiburg, Ger.: Alber, 1988.

——. "Medialität und Meontik: Eugen Finks spekulativer Entwurf." *Internationale Zeitschrift für Philosophie*, no. 1 (1998): 85–93.

——. "Totalhorizont—Zeitspielraum: Übergänge in Husserls und Finks Bestimmung von Welt." In *Eugen Fink: Sozialphilosophie—Anthropologie—Kosmologie—Pädagogik—Methodik*. Ed. Anselm Böhmer, 154–72. Würzburg, Ger.: Königshausen & Neumann, 2006.

Serres, Michel. *The Parasite*. Trans. Lawrence R. Schehr. Baltimore, Md.: Johns Hopkins University Press, 1982.

Shannon, Claude Elwood. *Collected Papers*. Ed. N. J. A. Sloane and A. D. Wyner. New York: IEEE, 1993.

Siegel, Steffen. "Die Kunst der Ostentatio: Zur frühneuzeitlichen Bildgeschichte des Selbstverweises." In *Deixis: Vom Denken mit dem Zeigefinger*, ed. Heike Gfrereis and Marcel Lepper, 38–61. Göttingen, Ger.: Wallstein, 2007.

Simmel, Georg. "The Picture Frame: An Aesthetic Study." Trans. Mark Ritter. *Theory, Culture & Society* 11, no. 1 (February 1994): 11–17.

Simon, Gérard. *Le regard, l'être et l'apparence dans l'optique de l'Antiquité*. Paris: Seuil, 1988.

Simplicius. *In Aristotelis de Caelo commentaria*. Ed. J. L. Heiberg. Berlin: Reimer, 1894.

——. *On Aristotle on the Soul 2.5–12*. Trans. Carlos Steel in coll. with J. O. Urmson. In *Priscian on Theophrastus' "On Sense-Perception" with "Simplicius' On Aristotle's on the Soul," 2.5–12*. Ithaca, N.Y.: Cornell University Press, 1997.

Smith, A. Mark. "Ptolemy, Alhazen and Kepler on the Problem of Optical Images." *Arabic Sciences and Philosophy* 8, no. 1 (March 1998): 9–44

Sorabji, Richard. "Aristotle on Demarcating the Five Senses." In *Articles on Aristotle*, vol. 4: *Psychology and Aesthetics*, ed. Jonathan Barnes, Malcolm Schofield, and Richard Sorabji, 76–92. London: Duckworth, 1979.

——, ed. *Aristotle Transformed: The Ancient Commentators and Their Influence*, 305–24. Ithaca, N.Y.: Cornell University Press, 1990.

——. "From Aristotle to Brentano: The Development of the Concept of Intentionality." In *Aristotle and the Later Tradition*, ed. Henry Blumenthal and Howard Robinson, 227–59. Oxford: Clarendon, 1991.

——. *The Philosophy of the Commentators 200–600 A.D.: A Sourcebook*. Vol. 1: *Psychology*. Ithaca, N.Y.: Cornell University Press, 2005.

Speer, Andreas. "Physics or Metaphysics? Some Remarks on Theory of Science and Light in Robert Grosseteste." In *Aristotle in Britain During the Middle Ages*, ed. John Marenbon, 73–90. Turnhout, Belg.: Brepols, 1996.

Spencer Brown, George. *Laws of Form/Gesetze der Form*. Trans. Thomas Wolf. Lübeck, Ger.: Bohmeier, 1997.

Spiegelberg, Herbert. "Der Begriff der Intentionalität in der Scholastik, bei Brentano und bei Husserl." *Philosophische Hefte* 5, no. 1/2 (1936): 75–91.

Spitzer, Leo. "Milieu and Ambiance: An Essay in Historical Semantics." *Philosophy and Phenomenological Research* 3, nos. 1 and 2 (September and December 1942): 1–42 and 169–218.

Staudigl, Michael. *Die Grenzen der Intentionalität: Zur Kritik der Phänomenalität nach Husserl.* Würzburg, Ger.: Königshausen & Neumann, 2003.

Steer, Georg. "Predigt 101: 'Dum medium silentium tenerent omnia.'" In *Lectura Eckhardi: Predigten Meister Eckharts von Fachgelehrten gelesen und gedeutet,* ed. Georg Steer, Loris Sturlese, and Dagmar Gottschall, vol. 1, 247–88. Stuttgart: Kohlhammer, 1998.

Stephanus (Henri Estienne). s.v. "Ἐπαλλάξις, Alternatio." In *Thesaurus Graecae linguae,* vol. 1, 353–54. Geneva: Stephanus, 1572.

Stock, Wiebke-Marie. *Theurgisches Denken: Zur kirchlichen Hierarchie des Dionysius Areopagita.* Berlin: de Gruyter, 2008.

Suárez, Francisco. *Commentaria una cum quaestionibus in libros Aristotelis DE ANIMA.* Vol. 2. Ed. Salvador Castellote. Madrid: Labor, 1981.

Tellkamp, Jörg Alejandro. *Sinne, Gegenstände und Sensibilia: Zur Wahrnehmungslehre des Thomas von Aquin.* Leiden: Brill, 1999.

Tengelyi, László. "Finks 'Fenster ins Absolute.'" *Phänomenologische Forschungen* 30: Die Freiburger Phänomenologie (1996): 65–87.

Thảo, Trân Đức. *Phenomenology and Dialectical Materialism.* Ed. Robert S. Cohen. Trans. Daniel J. Herman and Donald V. Morano. Dordrecht: Reidel, 1986.

Themistius. *On Aristotle's On the Soul.* Trans. Robert B. Todd. Ithaca, N.Y.: Cornell University Press, 1996.

——. *Paraphrase de la métaphysique d'Aristote, livre Lambda.* Ed. Rémi Brague. Paris: Vrin, 1999.

Theon of Smyrna. *Exposition des connaissances mathématiques utiles pour la lecture de Platon.* Trans. J. Dupuis. Paris: Hachette, 1892.

——. *Theonis smyrnaei Platonici Liber de Astronomia.* Ed. H. Martin. Paris: e Reipublicae typographeo, 1849.

Theophrastus. *De sensibus.* Ed. and trans. George Malcolm Stratton. London: Allen & Unwin, 1917.

Thiel, Detlef. "Der Phänomenologe in der Galerie: Husserl und die Malerei." *Phänomenologische Forschungen, Neue Folge* 2, no. 1 (1997): 61–103.

——. "Husserls Phänomenographie." *Recherches husserliennes,* no. 19 (2003): 67–108.

Thurmann-Moe, Jan. *Munchs "Roßkur": Experimente mit Technik und Material.* Hamburg, Ger.: Dölling und Galitz, 1994.

Trendelenburg, Friedrich Adolf, ed. *Aristotelis De anima libri tres* by Aristotle. Berlin: Weber, 1877.

Tugendhat, Ernst. *Der Wahrheitsbegriff bei Husserl und Heidegger.* Berlin: de Gruyter, 1967.

Tyradellis, Daniel. *Untiefen: Husserls Begriffsebene zwischen Formalismus und Lebenswelt.* Würzburg, Ger.: Königshausen & Neumann, 2006.

Tzetzes, John. "Concerning Alcamenes." Trans. Vasiliki Dogani. In *Chiliades or Book of Histories.* https://archive.org/details/TzetzesCHILIADES.

Valéry, Paul. *Tel Quel, Œuvres.* Ed. Jean Hytier. Paris: Gallimard, 1957–1960.

Vanni Rovighi, Sofia. "Una fonte remota della teoria husserliana dell'intenzionalità." In *Studi di filosofia medioevale,* vol. 2: *Secoli XIII e XIV,* 283–98. Milano: Vita e pensiero, 1978.

Vasari, Giorgio. *The Lives of the Artists.* Trans. Julia Conaway Bondanella and Peter E. Bondanella. Oxford: Oxford University Press, 2008.

Vasiliu, Anca. *Du Diaphane: Image, milieu, lumière dans la pensée antique et médiévale.* Paris: Vrin, 1997.

——. "Le mot et le verre: Une definition médiévale du *diaphane*." *Journal des savants,* no. 1994/1 (1994): 135–62.

Verbeke, Gérard, and José Rafael Moncho-Pascual. "L'anthropologie de Némésius." In *De natura hominis* by Nemesius, ix–lxxxv. Leiden: Brill, 1975.

Vernant, Jean-Pierre. "From the 'Presentification' of the Invisible to the Imitation of Appearance." In *Mortals and Immortals: Collected Essays*, ed. and trans. Froma I. Zeitlin, 151–63. Princeton, N.J.: Princeton University Press, 1991.

Vinciguerra, Laurent. *Archéologie de la perspective: Sur Piero della Francesca, Vinci et Dürer*. Paris: Presses universitaires de France, 2007.

Vitruvius. *On Architecture*. Trans. Frank Granger. 2 vols. Cambridge, Mass.: Harvard University Press, 1998.

Volonté, Paolo. *Husserls Phänomenologie der Imagination: Zur Funktion der Phantasie bei der Konstitution von Erkenntnis*. Freiburg, Ger.: Alber, 1997.

Volpi, Franco. "War Franz Brentano ein Aristoteliker? Zu Brentanos und Aristoteles' Auffassung der Psychologie als Wissenschaft." *Brentano Studien* 2 (1989): 13–29.

Voltaire. s.v. "Dionysius, St. (The Areopagite), and the Famous Eclipse." In *A Philosophical Dictionary*, trans. Abner Kneeland, vol. 1, 265–66. Boston: Mendum, 1865.

Walde, Alois. *Vergleichendes Wörterbuch der indogermanischen Sprachen*. Ed. Julius Pokorny. 3 vols. Berlin: de Gruyter, 1927–32.

Waldenfels, Bernhard. *Bruchlinien der Erfahrung: Phänomenologie, Psychoanalyse, Phänomenotechnik*. Frankfurt: Suhrkamp, 2002.

——. *Einführung in die Phänomenologie*. Munich: Fink, 1992.

——. "Das Paradox des Ausdrucks." In *Deutsch-französische Gedankengänge*, 105–23. Frankfurt: Suhrkamp, 1995.

——. "Das Rätsel der Sichtbarkeit: Kunstphänomenologische Betrachtungen im Hinblick auf den Status der modernen Malerei." In *Der Stachel des Fremden*, 204–24. Frankfurt: Suhrkamp, 1998.

——. *Phenomenology of the Alien: Basic Concepts*. Trans. Alexander Kozin and Tanja Stähler. Evanston, Ill.: Northwestern University Press, 2011.

——. "Verkörperung im Bild." In *Phänomenologie der Aufmerksamkeit*, 205–22. Frankfurt: Suhrkamp, 2004.

——. "Von der Wirkmacht und Wirkkraft der Bilder." In *Movens Bild: Zwischen Evidenz und Affekt*, ed. Gottfried Boehm, Birgit Mersmann, and Christian Spies, 47–63. Munich: Fink, 2008.

Walton, Kendall L. "Transparent Pictures: On the Nature of Photographic Realism." *Critical Inquiry* 11, no. 2 (December 1984): 246–77.

Warburg, Aby. "Sandro Botticellis 'Geburt der Venus' und 'Frühling,'" 1893. In *Werke in einem Band*, ed. Martin Treml, Sigrid Weigel, and Perdita Ladwig, 39–123. Berlin: Suhrkamp, 2010.

Wedin, Michael V. *Mind and Imagination in Aristotle*. New Haven, Conn.: Yale University Press, 1988.

Welsch, Wolfgang. *Aisthesis: Grundzüge und Perspektiven der aristotelischen Sinneslehre*. Stuttgart: Klett-Cotta, 1987.

Welton, Donn. *The Other Husserl: The Horizons of Transcendental Phenomenology*. Bloomington: Indiana University Press, 2002.

Wertheimer, Max. *Productive Thinking*. New York: Harper, 1945.

Wians, William. "Saving Aristotle from Nussbaum's Phainomena." In *Essays in Ancient Greek Philosophy*, vol. 5: *Aristotle's Ontology*, ed. Anthony Preus and John P. Anton, 133–49. Albany: State University of New York Press, 1992.

Wiesing, Lambert. *Artificial Presence: Philosophical Studies in Image Theory*. Trans. Nils F. Schott. Stanford, Calif.: Stanford University Press, 2010.

——. "Bilder—Collage—Videoclips: Das Materialkonzept von Kurt Schwitters." In *Stoffe: Zur Geschichte der Materialität in Künsten und Wissenschaften*, ed. Barbara Naumann, Thomas Strässle, and Caroline Torra-Mattenklott, 247–59. Zurich: vdf, 2006.

——. *Phänomene im Bild*. Munich: Fink, 2000.

——. *The Visibility of the Image: History and Perspectives of Formal Aesthetics*. Trans. Nancy Ann Roth. London: Bloomsbury, 2016.

Wild, Markus. "Begrifflicher und nichtbegrifflicher Gehalt der Wahrnehmung." In *Poetiken der Materie*, ed. Thomas Strässle and Caroline Torra-Mattenklott, 245–62. Freiburg, Ger.: Rombach, 2005.

Wittgenstein, Ludwig. *Philosophical Investigations*. Ed. P. M. S. Hacker and Joachim Schulte, trans. G. E. M. Anscombe, P. M. S. Hacker, and Joachim Schulte. 4th ed. Chichester: Wiley, 2009.

——. *Remarks on Colour*. Ed. G. E. M. Anscombe, trans. Linda L. McAlister and Margarete Schättle. Oxford: Blackwell, 1978.

——. *Zettel*. Ed. G. E. M. Anscombe and Georg Henrik von Wright, trans. G. E. M. Anscombe. 2nd ed. Oxford: Blackwell, 1981.

Wöhrle, Georg, ed. and trans. *De coloribus* by Aristotle. Vol. 18/5 of *Werke in deutscher Übersetzung*. Berlin: Akademie, 1956–.

Wolfson, Harry Austryn. "The Internal Senses in Latin, Arabic, and Hebrew Philosophic Texts." *Harvard Theological Review* 28, no. 2 (April 1935): 69–133.

Wollheim, Richard. *Art and Its Objects*. Cambridge: Cambridge University Press, 1980.

Woolf, Raphael. "The Coloration of Aristotelian Eye-Jelly: A Note on *On Dreams* 459b–460a." *Journal of the History of Philosophy* 37, no. 3 (July 1999): 385–91.

Wüstenberg, Klaus. *Die Konsequenz des Phänomenalismus: Erkenntnistheoretische Untersuchungen in kritischer Auseinandersetzung mit Hume, Brentano und Husserl*. Würzburg, Ger.: Königshausen & Neumann, 2004.

Xenophon. *Memorabilia*. In *Memorabilia. Oeconomicus. Symposium. Apology*. Trans. E. C. Marchant, rev. Jeffrey Henderson, 1–377. Cambridge, Mass.: Harvard University Press, 2013.

Zahavi, Dan, and Frederik Stjernfelt, eds. *One Hundred Years of Phenomenology: Husserl's "Logical Investigations" Revisited*. Dordrecht: Springer, 2002.

Index

COLUMBIA THEMES IN PHILOSOPHY,
SOCIAL CRITICISM, AND THE ARTS

Lydia Goehr and Gregg M. Horowitz, Editors

Lydia Goehr and Daniel Herwitz, eds., *The Don Giovanni Moment: Essays on the Legacy of an Opera*

Robert Hullot-Kentor, *Things Beyond Resemblance: Collected Essays on Theodor W. Adorno*

Gianni Vattimo, *Art's Claim to Truth*, edited by Santiago Zabala, translated by Luca D'Isanto

John T. Hamilton, *Music, Madness, and the Unworking of Language*

Stefan Jonsson, *A Brief History of the Masses: Three Revolutions*

Richard Eldridge, *Life, Literature, and Modernity*

Janet Wolff, *The Aesthetics of Uncertainty*

Lydia Goehr, *Elective Affinities: Musical Essays on the History of Aesthetic Theory*

Christoph Menke, *Tragic Play: Irony and Theater from Sophocles to Beckett*, translated by James Phillips

György Lukács, *Soul and Form*, translated by Anna Bostock and edited by John T. Sanders and Katie Terezakis with an introduction by Judith Butler

Joseph Margolis, *The Cultural Space of the Arts and the Infelicities of Reductionism*

Herbert Molderings, *Art as Experiment: Duchamp and the Aesthetics of Chance, Creativity, and Convention*

Whitney Davis, *Queer Beauty: Sexuality and Aesthetics from Winckelmann to Freud and Beyond*

Gail Day, *Dialectical Passions: Negation in Postwar Art Theory*

Ewa Płonowska Ziarek, *Feminist Aesthetics and the Politics of Modernism*

Gerhard Richter, *Afterness: Figures of Following in Modern Thought and Aesthetics*

Boris Groys, *Under Suspicion: A Phenomenology of the Media*, translated by Carsten Strathausen

Michael Kelly, *A Hunger for Aesthetics: Enacting the Demands of Art*

Stefan Jonsson, *Crowds and Democracy: The Idea and Image of the Masses from Revolution to Fascism*

Elaine P. Miller, *Head Cases: Julia Kristeva on Philosophy and Art in Depressed Times*

Lutz Koepnick, *On Slowness: Toward an Aesthetic of Radical Contemporaneity*

John Roberts, *Photography and Its Violations*

Hermann Kappelhoff, *The Politics and Poetics of Cinematic Realism*

Cecilia Sjöholm, *Doing Aesthetics with Arendt: How to See Things*

Owen Hulatt, *Adorno's Theory of Philosophical and Aesthetic Truth: Texture and Performance*

James A. Steintrager, *The Autonomy of Pleasure: Libertines, License, and Sexual Revolution*

Paolo D'Angelo, *Sprezzatura: Concealing the Effort of Art from Aristotle to Duchamp*

Fred Evans, *Public Art and the Fragility of Democracy: An Essay in Political Aesthetics*

Maurizio Lazzarato, *Videophilosophy: The Perception of Time in Post-Fordism*, translated by Jay Hetrick

Monique Roelofs, *Arts of Address: Being Alive to Language and the World*

Barbara Carnevali, *Social Appearances: A Philosophy of Display and Prestige*

Jason Miller, *The Politics of Perception and the Aesthetics of Social Change*